Lecture Notes in Artificial Intelligence   7268

Subseries of Lecture Notes in Computer Science

LNAI Series Editors

Randy Goebel
University of Alberta, Edmonton, Canada
Yuzuru Tanaka
Hokkaido University, Sapporo, Japan
Wolfgang Wahlster
DFKI and Saarland University, Saarbrücken, Germany

LNAI Founding Series Editor

Joerg Siekmann
DFKI and Saarland University, Saarbrücken, Germany

Leszek Rutkowski   Marcin Korytkowski
Rafał Scherer   Ryszard Tadeusiewicz
Lotfi A. Zadeh   Jacek M. Zurada (Eds.)

Artificial Intelligence and Soft Computing

11th International Conference, ICAISC 2012
Zakopane, Poland, April 29 - May 3, 2012
Proceedings, Part II

 Springer

Series Editors

Randy Goebel, University of Alberta, Edmonton, Canada
Jörg Siekmann, University of Saarland, Saarbrücken, Germany
Wolfgang Wahlster, DFKI and University of Saarland, Saarbrücken, Germany

Volume Editors

Leszek Rutkowski
Marcin Korytkowski
Rafał Scherer
Częstochowa University of Technology, Poland
E-mail: lrutko@kik.pcz.czest.pl,
{marcin.korytkowski, rafal.scherer}@kik.pcz.pl

Ryszard Tadeusiewicz
AGH University of Science and Technology, Kraków, Poland
E-mail: rtad@agh.edu.pl

Lotfi A. Zadeh
University of California, Berkeley, CA, USA
E-mail: zadeh@cs.berkeley.edu

Jacek M. Zurada
University of Louisville, KY, USA
E-mail: jacek.zurada@louisville.edu

ISSN 0302-9743   e-ISSN 1611-3349
ISBN 978-3-642-29349-8   e-ISBN 978-3-642-29350-4
DOI 10.1007/978-3-642-29350-4
Springer Heidelberg Dordrecht London New York

Library of Congress Control Number: 2012934672

CR Subject Classification (1998): I.2, H.3, F.1, I.4, H.4, I.5

LNCS Sublibrary: SL 7 – Artificial Intelligence

Typesetting: Camera-ready by author, data conversion by Scientific Publishing Services, Chennai, India

Printed on acid-free paper

Springer is part of Springer Science+Business Media (www.springer.com)

Preface

This volume constitutes the proceedings of the 11th International Conference on Artificial Intelligence and Soft Computing, ICAISC 2012, held in Zakopane, Poland, from April 29 to May 3, 2012. The conference was organized by the Polish Neural Network Society in cooperation with the SWSPiZ Academy of Management in Łódź, the Department of Computer Engineering at the Czestochowa University of Technology, and the IEEE Computational Intelligence Society, Poland Chapter. The previous conferences took place in Kule (1994), Szczyrk (1996), Kule (1997) and Zakopane (1999, 2000, 2002, 2004, 2006, 2008, 2010) and attracted a large number of papers and internationally recognized speakers: Lotfi A. Zadeh, Igor Aizenberg, Shun-ichi Amari, Daniel Amit, Piero P. Bonissone, Jim Bezdek, Zdzisław Bubnicki, Andrzej Cichocki, Włodzisław Duch, Pablo A. Estévez, Jerzy Grzymala-Busse, Martin Hagan, Akira Hirose, Kaoru Hirota, Janusz Kacprzyk, Jim Keller, Laszlo T. Koczy, Soo-Young Lee, Robert Marks, Evangelia Micheli-Tzanakou, Erkki Oja, Witold Pedrycz, Jagath C. Rajapakse, Sarunas Raudys, Enrique Ruspini, Jorg Siekman, Roman Slowinski, Igor Spiridonov, Ryszard Tadeusiewicz, Shiro Usui, Jun Wang, Ronald Y. Yager, Syozo Yasui and Jacek Zurada. The aim of this conference is to build a bridge between traditional artificial intelligence techniques and novel soft computing techniques. It was pointed out by Lotfi A. Zadeh that "soft computing (SC) is a coalition of methodologies which are oriented toward the conception and design of information/intelligent systems. The principal members of the coalition are: fuzzy logic (FL), neurocomputing (NC), evolutionary computing (EC), probabilistic computing (PC), chaotic computing (CC), and machine learning (ML). The constituent methodologies of SC are, for the most part, complementary and synergistic rather than competitive." This volume presents both traditional artificial intelligence methods and soft computing techniques. Our goal is to bring together scientists representing both traditional artificial intelligence approach and soft computing techniques. This volume is divided into seven parts:

- Data Mining
- Hardware Implementation
- Bioinformatics, Biometrics and Medical Applications
- Concurrent Parallel Processing
- Agent Systems, Robotics and Control
- Artificial Intelligence in Modeling and Simulation
- Various Problems of Artificial Intelligence

The conference attracted a total of 483 submissions from 48 countries and after the review process 212 papers were accepted for publication. ICAISC 2012 hosted the Symposium on Swarm Intelligence and Differential Evolution, the Symposium on Evolutionary Computation and the 4th International Workshop

on Engineering Knowledge and Semantic Systems (IWEKSS 2012). A special
theme of IWEKSS 2012 was "Nature-Inspired Knowledge Management Systems."
I would like to thank two main IWEKS 2012 organizers: Jason J. Jung from
Korea and Dariusz Krol from Poland. I would also like to thank our participants,
invited speakers and reviewers of the papers for their scientific and personal
contribution to the conference. Several reviewers were very helpful in reviewing
the papers and are listed herein.

Acknowledge

Finally, I thank my co-workers Łukasz Bartczuk, Agnieszka Cpałka, Piotr Dziwiński, Marcin Gabryel, Marcin Korytkowski and the conference secretary Rafał
Scherer, for their enormous efforts to make the conference a very successful event.
Moreover, I would like to acknowledge the work of Marcin Korytkowski, who designed the Internet submission system and Patryk Najgebauer, Tomasz Nowak
and Jakub Romanowski who created the web page.

April 2012   Leszek Rutkowski

Organization

ICAISC 2012 was organized by the Polish Neural Network Society in cooperation with the SWSPiZ Academy of Management in Łódź, the Department of Computer Engineering at Częstochowa University of Technology, and the IEEE Computational Intelligence Society, Poland Chapter.

ICAISC Chairs

Honorary Chairs	Lotfi Zadeh (USA)
	Jacek Żurada (USA)
General Chairs	Leszek Rutkowski (Poland)
Co-Chairs	Włodzisław Duch (Poland)
	Janusz Kacprzyk (Poland)
	Józef Korbicz (Poland)
	Ryszard Tadeusiewicz (Poland)

ICAISC Program Committee

Rafał Adamczak - Poland
Cesare Alippi - Italy
Shun-ichi Amari - Japan
Rafal A. Angryk - USA
Jarosław Arabas - Poland
Robert Babuska - The Netherlands
Ildar Z. Batyrshin - Russia
James C. Bezdek - USA
Marco Block-Berlitz - Germany
Leon Bobrowski - Poland
Leonard Bolc - Poland
Piero P. Bonissone - USA
Bernadette Bouchon-Meunier - France
James Buckley - Poland
Tadeusz Burczynski - Poland
Andrzej Cader - Poland
Juan Luis Castro - Spain
Yen-Wei CHEN - Japan
Wojciech Cholewa - Poland
Fahmida N. Chowdhury - USA
Andrzej Cichocki - Japan
Paweł Cichosz - Poland
Krzysztof Cios - USA

Ian Cloete - Germany
Oscar Cordón - Spain
Bernard De Baets - Belgium
Nabil Derbel - Tunisia
Ewa Dudek-Dyduch - Poland
Ludmiła Dymowa - Poland
Andrzej Dzieliński - Poland
David Elizondo - UK
Meng Joo Er - Singapore
Pablo Estevez - Chile
János Fodor - Hungary
David B. Fogel - USA
Roman Galar - Poland
Alexander I. Galushkin - Russia
Adam Gaweda - USA
Joydeep Ghosh - USA
Juan Jose Gonzalez de la Rosa - Spain
Marian Bolesław Gorzałczany - Poland
Krzysztof Grąbczewski - Poland
Garrison Greenwood - USA
Jerzy W. Grzymala-Busse - USA
Hani Hagras - UK
Saman Halgamuge - Australia

Enrique H. Ruspini - USA
Khalid Saeed - Poland
Dominik Sankowski - Poland
Norihide Sano - Japan
Robert Schaefer - Poland
Rudy Setiono - Singapore
Paweł Sewastianow - Poland
Jennie Si - USA
Peter Sincak - Slovakia
Andrzej Skowron - Poland
Ewa Skubalska-Rafajłowicz - Poland
Roman Słowiński - Poland
Tomasz G. Smolinski - USA
Czesław Smutnicki - Poland
Pilar Sobrevilla - Spain
Janusz Starzyk - USA
Jerzy Stefanowski - Poland
Pawel Strumillo - Poland
Ron Sun - USA
Johan Suykens Suykens - Belgium
Piotr Szczepaniak - Poland
Eulalia J. Szmidt - Poland
Przemysław Śliwiński - Poland
Adam Słowik - Poland
Jerzy Świątek - Poland
Hideyuki Takagi - Japan

Yury Tiumentsev - Russia
Vicenç Torra - Spain
Burhan Turksen - Canada
Shiro Usui - Japan
Michael Wagenknecht - Germany
Tomasz Walkowiak - Poland
Deliang Wang - USA
Jun Wang - Hong Kong
Lipo Wang - Singapore
Zenon Waszczyszyn - Poland
Paul Werbos - USA
Slawo Wesolkowski - Canada
Sławomir Wiak - Poland
Bernard Widrow - USA
Kay C. Wiese - Canada
Bogdan M. Wilamowski - USA
Donald C. Wunsch - USA
Maciej Wygralak - Poland
Roman Wyrzykowski - Poland
Ronald R. Yager - USA
Xin-She Yang - UK
Gary Yen - USA
John Yen - USA
Sławomir Zadrożny - Poland
Ali M.S. Zalzala - United Arab Emirates

SIDE Chairs

Janez Brest, University of Maribor, Slovenia
Maurice Clerc, Independent Consultant
Ferrante Neri, University of Jyväskylä, Finland

SIDE Program Chairs

Tim Blackwell, Goldsmiths College, UK
Swagatam Das, Indian Statistical Institute, India
Nicolas Monmarché, University of Tours, France
Ponnuthurai N. Suganthan, Nanyang Technological University, Singapore

SIDE Program Committee

Ashish Anand, India
Borko Boskovic, Slovenia
Jagdish Chand Bansal, India
Carlos Coello Coello, Mexico
Iztok Fister, Slovenia
Bogdan Filipic, Slovenia
Sheldon Hui, Singapore
Peter D. Justesen, Denmark
Nicolas Labroche, France
Jane Liang, China
Hongbo Liu, China
Efren Mezura Montes, Mexico
A. Nakib, France
Rammohan Mallipeddi, Korea
Slawomir Nasuto, UK
Jouni Lampinen, Finland

Mirjam Sepesy Maucec, Slovenia
Marjan Mernik, Slovenia
Godfrey Onwubolu, Canada
Jérôme Emeka Onwunalu, Canada
Quanke Pan, China
Gregor Papa, Slovenia
Boyang Qu, China
Shahryar Rahnamayan, Canada
Jurij Silc, Slovenia
Josef Tvrdik, Czech Republic
M. N. Vrahatis, Greece
Daniela Zaharie, Romania
Ales Zamuda, Slovenia
Qingfu Zhang, UK
Shizheng Zhao, Singapore

IWEKSS Program Committee

Jason J. Jung, Korea
Dariusz Krol, Poland
Ngoc Thanh Nguyen, Poland
Gonzalo A. Aranda-Corral, Spain
Myung-Gwon Hwang, Korea
Costin Badica, Romania
Grzegorz J. Nalepa, Krakow, Poland

ICAISC Organizing Committee

Rafał Scherer, Secretary
Łukasz Bartczuk, Organizing Committee Member
Piotr Dziwiński, Organizing Committee Member
Marcin Gabryel, Finance Chair
Marcin Korytkowski, Databases and Internet Submissions

Reviewers

R. Adamczak
M. Amasyal
A. Anand
R. Angryk
J. Arabas

T. Babczyński
M. Baczyński
C. Badica
Ł. Bartczuk
M. Białko

A. Bielecki
T. Blackwell
L. Bobrowski
A. Borkowski
L. Borzemski

B. Boskovic
J. Brest
T. Burczyński
R. Burduk
K. Cetnarowicz
M. Chang
W. Cholewa
M. Choraś
R. Choraś
K. Choros
P. Cichosz
R. Cierniak
P. Ciskowski
M. Clerc
O. Cordon
B. Cyganek
R. Czabański
I. Czarnowski
B. De Baets
J. de la Rosa
L. Diosan
G. Dobrowolski
W. Duch
E. Dudek-Dyduch
L. Dymowa
A. Dzieliński
P. Dziwiński
S. Ehteram
J. Emeka Onwunalu
N. Evans
A. Fanea
I. Fister
M. Flasiński
D. Fogel
M. Fraś
M. Gabryel
A. Gawęda
M. Giergiel
P. Głomb
F. Gomide
M. Gorzałczany
E. Grabska
K. Grąbczewski
W. Greblicki
K. Grudziński

J. Grzymala-Busse
R. Hampel
C. Han
Z. Hasiewicz
O. Henniger
F. Herrera
Z. Hippe
A. Horzyk
E. Hrynkiewicz
S. Hui
M. Hwang
A. Janczak
N. Jankowski
S. Jaroszewicz
J. Jung
W. Kacalak
W. Kamiński
A. Kasperski
W. Kazimierski
V. Kecman
E. Kerre
H. Kim
F. Klawonn
P. Klęsk
J. Kluska
A. Kołakowska
L. Kompanets
J. Konopacki
J. Korbicz
P. Korohoda
J. Koronacki
M. Korytkowski
M. Korzeń
W. Kosiński
J. Kościelny
L. Kotulski
Z. Kowalczuk
J. Kozlak
M. Kraft
D. Krol
R. Kruse
B. Kryzhanovsky
A. Krzyzak
J. Kulikowski
O. Kurasova

V. Kurkova
M. Kurzyński
J. Kusiak
H. Kwaśnicka
N. Labroche
S. Lee
Y. Lei
J. Liang
A. Ligęza
H. Liu
B. Macukow
K. Madani
K. Malinowski
R. Mallipeddi
J. Mańdziuk
U. Markowska-Kaczmar
A. Martin
J. Martyna
A. Materka
T. Matsumoto
V. Medvedev
J. Mendel
E. MezuraMontes
Z. Michalewicz
J. Michalkiewicz
Z. Mikrut
W. Mitkowski
W. Moczulski
W. Mokrzycki
N. Monmarche
T. Munakata
A. Nakib
G. Nalepa
S. Nasuto
E. Nawarecki
A. Nawrat
F. Neri
M. Nieniewski
A. Niewiadomski
R. Nowicki
A. Obuchowicz
M. Ogiela
G. Onwubolu
S. Osowski
M. Pacholczyk

Table of Contents – Part II

Part I: Data Mining

Part II: Hardware Implementation

Part III: Bioinformatics, Biometrics and Medical Applications

Part IV: Concurrent Parallel Processing

Part V: Agent Systems, Robotics and Control

Part VI: Artificial Intelligence in Modeling and Simulation

Part VII: Various Problems od Artificial Intelligence

Table of Contents – Part I

Part I: Neural Networks and Their Applications

Part II: Fuzzy Systems and Their Applications

Part III: Pattern Classification

Part IV: Computer Vision, Image and Speech Analysis

Part V: The 4th International Workshop on Engineering Knowledge and Semantic Systems

Part I

Data Mining

Dependency Analysis in Ontology-Driven Content-Based Systems

Yalemisew M. Abgaz, Muhammad Javed, and Claus Pahl

Centre for Next Generation Localization (CNGL),
School of Computing, Dublin City University, Dublin 9, Ireland
{yabgaz,mjaved,cpahl}@computing.dcu.ie

Abstract. Ontology-driven content-based systems are content-based systems (ODCBS) that are built to provide a better access to information by semantically annotating the content using ontologies. Such systems contain ontology layer, annotation layer and content layer. These layers contain semantically interrelated and interdependent entities. Thus, a change in one layer causes many unseen and undesired changes and impacts that propagate to other entities. Before any change is implemented in the ODCBS, it is crucial to understand the impacts of the change on other ODCBS entities. However, without getting these dependent entities, to which the change propagates, it is difficult to understand and analyze the impacts of the requested changes. In this paper we formally identify and define relevant dependencies, formalizing them and present a dependency analysis algorithm. The output of the dependency analysis serves as an essential input for change impact analysis process that ensures the desired evolution of the ODCBS.

Keywords: Dependency analysis, Change impact analysis, Content-based systems, Ontology-driven content-based systems.

1 Introduction

Ontology-driven content-based systems are content-based information systems that are built to provide a better access to information for both humans and machines by semantically enriching the content using ontologies. In such systems, using semantic annotation, the ontologies provide rich semantics to the content at hand [1][2][3]. To achieve this purpose, we proposed a layered framework [4] which contains the ontology, the annotation and the content layers. A continual change of entities in the layers causes the ODCBS to evolve dynamically [5].

Changes in ODCBS are complex as a result of the interdependence of the entities at different layers, the nature of the changes and the semantics involved in ODCBS. When an entity changes, the change propagates to other entities resulting intermediate changes to other dependent entities [6]. The propagation is towards the dependent entities of the changing entity. Because the interdependence between entities in the layers involves semantics, identifying the dependent entities is an arduous and complex and time consuming task. It is aggravated by

L. Rutkowski et al. (Eds.): ICAISC 2012, Part II, LNCS 7268, pp. 3–12, 2012.
© Springer-Verlag Berlin Heidelberg 2012

the evolution strategies [7] which require further analysis on the nature of the dependencies within and across the layers [4].

Understanding these dependencies and their nature is crucial for analyzing the impacts of changes in the ODCBS. A systematic and careful analysis for identifying dependent entities and analyzing the propagation of impacts to dependent entities is of vital importance in the evolution process [7][6]. Some key features of our approach are:

- providing the theoretical foundation for dependency analysis in ontology-driven content-bases systems.
- identifying the crucial and relevant dependencies that exist within and among the layers of the ODCBS. These dependencies are used to generate change operations [8] and to analyze impacts of change operations in ODCBS.
- providing formal definition of the identified relevant dependencies.
- providing algorithms to identify dependent entities for further analysis.

This research benefits us in different ways. It will serve as a vital input for generating change operations for different evolution strategies. It also serves as an input for change impact analysis process. It facilitates the visibility of the affected entities, improves the integrity of the ODCBS and makes the evolution process smooth and predictable.

This paper is organized as follows: Section 2 gives an overview of ODCBSs, its layered architecture and its graph based representation. In section 3, we present dependencies in ODCBS, their types and selected algorithms to identify dependent entities. Section 4 focuses on evaluation using empirical studies. Related work is given in section 5 and conclusion and future work in section 6.

2   Overview of Ontology-Driven Content-Based Systems

We represent an ODCBS using graph-based formalism. Graphs are selected for their known efficiency and similarity to ontology taxonomy. A full discussion of the ODCBS architecture is found in [4].

An ODCBS is represented as graph $G = G_o \cup G_a \cup Cont$ where: G_o is the ontology graph, G_a is the annotation graph and $Cont$ is the content set.

An *ontology* O is represented by a direct labelled graph $G_o = (N_o, E_o)$ where: $N_o = \{n_{o1}, n_{o2}, \ldots, n_{om}\}$ is a finite set of labelled nodes that represent classes, data properties, object properties etc. $E_o = \{e_{o1}, e_{o2} \ldots, e_{om}\}$ is a finite set of labelled edges and $e_{oi} = (n_1, \alpha, n_2)$ where: n_1 and n_2 are members of N_o and the label of an edge represented by $\alpha = \{$subclassOf, intersectionOf, minCardinality, maxCardinality...$\}$. The labels may indicate the relationship (dependency) between the nodes. A *content* represented by $Cont$ can be viewed as a set of documents $D = \{d_1, d_2, d_3 \ldots d_n\}$ where: d_i represents a single document or part of a document which can be mapped to nodes in the annotation graph. An *annotation* $Anot$ is represented by a direct labelled graph $G_a = (N_a, E_a)$ where: N_a and E_a are finite set of labelled nodes and edges respectively. An edge $E_a = (n_{a1}, \alpha_a, n_{a2})$ where $n_{a1} \in \{Cont\}$ as a subject, $n_{a2} \in \{Cont\} \cup \{O\}$ as

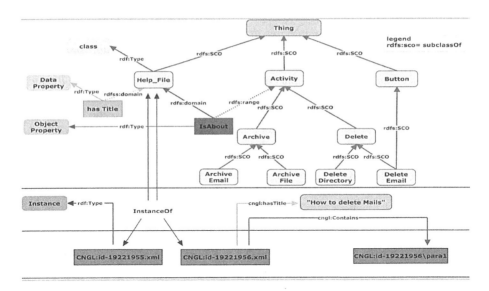

Fig. 1. Graph-based representation of sample ODCBS layered architecture

an object and $\alpha_a \in \{O\}$ as a predicate. The graph-based representation of an ODCBS is presented in (Fig. 1)and serves as a running example.

The type of a node is given by a function $type(n)$ that maps the node to its type (class, instance, data property, object property...). The label of any edge $e = (n_1, \alpha, n_2)$, which is α , is a string given by a function $label(e)$. All the edges of a node n are given by a function $edges(n)$. It returns all the edges as (n, α, m) where n is the target node and m is any node linked to n via α.

3   Dependency in ODCBSs

Characterization, representation and analysis of dependencies within and among the ontology, the annotation and the content layers is subtle and crucial aspect to perform impact analysis [9]. Using an empirical study [10] we discovered different types of dependencies that exist between entities within and among the layers.

Dependency is defined as a relationship between entities where the entities are related to each other by a given relation. Given a dependency between two entities (A and B) in the ODCBS, represented as $Dep(A, B)$, A is the dependent entity and B is the antecedent entity and there is a relationship that relates A to B. Dependency can be unidirectional or bidirectional. **Dependency Analysis** is a process of identifying the dependent entities of s given entity.

3.1   Dependency within Layers

In this section, we present the dependencies we identified in each layers of the ODCBS. The following list includes only frequently observed and useful dependencies and is not an exhaustive list.

1. **Concept-Concept Dependency:** Given two class nodes c_i and $c_j \in G_o$, c_i is dependent on c_j represented by $dep(c_i, c_j)$, if there exist an edge $e_i = (n_1, \alpha, n_2) \in G_o$ such that $(n_1 = c_i) \wedge (n_2 = c_j) \wedge (label(e_i) = \text{``subClassOf''}) \wedge (type(n_1) = type(n_2) = \text{``class''})$. Concept-concept dependency is transitive. For example, there is a concept-concept dependency between *Activity* and *Archive*. *Archive* depends on *Activity* because it is a subClass Of *Activity*.

2. **Concept-Axiom Dependency:** Given an axiom edge a_1 and a concept node $c_1 \in G_o$, a_1 is dependent on c_1 represented by $dep(a_1, c_1)$, if there exist an edge $e_i = (n_1, \alpha, n_2) \in G_o$ such that $(n_1 = c_1) \vee (n_2 = c_1) \wedge type(n_1) = type(n_2) = \text{``class''}$. For example, if we take the concept *Activity* there are three dependent *subClassOf* edges and one dependent *rdfs:range* edge.

3. **Concept-Restriction Dependency :** Given a restriction r_1 and a concept node $c_1 \in G_o$, r_1 is dependent on c_1 represented by $dep(r_1, c_1)$ if there exist an edge $e_i = (n_1, \alpha, n_2) = r_1 \in G_o$ such that $(n_2 = c_1) \wedge type(n_2) = \text{``class''}$. For example, if we have a restriction (*isAbout, allValuesFrom, Activity*), this specific restriction is dependent on the concept *Activity*.

4. **Property-Property Dependency:** Given two property nodes $p_1, p_2 \in G_o$, p_1 is dependent on p_2 represented by $dep(p_1, p_2)$ if there exist an edge $e_i = (n_1, \alpha, n_2) \in G_o$ such that $(n_1 = p_1) \wedge (n_2 = p_2) \wedge (label(e_i) = \text{``subPropertyOf''}) \wedge type(n_1) = type(n2) = \text{``property''}$. Here property refers to both data property and object property.

5. **Property-Axiom Dependency:** Given an axiom edge a_1 and a property node $p_1 \in G_o$, a_1 is dependent on p_1 represented by $dep(a_1, p_1)$ if there exist an edge $e_i = (n_1, \alpha, n_2) = a_1 \in G_o$ such that $(n_1 = p_1) \wedge type(n_1) = type(n_2) = \text{``property''}$.

6. **Property-Restriction Dependency:** Given a restriction edge r_1 and a property node $p_1 \in G_o$, r_1 is dependent on p_1 represented by $dep(r_1, p_1)$ if there exist an edge $e_i = (n_1, \alpha, n_2) \in G_o$ such that $(n_1 = p_1) \vee (n_2 = p_2) \wedge type(n_1) = type(n_2) = \text{``property''}$.

7. **Axiom-Concept Dependency:** Given an axiom edge a_1 and a concept node $c_1 \in G_o$, c_1 is dependent on a_1 represented by $dep(c_1, a_1)$ if there exist an edge $e_i = (n_1, \alpha, n_2) \in G_o$ such that $(n_1 = c_1) \wedge (label(e_i) = \text{``subClassOf''}) \wedge (type(n_1) = \text{``class''})$.

3.2   Dependency across Layers

We also observed entities in one layer depending on entities in another layer. These dependencies are treated separately and are discussed below.

Content-annotation dependency. An annotation a_i in the annotation layer is dependent on d_i in the content layer, represented by $dep(a_i, d_i)$, if there exist an edge $e_a = \{n_{ai}, \alpha_a, n_{aj}\} \in G_a$ such that $(n_{ai} = d_i) \vee (n_{aj} = d_i)$. This means a_i is dependent on document d_i if the document is used as a subject or an object of the annotation triple.

Ontology-annotation dependency. The relevant dependencies between entities in the annotation and the ontology layer are presented below.

1. **Concept-Instance Dependency:** Given an instance node i_1 and a concept node $C_1 \in G$, i_1 is dependent on C_1 represented by $dep(i_1, C_1)$ if there exist an edge $e_i = (n_1, \alpha, n_2) \in G$ such that $(n_1 = i_1) \wedge (n_2 = C_1) \wedge (label(e_i) =$ "$InstanceOf$"$) \wedge type(n_1) =$ "$Instance$" $\wedge type(n_2) =$ "$class$". For example, the instance $CNGL : id19221955.xml$ is dependent on the concept $Help\_file$ due to $(CNGL : id - 19221956.xml, instanceOf, Help\_file)$.

2. **Property-Instance property Dependency:** Given an instance property node ip_1 and a property node $p_1 \in G$, ip_1 is dependent on p_1 represented by $dep(ip_1, p_1)$ if there exist an edge $e_i = (n_1, \alpha, n_2) \in G$ such that $(label(e_i) = p) \wedge type(n_1) =$ "$instance$" $\vee type(n_2) =$ "$instance$". For example, in $(CNGL : id19221956.xml, cngl:hasTitle, How to delete Mails)$ the instance property $cngl:hasTitle$ is dependent on the property $hasTitle$ in the ontology layer.

3. **Axiom-Instance Dependency:** Given an instance node i_1 and an axiom edge $a_1 \in G$, i_1 is dependent on a_1 represented by $dep(i_1, a_1)$ if there exist an edge $e_i = (n_1, \alpha, n_2) \in G$ such that $(n_1 = i_1) \wedge (label(e_i) =$ "$instanceOf$"$) \wedge (type(i_1) =$ "$Instance$"$)$.

3.3 Types of Dependencies and Dependency Determination

Direct Dependency/Indirect Dependency. Direct dependency is the dependency that exist between two adjacent nodes(n_1, n_2). This means, there is an edge $e_i = (n_1, \alpha, n_2)$. Indirect dependency is a dependency of a node on another by a transitive or intermediate relationship. There exist a set of intermediate edges $(n_1, \alpha, n_x)(n_x, \alpha, n_y)...(n_z, \alpha, n_2)$ that link the two nodes.

Algorithm 1. getDirectDependentClasses(G,c)

1: **Input:** Graph G, Class node c
2: **Output:** direct dependent classes$=d$
3: $d \leftarrow \emptyset$
4: **if** the node c exists in G **then**
5:    **for** each edge $e_i = (m, \alpha, c)$ directed to c **do**
6:       **if** $label(e_i) =$ "$subClassOf$" $\wedge type(m) =$ "$class$" **then**
7:          add m to d
8:       **end if**
9:    **end for**
10: **end if**
11: return d

A node is considered as dependent node only when it satisfies one or more of the dependencies defined in section 3.1 and 3.2. Algorithm 1 identifies direct dependent entities and it focuses only on class nodes. However, it is implemented for all node types. To get both direct and transitive dependent entities, we expand algorithm 1 to include the transitive dependent entities. Algorithm 2 identifies all direct and transitive dependencies.

Total Dependency/Partial Dependency. Total dependency refers to a dependency when a target node depends only on a single node (articulation node).

That means, there is no other entity that gives meaning to the target entity except the antecedent. Algorithm 3 returns all total dependent classes.

Given two nodes $n_1, n_2 \in G$, n_1 is totally dependent on n_2 represented by $Tdep(n_1, n_2)$ if and only if, $\exists(dep(n_1, n_2)) \wedge \not\exists(dep(n_1, n_3))$, where $(n_2 \neq n_3)$. Partial dependency refers to a dependency when the existence of a node depends on more than one node. Two nodes n_1 and $n_2 \in G$, are partially dependent represented by $Pdep(n_1, n_2)$ if and only if, $\exists dep(n_1, n_2) \wedge \exists dep(n_1, n_3)$, where $(n_2 \neq n_3)$. We can reuse algorithm 3 to return the partial dependent classes.

Algorithm 2. getAllDependentClasses(G,c)

1: **Input** : Graph G, Class node c
2: **Output:** all dependent classes=d
3: $d \leftarrow \emptyset$
4: **Queue** Q
5: **if** the node c exists in G **then**
6:     DirectDep $\leftarrow$ getDirectDependentClasses(G,c)
7:     **for** each concept c_i in DirectDep **do**
8:         $Q.push(c_i)$
9:         **if** c_i not in d **then**
10:            add c_i to d
11:         **end if**
12:     **end for**
13:     **while** Q is not empty **do**
14:         $Temp = Q.peek()$
15:         getAllDependentClasses(G,Temp)
16:         $Q.remove()$
17:     **end while**
18: **end if**
19: return d

Total and partial dependency plays a major role in determining the impacts of a change operation. If a class is totally dependent on the changing class, that class is affected by the change. It becomes orphan concept. But, if that class is partially dependent, the deletion of the class causes only semantic impact. The change makes the partial class neither orphan nor cyclic.

Direct Total and Partial Dependent Entities. Direct total dependent entities are entities that are the result of the intersection between total dependent and direct dependent entities. The intersection of the results of algorithm 1 and algorithm 3 gives us the direct total dependent entities. Direct partial dependent entities are entities that are both directly dependent but which are partially dependent entities. These entities play a major role in the impact analysis process.

Limitation of the Algorithm. The limitation of the dependency analysis algorithm is related to complex class expressions. The algorithm that separates the partial and total dependencies in such expressions is not fully covered and the algorithm only identifies such expressions as total dependent expressions.

Algorithm 3. getTotalDependentClass(G,c)

1: **Input** : Graph G, Class node c
2: **Output:** all total dependent classes=d
3: $d \leftarrow \emptyset$, contained=true
4: Set depCls=$\emptyset$,totalDepCls=$\emptyset$,partialDepCls=$\emptyset$, super=$\emptyset$
5: depCls$\leftarrow$ getAllDependentClasses(G,c)
6: **for** each concept c_i in depCls **do**
7:    **if** count(getSuperClasses(c_i)=1 **then**
8:       super $\leftarrow$ getSuperClasses(G, c_i)
9:       **if** super not in partialDepcls **then**
10:          add c_i to totalDepCls
11:       **end if**
12:    **else**
13:       super $\leftarrow$ getSuperClasses(G, c_i)
14:       contained=true
15:       **for** each sc in super **do**
16:          **if** sc not in depCls **then**
17:             contained=false
18:          **end if**
19:       **end for**
20:    **end if**
21:    **if** contained=true **then**
22:       add c_i to totalDepCls
23:    **else**
24:       add c_i to partialDepCls
25:    **end if**
26: **end for**
27: return totalDepCls

---

4   Evaluation

We used the empirical study [10] to evaluate the completeness, accuracy, the adequacy, the transferability and the practical applicability of the solution. The evaluation uses a content-based system built for software help management system to semantically enrich software help files. We used frequent change operations which are used to evolve the ODCBS. For each change, we conducted dependency analysis manually and using the proposed method separately. A comparative result of the dependency analysis conducted for one selected change operation, *delete concept (Activity)*, is presented in table 1. The operation deletes a concept *"Activity"*, but the change propagates to other dependent entities.

The result shows that the proposed method is accurate in that it identified all the dependent entities identified by the manual method. It further identifies entities that are not identified by the manual analysis too. This is mainly attributed to dependent axioms that the manual analysis overlooked or failed to recognize. A similar result is observed in the other selected change operations however, due to space constraint we do not present all of them here.

The solution applied in other domain (university administration) shows a fairly similar result to the results in table 1. It identifies all the dependent entities that are manually identified and more axioms than the manual method. This shows that the dependency analysis is adequate and transferable to other similar domains. The algorithm gives us a complete list of all the dependent entities that are identified manually. This makes it complete and guarantees to return all dependent entities. The algorithm can be customized to find dependency to a certain level of depth, which makes it suitable for n-level cascading which seeks dependent entities of a given entity within n node distance.

Table 1. Comparison of the manual and automatic method

Entity	Automatic			Manual
	Total Dependent	Direct Dependent	All Dependent	All Dependent
Concepts	5	2	6	6
Axioms	14	5	14	9
Instances	1	2	2	2
Properties	0	0	0	0

We can use these entities to analyze change propagation, and to identify impacts of a change operation in different evolution strategies. This allows the users to see which entities are affected, how and why they are affected.

5   Related Work

A closely related work is given by [11]. They conducted a study on validating data instances against ontology evolution to evaluate the validity of data instances. In their research they identify 5 dependencies and two independencies to detect implicit semantic changes and generating semantic views. Our work focuses on dependency analysis to identify all affected entities using the current version and the change operations before they are permanently implemented in the ODCBS.

A related work [12] from a software domain conducted analysis and visualization of behavioural dependencies in UML model. They defined structural and behavioural dependencies, direct and transitive dependences to analyze how one entity depends on another. Their work focuses on identifying and measuring dependencies in UML models. An interesting work done by [13] focuses on dependency analysis using conceptual graphs. Even if the work is more conceptual, it has interesting similarity to our work. They identified dependent and antecedent entities, and further identify impact as an attribute of dependency.

6   Conclusion and Future Work

In this work, we identified relevant dependencies within and across ODCBS layers. We formalized each of the dependencies using graph based formalization.

We further developed algorithm that identifies these dependencies which will be used as an input for other phases of ODCBS evolution. The proposed method identifies the relevant dependent entities and the nature of the dependency.

This work is one phase of the bigger change impact analysis research we are conducting for ODCBS systems. The output of this phase will be used as an input for change operation generation, and further for change impact analysis process. It will be used for analysing optimal implementation of change operations, and change operation orchestration. Our future work will be applying the results of the dependency analysis process for change impact analysis.

Acknowledgment. This material is based upon works supported by the Science Foundation Ireland under Grant No. 07/CE/I1142 as part of the Centre for Next Generation Localisation (www.cngl.ie) at Dublin City University (DCU).

References

1. Gruber, T.R.: A translation approach to portable ontology specifications. Knowledge Acquisition 5(2), 199–220 (1993)
2. Reeve, L., Han, H.: Survey of semantic annotation platforms. In: SAC 2005: Proceedings of the, ACM Symposium on Applied Computing, pp. 1634–1638 (2005)
3. Uren, V., Cimiano, P., Iria, J., Handschuh, S., Vargas-Vera, M., Motta, E., Ciravegna, F.: Semantic annotation for knowledge management:requirements and survey of the state of the art. Web Semantics: Science, Services and Agents on World Wide Web 4 (1), 14–28 (2006)
4. Abgaz, Y.M., Javed, M., Pahl, C.: A Framework for Change Impact Analysis of Ontology-Driven Content-Based Systems. In: Meersman, R., Dillon, T., Herrero, P. (eds.) OTM-WS 2011. LNCS, vol. 7046, pp. 402–411. Springer, Heidelberg (2011)
5. Gruhn, V., Pahl, C., Wever, M.: Data Model Evolution as Basis of Business Process Management. In: Papazoglou, M.P. (ed.) OOER 1995. LNCS, vol. 1021, pp. 270–281. Springer, Heidelberg (1995)
6. Plessers, P., De Troyer, O., Casteleyn, S.: Understanding ontology evolution: A change detection approach. Web Semantics: Science, Services and Agents on the World Wide Web 5(1), 39–49 (2007)
7. Stojanovic, L.: Methods and tools for ontology evolution. PhD thesis, University of Karlsruhe (2004)
8. Javed, M., Abgaz, Y., Pahl, C.: A Pattern-Based Framework of Change Operators for Ontology Evolution. In: Meersman, R., Herrero, P., Dillon, T. (eds.) OTM 2009 Workshops. LNCS, vol. 5872, pp. 544–553. Springer, Heidelberg (2009)
9. Ren, X., Shah, F., Tip, F., Ryder, B.G., Chesley, O.: Chianti: a tool for change impact analysis of java programs. SIGPLAN Not. 39, 432–448 (2004)
10. Abgaz, Y.M., Javed, M., Pahl, C.: Empirical Analysis of Impacts of Instance-Driven Changes in Ontologies. In: Meersman, R., Dillon, T., Herrero, P. (eds.) OTM 2010. LNCS, vol. 6428, pp. 368–377. Springer, Heidelberg (2010)

11. Qin, L., Atluri, V.: Evaluating the validity of data instances against ontology evolution over the semantic web. Information and Software Technology 51(1), 83–97 (2009)
12. Garousi, V., Briand, L., Labiche, Y.: Analysis and Visualization of Behavioral Dependencies Among Distributed Objects Based on UML Models. In: Nierstrasz, O., Whittle, J., Harel, D., Reggio, G. (eds.) MoDELS 2006. LNCS, vol. 4199, pp. 365–379. Springer, Heidelberg (2006)
13. Cox, L., Harry, D., Skipper, D., Delugach, H.S.: Dependency analysis using conceptual graphs. In: Proceedings of the 9th International Conference on Conceptual Structures, ICCS 2001. Springer, Heidelberg (2001)

Measuring Web Page Similarity
Based on Textual and Visual Properties

Vladimír Bartík*

Brno Universtiy of Technology, Faculty of Information Technology,
IT4Innovations Centre of Excellence,
Božetěchova 2, 612 66 Brno, Czech Republic
bartik@fit.vutbr.cz

Abstract. Measuring web page similarity is a very important task in the area of web mining and information retrieval. This paper introduces a method for measuring web page similarity, which considers both textual and visual properties of pages. Textual properties of a page are described by means of modified weight vector space model. General visual properties are captured via segmentation of a page, which divides a page into visual blocks, properties of which are stored into a vector of visual properties. These both vectors are then used to compute the overall web page similarity. This method will be described in detail and results of several experiments are also introduced in this paper.

Keywords: Web Page Similarity, Clustering, Vector Space Model, Vector Distance, Term Weighting, Visual Blocks.

1 Introduction

The amount of documents stored on the Web is still growing rapidly. There is a growing need for effective and reliable methods of information retrieval on the Web. The other important task is to organize and navigate the information. Therefore, we need to develop methods for web content mining.

This paper is focused on measuring similarity of web pages. The results can be used to search on the web, web page clustering or to reveal phishing web pages. If we are able to store web pages, which are frequently accessed by a user, it is possible to warn user, if a phishing page is visited by the same user.

There are several factors, which affect similarity of web pages. At first, we have to mention the hyperlink structure of web pages, which is the most frequently used factor to measure the similarity. There is also text content and visual structure of a document used for this purpose.

The main idea of the method proposed here is that the pages are similar only if their text content and visual properties are similar simultaneously. A new measure based on these two factors is introduced. To represent text contents

---

* This work was supported by the research programme MSM 0021630528 and the IT4Innovations Centre of Excellence CZ.1.05/1.1.00/02.0070.

L. Rutkowski et al. (Eds.): ICAISC 2012, Part II, LNCS 7268, pp. 13–21, 2012.

of the pages, we use the vector space model with the modified TF-IDF weights for text terms. The visual properties of a web page are represented as another vector of properties. If we have these both vectors, we can compute the textual and visual similarity of web documents. The combination of both similarity measures forms the aggregate similarity of web pages.

In the first part of the paper, the way of getting necessary information from web pages and its representation is introduced. Then, the measures, which are used to compute the similarity from the information obtained by the previous step, are described. Finally, some results of experiments are proposed.

2   Related Work

The methods developed to count web page similarity differ in the information, which is used to compute it. In most of methods, hyperlink structure of a web document is used. In [1], to represent a page, keywords from all pages linking to a given page, are extracted and used for clustering algorithm. In [2], the hyperlink information is used to find related pages on the web, i.e. pages with similar topic.

Another possibility to represent web page content is to extract its textual information and use some of text mining methods. Typically, the Vector Space Model is used to represent text content. For example, TF-IDF can be used as a weighting method to express the term's significance [3]. A method, which uses only the proper names from the text, is proposed in [4]. Proper names are presented as more significant for the task of similarity search in this paper.

The visual layout of the page is also very important aspect of web page content. The basic idea is that similar pages would also have a similar visual layout and structure. In [5], the visual similarity is deduced from frequencies of individual HTML tags. Here, the information about general web page's structure and layout is acquired in a form of tag frequency. This brings some interesting results, but it does not affect the order in which tags appear in pages. In the visual representation based approach proposed in [6], a tree representation of the HTML structure is used as the input to count web page similarity.

Another possibility to extract visual information of web pages is to use page segmentation methods. Segmentation is a process, which divides a web page into visual blocks that are separated from each other. Segmentation algorithms usually work in hierarchical manner. This means that in the beginning, a page is divided into a few blocks, which are divided furthermore into smaller ones (top-down); or a small pieces of a page are joined together to form the greater ones (bottom-up). Probably the most popular segmentation algorithm working in top-down manner is VIPS (Vision-based Page Segmentation) [7]. Another segmentation method, which works in bottom-up manner, is presented in [8].

The tree of visual blocks obtained by segmentation can also be used to determine the web page similarity. Some results of this approach and comparison of different segmentation methods are presented in [9].

As the results of above mentioned methods are not suitable, several proposed methods focus on the combination of the above mentioned approaches to represent the web page content. Such approaches typically try to combine the information about hyperlink structure and textual contents of web pages. One of these methods [10] creates a vector with information about text content and links with different weights. This is used as an input to cluster pages.

This paper presents a new method, which uses a representation of web page content, which is combination of text content and visual structure extraction. An approach regarding this combination has been described in [11]. The structural information is taken also from HTML tags. Tags are divided into several classes. A weight is set for each class, according to its importance.

In our paper, we use information obtained by web page segmentation instead of HTML tags, because of the fact that the formation of various web pages is different and the same information can be represented in different ways in HTML. To represent textual contents of a page in a form of weight vectors, we use the modified TF-IDF weights, which affect the visual blocks, in which the text terms appear. This technique has been used for web page classification and it has brought some improvement of classification accuracy [12].

3   Description of the Page Similarity Method

The proposed method uses two vectors to measure similarity. The first one is the vector of modified TF-IDF weights, which reflects the textual content of a page. The second one is the vector of visual properties obtained by the segmentation.

3.1   Method Overview

At first, it is necessary to perform web page rendering, which takes the page source code and returns its visual layout. Then, this visual layout is an input for web page segmentation. The output of the segmentation process is a set of visual blocks, each of which has a set of properties assigned. This includes its position on the page, some other visual properties and text contained in the block.

This is then used to perform visual block classification, which is used to assign a class for each visual block. Each class has different significance for the web page representation. The results are then used to compute the modified TF-IDF weights for text of all visual blocks from the whole web page.

If we are able to create these vectors for each page, it is possible to count the textual similarity of pages. Some visual properties taken from the results of web page segmentation process are used to count the visual similarity of pages. According to some experiments, a set of suitable properties has been chosen. These properties are stored in a form of the second vector called visual vector.

Finally, we can combine these two similarities into the aggregate web page similarity, which is the main result of our method.

3.2   Visual Block Clasification

The first step of the process is using of a web page rendering machine, which interprets an input document and shows its final form. This allows analyzing the visual properties of component blocks of a page and obtaining necessary information about them.

Information about visual blocks is obtained by a segmentation method that produces hierarchical structure of visual blocks. A visual block represents a rectangular region in the page that is visually separated from other parts of the page. Our segmentation algorithm presented in [8] works in a bottom-up manner.

The resultant tree of visual blocks is created recursively: if a block is visually separated, a new corresponding block is added to a tree. Then, the same is applied to the child boxes. After that, the blocks are clustered - we find all visual blocks that are placed in the adjoining cells and are not visually separated from each other. Such areas are joined into a single area. This step corresponds to the detection of content blocks (for example text paragraphs) that consist of several boxes. Finally, we look for areas that are not separated but they are delimited with the visually separated areas around. These blocks are also clustered.

For each detected visual block, we can determine its visual properties, which are then used for classification of the blocks as input attributes. These attributes include: text font size, dominating text weight and style, count of text/number characters, count of lower/upper case/space characters, average luminosity, background color, contrast of the text and position of visual block.

If we have this set of attributes obtained, we can use arbitrary classification method to perform visual blocks classification. Our experiments presented in [14] showed that the classification accuracy is above 90%. This can be a good foundation for further processing of this data. The best results have been achieved by decision tree based methods. Here is the list of classes assigned to visual blocks:

- Heading - The main heading and subheadings of a page.
- Main Text - The main text content.
- Links - Links to other related web pages, some of them may be irrelevant.
- Navigation - Link to other sections of the web site.
- Date/Authors - Information about date and authors of a page.
- Others - Other unimportant parts, such as advertisement, caption etc.

Textual Similarity Measuring. It is obvious that different classes of visual blocks have different significance for representation of page content. This is reflected by our weighting method.

In the beginning, the text information is stored for each visual block. After the visual block classification, a class for each block is known. Then we have to perform two standard preprocessing procedures for the text contents of all visual blocks - stop words removal and stemming. If we set a significance coefficient for each class, it could be reflected in the text term weighting.

This is ensured by modified TF-IDF weighting, description of which follows. Let us denote an input set of web documents as $D = \{d_1, ..., d_n\}$ and a set of terms $T = \{t_1, ..., t_m\}$, which appear in documents from the set D.

It is possible to divide each document into several visual blocks, each of which can be classified. Let us denote a vector of all class labels as $C = (c_1, ..., c_k)$. Each class label is evaluated by a coefficient according to its importance for representation of page contents. We can represent it as a vector of coefficients $V = (v_1, ..., v_k)$, where v_j is the coefficient of a class label c_j. The modified document frequency of a term $t \epsilon T$ in a document $d \epsilon D$ is defined as:

$$MTF(t, d) = \sum_{i=1}^{k} v_i * F(t, d, c_i) \qquad (1)$$

where $F(t, d, c_i)$ is a frequency of term t in all blocks with class label c_i in a document d. The MTF weight is obtained as a summarization of all weights for visual blocks, in which the term is present. This weight should be normalized, as it is usually done for the TF weight. Modified IDF weight is obtained as:

$$MIDF(t) = 1 + \log(\frac{n}{k_V}) \qquad (2)$$

where t is a term from the set of terms T, n is the count of all documents and k_V is the count of documents, in which content visual blocks at least once contain the term t. The resultant modified TF-IDF weight is obtained as a multiplication of modified TF and modified IDF weight.

This allows us to omit the non-content parts of a web page, if we set zero significance coefficients for respective class of visual blocks. We can mention "Navigation" as an example of a non-content block. On the other hand, "links" are considered as content block class with lower significance coefficient. A suitable setting of significance coefficients has been suggested in [12].

The textual similarity of two web documents represented as modified TF-IDF weight vectors can be computed by means of some similarity measure. We use the Cosine similarity, which is typically recommended for this purpose.

Visual Similarity Measuring. To represent visual layout and structure of a page, we use the results of the visual block classification. These results include information about position, visual properties and class of each individual visual block. This is used to create a vector of visual properties containing attributes that characterize overall layout of a page. Here is the list of properties used:

- Font size, font name and color of the main heading - the main heading is discovered as a block of class "Heading" with the highest font size.
- Font size, font name and color of the main text - dominating values among all blocks of the class "Main text".
- Top-left position of the main heading and the main text.
- Amount of main text and the heading text, both expressed as the count of all characters inside these blocks.
- Length of the main heading and the count of all headings placed on the page.
- Dominating color of the main text background.
- Co-ordinates of the bottom-right corner of the main text, obtained as maximum value of co-ordinates between all "Main text" blocks.
- Minimum and maximum positions of the "Links" blocks - co-ordinates of top-left and bottom-right links.

- Amount of links expressed as the count of characters, which occur in all blocks of the "Link" class.
- Amount of text (number of characters) on the whole page (including the non-content visual blocks) and number of digit characters on the whole page.
- Number of different background colors and text colors on the whole page, including all content and non-content blocks.
- The "height" of the page, expressed as the maximum horizontal co-ordinate of any visual block of the page.

Then, the vectors consisting of all these properties can be used to measure the visual similarity of web pages. We can use arbitrary distance metric for this purpose, for example the Cosine similarity mentioned above.

3.3 Aggregate Web Page Similarity Computation

In the next phase, we have to aggregate both similarities into one similarity measure reflecting both visual and textual properties of pages. If these two similarity values are comparable, it is straightforward - we have to count up those two values to obtain the aggregate similarity measure. But during experiments, it turned out that the differences between values of textual similarity are much smaller than between values of visual similarity. That's why the aggregate similarity was more reflected by the visual similarity value.

We have to adjust the influence of both similarities to the aggregate similarity. This is enforced by the different powers applied to these two measures. Therefore, the aggregate similarity of two different web pages is defined as:

$$Agg\_Sim = Text\_Sim^M * Vis\_Sim^N \qquad (3)$$

where Text_Sim and Vis_Sim are the textual and visual similarity values, M and N are the powers to be applied on them. The higher is the value of power; the lower is the influence of that value to the aggregate similarity value.

4   Results of Experiments

Experimental phase of our project consists of two parts. In the first one, we use a dataset of web pages coming from news web servers (CNN.com, usatoday.com, reuters.com, nytimes.com). This dataset contains approximately 500 web pages of various topics.

The second dataset is a small dataset of phishing pages taken from a Phish-Tank database. This experiment is only used to verify that our approach is applicable to discover this type of fraudulent web pages.

4.1 Experiments with News Web Pages

As mentioned above, this dataset comes from several news web sites and covers several topics. It is clear that this dataset is suitable to perform experiments regarding both textual and visual similarity.

Experiments of Textual Similarity. There are many topics of web pages in our dataset, but there is a subset of pages about specific topics, which are expected to form clusters. There is a set of pages about war in Libya, earthquake in Japan and NHL playoffs. In our experiment, we will test if these three groups will form clusters. Other pages should be significantly different from these ones.

Our modified weighting approach will be compared to a simple text extraction with classical TF-IDF weighting. Because some text on the web page is non-content, it is expected that our approach will bring some improvement.

This experiment will be evaluated as follows: as queries, we will specify documents from those three clusters mentioned above. The ideal result of this experiment would be a response of exactly those (approximately 20) documents from the same cluster. In Table 1, the values of precision and recall values are compared for each of three clusters separately.

Table 1. Textual Similarity Experiment Results

Cluster	$MTF-IDF$		$TF-IDF$	
	Precision	Recall	Precision	Recall
Cluster 1 - Earthquake in Japan	91.2%	90.0%	77.5%	68.0%
Cluster 2 - Libya war	88.2%	86.0%	73.5%	66.8%
Cluster 3 - NHL playoffs	84.8%	89.9%	62.2%	60.0%

As we can see from the table, modified weighting of text terms brings significantly better results in measuring textual similarity. This is primarily caused by ignoring text from the non-content blocks of pages, even though the visual block classification could produce a small number of mistakes. Slightly worse results for the third cluster are caused by some web pages about other kinds of sport, which have been determined as similar to those pages from cluster 3.

It is evident from these results that this representation without computing visual similarity could be used to measure web page similarity because of higher precision and recall values.

Experiments of Visual Similarity. In this experiment, we assume that pages from the same web site have also high visual similarity. This assumption could not be valid for some attributes reflecting amounts of text mentioned in Section 3.4. These attributes will be omitted in this experiment, although they are important in the general process of measuring the similarity of web pages.

Here we assume three clusters - cluster of pages from CNN.com, pages from usatoday.com and reuters.com. The results are shown in Table 2. From the table we can see that this computation cannot be used independently to detect similarity of web pages. But it is applicable as a supporting mean in combination with textual similarity. In addition, worse values of precision and recall are partially caused by much wider clusters of pages than in the first experiment. This experiment has been evaluated in the same way as the previous experiment.

Table 2. Visual Similarity Experiment Results

Cluster	Precision	Recall
Cluster 1 - CNN.com	84.4%	71.2%
Cluster 2 - usatoday.com	71.0%	69.4%
Cluster 3 - reuters.com	73.5%	70.4%

Experiments with Aggregate Similarity. In our manually created dataset, there are also some clusters which have the same topic, i.e. documents have high textual similarity and concurrently they are from the same web site.

The results presented in Table 3 show the results for three clusters having these properties. The way of evaluation is the same as in the previous two subsections. We can see that there are slightly better results than that achieved by the textual similarity measure. These results are measured, if the coefficients M and N from the formula (4) both have the value 1.

Table 3. Aggregate Similarity Experiment Results

Cluster	Precision	Recall
Cluster 1 - Japan, CNN	92.5%	90.6%
Cluster 2 - Libya, Reuters	90.5%	84.3%
Cluster 3 - NHL, usatoday	89.6%	93.4%

4.2 Experiment with Phishing Web Pages

We have made only a small experiment with phishing pages. It is clear that text and visual layout of phishing page and original page should be very similar. The only objective of this experiment is to prove that our similarity measure will reach significantly higher values for pairs of phishing and original pages than for other pairs of pages used to login into some internet banking applications. The values of both textual and visual similarity between the original and phishing login page have been significantly higher (close to 1.0) than both similarities for two different pages.

5   Conclusion and Future Works

In this paper, we have presented a new way to measure similarity of web pages. The main idea is to compute textual and visual similarity of pages separately and then to join them into the aggregate similarity reflecting both similarities. To compute textual similarity, we use the modified text term weighting, which reflects the blocks, in which the text appears. Visual similarity is obtained by means of vectors of visual attributes. These attributes are obtained with use of rendering machine and web page segmentation algorithm.

In our future works, we are going to use web page representations proposed here to perform other web mining tasks. Another possibility is to extend our representation with hyperlink information.

We are also going to find some optimal settings for our method. This includes settings of coefficients M and N, which should be different for various types of pages and selection of suitable similarity measure for both similarities mentioned.

Finally, it may be convenient to find some better representation of visual layout, because the representation proposed here can be used only as a supporting mean, but not as an independent measure of similarity.

References

1. Halkidi, M., Nguyen, B., Varlamis, I., Vazirigiannis, M.: Thesus: Organizing web document collections based on link semantics. VLDB Journal 12(4), 320–332 (2003)
2. Dean, J., Henzinger, M.: Finding related pages in the World Wide Web. In: Proceedings of the 8th WWW Conference, Toronto, Canada, pp. 1467–1479 (1999)
3. Salton, G., Buckley, C.: Term weighting approaches in automatic text retrieval. Information Processing and Management 24, 513–523 (1998)
4. Sannella, M.J.: Constraint Satisfaction and Debugging for Interactive User Interfaces. PhD. Thesis. UMI Order No. GAX95-09398, University of Washington (1994)
5. Cruz, I.F., Borisov, S., Marks, M.A., Webb, T.R.: Measuring structural similarity among web documents: preliminary results. In: Proceedings of the 7th International Conference on Electronic Publishing, pp. 513–524. ICCC Press, Washington D.C. (1998)
6. Joshi, S., Agrawal, N., Krishnapuram, R., Negi, S.: A bag of paths model for measuring structural similarity in web documents. In: Proceedings of the 9th ACM SIGKDD Conference, pp. 577–582. ACM, Washington D.C (2003)
7. Cai, D., Yu, S., Wen, J.-R., Ma, W.-Y.: VIPS: a Vision-based Page Segmentation Algorithm. Technical Report MSR-TR-2003-79, Microsoft (2004)
8. Burget, R.: Automatic Document Structure Detection for Data Integration. In: Abramowicz, W. (ed.) BIS 2007. LNCS, vol. 4439, pp. 391–397. Springer, Heidelberg (2007)
9. Cai, D., Yu, S., Wen, J.-R., Ma, W.-Y.: Block-based Web Search. In: The 27th Annual International ACM SIGIR Conference on Information Retrieval, pp. 440–447. ACM, Sheffield (2004)
10. Modha, D.S., Spangler, W.S.: Clustering hypertext with applications to web searching. In: Proceedings of the 11th ACM Conference on Hypertext and Hypermedia, pp. 143–152. ACM, San Antonio (2000)
11. Cutler, M., Deng, H., Maniccam, S.S., Meng, W.: A new study on using html structures to improve retrieval. In: Proceedings of the 11th IEEE International Conference on Tools with Artificial Intelligence, pp. 406–409. IEEE, Chicago (1999)
12. Bartik, V.: Text-Based Web Page Classification with Use of Visual Information. In: International Symposium on Open Source Intelligence & Web Mining. IEEE, Odense (2010)

New Specifics for a Hierarchial Estimator Meta-algorithm

Stanisław Brodowski[1] and Andrzej Bielecki[2]

[1] Faculty of Physics, Astronomy and Applied Computer Science,
Jagiellonian University, Krakow, Poland
stanislaw.brodowski@uj.edu.pl
[2] Institute of Computer Science, Faculty of Mathematics and Computer Science,
Jagiellonian University, Krakow, Poland
andrzej.bielecki@ii.uj.edu.pl

Abstract. Hierarchical Estimator is a meta-algorithm presented in [1] concerned with learning a nonlinear relation between two vector variables from training data, which is one of the core tasks of machine learning, primarily for the purpose of prediction. It arranges many simple function approximators into a tree-like structure in order to achieve a solution with a low error.

This paper presents a new version of specifics for that meta-algorithm – a so called training set division and a competence function creation method. The included experimental results show improvement over the methods described in [1]. A short recollection of Hierarchical Estimator is also included.

Keywords: machine learning, function approximation, hierarchical, estimator.

1 Introduction

Hierarchical Estimator [1,2], a machine learning solution that this article relates to, is concerned with learning a possibly complicated, nonlinear relation (function) f

$$Y = f(X) + \varepsilon, \qquad (1)$$

where Y and X are variables with values, respectively, in $\mathcal{Y} \subset \mathbb{R}^r$ and $\mathcal{X} \subset \mathbb{R}^p$, ε is an error function with certain properties (e.g. 0 expected value). This learning is based on a training set of pairs (input, output) $T = \{(x^{(k)}, y^{(k)}), k \in \{1 \ldots |T|\}, \forall k : x^{(k)} \in \mathcal{X}, y^{(k)} \in \mathcal{Y}\}$. The primary goal is to be able to predict values of Y with acceptable errors for values of X not present in the training set. As in some other methods, it is done by approximating the relation on the training set, so *generalization* (good performance on unseen data) and avoiding *overfitting* (much worse performance on unseen data than on the training set) are core questions [3,4].

L. Rutkowski et al. (Eds.): ICAISC 2012, Part II, LNCS 7268, pp. 22–29, 2012.
© Springer-Verlag Berlin Heidelberg 2012

Related techniques. The scope of methods employed to solving the general problem described above is quite broad including many statistical methods [5,3], artificial neural networks [3,6,4,7], fuzzy systems [8], decision trees [9]. Because Hierarchical Estimator [1,2] tries to combine many simpler solutions into one more accurate, it is related to boosting [3,10,11] (e.g. AdaBoost), a notion of weak learn ability [12], committees [13]. As it arranges such simple solutions into a tree and divides the problem into subproblems, it bears some resemblance to Hierarchical Mixture of Experts with a creation algorithm [14,15] and to regression trees like M5 [9]. It shares previously mentioned properties, as well as other basic premises like using outputs and errors of existing parts to aid further construction and overlapping subproblems, also with Hierarchical Classifier [16] (HC), but since the concept of a class is crucial for HC, the differences are significant.

2   Hierarchical Estimator

This section describes Hierarchical Estimator directly after [1,2], with the nearly identical notation.

2.1   Basic Definitions

Hierarchical Estimator, on the most abstract level, is a function $HE : \mathcal{X} \longrightarrow \mathcal{Y}$, based on a tree structure constructed during learning (see 2.2).

The index set of the nodes of that tree is denoted I and the number of children (possibly 0) of the tree node with index i (called shortly " node i") – $N(i)$. $P : I \times \mathbb{N} \to I$ is the function that returns the global node index of a child based on the parent's index and that child number, i.e., $P(i,j)$ gives the index of the j-th child of node i.

Two functions are assigned to each node existing in the tree [1,2]:

1. A function estimator (approximator) $g_i : \mathcal{X} \longrightarrow \mathcal{Y}$ constructed to solve some subproblem of the original problem. In [1] feed forward neural networks with the low number of hidden neurons are used.
2. *Competence function* $C_i : \{0, \ldots, N(i)\} \times \mathcal{X} \longrightarrow [0, 1]$ used as the weight function when combining the results of certain nodes, see Eq. (2).

Definition 1 (Hierarchical Estimator node response). *For node i in the trained estimator, on input vector x, the response is obtained in the following recursive manner [1]:*

$$\widetilde{g}_i(x) = \sum_{j=1}^{N(i)} \widetilde{g}_{P(i,j)}(x) \cdot C_i(j,x) + C_i(0,x) \cdot g_i(x) \ , \quad \textit{where} \ \sum_{j=0}^{N(i)} C_i(j,x) = 1 \ . \ (2)$$

Definition 2 (Hierarchical Estimator response). *The response of the whole solution is the response of the root (node "r") of the tree, achieved using the above formula:* $HE(x) = \widetilde{g}_r(x)$.

Of course, in a leaf, $C_i(0, x) = 1$ and $\widetilde{g}_i(x) = g_i(x)$.

The definition of the response in [1,2] is usually conveniently compacted by replacing $g_i(x)$ with a result of a "virtual" zeroth child $\widetilde{g}_{P(i,0)}$:

$$\widetilde{g}_i(x) = \sum_{j=0}^{N(i)} \widetilde{g}_{P(i,j)}(x) \cdot C_i(j, x) \ .$$

An example being evaluated during work or testing is first propagated down the tree starting from the root. At each node, weights are proposed for each child and only the branches that were assigned non-zero competence for *this* example are used. The propagation locally stops if it reaches a node where only the estimator in the given node has non-zero competence ($C_i(0, x) = 1$), usually it is the leaf. Typically, the example is not propagated through the whole tree, but only certain paths and branches. Finally, responses of the nodes are returned up the tree and combined using Eq.(2).

Because function C generally depends on the example being evaluated, Hierarchical Estimator is not a linear combination of the estimators in the nodes even though each response of the root is a linear combination of responses of certain estimators in the tree.

Below, two definitions from [1] and [2], very useful for discussing Hierarchical Estimator, are cited:

Definition 3 (Competence area). *A competence area of a node is the set of all feature vectors that a given node may possibly be required to evaluate.*

Definition 4 (Competence set). *A competence set contains all examples from a given set (also if that set is only known from the context of discussion) that fall into the competence area of the node.*

An example belongs to the competence set or competence area of a node if the node is the root and it is a valid feature vector, or if the competence function in the parent node assigns this node and this vector a non-zero value. In the latter case such a set is denoted $\mathcal{S}_{P(i,j)} = \{(x^{(k)}, y^{(k)}) | (x^{(k)}, y^{(k)}) \in \mathcal{S} \land C_i(j, x^{(k)}) > 0\}$ (for a *jth* child of node i). This applies also to "virtual" child 0.

2.2   Training

The exact structure of Hierarchical Estimator varies between tasks and is found by learning from examples. Apart from learning data, the algorithm takes two basic parameters, concerned with the accuracy vs. learning time tradeoff. The main parameter is the error rate to achieve on a learning set in any given partial estimator, the second is tied to the maximum complexity of the tree – simply the maximum allowable tree depth in current versions.

The generic learning algorithm on a training set T is [1,2]:

1. Create a root and assign T as its training set. The root becomes the processed node.
2. Build a function estimator in the processed node (called also node i). In [1] simple feed-forward neural networks with the severely restricted number of hidden neurons were used. The exact way of creating those networks can also be found in [1].

3. Compute an error measure, e.g. a mean absolute error $|E|(\mathcal{S}_i, g_i)$ for the processed node and its competence set (which is often not identical to training set T_i). If it is smaller than the main parameter or this node causes the tree to meet the maximum complexity condition set in the second parameter, then the algorithm ends for this node. If that error is greater than both: the parameter and the error of its parent *on the same set*, the algorithm is stopped, but the node we are processing is also deleted. Instead of instantly deleting, the algorithm may be set to retrain the estimator and delete the node only if its error is still greater.

4. Build
   (a) Training sets for the children nodes $\{T_{P(i,1)} \ldots T_{P(i,N(i))}\}$ (exact $N(i)$ is not preset, but also to be found).
   (b) Competence function C_i.
   These tasks are closely related, and usually performed together.

5. Run this algorithm for the children of the given node from point 2.

This is a meta-algorithm, because two important steps must be yet described in detail. One is the creation of training sets for children and a competence function. It is possibly the most important step and it is the focus of this paper. The second is the creation of function estimators in nodes. Several detailed versions of both steps were presented in [1].

3   Training Set Division and Competence Function

In both [1] and [2] some theorems about Hierarchical Estimator were proven. Their interpretations and conclusions concerning the task of creating training sets and a competence function can be summarized as:

1. For each example, responses of more than one node should be taken into account.
2. The decrease of the error is greater if the responses of nodes used for a given example differ significantly from each another. One way to increase such difference is to make training sets for child nodes differ.
3. Competence areas and training sets for children should be made easier to learn by making them less diverse i.e., the examples within one such area or set should be in some way similar to each another.

The versions of the solution for this task described in [1] were based primarily on the responses of the estimator in the node and its errors. As goals 2 and 3 are similar to those of clustering with overlapping groups or fuzzy clustering (e.g. Fuzzy C-Means), those techniques were widely used.

3.1   A New Method

In this paper a new method of constructing training sets and a competence function is proposed. It stems from the intermediate goals mentioned above and its base is similar to the technique called "association matrix" in [1] but it includes serious enhancements as well.

The general algorithm is as follows:

1. Cluster the outputs of the estimator in a given node (g_i) achieved on its competence set with fuzzy clustering. Let co_j represent a membership function of the $j-th$ cluster. Apply thresholding (based on the rule of thumb that, on average, about two children nodes should be selected for each example, see [1]) and normalize (to obtain sum of 1) the membership functions. Let the transformed function of the $j-th$ cluster be called $\overline{co}_j$.

2. Apply the analogical procedure to the true output values from the training set of this node. Let ct_j and $\overline{ct}_j$ be functions analogical to co_j and $\overline{co}_j$, respectively.

3. For each cluster k in estimator outputs do:
   (a) Sort clusters in true values with respect to their centroid distances to the centroid of cluster k.
   (b) Initialize a competence set for k-kth child as samples with $\overline{co}_k > 0$.
   (c) For each cluster j in true values, in order from the closest to the farthest, do:
      i. Check if adding cluster j would cause the training set to be over 95% of the parent set. If yes, stop this loop.
      ii. Calculate function $H = \dfrac{a}{n_k} \cdot \sqrt{\dfrac{s}{n}} + \dfrac{(E_{ik} - a)}{n_k} \cdot \left(\dfrac{n}{s}\right)^2$, where E_{ik} is the error of the parent estimator on examples with $\overline{co}_k > 0$, n and n_k are the numbers of samples in the parent training set and with $\overline{co}_k > 0$, respectively, a is the sum of the parent estimator errors on examples with $\overline{ct}_l > 0$ for all such l that cluster l has been added to the training set (including cluster j), s is the size of the current training set, including cluster j. Dynamical programming can reduce the amount of computation for this step.
      iii. If H has decreased since last cycle (or this is the first cycle), add cluster j to the training set of child k, else stop the innermost loop.
   (d) Check if the value calculated analogically to that from 3(c)ii for any cluster m other than k is less than, corresponding, $E_{im}/2$. If yes, add them to the competence area of the k-th child.

The competence function for the k-th child and a given example x is quite simple: $\max(\overline{co}(x)_j)$ of all clusters j that were included to competence of the k-th child (k-th cluster and possibly others added in pt. 3d of the algorithm).

Ad 1. Preliminary tests showed that the cluster number should be rather low for better generalization and shorter training time. In experiments below, Fuzzy C-means [17] was used with the automatic cluster number selection procedure described in [18]. The range of possible cluster numbers was narrow (three adjacent numbers) to speed up the calculations. Because in all presented experiments the output was just a real value, the range of the cluster numbers began at span of values divided by "large error" which, for the number of samples m, was the $\lfloor ln(m) \rfloor$-th largest error.

Ad 2. Here the number of clusters should be much higher (for shorter training times) and high accuracy is not needed. "Crisp" clustering can be applied. It serves mostly to provide some broader learning "context". The rationale behind this is that if we include some example into a training set of a child, we usually should also include examples with very similar desired outputs for better generalization. It also decreases amount of computation needed in other steps. A fast and inaccurate clustering algorithm based on Dignet [19] and described in [20] was applied here with a cluster width parameter set to the target error.

As for the function H from 3(c)ii, it can be seen as a very rough guess of a child node error. The terms involving the number of samples correspond to two assumptions. First, that the reduced set should be easier to learn, and the children errors lower. Second, that on samples still present in the competence area but without a given appropriate "context" (see above), errors can be much higher. Therefore maximizing a – including every cluster in true outputs that has any common example with the processed cluster in estimator outputs – is usually a good strategy, unless it would demand a drastic increase in the size of the training set. The exact formula was chosen mainly due to simplicity and proper border behavior.

4   Experiments

The experiments were done using the identical method and data as in [1].

Datasets. Three data sets were used. Two of them were rather small and simple: *housing* and *auto-mpg* freely available from [21]. They have, respectively, 506 instances for 13 attributes and 393 instances for 8 attributes (after removing missing values). The third represents a larger problem – predicting a power load in the country-wide power grid for 168 hours in future based on the current load and temperature, some historical load and temperature data and data about time of the week, day, holidays etc. It has 26115 instances and 22 attributes. All data were normalized to fit the preset interval ([0..1] or [-1..1] for some attributes), the exact description can be found in [1].

Testing method. The performance on simple data sets (*housing* and *auto-mpg*) was tested with 10-fold cross-validation. The whole cycle was repeated 10 times yielding 100 learning-test cycles. For the power load, the solution was trained on first three years of available data, and tested on remaining examples (from over a year). The whole procedure was repeated 5 times. The errors (including relative ones) were calculated after decoding the output.

The error measures used are:

1. $|E|$ – the mean absolute error: $\frac{1}{|T|} \sum_{k=1}^{|T|} |HE(x^{(k)}) - y^{(k)}|$, where T is the test set and $|T|$ is the number of its examples.

2. $MAPE$ – the mean absolute percentage error: $\frac{1}{|T|} \sum_{k=1}^{|T|} \left| \frac{HE(x^{(k)}) - y^{(k)}}{y^{(k)}} \right|$.

3. APE_{max} – the maximum absolute percentage error.

Prefix *max* means that a value is the maximum on 10 (or 5 in the case of power load prediction) main cycles, prefix *avg*, that this is a mean.

Estimators used. Estimators in tests used the competence and training set division function described in this article. Simple neural networks were used as estimators in the nodes, having up to 5 hidden neurons (the calculation of the exact number is built into the solution, see [1]) and learned with the Levenberg-Marquardt algorithm for 100 turns. If the child estimator performed worse than its parent, it was retrained twice (for smaller data sets) or once (for a power load, to reduce learning time). The stop condition was set to 0.013 for a power load and 0.03 for other data sets and the maximum level of the tree was set to 4 (exactly as in [1]).

Results. The results on the testing part of the data are in Table 1.

Table 1. Errors on test sets

dataset	$avg|E|$	$avgMAPE$	$maxMAPE$	$avgAPE_{max}$	$maxAPE_{max}$
Power load	288	1.83%	1.86%	23.8%	24.6%
housing	2.18	11.1%	11.7%	151%	371%
auto-mpg	1.98	8.51%	8.57%	44.2%	54.0%

5   Conclusion

The version of a hierarchical estimator described in this paper has a lower error on the power load data set than any of the versions found in [1]. The lowest error reported in [1] was 1.88% of $avgMAPE$, 1.91% of $maxMAPE$, 23.9% of $avgAPE_{max}$ and 25.2 % of $maxAPE_{max}$. What is more, the version that achieved such error did much worse than the current one on simple data sets (2.45 of $avg|E|$ on *housing* and 2.33 for *auto-mpg*) so the improvement over that technique is significant. Two out of six estimators described in [1] achieved better results for simple data sets (2.08 to 2.11 of $avg|E|$ for *housing* and 1.93 to 1.94 for *auto-mpg*), but their errors on the power load data set were higher: 2.19% to 2.20% of $avgMAPE$, so neither of them could be described as better than the current one. The advantage of the method described in this article on the power load data set is relatively greater that its disadvantage on simple data sets and as the power load data set represents a bigger and perhaps more important problem, therefore, for other tasks, we would recommend using the training set split and competence function creation method introduced in this article in place of any method introduced earlier.

The search for new and better ways of dividing training set and competence areas among children is still a main task in developing Hierarchical Estimator. It might be the case that the easiest way for doing that would be to improve the rough guess of the error used in this paper, although partially due to the characteristics of Neural Networks and partially due the nature of the learning task itself, it could be extremely hard to find a significantly more accurate one. If so, decreasing the dependence on such guesses (even if the current dependence is not overwhelming) would be desirable.

References

1. Brodowski, S., Podolak, I.T.: Hierarchical estimator. Expert Systems with Applications 38(10), 12237–12248 (2011)
2. Brodowski, S.: On mean squared error of hierarchical estimator. Schedae Informaticae 20 (2011) (accepted)
3. Hastie, T., Tibshirani, R., Friedman, J.: The Elements of Statistical Learning, 2nd edn. Springer, New York (2009)
4. Haykin, S.: Neural networks, a comprehensive foundation., 3rd edn. Prentice Hall (2009)
5. Russell, S.J., Norvig, P.: Artificial Intelligence: A Modern Approach (2002)
6. Hand, D., Mannila, H., Smyth, P.: Principles of Data Mining. MIT Press (2001)
7. Riedmiller, M., Braun, H.: Rprop - a fast adaptive learning algorithm. In: Proceedings of the International Symposium on Computer and Information Science VII (1992)
8. Bezdek, J.C., Keller, J.M., Krishnapuram, R., Pal, N.R.: Fuzzy Models and Algorithms for Pattern Recognition and Image Processing. Springer (1999)
9. Quinlan, J.R.: Learning with continuous classes. In: Proceedings of the 5th Australian Conference on Artificial Intelligence, AI 1992, pp. 343–348. World Scientific (1992)
10. Freund, Y., Schapire, R.: A decision theoretic generalization of online learning and an application to boosting. Journal of Computer and System Sciences 55, 119–139 (1997)
11. Bartlett, P.L., Traskin, M.: Adaboost is consistent. Journal of Machine Learning Research 8, 2347–2368 (2007)
12. Schapire, R.E.: The strength of weak learnability. Machine Learning 5(2), 197–227 (1990)
13. Tresp, V.: Committee machines. In: Hu, Y.H., Hwang, J.N. (eds.) Handbook for Neural Network Signal Processing. CRC Press (2001)
14. Jordan, M.I., Jacobs, R.A.: Hierarchical mixtures of experts and the em algorithm. Neural Computation, 181–214 (1994)
15. Saito, K., Nakano, R.: A constructive learning algorithm for an hme. In: IEEE International Conference on Neural Networks, vol. 3, pp. 1268–1273 (1996)
16. Podolak, I.T.: Hierarchical classifier with overlapping class groups. Expert Systems with Applications 34(1), 673–682 (2008)
17. Pal, N., Bezdek, J.: On cluster validity for the fuzzy c-means model. IEEE Transactions on Fuzzy Systems 3(3), 370–379 (1995)
18. Brodowski, S.: A Validity Criterion for Fuzzy Clustering. In: Jedrzejowicz, P., Nguyen, N.T., Hoang, K. (eds.) ICCCI 2011, Part I. LNCS (LNAI), vol. 6922, pp. 113–122. Springer, Heidelberg (2011)
19. Wann, C.-D., Thomopoulos, S.C.A.: A comparative study of self-organizing clustering algorithms dignet and art2. Neural Networks 10(4), 737–753 (1997)
20. Brodowski, S.: Adaptujący się hierarchiczny aproksymator, MSc thesis (2007) (in polish)
21. Asuncion, A., Newman, D.: UCI machine learning repository (2007)

Fast Plagiarism Detection by Sentence Hashing

Dariusz Ceglarek[1] and Konstanty Haniewicz[2]

[1] Poznan School of Banking, Poland
`dariusz.ceglarek@wsb.poznan.pl`
[2] Poznan University of Economics, Poland
`konstanty.haniewicz@ue.poznan.pl`

Abstract. This work presents a Sentence Hashing Algorithm for Plagiarism Detection - SHAPD. To present a user with the best results the algorithm makes use of special trait of the written texts - their natural sentence fragmentation, later employing a set of special techniques for text representation. Results obtained demonstrate that the algorithm delivers solution faster than the alternatives. Its algorithmic complexity is logarithmic, thus its performance is better than most algorithms using dynamic programming used to find the longest common subsequence.

Keywords: plagiarism, plagiarism detection, longest common subsequence, semantic compression, SEIPro2S.

1 Introduction

This work presents the results of the ongoing research on a Semantically Enhanced Intellectual Property Protection System [4]. Throughout research activities, a need of a new algorithm that can boost the overall performance of the system arose.

Previous efforts were accomplished by building the system characterised with a high level of satisfaction with the quality of results. It was possible thanks to employment of semantic compression (please refer to [5] and [6]). The semantic compression enabled the system to discover similar thoughts encoded in different wording, thus enabling it to highlight passages of text that borrowed from the original document with considerable amount of altered yet unoriginal content.

The main challenge with available solution was time efficiency. The number of operations and its level of complexity prevented authors from offering the solution in a online form on available computing platform due to the considerably large number of documents that have to be processed in order to present a viable plagiarism report. This directly created a need for a new algorithm that could deliver results faster.

The outlined need is catered for by the presented algorithm that allows for text processing up to 40 times faster for long texts than its predecessor and available alternatives. In general, algorithm runs in approximately linear time on the experimental corpus of documents (Reuter's corpus was used). The algorithm has some traits in common with the revised version of Smith-Waterman algorithm [7]. The most important are those that allow for not loosing information

L. Rutkowski et al. (Eds.): ICAISC 2012, Part II, LNCS 7268, pp. 30–37, 2012.
© Springer-Verlag Berlin Heidelberg 2012

on long common sequences where some minor inclusions are present and a word order is not preserved. As to be found in previously cited work [7] and previous publications of authors [4], such an algorithm as presented here has a number of applications. First and foremost, the core interest of a longest common subsequence matching in text processing is fighting plagiarism. It is essential task in times, where access to information is nearly unrestricted and culture for sharing without attribution is a recognized problem (see [11] and [10]).

The presented algorithm is an important example of a case when a task of matching the longest common subsequence has a time complexity lower than $O(n * m)$. The question whether it is possible was stated first by Knuth in [1]. First affirmative answer was given in [3] with time complexity $O((m * n)/ log(n))$ for case when $m < n$ and they pertain to a limited sequence. Another special case with an affirmative answer was given in [2] with time complexity of $O((n + m) * log(n + m))$.

This paper is organized as follows. Following introduction, a discussion on the method used to transform input text is introduced. Later on, an algorithm based on this description is introduced with addition of pseudo code and example. It is followed by a section on the algorithm performance and comparison with alternatives.

2   Sentence Hashing

The core advantage of the discussed algorithm stems from the application of hashing technique to sentences of processed document.

First of all, every document is seen as a number of sentences separated by a full stop. While processing text, there is a number of mechanisms that take care for the acronym detection or decimal points in numbers (for more details please consult [8]). This is important as many techniques start with normalization of the text. The performance of algorithm is affected very slightly by not normalizing input data in general, and saving the sentence structure is crucial to its success. Similar strategy, underlining the value of a sentence for automatic text summarisation was presented by [9]. Of course, a text can contain a number of unstructured text passages such as enumerations and lists. Therefore, a notion of frame makes it possible to manage a situation where a natural full stop at the end of sentence is not available.

Second, a length of hash frame is chosen for the whole system. Hash frame is constructed of a number of subsequent terms obtained from the processed document. The length of this frame is very important, as it's in direct relation with algorithm performance. This frame steers the production of consequent hashes. It shall not be too short as the bookkeeping costs will overwhelm the positive aspects of hashing in the later phases of algorithm, yet it shall not be too long as it effectiveness of search for a longest common sequence drops drastically.

Hashing procedure is driven by two parameters: α and β. When processing text, a sequence of terms is treated as a single text frame to be hashed when its total length is less than the value of parameter α, otherwise the sequence is divided into a number of text frames which length is β. Whether a result of division has a reminder (which length is less than the value of α) it is processed according to the first part of the rule.

Every term in frame is mapped onto some unique term, then a value for given frame is computed as a sum of numbers representing given terms. Therefore, it makes the procedure resilient to word order of the captured terms which is of great value in plagiarism detection tasks. Whole text is processed in order to come up with a sequence of numbers representing a document.

Consider following example with parameters α and β set to 9 and 1.5. The values should be interpreted as such that a sentence up to 13 words long is treated as a single text frame ($\alpha * \beta$) and those longer than this value are partitioned in frames 9 terms long.

Table 1. Example

On Tuesday Huntsman Corporation informed that it had revoked a bid worth \$460 million for Rexene Corp. due to double rejection of its bids by the chemical company from Dallas.
On → 742 Tuesday → 110226 Huntsman → 289972 Corporation → 88818 informed → 57582 that → 66940 it → 956 had → 7532 revoked → 81758 a → 97
Frame hash: 704623
bid → 7212 worth → 161187 \$460 → 22240 million → 33767 for → 7530 Rexene → 38381 Corp → 42432 due → 7437 to → 1039 double → 276024
Frame hash: 597249
rejection → 169746 of → 990 its → 7763 bids → 57811 by → 905 the → 8357 chemical → 337263 company → 354349 from → 60517 Dallas → 340253
Frame hash: 1337954

3   The Core Algorithm

The hashing procedure described in the previous section is the necessary step in the algorithm as it enables for tremendous savings when comparing two documents.

To present fully the idea, lets assume that the general task is to compare a document (to be referred as **D**) which is suspected to contain a number of phrases copied without attribution from external sources with a set Δ of n documents (where any given member document $\delta_i \in \Delta, i = 1, ..., n$) obtained from document repository. The algorithm to achieve it is twofold.

First of all, for every δ_i there is a file with consequently hashed text frames. To advance to the next step, document **D** must undergo described procedure of text frame hashing. As a result a associative array **T** is built where every key denotes a hash of a text frame and value associated is a tuple filled with the following entries: frame number, local maxima and continuity maxima.

$$T = \begin{pmatrix} t_1 \rightarrow \langle n, m_l, m_c \rangle \\ t_2 \rightarrow \langle n, m_l, m_c \rangle \\ \vdots \\ t_n \rightarrow \langle n, m_l, m_c \rangle \end{pmatrix}$$

Associative array **T** is loaded to the memory once for all tests, the only process that is repeated is the zeroing values of the values for all the keys between checks of document **D** with subsequent members of the Δ set.

First phase concludes in loading subsequent hash values for document **D**, where n is filled with a frame number and local maxima and continuity maxima are set to 0. A description in pseudocode is given in algorithm 1.

Second, matching of common subsequences commences. Sequences of hashes from documents forming the Δ set are compared with sequences from the document **D**. Document **D** has to have its associative array T_i zeroed for both maxima. Document δ_i is compared by taking subsequent hashes $\delta_i t_j$ (where i identifies document in set Δ and j identifies a hash key in its associative array). Whether $\delta_i t_j$ exists in Dt_j, then a values from matching hash are updated in **D** according to the following rules.

When value representing local minimum ($Dt_j \rightarrow m_l$ for a key matched from document δ_i is equal to zero, it means that a beginning of a common sequence has been just detected. Therefore, $Dt_j \rightarrow n$ is updated to the number of matching frame from document δ_i and $Dt_j \rightarrow m_l = 1$, $Dt_j \rightarrow m_c = 1$.

When $Dt_j \rightarrow m_l$ is nonzero and $Dt_j \rightarrow n$ equals $i - 1$, this means that compared hash of a text frame was preceded by a previously matched hash of a text frame in both **D** and D_i. Hence, a continuation of same text was found. $Dt_j \rightarrow n$ and $Dt_j \rightarrow m_l$ are incremented each by one. Weather $Dt_j \rightarrow m_l$ is greater then $Dt_j \rightarrow m_c$, $Dt_j \rightarrow m_c$ is incremented by one, as the longest common subsequence has just been found to be one frame longer.

If $Dt_j \rightarrow n$ is not equal $i - 1$, it means that the ongoing match was disrupted, so $Dt_j \rightarrow m_l$ has to be decreased by one and $Dt_j \rightarrow n$ must be updated to the number of matching frame from δ_i. Depending on the value of $Dt_j \rightarrow m_l$ being greater then zero, one is still awaiting for continuation of the matching sequence. Otherwise, a value of $Dt_j \rightarrow m_c$ is the number informing of the longest match for a sequence.

Having examined document δ_i, one can examine associative array **T** row by row in order to come up with the highest values of $Dt_j \rightarrow m_c$. A description in pseudocode is given in algorithm 2, for exemplary documents, please refer to table 2 for document **D** and table 3 for document δ_i.

Table 2. Exemplary document **D**

692254	Huntsman's first bid of $14 per share was rejected by Rexene on July
85790	Rexene on July 22
574311	It then sweetened the offer to $15 per share on Aug
405972	Rexene rejected that bid as well
828756	The unsolicited bid also included the assumption of $175 million of debt
902783	Rexene did not have any immediate comment on Huntsman's decision
1670207	But Rexene's stock, which had risen sharply after Huntsman first launched its bid

Table 3. Exemplary document δ_i, first hash of a common frame is underlined

704623	On Tuesday Huntsman Corporation informed that it had revoked a	
597249	bid worth \$460 million for Rexene Corp. due to double	
1337954	rejection of its bids by the chemical company from Dallas	
692254	Huntsman's first bid of \$14 per share was rejected by	$m_l = 1, m_c = 1$
85790	Rexene on July 22	$m_l = 2, m_c = 2$
574311	It then sweetened the offer to \$15 per share on Aug	$m_l = 3, m_c = 3$
405972	Rexene rejected that bid as well	$m_l = 4, m_c = 4$
828756	The unsolicited bid also included the assumption of \$175 million of debt	$m_l = 5, m_c = 5$
1005759	The announcement from Huntsman was delivered after the closing of the market.	$m_l = 4, m_c = 5$

4   Experiments

In order to measure efficiency of described algorithm an implementation was prepared of both the algorithm and revised version of Smith-Waterman algorithm (as described in [7]). Table 4 summarizes the performance comparison of both algorithms. It is easy to observe that performance of the presented algorithm beats benchmarked algorithm. This is possible by the fact that SHAPD complexity is a logarithmic one, while S&W variations and extensions are approximately quadratic. Accuracy and completeness of the described algorithm is 100%. English was the language of all the documents.

Data gathered describe performance of both algorithms in two cases. First case, covers a long article whose length expressed in words was 412. Second one is for a long article of 3255 words. Each run of the test covered a comparison of one of the three given documents with a corpus of 1000 documents whose length was incrementally augmented from 1000 bytes to 6000 bytes (1000 bytes is on the average 232 words).

Table 4. Results on experiment benchmarking Smith-Waterman algorithm and Sentence Hashing Algorithm for Plagiarism Detection - (SHAPD). The detailed description of content is given in the beginning of the experiment section. Number of bytes is expressed for every batch of 1000 documents taken from the Reuter's corpus. Time is expressed in milliseconds.

Number of bytes p. doc.	1 000	2 000	3 000	4 000	5 000	6 000
Document - 412 words						
SHAPD	2 940.00	6 238.36	9 989.58	13 121.75	16 552.54	21 724.30
S&W	7 560.01	16 129.92	23 417.34	34 633.56	42 754.44	54 805.13
DIFF.	2.57	2.59	2.42	2.64	2.58	2.52
Document - 3255 words						
SHAPD	2 667.15	6 039.34	9 554.21	12 802.04	16 424.06	19 784.12
S&W	45 257.59	91 033.21	141 361.62	191 598.61	228 094.09	283 437.67
DIFF.	16.97	15.07	14.80	14.97	13.89	14.33

Of interest to the ongoing research is the optimal length of text frame depending on the language of document and its domain. It is believed that the number used in experiments can vary and additional research must be performed in order to present the conclusions. Results of experiments are outlined in the visualisation available in figure 1, calculated parameters for $\alpha = 9$ and $\beta = 2.25$.

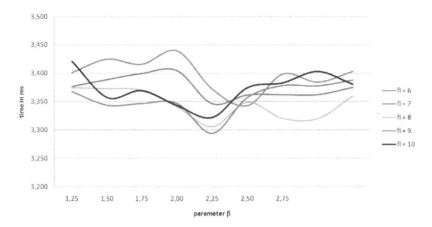

Fig. 1. Results of experiments on frame length. The best results for English measured on the Reuter's corpus are when parameter α is set to 9 (the length of a frame) and parameter β is set to 2.25.

Algorithm 1. Phase one of the algorithm: Sentence hashing

```
for all Sentence ∈ Document do
    //l - number of words in Sentence
    if l > α * β then
        k = 0, h = 0
        for all Word ∈ Sentence do
            h = h + Hash(w)
            if k > α then
                write(h), k = 0, h = 0
            end if
        end for
        if k > 0 then
            write(h)
        end if
    else
        h = 0
        for all Word ∈ Sentence do
            h = h + Hash(w)
        end for
        write(h)
    end if
end for
```

Algorithm 2. Phase two of the algorithm: Document matching

```
for all δᵢ ∈ Δ do
    Dtⱼ → n = 0, Dtⱼ → mₗ = 0, Dtⱼ → m_c = 0
    for all δᵢtⱼ ∈ δᵢ do
        if δᵢtⱼ ∈ T then
            if Dtⱼ → mₗ > 0 then
                if δtⱼ → n = Dtⱼ → n + 1 then
                    inc(Dtⱼ → n), inc(Dtⱼ → mₗ)
                    if Dtⱼ → mₗ > Dtⱼ → m_c then
                        Dtⱼ → m_c = Dtⱼ → mₗ
                    end if
                else
                    dec(Dtⱼ → mₗ)
                    if Dtⱼ → mₗ = 0 then
                        if Dtⱼ → m_c > Treshold then
                            write(Dtⱼ → m_c, Dtⱼ → n), Dtⱼ → m_c = 0, Dtⱼ → n = 0
                        end if
                    end if
                end if
            else
                Dtⱼ → n = δᵢtⱼ → n, Dtⱼ, → mₗ = 1, → m_c = 1
            end if
        else
            if Dtⱼ → mₗ > 0 then
                dec(Dtⱼ → mₗ)
                if Dtⱼ → m_c > Treshold then
                    write(Dtⱼ → m_c, Dtⱼ → n), Dtⱼ → m_c = 0, Dtⱼ → n = 0
                else
                    inc(Dtⱼ → n)
                end if
            end if
        end if
    end for
end for
```

5   Summary

The presented novel algorithm yields exceptionally good results in its core application extremely boosting the process of plagiarism detection in comparison with S&W algorithm. The results presented are taking into account a initial version of the prepared algorithm.

There is a number of performance extensions that can be applied in order to yield even better effects. The most obvious is normalization of text that shall diminish the overall length of vector storing hashed frames. A less obvious extension is application of semantic compression to even more diminish discussed vector. In addition, application of semantic compression shall improve the plagiarism detection due to the fact that more techniques used by those willing to commit plagiary, shall be vulnerable.

Additional modifications are already designed, yet due to the space constraints will be addressed in separate publications.

References

1. Chvatal, V., Klarner, D.A., Knuth, D.E.: Selected Combinatorial Research Problems. Technical Report, Stanford University, Stanford, CA, USA (1972)
2. Szymanski, T.G.: A special case of the maximal common subsequence problem. Technical Report TR-170, Computer Science Laboratory, Princeton University (1975)
3. Masek, W.J., Paterson, M.S.: A faster algorithm computing string edit distances. Journal of Computer and System Sciences 20 (1980)
4. Ceglarek, D., Haniewicz, K., Rutkowski, W.: Semantically Enhanced Intellectual Property Protection System - SEIPro2S. In: Nguyen, N.T., Kowalczyk, R., Chen, S.-M. (eds.) ICCCI 2009. LNCS, vol. 5796, pp. 449–459. Springer, Heidelberg (2009)
5. Ceglarek, D., Haniewicz, K., Rutkowski, W.: Semantic Compression for Specialised Information Retrieval Systems. In: Nguyen, N.T., Katarzyniak, R., Chen, S.-M. (eds.) Advances in Intelligent Information and Database Systems. SCI, vol. 283, pp. 111–121. Springer, Heidelberg (2010)
6. Ceglarek, D., Haniewicz, K., Rutkowski, W.: Quality of Semantic Compression in Classification. In: Pan, J.-S., Chen, S.-M., Nguyen, N.T. (eds.) ICCCI 2010. LNCS, vol. 6421, pp. 162–171. Springer, Heidelberg (2010)
7. Irving, R.: Plagiarism and collusion detection using the Smith-Waterman algorithm. Technical Report TR-2004-164, University of Glasgow, Computing Science Departament Research Report (2004)
8. Yeates, S.: Automatic Extraction of Acronym from Text. In: Proceedings of the Third New Zealand Computer Science Research Students Conference. University of Waikato, New Zealand (1999)
9. Alonso, L., et al.: Approaches to text summarization: Questions and answers. Inteligentia Artificial. Revista Iberoamericana de Inteligencia Artificial (20), 34–52 (2003)
10. Burrows, S., Tahaghoghi, S.M.M., Zobel, J.: Efficient plagiarism detection for large code repositories. Softw. Pract. Exper. 37, 151–175 (2007)
11. Ota, T., Masuyama, S.: Automatic plagiarism detection among term papers. In: Proceedings of the 3rd International Universal Communication Symposium, pp. 395–399. ACM, New York (2009)

Enriching Domain-Specific Language Models Using Domain Independent WWW N-Gram Corpus

Harry Chang

AT&T Labs, Austin, TX USA
http://www.research.att.com

Abstract. This paper describes the new techniques developed to extract and compute the domain-specific knowledge implicitly embedded in a highly structural ontology-based information system for TV Electronic Programming Guide (EPG). The domain knowledge represented by a set of mutually related n-gram data sets is then enriched by exploring the explicit structural dependencies and implicit semantic association between the data entities in the domain and the domain-independent texts from the Google 1 trillion 5-grams corpus created from general WWW documents. The knowledge-based enrichment process creates the language models required for a natural language based EPG search system that outperform the baseline model created only from the original EPG data source by a significant margin measured by an absolute improvement of 14.1% on the model coverage (recall accuracy) using large-scale test data collected from a real-world EPG search application.

Keywords: Knowledge engineering, natural language processing, text mining, WWW, speech recognition.

1 Introduction

Developing a natural language (NL) based search interface for an information system with fast changing content requires a deep knowledge of both its domain and its target user population. For some domains, obtaining an adequate training corpus for the knowledge acquisition is often difficult. To address the issue of sparse data, researchers use smoothing techniques to improve the maximum likelihood estimate (MLE) technique [1], [2], [3], [4]. For other domains, the opposite becomes a major issue when the amount of training sentences is in the tens of millions. To improve the effectiveness of their training process, researchers discovered various discriminative training techniques [5], [6]. One known weakness with both types of techniques is the complexity of its training process and the cost of human labors required for preparing hand-labeled training sentences.

In this paper, we explore a new knowledge driven and soft computing process for creating the domain-specific *language models* (LMs) through loading of a domain-specific ontology and then enriching it through a domain-independent text corpus. Our research objective is to develop a NL-based search interface for

L. Rutkowski et al. (Eds.): ICAISC 2012, Part II, LNCS 7268, pp. 38–46, 2012.

the domain of TV EPG [7]. The most unique characteristic of this domain is that the target content is constantly changing. Thus, it is impractical to collect an adequate training corpus from the TV viewing public and then spend weeks to build the n-gram LMs before it becomes obsolete. To solve this problem, we create a 2-step training process: 1) construct an optimal sub-tree with the nodes carrying the important domain knowledge using an EPG taxonomy tree [8] and 2) expand the diversity of the underlying LMs created from the domain data using a domain-independent text corpus from Web documents. Figure 1 shows a flattened data view of a simplified EPG taxonomy tree with the 7 leaf nodes.

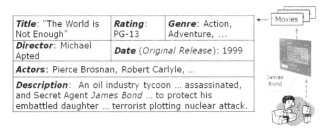

Fig. 1. Visual representation of a structured data record instance of a generic TV EPG

An Ontology of TV EPG. When average TV viewers construct their search expressions, they generally don't know how the underlying EPG content is structured. Consequently, they do not express their search intention in a well-formed query according to the taxonomy of an EPG data feed. Through analyzing the user data collected for our prior study [9], we empirically discover that the users' query language for TV EPG can be effectively modeled by a rather compact EPG ontology with as few as 6 semantic concepts as depicted in Figure 2.

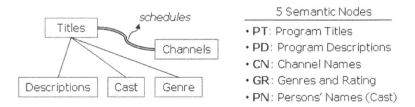

Fig. 2. The EPG ontology used to construct the knowledge framework for the study

It is a common knowledge that the users' language model (spoken or typed words) for expressing their search intention are shaped by many other types of public media such as radio, newspapers, magazines, and web sites. For example, the text string '007' does not always occur in the descriptions of all "*James Bond's movies*" such as the "The World Is Not Enough" example in Figure 1. To address this inherited limitation in an EPG data source, we develop a set of knowledge-based rules to discover the implicit semantic associations between the data elements in an EPG text corpus and their "peers" in a domain-independent WWW-based text corpus using various text mining techniques similar to those reported by others [10], [11]. The Google 1-trillion 5-grams corpus [12] is selected for this study for the two main reasons: *a)* it is the largest domain-independent text corpus from the web documents and *b)* it has the same n-gram data format as that used in our framework.

2   Construct Baseline Model from the EPG Data Source

The EPG corpus used for this study is constructed from a series of the EPG data feed for 59 TV markets in the U.S. over a 32-month period. The text corpus can be viewed as a stack of daily TV Guide pages where each page holds the information for all TV programs and their schedules on various channels on a given day in a highly structured XML file. The text corpus, referred to as the EPG59 corpus, consists of over 500,000 unique sentences with a vocabulary of approximately 210,000 words. Altogether, the EPG59 corpus contains over 1.8 billion word tokens.

2.1   Generating n-Grams Based Semantic Classes from EPG

Definition of N-gram Words. A syntactically-constrained n-gram selection method [7] is used for this study. For example, a program title such as "*Tonight Show with Jay Leno*" only contains 4 *bigrams* and 3 *trigrams*, and etc. We limit the n-grams generation to the first *four* orders for the PT node: PT_i ($i \leq 4$). For all other nodes, we limit the n-grams generation to the first *three* orders: PD_j, CN_j, GR_j, and PN_j ($j \leq 3$).

Populating the EPG Ontology. We develop a simple parser to extract various data elements in the EPG59 corpus and populate the 5 semantic nodes as defined in Figure 2. The relationships between different semantic nodes are represented by their links with one or more properties. The semantic node *schedules* is implicitly encoded as a property associated with the link between the PT and CN node. Thus, after populating the EPG ontology, a property value for the schedule frequency $P_{freq}^{CN}($"$Seinfeld$" $\in PT) = 685$ represents the accumulative frequency for the show aired on all channel instances of the CN node during the lifetime of the corpus.

2.2   Computing n-Gram Weights Using Semantic Nodes

PT Node. Each n-gram string w generated from a PT sentence s is assigned with a weight, p^{PT}, based on its value for the schedule property associated with all link instances between the PT instance s and the CN node using (1). The function $TF(w)$ is a widely-used *Term Frequency* function for the PT set. The constant c is a *primetime* factor, equal to 4 if the schedule instance for the program s occurs during a specific time period of day known to the TV industry as the primetime and equal to 1 otherwise. This method effectively adds a positive bias to the probability weighting of the applicable n-grams in the PT datasets to reflect the domain knowledge.

$$p^{PT}(w) = c * TF(w)|w \in s^{PT} \tag{1}$$

PD Node. The language style used to describe TV programs is generally informal and short in order to fit on a single TV screen. A description text may contain a single sentence of a few words or a loosely structured paragraph with as many as 80 words. The parser extracts approximately 400,000 unique sentences from the description fields. From these sentences, approximately 5 million trigrams and 2.5 million bigrams are generated from the PD subset. Their weight function, p^{PD}, is defined by (2).

$$p^{PD}(w) = c * TF(w)|w \in s^{PD} \tag{2}$$

CN Node. The EPG59 corpus covers the TV programs aired on 446 English channels. Each channel has a unique callsign such as HBO and a full name such as "Home Box Office". The parser extracts approximately 1300 sentences from the corpus to create the CN set and then generates their corresponding n-grams ($n \leq 3$). The weights for the n-grams in the CN set are computed based on a hidden relationship between a channel name and its *diversity* – the count of unique TV shows s aired on the channel c represented by the function $u(c)$, as shown in (3).

$$p^{CN}(w) = \sum_{c}^{446} u(c)|w \in s^{CN} \tag{3}$$

GR Node. Most TV programs in the EPG59 corpus contain a few special data attributes such as genre and rating. In this study, we combine these two data elements to form a single concept as GR (Genres and Rating). The parser extracts 196 phrases from the GR related data fields in the corpus. For simplicity, the probability weighting, $p^{GR}(w) = k$, for all n-grams in the GR set is assigned to a constant ($k = 100$).

PN Node. For a program title, the EPG59 corpus contains two attributes known as cast and director. Altogether, approximately 151,000 names are extracted from the corpus. To achieve a reasonable *word error rate* (WER) for the speech recognition application contemplated for the domain, we decide to reduce the size of this name list using a simple rating scheme to model the popularity of TV cast/directors as follows: for each show title s where a name is listed as a cast member or a director, the person is given one credit (e.g., $cast_s(w) = 1$). For this study we select the 65,000 names with the highest credit rating, which forms the final PN n-gram datasets. The weight for a name n-grams, w, in the PN set is calculated based on the total credits given to the name using (4).

$$p^{PN}(w) = \sum_{s}(cast_s(w) + director_s(w))\,|\,s \in PT \tag{4}$$

Approximately 7 million n-grams ($n \leq 4$) w_n are generated from the EPG59 corpus to form the baseline model (denoted as $\mathbb{B}$) where w may be linked to multiple semantic nodes in the EPG ontology as shown in Figure 2. The overall weight function p for each n-gram w in the baseline model is then the accumulative weight for w over the five semantic nodes where there is a relationship.

3   Model Enrichment through the Google Corpus

There are two main objectives for the enrichment process: a) expand the baseline model by finding new n-grams in the Google 1 Trillion n-grams corpus (G1T) that are deemed *relevant* to our domain and b) adjust the weights of all n-grams in the baseline model that also occur in the G1T corpus. We know from our previous study [9]: there is little accuracy improvement in the speech recognition experiments by including any higher-order n-grams beyond $n=4$. Therefore, only the first four n-gram data sets in the G1T corpus are used in the enrichment process. Table 1 summarizes the basic statistics of the G1T corpus.

Table 1. The data summary of the n-gram sets in the Google 1 trillion 5-gram corpus

Set ID	Types	Set Size	Freq Function
G1T$_{NG1}$	unigrams	13,588,391	$F(w_1)$
G1T$_{NG2}$	bigrams	314,843,401	$F(w_1 w_2)$
G1T$_{NG3}$	trigrams	977,069,902	$F(w_1 w_2 w_3)$
G1T$_{NG4}$	4-gram	1,313,818,354	$F(w_1 w_2 w_3 w_4)$
G1T$_{NG5}$	5-gram	1,176,470,663	*not used*

The enrichment process is a simple recurring procedure starting with the lowest-order n-grams ($n=1$) in the baseline model $\breve{B}$ and using them to find their *relevant* counterparts in the G1T corpus. After all relevant i-grams w_i in the G1T corpus are added to the newly enriched n-gram set $\breve{E}$, the process repeats for the next higher order n-grams in the G1T corpus until $n=4$.

1. Initialize the enriched model $\breve{E}$ with the n-grams in the baseline model $\mathbb{B}$.
2. For $i=1,2,3,4$ repeat the following steps
   (a) Select relevant i-grams $\breve{w}_i$ in $\bigcup$ GIT$_{NGj}$ | $i{\leq}j$
   (b) Add $\breve{w}_i$ to the enriched model $\breve{E}$

The relevance is computed based on the principles of the most common edit-distance algorithms [13], [14]. Any unknown i-gram w_i in the G1T corpus is deemed *relevant* to the domain *if* one of its subordinate j-grams w_j ($w_j \in w_i$) has an edit distance $d \leq \lambda$ to at least one semantic node defined in Figure 2. The value λ is set to 1 for G1T$_{NG1}$ and G1T$_{NG2}$ and increased to 2 for G1T$_{NG3}$ and G1T$_{NG4}$. Thus, any unknown fourgram w_4 containing the name "*James Bond*" would be considered relevant to the domain because it has an edit distance $d(w_4, \text{``}James\ Bond\text{''} \in PD_2) \leq 2$ to the semantic node PD. The weight function f of an n-gram $\breve{w}$ in the enriched model $\breve{E}$ is based on the greater value of the two functions, $F(\breve{w})$ and $p(\breve{w})$ using (5).

$$f^{\mathcal{X}}(\breve{w}) = max(F(\breve{w}, p^{\mathcal{X}}(\breve{w})) \,|\, \mathcal{X} \in \{PT, PD, CN, GR, PN\} \qquad (5)$$

The enrichment process expands the baseline model by two orders of magnitudes as shown in Table 2. To study if the expansion algorithm is too greedy or over-constrained, we rank all n-grams in the enriched model $\breve{E}$ based on their weight function f and then create three smaller *nested* subsets whose n-grams have a weight higher than a certain threshold that is empirically determined. Table 2 shows the sizes of the n-gram datasets within the enrichment model $\breve{E}$ and its three subsets: *small*, *medium*, and *large*.

Table 2. The n-gram dataset summary for the model $\mathbb{B}$ and the enhanced models

n-gram	Model $\mathbb{B}$	Model $\breve{E}$	$\breve{E}_{small}$	$\breve{E}_{medium}$	$\breve{E}_{large}$
n=1	137,764	1,078,118	167,565	300,389	889,222
n=2	1,435,673	71,535,612	6,453,393	8,767,176	14,589,380
n=3	2,637,036	257,109,225	5,393,306	12,089,203	47,646,227
n=4	2,760,003	285,002,030	28,434,955	58,498,012	103,888,021
all	6,970,476	613,817,714	40,431,219	79,654,780	167,012,856

4   Evaluations and Results

The effectiveness of the enrichment process described in Section 3 is evaluated from two perspectives, NL Processing (NLP), and Automatic Speech Recognition (ASR). The NLP-oriented performance is measured using the standard recall accuracy (the percentage of all test sentences that found a match in the LMs) and precision accuracy (the percentage of all test sentences *correctly* mapped to the LMs). For the ASR test, the common WER metric is used to measure the performance of a statistical language model (SLM) based ASR engine trained from the n-grams based sentences.

4.1   Coverage Analysis on Typed Queries (TQ)

Test Data. Approximately 1.5 million typed search texts were collected from an EPG website with an estimated user population of over 50,000. The raw text data was filtered with a domain-specific automatic spell check dictionary and then compared to the full program titles in the PT data set. All search queries that mapped to an exact program title (*24, American Idol, Seinfeld*, etc) were considered too simplistic and excluded from this study. The remaining set containing 34,589 unique search texts are considered as a harder test set because they reflect worse-than-average scenarios in terms of low-frequency words and query complexity.

Text Search Engine. A simple text search engine is built with an n-gram based scoring procedure. To minimize complexities in computing precision accuracy, the following search and scoring procedure is used: all test queries with exactly one word (count=8,656) are only compared with the unigrams used to train the search engine; similarly, the test queries with exactly two words (count=14,627) are only submitted to their corresponding bigrams models, and so on. Therefore, the precision accuracy for all matched queries consisting of four words or less is always 100 percent. The percentages of exact matches produced by the search engine trained with the different models are shown in Table 3, grouped by the lengths of the test queries. All three enrichment models clearly outperform the baseline model $\mathbb{B}$ by a significant margin, especially for n=2 and 3.

Table 3. The recall accuracies: the baseline model vs enhanced models

TQ Test Subset	$\mathbb{B}$	$\breve{E}_{small}$	$\breve{E}_{medium}$	$\breve{E}_{large}$
1-word queries	87.0%	90.7%	92.0%	94.3%
2-word queries	51.4%	75.1%	76.8%	78.9%
3-word queries	47.5%	59.0%	62.6%	75.0%
4-word queries	14.7%	18.9%	22.0%	25.0%

TQ Test Set (N=34,859)	$\mathbb{B}$	$\breve{E}_{small}$	$\breve{E}_{medium}$	$\breve{E}_{large}$
Recall Accuracy	56.3%	70.4%	72.5%	75.9%
Model Size (millions)	6.97	40.43	79.65	167.01
Vocabulary Size	137K	167K	300K	889K

For the test queries with 5 words or more (4.3%), there is no exact match possible by the search engine. A simple divide-and-conquer method is used for these longer test queries. For those longer test queries, w_i, if any of its bigrams, trigrams, or fourgrams score a match by the search engine, it is counted as a recall. The overall improvement of recall accuracy across all five subsets in the TQ test set is shown in Table 3. Even the smallest enriched model, $\breve{E}_{small}$, outperforms the baseline model $\mathbb{B}$ by 14.1% absolute in terms of recall accuracy.

4.2   ASR Performance on Spoken Queries (SQ)

Discriminative Selection of Training N-grams. The vocabulary size of the enriched LMs is rather high for the target search applications. To reduce it, we develop a method for selecting those n-grams of the highest probabilities for appearing in a spoken expression by average users. First, we apply a common NLP technique known as the *Term Frequency and Inverse Document Frequency* (TF-IDF) based title ranking [9] but only to the unigrams and bigrams in the PT subset. This rating process excludes those PT unigrams and bigrams with the highest or lowest TF-IDF values using a threshold determined empirically. The surviving unigrams and bigrams in the original PT set are called the *anchoring* sets: PT_{1a} and PT_{2a}. We then increase discriminatively the weight of those n-grams in all four models listed in Table 3 *only if* it contains a text string in the PT_{1a} and PT_{2a} anchoring sets. Finally, we re-rank the weight of all n-grams in the four models and eliminate those ranked below the bottom 10 percentile within their corresponding n-gram sets. This process creates the final four sets: B^*, E^*_{small}, E^*_{medium}, and E^*_{large}, which are then used to train a statistical language model (SLM) based speech recognition engine. Table 4 shows the size of the final training sets used for the ASR tests in this study.

Testing Data and Results. Two groups of employee-based users participated in this SQ study. They interacted with an experimental EPG system using a multi-modal TV remote with speech input capabilities, producing 1,585 spoken queries for the domain. The larger user group (50 speakers) used more well-formed search queries with an average term length of 3.4 words while the smaller user group (5 families) used the prototype in their homes, producing slightly shorter, yet spontaneous spoken queries with an average term length of 2.9 words. Average sentence length for the spoken queries is 3.1 words. Table 4 shows the WER statistics generated by the same speech recognition system using the different SLMs compiled from the n-grams in the four different training sets.

Table 4. The performance comparison: the baseline model vs enhanced models

Training Set	Vocab	N-gram Size	WER
B^*	123,680	4,331,934	22.8%
E_{small}^*	126,369	5,269,354	22.8%
E_{medium}^*	126,561	6,944,184	22.5%
E_{large}^*	124,256	9,119,511	22.5%

Table 4 shows that the expanded n-gram sets from the enrichment process do not produce a higher WER. In fact, the enrichment models E_{medium}^* and E_{large}^* outperform the baseline line model B^* by a small margin. The small reduction in WER is primarily due to the fact that some of the spoken queries in the SQ test set are not covered by the baseline model.

5 Discussions and Future Research

Using a domain-specific ontology system populated from the system-generated domain data, we have created a highly automated process for enriching the language model through the knowledge-driven text mining techniques on the Google 1 trillion n-gram corpus. The enriched LMs outperform the baseline model by a significant margin in terms of recall accuracy (70.4% from the smallest enrichment model versus 56.3% on the baseline model) when tested on large-scale field data collected from a real world EPG application.

The ASR test on a small set of spoken queries collected from an experimental EPG search system with a spoken interface shows that the enriched models can achieve the same or slightly better WER metric vs the baseline model. It is worth emphasizing that the SQ test set has a very small vocabulary of approximately 1200 words and that a majority of spoken sentences are considered well formed. Had the SQ test set contained as many complex queries as found in the TQ test, we would expect a much higher WER from the baseline model.

One potential improvement to the enrichment process is the introduction of penalties for the n-grams with a very low in-domain frequency count. For example, the testing utterance "HBO" was mis-recognized as "Eight DEO". The main reason for the word DEO to remain in the final training set is that the word carries a fairly high weight, which is almost entirely contributed from the Google corpus (it contains over 10 million instances of the word). However, the word only has 2 instances in the original EPG59 corpus which contains over 1.8 billion word tokens. Another future improvement could incorporate a recency factor in determining the weight for the name entries in the PN set based on the frequency of their movie appearances on TV during the last X months.

References

1. Katz, S.M.: Estimation of Probabilities from Sparse Data for the Language Model Component of a Speech Recognizer. IEEE Trans. ASSP 35(3), 400–401 (1987)
2. Eseen, H.N., Kneser, R.: On Structuring Probabilistic Dependencies in Stochastic Language Modeling. Computer, Speech, and Language 8, 1–38 (1994)
3. Kneser, R., Ney, H.: Improved Backing-off for M-gram Language Modeling. In: Proc. of ICASSP, vol. 1, pp. 181–184 (1995)
4. Chen, S.F., Goodman, J.: An Empirical Study of Smoothing Techniques for Language Modeling. Technical Report TR-10-98, Harvard University Center for Research in Computing Technology (1998)
5. Chelba, C., Acero, A.: Discriminative Training of N-gram Classifier for Speech and Text Routing. In: Proc. of Eurospeech, pp. 1–4 (2003)
6. Chen, Z., Lee, K.F., Li, M.J.: Discriminative Training on Language Models. In: Proc. of ICSLP (2000)
7. Chang, H.M.: Conceptual Modeling of Online Entertainment Programming Guide for Natural Language Interface. In: Hopfe, C.J., Rezgui, Y., Métais, E., Preece, A., Li, H. (eds.) NLDB 2010. LNCS, vol. 6177, pp. 188–195. Springer, Heidelberg (2010)
8. Chang, H.M.: Constructing N-gram Rules for Natural Language Models through Exploring the Limitations of the Zipf-Mandelbrot Law. Computing 91, 241–264 (2011)
9. Chang, H.M.: Topics Inference by Weighted Mutual Information Measures Computed from Structured Corpus. In: Muñoz, R., Montoyo, A., Métais, E. (eds.) NLDB 2011. LNCS, vol. 6716, pp. 64–75. Springer, Heidelberg (2011)
10. Ng, T., Ostendorf, M., Hwang, M.Y., Manhung, S., Bulyko, I., Xin, L.: Web-data Augmented Language Models for Mandarin Conversational Speech Recognition. In: Proc. of ICASSP, pp. 589–592 (2005)
11. Tsiartas, A., Tsiartas, P., Narayanan, S.: Language Model Adaptation Using WWW Docuements Obtained by Utterance-based Queries. In: ICASSP (2010)
12. Brants, T., Franz, A.: Web 1T 5-gram Corpus Version 1.1. Technical Report, Google Research (2006)
13. Bille, P.: A Survey on Tree Edit Distance and Related Problems. Theor. Computing Sci. 331(1-3), 217–239 (2005)
14. Dalamagas, T., Cheng, T., Wintel, K.J., Sellis, T.: A Methodology for Clustering XML Documents by Structure. Information System 31(3), 187–228 (2006)

On the Structure of Indiscernibility Relations Compatible with a Partially Ordered Set

Pietro Codara

Università degli Studi di Milano,
Dipartimento di Informatica e Comunicazione,
Via Comelico 39, I-20135, Milan, Italy
codara@dico.unimi.it

Abstract. In a recently published work the author investigates indiscernibility relations on information systems with a partially ordered universe. Specifically, he introduces a notion of compatibility between the (partially ordered) universe and an indiscernibility relation on its support, and establishes a criterion for compatibility. In this paper we make a first step in the direction of investigating the structure of all the indiscernibility relations which satisfy such a compatibility criterion.

Keywords: Indiscernibility Relation, Partially Ordered Set, Partition, Rough Set.

1 Introduction

As stated by Pawlak in [13], the notion of indiscernibility relation stands at the basis of the theory of rough sets. In a recently published paper ([3]), the author investigates the indiscernibility relation in an information system where the universe is partially ordered. After introducing appropriate notions of partition of a partially ordered set (*poset*, for short), a relation between partitions and indiscernibility relations is established. More specifically, the author introduces a notion of compatibility between a poset and an indiscernibility relation on its support, based on the definition of partition of a poset. Further, a criterion for compatibility is established and proved.

In this paper, we make a first step in the direction of investigating the structure of all the indiscernibility relations which are compatible with a poset. To this end, indeed, we need first to learn about the structure of all the partitions of a poset.

Some of the mathematical concepts used in this paper have been developed by the author in [1] and [2]. In these works, the author provides two different notions of partition of a poset, namely, *monotone partition* and *regular partition*. We recall this concepts in Section 2.

Our main results are contained in Section 4, where we describe the lattice structure of monotone and regular partitions of a poset.

In Section 3 we recall the results obtained in [3]. Such results are used in Section 5 to obtain, by way of an example, the structure of all indiscernibility relations compatible with a poset in a specific case.

L. Rutkowski et al. (Eds.): ICAISC 2012, Part II, LNCS 7268, pp. 47–55, 2012.

2 Preorders and Partitions of a Partially Ordered Set

A partition of a set A is a collection of nonempty, pairwise disjoint subsets, often called *blocks*, whose union is A. Equivalently, partitions can be defined by means of *equivalence relations*, by saying that a partition of a set A is the set of equivalence classes of an equivalence relation on A. A third definition of a partition can be given in terms of *fibres* of a surjection: a partition of a set A is the set $\{f^{-1}(y) \mid y \in B\}$ of fibres of a surjection $f : A \to B$.

In [1] and [2], the notion of partition of a poset is investigated. Starting by providing definitions of partition in terms of *fibres* (such kind of definition arise naturally when thinking in terms of categories, *i.e.*, in terms of objects and maps between them), the author provides the corresponding definitions in terms of *blocks*, and in terms of *relations*. In this section, we only present the third kind of definitions, the ones given in terms of relations. Full results and proofs are contained in [1] and [2].

2.1 Two Different Kinds of Partition?

In the case of posets, and in contrast with classical sets, we can derive two different notions of partition. To justify this fact, some remarks on the categories having sets and posets, respectively, as objects, are needed. For background on category theory we refer, *e.g.*, to [9]. Let Set be the category having sets as objects and functions as morphisms. To define a partition of a set in terms of fibres, one makes use of a special class of morphisms of the category Set. In fact, such definition exploits the notion of surjection, which can be shown to coincide in Set with the notion of *epimorphism*. Moreover, in Set, injections coincide with monomorphisms. The well-known fact that each function factorises (in an essentially unique way) as a surjection followed by an injection can be reformulated in categorical terms by saying that the class epi of all epimorphisms and the class mono of all monomorphisms form a factorisation system for Set, or, equivalently, that (epi,mono) is a factorisation system for Set.

Consider the category Pos of posets and *order-preserving maps* (also called *monotone maps*), *i.e.*, functions $f : P \to Q$, with P, Q posets, such that $x \leqslant y$ in P implies $f(x) \leqslant f(y)$ in Q, for each $x, y \in P$. In Pos, (epi,mono) is not a factorisation system; to obtain one we need to isolate a subclass of epimorphisms, called regular epimorphisms. While in Set regular epimorphisms and epimorphisms coincide, that is not the case in Pos. The dual notion of regular epimorphism is *regular monomorphism*. It can be shown (see, *e.g.*, [1, Proposition 2.5]) that (regular epi,mono) is a factorisation system for the category Pos. A second factorisation system for Pos is given by the classes of epimorphisms and regular monomorphisms. In other words, each order-preserving map between posets factorises in an essentially unique way both as a regular epimorphism followed by a monomorphism, and as an epimorphism followed by a regular monomorphism.

The existence of two distinct factorisation systems in Pos leads to two different notions of partition of a poset: the first, we call *monotone partition*, is based on the use of epimorphisms, the second, we call *regular partition*, is based on the use of regular epimorphisms.

Remark 1. Another, distinct, notion of partition of a poset can be derived by taking into account the category of posets and *open maps*, instead of the category Pos we are considering. Such kind of partition is called *open partition* (see [2, Definition 4.8]). An application of the notion of open partition can be found in [4].

2.2 Partitions of Partially Ordered Sets

Notation. If π is a partition of a set A, and $a \in A$, we denote by $[a]_\pi$ the block of a in π. When no confusion is possible, we shall write $[a]$ instead of $[a]_\pi$. Further, let us stress our usage of different symbols for representing different types of binary relations. The symbol $\leqslant$ denotes the partial order relation between elements of a poset. A second symbol, $\lesssim$, denotes *preorder relations*, sometimes called *quasiorders*, *i.e*, reflexive and transitive relations.

A preorder relation $\lesssim$ on a set A induces on A an equivalence relation $\equiv$ defined as

$$x \equiv y \text{ if and only if } x \lesssim y \text{ and } y \lesssim x, \text{ for any } x, y \in A. \tag{1}$$

The set π of equivalence classes of $\equiv$ is a partition of A.

Notation. In the following we denote by $[x]_\lesssim$ the equivalence class (the block) of the element x induced by the preorder $\lesssim$ via the equivalence relation defined in (1).

Further, the preorder $\lesssim$ induces on π a partial order $\preccurlyeq$ defined by

$$x \lesssim y \text{ if and only if } [x]_\lesssim \preccurlyeq [y]_\lesssim, \text{ for any } x, y \in A. \tag{2}$$

We call $(\pi, \preccurlyeq)$ *the poset of equivalence classes induced by* $\lesssim$.

This correspondence allows us to define partitions of a poset (more precisely, monotone and regular partitions) in terms of preorders.

Definition 1 (Monotone partition). *A monotone partition of a poset* $(P, \leqslant)$ *is the poset of equivalence classes induced by a preorder* $\lesssim$ *on P such that* $\leqslant \subseteq \lesssim$.

Definition 2 (Regular partition). *A regular partition of a poset* $(P, \leqslant)$ *is the poset of equivalence classes induced by a preorder* $\lesssim$ *on P such that* $\leqslant \subseteq \lesssim$, *and satisfying*

$$\lesssim = \text{tr}(\lesssim \setminus \rho), \tag{3}$$

where tr(R) *denotes the transitive closure of the relation R, and ρ is a binary relation defined by*

$$\rho = \{(x, y) \in P \times P \mid x \lesssim y, x \not\leqslant y, y \not\leqslant x\}. \tag{4}$$

Example 1. We refer to Figure 1, and consider the poset P. One can check, using the characterisations of poset partitions provided in Definitions 1 and 2, that the following hold.

- π_1 is a monotone partition of P, but it is not regular.
- π_2 and π_3 are regular partitions of P, thus monotone ones.

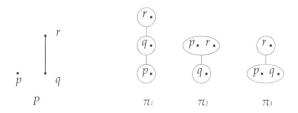

Fig. 1. Example 1

3 Indiscernibility Relations Compatible with a Partially Ordered Set

Denote by $\mathcal{P} = (P, A)$ the information system having as universe the finite poset $P = (U, \leqslant)$, where U is the collection of objects (the *universe*), $\leqslant$ is a partial order on U, and A is a set of *attributes*.

As in the 'classical' rough set theory, with a subset of attributes $B \subseteq A$ we associate an *indiscernibility relation* on the underlying set of P, denoted by I_B and defined by

$$(x, y) \in I_B \text{ if and only if } a(x) = a(y),$$

for each $a \in A$, and for each $x, y \in P$. Clearly, I_B is an equivalence relation on the underlying set U of P, and thus induces on U a partition $\pi = U/I_B$. We can look at the relation I_B as a way to express the fact that we are unable to observe (to distinguish) individual objects, but we are forced, instead, to think in terms of *granules*, *i.e.*, in terms of blocks of a partition (see, *e.g.*, [10,14,15]). In symbols, if $x, y \in P$, x is distinguishable from y if and only if $[x]_\pi \neq [y]_\pi$.

The partition π has no reason to be the underlying set of a partition of P in the sense of Definitions 1 or 2. When it is the case, we say that π *is compatible with the poset*.

In [3] we formalise the notion of compatibility, and proof a criterion for an indiscernibility relation to be compatible with a partially ordered universe. We briefly recall these results.

Definition 3. *Let $P = (U, \leqslant)$ be a poset, let I_B be an indiscernibility relation on U and let $\pi = U/I_B$. We say I_B is* compatible *with P if there exists a monotone partition $(\pi, \leqslant)$ of P. Further, if I_B is compatible with P we say that π admits an* extension *to a monotone partition of P.*

The question arises, under which conditions π can be *extended* to a monotone or regular partition of P, by endowing π with a partial order relation $\leqslant$. In order to give an answer we need a further definition.

Definition 4 (Blockwise preorder). *Let $(P, \leqslant)$ be a poset and let π be a partition of the set P. For $x, y \in P$, x is blockwise under y with respect to π, written $x \lesssim_\pi y$, if and only if there exists a sequence $x = x_0, y_0, x_1, y_1, \ldots, x_n, y_n = y \in P$ satisfying the following conditions.*

(1) For all $i \in \{0, \ldots, n\}$, $[x_i] = [y_i]$.
(2) For all $i \in \{0, \ldots, n-1\}$, $y_i \leqslant x_{i+1}$.

Corollary 1 (Compatibility Criterion). *Let $P = (U, \leqslant)$ be a poset, let I_B be an indiscernibility relation on U and let $\pi = U/I_B$. Then, I_B is compatible with P if and only if, for all $x, y \in P$,*

$$x \leqslant_\pi y \text{ and } y \leqslant_\pi x \text{ imply } [x]_\pi = [y]_\pi . \tag{5}$$

For regular partitions one can say more: a set partition of P admits at most one extension to a regular partition of the poset P.

Corollary 2. *Let $P = (U, \leqslant)$ be a poset, let I_B be an indiscernibility relation on U and let $\pi = U/I_B$. If π is compatible with P, then π admits a unique extension to a regular partition of P.*

The uniqueness property of regular partitions does not hold, in general, for monotone partitions; cf. Figure 2, which shows three distinct monotone partitions of a given poset P having the same underlying set.

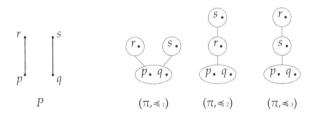

Fig. 2. Distinct monotone partitions with the same support π

4   The Lattices of Partitions of a Partially Ordered Set

In the light of Definitions 1 and 2, we can think at partitions of a poset as preorders. More precisely, each preorder $\lesssim$ such that $\leqslant \subseteq \lesssim \subseteq P \times P$ defines a unique monotone partition of $(P, \leqslant)$. Moreover, when (and only when) $\lesssim$ satisfies Condition (3) in Definition 2, then $\lesssim$ defines a regular partition of $(P, \leqslant)$. We can endow the set of all monotone (regular) partitions of a poset with a partial order by considering the set-theoretic inclusion between the associated preorders.

Proposition 1. *The collection of monotone partitions of $(P, \leqslant)$ is a lattice when partially ordered by set-theoretic inclusion between the corresponding preorders.*

Specifically, let π_1 and π_2 be the monotone partitions of $(P, \leqslant)$, induced by the preorders $\lesssim_1$ and $\lesssim_2$, respectively. Then $\pi_1 \wedge_m \pi_2$ and $\pi_1 \vee_m \pi_2$ (the lattice meet and join) are the partitions induced, respectively, by the preorders:

$$\lesssim_1 \wedge_m \lesssim_2 = \lesssim_1 \cap \lesssim_2 , \quad \lesssim_1 \vee_m \lesssim_2 = \mathrm{tr}(\lesssim_1 \cup \lesssim_2).$$

Proof. We observe that if $\leqslant \subseteq \lesssim_1$ and $\leqslant \subseteq \lesssim_2$, then $\leqslant \subseteq \lesssim_1 \cap \lesssim_2$, and $\leqslant \subseteq \lesssim_1 \cup \lesssim_2$. We also notice that $\lesssim_1 \cap \lesssim_2 = \lesssim_1$ if and only if $\lesssim_1 \subseteq \lesssim_2$. Moreover, both $\wedge_m$ and $\vee_m$ are idempotent, commutative, and associative, because intersection and union are. Finally, the absorption laws

$$\lesssim_1 \wedge_m (\lesssim_1 \vee_m \lesssim_2) = \lesssim_1 \text{ and } \lesssim_1 \vee_m (\lesssim_1 \wedge_m \lesssim_2) = \lesssim_1$$

trivially hold.   □

The class of regular partitions also carries a lattice structure.

Proposition 2. *The collection of regular partitions of $(P, \leqslant)$ is a lattice when partially ordered by set-theoretic inclusion between the corresponding quasiorders.*

Specifically, let π_1 and π_2 be the regular partitions of $(P, \leqslant)$, induced by the preorders $\lesssim_1$ and $\lesssim_2$, respectively, and let $\tau = \{(x, y) \in (\lesssim_1 \cap \lesssim_2) \setminus \leqslant \mid y \not\lesssim_1 x \text{ or } y \not\lesssim_2 x\}$ Then $\pi_1 \wedge_r \pi_2$ and $\pi_1 \vee_r \pi_2$ (the lattice meet and join) are the partitions induced, respectively, by the preorders:

$$\lesssim_1 \wedge_r \lesssim_2 = \mathrm{tr}((\lesssim_1 \cap \lesssim_2) \setminus \tau), \quad \lesssim_1 \vee_r \lesssim_2 = \mathrm{tr}(\lesssim_1 \cup \lesssim_2).$$

Proof. By construction, $\lesssim_1 \wedge_r \lesssim_2$ induces a regular partition. We now prove that the preorder $\lesssim_1 \vee_r \lesssim_2$ induces a regular partition, too. Consider $\lesssim_{12} = \lesssim_1 \cup \lesssim_2$, and let $\tau_{12} = \{(x, y) \in \lesssim_{12} \mid x \not\leqslant y, y \not\lesssim_{12} x\}$. Suppose $(p, q) \in \tau_{12}$. Say, without loss of generality, $p \lesssim_1 q$. Then, by Definition 2, there exists a sequence $p = z_0 \lesssim_1 z_1 \lesssim_1 \cdots \lesssim_1 z_r = q$ of elements of P such that $(z_i, z_{i+1}) \in \lesssim_1 \setminus \tau_1$ for all $i = 0, \ldots, r$, and $\tau_1 = \{(x, y) \in \lesssim_1 \mid x \not\leqslant y, y \not\lesssim_1 x\}$. But if $(z_i, z_{i+1}) \notin \tau_1$, then $z_i \leqslant z_{i+1}$, or $z_{i+1} \lesssim_1 z_i$. In both cases $(z_i, z_{i+1}) \notin \tau_{12}$, and thus $(z_i, z_{i+1}) \in \lesssim_{12} \setminus \tau_{12}$ for all i, and $(p, q) \in \mathrm{tr}((\lesssim_1 \cup \lesssim_2) \setminus \tau_{12})$. Hence, $\mathrm{tr}(\lesssim_1 \cup \lesssim_2)$ corresponds to a regular partition.

We can easily check, by the properties of intersection and union, that $\wedge_r$ and $\vee_r$ are idempotent, commutative, associative, and satisfy the absorption laws. It remains to show that $\lesssim_1 \wedge_r \lesssim_2 = \lesssim_1$ if and only if $\lesssim_1 \subseteq \lesssim_2$. Suppose $\lesssim_1 \subseteq \lesssim_2$. Then, $\lesssim_1 \cap \lesssim_2 = \lesssim_1$ and, since $\lesssim_1$ is regular, $\mathrm{tr}((\lesssim_1 \cap \lesssim_2) \setminus \tau) = \mathrm{tr}(\lesssim_1 \setminus \tau) = \lesssim_1$. Suppose now that $\mathrm{tr}((\lesssim_1 \cap \lesssim_2) \setminus \tau) = \lesssim_1$ and let $x \lesssim_1 y$. Then either $(x, y) \in (\lesssim_1 \cap \lesssim_2) \setminus \tau$, or (x, y) is a pair arising from the transitive closure of $(\lesssim_1 \cap \lesssim_2) \setminus \tau$. In any case, since $(\lesssim_1 \cap \lesssim_2) \setminus \tau \subseteq \lesssim_2$ and $\lesssim_2$ is transitive, we have that $x \lesssim_2 y$, proving that if $\mathrm{tr}((\lesssim_1 \cap \lesssim_2) \setminus \tau) = \lesssim_1$, then $\lesssim_1 \subseteq \lesssim_2$. $\square$

We will call *monotone partition lattice* and *regular partition lattice* the lattices of monotone and regular partitions of a poset, respectively.

5   Structure of Indiscernibility Relations Compatible with a Partially Ordered Set: An Example

Following the example introduced in [3], we show how to obtain the structure of indiscernibility relations compatible with a partially ordered set. Consider the following table, reporting a collection of houses for sale in the city of Merate, Lecco, Italy.

House	Price (€)	Size (m^2)	District	Condition	Rooms
a	200.000	50	Centre	excellent	2
b	170.000	70	Centre	poor	3
c	185.000	53	Centre	very good	2
d	190.000	68	Sartirana	very good	3
e	140.000	60	Sartirana	good	2
f	155.000	65	Novate	good	2
g	250.000	85	Novate	excellent	3
h	240.000	75	Novate	excellent	3

In this simple information table eight distinct houses are characterised by five attributes: Price, Size, District, Condition, and Rooms. Let $U = \{a, b, c, d, e, f, g, h\}$ be the set of all houses. We choose the subset of attributes $O = \{Price, Size\}$ to define on U a partial order $\leqslant$ as follow. For each $x, y \in U$,

$$x \leqslant y \text{ if and only if Price}(x) \leqslant \text{Price}(y), \text{Size}(x) \leqslant \text{Size}(y).$$

We obtain the poset $P = (U, \leqslant)$ displayed in Figure 3.

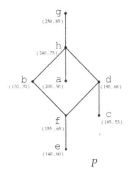

Fig. 3. $P = (U, \leqslant)$

We denote by $\mathcal{P}(P, \bar{A})$ the information system having P as universe, and $\bar{A} = \{$District, Condition, Rooms$\}$ as the set of attributes. Let $D = \{$District$\}$, $C = \{$Condition$\}$, and $R = \{$Rooms$\}$, and denote by π_D, π_C, and π_R the partitions U/I_D, U/I_C, and U/I_R respectively. Moreover, let $DR = D \cup R, CR = C \cup R, DC = D \cup C, DCR = D \cup C \cup R$ and let $\pi_{DR} = U/I_{DR}, \pi_{CR} = U/I_{CR}, \pi_{DC} = U/I_{DC}, \pi_{DCR} = U/I_{DCR}$. We have:

$\pi_D = \{\{a, b, c\}, \{d, e\}, \{f, g, h\}\}$;
$\pi_C = \{\{a, g, h\}, \{b\}, \{c, d\}, \{e, f\}\}\}$;
$\pi_R = \{\{a, c, e, f\}, \{b, d, g, h\}\}$;
$\pi_{DR} = \{\{a, c\}, \{b\}, \{d\}, \{e\}, \{f\}, \{g, h\}\}$;
$\pi_{CR} = \{\{a\}, \{b\}, \{c\}, \{d\}, \{e, f\}, \{g, h\}\}$;
$\pi_{DC} = \pi_{DCR} = \{\{a\}, \{b\}, \{c\}, \{d\}, \{e\}, \{f\}, \{g, h\}\}$.

Furthermore,

$\pi_0 = U/I_0 = \{\{a, b, c, d, e, f, g, h\}\}$.

Figure 4 represents on P all the partitions listed above.

It can be checked, using Corollary 1, that all the partitions, expect π_D, are compatible with P. Figure 5 shows the structure of the indiscernibility relations which are compatible with P.

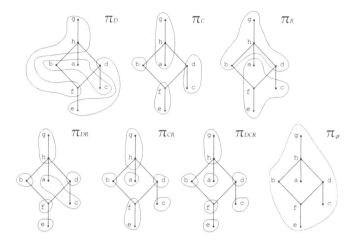

Fig. 4. Partitions of P induced by indiscernibility relations

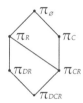

Fig. 5. Structure of the indiscernibility relations compatible with P

6   Conclusion

Rough sets were introduced in the early 1980s by Pawlak ([12]). Since then, lot of works have been published, developing and enriching the theory of rough sets (see, *e.g.*, [8,11,14,16]), and showing how the notion of rough set is suited to solve several problems in different fields of application (see, *e.g.*, [5,6,7]). The notion of indiscernibility relation stand at the basis of the theory of rough sets.

The results presented in this paper are preparatory to a deeper understanding of the structure of the indiscernibility relations on a partially ordered universe P which satisfies the compatibility criterion introduced in [3]. The main results are Propositions 1 and 2, where we prove that monotone and regular partitions of a poset carry a lattice structure. By way of an example, in Section 5 we show the structure of indiscernibility relations compatible with a specific poset.

References

1. Codara, P.: A theory of partitions of partially ordered sets. PhD thesis, Università degli Studi di Milano, Italy (2008)
2. Codara, P.: Partitions of a Finite Partially Ordered Set. In: Damiani, E., D'Antona, O., Marra, V., Palombi, F. (eds.) From Combinatorics to Philosophy. The Legacy of G.-C. Rota, pp. 45–59. Springer, US (2009)

3. Codara, P.: Indiscernibility Relations on Partially Ordered Sets. In: IEEE International Conference on Granular Computing, GrC 2011, pp. 150–155 (2011)
4. Codara, P., D'Antona, O.M., Marra, V.: Open Partitions and Probability Assignments in Gödel Logic. In: Sossai, C., Chemello, G. (eds.) ECSQARU 2009. LNCS (LNAI), vol. 5590, pp. 911–922. Springer, Heidelberg (2009)
5. Greco, S., Matarazzo, B., Slowinski, R.: Rough sets theory for multicriteria decision analysis. European Journal of Operational Research 129(1), 1–47 (2001)
6. Jelonek, J., Krawiec, K., Slowinski, R.: Rough set reduction of attributes and their domains for neural networks. Computational Intelligence 11, 339–347 (1995)
7. Kryszkiewicz, M.: Rough set approach to incomplete information systems. Inform. Sci. 112(1-4), 39–49 (1998)
8. Liu, G., Zhu, W.: The algebraic structures of generalized rough set theory. Inform. Sci. 178(21), 4105–4113 (2008)
9. Mac Lane, S.: Categories for the working mathematician, 2nd edn. Graduate Texts in Mathematics, vol. 5. Springer, New York (1998)
10. Orłowska, E. (ed.): Incomplete information: rough set analysis. STUDFUZZ, vol. 13. Physica-Verlag, Heidelberg (1998)
11. Pagliani, P., Chakraborty, M.: A geometry of approximation. Trends in Logic—Studia Logica Library, vol. 27. Springer, New York (2008)
12. Pawlak, Z.: Rough sets. Internat. J. Comput. Inform. Sci. 11(5), 341–356 (1982)
13. Pawlak, Z.: Rough set approach to knowledge-based decision support. European Journal of Operational Research 99, 48–57 (1995)
14. Pawlak, Z., Skowron, A.: Rudiments of rough sets. Inf. Sci. 177(1), 3–27 (2007)
15. Yao, Y.Y.: Information granulation and rough set approximation. Int. J. Intell. Syst. 16(1), 87–104 (2001)
16. Yao, Y.Y.: Two views of the theory of rough sets in finite universes. International Journal of Approximate Reasoning 15, 291–317 (1996)

On Pre-processing Algorithms for Data Stream

Piotr Duda, Maciej Jaworski, and Lena Pietruczuk

Department of Computer Engineering, Czestochowa University of Technology,
Czestochowa, Poland
{pduda,maciej.jaworski,lena.pietruczuk}@kik.pcz.pl

Abstract. Clustering is a one of the most important tasks of data mining. Algorithms like the Fuzzy C-Means and Possibilistic C-Means provide good result both for the static data and data streams. All clustering algorithms compute centers from chunk of data, what requires a lot of time. If the rate of incoming data is faster than speed of algorithm, part of data will be lost. To prevent such situation, some pre-processing algorithms should be used. The purpose of this paper is to propose a pre-processing method for clustering algorithms. Experimental results show that proposed method is appropriate to handle noisy data and can accelerate processing time.

Keywords: data streams, fuzzy clustering, pre-processing.

1 Introduction

A data stream is a massive unbounded sequence of data elements continuously generated at a rapid rate. Due to limited memory space every data should be scanned by only one pass On way is to sacrifice the performance of algorithm result for fast processing time. Other way is to use some pre-processing. In literature there are many different techniques like: sliding windows, sketching, sampling, wavelets, histograms, aggregations or load shedding [4], [6], [7], [9], [17], [31].

All created clustering algorithms, like C-Means, Fuzzy C-Means, Possibilistic C-Means and entropy based C-Means, do not work on every single data. All of them should operate on data chunk. Every clustering algorithm for data stream computes clusters centers from chunk of data and creates new chunk from incoming data. It is obvious that, when rate of incoming data is faster than speed of algorithm, then all available memory can be overflowed and then part of data must be lost. To prevent this situation we propose to use same kind of aggregation, which we called *equi-width cubes*. This method splits data space into some number of cubes, which depends on data dimension and memory limit. When new data comes it is included to one of the cubes. When algorithm computes cluster center from previous chunk, new chunk (created from all cubes) is sent to cluster algorithm. This solution ensures that the number of data will never fill up all available memory space and because used pre-processing methods are faster than algorithm speed, loss due to rate of data coming is smaller.

L. Rutkowski et al. (Eds.): ICAISC 2012, Part II, LNCS 7268, pp. 56–63, 2012.

The rest of this paper is organized as follows: section 2 surveys related work. Section 3 shows the pre-processing method. Section 4 shows experimental result on synthetic data. Subsection 4.1 shows data without noise and Subsection 4.2 shows data with noise. Subsection 4.3 compares previous subsections. Finally in section 5 we draw conclusions.

2   Related Work

Since 1967, when MacQueen proposed the C-Means algorithm in [12], clustering become one of major task in data mining. In 1981 Bezdek presented Fuzzy C-Means algorithm in [5]. In 1993 Krishnapuram and Keller proposed Possibilistic C-Means algorithm in [10]. Until today all these algorithms are the most popular tools. More about fuzzy sets and fuzzy clustering can be found in [8], [13], [22].

In 2002 O'Callaghan, et al. proposed modification of the C-Means algorithm for data streams [16]. From this time many improvements of this procedure were created. A special attention deserves CluSTREAM proposed by Aggarwal, et al. in [1]. Domingos and Hulton proposed another modification in [3] called VFKM.

In [30] a modification of the Fuzzy C-Means algorithm for data streams was proposed.

Another approach described in the literature is so called density-based clustering [2], [11], [14]. This paper combines approaches used so far in the centroid-based clustering and density-based clustering.

3   Pre-processing Procedures

In this section we propose pre-processing algorithms called *equi-width cubes*. This method can be used only for numerical attributes. We assume that the incoming data are D-dimensional. Data space is partitioning into a certain number N of cubes. The division of space is made by partition every axis into the some number of bins; for axis i we indicate it by B_i, for $i \in \{1, \ldots, D\}$. Of course $N = B_1 \cdot B_2 \cdot \ldots \cdot B_D$.

In order to use this method we have to assume possible minimum and maximum values of data stream, for all dimensions. After fixing the number of bins for each axis, algorithm partitions this axis into bins of equal width. Width of bins do not have to be equal in different axes. Cubes are created by crossing all dimensions. An exemplary, two-dimensional cube, is presented in Fig. 1, where $B_1 = h$ and $B_2 = m$.

For every cube C_{ij} we store the following values: n - number of elements in the cube, $\bar{A}_i$ - mean value of data elements in the cube, on the axis i, for $i = 1, \ldots, D$. This means that C_{ij} is $D+1$ dimensional vector.

When new data $x = [x_1, \ldots, x_D]$ comes, algorithm checks to which bins it belongs. Then it updates given cube by increasing n by one , and updates value $\bar{A}_i$ for all $i \in \{1, \ldots, D\}$, according to the formula:

$$\bar{A}_i = \frac{\bar{A}_i \cdot n + x_i}{n + 1}, \tag{1}$$

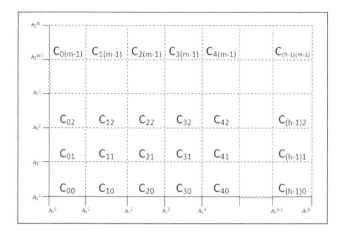

Fig. 1. Equi-width cubes

where n is value before adding current data.

Until clustering algorithm works new data are added to *equi-width cubes*. After computing clusters centers, cubes became a new chunk of data, to be processed by the clustering algorithm.

The biggest advantage of this method is that any number of elements coming from the stream can be stored in fix amount of memory. In no pre-processing case, cluster algorithms, like *FCM* or *PCM* work on the data chunk of such size as the data arrives. With *equi-width cubes* method there exists maximum value of cube on with cluster algorithm would be work.

In practice noisy data may hinder performance of the clustering algorithm. In the next section two cases will be considered:

- *all cubes* - all cubes, created at *equi-width cubes* methods, are sent to clustering algorithm.
- *most of cubes* - cubes with the value of n higher with some constant, are sent to clustering algorithm.

The *most of cubes* method reduces the effects of noisy data, but also accelerates the work of the algorithm.

4   Experimental Result

In this section the result of the *equi-width cubes method* is shown. The results obtained by the *all cubes method* are compared with results of the *most of cubes*. Simulations are performed on the two dimensional synthetic noisy data and data without noise. There are 100000 data without noise and additionally 1000 for noisy data.

4.1   Data without Noise

One of the key assumptions underlying the user side is to determine the number of bins for one dimension. Figure 2 shows change of the precision for different

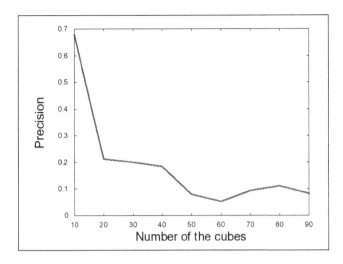

Fig. 2. Average distances from the centers of clusters to distributed centers

number of bins. Number of bins in all dimension is equal. Precision is an average of Euclidean distances from the true cluster center and determined by the FCM. As we can see too low amount of bins (and consequently cubes) leads to worse results. Best results are obtained for 60 bins. This amount will be used in further simulations.

Precision in 60 bins case is equal to $0,041$. In this case all cubes were sent to FCM. If we sent only cubes with number of elements higher than 100 then precision is $0,053$. Original data and computed centers of cluster are depicted in Fig. 3. All four clusters centers are almost in the same place for both methods.

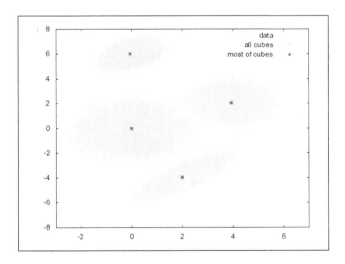

Fig. 3. Data and the calculated clusters centers

4.2 Noisy Data

To 100000 data used in previous subsection we added 1000 new data. New data were generated from uniform distribution on $[-3, 7] \times [-8, 8]$. All 101000 data were used for both methods, *all cubes* and *most of cubes*. Precision obtained by these method is $0,0419$ and $0,0536$, respectively. Original data and computed centers of clusters are depicted in Fig. 4.

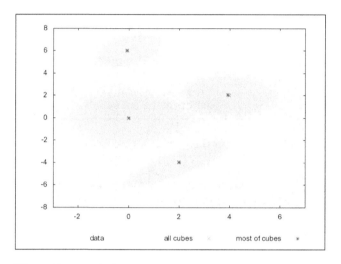

Fig. 4. Data and the calculated clusters centers - noisy data

4.3 Comparison

Both methods give similar results for noisy data and data without noise. Number of cubes sent to FCM are depicted in Fig. 5. One can see that cubes with

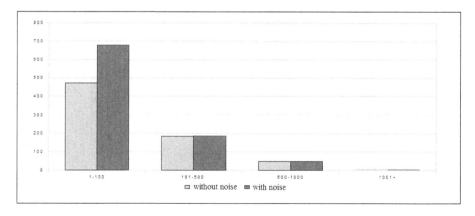

Fig. 5. Number of used cubes

number of elements lower than 101 is 66% for data without noise and 74% for noisy data. It shows that, the *most of cubes method*, required memory can be strongly reduced with little loss of accuracy.

5 Conclusions

In this paper we proposed pre-processing method for stream data mining. The analysis shows that results of method are satisfactory. Differences between clusters centers computed from original data and aggregate data are small in both proposed version.

Presented solutions are not exhaustive. It is necessary to create new, faster algorithms, that will provide greater accuracy.

Presented solutions are not suitable for the high dimensional data. If we have only 10 dimensions and partition all axis into two bins, we must keep in memory 1024 cubes. If we have 35 dimensions, there will be 17179869184 cubes.

Our current research is devoted to developing pre-processing techniques for neuro-fuzzy systems [15], [23], [24], [25], [26], [27], [28] and probabilistic neural networks [18], [19], [20], [21], [29] to deal with data streams.

Acknowledgments. The paper was prepared under project operated within the Foundation for Polish Science Team Programme co-financed by the EU European Regional Development Fund, Operational Program Innovative Economy 2007-2013, and also supported by National Science Center NCN.

References

1. Aggarwal, C.C., Han, J., Wang, J., Yu, P.S.: A framework for clustering evolving data streams. In: Proceedings of 29th International Conference on Very Large Data Bases, pp. 81–92 (2003)
2. Birant, D., Kut, A.: ST-DBSCAN: An algorithm for clustering spatial-temporal data. In: Data and Knowledge Engineering, pp. 208–221 (2007)
3. Domingos, P., Hulton, G.: A general method for scaling up machine learning algorithms and its application to clustering. In: Proceedings of the 18th International Conference on Machine Learning, pp. 106–113 (2001)
4. Babcook, B., Badu, S., Datar, M., Motwani, R., Widom, J.: Models and Issues in Data Stream Systems. In: International Conference on Management of Data and Symposium on Principles Database and Systems Madison (2002)
5. Bezdek, J.C.: Pattern Recognition with Fuzzy Objective Function Algoritms. Plenum Press, New York (1981)
6. Golab, L., Ozsu, T.: Issue in Data Stream Management. SIGMOD Record 32(2) (2003)
7. Guha, S., Koudas, N., Shim, K.: Data-Streams and Histograms. STOC 2001, Hersonissos, Crete, Greece (2001)
8. Hoppner, F., Klawonn, F., Kruse, R., Runkler, T.: Fuzzy Cluster Analysis. In: Method For Classification, Data Analysis and Image Recognition. John Wiley & Sons, Ltd. (1999)

9. Jagadish, H.V., Koudas, N., Muthukrishnan, S., Poosala, V., Sevcik, K., Suel, T.: Optimal Histograms with Quality Guarantees. In: Proceeding of the 24th VLBD Conference, New York, USA (1998)

10. Krishnapuram, R., Keller, J.: A possibilistic approach to clustering. IEEE Trans. Fuzzy Syst. 1(2), 98–110 (1993)

11. Tu, L., Chen, Y.: Stream Data Clustering based on Grid Density and Attraction. ACM Transactions on Computional Logic 1, 1–26 (2008)

12. MacQueen, J.B.: Some Methods for classification and Analysis of Multivariate Observations. In: Proceedings of 5th Berkeley Symposium on Mathematical Statistics and Probability, vol. 1, pp. 281–297. University of California Press, Berkeley (1967)

13. Miyamoto, S., Ichihashi, H., Honda, K.: Algorithms for Fuzzy Clustering. Methods in C-Means Clustering with Applications. Springer (2008)

14. Park, N.H., Lee, W.S.: Statistical Grid-based Clustering over Data Streams. SIGMOD Record 33(1) (2004)

15. Nowicki, R.: Nonlinear modelling and classification based on the MICOG defuzzifications. Journal of Nonlinear Analysis, Series A: Theory, Methods and Applications 7(12), 1033–1047 (2009)

16. O' Chalaghan, L., Mishra, N., Meyerson, A., Guha, S., Motwani, R.: Streaming data algorithms for high quality clustering. In: Proceedings of the 18th International Conference on Data Engineering, pp. 685–694 (2002)

17. Poosala, V., Ioannidis, Y.E., Haas, P.J., Shekita, E.J.: Improved Histograms for Selectivity Estimation of Range Predicates. In: Proc. of ACM SIGMOD Conf., pp. 294–305 (1996)

18. Rutkowski, L.: The real-time identification of time-varying systems by nonparametric algorithms based on the Parzen kernels. International Journal of Systems Science 16, 1123–1130 (1985)

19. Rutkowski, L.: Sequential pattern recognition procedures derived from multiple Fourier series. Pattern Recognition Letters 8, 213–216 (1988)

20. Rutkowski, L.: An application of multiple Fourier series to identification of multivariable nonstationary systems. International Journal of Systems Science 20(10), 1993–2002 (1989)

21. Rutkowski, L.: Nonparametric learning algorithms in the time-varying environments. Signal Processing 18, 129–137 (1989)

22. Rutkowski, L.: Computational Intelligence: Methods and Techniques. Springer (2008)

23. Rutkowski, L., Cpałka, K.: A general approach to neuro - fuzzy systems. In: Proceedings of the 10th IEEE International Conference on Fuzzy Systems, Melbourne, December 2-5, vol. 3, pp. 1428–1431 (2001)

24. Rutkowski, L., Cpałka, K.: A neuro-fuzzy controller with a compromise fuzzy reasoning. Control and Cybernetics 31(2), 297–308 (2002)

25. Scherer, R.: Boosting Ensemble of Relational Neuro-fuzzy Systems. In: Rutkowski, L., Tadeusiewicz, R., Zadeh, L.A., Żurada, J.M. (eds.) ICAISC 2006. LNCS (LNAI), vol. 4029, pp. 306–313. Springer, Heidelberg (2006)

26. Scherer, R.: Neuro-fuzzy Systems with Relation Matrix. In: Rutkowski, L., Scherer, R., Tadeusiewicz, R., Zadeh, L.A., Zurada, J.M. (eds.) ICAISC 2010. LNCS (LNAI), vol. 6113, pp. 210–215. Springer, Heidelberg (2010)

27. Starczewski, J., Rutkowski, L.: Interval type 2 neuro-fuzzy systems based on interval consequents. In: Rutkowski, L., Kacprzyk, J. (eds.) Neural Networks and Soft Computing, pp. 570–577. Physica-Verlag, Springer-Verlag Company, Heidelberg, New York (2003)

28. Starczewski, J.T., Rutkowski, L.: Connectionist Structures of Type 2 Fuzzy Inference Systems. In: Wyrzykowski, R., Dongarra, J., Paprzycki, M., Waśniewski, J. (eds.) PPAM 2001. LNCS, vol. 2328, pp. 634–642. Springer, Heidelberg (2002)
29. Vivekanandan, P., Nedunchezhian, R.: Mining Rules of Concept Drift Using Genetic Algorithm. Journal of Artificial Inteligence and Soft Computing Research 1(2), 135–145 (2011)
30. Wan, R., Yan, X., Su, X.: A Weighted Fuzzy Clustering Algorithm for Data Stream. In: ISECS International Colloquium on Computing, Communication, Control, and Management (2008)
31. Zhang, D., Gunopulos, D., Tsotras, V.J., Seeger, B.: Temporal and spatio-temporal aggregations over data streams using multiple time granularities. Journal Information Systems 28(1-2) (2003)

Simple Incremental Instance Selection Wrapper for Classification

Marek Grochowski

Department of Informatics, Nicolaus Copernicus University, Toruń, Poland
grochu@is.umk.pl

Abstract. Instance selection methods are very useful data mining tools for dealing with large data sets. There exist many instance selection algorithms capable for significant reduction of training data size for particular classifier without generalization degradation. In opposition to those methods, this paper focuses on general pruning methods which can be successfully applied for arbitrary classification method. Simple but efficient wrapper method based on generalization of Hart's Condensed Nearest Neighbors rule is presented and impact of this method on classification quality is reported.

Keywords: instance selection, condensed nearest neighbors, classification.

1 Introduction

Datasets with enormous amount of instances become great challenge nowadays. Storage requirements and computational cost of many commonly used machine learning algorithms, especially when dealing with large datasets, cause the need for investigating techniques capable of reducing the size of data set without degradation in quality of inherent information. This paper focuses on effect of instance selection techniques used for classification algorithms, thus the main requirement for instance selection is to preserve generalization abilities of classifier trained on reduced data set.

Many instance selection methods based on various assumptions and strategies was developed. These methods can be grouped into three types based on applications: noise filters, condensation algorithms and prototype selection methods.

Noise Filters (or edited methods) prune outliers and instances recognized as noise. Removing of noisy vectors is crucial for algorithms that are sensitive for noise and usually lead to improvement in generalization and increase decision boundaries smoothness. Typically noise filters are decremental methods. For example Wilson's Edited Nearest Neighbors [12] remove instances whose class labels does not agree with majority class of its neighbors.

Condensation Algorithms are used for decreasing the size of training data to reduce storage requirements and improve computation speed of classifiers without lose in competence. Those methods attempt to select a subset of data from training set which include most informative samples sufficient to fully reproduce solution generated by classifiers trained on whole training data set. Typically condensation methods are incremental. For example, probably the first instance selection method and one of the

L. Rutkowski et al. (Eds.): ICAISC 2012, Part II, LNCS 7268, pp. 64–72, 2012.
© Springer-Verlag Berlin Heidelberg 2012

simplest one is Hart's Condensed Nearest Neighbor rule [6] which build up reference set by adding sequentially instances that cannot be correctly handled by nearest neighbors from current reference set.

Prototype Selection methods reduce training set to few highly representative samples. Usually those prototypes are not drawn from training data but become created in centers of clusters containing instances associated with single class. In most cases of prototype based methods the number of resulting prototypes must be determined explicitly by user.

Some methods combine this instance selection approaches by searching for a very small, noise-free reference sets that not only preserve generalization capabilities of classifier training on whole dataset but even are able to increase its performance. For in-depth review and comparison of instance selection methods refer to [8,7,4,13].

Related research has mainly focused on instances selection techniques for nearest neighbors classification, which is understandable due to the significant storage requirement of NN methods. Most of them are embedded models and use prior knowledge about neighbors relations or shape of decision boundary created by kNN classifier to build efficient pruning strategy therefore the application of these methods for reducing training dataset for non-case based classifiers is usually inappropriate. Detailed comparison of instance selection techniques applied to training data set reduction for several different type of classifiers is refereed in [7,4]. Furthermore, one should not expect that there exist one general instance selection method suitable for all classifiers and for all classification problems. An attempt to automate the process of choosing a proper selection technique suitable for particular classification task using meta-learning is discussed in [11]. However, some general strategies suitable in common applications can be considered. This paper focuses on discovering of such instance selection methods capable for significant training data set size reduction without significant lose in generalization for arbitrary classification learning machine.

2   General Instance Selection Methods

Each classification algorithm make some specific assumptions about relations inherent in data which is tend to discover. Methods based on statistical principles (e.g. SVM, Naive Bayes, RBF, Bayesian Networks) require proper density of samples to discover accurate solution. Therefore, prototype based selection methods, by reducing training data do few samples, are not applicable here and may only lead to lose in generalization. For case-based classifiers like kNN removing of all clusters internals leaving only samples close to decision boundary is appropriate. But also opposite strategy that remove vectors placed near decision boundaries and leaving only few representative samples placed near class centers may act here very well. If optimal condensation is required, i.e. there is strong need for obtaining reduced training set with minimal possible size without any degradation in classification quality, then each classifier might require its own special designed instance selection strategy. General selection algorithm should not have prior knowledge about classifier for witch it was applied. Therefore, one should not expect that such approach will lead to best possible instance selection solution for given classifier, however if only such selection will lead to heavy reduction in training data size and if only lose in generalization will not be significant then gain in storage requirement and possible acceleration of classification speed will justify such approach.

Analogous to feature selection algorithms, general instance selection method, applicable for arbitrary classification machine, can be broken into two major types: wrapper selection methods and filters. **Wrapper methods** perform searching trough space of possible training data subsets and use classifier to evaluate usefulness of each subset. For example Skalak proposed Monte Carlo method [10] where nearest neighbors method was used for evaluation of sampled subsets of k prototypes. Similar method EkP, where searching was made by simplex optimization, was introduced by Grudziński in [5] and used for training of decision trees. Unfortunately, both those methods use fixed number of reference vectors. Identification of proper reference set size is major challenge that should be stressed by general selection algorithm. Wrapper methods can be computationally expensive and have tend to overfit. **Filters** do not depend on any classification method and use only information gained from data structure (e.g. basic statistics) to identify vectors that can be safely removed from training data without significant lose of relevant information supplied by dataset. There are many data squashing techniques [2] that attempts to preserve statistical informations, e.g. likelihood function profile or data moments. In case of classification such filter methods should provide proper inner-class density preservation.

Searching trough possible interesting subsets of training data without proper strategy might become impracticable due to time limitations, especially for wrapper methods where given classifier have to be used many times for evaluation. Therefore, incremental searching strategies should be preferred where most of evaluations, especially at the beginning of growing phase, are performed on small number of instances.

3   Using Modified CNN Rule as Instance Selection Wrapper

One of the most simplest incremental instance selection method is Hart's Condensed Nearest Neighbors [6] rule. Although, the algorithm was designed for nearest neighbors classification it can be easy adopted for arbitrary classifier. Algorithm 1 present modified CNN algorithm which act as wrapper. Growing procedure sequentially puts, to initially empty reference set, vectors misclassified by classifier trained on current reference set S. In case of nearest neighbors rule used for classification this algorithm is equivalent to Hart's CNN method.

The main advantage of this approach is that the size of resulting reference set is chosen automatically. The stop criterion is clearly stated: reference set will continue to grow if there still exists some misclassified instances that do not belong to reference set. This means that the search process continues as long as the reference set is still not representative enough to cover all class relations in training data. Therefore, in cases where all important information should remain in compressed dataset, this method is beneficial over most of general instance selection methods, which require explicit specification of number of reference vectors. In contrast to sampling algorithms proposed by Skalak [10] or EkP method [5] presented here incremental algorithm lead to creation of condensed training data set which size is strictly suited to given classifier in automatic way.

Algorithm 1. Incremental instance selection wrapper algorithm

---

```
1  begin
       Data: training dataset T
       Result: reference dataset S ⊂ T
2      Initialization: add to S one random instance from each class
3      repeat
4          foreach instance x ∈ T \ S do
5              if x is misclassified by classifier trained on S then
6                  │   S ← S ∪ {x}
7              end
8          end
9      until there exist misclassified instance x ∈ T \ S
10     return S
11 end
```

Content of the final training set depend on initialization and on the order of instance presentation. Most important disadvantage of this approach is strong influence of noise and data artifact on quality of solution. Noisy instances always will be included in the final reference set, therefore, this method do not provide minimal possible accurate condensation. Figure 1 illustrate the process of training of presented instance selection algorithm for few different types of classifiers on two real world datasets taken from UCI [1] repository. Dependence of accuracy measured on training dataset during incremental searching is presented for kNN classifier (with euclidean metric and $k = 1$), Separability of Split Value (SSV) decision tree [3], SVM with Gaussian and linear kernel. In case of nearest neighbors method learning is stable, each newly added instance make only local change of decision boundary, therefore training accuracy is evenly growing while algorithm proceed. For all other considered classifiers the learning process may become highly unstable at the beginning of reference set growing phase. Each newly added instance may influent on classifier significant and may create totally different decision boundaries comparing to previous iteration. However, during further

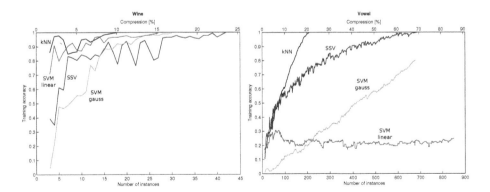

Fig. 1. Variability of training accuracy during growing phase of condensed instance selection algorithm

training error function is stabilizing and even if atypical and noisy instanced was added previously to reference set the vectors considered as eligible finally will predominate leading to decrease of training error. In vast majority of trials presented approach lead to significant training dataset reduction and the most typical behavior is the one shown for the Wine dataset (see Fig. 1), where accuracy increases rapidly at the beginning and after few iterations training error stabilize.

3.1   Condensed Dataset Visualization

For given training data different set of data point that mater the most to a classifier will be generated by instance selection. This is shown in toy example on Fig. 2 where scatter plots of three simple artificial dataset are presented. Sequential pictures (from top to bottom) present visualizations of original dataset and condensed dataset obtained by instance selection applied for kNN, SSV and SVM classifiers accordingly. In most cases only instances placed near the decision border are selected. Resulting reference sets differ mostly in size for each type of classification method. Nearest neighbor classifier need only few data point to cover whole clusters of vectors with the same class label. Only overlapping regions remain dense. Solutions generated by SSV decision tree and SVMs depend on greater number of critical points and more instances placed close to class centers are selected. In case of data that are not linear separable presented instance selection method applied to linear machine (SVM with linear kernel) lead to selection of almost all data points (see left column of Fig. 2). This shows weeknights of that method where many irrelevant instances which can be safely pruned without lose in generalization still remain in reference set.

3.2   Generalization Test

Numerical experiments have been performed on several real-world classification problems from the UCI repository [1]. Presented in this paper Incremental Instance Selection Wrapper (IISW) has been used to perform training dataset compression for few different types of classifiers: kNN (with $k = 1$ and Euclidean metric), SSV decision tree, SVM with Gaussian kernel ($\sigma = 0.1$ and $C = 1.0$) and SVM with linear kernel ($C = 1.0$). Due the space limitations only results for SSV decision tree (Tab. 1) and SVM with Gaussian kernel (Tab. 2) are presented. Average classification accuracy was estimated using 10-fold stratified cross-validation tests repeated 10 times. For each training data sampled with cross-validation all missing values have been replaced by average attribute values taken from all non-missing feature values (for ordered features) or by mode value (for unordered features). Then all contiguous features have been standardized and finally instance selection method was applied and classifier was trained on resulting condensed dataset. To compare generalization of classifiers trained with and without instance selection algorithm for each dataset corrected resampled t-test was used, which is suitable statistical test for model comparison in classification evaluation [9].

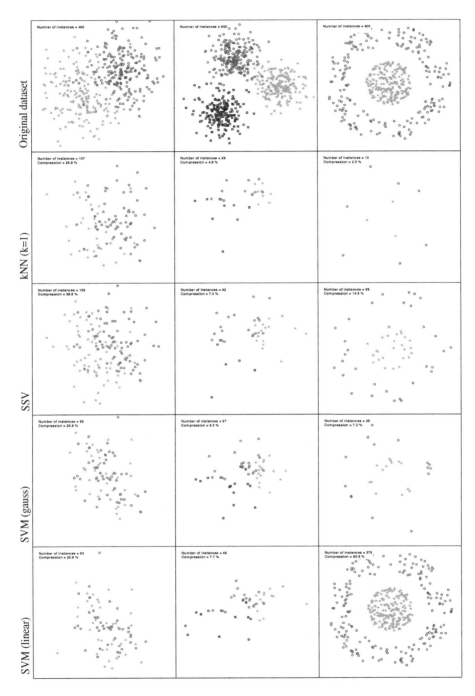

Fig. 2. Scatter plots of artificial toy data before (top line) and after instance selection applied to kNN, SSV decision tree and SVM with Gaussian and linear kernel

Table 1. Average accuracy, overall time of computations and dataset compression achieved in the 10x10 stratified CV test for SSV decision tree

Dataset	SSV		IISW(SSV)		
	accuracy [%]	time [s.]	accuracy [%]	time [s.]	compression [%]
appendicitis	81.4 ± 10.2	6.3	79.9 ± 10.2	88.6	49.0 ± 5.5
dermatology	91.4 ± 4.1	12.9	91.7 ± 4.9	276.8	36.8 ± 3.3
glass	67.8 ± 9.5	9.2	69.7 ± 10.2	403.3	68.6 ± 4.6
heart-statlog	75.9 ± 8.5	9.3	74.0 ± 9.1	641.1	64.6 ± 3.0
ionosphere	81.3 ± 8.5	15.2	81.4 ± 9.2	653.3	62.3 ± 5.2
labor	82.8 ± 13.4	4.8	83.1 ± 15.8	47.2	44.2 ± 6.8
lymph	76.7 ± 9.8	5.8	74.0 ± 12.0	184.7	59.2 ± 4.6
sonar	76.1 ± 9.1	33.6	73.4 ± 9.5	5016.7	74.4 ± 4.1
voting	93.3 ± 3.4	7.8	93.1 ± 3.7	189.7	20.1 ± 1.8
wine	91.7 ± 6.5	12.8	94.1 ± 5.5	97.1	30.6 ± 3.9
zoo	90.6 ± 8.5	6.5	90.7 ± 8.1	52.2	27.9 ± 3.0
Average	82.6	11.3	82.3	695.5	48.9
t Test Win/Tie/Lose			0/11/0		
Wilcoxon p-value			0.369		

Table 2. Average accuracy, overall time of computations and dataset compression achieved in the 10x10 stratified CV test for SVM with Gaussian kernel

Dataset	SVM gauss		IISW(SVM gauss)		
	accuracy [%]	time [s.]	accuracy [%]	time [s.]	compression [%]
appendicitis	87.0 ± 8.7	6.9	86.0 ± 9.4	161.5	28.6 ± 2.1
dermatology	94.8 ± 3.4	32.7	89.5 ± 5.1	1773.8	27.2 ± 0.9
glass	56.3 ± 9.1	30.1	41.2 ± 9.3	2192.3	78.9 ± 1.5
heart-statlog	83.4 ± 6.7	12.1	82.0 ± 7.5	335.3	37.5 ± 1.6
ionosphere	91.8 ± 6.1	8.1	90.2 ± 6.2	135.9	24.4 ± 1.8
labor	94.6 ± 9.2	8.8	92.5 ± 10.0	50.7	30.3 ± 4.2
lymph	76.2 ± 9.8	17.4	73.0 ± 11.2	759.9	50.9 ± 2.2
sonar	78.5 ± 6.5	10.3	84.3 ± 7.4	364.0	49.7 ± 3.3
voting	95.6 ± 2.8	10.1	95.9 ± 2.9	154.6	11.9 ± 0.8
wine	98.3 ± 2.9	16.4	95.2 ± 5.0	247.9	17.7 ± 1.4
zoo	37.2 ± 11.2	22.6	32.4 ± 11.3	1645.6	85.2 ± 1.6
Average	81.2	16.0	78.4	711.0	40.2
t Test Win/Tie/Lose			0/11/0		
Wilcoxon p-value			0.027		

Presented instance selection method was able to reduce the size of training data for SSV decision tree in average up to 48.9 % of original dataset size without degradation in generalization. Even higher average compression (40.2 %) was achieved in case of SVM classifier. In most cases average accuracy slightly decreased after dataset condensation, however the differences are always in the range of standard deviation. Therefore t-test shows no significant difference in generalization of classifiers applied after instance selection and classifiers trained on original data (11 ties obtained by t-test with level of significance equal to 5%). Similar results was obtained for kNN and SVM with linear kernel where average reduction of training data size reached 33.7% and 34.1% accordingly, without significant loss in accuracy. The Wilcoxon's signed-rank test confirms that there is no significant difference (p-value equal to 0.369) between distributions of average accuracies for SSV trained on whole dataset and after dataset reduction. In case of SVM Wilcoxon's test give p-value equal to 0.027, however still the hypothesis that distribution of accuracies is identical in both cases can not be rejected at the level of significance equal to 1%. Presented results reveals also another weakens of this approach that is significant increase of overall training time which limits its applications to situations where storage requirements are highly preferred over computation complexity.

4 Conclusions

Data condensation is very useful tool for dealing with very large datasets. Smaller training data tend to create less complex classification models which lead to simplification of solution and facilitate model interpretation. Simple but efficient instance selection method has been proposed in this paper that can be used for data condensation for any arbitrary classifier. Presented method lead to significant reduction of training data size while comparison of classification accuracy achieved on original dataset and on condensed data shows no significant difference. Like in case of most of wrappers this method also suffer for requirements for time of computations which might make this method impractical for computational expensive classifiers. However, the requirement for time can be relaxed because in many applications instance selection is performed once in a while.

Acknowledgment. This work was supported by the Polish Ministry of Higher Education under research grant no. N N516 500539.

References

1. Asuncion, A., Newman, D.J.: UCI machine learning repository (2007),
   http://www.ics.uci.edu/~mlearn/MLRepository.html
2. DuMouchel, W.: Data squashing: constructing summary data sets. In: Handbook of Massive Data Sets, pp. 579–591. Kluwer Academic Publishers, Norwell (2002)
3. Grąbczewski, K., Duch, W.: The separability of split value criterion. In: Proceedings of the 5th Conf. on Neural Networks and Soft Computing, pp. 201–208. Polish Neural Network Society, Zakopane (2000)

4. Grochowski, M., Jankowski, N.: Comparison of Instance Selection Algorithms II. Results and Comments. In: Rutkowski, L., Siekmann, J.H., Tadeusiewicz, R., Zadeh, L.A. (eds.) ICAISC 2004. LNCS (LNAI), vol. 3070, pp. 580–585. Springer, Heidelberg (2004)
5. Grudziński, K., Grochowski, M., Duch, W.: Pruning Classification Rules with Reference Vector Selection Methods. In: Rutkowski, L., Scherer, R., Tadeusiewicz, R., Zadeh, L.A., Zurada, J.M. (eds.) ICAISC 2010. LNCS, vol. 6113, pp. 347–354. Springer, Heidelberg (2010)
6. Hart, P.E.: The condensed nearest neighbor rule. IEEE Transactions on Information Theory 14, 515–516 (1968)
7. Jankowski, N., Grochowski, M.: Comparison of Instances Seletion Algorithms I. Algorithms Survey. In: Rutkowski, L., Siekmann, J.H., Tadeusiewicz, R., Zadeh, L.A. (eds.) ICAISC 2004. LNCS (LNAI), vol. 3070, pp. 598–603. Springer, Heidelberg (2004)
8. Liu, H., Motoda, H.: Instance Selection and Construction for Data Mining. Kluwer Academic Publishers, Norwell (2001)
9. Nadeau, C., Bengio, Y.: Inference for the generalization error. Machine Learning 52(3), 239–281 (2003)
10. Skalak, D.B.: Prototype and feature selection by sampling and random mutation hill climbing algorithms. In: Proc. 11th International Conference on Machine Learning, pp. 293–301 (1994)
11. Smith-Miles, K., Islam, R.: Meta-learning for data summarization based on instance selection method. In: IEEE Congress on Evolutionary Computation, pp. 1–8 (2010)
12. Wilson, D.L.: Asymptotic properties of nearest neighbor rules using edited data. IEEE Trans. Systems, Man and Cybernetics 2, 408–421 (1972)
13. Wilson, D.R., Martinez, T.R.: Reduction techniques for instance-based learning algorithms. Machine Learning 38(3), 257–286 (2000)

Mining of Multiobjective Non-redundant Association Rules in Data Streams

Anamika Gupta, Naveen Kumar, and Vasudha Bhatnagar

Department of Computer Science, University of Delhi, India
{agupta,nk,vbhatnagar}@cs.du.ac.in

Abstract. Non-redundant association rule mining requires generation of both closed itemsets and their minimal generators. However, only a few researchers have addressed both the issues for data streams. Further, association rule mining is now considered as multiobjective problem where multiple measures like correlation coefficient, recall, comprehensibility, lift etc can be used for evaluating a rule. Discovery of multiobjective association rules in data streams has not been paid much attention.

In this paper, we have proposed a 3-step algorithm for generation of multiobjective non-redundant association rules in data streams. In the first step, an online procedure generates closed itemsets incrementally using state of the art CLICI algorithm and stores the results in a lattice based synopsis. An offline component invokes the proposed genMG and genMAR procedures whenever required. Without generating candidates, genMG computes minimal generators of all closed itemsets stored in the synopsis. Next, genMAR generates multiobjective association rules using non-dominating sorting based on user specified interestingness measures that are computed using the synopsis. Experimental evaluation using synthetic and real life datasets demonstrates the efficiency and scalability of the proposed algorithm.

1 Introduction

Association Rule Mining (ARM), an important data mining task, discovers meaningful associations amongst items using association rules of the form $X \rightarrow Y$ where X and Y are independent sets of items. X is called the antecedent and Y is called the consequent of the rule [1]. Algorithms for ARM essentially perform two distinct tasks: 1) Discover frequent item-sets (FIs). 2) Generate strong rules from frequent item-sets. However, the set of rules so generated is too large to be comprehensible by the user even for small datasets having only hundreds of transactions. Further, the generated rulesets have lot of redundant rules. Traditional association rule mining algorithms use support and confidence as interestingness measures to prune the set of discovered rules [1].

In the last decade, researchers have explored the idea of mining frequent closed itemsets (FCIs) instead of frequent itemsets for association rules [13,15,20]. There are two major advantages of mining FCIs over FIs. The set of FCIs has been shown to be loss-less and reduced representation of set of FIs [13,20] and the

L. Rutkowski et al. (Eds.): ICAISC 2012, Part II, LNCS 7268, pp. 73–81, 2012.

rules discovered are non-redundant in nature [11,18,21]. Mining of non-redundant association rules using FCIs involves three sub-tasks [11,18,21]: generation of i) closed itemsets (CIs) ii) minimal generators (MGs) iii) non-redundant association rules (NARs).

Mining of closed itemsets in static datasets [7] as well as data streams [3] has received much attention during last decade. Several algorithms like Closet, Charm, Closet+, CHARM-L, FP-Close, and DCI-Closed [7] have been proposed to generate CIs in static datasets. Algorithms like Moment [19], CFI-Stream [10], Newmoment [12], and CLICI [6] address the issue of mining CIs in data streams. Generation of minimal generators (MGs), although an important subtask of non-redundant association rule mining, has not been paid much attention. Only a few methods have been proposed for extracting FCIs and MGs in static datasets e.g. Titanic [15], Charm-L [21], Talky-G [16].

In today's world, more and more applications such as traffic monitoring, web-click analysis, military sensing and tracking generate a large amount of high speed streaming data. Thus the need arises for efficient mining of association rules in such streams. However, the algorithms designed for static datasets scan the dataset multiple times and hence are not suitable for streams. Incremental algorithms proposed by Tan et al. [17] and Shin et al. [14] for discovery of association rules in streams are based on frequent itemsets and generate a lot of redundant rules. CARM proposed by Jiang et al. [11] generates a small subset of association rules using closed itemsets which are used in estimating missing values in sensor data. However, discovering rules in data streams using efficient methods has not been paid enough attention.

Another issue in ARM is the choice of appropriate interestingness measure (IM) for pruning the set of generated rules. The commonly used IMs, support and confidence, may not be appropriate for the application in hand. For example, for an application requiring negative association rules, it may be better to use correlation coefficient as an IM. Other rule evaluation measures like recall, certainty factor, variance, laplace, and information gain have been proposed in literature [5,8] which may be useful in different applications of ARM. Further, it has been observed that association rule mining is a multiobjective problem rather than a two objective problem where various rule evaluation measures act as different objectives [9].

In this paper, we address the issue of mining multiobjective non-redundant association rules in data streams and propose a three step algorithm, MARM_DS. The online component of MARM_DS uses state of the art algorithm CLICI [6] for extraction of recent closed itemsets in data stream and maintains a lattice based synopsis data structure for storing all recent closed itemsets and their support. An offline component invokes the proposed genMG procedure which traverses the synopsis once to discover minimal generators of all closed itemsets. Use of synopsis for computation of various interestingness measures (IMs) is demonstrated. User specified IMs serve as objective functions for non-dominated sorting [4] and multiobjective association rules are discovered using the proposed genMAR procedure.

Organization of the Paper. Rest of the paper is organized as follows: section 2 presents the related work, section 3 introduces non-redundant association rule mining and gives an overview of the CLICI algorithm, section 4 describes the proposed MARM_DS algorithm for generation of multiobjective non-redundant association rules and section 5 presents the experimental results. Finally section 6 concludes the paper.

2   Related Work

Algorithms for ARM Using CIs in Static Datasets. Charm-L algorithm mines association rules in static datasets [21]. It traverses the dataset in a vertical format and generates closed itemsets along with associated transactions that are stored in a lattice. Later, the lattice is traversed and minimal generators of each closed itemset are generated in an apriori style generating all candidates. Lattice is further traversed to generate association rules. MG-Charm [18] algorithm modifies Charm-L algorithm by integrating the generation of MGs along with the generation of CIs, hence generates no candidates. Touch [16] algorithm generates CIs and MGs separately as two independent tasks. While generation of CI is performed by Charm-L algorithm, a stand-alone method Talky-G is proposed for generation of MGs. Later, Touch algorithm associates MGs to their respective CIs. Being based on vertical traversal of the dataset, all the aforementioned algorithms can work only on static datasets.

Algorithms for ARM in Data Streams. Several algorithms have been proposed for mining association rules in data streams using frequent itemsets [3]. Being based on frequent itemsets, the generated set of rules contains a lot of redundancy and is very large in size. Algorithms like Moment [19], CFI-Stream [10], Newmoment [12], and CLICI [6], mine closed itemsets in data stream but do not address the issue of mining association rules. Nan et al. proposed CFI-Stream algorithm [11] for mining CIs in data stream and claim that the same can be used to mine subsets of association rules for datasets having missing values.

3   Background

First we introduce some terminology. Let $I = \{i_1, i_2, ..., i_n\}$ be a set of n items. Let D denote the set of transactions (the dataset). A transaction $t \in D$ is a set of items. A set of one or more items is termed as an itemset. The support count of an itemset X is defined as the number of transactions in which X occurs. An itemset X is called **closed itemset** if there does not exist a proper superset Y of X such that support of Y is same as that of X.

An association rule is an implication of the form $R : X \to Y$, where $X \subset I$, $Y \subset I$ and $X \cap Y = \emptyset$. X and Y are termed antecedent and consequent respectively of the rule. A rule is said to have support s if $s\%$ of transactions in D contain $X \cup Y$ and is said to have confidence c if $c\%$ of transactions in D that contain X also contain Y. Association rule mining aims to discover all rules that have support and confidence greater than the user-specified minimum support and minimum confidence threshold.

Non-redundant Association Rules. A rule R_1 is said to be more general than another rule R_2 if support and confidence of both R_1 and R_2 are equal and R_2 can be generated by adding additional items to either the antecedent or consequent of R_1. Let $\mathcal{R} = R_1, R_2, ..., R_n$ be a set of n rules having same support and confidence. Then a rule R_i is **redundant** if there exists a more general rule than R_j in $\mathcal{R}$.

An itemset G is called a generator of a closed itemset X if and only if (1) $G \subset X$ and (2) support$(G) =$ support(X). Let $\mathcal{G}(X)$ denote the set of generators of X. $G \in \mathcal{G}(X)$ is a **minimal generator** if it has no proper subset in $\mathcal{G}(X)$. Let $\mathcal{G}^{min}(X)$ denote the set of all minimal generators of X. Let X and Y denote two closed itemsets such that $X \subset Y$. Let $G' \in \mathcal{G}^{min}(X)$ and $G'' \in \mathcal{G}^{min}(Y)$. Rules of the form $G' \rightarrow G''$ are $< 100\%$ **confident rules** . Rules of the form $G'' \rightarrow G'$ are 100% **confident rules** [21].

Discovery of Closed Itemsets. In [6], Gupta et al. have proposed an incremental algorithm, CLICI, for discovery of all recent closed itemsets in a given dataset. The discovered closed itemsets are stored in a synopsis, called CILattice. CILattice has two components: a lattice $\mathcal{L}$ and a table ITable that maps item i to its minimal node (denoted by F_i) in the lattice. A node X of $\mathcal{L}$ represents a closed itemset I_X and stores its frequency f_X along with links to its parents and child nodes. CLICI fades out the obsolete information of old transactions using a decay function [2] and later prunes the decayed information, thereby ensuring the recency of closed itemsets and in turn keeping size of the synopsis under control.

Fig. 1 shows the example dataset and corresponding $< \mathcal{L}, Itable >$. For details of procedures for insert, delete and search in $\mathcal{L}$, please refer to [6].

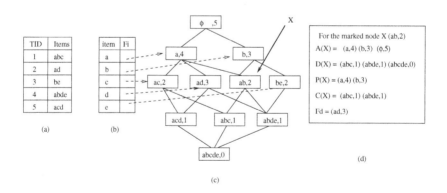

Fig. 1. (a) A toy dataset (b) Header table with items i and pointer to their minimal node F_i in $\mathcal{L}$ (c) $\mathcal{L}$ with nodes having closed itemset and its support (d) List of ancestors $A(X)$, descendents $D(X)$, parents $P(X)$ and children $C(X)$ for node X and F_i for $i = d$

4   MARM_DS Algorithm

The proposed algorithm for multiobjective association rule mining in data streams (MARM_DS) is a 3-step algorithm. The online component of MARM_DS uses state of the art algorithm CLICI [6] for extraction of recent closed itemsets in data stream and maintains a lattice based synopsis, CILattice, for storing all recent closed itemsets and their support. An offline component invokes the proposed genMG procedure which traverses the synopsis once to discover minimal generators of all closed itemsets. Based on user specified IMs, multiobjective association rules are discovered using the proposed genMAR procedure.

CLICI algorithm for generation of all recent closed itemsets in data streams has already been described in section 3. We now describe the procedures genMG and genMAR for generation of minimal generators and multiobjective association rules respectively.

4.1   genMG Procedure

Before describing the algorithm, we make some observations about minimal generators. Let $\mathcal{G}(X)$ denote the set of generators and $\mathcal{G}^{min}(X)$ denote the set of minimal generators of node X in $\mathcal{L}$. Let $\mathcal{G}^{min}(P(X))$ denote the set of minimal generators of all parents of X.

Observation 1. *Let X be a node in $\mathcal{L}$, for each $i \in I$ such that $F_i = X$, $i \in \mathcal{G}^{min}(X)$.*

Observation 2. *For a node X of $\mathcal{L}$, $Y \in P(X)$, $G \in \mathcal{G}^{min}(P(X))$, for each $i \in I_X$ such that $i \notin I_Y$, $\{G \cup \{i\}\} \in \mathcal{G}(X)$.*

Algorithm. genMG traverses $\mathcal{L}$ starting from the top node $\top$. Minimal generator of $\top$ is same as items present in $I_\top$. Next, ITable is searched to find the F_i corresponding to each item $i \in I$ and that item is assigned as the minimal generators of the corresponding F_i (ref. Observation 1).

Next, for each node X of $\mathcal{L}$, minimal generators of $\mathcal{G}^{min}(P(X))$ (i.e. minimal generators of parent Y of X) are considered. For each minimal generator G of $\mathcal{G}^{min}(P(X))$, we consider the set $G \cup \{i\}$ where i is an item of X but not present in Y. According to observation 2, $G \cup \{i\}$ is a generator of X, but it may not necessarily be a minimal generator. We apply the following steps to find whether $G \cup \{i\}$ is a minimal generator.

1. if $G \cup \{i\}$ has no subset in $\mathcal{G}^{min}(X)$ then $G \cup \{i\} \in \mathcal{G}^{min}(X)$
2. if $G \cup \{i\}$ is same as a generator in $\mathcal{G}^{min}(X)$ then no action is performed
3. if $G \cup \{i\}$ is subset of a generator G' in $\mathcal{G}^{min}(X)$ then $G \cup \{i\}$ is added to $\mathcal{G}^{min}(X)$ and G' is removed from $\mathcal{G}^{min}(X)$

For the bottom node, minimal generators are generated only if the support of bottom is greater than zero. The algorithm stops when all nodes are visited. We now formally present the algorithm for generating minimal generators of all closed itemsets given in $\mathcal{L}$.

4.2   genMAR Procedure

Once sets of minimal generators of node X and its parent node Y are computed, genMAR procedure generates association rules between minimal generators of X and Y. For each minimal generator $G'' \in \mathcal{G}^{min}(Y)$ and minimal generator $G' \in \mathcal{G}^{min}(X)$ such that $G' \cap G'' = \emptyset$, following rules are generated:

1. $R_1 : G' \to G''$
2. $R_2 : G'' \to G'$

Input: $\mathcal{L}$ - Lattice of closed itemsets (CIs)
Output: Minimal Generators of all nodes of $\mathcal{L}$

$\mathcal{G}^{min}(\top)$ = set of all items in $I_\top$
for all items i in ITable **do**
  if $F_i = X$ **then**
    add i to $\mathcal{G}^{min}(X)$.
  end if
end for
for all nodes X of $\mathcal{L}$ **do**
  if X is bottom and support of X is 0 **then**
    do nothing
  else
    for all parent nodes Y of X **do**
      for all generators G of Y **do**
        compute $G \cup \{k\}$, where $k \in X$ but $k \notin Y$
        if $G \cup \{k\}$ has no subset in $\mathcal{G}^{min}(X)$ **then**
          add $G \cup \{k\}$ to $\mathcal{G}^{min}(X)$
        else
          if $G \cup \{k\}$ is subset of a generator G' in $\mathcal{G}^{min}(X)$ **then**
            add $G \cup \{k\}$ to $\mathcal{G}^{min}(X)$
            remove G' from $\mathcal{G}^{min}(X)$
          end if
        end if
      end for
    end for
  end if
end for

Algorithm 1. genMG Procedure

Computation of Interestingness Measures. We demonstrate the use of synopsis for computation of various interestingness measures. The following observations are obvious w.r.t rules R_1 and R_2 mentioned above:

1. Support(G'') = Support(Y)
2. Support(G') = Support(X)
3. Support($G' \cup G''$) = Support(G') = Support(X)

In the table 1, we show the computation of some interestingness measures (IMs) for the generated rules in terms of support of X and Y. Several other IMs can be expressed similarly but because of lack of space, we show only a few.

Table 1. Interestingness Measures

IM	$R_1 : G' \to G''$	$R_2 : G'' \to G'$
Support	$Support(X)$	$Support(X)$
Confidence	100%	$\frac{Support(X)}{Support(Y)}$
Coverage	$Support(X)$	$Support(Y)$
Prevalence	$Support(X)$	$Support(Y)$
Recall	$\frac{Support(X)}{Support(Y)}$	100%
Lift	$\frac{1}{Support(Y)}$	$\frac{1}{Support(Y)}$
Certainty factor	100%	$\frac{Support(X)-Support(Y)^2}{Support(Y)*(1-Support(Y))}$
Cosine	$\sqrt{\frac{Support(X)}{Support(Y)}}$	$\sqrt{\frac{Support(X)}{Support(Y)}}$

5 Experimental Results

We implemented the proposed MARM_DS algorithm in C++ and conducted experiments on a 2.1 GHz AMD Dual-Core PC running Red Hat Linux with 4 GB of memory. Experiments were conducted to study the efficiency and scalability of MARM_DS on synthetic datasets generated using IBM data generator[1] and real life datasets from UCI repository[2].

Since there is no algorithm available for generating recent closed itemsets, their minimal generators and the associated rules on data streams, still we compare MARM_DS with state of the art Charm-L[3] algorithm [21]. Whereas Charm-L generates closed itemsets in static datasets and use support and confidence thresholds to prune the set of CIs, MARM_DS decays older information and generates recent CIs in data streams. Even though the closed itemset generation procedure in both the algorithms is not comparable, both the algorithms use lattice of generated closed itemsets for generating minimal generators and rules and hence are comparable if the same set of closed itemsets is given as input.

We run Charm-L (with no pruning) and MARM_DS (with no decay mechanism) on the datasets mentioned in Table 2 and generate all closed itemsets. We compared execution time of Charm-L and MARM_DS for generating MGs and rules. It can be observed from Table 2 that MARM_DS is more efficient than Charm-L on all the datasets.

To demonstrate scalability of the proposed MARM_DS algorithm, we generated four different datasets T3I4D100K, T5I6D100K, T8I8D100K, T12I10D100K using IBM data generator [1]. Three numbers in each dataset denote the average transaction length (T), average maximum potential frequent itemset size (I) and

---

[1] http://www.almaden.ibm.com/software/quest/Resources/

[2] ftp://ftp.ics.uci.edu/pub/machine-learning-databases/

[3] http://www.cs.rpi.edu/~zaki/www-new/pmwiki.php/Software/

Table 2. Comparison on Small Datasets

Dataset	#Trans	#Items	#CIs	#MGs	Charm-L (sec)	MARM_DS (sec)
Australian	690	14	17345	46676	9.56	2.38
Breast-Cancer-W	699	9	5805	13967	3.27	0.56
Crx	690	15	27081	215287	201.15	54.73
Diabetes	768	8	14741	44760	16.16	1.70
Glass	214	9	1935	9784	1.78	0.54
Heart	270	13	13084	66495	116.13	9.64

the total number of transactions (D) respectively. Transactions of each dataset are examined one by one in sequence to simulate the environment of an online data stream. Since generation of all closed itemsets is a daunting task in view of the large size of the dataset involved, MARM_DS was used to generate lattice of recent closed itemsets only and the lattice so generated was passed on to Charm-L for generation of MGs and rules. Table 3 summarizes the execution time (excluding I/O) of MARM_DS and Charm-L for generation of MGs and rules. It was observed that MARM_DS is more efficient than Charm-L in all the cases. The resulting efficiency is in borne by the fact that while MARM_DS generates no candidates of the closed itemsets while generating minimal generators, Charm-L generates all candidates.

Table 3. Comparison on Large Datasets

Dataset	#CIs	#MGs	Charm-L (sec)	MARM_DS (sec)
T3I4D100K	34135	435220	81.75	36.13
T5I6D100K	89232	1098762	423.09	64.67
T8I8D100K	151289	1614840	953.9	152.16
T12I10D100K	244814	2475933	1520.23	237.12

6   Conclusions

In this paper, we have proposed an algorithm for generation of multiobjective non-redundant association rules in data streams. The proposed genMG procedure generates no candidates and efficiently computes minimal generators from the set of closed itemsets. Another contribution of this paper is the use of synopsis data structure for computation of various interestingness measures which are further used in selecting non-dominated associations rules on the basis of the multiobjective interestingness criteria.

References

1. Agarwal, R., Srikant, R.: Fast Algorithms for Mining Association Rules. In: 20th International Conference on Very Large Databases, pp. 487–499 (1994)
2. Chang, J., Lee, W.: Finding Recent Frequent Itemsets Adaptively over Online Data stream. In: 9th ACM SIGKDD, pp. 487–492. ACM Press, New York (2003)

3. Cheng, J., Ke, Y., Ng, W.: A Survey on Algorithms for Mining Frequent Itemsets over Data stream. KAIS Journal 16(1), 1–27 (2008)
4. Deb, K., Pratap, A., Agarwal, S., Meyarivan, T.: A Fast and Elitist Multiobjective Genetic Algorithm: NSGA-II. IEEE Transaction on Evolutionary Computation 6(2), 181–197 (2002)
5. Geng, L., Hamilton, H.J.: Interestingness Measures for Data Mining: A Survey. ACM Computing Surveys, 38(3), Article 9 (2006)
6. Gupta, A., Bhatnagar, V., Kumar, N.: Mining Closed Itemsets in Data Stream Using Formal Concept Analysis. In: Bach Pedersen, T., Mohania, M.K., Tjoa, A.M. (eds.) DAWAK 2010. LNCS, vol. 6263, pp. 285–296. Springer, Heidelberg (2010)
7. Han, J., Cheng, H., Xin, D., Yan, X.: Frequent Pattern Mining: Current Status and Future Directions. Journal of DMKD 15, 55–86 (2007)
8. Heravi, M.J., Zaiane, O.R.: A Study on Interestingness Measures for Associative Classifiers. In: ACM Symposium on Applied Computing (2010)
9. Ishibuchi, H., Kuwajima, I., Nojima, Y.: Multiobjective Association Rule Mining. In: PPSN Workshop on Multiobjective Problem Solving from Nature (2006)
10. Jiang, N., Gruenwald, L.: CFI-Stream: Mining Closed Frequent Itemsets in Data stream. In: ACM SIGKDD, Poster Paper, pp. 592–597. ACM Press, New York (2006)
11. Jiang, N., Gruenwald, L.: Estimating Missing Data in Data Streams. In: International Conference on Database Systems for Advanced Applications, pp. 981–987 (2007)
12. Li, H., Ho, C., Lee, S.: Incremental Updates of Closed Frequent Itemsets Over Continuous Data stream. Expert Systems with Applications 36, 2451–2458 (2009)
13. Pasquier, N., et al.: Efficient Mining of Association Rules using Closed Itemset Lattices. Journal of Information Systems 24(1), 25–46 (1999)
14. Shin, S.J., Lee, W.S.: An On-line Interactive Method for Finding Association Rules Data Streams. ACM CIKM (2007)
15. Stumme, G., et al.: Computing Iceberg Concept Lattices with Titanic. Journal on Knowledge and Data Engineering 42(2), 189–222 (2002)
16. Szathmary, L., Valtchev, P., Napoli, A., Godin, R.: Efficient Vertical Mining of Frequent Closures and Generators. In: Adams, N.M., Robardet, C., Siebes, A., Boulicaut, J.-F. (eds.) IDA 2009. LNCS, vol. 5772, pp. 393–404. Springer, Heidelberg (2009)
17. Tan, J., Bu, Y., Zhao, H.: Incremental Maintenance of Association Rules Over data Streams. In: International Conference on Networking and Digital Society (2010)
18. Vo, B., Le, B.: Fast algorithm for mining Minimal generators of FCI and their applications. In: IEEE International Conference on Computers and Industrial Engineering, pp. 1407–1411 (2009)
19. Chi, Y., Wang, H., Yu, P.S., Muntz, R.R.: Catch the Moment: Maintaining Closed Frequent Itemsets over a Stream Sliding Window. Journal of Knowledge and Information Systems 10, 265–294 (2006)
20. Zaki, M.J.: Generating Non-Redundant Association Rules. In: 6th ACM SIGKDD International Conference on Knowledge Discovery and Data Mining, pp. 34–43. ACM Press, New York (2000)
21. Zaki, M.J.: Mining Non-Redundant Association Rules. In: Data Mining and Knowledge Discovery, vol. 9, pp. 223–248 (2004)

On Fuzzy Clustering of Data Streams
with Concept Drift

Maciej Jaworski, Piotr Duda, and Lena Pietruczuk

Department of Computer Engineering, Czestochowa University of Technology,
Armii Krajowej 36, 42-200 Czestochowa, Poland
{maciej.jaworski,pduda,lena.pietruczuk}@kik.pcz.pl

Abstract. In the paper the clustering algorithms based on fuzzy set theory are considered. Modifications of the Fuzzy C-Means and the Possibilistic C-Means algorithms are presented, which adjust them to deal with data streams. Since data stream is of infinite size, it has to be partitioned into chunks. Simulations show that this partitioning procedure does not affect the quality of clustering results significantly. Moreover, properly chosen weights can be assigned to each data element. This modification allows the presented algorithms to handle concept drift during simulations.

1 Introduction

In literature a lot of clustering algorithms has been proposed. The most popular are k-means algorithm [15], DBSCAN [8] or COBWEB [9]. Given a set $\mathbb{X} = \{\mathbf{x}_1, \ldots, \mathbf{x}_N\}$ of data elements, the aim of the clustering procedure is to divide the set $\mathbb{X}$ into K disjoint clusters. The clusters are described by their centers. The set of cluster centers is denoted by $\mathbf{V} = \{\mathbf{v}_1, \ldots, \mathbf{v}_K\}$. The algorithms mentioned above are designed for crisp clustering. In this type of methods every data element can belong to only one of existing clusters. An alternative approach is the fuzzy clustering. In this case, the membership degree U_{ij} of data element $\mathbf{x}_j$ to the cluster center $\mathbf{v}_i$ takes values in interval $[0; 1]$. All the membership degrees can be represented by a membership matrix $\mathbf{U} = [U_{ij}]_{K \times N}$. The most known fuzzy clustering method is the Fuzzy C-Means (FCM) algorithm [5], [7], which is based on the k-Means algorithm. In this case the following objective function is minimized

$$J_{FCM} = \sum_{i=1}^{K} \sum_{j=1}^{N} (U_{ij})^m \|\mathbf{v}_i - \mathbf{x}_j\|^2, \tag{1}$$

with respect to the U_{ij}, $\mathbf{v}_i$, $i = 1, \ldots, K$, $j = 1, \ldots, N$, where $m > 1$ is a fuzzifier parameter. Moreover, the membership values U_{ij} should obey the following conditions

$$\sum_{i=1}^{K} U_{ij} = 1, \forall j \in \{1, \ldots, N\}. \tag{2}$$

L. Rutkowski et al. (Eds.): ICAISC 2012, Part II, LNCS 7268, pp. 82–91, 2012.

Many modifications of the FCM algorithm have been proposed in literature [4], [16], [22]. The Possibilistic C-Means (PCM) algorithm [14] is particularly interesting, since it is insensitive to outliers. The membership values U_{ij} do not have to satisfy conditions (2). The appropriate objective function, to be minimized, is given by

$$J_{PCM} = \sum_{i=1}^{K}\sum_{j=1}^{N}(U_{ij})^{m}\|\mathbf{v}_i - \mathbf{x}_j\|^2 + \sum_{i=1}^{K}\eta_i\sum_{j=1}^{N}(1 - U_{ij})^{m}. \tag{3}$$

To ensure the convergence of the algorithm, the starting points for cluster centers should be chosen very carefully. Therefore, the FCM algorithm is usually performed at the beginning of the PCM algorithm. The convergence is also dependent on the values of parameters η_i, which represent the sizes of data clusters.

The mentioned algorithms are applicable only for static data. To deal with data streams they should be radically modified. Data streams [1], [6] are of infinite size and the concept of data can evolve in time. Therefore, appropriate algorithms should process data continuously online and be able to detect any kind of concept drift [29]. The clustering of data streams is a very challenging research issue [13]. Several algorithms has been proposed so far, e.g. the STREAM algorithm [11], the CluStream system [2] and the HPStream algorithm [3].

In this paper, following the idea proposed in [12], the modification of the FCM algorithm is presented. The modified algorithm is applicable for data streams. The same idea is then applied to the PCM algorithm. Both algorithms are presented in section {refsec2. The method for concept drift handling is considered in section 3. In section 4 the experimental results are presented. Conclusions are drawn in section 5.

2   The wFCM and the wPCM Algorithms

The FCM algorithm cannot be directly applied to the data streams. Significant modifications are needed. An interesting solution, called the weighted Fuzzy C-Means algorithm (wFCM), was proposed in [12]. The block diagram of the wFCM algorithm is depicted in Fig. 1.

Data stream is divided into chunks $\mathbf{S}_p = \{\mathbf{x}_1^p, \ldots, \mathbf{x}_{n_p}^p\}$, $p = 1, 2, \ldots$. Data elements for the p-th chunk are collected in a buffer, while the $(p-1)$-th chunk is processed. Each data element $\mathbf{x}_j^p$ is accompanied with a weight w_j^p. The way of assigning the weights is described in details in section 3. The idea of the wFCM algorithm is to perform clustering on the subsequent data parts, which are associated with data chunks.

The first part of data, denoted by $\mathbf{X}_1$, is equivalent to the first chunk

$$\mathbf{X}_1 = \mathbf{S}_1 = \{\mathbf{x}_1^1, \ldots, \mathbf{x}_{n_1}^1\}. \tag{4}$$

Each next data part $\mathbf{X}_p$, $p > 1$, is formed by merging the data chunk $\mathbf{S}_p$ and the set of cluster centers $\mathbf{V}_{p-1} = \{\mathbf{v}_1^{p-1}, \ldots, \mathbf{v}_K^{p-1}\}$, obtained for previous data part

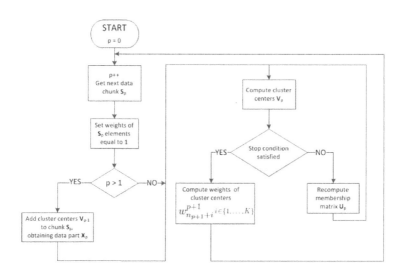

Fig. 1. Convergence of the estimator $\hat{a}_n$ to the actual value of parameter a

$$\mathbf{X}_p = \mathbf{S}_p \cup \mathbf{V}_{p-1} = \{\underbrace{\mathbf{x}_1^p, \ldots, \mathbf{x}_{n_p}^p}_{\mathbf{S}_p}, \underbrace{\mathbf{x}_{n_p+1}^p, \ldots, \mathbf{x}_{n_p+K}^p}_{\mathbf{V}_{p-1}}\}, \, p > 1, \tag{5}$$

where $x_{n_p+1}^p = v_1^{p-1}, \ldots, x_{N_p+K}^p = v_K^{p-1}$. Summarizing, the size N_p of data part $\mathbf{X}_p$ is equal to

$$N_p = \begin{cases} n_p, & p = 1, \\ n_p + K, & p > 1. \end{cases} \tag{6}$$

The weights $w_{n_p+i}^p$ $\left(\text{for } \mathbf{x}_{n_p+i}^p = \mathbf{v}_i^p\right)$ are computed using the following formula

$$w_{n_p+i}^p = \sum_{j=1}^{N_{p-1}} U_{ij}^{p-1} w_j^{p-1}, \, i = 1, \ldots, K, \, p > 1, \tag{7}$$

For each data part $\mathbf{X}_p$, the membership matrix $\mathbf{U}_p$ and the set of cluster centers are calculated iteratively. The aim is to minimize the following objective function

$$J_{wFCM}^p = \sum_{i=1}^{K} \sum_{j=1}^{N_p} w_j^p \left(U_{ij}^p\right)^m \|\mathbf{v}_i^p - \mathbf{x}_j^p\|^2, \, p \geq 1. \tag{8}$$

This leads to the following formulas for the membership values

$$U_{ij}^p = \left(\sum_{k=1}^{K} \left(\frac{\|\mathbf{v}_i^p - \mathbf{x}_j^p\|}{\|\mathbf{v}_k^p - \mathbf{x}_j^p\|}\right)^{\frac{2}{m-1}}\right)^{-1}, \, i = 1, \ldots, K, \, j = 1, \ldots, N_p \tag{9}$$

and for the cluster centers

$$\mathbf{v}_i^p = \frac{\sum_{j=1}^{N_p} w_j^p \left(U_{ij}^p\right)^m \mathbf{x}_j^p}{\sum_{j=1}^{N_p} w_j^p \left(U_{ij}^p\right)^m}, \; i = 1, \ldots, K. \tag{10}$$

Processing of the data part $\mathbf{X}_p$ stops if the value of function (8) changes insignificantly.

The above schema can be also applied to the PCM algorithm, adopting it to deal with data streams. An appropriate objective function is given by

$$J_{wPCM}^p = \sum_{i=1}^{K} \sum_{j=1}^{N_p} w_j^p \left(U_{ij}^p\right)^m \|\mathbf{v}_i^p - \mathbf{x}_j^p\|^2 + \sum_{i=1}^{K} \eta_i^p \sum_{j=1}^{N_p} w_j^p \left(1 - U_{ij}^p\right)^m, \; p \geq 1. \tag{11}$$

The formulas for cluster centers $\mathbf{v}_i^p$ and for the weights $w_{n_p+i}^p$ are exactly the same as formulas (10) and (7), respectively. The formula for the membership values states as follows

$$U_{ij}^p = \left(1 + \left(\frac{\|\mathbf{v}_i^p - \mathbf{x}_j^p\|^2}{\eta_i^p}\right)^{\frac{1}{m-1}}\right)^{-1}, \; i = 1, \ldots, K, \; j = 1, \ldots, N. \tag{12}$$

For the parameters η_i^p the following form is proposed

$$\eta_i^p = \frac{\sum_{j=1}^{n_p} \left(U_{ij}^p\right)^m \|\mathbf{v}_i^p - \mathbf{x}_j^p\|^2}{\sum_{j=1}^{n_p} \left(U_{ij}^p\right)^m}, \; i = 1, \ldots, K. \tag{13}$$

3   Assigning Weights to Data Elements

One of the key points of the wFCM and the wPCM algorithms is the assignment of weights to the incoming data elements. If the concept drift is absent, the simplest solution is to set weights equal to 1 for all data elements

$$w_j^p = 1, \; p \geq 1, \; j = 1, \ldots, n_p. \tag{14}$$

However, data streams are usually time-varying in their nature. In this case the concept drift may occur, therefore the values of weights should increase for subsequent data elements. For data chunk $\mathbf{S}_p$ weights values can be chosen to obey the following recurrent formula

$$w_{j+1}^p = w_j^p 2^\lambda, \; w_1^p = 1, \; p \geq 1, \; j = 1, \ldots, n_p - 1, \tag{15}$$

where $\lambda > 0$ is a decay rate parameter. The value of λ reflects the speed of forgetting the influence on the clustering result of the old data elements. Note that if $\lambda = 0$ then equation (15) becomes equivalent to equation (14).

The last element of data chunk $\mathbf{S}_{p-1}$ receives weight $w_{n_{p-1}}^{p-1} = 2^{(n_{p-1}-1)\lambda}$. After the clustering of data part $\mathbf{X}_{p-1}$ is done, all weights of current cluster centers $\mathbf{V}_{p-1}$ (which are included into data part $\mathbf{X}_p$ according to (5)) are divided by $2^{n_p\lambda}$. This operation ensures that the weights of the first data element from chunk $\mathbf{S}_p$ is 2^λ times larger than the weight of the last element from chunk $\mathbf{S}_{p-1}$.

4   Experimental Results

Evaluating the accuracy of clustering results is a very difficult task. In literature, several validity measures have been proposed so far. For fuzzy clustering approach, one of the most effective are:

- Sum of covariance matrices determinants [10],
- Xie-Beni's index [30].

The first one, for the needs of this paper, is defined for each data chunk $\mathbf{S}_p$ as follows

$$W_{Det}^p = \sum_{i=1}^{K} det(\mathbf{F_i}^p), \ p \geq 1 \tag{16}$$

where $\mathbf{F_i^p}$ is the covariance matrix of the i-th cluster for the p-th chunk. Matrices $\mathbf{F_i^p}$ are defined in the following way

$$\mathbf{F_i}^p = \frac{\sum_{j=1}^{n_p} w_j^p \left(U_{ij}^p\right)^m \left(\mathbf{v}_i^p - \mathbf{x}_j^p\right) \cdot \left(\mathbf{v}_i^p - \mathbf{x}_j^p\right)^T}{\sum_{j=1}^{n_p} w_j^p \left(U_{ij}^p\right)^m}, \ i = 1, \ldots, K, \ p \geq 1. \tag{17}$$

The modified Xie-Beni's index is given by

$$W_{XB}^p = \frac{\sum_{i=1}^{K} \sum_{j=1}^{n_p} w_j^p \left(U_{ij}\right)^m \left\|\mathbf{v}_i^p - \mathbf{x}_j^p\right\|^2}{\sum_{j=1}^{n_p} w_j^p \min_{q,r} \left\|\mathbf{v}_q^p - \mathbf{v}_r^p\right\|^2}, \ p \geq 1. \tag{18}$$

Note that the values of both W_{Det}^p and the W_{XB}^p indices decrease with the increasing accuracy of the clustering results.

To investigate the performance of the wFCM and the wPCM algorithms and to compare them with the FCM and the PCM algorithms, 8-dimensional synthetic dataset was generated. The dataset consists of 250000, forming four gaussian clusters. The dataset is static, i.e. no concept drift is occurring in it. Therefore the weights are assigned by making use of formula (14). The dataset was partitioned into $P = 1$, $P = 5$, $P = 10$ and $P = 100$ data chunks of equal size ($n_p = 250000/P, p = 1, \ldots, P$). Note that for $P = 1$ the wFCM (wPCM) algorithm is equivalent to the FCM (PCM) algorithm. For the needs of this paper, the average sum of covariance matrices W_{Det} and the average Xie-Beni's index have to be defined

$$W_{Det} = \frac{1}{P} \sum_{p=1}^{P} W_{Det}^p, \ W_{XB} = \frac{1}{P} \sum_{p=1}^{P} W_{XB}^p. \tag{19}$$

Values of the W_{Det} coefficient and the W_{XB} index, obtained in simulations for the wFCM algorithm, are presented in Fig. 2.

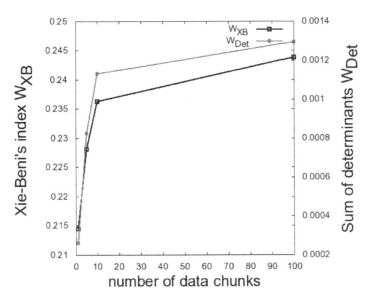

Fig. 2. Values of the W_{Det} coefficient and the W_{XB} index for different numbers P of data chunks (the wFCM algorithm)

The presented results show that the accuracy of clustering results decreases as the number of data chunks P increases. Similar experiments were performed for the wPCM algorithm. Obtained values of the W_{Det} coefficient and the W_{XB} index are depicted in Fig. 3.

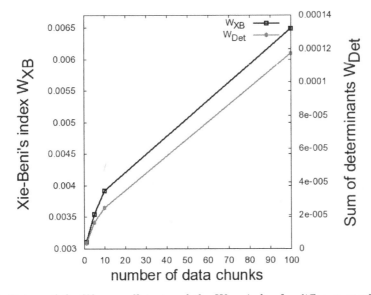

Fig. 3. Values of the W_{Det} coefficient and the W_{XB} index for different numbers P of data chunks (the wPCM algorithm)

Both the wFCM and the wPCM algorithms demonstrate worse accuracy than their base algorithms for static data (FCM and PCM respectively), although it still remains satisfactory.

To present the mechanism of handling the concept drift, using the wFCM and the wPCM algorithms, another synthetic dataset was generated. This dataset consists of 250000 two-dimensional data elements. It forms three clusters, which change their positions as the time goes on. The dataset was partitioned into $P = 25$ data chunks of equal size. Three simulations were performed on the dataset

- the wFCM algorithm for $\lambda = 0.0001$,
- the wFCM algorithm for $\lambda = 0.001$,
- the wPCM algorithm for $\lambda = 0.001$.

The results, presenting four different moments of clusters movement, are shown in Fig. 4. The cluster centers obtained for $\lambda = 0.0001$ follows the original clusters slowly. In the case of $\lambda = 0.001$, both the wFCM and the wPCM algorithms give similar results for almost the whole simulation time. A difference occurs at the end, when the small perturbation of the cluster at the bottom appears.

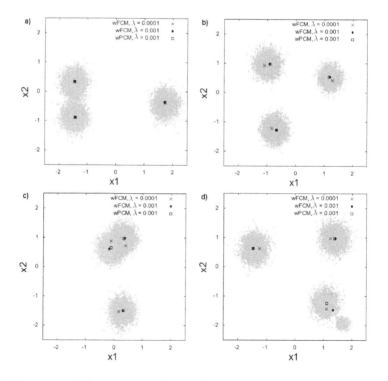

Fig. 4. Clusters and cluster centers obtained with the wFCM algorithm for $\lambda = 0.0001$, the wFCM algorithm for $\lambda = 0.001$ and the wPCM algorithm for $\lambda = 0.001$ at four different moments of the simulation: a) $p = 1$, b) $p = 9$, c) $p = 17$ and $p = 25$

The outliers affect the results of the wFCM algorithm, while the wPCM algorithm remains insensitive. Since the dataset is synthetic, the true positions of cluster centers $\tilde{\mathbf{v}}_1^p$, $\tilde{\mathbf{v}}_2^p$ and $\tilde{\mathbf{v}}_3^p$ are known for each data chunk $p = 1, \ldots, 25$. This fact can be used to validate the clustering results more precisely. Let us define the following validity measure for data chunk $\mathbf{S}_p$

$$V_p = \frac{1}{3} \sum_{i=1}^{3} \|\tilde{\mathbf{v}}_i^p - \mathbf{v}_i^p\|, \ p \geq 1. \tag{20}$$

The values of V_p as a function of processed data elements is shown in Fig. 5. The case of the wFCM algorithm for $\lambda = 0.0001$ gives the worst results during all the simulation time. In the middle of the simulation, when the two clusters at the top overlap, the wPCM algorithm for $\lambda = 0.001$ loses some accuracy with respect to the wFCM algorithm ($\lambda = 0.001$). Then it returns back to the satisfactory level and at the end, when the outliers appear, it outperforms the wFCM algorithm.

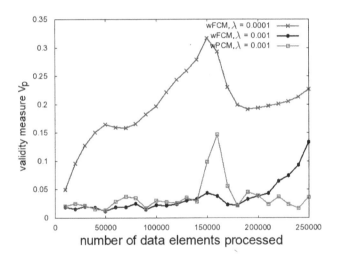

Fig. 5. The validity measure V_p as a function of processed data elements, obtained with the wFCM algorithm for $\lambda = 0.0001$, the wFCM algorithm for $\lambda = 0.001$ and the wPCM algorithm for $\lambda = 0.001$

5   Conclusions and Future Work

In this paper the modified variants of the Fuzzy C-Means (wFCM) and the Possibilistic C-Means (wPCM) algorithms were considered. It was shown how the partitioning the data stream into chunks allows to perform fuzzy clustering on it online. Simulations demonstrated that this procedure decreases the quality of clustering results slightly. However, the change of accuracy is on the acceptable level. The concept drift handling, using both the wFCM and the wPCM algorithms, was studied as well. Simulations showed that the algorithms are appropriate tools for detecting evolving changes of data. In our ongoing research we are working on applications of algorithms developed in this paper to adapting various soft computing techniques [17]-[21], [23]-[28] to deal with data streams.

Acknowledgments. The paper was prepared under project operated within the Foundation for Polish Science Team Programme co-financed by the EU European Regional Development Fund, Operational Program Innovative Economy 2007-2013, and also supported by National Science Centre NCN.

References

1. Aggarwal, C.: Data Streams: Models and Algorithms. Springer, LLC (2007)
2. Aggarwal, C., Han, J., Wang, J., Yu, P.S.: A Framework for Clustering Evolving Data Streams. In: Proc. of the 29th Conference on Very Large Data Bases, Berlin, Germany (2003)
3. Aggarwal, C., Han, J., Wang, J., Yu, P.S.: A Framework for Projected Clustering of High Diensional Data Streams. In: Proc. of the 30th Conference on Very Large Data Bases, Toronto, Canada (2003)
4. Babuska, R.: Fuzzy Modeling for Control. Kluwer Academic Press, Dordrecht (1998)
5. Bezdek, J.C.: Pattern Recognition with Fuzzy Objective Function Algorithms. Kluwer Academic Publishers, Norwell (1981)
6. Bifet, A.: Adaptive Stream Mining: Pattern Learning and Mining from Evolving Data Streams. IOS Press BV, Netherlands (2010)
7. Dunn, J.C.: A Fuzzy Relative of the ISODATA Process and Its Use in Detecting Compact Well-Separated Clusters. Cybernetics and Systems 3(3), 32–57 (1973)
8. Ester, M., Kriegel, H.P., Sander, J., Xu, X.: A Density-Based Algorithm for Discovering Clusters in Large Spatial Databases with Noise. In: Proc. of 2nd International Confrence on Knowledge Discovery and Data Mining, pp. 226–231. AAAI Press (1996)
9. Fisher, D.H.: Knowledge Acquisition via Incremental Conceptual Clustering. Machine Learning 2(2), 139–172 (1987)
10. Gath, I., Geva, A.B.: Unsupervised Optimal Fuzzy Clustering. IEEE Transactions on Pattern Analysis and Machine Intelligence 11(7), 773–781 (1989)
11. Guha, S., Mishra, N., Motwani, R., O'Callaghan, L.: Clustering Data Streams. In: Proc. of 41st Annual Symposium on Foundations of Computer Science, Redondo Beach, CA, USA (2000)
12. Hore, P., Hall, L.O., Goldgof, D.B.: Single Pass Fuzzy C Means. In: Proc. of the IEEE International Conference on Fuzzy Systems, London, July 23-26 (2007)
13. Khalilian, M., Mustapha, N.: Data Stream Clustering: Challenges and Issues. In: Proc. of the International Multiconference of Engineers and Computer Scientists, HongKong, vol. I (2010)
14. Krishnapuram, R., Keller, J.M.: A Possibilisic Approach to Clustering. IEEE Transactions on Fuzzy Systems 1(2), 98–110 (1993)
15. McQueen, J.B.: Some Methods for Classification and Analysis of Multivariate Observations. In: Proc. of 5th Berkeley Symposium on Mathematical Statistics and Probability, vol. 1, pp. 281–297. University of California Press, Berkeley (1967)

16. Miyamoto, S., Ichihashi, H., Honda, K.: Algorithms for Fuzzy Clustering. Springer, Heidelberg (2008)
17. Nowicki, R.: Nonlinear modelling and classification based on the MICOG defuzzifications. Journal of Nonlinear Analysis, Series A: Theory, Methods and Applications 7(12), 1033–1047 (2009)
18. Rutkowski, L.: The real-time identification of time-varying systems by nonparametric algorithms based on the Parzen kernels. International Journal of Systems Science 16, 1123–1130 (1985)
19. Rutkowski, L.: Sequential pattern recognition procedures derived from multiple Fourier series. Pattern Recognition Letters 8, 213–216 (1988)
20. Rutkowski, L.: An application of multiple Fourier series to identification of multivariable nonstationary systems. International Journal of Systems Science 20(10), 1993–2002 (1989)
21. Rutkowski, L.: Nonparametric learning algorithms in the time-varying environments. Signal Processing 18, 129–137 (1989)
22. Rutkowski, L.: Computational Intelligence. Springer (2008)
23. Rutkowski, L., Cpałka, K.: A general approach to neuro - fuzzy systems. In: Proceedings of the 10th IEEE International Conference on Fuzzy Systems, Melbourne, December 2-5, vol. 3, pp. 1428–1431 (2001)
24. Rutkowski, L., Cpałka, K.: A neuro-fuzzy controller with a compromise fuzzy reasoning. Control and Cybernetics 31(2), 297–308 (2002)
25. Scherer, R.: Boosting Ensemble of Relational Neuro-fuzzy Systems. In: Rutkowski, L., Tadeusiewicz, R., Zadeh, L.A., Żurada, J.M. (eds.) ICAISC 2006. LNCS (LNAI), vol. 4029, pp. 306–313. Springer, Heidelberg (2006)
26. Scherer, R.: Neuro-fuzzy Systems with Relation Matrix. In: Rutkowski, L., Scherer, R., Tadeusiewicz, R., Zadeh, L.A., Zurada, J.M. (eds.) ICAISC 2010. LNCS (LNAI), vol. 6113, pp. 210–215. Springer, Heidelberg (2010)
27. Starczewski, J., Rutkowski, L.: Interval type 2 neuro-fuzzy systems based on interval consequents. In: Rutkowski, L., Kacprzyk, J. (eds.) Neural Networks and Soft Computing, pp. 570–577. Physica-Verlag, Springer-Verlag Company, Heidelberg, New York (2003)
28. Starczewski, J.T., Rutkowski, L.: Connectionist Structures of Type 2 Fuzzy Inference Systems. In: Wyrzykowski, R., Dongarra, J., Paprzycki, M., Waśniewski, J. (eds.) PPAM 2001. LNCS, vol. 2328, pp. 634–642. Springer, Heidelberg (2002)
29. Vivekanandan, P., Nedunchezhian, R.: Mining Rules of Concept Drift Using Genetic Algorithm. Journal of Artificial Inteligence and Soft Computing Research 1(2), 135–145 (2011)
30. Xie, X.L., Beni, G.: A Validity Measure for Fuzzy Clustering. IEEE Transactions on Pattern Analysis and Machine Intelligence 13(4), 841–846 (1991)

On Resources Optimization in Fuzzy Clustering of Data Streams

Maciej Jaworski, Lena Pietruczuk, and Piotr Duda

Department of Computer Engineering, Czestochowa University of Technology,
Armii Krajowej 36, 42-200 Czestochowa, Poland
{maciej.jaworski,lena.pietruczuk,pduda}@kik.pcz.pl

Abstract. In this paper the resource consumption of the fuzzy cluster-ing algorithms for data streams is studied. As the examples, the wFCM and the wPCM algorithms are examined. It is shown that partitioning a data stream into chunks reduces the processing time of considered al-gorithms significantly. The partitioning procedure is accompanied with the reduction of results accuracy, however the change is acceptable. The problems arised due to the high speed data streams are presented as well. The uncontrolable growth of subsequent data chunk sizes, which leads to the overflow of the available memory, is demonstrated for both the wFCM and wPCM algorithms. The maximum chunk size limit modifi-cation, as a solution to this problem, is introduced. This modification ensures that the available memory is never exceeded, what is shown in the simulations. The considered modification decreases the quality of clustering results only slightly.

1 Introduction

Data stream mining [2], [7], [31] raises many challenging tasks in data mining community. The main characteristics of data streams is that they are of infi-nite size and usually data elements income with very high rates. Algorithms developed to deal with data streams should be resource-aware from one side and ensure as best accuracy as possible from the other side. From the data stream mining point of view, the most important hardware resources are the available memory and the computational power. The memory is always not enough to store all the incoming data elements. Therefore, some synopsis structures, like wavelets or histograms, should be used. Additionally, data stream mining algo-rithms have to be scalable to work with different amounts of available memory, since they are usually designed to run on various devices. Computational power is very important hardware resource in mining high speed data streams. Algo-rithms have to process data as fast as possible, performing at most one scan for each data element. If the processing time is greater than the speed of data stream, some data elements have to be rejected. The rejection may be conducted in an intelligent way, by making use of load shedding techniques [5], [8].

It is obvious that low computational power and small amount of available memory are accompanied with worse accuracy of results. There is always a

L. Rutkowski et al. (Eds.): ICAISC 2012, Part II, LNCS 7268, pp. 92–99, 2012.

trade-off between the hardware resources in a device from one side, and the performance of the algorithm on the other side. In literature, several resource-aware methods of data stream mining have been proposed so far [30], [1]. The Algorithm Output Granularity (AOG) approach, described in [10], [12], seems to be one of the most promising. Based on the AOG technique, several algorithms were developed [11], e.g. the LWClass algorithm for classification, the LWF algorithm for frequent pattern mining or the LWC algorithm, designed for data clustering.

Clustering of data streams is the main scope of this paper. Beside the LWC algorithm, several other data stream clustering methods have been proposed so far in literature [14], [17]. Commonly known are the STREAM algorithm [15], the CluStream system [3], and the HPStream algorithm [4]. The mentioned algorithms are examples of crisp clustering. An alternative method is a fuzzy clustering approach, in which a data element can belong to more than one cluster, with different membership degrees. The most popular fuzzy clustering algorithm, designed for static data, are the Fuzzy C-Means algorithm (FCM) [6], [9] and the Possibilistic C-Means algorithm (PCM) [18]. In [16] the authors proposed an interesting modification of the FCM algorithm called the weighted Fuzzy C-Means algorithm (wFCM), adapting it to deal with data streams. The key point of this modification is to perform the fuzzy clustering procedures on data chunks of finite sizes. The same schema can be applied to the PCM algorithm. Analogously, the stream version is further called the wPCM algorithm.

In section 2 the time and memory consumption of the wFCM and the wPCM algorithms is analyzed. Some resource-aware variants of considered methods are discussed in section 3. A maximum size of data chunk is introduced as an example solution. The influence of proposed modification on the clustering algorithms performance is investigated. Final remarks are drawn in section 4.

2   Processing Time and Memory Consumption Analysis

The idea of the wFCM and the wPCM algorithms is to perform clustering sequentially on data chunks. Clustering procedures are performed sequentially on data chunks of finite sizes. It seems to be obvious that the larger the size of data chunk is, the slower it is processed. Let us consider a dataset of size N, partitioned into P chunks of equal size N/P. In the following experiment, the processing time of the wFCM and the wPCM algorithms as a function of P will be investigated. For this purpose a 8-dimensional synthetic dataset was generated. The dataset consists of 250000 elements, forming 4 distinct clusters of gaussian shape. The wFCM and the wPCM algorithms were run with four different numbers of data chunks P: $P = 1$, $P = 5$, $P = 10$ and $P = 100$ (note that the case with $P = 1$ is equivalent to the FCM and the PCM algorithms). The obtained results of processing time are depicted in Fig. 1.

Partitioning of the data stream into data chunks provides a significant reduction of processing time of the wFCM and wPCM algorithms. On the other side, one should expect that this procedure may reduce the quality of clustering results.

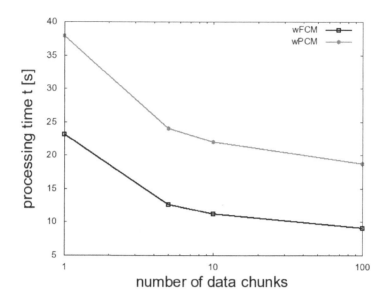

Fig. 1. Processing time of the wFCM and the wPCM algorithms for four different numbers of data chunks: $P = 1$, $P = 5$, $P = 10$ and $P = 100$

Validation of clustering results is a difficult task, however several validity measures have been proposed in literature so far. For fuzzy clustering one can use the sum of covariance matrices determinants W_{Det}, proposed in [13]. The lower the value of the W_{Det} measure is, the better the clustering results are. The values of W_{Det}, obtained in the considered experiment, are collected in Tab. 1. The accuracy of clustering results indeed decrease with the increasing number of data chunks. However the changes are at the acceptable level.

Table 1. The sum of covariance matrices determinants W_{Det} obtained for the wFCM and the wPCM algorithms

	$P = 1$	$P = 5$	$P = 10$	$P = 100$
wFCM	$2,61 \times 10^{-4}$	$8,24 \times 10^{-4}$	$11,32 \times 10^{-4}$	$12,94 \times 10^{-4}$
wPCM	$0,03 \times 10^{-4}$	$0,15 \times 10^{-4}$	$0,24 \times 10^{-4}$	$1,17 \times 10^{-4}$

In the previous experiment the dataset was partitioned artificially into chunks of equal size. However, in real life applications sizes of data chunks are not known a priori. Data elements of the i-th chunk are collected in a buffer while the previous $(i-1)$-th chunk is processed. If the incoming data rate ν is relatively low, then the sizes of subsequent chunks oscillate around some average value. The available memory in the buffer is never overflowed. Problems arise if the speed of data stream is high with respect to the computational power of the system. While a data chunk is processed, a large number of elements is collected in the buffer for the next chunk. In consequence, the processing time of this next chunk becomes longer. A kind of positive feedback leads to the uncontrollable increase of the sizes of subsequent data chunks. The available memory is exceeded finally and the significant part of data is lost. To illustrate this effect the following simulations were performed. The wFCM algorithm was run three times, using the dataset mentioned before, for three different data stream rates: $\nu = 20/ms$, $\nu = 30/ms$ and $\nu = 40/ms$. the sizes of subsequent data chunks, obtained in these simulations, are shown in Fig. 2. A similar experiment was performed with the wPCM algorithm, for $\nu = 10/ms$, $\nu = 15/ms$ and $\nu = 20/ms$. Results are presented in Fig. 3.

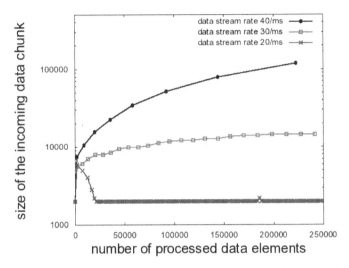

Fig. 2. The sizes of subsequent data chunks obtained for the wFCM algorithm, applied to data streams with three different data rates: $\nu = 20/ms$, $\nu = 30/ms$ and $\nu = 40/ms$

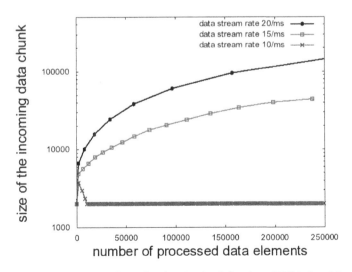

Fig. 3. The sizes of subsequent data chunks obtained for the wPCM algorithm, applied to data streams with three different data rates: $\nu = 10/ms$, $\nu = 15/ms$ and $\nu = 20/ms$

3   Resource-Aware Modifications of the wFCM and the wPCM Algorithms

As it was presented in the previous section, the wFCM and the wPCM algorithms are not directly applicable for extremely high speed data streams. Some resource-aware modifications are needed to adapt them for devices with limited memory and computational power. The simplest solution is to reject part of the data stream, e.g. by making use of the load shedding techniques. However, in this case a fraction of data elements does not participate in clustering procedures. In some cases it can reduce the accuracy of results significantly. An alternative solution is to divide the data values space into hypercubes. Each hypercube is assigned a weight, which is equal to the number of original elements belonging to it. Then, in the wFCM (or wPCM) algorithm each hypercube is treated as a single data element. However, in this modification the minimum and maximum values for each dimension have to be known a priori. Moreover, this solution is impractical for high dimensional data streams, since the enormous number of hypercubes should be created in this case.

In this paper, the another resource-aware variant of the wFCM and the wPCM algorithms is proposed. To avoid the overflow of the available memory, the maximum chunk size N_{max} limit is introduced. If the N_{max} data elements are collected in the buffer for the next data chunk, then clustering of the currently processed chunk is stopped immediately. It means that each data chunk is processed no longer than $T_{max} = N_{max}/\nu$, where ν denotes the rate of data stream. The maximum chunk size (processing time) limit ensures that the available

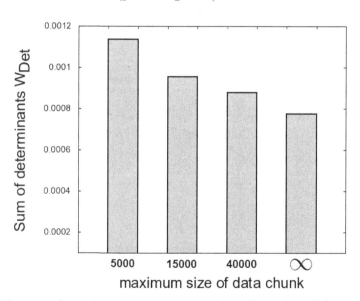

Fig. 4. The sum of covariance matrices traces obtained for three different values of maximum chunk size limit: $N_{max} = 5000$, $N_{max} = 15000$ and $N_{max} = 40000$. The case with no limit is denoted by the infinity symbol ($N_{max} = \infty$).

memory is never exceeded. In the following experiment the influence of the proposed modification on the accuracy of clustering results is investigated. Simulations for the wFCM algorithm were performed on the dataset described in section 2, for three different values of N_{max}: $N_{max} = 5000$, $N_{max} = 15000$ and $N_{max} = 40000$. For comparison, the simulation with no limit for maximum chunk size was performed as well. The data stream rate was set to $\nu = 40/ms$. Obtained results are shown in Fig. 4. The accuracy, expressed by the W_{Det} measure, decreases with the decreasing value of the limit N_{max}. However, the changes are insignificant.

4   Final Remarks and Future Work

In this paper the resource awarness of the wFCM and the wPCM algorithms were investigated. Simulations showed that the processing time of the considered algorithms decreases if the clustering is performed sequentially on data chunks. Simultaneously, partitioning of the data stream leads to the decrease of the clustering quality, however the changes are at the acceptable level. It was also shown that the available memory can be exceeded, if the rate of data stream is very high with respect to the computational power. As a solution to this problem, a modification of maximum data chunk size limit was proposed. Considered modification reduces the accuracy of clustering results insignificantly. In future work we will investigate the problem of resources optimization for various soft-computing techniques (see [19]-[29]) applied to data streams.

Acknowledgments. The paper was prepared under project operated within the Foundation for Polish Science Team Programme co-financed by the EU European Regional Development Fund, Operational Program Innovative Economy 2007-2013, and also supported by National Science Centre NCN.

References

1. Agarwal, I., Krishnaswamy, S., Gaber, M.M.: Resource-Aware Ubiquitous Data Stream Querying. In: Proc. of the International Conference on Information and Automation, Colombo, Sri Lanka (2005)
2. Aggarwal, C.: Data Streams: Models and Algorithms. Springer, LLC (2007)
3. Aggarwal, C., Han, J., Wang, J., Yu, P.S.: A Framework for Clustering Evolving Data Streams. In: Proc. of the 29th Conference on Very Large Data Bases, Berlin, Germany (2003)
4. Aggarwal, C., Han, J., Wang, J., Yu, P.S.: A Framework for Projected Clustering of High Diensional Data Streams. In: Proc. of the 30th Conference on Very Large Data Bases, Toronto, Canada (2004)
5. Babcock, B., Datar, M., Motwani, R.: Load Shedding for Aggregation Queries over Data Streams. In: Proc. of the 20th International Conference on Data Engineering, Boston, MA, USA (2004)
6. Bezdek, J.C.: Pattern Recognition with Fuzzy Objective Function Algorithms. Kluwer Academic Publishers, Norwell (1981)
7. Bifet, A.: Adaptive Stream Mining: Pattern Learning and Mining from Evolving Data Streams. IOS Press BV, Netherlands (2010)

8. Chi, Y., Yu, P.S., Wang, H., Muntz, R.R.: Loadstar: A Load Shedding Scheme for Classifying Data Streams. In: Proc. of the SIAM International Conference on Data Mining, Newport Beach, CA, USA, (2005)
9. Dunn, J.C.: A Fuzzy Relative of the ISODATA Process and Its Use in Detecting Compact Well-Separated Clusters. Cybernetics and Systems 3(3), 32–57 (1973)
10. Gaber, M.M., Krishnaswamy, S., Zaslavsky, A.: Adaptive Mining Techniques for Data Streams Using Algorithm Output Granularity. In: The Australasian Data Mining Workshop, Canberra, Australia (2003)
11. Gaber, M.M., Krishnaswamy, S., Zaslavsky, A.: On-board Mining of Data Streams in Sensor Networks. In: Badhyopadhyay, S., Maulik, U., Holder, L., Cook, D. (eds.) Advanced Methods of Knowledge Discovery from Complex Data. Springer (2005)
12. Gaber, M.M., Krishnaswamy, S., Zaslavsky, A.: Resource-aware Mining of Data Streams. Journal of Universal Computer Science 11(8), 1440–1453 (2005)
13. Gath, I., Geva, A.B.: Unsupervised Optimal Fuzzy Clustering. IEEE Transactions on Pattern Analysis and Machine Intelligence 11(7), 773–781 (1989)
14. Guha, S., et al.: Clustering Data Streams: Theory and Practice. IEEE Transactions on Knowledge and Data Engineering 15(3), 515–528 (2003)
15. Guha, S., Mishra, N., Motwani, R., O'Callaghan, L.: Clustering Data Streams. In: Proc. of 41st Annual Symposium on Foundations of Computer Science, Redondo Beach, CA, USA (2000)
16. Hore, P., Hall, L.O., Goldgof, D.B.: Single Pass Fuzzy C Means. In: Proc. of the IEEE International Conference on Fuzzy Systems, London, July 23-26 (2007)
17. Khalilian, M., Mustapha, N.: Data Stream Clustering: Challenges and Issues. In: Proc. of the International Multiconference of Engineers and Computer Scientists, HongKong, vol. I (2010)
18. Krishnapuram, R., Keller, J.M.: A Possibilisic Approach to Clustering. IEEE Transactions on Fuzzy Systems 1(2), 98–110 (1993)
19. Nowicki, R.: Nonlinear modelling and classification based on the MICOG defuzzifications. Journal of Nonlinear Analysis, Series A: Theory, Methods and Applications 7(12), 1033–1047 (2009)
20. Rutkowski, L.: The real-time identification of time-varying systems by nonparametric algorithms based on the Parzen kernels. International Journal of Systems Science 16, 1123–1130 (1985)
21. Rutkowski, L.: Sequential pattern recognition procedures derived from multiple Fourier series. Pattern Recognition Letters 8, 213–216 (1988)
22. Rutkowski, L.: An application of multiple Fourier series to identification of multivariable nonstationary systems. International Journal of Systems Science 20(10), 1993–2002 (1989)
23. Rutkowski, L.: Nonparametric learning algorithms in the time-varying environments. Signal Processing 18, 129–137 (1989)
24. Rutkowski, L., Cpałka, K.: A general approach to neuro - fuzzy systems. In: Proceedings of the 10th IEEE International Conference on Fuzzy Systems, Melbourne, December 2-5, vol. 3, pp. 1428–1431 (2001)
25. Rutkowski, L., Cpałka, K.: A neuro-fuzzy controller with a compromise fuzzy reasoning. Control and Cybernetics 31(2), 297–308 (2002)
26. Scherer, R.: Boosting Ensemble of Relational Neuro-fuzzy Systems. In: Rutkowski, L., Tadeusiewicz, R., Zadeh, L.A., Żurada, J.M. (eds.) ICAISC 2006. LNCS (LNAI), vol. 4029, pp. 306–313. Springer, Heidelberg (2006)
27. Scherer, R.: Neuro-fuzzy Systems with Relation Matrix. In: Rutkowski, L., Scherer, R., Tadeusiewicz, R., Zadeh, L.A., Zurada, J.M. (eds.) ICAISC 2010. LNCS (LNAI), vol. 6113, pp. 210–215. Springer, Heidelberg (2010)

28. Starczewski, J., Rutkowski, L.: Interval type 2 neuro-fuzzy systems based on interval consequents. In: Rutkowski, L., Kacprzyk, J. (eds.) Neural Networks and Soft Computing, pp. 570–577. Physica-Verlag, Springer-Verlag Company, Heidelberg, New York (2003)

29. Starczewski, J.T., Rutkowski, L.: Connectionist Structures of Type 2 Fuzzy Inference Systems. In: Wyrzykowski, R., Dongarra, J., Paprzycki, M., Waśniewski, J. (eds.) PPAM 2001. LNCS, vol. 2328, pp. 634–642. Springer, Heidelberg (2002)

30. Teng, W.G., Chen, M.S., Yu, P.S.: Resource-Aware Mining with Variable Granularities in Data Streams. In: Proc. of the Fourth SIAM International Conference on Data Mining, Lake Buena Vista, Florida (2004)

31. Vivekanandan, P., Nedunchezhian, R.: Mining Rules of Concept Drift Using Genetic Algorithm. Journal of Artificial Inteligence and Soft Computing Research 1(2), 135–145 (2011)

A Comparison of Complexity Selection Approaches for Polynomials Based on: Vapnik-Chervonenkis Dimension, Rademacher Complexity and Covering Numbers[*]

Przemysław Klęsk

Department of Methods of Artificial Intelligence and Applied Mathematics,
West Pomeranian University of Technology,
ul. Żołnierska 49, 71-210, Szczecin, Poland
pklesk@wi.zut.edu.pl

Abstract. We compare and give some practical insights about several complexity selection approaches (under PAC model) based on: well known VC-dimension, and more recent ideas of Rademacher complexity and covering numbers. The classification task that we consider is carried out by polynomials. Additionally, we compare results of non-regularized and L_2-regularized learning and its influence on complexity.

1   Introduction

Life shows that the cross-validation is still the most popular complexity selection approach in practical applications. It is commonly known that probabilistic approaches (PAC model [8]) like e.g. *Structural Risk Minimization* introduced by Vapnik [10,11] can speed up the complexity selection. In general, these approaches require $O(n)$ less computational time than the n-fold cross-validation. Even so, practitioners somehow prefer not to use them. One of the reasons might be the fact that historic proposition of the SRM involved overly pessimistic *bounds on true errors*. These bounds were usually based on VC-dimension [11,5] as a combinatorial concept describing the capacity (richness) of the set of functions used for learning. In effect of too pessimistic bounds, the selected complexity was often an underestimation of optimal complexity.

In recent years studies within statistical learning have been strongly focused around: covering numbers [1,13], data-driven capacity concepts like Rademacher complexity [3] and regularization techniques (e.g. L_1, L_2, elastic net) [14,9]. Some of new theoretical results might potentially facilitate the complexity selection. In the paper we gather several such results, compare them, and point out advantages and difficulties in their practical usage.

[*] This work has been financed by the Polish Government, Ministry of Science and Higher Education from the sources for science within years 2010–2012. Research project no.: N N516 424938.

L. Rutkowski et al. (Eds.): ICAISC 2012, Part II, LNCS 7268, pp. 100–110, 2012.

As regards asymptotics, all compared approaches (actually *all* known approaches) are similar in such sense that the bounds on true errors tighten at the rate $\sim 1/\sqrt{m}$, where m stands for the sample size. This is a common property of many large-number-laws. The differences (and potential gains) can only lie in the constants and capacity terms which either make probabilistic bounds sufficiently tight or too loose for given conditions of experiment.

2 Approaches to Be Compared

In this section we briefly remind concepts and point out known results related to the approaches we want to compare. In all cases we use the following notation. The data sample $\mathbf{z} = \{(\mathbf{x}_1, y_1), \ldots, (\mathbf{x}_m, y_m)\}$ is drawn in the i.i.d. manner from some unknown joint distribution P defined over $\mathbf{X} \times \{0, 1\}$, where $\mathbf{X} \subset \mathbb{R}^n$ stands for the input domain.

2.1 Approach 1 — Based on Vapnik-Chervonenkis Dimension

In this approach we remain in the traditional setting of the classification problem where a set F of functions used for learning contains *indicator* functions. The *true error* of a function f with respect to P is defined as

$$\mathrm{er}_P(f) = \int_{\mathbf{x} \in \mathbf{X}} \sum_{y \in \{0,1\}} [f(\mathbf{x}) \neq y] dP(\mathbf{x}, y), \tag{1}$$

where $[\cdot]$ returns 1 if its argument is true and 0 otherwise. The true error is the probability of misclassification. Obviously, in practice this quantity is unknown. The *sample error* which ought to be minimized by the learning algorithm is $\widehat{\mathrm{er}}_{\mathbf{z}}(f) = 1/m \sum_{i=1}^{m} [f(\mathbf{x}_i) \neq y_i]$.

We start by reminding the following uniform convergence result — one of the keystones in the learning theory.

Theorem 1. *(Vapnik & Chervonenkis [12]) Let F be a set of indicator functions with VC-dimension equal d. Then*

$$P_m \left(\sup_{f \in F} |\mathrm{er}_P(f) - \widehat{\mathrm{er}}_{\mathbf{z}}(f)| \geq \epsilon \right) \leq 4 \exp \left(d \left(1 + \ln \frac{2m}{d} \right) - m\epsilon^2/8 \right). \tag{2}$$

By substituting the right-hand-side of (2) with a small probability $\delta > 0$ and solving for ϵ, one obtains the following bound on true error

$$\mathrm{er}_P(f) \leq \widehat{\mathrm{er}}_{\mathbf{z}}(f) + \sqrt{\frac{d(1 + \ln(2m/d)) - \ln(\delta/4)}{m/8}}, \tag{3}$$

which holds true with probability at least $1 - \delta$ for all functions $f \in F$. Inequality (3) can readily be applied for complexity selection according to the SRM procedure. By increasing d one generates a sequence of more and more rich sets of functions. In the end, one chooses such d^* for which the right-hand-side of (3) is the smallest (i.e. the guaranteed bound on true error is the smallest).

2.2 Approach 2 — Based on Rademacher Complexity

Given a sample $\{\mathbf{x}_1, \ldots, \mathbf{x}_m\}$, the *empirical Rademacher complexity* of a set F of indicator functions is defined as

$$\widehat{C}(F|\mathbf{x}_1, \ldots, \mathbf{x}_m) = \mathbb{E}\sup_{f \in F} \left| \frac{2}{m}\sum_{i=1}^{m}\sigma_i f(\mathbf{x}_i) \right|, \tag{4}$$

where σ_i are independent random variables, such that $\Pr(\sigma_i = \pm 1) = 1/2$, and the expectation is taken with respect to the joint distribution of $(\sigma_1, \ldots, \sigma_m)$.[1] Then, the *Rademacher complexity* is defined as the expectation of $\widehat{C}$ taken with respect to all m-sized samples drawn from the distribution P^m:

$$C_m(F) = \mathbb{E}_{P^m}\,\widehat{C}(F|\mathbf{x}_1, \ldots, \mathbf{x}_m). \tag{5}$$

As one can notice, calculating $\widehat{C}(F|\mathbf{x}_1, \ldots, \mathbf{x}_m)$ seems to require 2^m optimizations over the set of functions. Two theorems are important in this context.

Theorem 2. *(Bartlett & Mendelson [3]) With probability at least $1-\delta$, for every function in F the following bound on true error holds:*

$$er_P(f) \leq \widehat{er}_\mathbf{z}(f) + C_m(F)/2 + \sqrt{-\ln\delta/(2m)}. \tag{6}$$

Theorem 3. *(Bartlett & Mendelson [3]) For a set of functions F mapping to $[-1, 1]$ true are inequalities:*

$$P\left(\left|C_m(F) - \widehat{C}(F|\mathbf{x}_1, \ldots, \mathbf{x}_m)\right| \geq \epsilon\right) \leq 2\exp(-m\epsilon^2/8)$$

$$P\left(\left|C_m(F) - \sup_{f \in F}\left|\frac{2}{m}\sum_{i=1}^{m}\sigma_i f(\mathbf{x}_i)\right|\right| \geq \epsilon\right) \leq 2\exp(-m\epsilon^2/8). \tag{7}$$

Theorem 3 is a consequence of Hoeffding (or McDiarmid) inequality and implies that in practice we can estimate Rademacher complexity from a single sample and a single realization of $\sigma_1, \ldots, \sigma_m$ variables put in the place of former output values $y_1, \ldots, y_m$. So it does not require $O(2^m)$ work. By using a one-sided version of (7) and substituting the right-hand-side with a small δ, it is easy to check that:

$$C_m(F) \leq \sup_{f \in F}\left|\frac{2}{m}\sum_{i=1}^{m}\sigma_i f(\mathbf{x}_i)\right| + \sqrt{\frac{-8\ln\delta}{m}} \tag{8}$$

holds equivalently true with probability at least $1-\delta$. Finally, by joining (2) and (8) and by inserting $\delta := \delta/2$, we obtain the bound:

$$er_P(f) \leq \widehat{er}_\mathbf{z}(f) + \sup_{f \in F}\left|\frac{1}{m}\sum_{i=1}^{m}\sigma_i f(\mathbf{x}_i)\right| + \sqrt{\frac{-2\ln(\delta/2)}{m}} + \sqrt{\frac{-\ln(\delta/2)}{2m}}, \tag{9}$$

which holds true with probability at least $1 - \delta$.

---

[1] A known variant of this quantity is *empirical Gaussian complexity* where σ_i are drawn from normal distributions $N(0,1)$.

2.3   Approach 3 — Based on Covering Numbers for Classification with Margin

In this approach we move to *real-valued* functions $f \colon \mathbf{X} \to [0, 1]$ and change the problem posing to *classification with margin*. Let $\text{sgn}(\alpha) = 1$ when $\alpha > 0$ and 0 otherwise. The true error (probability of misclassification) is now:

$$\text{er}_P(f) = \int_{\mathbf{x} \in \mathbf{X}} \sum_{y \in \{0,1\}} [\text{sgn}\,(f(\mathbf{x}) - 1/2) \neq y] dP(\mathbf{x}, y). \tag{10}$$

The *margin* is defined as

$$\text{margin}(f(\mathbf{x}), y) = \begin{cases} f(\mathbf{x}) - \frac{1}{2}, & \text{dla } y = 1; \\ \frac{1}{2} - f(\mathbf{x}), & \text{dla } y = 0. \end{cases} \tag{11}$$

Probability of margin smaller than γ is

$$\text{er}_P^\gamma(f) = \int_{\mathbf{x} \in \mathbf{X}} \sum_{y \in \{0,1\}} [\text{margin}(f(\mathbf{x}), y) < \gamma] dP(\mathbf{x}, y), \tag{12}$$

and the corresponding frequency of margin smaller than γ is $\widehat{\text{er}}_{\mathbf{z}}^\gamma(f) = \frac{1}{m} \sum_{i=1}^{m} [\text{margin}\,(f(\mathbf{x}_i), y_i) < \gamma]$. In this approach we take advantage of the following uniform convergence result.

Theorem 4. *(Bartlett [2]) Suppose that F is a set of real-valued functions defined on $\mathbf{X}$. Let P by any probability distribution defined on $\mathbf{Z} = \mathbf{X} \times \{0, 1\}$, let $\epsilon \in (0, 1)$ and $\gamma > 0$. Then*

$$P_m \left(\sup_{f \in F} \text{er}_P(f) - \widehat{\text{er}}_{\mathbf{z}}^\gamma(f) \geq \epsilon \right) \leq 2 \mathcal{N}_\infty(\gamma/2, F, 2m) \exp(-m\epsilon^2/8). \tag{13}$$

For the definition of covering numbers $\mathcal{N}(\cdot)$ we refer the reader e.g. to [1,13]. A more convenient bound-like form of the theorem is that with probability at least $1 - \delta$ for all functions $f \in F$ we have

$$\text{er}_P(f) \leq \widehat{\text{er}}_{\mathbf{z}}^\gamma(f) + \sqrt{\frac{\ln \mathcal{N}_\infty(\gamma/2, F, 2m) - \ln(\delta/2)}{m/8}}. \tag{14}$$

To use the above inequality one needs to bound the covering number in it. To do this we shall use the next result, which bounds the covering number by means of the pseudo-dimension d. The pseudo-dimension, although formally defined for real-valued functions, can as a quantity be identified with the VC-dimension defined for indicator functions, see e.g. [1]. For polynomials, that we consider later on, both VC-dimension and pseudo-dimension will be equal to the number of terms in the polynomial.

Theorem 5. *(Haussler and Long [7]) Let F be a set of real-valued functions mapping to $[0, A]$, with pseudo-dimension equal d. Then for all $\epsilon > 0$*

$$\mathcal{N}_\infty(\epsilon, F, m) \leq \sum_{i=0}^{d} \binom{m}{i} (A/\epsilon)^i \leq \left(\frac{mAe}{\epsilon d} \right)^d. \tag{15}$$

The insertion of (15) with $A := 1$ into (14) leads to a bound that we can practically apply for complexity selection:

$$\mathrm{er}_P(f) \leq \widehat{\mathrm{er}}_{\mathbf{z}}^{\gamma}(f) + \sqrt{\frac{d\ln(1 + 4m/(\gamma d)) - \ln(\delta/2)}{m/8}}. \tag{16}$$

We remark that there exist other bounds on covering numbers than (15), not necessarily derived via pseudo-dimension. However, for our purposes the selection of this particular bound makes the comparison of approach 1 and approach 3 interesting and more competent. Although bounds (3) and (16) refer to different problem posing (indicator vs. real-valued functions), they now both are backed by the same combinatorial capacity concept underneath.

2.4   Approach 4 — Based on Covering Numbers with Regularization

In this approach we want to take advantage of an attractive result due to Zhang. It states that for regularized learning the covering number (in 2-norm) scales only linearly (not exponentially) with the number of attributes[2].

Theorem 6. *(Zhang [13]). Let F be a set of real-valued functions linear in parameters of form $f(\mathbf{x}) = \sum_{j=1}^{M} w_j g_j(\mathbf{x})$ with basis functions g_j. Let the learning algorithm put the L_q regularization on weights so that we have $\|w\|_q \leq a$, for an imposed $a > 0$. Assume the data is bounded in p-norm, i.e. $\|\mathbf{x}\|_p \leq b$ for all i, where $1/p + 1/q = 1$ (conjugate norms) and $2 \leq p \leq \infty$. Then for all $\epsilon > 0$*

$$\mathcal{N}_2(\epsilon, F, m) \leq (2M + 1)^{\lceil a^2 b^2/\epsilon^2 \rceil}. \tag{17}$$

Since $\mathcal{N}_1 \leq \mathcal{N}_2 \leq \mathcal{N}_\infty$ (due to the definition of metrics for covering numbers), the result unfortunately cannot be applied in (14). A possible thing to do is to once again change the problem posing, and perform classification via regression estimation. In that case error measures become

$$\mathrm{er}_P(f) = \iint_{\mathbf{X} \times [0,1]} (f(\mathbf{x}) - y)^2 \, dP(\mathbf{x}, y), \quad \widehat{\mathrm{er}}_{\mathbf{z}}(f) = \frac{1}{m} \sum_{i=1}^{m} (f(\mathbf{x}_i) - y_i)^2, \tag{18}$$

and there exists the following useful result [1]:

Theorem 7. *Suppose that F is a set of real-valued functions mapping from $\mathbf{X}$ to $[0,1]$. Let P be any probability distribution defined on $\mathbf{X} \times [0,1]$. Then*

$$P_m \left(\sup_{f \in F} |\mathrm{er}_P(f) - \widehat{\mathrm{er}}_{\mathbf{z}}(f)| \geq \epsilon \right) \leq 4\mathcal{N}_1(\epsilon/16, F, 2m) \exp(-\epsilon^2 m/32). \tag{19}$$

We insert (17) into (19) and want to solve the right-hand-side for ϵ. Note however that now ϵ is not only involved in the $\exp(\cdot)$ factor as in former uniform

---

[2] This allows for good generalization from small samples with many attributes.

convergence results, it is also involved in the covering number. Note too that in the approach 3 we had an independent parameter γ instead of ϵ in the covering number $\mathcal{N}_\infty(\cdot)$, which made matters easier. After some algebra[3] one obtains $\epsilon(A, B, C) = \left((-B + \sqrt{B^2 - 4AC})/(2A)\right)^{1/2}$, with constants $A = m/32$, $B = \ln(\delta/4) - \ln(2M+1)$, $C = -256a^2b^2 \ln(2M+1)$. And finally, with probability at least $1 - \delta$ true is the bound:

$$\mathrm{er}_P(f) \leq \hat{\mathrm{er}}_{\mathbf{z}}(f) + \epsilon(A, B, C). \tag{20}$$

3 Experiments

3.1 Polynomials and Learning Algorithm

We consider general multivariate polynomials with n variables and order q:

$$f(\mathbf{x}) = f(x_1, \ldots, x_n) = \sum_{j=0}^{q} \sum_{\substack{0 \leq k_1, k_2, \ldots, k_n \leq j \\ k_1 + k_2 + \cdots + k_n = j}} a_{k_1, k_2, \ldots, k_n} x_1^{k_1} x_2^{k_2} \cdots x_n^{k_n}. \tag{21}$$

The number of all terms is $M = \binom{n+q}{n}$. Note that this number is also the VC/pseudo-dimension since our set of functions is linear in parameters. To simplify the notation let the form above be rewritten to $f(\mathbf{x}) = \sum_{j=1}^{M} w_j g_j(\mathbf{x})$, where g_j denotes some polynomial basis and w_j coefficient corresponds to some $a_{k_1, k_2, \ldots, k_n}$. We assume the terms to be variable-wise ordered as in the following example for $n = 2$, $q = 3$:

$$w_1 + w_2 x_1 + w_3 x_2 + w_4 x_1^2 + w_5 x_1 x_2 + w_6 x_2^2 + w_7 x_1^3 + w_8 x_1^2 x_2 + w_9 x_1 x_2^2 + w_{10} x_2^3. \tag{22}$$

The learning algorithm we choose is the least squares minimization. For non-regularized learning the solution is $w = (G^T G)^{-1} G^T Y$, where G denotes the matrix of bases values calculated at data points, i.e. $G_{ij} = g_j(\mathbf{x}_i)$ and Y is the column of class $\{0, 1\}$ labels. For learning with regularization the solution is $w = (G^T G + \lambda \mathbf{1})^{-1} G^T Y$, where λ is the regularization parameter and $\mathbf{1}$ is the identity matrix[4], see e.g. [4,6].

3.2 Experiments Settings

In experiments we look for classifiers of a $N \times N$ chessboard pattern, see Fig. 1. Training pairs are drawn from P with density function $p(\mathbf{x}, y) = p(\mathbf{x})P(y|\mathbf{x}) = 1/N^2 P(y|x)$, with the conditional probabilities for $y \in \{0, 1\}$ defined as

$$P\Big(y|(x_1, x_2)\Big) = |y - r(x_1, x_2)| + \frac{(-1)^{|y - r(x_1, x_2)|}}{1 + e^{-\beta s(x_1, x_2)}}, \tag{23}$$

---

[3] First using $\lceil a^2 b^2/\epsilon^2 \rceil \leq a^2 b^2/\epsilon^2 + 1$, then solving a quadratic equation.

[4] Often, the coefficient w_1 is not to be regularized so that vertical shifts of output can be done freely. In that case, one imposes $\mathbf{1}_{1,1} := 0$.

(a)   (b)   (c)

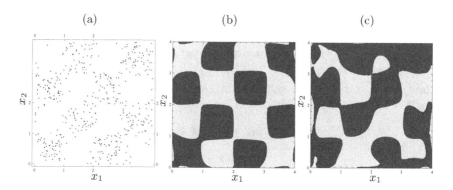

Fig. 1. (a) Sample of data for $m = 10^3$, $\beta = 20$. (b) Exemplary well-fit polynomial model. (c) Exemplary overfitted model.

where $s(x_1, x_2) = \min\{x_1 - \lfloor x_1 \rfloor, \lceil x_1 \rceil - x_1, x_2 - \lfloor x_2 \rfloor, \lceil x_2 \rceil - x_2\}$ and $r(x_1, x_2) = (\lfloor x_1 \rfloor + \lfloor x_2 \rfloor)$ mod 2 is the perfect function. The coefficient $\beta > 0$ in (23) influences how strong is the 'random overlapping' of classes. With $\beta \to 0_+$ we obtain classes strongly mixed (large noise), and with $\beta \to \infty$ well separated.

For the described conditions we carried out a series of complexity selection experiments, in which we manipulated with: pattern size $N = 3, 4$, noise parameter $\beta = 10, 20$, sample size $m = 10^3, 10^4$. In non-regularized learning the full polynomial form consisted of $M = 105$ terms (10-th order polynomial of two variables). In each experiment the complexity was being increased via the number of terms starting from 5 and jumping by 10 terms, $M = 5, 15, 25, \ldots, 105$. In L_2-regularized learning, we tried 'larger' polynomials consisting at maximum of $M = 136$ terms (13-th order). We did it to check if despite more terms the regularization could still prevent from overfitting to noises.

3.3   Results of Experiments (without Regularization)

In this section we show results of experiments comparing approaches 1, 2 and 3. All detailed results are presented in Tab. 1a. Exemplary plots of single experiments are graphed in the Tab. 1b. In the plots, the number of terms M in the polynomial is put along arguments axis. We also write the following symbols: 'VC' to denote the bound (3) VC-dim-based, 'RC' for bound (9) based on Rademacher complexity and 'CN' for bound (15) based on the covering number. Please note also that for approach 2 we used the value of margin $\gamma = 0.1$.

Comments to Result. (i) Approach 2 using Rademacher complexity turned out clearly the best and most accurate. It indicated complexities close to the true optimum or agreeing with it. (ii) The numerical values of Rademacher bound were very close to the true error values. This makes them meaningful in contrast to bounds from approaches 1, 3, where values often exceeded 1.0 (trivial). In such cases bounds can only be interpreted as heuristic scores for complexity selection. (iii) Approach 3 based on covering numbers worked well

Table 1. (a) Results of all experiments for approaches 1, 2, 3. (b) Exemplary plots of complexity selection runs.

(a)

(b)

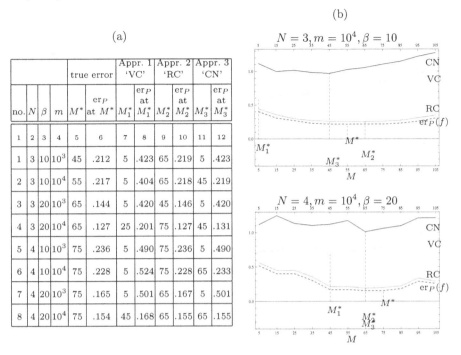

no.	N	β	m	M*	erP at M*	M1*	erP at M1*	M2*	erP at M2*	M3*	erP at M3*
						Appr. 1 'VC'		Appr. 2 'RC'		Appr. 3 'CN'	
1	2	3	4	5	6	7	8	9	10	11	12
1	3	10	10^3	45	.212	5	.423	65	.219	5	.423
2	3	10	10^4	55	.217	5	.404	65	.218	45	.219
3	3	20	10^3	65	.144	5	.420	45	.146	5	.420
4	3	20	10^4	65	.127	25	.201	75	.127	45	.131
5	4	10	10^3	75	.236	5	.490	75	.236	5	.490
6	4	10	10^4	75	.228	5	.524	75	.228	65	.233
7	4	20	10^3	75	.165	5	.501	65	.167	5	.501
8	4	20	10^4	75	.154	45	.168	65	.155	65	.155

only for large samples of size $m = 10^4$. But still, the indicated complexity was always an underestimation of the optimal. For samples of size $m = 10^3$ the bound was immediately too loose, indicating the minimum for $M = 5$. (iv) It should be also remarked that approach 3 might be sensitive to the choice of margin γ. In Fig. 2 we show two illustrations where the position of minimum depends on the choice of γ. (v) Approach 1 based on VC-dimension worked only for large samples and additionally with little noise — $\beta = 20$. The results were worse underestimations than in Approach 3. In all other cases the bound was immediately too loose, indicating minimum at $M = 5$.

3.4   Results of Experiments with L_2-Regularization

In this section we show results of experiments comparing approaches 2 and 4, *both* using L_2-regularization. When learning with regularization a question arises how to choose the penalty coefficient λ. We remind that the higher is λ the tighter bound the algorithm puts on the norm $\|w\|$. In our experiments, separately for each M, the suitable λ was validated-out by means of a testing set. We split the data into a training set (70%) and a testing set (30%) and we tried successive values for λ in a 'divide-and-conquer'-like manner: $\lambda := 10^4 \cdot 2^{1-i}, i = 1, 2, \ldots, 20.$, see Tab. 2b. Errors obtained on the testing set were memorized

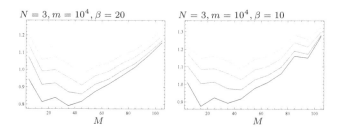

$N = 3, m = 10^4, \beta = 20$ $N = 3, m = 10^4, \beta = 10$

M M

Fig. 2. Illustration of sensitivity of approach 3 (based on covering numbers) to the choice of γ — minima attained for different M values. The levels of gray represent different $\gamma = 0.05, 0.1, \ldots, 0.25$, with the darkest gray for the smallest value.

and the 'best' λ^* with smallest testing was determined. Afterwards, the final training was performed, this time using the whole data set and λ^*. Results of all experiments are shown in Tab. 2a.

Table 2. (a) Results of experiments with L_2-regularization for approaches 2, 4. $M^*, \lambda^*, \|w^*\|$ stand for relevant quantities for which the minimum of given approach was attained. (b) Exemplary plot of errors along decreasing λ (which increases the complexity).

(a)

						Appr. 2 "Rademacher"			Appr. 4 "covering numbers"		
						true error					
						er_P at			er_P at		
N	β	m	M^*	M^*	$\|w^*\|$	M_2^*	M_2^*	$\|w^*\|$	M_4^*	M_4^*	$\|w^*\|$
1	2	3	4	5	6	7	8	9	10	11	12
3	10	10^3	105	.243	23.9	85	.244	16.2	5	.436	0.40
3	10	10^4	85	.222	31.3	85	.222	31.3	5	.404	0.43
3	20	10^3	75	.141	20.1	55	.148	20.4	5	.404	0.49
3	20	10^4	105	.125	57.7	75	.132	42.2	5	.386	0.45
4	10	10^3	85	.241	9.4	115	.258	0.92	5	.462	0.47
4	10	10^4	105	.231	19.2	105	.231	19.2	5	.519	0.42
4	20	10^3	95	.167	19.4	75	.177	28.4	5	.521	0.43
4	20	10^4	75	.151	20.1	55	.148	20.4	5	.404	0.49

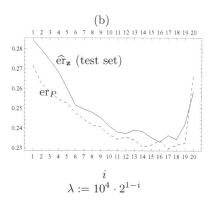

(b)

$\widehat{\mathrm{er}}_{\mathbf{z}}$ (test set)

er_P

i

$\lambda := 10^4 \cdot 2^{1-i}$

Comments to Results with L_2-regularization. (i) Approach 2 again performed best with fairly accurate indications. (ii) Approach 4 turned out to be unapplicable in practice. Despite the qualitative correctness of Zhang's bound (17), it seems that constants related to it and to result (19) make the bound too loose for given conditions of experiments. (iii) As one may note the process of complexity selection with regularization is two-fold: we manipulate with number of terms M and also with penalty coefficients λ. Both these quantities surely affect the generalization performance. In authors opinion this process can be reduced only to manipulations on λ, while M can be kept maximal. In Tab. 2b we illustrate as an example complexity selection carried out solely by means of λ. Note that errors on the testing set were very close to true errors, which helps to indicate the minimum correctly.

4 Summary

Probabilistic bounds on true errors must be quantitatively tight to be applied in practice for complexity selection. In the paper we demonstrate on a simple and non-demanding experiment (only two variables and large samples of sizes 10^3, 10^4) that most of compared approaches fail to be applicable.

In particular we have shown approaches based on the VC-dimension directly or on a $\mathcal{N}_\infty$ covering number (built upon the VC-dimension) required large samples and both underestimated optimal complexity, with a slightly better performance of the latter. An additional difficulty is that the approach using the $\mathcal{N}_\infty$ covering number requires that we specify the value of margin γ as a parameter. It turns out that results of complexity selection are sensitive to the choice of γ and there it is unclear what kind of heuristic can be proposed here.

We have also considered learning with L_2-regularization. In that case we proposed a bound (20) taking advantage of a result by Zhang. Unfortunately the bound also proved to be practically unsatisfactory for polynomials in the case when complexity selection was parametrized both by the number M of polynomial terms and the penalty coefficient λ. A much better approach is to use λ alone and to use a single testing set rather than probabilistic bounds.

The approach based on data-driven Rademacher complexity turned out to be the best for all experimental conditions. Probabilistic bounds based on that quantity proved to be sufficiently tight. The cost of this approach is an additional execution of the learning algorithm, so that an estimate of Rademacher complexity can be calculated.

References

1. Anthony, M., Bartlett, P.L.: Neural Network Learning: Theoretical Foundations. Cambridge University Press, Cambridge (2009)
2. Bartlett, P.L.: The sample complexity of pattern classification with neural networks: the size of the weights is more important than the size of the network. IEEE Transactions on Information Theory 44(2), 525–536 (1998)
3. Bartlett, P.L., Mendelson, S.: Rademacher and gaussian complexities: Risk bounds and structural results. Journal of Machine Learning Research 3, 463–482 (2002)
4. Bishop, C.M.: Pattern Recognition and Machine Learning. Springer, New York (2006)
5. Cherkassky, V., Mulier, F.: Learning from data. Adaptive and Learning Systems for Signal Processing, Communications and Control. John Wiley & Sons, Inc. (1998)
6. Hastie, T., Tibshirani, R., Friedman, J.: The Elements of Statistical Learning. Springer, New York (2009)
7. Haussler, D., Long, P.: A generalization of Sauer's lemma. Journal of Combinatorial Theory, Series A 71(2), 219–240 (1995)

8. Holden, S.B.: Cross-validation and the PAC learning model. Technical report, Dept. of CS, University College, London, Research Note, RN/96/64 (1996)
9. Ng, A.Y.: Feature selection, l1 vs. l2 regularization, and rotational invariance. In: ICML 2004: Proceedings of the Twenty-First International Conference on Machine Learning, p. 78. ACM, New York (2004)
10. Vapnik, V.N.: The Nature of Statistical Learning Theory. Springer, New York (1995)
11. Vapnik, V.N.: Statistical Learning Theory: Inference from Small Samples. Wiley, New York (1995)
12. Vapnik, V.N., Chervonenkis, A.J.: On the uniform convergence of relative frequencies of events to their probabilities. Theory of Probability and its Applications 16(2), 264–280 (1971)
13. Zhang, T.: Covering number bounds of certain regularized linear function classes. Journal of Machine Learning Research 2, 527–550 (2002)
14. Zou, H., Hastie, T.: Regularization and variable selection via the elastic net. J. R. Statist. Soc. B 67(2), 301–320 (2005)

Sample Complexity of Linear Learning Machines with Different Restrictions over Weights*

Marcin Korzeń and Przemysław Klęsk

Faculty of Computer Science and Information Technology,
West Pomeranian University of Technology,
ul. Żołnierska 49, 71-210, Szczecin, Poland
{mkorzen,pklesk}@wi.ps.pl

Abstract. Known are many different capacity measures for learning machines like: Vapnik-Chervonenkis dimension, covering numbers or fat dimension. In this paper we present experimental results of sample complexity estimation, taking into account rather simple learning machines linear in parameters. We show that, sample complexity can be quite different even for learning machines having the same VC-dimension. Moreover, independently from the capacity of a learning machine, the distribution of data is also significant. Experimental results are compared with known theoretical results for sample complexity and generalization bounds.

1 Introduction

In the papers [6], [18] the following question is considered: which model should we prefer if two models have the same test error and they are different in the complexity? Authors give some experimental evidences showing that the connection between generalization error and model complexity is *not* clear. Model complexity is a fairly intuitive concept, typically associated with the number of model parameters. Formally, known are many capacity measures like: Vapnik-Chervonenkis dimension [15], Rademacher complexity [2], covering numbers, fat dimension [1] or other. All these capacity concepts can lead to different bounds on sample complexity.

In this paper we consider a rather simple class of classifiers, for which the decision is a linear combination of attributes. From the theoretical point, such classifiers are equally rich in the sense that they have the same Vapnik-Chervonenkis dimension – which is equal to $n + 1$ where n is the number of attributes. Thus they are comparable with respect toVapnik bounds on true error (generalization bounds) [15] show that all methods give near-to-optimal results when sample size grows large. These bounds tighten proportionally to $1/\sqrt{m}$, where m is the sample size. However, in practice for a fixed size of data, we know that those

---

* This work has been financed by the Polish Government, Ministry of Science and Higher Education from the sources for science within years 2010–2012. Research project no.: N N516 424938.

L. Rutkowski et al. (Eds.): ICAISC 2012, Part II, LNCS 7268, pp. 111–119, 2012.

methods give quite different results and generalization bounds can be relatively loose. This situation is especially noticeable when the sample size is relatively small compared to the number of attributes.

We introduce the following notation. Let $S = \{(X_i, d_i), i = 1, \ldots, m\}$ be the sample (dataset), where $X_i \in \mathbb{R}^n$ and $d_i \in \{0, 1\}$. Consider the class of linear learning machines with the classification rule:

$$\mathcal{L}(x; w, b) = \begin{cases} 1, & \text{for} \quad w^T x + b \geq 0, \\ 0, & \text{for} \quad w^T x + b < 0. \end{cases}$$

In the above expression weights can be made arbitrary large during the learning process. Such situation is disadvantageous due to numerical restrictions or other (e.g. dependant on the dataset). Some learning algorithms add to this class different types of restrictions (regularization) over the norm of weights like e.g.:

$$\|w\|_1 = \sum_i |w_i| < a_1,$$

$$\|w\|_2 = \sqrt{\sum_i w_i{}^2} < a_2.$$

Even in such a simple case there exist many well known learning algorithms and techniques. Generally there are three main groups of approaches:

Methods minimizing the MSE criterion this group contains most of neural networks techniques also including weight decay or regularization [11], [1].

Methods maximizing the likelihood function which include logistic regression and its variants: ridge regression (L^2 regularization over weights), lasso (L^1-regularization over weights) [17,14], elastic-net (mixed L^1 and L^2) and others [9], [7].

Methods based on separation margin maximization this group contains SVM methods and its variants [15], [3].

These methods differ considerably with regard to the manner of attributes selection and grouping of correlated attributes. In particular, methods with L^2 regularization over weights give a grouping effect [20]. On the other hand L^1 regularization term leads to a strong selection of attributes (a shrinkage effect) [20] and a small sample complexity [13].

2   Motivation

The variables selection problem for linear models is considered one of the most important in statistical inference, see e.g. [9]. Recently, many methods for that purpose became well-known [8], [20]. Regularizations like L^2, L^1 lead to minimal models in the sense of norm of weights or small number of applied attributes, and therefore can be regarded (especially L^1) as a convenient way for attributes selection. Weight decay techniques commonly used in neural networks [1,11] can also be considered as L^2 regularization techniques with the mean squared loss function (instead of the likelihood function used in logistic regression). SVM techniques have a geometric rather than a probabilistic motivation. We remark that the SVM criterion uses a constraint which makes the product of margin and norm of weights equal to 1. Then, the minimization of norm of weights leads to a large margin. Therefore, this approach can also be considered as a kind of L^2 regularization on weights.

In the paper we want to present a simple experimental results, showing that different regularization techniques can be worse or better depending on the unknown data distribution. The reason we choose only linear classifiers is that it makes experiments dependent only on the loss function and the regularization term, and additionally for those classifiers known are theoretical capacity measures and bounds on true error.

Additionally, we compare linear classifiers with a known k-NN classifier. It is worth to remark that 1-NN can be regarded as a large margin classifier with respect to a non-linear decision boundary [16]. When the fraction of nearest neighbors is fixed as α then the VC-dimension is approximately $2/\alpha$ [10,8].

3   Generalization and Sample Complexity

For classification, the classical uniform convergence result is dedicated to sets of indicator functions ($\{0, 1\}$-valued functions) and uses the VC-dimension as the capacity concept. Because in fact, we want to compare different regularization techniques, it is more convenient for us to use the following uniform convergence result [1, theorem 17.1] dedicated for real-valued functions. It bounds the difference between the true error er_P and the observed error on the sample $\widehat{er}_S$ and uses a somewhat more sensitive capacity concept i.e. covering numbers. Moreover, there exist useful results which bound covering numbers for both unregularized and regularized learning. We remark that there are no corresponding results for indicator functions. Therefore, we want to look at classification by means of regression estimation.

Theorem 1. *Let F be a set of learning functions mapping from $\mathbf{X}$ to $[0, 1]$. Let P denote the probability distribution defined on $\mathbf{X} \times [0, 1]$. Then for all $f \in F$:*

$$P_m \left(|er_P(f) - \widehat{er}_S(f)| \geq \epsilon \right) \leq 4\mathcal{N}_1(\epsilon/16, F, 2m) \exp(-\epsilon^2 m/32),$$

for any $0 < \epsilon < 1$.

For the unregularized learning we shall use the bound on the covering number $\mathcal{N}_1(\cdot)$ given in terms of the VC-dimension h [1, theorem 18.4]:

$$\mathcal{N}_1(\epsilon, F, m) \leq e(h+1) \left(\frac{2e}{\epsilon} \right)^h.$$

We remind that in our case of linear classifiers $h = n + 1$.

For the regularized learning we shall use the following bound on the covering number [19, theorem 3]:

$$\mathcal{N}_2(\epsilon, F, m) \leq (2n + 1)^{\lceil a^2 b^2 / \epsilon^2 \rceil},$$

where a is the constraint on weights implied by the regularization in q-norm, $\|w\|_q \leq a$, b is the bound on data in p-norm, $\|x\|_p \leq b$ and $1/p + 1/q = 1$. Note also that by definition of covering numbers $\mathcal{N}_2(\cdot) \geq \mathcal{N}_1(\cdot)$.

By combining bounds on covering numbers with the uniform convergence Theorem 1 we derive the following two bounds on the sample complexity, respectively for unregularized and regularized learning (both hold true with probability at least $1 - \delta$):

$$m_{\mathrm{VC}}(\epsilon, \delta) \geq \frac{128 \left(\ln(16/\delta) + 2(1 + n) \ln(34/\epsilon)\right)}{\epsilon^2} \tag{1}$$

$$m_{\mathrm{REG}}(\epsilon, \delta) \geq \frac{128 \left(1024 a^2 b^2 \ln(1 + 2n) + \epsilon^2 \ln(4(1 + 2n)/\delta)\right)}{\epsilon^4} \tag{2}$$

Let us look at qualitatively on both these expressions. The first expression grows with $1/\epsilon^2$ and the second with $1/\epsilon^4$. Also, the constant term in the second expression is larger: $128 \cdot 1024$ instead of 128. But the main advantage of the second expression is a weaker dependency on the number of attributes n. It means that m_{REG} grows at rate $O(\log(n))$ with the number of attributes while m_{VC} grows at rate $O(n)$. When constants a and b are small then the second expression gives tighter bounds on the sample size. Finally, we would like to stress that the sample complexity bounds are valid for *all* datasets, thus it should be clear, that in a fixed situation they can give pessimistic values.

In the next section we want to present some experimental results showing that norms of weights are really connected with the generalization error and a properly regularized model gives better predictions. Moreover independently from sample complexities there are strong (dependent on the particular dataset) motivations preferring such or other regularization term.

4   Experimental Results

We use a learning and testing procedure shown in the figure 1. All models are trained and tested 100 times. Outer loop is responsible for the change of the fraction φ which indicates how large part of the whole dataset will form the learning set, the remaining part is treated as the test data set. The fraction φ changes from 1% to 50%. Before testing we choose proper regularization parameters, with two exceptions: log reg remains unregularized, and in the case of msereg the regularization parameter is set to $\frac{1}{9}$ of the MSE criterion.

All experiments were done using MATLAB. We compare the following methods:

α–**NN:** k nearest neighbors algorithm with fixed fraction of nearest points ($k = \alpha \cdot m$), this way we maintain fixed complexity,

```
 1: for all φ = {0.01, . . . , 0.5} do
 2:     for all model M ∈ {α − NN, L1 reg, L2 reg, linSVM} do
 3:         choose regularization parameters, α (in α-NN) and C in linSVM using re-
   sampling procedure with factor φ.
 4:     end for
 5:     for i = 1, . . . , 100 do
 6:         choose randomly data-subsets L and T using factor φ
 7:         for all model M ∈ {α − NN, L1 reg, L2 reg, linSVM, msereg, log reg} do
 8:             fit each M on L and evaluate M on T
 9:         end for
10:     end for
11: end for
```

Fig. 1. Experimental scheme with resampling

log reg: pure logistic regression implemented in the `netlab` package[1],

msereg: MATLAB package in neural networks toolbox using 1-layer network with the learning method `trainscg` and the `mesreg` criterion: `mse` and L^2 regularization over weights,

linSVM: the libSVB library [5] for SVM's with linear kernels, with the use of the Matlab interface[2],

L1 reg and L2 reg: our own implementations in MATLAB of logistic regressions with L^1 and L^2 regularization over weights. In the case of L^2 it use conjugate gradients [12], in the case of L^1 also conjugate gradient are used but together with techniques described in [4].

Experiment 1: Few Significant and Many Redundant Attributes Consider a situation when we have only few significant attributes and many insignificant attributes containing only noises. In this case the selection of attributes is very important, nevertheless we omit this step and we hope that the model itself discovers good attributes by assigning some positive weights to them.

Artificial datasets (with 2000 instances, 3 significant attributes and 400 noise-attributes) were generated by the following MATLAB code:

```
m = 2000;   % size of data set
n = 400;    % number of insignificant attributes
k = 3;      % number of hidden values
H = randn(m, k);                            % hidden signals
Dorg = H  * [-3 -2 3]';                     % original output
X = [H randn(m, n)];                        % observed signals
D = (Dorg + randn(size(Dorg)) * 0.2) < (mean(Dorg) - 0.5); % noised output
```

In the figure 2, we present results – mean values of: classification error, mean squared error (MSE), and area under ROC (AUC). In such a setting the logistic regression

---

[1] Available at `http://www.ncrg.aston.ac.uk/netlab/index.php`

[2] Available at
`http://pc228.rt.e-technik.tu-darmstadt.de/~vogt/de/software.html`

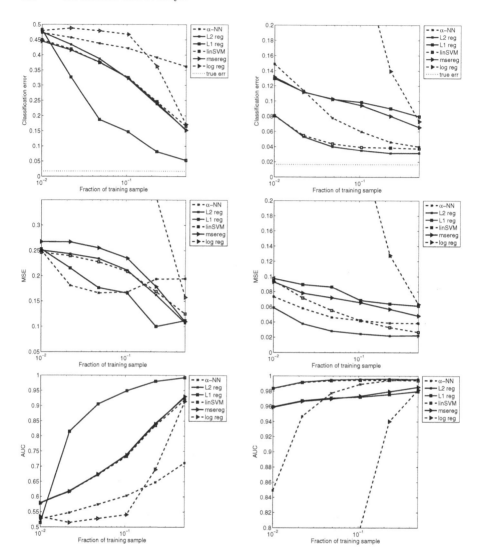

Fig. 2. Experiment 1: few significant and many redundant attributes, mean values over 100 traials

Fig. 3. Experiment 2: many significant attributes and many correlations, mean values over 100 traials

model with L^1 regularization has the smallest sample complexity and gives the best results[3]. There are no statistically significant differences between models: L2 reg, linSVM and msereg. The result is consistent with [13] where it has been shown that logistic regression has smaller sample complexity when there is only a small number of significant attributes.

---

[3] The result is statistically significant using Wilcoxon rank sum test for equality of medians in two populations p-value is less then 10^{-4}.

Table 1. The L^1 and L^2 bounds on samples

	exp. 1	exp. 2
$b_1 = \|X\|_1$	4.93	2.99
$b_2 = \|X\|_2$	22.42	30.65
VC(lin) $= n + 1$	404	151

Table 2. Sufficient sample size based on equations (1) and (2) for m_{VC} and m_{REG} with $\epsilon = 0.2$, $\delta = 0.05$ and experiment 1

	L1 reg	L2 reg	msereg	linSVM	logreg	α-NN
m_{VC}	$1 \cdot 10^7$	$1 \cdot 10^7$	$1 \cdot 10^7$	$1 \cdot 10^7$	$1 \cdot 10^7$	$5 \cdot 10^5$
m_{REG}	$4 \cdot 10^9$	$9 \cdot 10^{10}$	$9 \cdot 10^{11}$	$4 \cdot 10^{10}$	$5 \cdot 10^{15}$	—

Table 3. Exemplary norms of weights for fraction $\varphi = 0.05$ in each experiment

	exp. 1	exp. 2
$a_1 = \|w\|_1$ L1 reg	0.601	34.46
$a_2 = \|w\|_2$ L2 reg	0.629	4.01
$a_2 = \|w\|_2$ msereg	1.973	3.48
$a_2 = \|w\|_2$ linSVM	0.487	1.25
$a_2 = \|w\|_2$ logreg	148.2	232.42

Experiment 2: Many Significant and Many Correlations. The next experiment concerns a much different situation. We have three hidden attributes and each of them is the repeated 100 times. Intuitively, it is understandable that a better approach is to take an *average* of these attributes in each group than to remove most of them leaving only a few. Groups of course are unknown to the learning algorithms. Here is sample code generating the second artificial dataset:

```
m = 2000;               % size of data set
n = 100;                % number of attributes in the each group
k = 3;                  % number of hidden values
H = randn(m, k);        % hidden signals
Dorg = H * [-5; -1; 3]; % original output
X = [];
for i = 1 : k
    X = [X [H(:,i) * ones(1, n) + randn(m, n)]];      % observed signals
end
D = (Dorg + randn(size(Dorg)) * 0.2) < (mean(Dorg) - 0.5); % noised output
```

This experiment shows that L^2 regularization techniques (L2 reg and linSVM) gives quite good solutions when dataset contains many correlated attributes. In this case also α-NN algorithm gives good, but slightly worse results. Differences between L2 reg and linSVM or α-NN for fraction $\varphi = 0.5$ are statistically significant (p-value=0.0063 using Wilcoxon rank sum test). The msereg method works much weaker in this case, it may be caused by the mean squared error term rather than the regularization term. Other methods give much worse results, but as the size of the learning set grows the true error decreases. Tables 1, 3 present exemplary values of norm of weights and the radius of data for a fixed fraction of learning sample $\varphi = 0.05$. In the table 2 shown are calculated minimal sample sizes sufficient to learn with accuracy ϵ and with probability at least $1 - \delta$. We can treat this number only qualitatively and it shows that L^1 regularization has really the smallest bound on sample complexity. It is also worth to remark that as regards the m_{VC} sample complexity, the α-NN turned out to have the smallest value. This was caused by discovering the best $\alpha \approx 0.1$ in experiments, which implied that the VC-dimension was $2/\alpha \approx 20$.

5   Conclusions

The paper contains experimental results concerning the sample complexity of a simple classifiers. We want to show that regularization facilitates the learning process, and it is helpful especially for small learning samples. Unfortunately, distribution dependent factors like noises or correlations prefer different kind of regularization and it is unclear a priori which one should be used. Newer models like *elastic-net* [20] try to combine both approaches. The common (unregularized) logistic regression has an unfavourable sample complexity and should be used only for larger datasets. According to the works of [18] and [6] we want to note that factors dependent upon distribution should decide in the practical cases.

References

1. Anthony, M., Bartlett, P.L.: Neural Network Learning: Theoretical Foundations. Cambridge University Press (1999)
2. Bartlett, P.L., Mendelson, S.: Rademacher and gaussian complexities: risk bounds and structural results. J. Mach. Learn. Res. 3, 463–482 (2003)
3. Burges, C.J.C.: A tutorial on support vector machines for pattern recognition. Data Min. Knowl. Discov. 2(2), 121–167 (1998)
4. Cawley, G.C., Talbot, N.L.C.: Gene selection in cancer classification using sparse logistic regression with bayesian regularisation. Bioinformatics 22(19), 2348–2355 (2006)
5. Chang, C.C., Lin, C.J.: LIBSVM: a library for support vector machines (2001), Software available at, http://www.csie.ntu.edu.tw/cjlin/libsvm
6. Domingos, P.: The role of occam's razor in knowledge discovery. Data Mining and Knowledge Discovery 3, 409–425 (1999)
7. Efron, B., Hastie, T., Johnstone, I., Tibshirani, R.: Least angle regression. Annals of Statistics 32(2), 407–451 (1996)
8. Hastie, T., Tibshirani, R., Friedman, J.: The Elements of Statistical Learning: Data Mining, Inference, and Prediction. Springer (2009)
9. Hesterberg, T., Choi, N.H., Meier, L., Fraley, C.: Least angle and l_1 penalized regression: A review. Statistics Surveys 2, 61–93 (2008)
10. Klęsk, P., Korzeń, M.: Sets of approximating functions with finite vapnik-chervonenkis dimension for nearest-neighbors algorithms. Pattern Recognition Letters 32(14), 1882–1893 (2011)
11. MacKay, D.J.C.: Information theory, inference, and learning algorithms. Cambridge University Press (2003)
12. Minka, T.P.: A comparison of numerical optimizers for logistic regression. Technical report, Dept. of Statistics, Carnegie Mellon Univ. (2003)
13. Ng, A.Y.: Feature selection, l1 vs. l2 regularization, and rotational invariance. In: ICML 2004: Proceedings of the Twenty-First International Conference on Machine Learning, p. 78. ACM, New York (2004)
14. Tibshirani, R.: Regression shrinkage and selection via the lasso. Journal of the Royal Statistical Society, Series B 58(1), 267–288 (1996)

15. Vapnik, V.: Statistical learning theory. Wiley (1998)
16. Vincent, P., Bengio, Y.: K-local hyperplane and convex distance nearest neighbors algorithms. In: Advances in Neural Information Processing Systems, pp. 985–992 (2001)
17. Williams, P.M.: Bayesian regularisation and pruning using a laplace prior. Neural Computation 7, 117–143 (1994)
18. Zahálka, J., Železný, F.: An experimental test of occam's razor in classification. Machine Learning 82, 475–481 (2011)
19. Zhang, T.: Covering number bounds of certain regularized linear function classes. Journal of Machine Learning Research 2, 527–550 (2002)
20. Zou, H., Hastie, T.: Regularization and variable selection via the elastic net. J. R. Statist. Soc. B 67(2), 301–320 (2005)

A Clustering Algorithm Based on Distinguishability for Nominal Attributes

Maciej Krawczak[1,2] and Grażyna Szkatuła[1]

[1] Systems Research Institute, Polish Academy of Sciences,
Newelska 6, Warsaw, Poland
[2] Warsaw School of Information Technology,
Newelska 6, Warsaw, Poland
{krawczak,szkatulg}@ibspan.waw.pl

Abstract. In this paper we developed a new methodology for grouping objects described by nominal attributes. We introduced a definition of condition's domination within each pair of cluster, and next the measure of ω-distinguishability of clusters for creating a junction of clusters. The developed method is hierarchical and agglomerative one and can be characterized both by high speed of computation as well as extremely good accuracy of clustering.

Keywords: cluster analysis, nominal attributes, sets theory.

1 Introduction

Nowadays there are collected data characterized by huge number of objects and each object is characterized by a number of attributes, often of categorical (nominal) nature. Often nominal attributes are considered in a symbolic way.

In this paper we will consider a clustering problem. Our aim is to group a set of objects using the new symbolic representation. To do that we developed a new technique based on introduced relation of dominance between the clusters.

However, there are algorithms specialized to analysis of long chains of symbols, the algorithms found applications in text analysis or in bioinformatics ([1], [5], [9]). Generally, algorithms dealing with symbolic data are based on introduction of some distance between objects, e.g. [11].

Our approach to cluster analysis with symbolic data differs from algorithms known in the literature and the efficiency of it seems to be higher than those known in literature.

The developed algorithm has several features common with standard ones, namely our algorithm is hierarchical and agglomerative ("bottom-up") one. Hierarchical clustering (defined by [6] in 1967) is starting with N clusters (each containing one object). This kind of algorithms can find the closest (most similar) pair of clusters and merge them into a single cluster. This kind of hierarchical clustering is called *agglomerative* because it merges clusters iteratively. The main weaknesses of agglomerative clustering methods are that they can never undo what was done previously. In our algorithm instead of measure of distance between objects, in

L. Rutkowski et al. (Eds.): ICAISC 2012, Part II, LNCS 7268, pp. 120–127, 2012.
© Springer-Verlag Berlin Heidelberg 2012

the paper, we introduced a definition of the condition's dominance which allowed merging smaller clusters in order to get larger ones.

2   Basic Elements of the Applied Approach

Let us consider a finite set of objects $U = \{e_n\}$, $n = 1, 2, \ldots, N$. The objects are described in the form of conditions associated with the finite set of K attributes $A = \{a_1, \ldots, a_K\}$. The set $V_{a_j} = \{v_{j,1}, v_{j,2}, \ldots, v_{j,L_j}\}$ is the domain of the attribute $a_j \in A$, $j = 1, \ldots, K$, where L_j denotes the number of nominal values of the j-th attribute. Each object $e_n \in U$ is represented by K conditions in the following manner

$$e_n = (a_1 \in \{v_{1,t(1,n)}\}) \wedge \ldots \wedge (a_K \in \{v_{K,t(K,n)}\}) \tag{1}$$

where $v_{j,t(j,n)} \in V_{a_j}$ and $j = 1, \ldots, K$. The index $t(j,n)$ for $j \in \{1, 2, \ldots, K\}$ and $n \in \{1, 2, \ldots, N\}$ denotes that the attribute a_j takes the value $v_{j,t(j,n)}$ in the object e_n. For instance, for the attribute a_j and $L_j = 4$, using letters of the alphabet the set V_{a_j} can have the following nominal form $V_{a_j} = \{a, b, c, d\}$. An exemplary data object for a given $n \in \{1, \ldots, N\}$ and $K = 4$ can be written as follows:

$$e_n = (a_1 \in \{b\}) \wedge (a_2 \in \{d\}) \wedge (a_3 \in \{a\}) \wedge (a_4 \in \{c\}) \text{ or shortly } e_n = [b, d, a, c].$$

The task of clustering can be formulated as follows: we want to split the set of objects U into non-empty, disjoint subsets (called *clusters*) $C_{g_1}, C_{g_2}, \ldots, C_{g_C}$, $\overset{C}{\underset{i=1}{\cup}} C_{g_i} = U$ and $C_{g_u} \cap C_{g_w} = \emptyset$, for $u \neq w$, in such a way that objects in each cluster are 'similar' in some sense, and the objects from different clusters should be 'dissimilar'. The set of clusters on U is denoted by $C(U)$.

In the new proposed method *a measure of clusters' distinguishability* is introduced, it describes in some sense clusters' similarity and/or clusters' dissimilarity. The proposed algorithm belongs to a family of hierarchical clustering algorithms.

The procedure starts with N objects as individual clusters and proceed to find the whole set U as one cluster. A pair of clusters described by the lowest value of clusters' distinguishability measure is coupled and in such a way a new cluster is created – this way the number of clusters is decreased by one. The procedure is stopped when a fixed number of clusters C, $C < N$ is found.

By assumption, if a certain object belongs to a definite cluster then it could not be included in another cluster. The basic elements of proposed method were introduced below.

Let us consider an attribute a_j, $j \in \{1, \ldots, K\}$ and no empty sets $A_{j,t(j,k)}$ and $A_{j,t(j,n)}$, where $A_{j,t(j,k)} \subseteq V_{a_j}$, $A_{j,t(j,n)} \subseteq V_{a_j}$, V_{a_j} is the domain of the attribute a_j. The *elementary condition* is described by

$$\left(a_j \in A_{j,t(j,k)}\right)$$

where $card(A_{j,t(j,k)}) \geq 1$ means that the attribute a_j takes values from the set $A_{j,t(j,k)}$. For instance, the condition $(a_j \in \{a, b, f\})$ means that the clause $(a_j \in \{a\}) \vee (a_j \in \{b\}) \vee (a_j \in \{f\})$ is satisfied.

Now, on the base of conditions, we introduce a definition of relation of dominance of one condition over another one.

Definition 1. *Elementary condition $(a_j \in A_{j,t(j,k)})$ dominates another elementary condition $(a_j \in A_{j,t(j,n)})$ if the clause $A_{j,t(j,k)} \supseteq A_{j,t(j,n)}$ is satisfied, denoted by $(a_j \in A_{j,t(j,k)}) \succeq (a_j \in A_{j,t(j,n)})$.*

It easy to notice that the condition $(a_j \in \{a, b, f\})$ dominates the condition $(a_j \in \{a, f\})$, and this is denoted as $(a_j \in \{a, b, f\}) \succeq (a_j \in \{a, f\})$.

It is important to mention that dominance is a transitive relation, and the following conditions are satisfied:

IF $(a_j \in A_{j,t(j,k)}) \succeq (a_j \in A_{j,t(j,n)})$ and $(a_j \in A_{j,t(j,n)}) \succeq (a_j \in A_{j,t(j,m)})$

THEN $(a_j \in A_{j,t(j,k)}) \succeq (a_j \in A_{j,t(j,m)})$.

We assume that there is *a lack of mutual dominance* of two elementary conditions $(a_j \in A_{j,t(j,k)})$ and $(a_j \in A_{j,t(j,n)})$ if the first condition does not dominates the second, and the second condition does not dominates the first one. Such situation we will denote as $(a_j \in A_{j,t(j,k)}) \prec\!\!\succ (a_j \in A_{j,t(j,n)})$. In the following case of two conditions $(a_j \in \{a, b, f\})$ and $(a_j \in \{a, c\})$ there is a lack of mutual dominance of two conditions, i.e. $(a_j \in \{a, b, f\}) \prec\!\!\succ (a_j \in \{a, c\})$.

Using the term of an elementary condition, *a cluster C_g* can be expressed as follows:

$$C_g = (a_1 \in A_{1,t(1,g)}) \wedge \ldots \wedge (a_K \in A_{K,t(K,g)}) \tag{2}$$

where $A_{j,t(j,g)} \subseteq V_{a_j}$, for $j = 1, \ldots, K$, $card(A_{j,t(j,g)}) \geq 1$.

We say that the object $e_n = (a_1 \in \{v_{1,t(1,n)}\}) \wedge \ldots \wedge (a_K \in \{v_{K,t(K,n)}\})$ *belongs to the cluster C_g* if the following conditions:

$$(a_1 \in A_{1,t(1,g)}) \succeq (a_1 \in v_{1,t(1,n)})$$

$$\vdots$$

$$(a_K \in A_{K,t(K,g)}) \succeq (a_K \in v_{K,t(K,n)}) \tag{3}$$

are satisfied.

Now we will introduce the definition of *distinguishability* for two clusters

$$C_{g_1} : (a_1 \in A_{1,t(1,g_1)}) \wedge \ldots \wedge (a_K \in A_{K,t(K,g_1)}) \text{ and}$$
$$C_{g_2} : (a_1 \in A_{1,t(1,g_2)}) \wedge \ldots \wedge (a_K \in A_{K,t(K,g_2)}),$$

while $A_{j,t(j,g_1)} \subseteq V_{a_j}$, $A_{j,t(j,g_2)} \in V_{a_j}$, $j = 1, \ldots, K$. First, let us introduce the following definition of *distinguishability measure* of two clusters.

Definition 2. *Measure of distinguishable two clusters C_{g_1} and C_{g_2} is defined in the following manner*

$$\omega(C_{g_1}, C_{g_2}) = \sum_{j=1}^{K} \begin{cases} 1 & \text{if} \quad (a_j \in A_{j,t(j,g_1)}) \prec\!\!\succ (a_j \in A_{j,t(j,g_2)}) \\ 0 & \text{otherwise} \end{cases} \tag{4}$$

We say that the cluster C_{g_1} and the cluster C_{g_2} are *ω-distinguishable* for the set of attributes $\{a_j : j \in I_k\}$, $card(I_k) = \omega$, if two conditions are satisfied:

1) $(a_j \in A_{j,t(j,g_1)}) \prec\succ (a_j \in A_{j,t(j,g_2)}), \forall j \in I_k$
2) $(a_j \in A_{j,t(j,g_1)}) \succeq (a_j \in A_{j,t(j,g_2)})$ or $(a_j \in A_{j,t(j,g_2)}) \succeq (a_j \in A_{j,t(j,g_1)})$,
$\forall j \in \{1, \ldots, K\} \setminus I_k.$ (5)

We assume that the cluster $C_{g_1} : \{e_n : e_n \in U, n \in J_{g_1} \subseteq \{1, 2, \ldots, N\}\}$ and the cluster $C_{g_2} : \{e_n : e_n \in U, n \in J_{g_2} \subseteq \{1, 2, \ldots, N\}\}$ are ω-*distinguishable* for the set of the attributes $\{a_j : j \in I_k\}$, $card(I_k) = \omega$.

Definition 3. *The junction of the two ω-distinguishable clusters is defined as follows:*

$$C_{g_1} \oplus C_{g_2} :=$$
$$\bigwedge_{j \in I_k} (a_j \in A_{j,t(j,g_1)} \cup A_{j,t(j,g_2)}) \bigwedge_{j \in \{1,2,\ldots K\} \setminus I_k} (a_j \in dom\{A_{j,t(j,g_1)}, A_{j,t(j,g_2)}\}) \quad (6)$$

where dom is meant as a dominant condition.

In result a new cluster $C_{g_3} : (a_1 \in A_{1,t(1,g_3)}) \wedge \ldots \wedge (a_K \in A_{K,t(K,g_3)})$ contains the following objects $\{e_n : e \in U, n \in J_{g_1} \cup J_{g_2}\}$, see Example 1.

Example 1. Let's consider two clusters C_{g_1} and C_{g_2} shown in Table 1. The cluster C_{g_1} contains objects $e1$ and $e2$. The cluster C_{g_2} contains objects $e3$, $e4$ and $e5$. Let us notice that the clusters C_{g_1} and C_{g_2} are 4-distinguishable for the set of attributes $\{a_j\}$, $j \in I_k = \{1, 4, 5, 10\}$, $card(I_k) = 4$.

The way of construction of a new cluster C_{g_3} is shown in Table 2.

Table 1.

Cluster\Attribute	a_1	a_2	a_3	a_4	a_5	a_6	a_7	a_8	a_9	a_{10}
$C_{g_1} : e1, e2$	e	e	g $\vee$ h	e $\vee$ d	d	g	g	f $\vee$ g	f	f
$C_{g_2} : e3, e4, e5$	f	e	g	f $\vee$ e	e	g	g	g	g $\vee$ f	g

Table 2.

Cluster\Attribute	a_1	a_2	a_3	a_4	a_5	a_6	a_7	a_8	a_9	a_{10}
$C_{g_3} :$ $e1, e2, e3, e4, e5$	e $\vee$ f	e	g $\vee$ h	e $\vee$ d $\vee$ f	d $\vee$ e	g	g	f $\vee$ g	f $\vee$ g	f $\vee$ g

The new cluster $C_{g_3} = (a_1 \in \{e, f\}) \wedge (a_2 \in \{e\}) \wedge \ldots \wedge (a_K \in \{f, g\})$ contains objects $e1$, $e2$, $e3$, $e4$ and $e5$.

3   Clustering Algorithm

3.1   Algorithm Description

We proposed a hierarchical agglomerative approach to cluster nominal data. The bottom level of the structure has singular clusters while the top level contains one cluster with all objects. During iteration two clusters are heuristically selected. These selected clusters are then merged to form a new cluster.

Assuming: U – set of objects, $card(U) = N$, K – number of attributes, C – waited number of clusters the basic elements of the proposed algorithm be described as follows.

Step 1. Each object creates one-element cluster in the initial set of clusters, i.e.

$$C\,(U) = \{\,C_{g_1},\,C_{g_2},\dots,C_{g_N}\,\},$$
$$C_{g_n} = (a_1 \in A_{1,t(1,g_n)}) \wedge \dots \wedge (a_K \in A_{K,t(K,g_n)}),\ \forall n = 1,2,\dots,N.$$

Step 2. We find ω^*-distinguishable clusters C_{g_i} and C_{g_j} that minimize the following criterion:

$$\omega^* = \min_{\substack{\forall i \in \{1,2,\dots,card(C(U)\} \\ \forall j \in \{1,2,\dots,card(C(U)\} \\ i < j,}} \omega(C_{g_i},C_{g_j})$$

Step 3. From pair of ω^*-distinguishable clusters we create new cluster in the set of clusters $C\,(U)$. The pair of ω^*-distinguishable clusters are removed from the set $C(U)$. Thus $card(C(U)) := card(C(U)) - 1$.

Step 4. If $card(C(U)) = C$, go to Step 6; otherwise, go to Step 5.

Step 5. If $\omega^* < K$, repeat Step 2; otherwise, go to Step 6.

Step 6. STOP.

3.2   Illustrating Example

Let us consider data shown in Table 3. The objects $e1,\dots,e6$ are described in the form of conditions associated with the set of attributes $\{a_1,\dots,a_5\}$.

Table 3.

Object\Attribute	a_1	a_2	a_3	a_4	a_5
e1	c	b	a	a	b
e2	b	a	b	a	c
e3	d	b	c	a	b
e4	d	a	a	b	a
e5	b	a	b	b	a
e6	d	b	c	a	b

Our aim is to group the objects into prescribed number of two clusters, $C = 2$. At the beginning we assume that each object creates one-element cluster in the initial set of clusters $C\,(U) = \{C_{g_1},C_{g_2},\dots,C_{g_6}\}$, $card(C(U)) = 6$, in the following way:

$$C_{g_1} : (a_1 \in \{c\}) \wedge (a_2 \in \{b\}) \wedge (a_3 \in \{a\}) \wedge (a_4 \in \{a\}) \wedge (a_5 \in \{b\}),$$

$$\vdots$$

$$C_{g_6} : (a_1 \in \{d\}) \wedge (a_2 \in \{b\}) \wedge (a_3 \in \{c\}) \wedge (a_4 \in \{a\}) \wedge (a_5 \in \{b\}).$$

From a pair of 0-distinguishable clusters C_{g_3} and C_{g_6} a new cluster C_{g_7} is created (Table 4). The newly formed cluster is shaded in the Table 4, while clusters C_{g_3} and C_{g_6} are removed from the set $C(U)$. Thus, $card(C(U)) := card(C(U)) - 1 = 5$.

Table 4.

Cluster\Attribute	a_1	a_2	a_3	a_4	a_5
$C_{g_1} : e1$	c	b	a	a	b
$C_{g_2} : e2$	b	a	b	a	c
$C_{g_4} : e4$	d	a	a	b	a
$C_{g_5} : e5$	b	a	b	b	a
$C_{g_7} : e3, e6$	d	b	c	a	b

Next, from each pair of 2-distinguishable clusters a new cluster is created, see Table 5, 6 and 7.

Table 5.

Cluster\Attribute	a_1	a_2	a_3	a_4	a_5
$C_{g_2} : e2$	b	a	b	a	c
$C_{g_4} : e4$	d	a	a	b	a
$C_{g_5} : e5$	b	a	b	b	a
$C_{g_8} : e1, e3, e6$	c ∨ d	b	a ∨ c	a	b

Table 6.

Cluster\Attribute	a_1	a_2	a_3	a_4	a_5
$C_{g_2} : e2$	b	a	b	a	c
$C_{g_8} : e1, e3, e6$	c ∨ d	b	a ∨ c	a	b
$C_{g_9} : e4, e5$	b ∨ d	a	a ∨ b	b	a

Table 7.

Cluster \Attribute	a_1	a_2	a_3	a_4	a_5
$C_{g_8} : e1, e3, e6$	c ∨ d	b	a ∨ c	a	b
$C_{g_{10}} : e2, e4, e5$	b ∨ d	a	a ∨ b	a ∨ b	a∨c

The required number of clusters has been already reached, $card(C(U)) = 2$, and we obtained the following set of clusters $C(U) = \{C_{g_8}, C_{g_{10}}\}$, where

$$C_{g_8} : (a_1 \in \{c, d\}) \wedge (a_2 \in \{b\}) \wedge (a_3 \in \{a, c\}) \wedge (a_4 \in \{a\}) \wedge (a_5 \in \{b\}),$$
$$C_{g_{10}} : (a_1 \in \{b, d\}) \wedge (a_2 \in \{a\}) \wedge (a_3 \in \{a, b\}) \wedge (a_4 \in \{a, b\}) \wedge (a_5 \in \{a, c\}).$$

The cluster C_{g_8} contains objects $e1$, $e3$ and $e6$, and the cluster $C_{g_{10}}$ contains objects $e2$, $e4$ and $e5$.

The hierarchical clustering dendrogram representing the entire process of clustering starting from individual objects and ending with two clusters and is shown below.

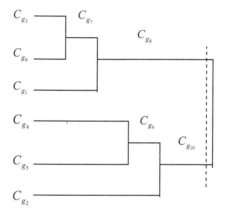

Fig. 1. Dendrogram of the algorithm

These descriptions can be also represented in a different form of rules of "IF *certain conditions are fulfilled* THEN *membership in a definite cluster takes place*" type. In our case, the conditional part of the rules will contain the disjunction of conditions related to the subset of attributes selected for the description of the objects. The obtained rules are shown below.

IF $(a_1 \in \{c\}) \vee (a_2 \in \{b\}) \vee (a_3 \in \{c\}) \vee (a_5 \in \{b\})$ THEN G_{g_8}
IF $(a_1 \in \{b\}) \vee (a_2 \in \{a\}) \vee (a_3 \in \{b\}) \vee (a_4 \in \{b\}) \vee (a_5 \in \{a, c\})$ THEN $G_{g_{10}}$.

4   Conclusions

In this paper we described a new approached for building clusters of objects described by nominal data. For such objects description we introduced and developed the algorithm based on the idea of dominations of conditions within each pair of clusters. Each cluster is described by a conjunction of conditions associated with nominal attributes describing objects. The introduced measure of distinguishability of two clusters allowed us to choose a pair of the most 'close' clusters in order to join them and create a new one.

The primary solved examples shows the efficiency of the proposed method which seems to be effective and elegant.

Acknowledgements. The research was partially supported by the Ministry of Science and Higher Education (Poland) under Grant Nr N N519 384936.

References

1. Apostolico, R., Bock, M.E., Lonardi, S.: Monotony of surprise in large-scale quest for unusual words. In: Proceedings of the 6th International Conference on Research in Computational Molecular Biology, Washington, DC, April 18-21, pp. 22–31 (2002)
2. Dunn, J.C.: A Fuzzy Relative of the ISODATA Process and Its Use in Detecting Compact Well-Separated Clusters. Journal of Cybernetics 3, 32–57 (1973)
3. Bezdek, J.C.: Pattern Recognition with Fuzzy Objective Function Algorithms. Plenum Press, New York (1981)
4. Dempster, A.P., Laird, N.M., Rubin, D.B.: Maximum Likelihood from Incomplete Data via the EM algorithm. Journal of the Royal Statistical Society, Series B 39, 1-3-8 (1977)
5. Gionis, A., Mannila, H.: Finding recurrent sources in sequences. In: Proceedings of the 7th International Conference on Research in Principles of Database Systems, Tucson, AZ, May 12-14, pp. 249–256 (2003)
6. Johnson, S.C.: Hierarchical Clustering Schemes. Psychometrika 2, 241–254 (1967)
7. Krawczak, M., Szkatuła, G.: On time series envelopes for classification problem. In: Developments of Fuzzy Sets, Intuitionistic Fuzzy Sets, Generalized Nets, vol. II, pp. 149–164 (2010)
8. Krawczak, M., Szkatuła, G.: Time series envelopes for classification. In: Proceedings of the Conference: 2010 IEEE International Conference on Intelligent Systems, London, UK, July 7-9, pp. 156–161 (2010)
9. Lin, J., Keogh, E., Wei, L., Lonardi, S.: Experiencing SAX: a Novel Symbolic Representation of Time Series. Data Min. Knowledge Disc. 2(15), 107–144 (2007)
10. MacQueen, J.B.: Some Methods for classification and Analysis of Multivariate Observations. In: Proceedings of 5th Berkeley Symposium on Mathematical Statistics and Probability, vol. 1, pp. 281–297. University of California Press, Berkeley (1967)
11. Wang, B.: A New Clustering Algorithm on Nominal Data Sets. In: Proceedings of International MultiConference on Engineers and Computer Scientists, IMECS 2010, Hong Kong, March 17-19 (2010)

Retrieving Informative Content from Web Pages with Conditional Learning of Support Vector Machines and Semantic Analysis

Piotr Ładyżyński[1] and Przemysław Grzegorzewski[1,2]

[1] Faculty of Mathematics and Computer Science,
Warsaw University of Technology,
Plac Politechniki 1, 00-661 Warsaw, Poland
[2] Systems Research Institute, Polish Academy of Sciences,
Newelska 6, 01-447 Warsaw, Poland
{p.ladyzynski,pgrzeg}@mini.pw.edu.pl

Abstract. We propose a new system which is able to extract informative content from the news pages and divide it into prescribed sections. The system is based on the machine learning classifier incorporating different kind of information (styles, linguistic information, structural information, content semantic analysis) and conditional learning. According to empirical results the suggested system seems to be a promising tool for extracting information from web.

Keywords: Conditional learning, machine learning, semantic analysis, sparse matrices, support vector machines, web information extraction.

1 Introduction

News web pages are organized in distinct segments such as menus, comments, advertisements areas, navigation bars and the main informative segments – article texts, summarizations, titles, authors names. Distinguishing informative content from redundant blocks plays enormous role in systems which require fast and online monitoring of thousands of published information (see Fig. 1). For example, imagine a system for predicting stock price fluctuations based on the analysis of content published in financial news web pages or social networking sites. Such a system should be supported with filtered texts. Another example is a system which gathers automatically morning business information from all important news pages, categorize it and present as one application. Retrieving such amount of information manually will by probably impossible and too expensive.

2 Related Work

The broad literature devoted to the problem is evidence of its importance. Most of the proposed systems are based on heuristics or templates prepared manually. Gujjar et al. [6] and Lin, Ho at al. [7] constructed a decision rule by examining

L. Rutkowski et al. (Eds.): ICAISC 2012, Part II, LNCS 7268, pp. 128–135, 2012.
© Springer-Verlag Berlin Heidelberg 2012

Fig. 1. An exemplar news web site from *wiadomosci.wp.pl.*Informative content (title, summary, article title) is selected within thick black lines areas.

node text content size and entropy. Castro Reis et al. [4] created extraction templates by the analysis of HTML tree structure and label text passages that match the extraction templates ([5] shows a similar approach). Another approach presenting matching unseen sites to the templates is proposed in [1] - [3].

Such solutions may work even well for one domain but have no ability to adapt to different sites (with different structure) without manual intervention to modify rules or templates. Moreover, such rigid rules will work properly for sites with well organized structure (for example large information portals where HTML tree structure is based on a machine generated code) but will behave poorly on sites which often change their layout (blogs, small hand-developed portals). Little modification of content structure in analyzed site often results in necessity of templates modification. Hence Ziegler et al. [10] extracted tree structure from HTML for linguistic and structural features and than used the Particle Swarm Intelligence machine learning technique to establish a classification rule.

In the present paper we propose a solution utilizing the support vector machine (SVM). By sequence learning algorithm and sparse matrix processing our system is able to handle a training set of 2 000000 examples each consisting of 25000 attributes (learning SVM on such matrix in classic way requires 400TB of RAM memory). Moreover, to extend classifier's ability to capture HTML tree structure we use conditional learning transferring information on parents classification to children node in the HTML tree. The construction of a training set is based on capturing thousands of features which makes the solution robust to page layout modifications.

3   System Architecture

3.1   Collecting Data

Our goal is to construct a system which is able to retrieve specified blocks for a given domain from WWW sites. We would like to extract the following article segments from the news web page: 1. noise (non-informative segments), 2. main content, 3. title, 4. summary, 5. author's name, 6. readers comments.

We have written a GUI application *(SegmentSelector)* in Java programming language for preparing a training set through manual classification of the nodes. More precisely, this application displays web page and unable a user to select text segments and assigning them to specified class (from 1 to 6). It is worth noting that our GUI application may help to make this process more even efficient. Namely, just after classifying manually only a few sites one may force the system to follow the process for successive sites keeping eye on the classification and reducing users activity to correct mistakes and misclassifications.

3.2   Attributes Selection

A typical web page in the form we can see in a browser is build from HTML code supported by styles files CSS. Each area in WWW page is represented in HTML source code tree by a certain node. Each node has a wide range (over 300) of attributes and layout features which we can obtain from the browser rendering engine. Examples are the font size, background color, position, height, width, margin, padding, border etc. Moreover, we also compute or aggregate some extra features along with feeding classifier with preprocessed text content of the node. Even the most sophisticated artificial intelligence method would work poorly if it would be fed with a feature set which do not separate learning examples. Therefore, when creating a training set, it is advisable to draw attention to the following aspects:

Styles Features. We can get styles attributes directly from a browser rendering engine. Some of them are quantitative - they are generally real numbers (position, font size, background color) while others are qualitative (bold, italic, text-decoration:none). For each node, Quantitative features for each node are collected in an array, while qualitative are stored as a string (which would be later transform into a sparse matrix required for the SVM classifier).

Structural Features. Structural features contain information on the structure of HTML tree:

- **tag-path, id-path, class-path** – For each node we define a string attribute by a sequence tag's names corresponding to given path (from the root to that node of the tree). Next we do the same for class and id parameters. The illustration is given in Fig. 2, where `html.div.p`, `0.main_article.kls_01` and `0.0.temat` correspond to **tag-path**), **id-path** and **id-path**, respectively. These three attributes of the node will be used in further processing. It is worth noting that these structural attributes remain unchanged even if the graphical layout of the page would be modified.

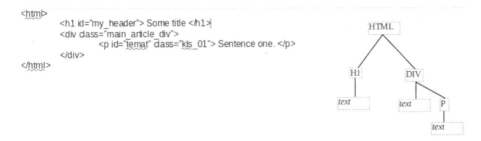

```
<html>
    <h1 id="my_header"> Some title </h1>
    <div class="main_article_div">
        <p id="temat" class="kls_01"> Sentence one. </p>
    </div>
</html>
```

Fig. 2. Tree structure of HTML source code of web page. Each node represents a specified segment in page layout.

- **anchor-ratio** – high value of this ratio indicates that the text node probably does not contain the main content.
- **format-tag-ratio** – formatting tags are HTML instructions (or set CSS styles) which change the text display format. We assume that main content nodes take higher value of this ratio.

Linguistic Features. We compute some word statistics in each examined node: **word-count** – number of words, **words-ratio** – fraction of words in the node beginning with uppercase (often in block containing author's name this feature is equal to 1), **letters-count** – number of letters in given node, **letters-ratio** – fraction of uppercase letters, **average-sentence-length** – the average of letters in the sentence.

Semantic Analysis. We will also try to teach our SVM classifier the meaning of some sort of text in node. SVM should recognize some groups of words typical for a given type of node. As an example we can consider an advertisement block which usually contains phrase "Google Ads".

It seems that the simplest way for including information stored in the text content corresponding to given node is to treat each word as a separate string feature and include it to the list of all string features of that node. However, such solution may result in adding too many unique words to the feature space. Fortunately we can reduce the dimension of the data by choosing only words which are in some sense more informative than others (e.g. word "molecular" is much more informative than word "are"). The importance of a word increases if it occurs many times. Let

$$tf_{i,j} = \frac{n_{i,j}}{\sum_k n_{k,j}}, \tag{1}$$

where $n_{i,j}$ shows how many times word i occurs in node j and $\sum_k n_{k,j}$ is the number of all words in node j. On the other hand the importance of word decreases when it is common in the language:

$$idf_i = \log \frac{|D|}{|\{j : t_i \in d_j\}|}, \tag{2}$$

where $|D|$ is the number of analyzed nodes containing text and $|\{j : t_i \in d_j\}|$ is the number of documents containing term i.

Now we can define a measure of importance of word i in node j:

$$(tf - idf)_{i,j} = tf_{i,j} \times idf_i. \tag{3}$$

This way we can reduce the dimension of data by choosing only words with high values of $(tf - idf)_{i,j}$ matrix. As an example, let us consider the portal *wiadomosci.wp.pl*. Using the distribution of importance we reduce the number of word attributes from 45471 to 10000.

3.3   Training Set Preparation

Let us consider a training set obtained from the news portals *wiadomosci.wp.pl* and *businessweek.com* by the manual indication of the text areas we would like to extract (class selection). Our web robot application collected articles from this sites for two months and displayed it in *(SegmentSelector)* for the manual classification. Each day after classification of new articles SVM classifier was retrained with new observations so each day the sites where classified better and only few small corrections were required. After two month we had 245000 nodes from *wiadomosci.wp.pl* and 180000 nodes from *businessweek.com*.

As we have mentioned above we collect two types of features for each node: quantitative (real-valued features) and qualitative (string features like tag-path, words from text content, etc.). For *wiadomoci.wp.pl* we obtained 46 real-valued attributes for each node. However, there were differences in the number of qualitative features for each node, e.g. we got $|F_{styl}| = 283$ different string features for styles, $|F_{struc}| = 8506$ string features for structural features and $|F_{sem}| = 10000$ string features for reduced dimensions from semantic analysis of the content. Next we gave a unique number (from 1 to 18789) for each string feature to generate the input training file in a **sparse matrix representation**. The results obtained for *businessweek.com* were similar.

3.4   Conditional Learning

An information that our observations are derived from the tree structure is crucial for the classifier. Going down the tree we can classify parent node first and consider the parents' class as a feature for the child nodes. Constructing the training set in this way we emulate a learning scheme which takes into consideration conditional *a-posteriori* distribution without direct estimation as in the case of the conditional random field (see. [8]).

3.5   SVM Sequence Learning with Sparse Matrices

As we have mentioned above the SVM classifier is the heart of our system. Let $\mathbf{y} = (y_1, \ldots, y_N)$ denote a class labels $y_i \in \{-1, 1\}$ and let $(\mathbf{x}_i)_{i=1}^N$ denote vectors of features. Training the SVM classifier is equivalent to finding the solution of the quadratic optimization problem:

$$\min_{w} \frac{||w||^2}{2} \tag{4}$$

under boundary conditions:

$$y_i(\mathbf{w}\mathbf{x}_i + b) \geq 1, \tag{5}$$

where $\mathbf{w}$ is a vector defining a separating hyperplane.

Due to the size of our data all usual solving techniques are useless. For training our SVM classifier we use the kernalized subgradient sequential algorithm (see [9]):

INPUT: S, λ, T
INITIALIZE: Set $\alpha_1 = 0$
    for $t = 1, 2, \ldots, T$ do
        Choose $i_t \in \{0, \ldots, |S|\}$ uniformly at random.
        for all $j \neq i_t$ do
          $\alpha_{t+1}[j] = \alpha_t[j]$
        end for
        if $y_{i_t} \sum_j \alpha_t[j] y_j K(x_{i_t}, x_j) \leq 0$ then
          $\alpha_{t+1}[i_t] = \alpha_t[i_t] + 1$
        else
          $\alpha_{t+1}[i_t] = \alpha_t[i_t]$
        end if
    end for
OUTPUT: α_{T+1}

where $K(.,.)$ is a kernel function (the gaussian kernel was successfully applied in our study).

This algorithm was applied for training a classifier with two classes only. To enable a multi-class performance we have used the *one-for-all* strategy.

Table 1. Crossvalidation tests for *wiadomosci.wp.pl* training set: (a) SVM without semantic analysis features and conditional learning, (b) SVM with Semantic Analysis features but without conditional learning, (c) SVM with full system architecture

(a)

	noise	content	Prec.
noise	200077	11213	0.946
content	1812	32569	0.947

(b)

	noise	content	Prec.
noise	201868	9422	0.955
content	1231	33150	0.964

(c)

	noise	content	Prec.
noise	209314	1976	0.991
content	221	34160	0.994

Table 2. Crossvalidation tests for *businessweek.com* training set: (a) SVM without semantic analysis features and conditional learning, (b) SVM with semantic analysis features but without conditional learning, (c) SVM with full system architecture, where: 1. noise content, 2. article main text 4, title, 3. summary, 5. author's name, 6. readers comments.

	1	2	3	4	5	6	Prec.
(a)							
1	152308	6	41	12	213	9011	0.943
2	12	20088	168	343	0	513	0.951
3	1	10	426	14	2	2	0.936
4	4	13	2	365	1	5	0.936
5	58	4	1	1	266	12	0.777
6	15	243	4	43	6	408	0.567
(b)							
1	154910	6	40	12	191	6432	0.959
2	12	20338	132	297	0	345	0.968
3	0	8	429	14	2	2	0.943
4	2	11	2	371	1	3	0.951
5	49	4	1	0	279	9	0.816
6	15	221	4	41	6	432	0.601
(c)							
1	160170	6	38	12	152	1213	0.991
2	8	20715	74	183	0	144	0.981
3	0	2	446	4	1	2	0.980
4	1	3	2	383	1	0	0.982
5	31	4	1	0	299	7	0.874
6	14	161	4	39	4	497	0.691

4   Results and Conclusions

We trained the SVM classifier with sparse features matrices of dimensions: 184621×18789 – for *businessweek.com* and 243474×18789 – for *wiadomosci.wp.pl* with the sparsity level equal to $0, 1\%$. With the grid search we found that $\sigma = 18$ for standard deviation in SVM Gauss kernel works well. Due to immense size of data we train SVM by only two passes through entire learning set which result in training time equal to about fourteen days on machine with $2, 4GHz$ processor.

Results for distinguishing informative content from non-informative task for *wiadomosci.wp.pl* are shown in Table 1 while the performance in labelling the informative nodes is given in Table 2. Both semantic analysis and conditional learning technique resulted in significant improvement of classification results. We can see that comments block as its semantic and style similarity to main content of article is difficult to extract.

Since a page structure varies for each domain it is extremely difficult to compare various systems trained on different data. However, the precision rate equal about 99% is quite promising in comparison of performance of systems proposed in previous works (e.g. 90% in [10] or 80% in [6]). That outstanding performance of the proposed system is a result the skilful application the SMV classifier implemented in a way that enables handling with immense training sets along with conditional learning and taking into consideration all possible types of features.

Although the performance of our system quite satisfactory, some further improvements would be desirable. Firstly, we should try to upgrade classifier using boosting technique. Secondly, a more sophisticated semantic analysis technique (e.g. semantic patterns recognition) seems to be promising. Finally, it would be interesting to examine the proposed system for retrieving information from more difficult, irregular and mutable sites such as blogs.

References

1. Arasu, A., Garcia-Molina, H., University, S.: Extracting structured data from web pages. In: ACM SIGMOD 2003, pp. 337–348. ACM (2003)
2. Crescenzi, V., Mecca, G., Merialdo, P.: Roadrunner: Towards automatic data extraction from large web sites. In: 27th International Conference on Very Large Databases, VLDB, pp. 109–118 (2001)
3. Lerman, K., Getoor, L., Minton, S., Knoblock, C.: Using the structure of web sites for automatic segmentation of tables. In: ACM SIGMOD 2004, pp. 119–130. ACM (2004)
4. Castro Reis, D., Golgher, P.B., Silva, A.S., Laenderl, A.H.F.: Automatic web news extraction using tree edit distance. In: Proceedings of the 13th International World Wide Web Conference, pp. 502–511. ACM Press, New York (2004)
5. Geng, H., Gao, Q., Pan, J.: Extracting Content for News Web Pages based on DOM. In: IJCSNS International Journal of Computer Science and Network Security, vol. 7(2) (2007)
6. Vineel, G.: Web Page DOM Node Characterization and its Application to Page Segmentation. In: Internet Multimedia Services Architecture and Applications (IMSAA). IEEE Press (2009)
7. Lin, S.H., Ho, J.M.: Discovering informative content blocks from web documents. In: KDD 2002 Proceedings of the Eighth ACM SIGKDD International Conference on Knowledge Discovery and Data Mining, pp. 588–593. ACM, New York (2002)
8. Lafferty, J.D., McCallum, A., Pereira, F.C.N.: Conditional random fields: Probabilistic models for segmenting nd labeling sequence data. In: Proceedings of the Eighteenth International Conference on Machine Learning, San Francisco, pp. 282–289 (2000)
9. Shalev-Shwartz, S., Singer, Y., Srebro, N.: Pegasos: Primal Estimated sub-GrAdient Solver for SVM. In: ICML 2007 Proceedings of the 24th International Conference on Machine Learning, New York, pp. 807–814 (2007)
10. Ziegler, C.N., Skubacz, M.: Content extraction from news pages using particle swarm optimization on linguistic and structural features. In: Web Intelligence, pp. 242–249. IEEE Computer Society (2007)

Enhancing Recognition of a Weak Class – Comparative Study Based on Biological Population Data Mining

Henryk Maciejewski[1], Ewa Walkowicz[2], Olgierd Unold[1], and Paweł Skrobanek[1]

[1] Institute of Computer Engineering, Control and Robotics,
Wroclaw University of Technology,
Wybrzeże Wyspiańskiego 27, 50-370 Wrocław, Poland
{henryk.maciejewski,olgierd.unold,pawel.skrobanek}@pwr.wroc.pl
[2] Department of Horse Breeding and Riding,
Wroclaw University of Environmental and Life Sciences,
Kożuchowska 6, 51-631 Wrocaw, Poland
ewa.walkowicz@up.wroc.pl

Abstract. This paper presents an overview of several methods that can be used to improve recognition of a weak class in binary classification problem. We illustrated this problem in the context of data mining based on a biological population data. We analyze feasibility of several approaches such as boosting, non-symmetric cost of misclassification events, and combining several weak classifiers (metalearning). We show that metalearning seems counter-productive if the goal is to enhance the recognition of a weak class, and that the method of choice would consist in combining boosting with the non-symmetric cost approach.

Keywords: Classification, weak class recognition, boosting, metalearning.

1 Introduction - Problem Formulation

Recent advances in machine learning techniques and development of sophisticated data mining tools make is feasible to model very complex relationships between variables in datasets provided by life sciences [5]. This work originated from an interdisciplinary project focused on application of machine learning to analysis of animal breeding databases. The purpose of analysis is to build predictive models of various characteristics of offspring in the breeding population based on parameters of their ancestors. This task has important practical applications for the breeding community, as such models allow to include into the breeding herd the most promising parents in terms of value of their future progeny. However, building successful predictive models from animal breeding data is a challenging task. In this work we focus on a specific problem often faced when mining biological population data which is related to unbalanced response of classification models in terms of sensitivity and specificity. More

L. Rutkowski et al. (Eds.): ICAISC 2012, Part II, LNCS 7268, pp. 136–143, 2012.

specifically, we often observe that different classifiers tend to predict one of the classes accurately and the other class very weakly. This problem is well known in data mining when learning from unbalanced data, ie. when one of the classes is severely underrepresented in the training data. Several solution have been proposed to tackle this issue ranging from oversampling to modifications of prior probabilities. However highly unbalanced responses also can also occur when learning from perfectly balanced data, as was the case of the animal breeding study which motivated this work. In this paper we analyze different techniques that can be attempted to improve recognition of the weak class. We illustrate these methods by a numerical study based on animal breeding data. Although presented in the context of mining biological data, these techniques can be regarded as generic hints to balance classifiers.

The paper is organized as follows. In the next section we describe the population database analyzed and the collection of classification models fitted to this data. Next we present different approaches that can be attempted to enhance recognition of the weak class. Finally we compare these methods in the numerical study.

2   Data and Methods

2.1   Data

In this study we analyzed the complete population of Silesian horses [8]. The purpose of analysis was to predict various zoometric features of progeny based on attributes of their parents. The attributes of parents used in this study include their zoometric features, family, race and affinity (inbreeding index). The specific task demonstrated here consists in predicting the height of a horse based on the knowledge about its parents. More specifically, we define a binary target with the value of 1 indicating height above the population mean and 0 - otherwise. The vector of predictors consisted of 20 variables related to 5 zoometric features of father and 5 features of mother as well as 5 features per father and mother related to family, race and inbreeding. The numbers of observations, including observations with at least one missing value are summarized in Tab. 1, separately for the two classes compared.

Table 1. The number of observations (N), observations with at least one missing value (NMISS), and percentage of observations with missing values (%MISS)

Target	N	NMISS	%MISS
0	2521	551	21.9
1	2333	566	24.3
total	4854	1117	23.0

2.2   Predictive Models

We attempted to model the target using different classification tree algorithms, neural network and logistic regression [1],[6]. Specific algorithms used in the study are summarized below.

- **CR:** Classification and Regression tree. This algorithm splits training records into subgroups aiming to obtain highest reduction in the impurity index. The splits are always binary, ie. the algorithm builds binary decision trees.
- **CHAID:** Chi-squared Automatic Interaction Detection. This algorithm selects predictors for consecutive splits based on the chi-square test of independence between the predictor and the target. Predictor with the smallest p-value of the test is used as the variable defining the next split. This method can build non-binary trees, hence CHAID trees will generally grow wider than binary trees.
- **QUEST:** Quick, Unbiased, Efficient Statistical Tree. This algorithm selects splits based on statistical tests of independence and uses a simplified method to find the splitting threshold as compared with the previous algorithms. Generally, it avoids exhaustive searches performed by previous methods (using discriminant analysis instead), and as such it can be regarded as a simplified version of the CR method. The trees built are binary.
- **C5.0** algorithm proposed by [7] splits records based on maximum information gain criterion. The resulting trees are also binary.
- **LOG** - Logistic regression.
- **NN** - Neural network (we use multilayer perceptron architecture with 1 hidden layer).

2.3 Methods of Enhancing Recognition of Weak Class

In order to improve recognition of the weak class we apply several techniques which can be broadly categorized as (i) modifications in training algorithms or (ii) combining several predictive models (metalearning). We used the following techniques:

1. Boosting. This method builds a sequence of models, where consecutive models focus on proper recognition of observations misclassified by the previous model [3],[4]. The final classification is done by using the whole collection of models. Individual models are combined by a voting procedure. In the boosting procedure we control the number of models built. Sensitivity of this parameter with regard to improving recognition of the weak class is analyzed in the numerical study shown in the next section.
2. Non-symmetric cost of misclassification events. In the model training algorithms which attempt to minimize the overall cost of misclassification events, we increase the cost associated with misclassification of the weak class. Thus we directly control the sensitivity vs specificity of the model created. In the following numerical study we analyze sensitivity of this parameter.
3. Boosting models with non-symmetric cost of misclassification events. This approach essentially consists in combining the two previous methods.
4. Combining several (weak) models. We build a metamodel by combining individual models described in the previous section. We build several metamodels and observe how different combinations of individual models affect sensitivity and specificity of the overall model. More specifically, we first rank the

individual model by decreasing sensitivity, which corresponds to the recognition rate of the weak class. The rank is shown in Tab. 2. The first metamodel combines two best models in terms of sensitivity (ie. CHAID and NN). The second metamodel is created by adding the next weak model, etc.

Table 2. Summary of performance of classifiers (models ranked by sensitivity)

Rank	Classifier	Sensitivity	Specificity	Accuracy	AUC
1	CHAID	0.627	0.713	0.670	0.706
2	NN	0.619	0.724	0.672	0.743
3	CR	0.568	0.773	0.672	0.735
4	QUEST	0.533	0.802	0.670	0.712
5	C5	0.528	0.801	0.666	0.708
6	LOG	0.503	0.595	0.549	0.737

3   Numerical Study

In this study we attempt to predict whether the height of a child horse will exceed the population average (this is related to the value of target=1). We define the *sensitivity* of classifiers with regard to this value of target, ie. sensitivity measures the proportion of correctly classified horses with the actual target value of 1. Similarly, *specificity* of the model is related to the proportion of correctly classified horsed with the value of target=0. The population database is split randomly into the training and test partitions. The performance of classifiers is summarized in Tab. 2 (result pertaining to the test partition), and graphically compared in Fig. 1 for the training and test partitions. We observe that the models are generally weak in terms of sensitivity (recognition of the value of 1). Even the best models (CHAID and NN) realize sensitivity around 60%, with sensitivity of the remaining models slightly above 50% (which essentially means that these models do not recognize the 1 class). It should be also noted that the models are very similar in terms of the overall error (or accuracy), with the exception of the logistic regression (this is the only model unable to classify observations with missing values, which, considering the number of missing values (Tab. 1), decreases its performance).

In order to increase sensitivity, we first tried boosting, with results shown in Fig. 2. Here we used boosting with the C5.0 algorithm. It is interesting to observe that increasing the number of boosting models initially brings significant improvement in sensitivity (up to 5 models), however further increase again brings deterioration in sensitivity. Often used default value of 10 boosting models proves non-optimal in our study, proving that it is worth fine-tuning this parameter in practical model building.

The next analysis consisted in specifying non-symmetric cost of misclassification events. We also used this method with the C5.0 algorithm. Specifically, we increased the cost of the '1 as 0' misclassification, as shown in Fig. 3.

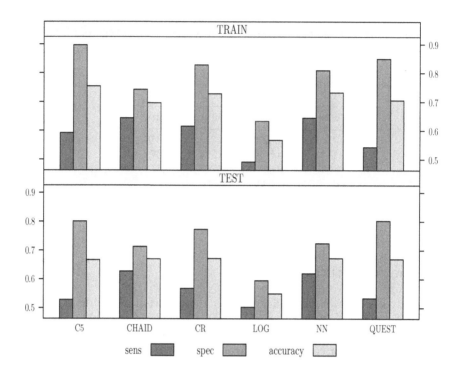

Fig. 1. Summary of performance of classification models

(The cost the '0 as 1' misclassification was kept constant as 1.) As expected, the non-symmetric cost directly controls the sensitivity-specificity ratio. However, this effect is non-linear: up to the value of cost equal 1.3 we observe little change, while further increase of the cost to 1.4 brings sudden change in sensitivity. This is apparently related to the non-linear nature of tree-based classifiers.

The effect of combining the two previous methods is illustrated in Fig. 4. With this approach we observe that the models are more responsive to the increase in the cost parameter, and we are able to balance sensitivity and specificity (at the cost of 1.3). It should be noted that this analysis was done for the fixed number of boosting models (equal 5, which realized best sensitivity in Fig. 2).

Finally, we tested the effect of metalearning, ie. combining several weak models, with results summarized in Fig. 5. The graph shows performance of a meta-model comprising 1, 2, etc. weak models as listed in Tab. 2. The first metamodel is essentially the CHAID model, the second - combines CHAID and NN, etc. Voting of the models is organized in the following way. We take the average of individual responses (coded as 0 or 1), and produce the final decision of 1 if the average is 0.5 or above. In this way we slightly favor the class 1, which can be clearly seen in the second metamodel, where we realize very high sensitivity of ca 0.75. This can be explained by the voting procedure, which in this case produces

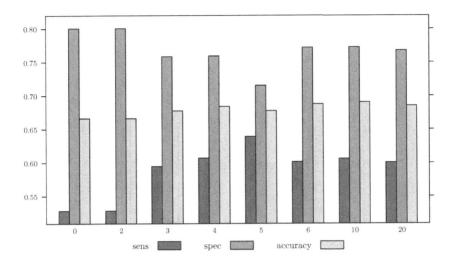

Fig. 2. Performance of the C5.0 model as a function of the number of boosting models generated

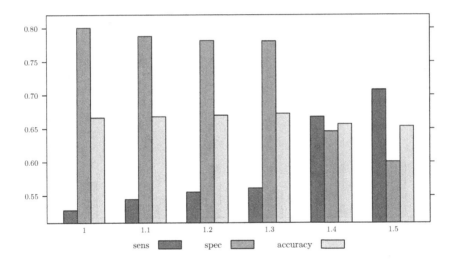

Fig. 3. Performance of the C5.0 model as a function of the cost of the '1 as 0' misclassification event

the response of 1 if any of the CHAID or NN models outputs a 1. However it is interesting to observe that metalearning based on 3 or more weak models is essentially counter-productive, as it leads to further decrease in sensitivity and to improvement in specificity - contrary to the goal of the study.

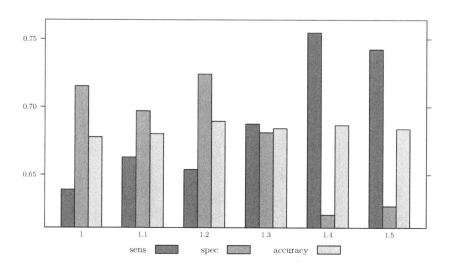

Fig. 4. Performance of the C5.0 with five-fold boosting as a function of the cost of the '1 as 0' misclassification event

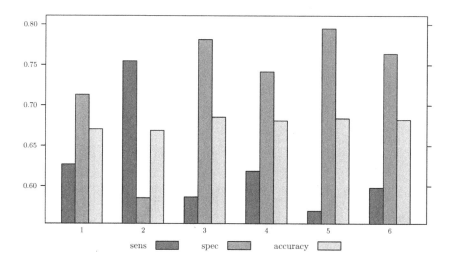

Fig. 5. Performance of the metamodel as a function of the number of models combined

4   Conclusions

In this work we demonstrated feasibility of several approaches commonly used in data mining to improve recognition of a weak class. The problem of unbalanced classifiers in terms of sensitivity and specificity often arises in datasets with highly nonlinear relationships between features and substantial number of observations with missing values, such as biological population datasets. We demonstrated boosting, non-symmetric cost based approaches and combining several weak models. Our study brings several practical conclusions. First, it seems that combining several weak models is useless if the goal is to improve recognition of a weak class. A voting collection of weak models generally brings further deteriorate of the weak class recognition, boosting recognition of the other class. Secondly, it seems that the method of choice would be cost based fine-tuning of the boosting model (as realized in Fig. 4). Finally, it is worth remembering that boosting itself is sensitive to the number of models generated, and that smaller number of models combined may well outperform the larger number of models, as shown in Fig. 5. Although this study originated from analysis of animal breeding datasets, model enhancement techniques illustrated here in the context of mining biological data can be attempted in any other applications of data mining.

Acknowledgment. This work was financed by the grant N516 415138 from the Ministry of Science and Higher Education.

References

1. Breiman, L., Friedman, J., Olshen, R., Stone, C.: Classification and regression trees. Wadsworth (1984)
2. Efron, B., Tibshirani, R.J.: An introduction to the bootstrap. Chapman and Hall, New York (1993)
3. Freund, Y.: Boosting a weak learning algorithm by majority. Information and Computation 121, 256–285 (1995)
4. Friedman, J., Hastie, T., Tibshirani, R.: Additive logistic regression: a statistical view of boosting. Annals of Statistics 28(4), 337–407 (2000)
5. Garner, S.R., Holmes, G., McQueen, R.J., Witten, I.H.: Machine learning from agricultural databases: practice and experience. J. Computing 6(1a), 69–73 (1997)
6. Hastie, T., Tibshirani, R., Friedman, J.: The Elements of Statistical Learning. In: Data Mining, Inference and Prediction. Springer (2002)
7. Quinlan, R.: C4.5: Programs for Machine Learning. Morgan Kaufmann (1993)
8. Walkowicz, E., Unold, O., Maciejewski, H., Skrobanek, P.: Zoometric indices in Silesian horses in the years 1945-2005. Ann. Anim. Sci. 11(4), 555–565 (2011)

Foundations of Rough Biclustering

Marcin Michalak

Silesian University of Technology, ul. Akademicka 16, 44-100 Gliwice, Poland
Marcin.Michalak@polsl.pl

Abstract. Amongst the algorithms for biclustering using some rough sets based steps none of them uses the formal concept of rough bicluster with its lower and upper approximation. In this short article the new foundations of rough biclustering are described. The new relation β generates $\beta-$description classes that build the rough bicluster defined with its lower and upper approximation.

Keywords: rough sets, biclustering, upper and lower approximation.

1 Introduction

Two significant branches of data analysis deals with the problem of finding values of unknown function on the basis of known values for some training data points. In the case of continuous function we say that it is the regression task and in the case of discrete function the problem is known as the classification task. In this second example we need to know the finite set of values, taken by the unknown dependance. Sometimes the cardinality of the set is unknown and that is the moment when the cluster analysis is performed.

The typical onedimensional cluster analysis gives the answer for two questions: how many groups are in the data and which training object belongs to which group (category, class, cluster). We may obtain the complete division of objects into classes (for example k-means algorithm [7]) or we may also have some ungrouped objects considered as the kind of background or noise (DB-SCAN [5]). But if we consider the noise as the class the both kinds of results are equivalent.

The extension of the clustering notion is biclustering. This problem was introduced in early 70's last century [6] and deals with the problem of grouping both subsets of rows and subsets of columns from the twodimensional matrices. Since then many biclustering algorithms were developed, especially for the purpose of microarray data analysis [13,11,1].

Almost ten years after the biclustering beginnings Pawlak introduced the rough sets theory as the different formal description of inexactness [9,10]. In this approach every set may be described with its lower and upper approximation. Lower approximation points which objects surely belong to the considered set and the complement of the upper approximation points which object surely not belong to the considered set. In the language of rough sets theory the set is exact iff its lower and upper approximations are equal.

L. Rutkowski et al. (Eds.): ICAISC 2012, Part II, LNCS 7268, pp. 144–151, 2012.

There are attempts to apply the rough sets theory to the biclustering. Some of them are based on the generalisation of k-means algorithm [12,4]. But there are no complete formal definition of rough bicluster on the basis of its approximations.

In this article the new complex rough approach for the biclustering is proposed. It starts with the generalisation (unification) of object and attribute notations. Then the special relation between matrix cells is defined (β−relation). This relation generates the set of β−description classes which sums and intersections give (respectively) upper and lower approximation of rough biclusters what fulfils the Pawlak definition of the rough set. The short example of finding rough biclusters in the discrete value matrix is also shown.

2   Rough Sets Based Description of Biclustering

Let us consider the binary matrix M with r rows and c columns. As the matrix can be rotated by 90 degrees without any loss of information we see that notions of „row" and „column" are subjective. From this point of view two other notions (already introduced in previous papers [8]) are more useful: feature and co-feature. If we consider feature as a row then every column is called co-feature and in the opposite way: if we consider feature as a column then every row is called co-feature. The set of features will be denoted as $\mathcal{F}$ and features will be denoted as f. The set of co-features will be denoted as $\mathcal{F}^*$ and co-features will be denoted as f^*. Generally all notions without the asterisk will be connected with features and all analogically notions for co-features will be marked with the asterisk. $M\{f, f^*\}$ is the value in the matrix M but it depends on the user assumptions whether $M\{f, f^*\} = M(f, f^*)$ or $M\{f, f^*\} = M(f^*, f)$.

Original table   Rows as features   Rows as co-features

Fig. 1. Illustration of features and co-features

2.1 β−Relation

Let us consider the draft of β−relation $\beta \subseteq (\mathcal{F} \times \mathcal{F}^*)^2$ that joins cells with the same value. It may be written non formally in the intuitive way as:

$$(f, f^*)\beta^v(g, g^*) \Leftrightarrow M\{f, f^*\} = M\{g, g^*\} = v$$

where $v \in V$ and V is the set of values from the matrix M. In the case where M is a binary one $v = 0$ or $v = 1$.

Now it is the time to precise this definition. We want this relation to be v−reflexive, symmetric and v−transitive. The v−reflexivity of this relation is implied by the equality $M\{f, f^*\} = M\{f, f^*\} = v$ and means that cell is in the β−relation with itself. The symmetry implies from the symmetry of the equality

$M\{f, f^*\} = M\{g, g^*\}$. The definition of v−transitivity is more complicated but is also intuitive. This property is the basis of the biclustering relation.

Let us start for the single cell from the matrix $M\{f, f^*\} = v$. For every $g^* \in \mathcal{F}^*$ that $M\{f, g^*\} = v$ we will claim that $(f, f^*)\beta^v(f, g^*)$. Also for every $g \in \mathcal{F}$ that $M\{g, f^*\} = v$ we will claim that $(f, f^*)\beta^v(g, f^*)$.

If we want two pairs $(f, f^*), (g, g^*)$, where $f \neq g$ and $f^* \neq g^*$ (two different cells from the matrix M) to be in the relation $\beta \subseteq (\mathcal{F} \times \mathcal{F}^*)^2$ we have to satisfy the following condition:

$$(f, f^*)\beta^v(g, g^*)|_{f \neq g, f^* \neq g^*} \Leftrightarrow (f, f^*)\beta^v(g, f^*) \wedge (f, f^*)\beta^v(f, g^*) \wedge$$
$$\wedge (f, g^*)\beta^v(g, g^*) \wedge (g, f^*)\beta^v(g, g^*)$$

Now let us extend the definition of the relation β^v for some subsets of features and co-features. Subset of features $F \subseteq \mathcal{F}$ and $F^* \subseteq \mathcal{F}^*$ are in the relation $\beta \subseteq (2^{\mathcal{F}} \times 2^{\mathcal{F}^*})^2$ iff every feature $f \in F$ is in the relation β^v with every co-feature $f^* \in F^*$.

$$F \beta^v F^* \Leftrightarrow \forall_{f \in F} \forall_{f^* \in F^*} f \beta^v f^*$$

So, if there is a set of features $F \subseteq \mathcal{F}$ and a subset of co-features $F^* \subseteq \mathcal{F}^*$ and $F \beta^v F^*$ then the cell $C = M\{k, k^*\}$ will be in the relation β^v with $F \times F^*$ iff:

$$\forall_{P \in F \times F^*} P \beta^v C$$

what will be written in the shorten way as:

$$(F \times F^*) \beta^v C$$

The final definition of v−transitivity has a form as follows:

$$(a, a^*)\beta^v(b, b^*) \wedge (b, b^*)\beta^v(c, c^*) \wedge (\{a, b\} \times \{a^*, b^*\})\beta^v(c, c^*) \Rightarrow (a, a^*)\beta^v(c, c^*)$$

2.2 β−Description Class

Apart from v−symmetry, reflexivity and v−transitivity the β−relation has another notion analogical for the equivalence relation: β−description class will be defined similarly as the equivalence class. The one thing that differs β−description class from the equivalence class is that every cell may have at least one but not only the one class. β−description class is defined as an ordered pair of subsets of $\mathcal{F}$ and $\mathcal{F}^*$ as follows:

$$[(f, f^*)]_{\beta^v} = (F, F^*), \quad F \subseteq \mathcal{F}, F^* \subseteq \mathcal{F}^*$$

iff:

i) $(f, f^*)\beta^v(F \times F^*)$
ii) $\forall_{e \notin F} \forall_{e^* \notin F^*} \neg [(f, f^*)\beta^v(F \cup \{e\}) \times (F^* \cup \{e^*\})]$

Table 1. Left: $\{f_2, f_3, f_4\} \times \{f_2^*, f_3^*, f_4^*, f_5^*\}$ is not in the relation β^1 with $\{f_6, f_7^*\}$. Right: $\{f_2, f_3, f_4\} \times \{f_2^*, f_3^*, f_4^*, f_5^*\}\beta^1\{f_6, f_7^*\}$.

	f_1	f_2	f_3	f_4	f_5	f_6	f_7		f_1	f_2	f_3	f_4	f_5	f_6	f_7
f_1^*	0	0	0	0	0	0	0	f_1^*	0	0	0	0	0	0	0
f_2^*	0	1	1	1	0	0	0	f_2^*	0	1	1	1	0	1	0
f_3^*	0	1	1	1	0	0	0	f_3^*	0	1	1	1	0	1	0
f_4^*	0	1	1	1	0	0	0	f_4^*	0	1	1	1	0	1	0
f_5^*	0	1	1	1	0	0	0	f_5^*	0	1	1	1	0	1	0
f_6^*	0	0	0	0	0	0	0	f_6^*	0	0	0	0	0	0	0
f_7^*	0	0	0	0	0	1	0	f_7^*	0	1	1	1	0	1	0
f_8^*	0	0	0	0	0	0	0	f_8^*	0	0	0	0	0	0	0

In other words it may be said that the β−description class are the largest (in the sense of inclusion) subset of features and co-features which Cartesian product gives cells that are all in the β^v relation with the given one cell. Now we see why it is possible for the cell to have more than one β−description class. The set of all β−description classes from matrix M will be called the dictionary: $\mathcal{D}_M$.

Let us consider the following relation $\mathcal{R}(\mathcal{D}_M^v) \subseteq \mathcal{D}_M^v \times \mathcal{D}_M^v$. Two β−description classes $d_1 = (F_1, F_1^*), d_2 = (F_2, F_2^*)$ are in the relation $\mathcal{R}(\mathcal{D}_M^v)$ when at least one of the following conditions is satisfied:

i) $F_1 \cap F_2 \neq \emptyset \wedge F_1^* \cap F_2^* \neq \emptyset$
ii) $\exists_{d_3 \in \mathcal{D}_M} \ d_1 \mathcal{R}(\mathcal{D}_M^v)d_3 \wedge d_3 \mathcal{R}(\mathcal{D}_M^v)d_2$

This relation is the equivalence relation: the symmetry and the reflexivity are given by the first condition and the transitivity is given by the second condition. The partition of $\mathcal{R}$ introduced by this relation will be denoted as:

$$\Pi_M^v = \{\pi_1, \pi_2, \cdots, \pi_p\}$$

This means that π_i is the set of β−description classes. For every π_i two sets may be defined, connected with predecessors and successors of pairs that are elements of π_i.

$$p(\pi_i) = \{F \subseteq \mathcal{F} : \exists_{F^* \subseteq \mathcal{F}^*} \ (F, F^*) \in \pi_i\}$$
$$s(\pi_i) = \{F^* \subseteq \mathcal{F}^* : \exists_{F \subseteq \mathcal{F}} \ (F, F^*) \in \pi_i\}$$

2.3   Rough Biclusters

Now we are able to define the rough sets based approach for the biclustering problem. Every π_i generates the one rough bicluster b_i in the following way:

i) lower bound: $\underline{b_i} = (\bigcap p(\pi_i), \bigcap s(\pi_i))$
ii) upper bound: $\overline{b_i} = (\bigcup p(\pi_i), \bigcup s(\pi_i))$

Bicluster b_i will be rough in the case when the sum and the join of the π_i will be different or exact otherwise. The only possibility for the b_i to be exact is that $card(\pi_i) = 1$.

3   Case Study

Let us consider the following discrete value matrix M presented in the Table 2. It contains ten rows and ten columns. Arbitrary rows are considered as co-features (that is why their labels are with asterisks) and columns are considered as features.

Table 2. Matrix M

	f_1	f_2	f_3	f_4	f_5	f_6	f_7	f_8	f_9	f_{10}
f_1^*	0	0	0	0	0	0	1	1	1	1
f_2^*	0	0	0	0	0	0	1	1	1	1
f_3^*	0	0	0	0	0	0	1	1	1	1
f_4^*	0	0	0	0	0	0	0	1	1	1
f_5^*	0	0	0	0	0	0	0	1	1	1
f_6^*	0	0	2	2	2	0	0	0	0	0
f_7^*	0	0	2	2	2	0	0	0	0	0
f_8^*	2	2	2	2	2	0	2	2	2	0
f_9^*	2	2	2	0	0	0	2	2	2	0
f_{10}^*	2	2	2	0	0	0	2	2	2	0

We are interested in finding biclusters of some subset of matrix values: biclusters of ones and twos. In the first step we are looking for β^1-description classes. We obtain the dictionary $\mathcal{D}_M^1$ that contain two classes:

$$\mathcal{D}_M^1 = \{(\{f_8, f_9, f_{10}\}, \{f_1^*, f_2^*, f_3^*, f_4^*, f_5^*\}), (\{f_6, f_7, f_8, f_9, f_{10}\}, \{f_1^*, f_2^*, f_3^*\})\}$$

Both classes are shown in Tables 3(a) and 3(b).

As we see the partition of $\mathcal{R}(\mathcal{D}_M^1)$ has only one element (both β^1-description classes has non-empty intersection), so we obtain just one rough bicluster and it form is:

$$\underline{b}_1 = (\{f_8, f_9, f_{10}\}, \{f_1^*, f_2^*, f_3^*\}) \quad \overline{b}_1 = (\{f_6, f_7, f_8, f_9, f_{10}\}, \{f_1^*, f_2^*, f_3^*, f_4^*, f_5^*\})$$

Table 3. The dictionary $\mathcal{D}_M^1$

(a) First β^1-description class.

	f_1	f_2	f_3	f_4	f_5	f_6	f_7	f_8	f_9	f_{10}
f_1^*	0	0	0	0	0	0	1	1	1	1	1
f_2^*	0	0	0	0	0	0	1	1	1	1	1
f_3^*	0	0	0	0	0	0	1	1	1	1	1
f_4^*	0	0	0	0	0	0	0	0	1	1	1
f_5^*	0	0	0	0	0	0	0	0	1	1	1
f_6^*	0	0	2	2	2	0	0	0	0	0
f_7^*	0	0	2	2	2	0	0	0	0	0
f_8^*	2	2	2	2	2	0	2	2	2	0
f_9^*	2	2	2	0	0	0	2	2	2	0
f_{10}^*	2	2	2	0	0	0	2	2	2	0

(b) Second β^1-description class.

	f_1	f_2	f_3	f_4	f_5	f_6	f_7	f_8	f_9	f_{10}
f_1^*	0	0	0	0	0	1	1	1	1	1
f_2^*	0	0	0	0	0	1	1	1	1	1
f_3^*	0	0	0	0	0	1	1	1	1	1
f_4^*	0	0	0	0	0	0	0	1	1	1
f_5^*	0	0	0	0	0	0	0	1	1	1
f_6^*	0	0	2	2	2	0	0	0	0	0
f_7^*	0	0	2	2	2	0	0	0	0	0
f_8^*	2	2	2	2	2	0	2	2	2	0
f_9^*	2	2	2	0	0	0	2	2	2	0
f_{10}^*	2	2	2	0	0	0	2	2	2	0

Now let us see the dictionary $\mathcal{D}_M^2$ – it also has two β–description classes (Tables 4(a) and 4(b)).

Table 4. The dictionary $\mathcal{D}_M^2$

(a) First β^2–description class.

	f_1	f_2	f_3	f_4	f_5	f_6	f_7	f_8	f_9	f_{10}
f_1^*	0	0	0	0	0	1	1	1	1	1
f_2^*	0	0	0	0	0	1	1	1	1	1
f_3^*	0	0	0	0	0	1	1	1	1	1
f_4^*	0	0	0	0	0	0	0	1	1	1
f_5^*	0	0	0	0	0	0	0	1	1	1
f_6^*	0	0	2	2	2	0	0	0	0	0
f_7^*	0	0	2	2	2	0	0	0	0	0
f_8^*	2	2	2	2	2	0	2	2	2	0
f_9^*	2	2	2	0	0	0	2	2	2	0
f_{10}^*	2	2	2	0	0	0	2	2	2	0

(b) Second β^2–description class.

	f_1	f_2	f_3	f_4	f_5	f_6	f_7	f_8	f_9	f_{10}
f_1^*	0	0	0	0	0	1	1	1	1	1
f_2^*	0	0	0	0	0	1	1	1	1	1
f_3^*	0	0	0	0	0	1	1	1	1	1
f_4^*	0	0	0	0	0	0	0	1	1	1
f_5^*	0	0	0	0	0	0	0	1	1	1
f_6^*	0	0	2	2	2	0	0	0	0	0
f_7^*	0	0	2	2	2	0	0	0	0	0
f_8^*	2	2	2	2	2	0	2	2	2	0
f_9^*	2	2	2	0	0	0	2	2	2	0
f_{10}^*	2	2	2	0	0	0	2	2	2	0

Also the partition of $\mathcal{R}(\mathcal{D}_M^2)$ has only one element and the rough bicluster has the form:

$$\underline{b}_2 = (\{f_3\}, \{f_8^*\}) \quad \overline{b}_2 = (\{f_1, f_2, f_3, f_4, f_5, f_7, f_8, f_9\}, \{f_6^*, f_7^*, f_8^*, f_9^*, f_{10}^*\})$$

The last one table (Table 5) shows all rough biclusters. Lower approximations are marked with the darker background and upper approximations are marked with the lighter background.

Table 5. Rough biclusters

	f_1	f_2	f_3	f_4	f_5	f_6	f_7	f_8	f_9	f_{10}
f_1^*	0	0	0	0	0	1	1	1	1	1
f_2^*	0	0	0	0	0	1	1	1	1	1
f_3^*	0	0	0	0	0	1	1	1	1	1
f_4^*	0	0	0	0	0	0	0	1	1	1
f_5^*	0	0	0	0	0	0	0	1	1	1
f_6^*	0	0	2	2	2	0	0	0	0	0
f_7^*	0	0	2	2	2	0	0	0	0	0
f_8^*	2	2	2	2	2	0	2	2	2	0
f_9^*	2	2	2	0	0	0	2	2	2	0
f_{10}^*	2	2	2	0	0	0	2	2	2	0

4 Rough and Exact Biclusters

We may see that from the formal point of view every β–description class may be also considered as the bicluster. Building rough biclusters from the partition of the dictionary gives the opportunity of generalisation and limitation the number of biclusters. It should depend from the user whether combine $\beta-$description classes into rough biclusters or just use exact ones. It also should be marked that if π_i in the partition of the relation $\mathcal{R}(\mathcal{D}_M^v)$ has the only one element the bicluster generated from this element will be also exact.

5   Conclusions

This article brings the new look for the rough description of the biclustering problem. In the opposition to other biclustering algorithms referring to the rough sets theory, this rough biclustering approach gives the formal definition of rough bicluster. The short example described in this article shows also two levels of interpreting the bicluster in the data: from the one hand we use the definition of rough bicluster and the possibility of generalisation (biclusters with their lower and upper approximation) and from the other hand we may stop the analysis at the step where the $\beta-$description classes are generated. This is the choice between lower number of more general inexact biclusters or bigger number of small exact ones.

Further works will focus on finding the algorithm of generating $\beta-$description classes what will make it possible to apply rough biclustering approach to the real data sets. If we consider the wide applicability of biclustering algorithm, especially the medical and bioinformatical ones, the potential of rough bicluster becomes really impressive.

Acknowledgements. This work was supported by the European Community from the European Social Fund.

References

1. Cheng, Y., Church, G.M.: Biclustering of expression data. In: Proc. of the 8th Int. Conf. on Intell. Syst. for Mol. Biol., pp. 93–103 (2000)
2. Emilyn, J.J., Ramar, K.: Rough Set Based Clustering of Gene Expression Data: A Survey. Int. J. of Eng. Sci. and Technol. 2(12), 7160–7164 (2010)
3. Emilyn, J.J., Ramar, K.: A Rough Set Based Gene Expression Clustering Algorithm. J. of Comput. Sci. 7(7), 986–990 (2011)
4. Emilyn, J.J., Ramar, K.: A Rough Set Based Novel Biclustering Algorithm for Gene Expression Data. In: Int. Conf. on Electron. Comput. Techn., pp. 284–288 (2011)
5. Ester, M., Kriegel, H.P., Sander, J., Xu, X.: A Density-Based Algorithm for Discovering Clusters in Large Spatial Databases with Noise. In: Proc. of 2nd Int. Conf. on Knowl. Discov. and Data Min., pp. 226–231 (1996)
6. Hartigan, J.A.: Direct Clustering of a Data Matrix. J. Am. Stat. Assoc. 67(337), 123–129 (1972)
7. MacQueen, J.: Some Methods for Classification and Analysis of Multivariate Observations. In: Proc. Fifth Berkeley Symp. on Math. Statist. and Prob., pp. 281–297 (1967)

8. Michalak, M., Stawarz, M.: Generating and Postprocessing of Biclusters from Discrete Value Matrices. In: Jedrzejowicz, P., Nguyen, N.T., Hoang, K. (eds.) ICCCI 2011, Part I. LNCS, vol. 6922, pp. 103–112. Springer, Heidelberg (2011)
9. Pawlak, Z.: Rough Sets. J. of Comput. and Inf. Sci. 5(11), 341–356 (1982)
10. Pawlak, Z.: Rough Sets: Theoretical Aspects of Reasoning About Data. Kluwer Academic Publishing (1991)
11. Pensa, R., Boulicaut, J.F.: Constrained Co-clustering of Gene Expression Data. In: Proc. SIAM Int. Conf. on Data Min., SDM 2008, pp. 25–36 (2008)
12. Wang, R., Miao, D., Li, G., Zhang, H.: Rough Overlapping Biclustering of Gene Expression Data. In: Proc. of the 7th IEEE Int. Conf. on Bioinforma. and Bioeng. (2007)
13. Yang, E., Foteinou, P.T., King, K.R., Yarmush, M.L., Androulakis, I.P.: A Novel Non-overlapping biclustering Algorithm for Network Generation Using Living Cell Array Data. Bioinforma. 17(23), 2306–2313 (2007)

ORG - Oblique Rules Generator

Marcin Michalak[1], Marek Sikora[1,2], and Patryk Ziarnik[1]

[1] Silesian University of Technology, ul. Akademicka 16, 44-100 Gliwice, Poland
{Marcin.Michalak,Marek.Sikora,Patryk.Ziarnik}@polsl.pl
[2] Institute of Innovative Technologies EMAG, ul. Leopolda 31, 40-189 Katowice,
Poland

Abstract. In this paper the new approach to generating oblique decision rules is presented. On the basis of limitations for every oblique decision rules parameters the grid of parameters values is created and then for every node of this grid the oblique condition is generated and its quality is calculated. The best oblique conditions build the oblique decision rule. Conditions are added as long as there are non-covered objects and the limitation of the length of the rule is not exceeded. All rules are generated with the idea of sequential covering.

Keywords: machine learning, decision rules, oblique decision rules, rules induction.

1 Introduction

Example based rules induction is, apart from decision trees induction, one of the most popular technique of knowledge discovery in databases. So-called decision rules are the special kind of rules. Sets of decision rules built by induction algorithms are usually designed for two basic aims. One is developing a classification system that exploits determined rules. Other aim is describing patterns in an analyzed dataset.

Apart from the number of algorithms that generate hyper-cuboidal decision rules it is worth to raise the question: Aren't the oblique decision rules more flexible to describe the nature of the data? On the one hand every simple condition like "parameter less/greater than value" may be interpreted in the intuitive way, but on the other hand the linear combination of the parameters "a_1* parameter $a_1 \pm a_2$ parameter $a_2 + a_0$ less/greater 0" may substitute several non-oblique decision rules with the cost of being a little less interpretable.

In this article we describe the method of generating oblique decision rules (Oblique Decision rules Generator − ORG) which is the kind of exhausting searching of oblique conditions in the space of oblique decision rule parameters. As oblique decision rules may be treated as the generalization of the standard decision rules the next part of the paper presents some achievements in the area of rules generalization. Then some basic notions that deal with oblique decision rules are presented. Afterwards the algorithm that generates oblique decision rules (ORG) is defined. The paper ends with comparison of results obtained on several our synthetic and some well known datasets.

L. Rutkowski et al. (Eds.): ICAISC 2012, Part II, LNCS 7268, pp. 152–159, 2012.

2 Related Works

The simplest method of generalization used by all induction algorithms is rules shortening consists in removing elementary conditions. Heuristic strategies are applied here (for example hill climbing) or exhaustive searching. Rules are shortened until a quality (e.g. precision) of the shortened rule drops below some fixed threshold. Such solution was applied, inter alia, in the RSES system [2] where rules are shortened as long as the rule precision does not decrease. In the case of unbalanced data introducing various threshold values of shortened rules quality leads to keeping better sensitivity and specificity of an obtained classifier. The other approach to rules generalization is concerned with decision rules joining algorithms that consists in merging two or more similar rules [10,16]. In [16] an iterative joining algorithm relying on merging ranges occurring in corresponding elementary conditions of input rules is presented. The merging ends when a new rule covers all positive examples covered by joined rules. Rule quality measures [1] are used for output rules quality assessment. Paper [10] presents a similar approach, where rules are grouped before joining [11] or the similarity between rules is calculated, and rules belonging to the same group or sufficiently similar are joined.

The special case of a rules joining algorithm is the algorithm proposed in [13], in which authors introduce complex elementary conditions in rules premises. The complex conditions are linear combinations of attributes occurring in simple elementary conditions of rules premises. The algorithm applies to the special kind of rules obtained in so-called dominance based rough set model [8] only, and is not fit for aggregation of classic decision rules, in which ranges of elementary conditions can be bounded above and below simultaneously.

Finally, also algorithms that make it possible to generate oblique elementary conditions during the model constructing are worth to be mentioned. One manages here with algorithms of oblique decision trees induction [5,9,12]. A special case of getting a tree with oblique elementary conditions is an application of the linear SVM in construction of the tree nodes [3]. For decision rules, an algorithm that enables oblique elementary conditions to appear during the rules induction is ADReD [14]. Considering obtained rules in terms of their description power we can say that, even though the number of elementary conditions in rules premises is usually less than in rules allowing no oblique conditions, unquestionable disadvantage of these algorithms is a very complicated form of elementary conditions in which all conditional attributes are frequently used. Other approach introducing oblique elementary conditions in rules premises consists in applying the constructive induction (especially the data driven constructive induction) and inputting new attributes depending on linear combinations of existing features, and next determining rules by the standard induction algorithm [4,17] based on the attributes set extended this way.

3 Oblique Decision Rules

Fundamentals. Decision rules with oblique conditions assume more complex form of descriptors than standard decision rules. The oblique condition is a condition in which a plane separating decision classes is a linear combination of conditional values of attributes $a_i \in A$ (elementary conditions) on the assumption that all of them are of numerical type: $\sum_{i=1}^{|A|} c_i a_i + c_0$ where $a_i \in A, c_i, c_0 \in \mathbb{R}$. The oblique condition can be defined as: $\sum_{i=1}^{|A|} c_i a_i + c_0 \geq 0$ or $\sum i = 1^{|A|} c_i a_i + c_0 < 0$ The oblique condition describes a hyperplane in a condition attributes space. The condition of the rule determines which elements from the decision class are covered by the given rule. Each oblique decision rule is defined by the intersection of oblique conditions.

Parameters of the Descriptor and Their Ranges - The Analysis. Let us define the space of all hyperplanes which are single oblique conditions. The $n-$dimensional hyperplane can be described with a linear equation of the following general form $A_1 x_1 + A_2 x_2 + ... + A_n x_n + C = 0$ where $A_i, C \in \mathbb{R}$ and at least one of the $A_i \neq 0$. In the proposed solution, instead of the general form, we can use the normal form of the hyperplane equation:

$$\alpha_1 x_1 + \alpha_2 x_2 + ... + \alpha_n x_n - \rho = 0$$

where α_i are the direction cosines ($\alpha_1{}^2 + \alpha_2{}^2 + ... + \alpha_n{}^2 = 1$) and ρ is the hyperplane distance from the origin of the coordinate system. This notation makes it possible to limit the range of every parameter.

To explain how to find a real value range of descriptor parameters we could consider a straight line in the plane defined by the following normal form:

$$x \cos \theta + y \sin \theta - \rho = 0$$

where θ is the angle of depression to the $x-$axis and ρ is the distance between the line and the origin as illustrated in Fig. 1.

Every line in the plane corresponds to a proper point in the parameters space. Determination of a straight line in (θ, ρ)-space could be realized by searching a chosen subset of that space using a grid method. The angle θ is naturally bounded, so it can be defined as $\theta \in [0, 2\pi)$. It is enough to determine a step of creating a grid for this variable. It is also possible to bound the values of

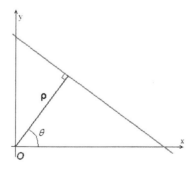

Fig. 1. The normal parameters for a line

parameter ρ. The lower bound is 0 and the upper bound could be calculated as follows: The set of points is finite so we could determine maximal values of each coordinate. If some values of variables are negative, data could be translated into such a coordinate system where all of coordinates are positive.

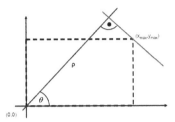

Fig. 2. The idea of the values of the parameter

The idea is to find a straight line which passes through the point and its distance from the origin is the longest one (Fig. 2.). This problem could be solved by searching the global maximum of a function of the distance between the line and the origin depending on the value of the angle θ:

$$\rho_{\max}(\theta_{opt}) = x_{\max} \cos\left(\arctan \frac{y_{\max}}{x_{\max}}\right) + y_{\max} \sin\left(\arctan \frac{y_{\max}}{x_{\max}}\right)$$

Having set boundary values for all parameters of the condition we only have to determine the resolution of searching of the parameter space - a step for each parameter for the grid method: $\theta \in [0, 2\pi)$, $\rho \in [0, \rho_{\max})$.

The solution could be used for each hyperplane using the dependency of the sum of the squares of the direction cosines, for example for planes in 3−dimensional and any n−dimensional space.

"Correct" Side of the Condition. Each oblique condition requires to define its "correct side". To determine this we can use a normal vector to a hyperplane (containing a considered condition) as follows: for n−dimensional space each hyperplane could be described with its normal vector $\boldsymbol{n}$ defined as $\boldsymbol{n} = [A_1, A_2, ..., A_n]$. We should calculate one vector more to find a correct side of a considered condition for a given point called T. The initial point P of such a vector could be any point lying on the hyperplane and the final point should be the point T. According to this, the second vector $\boldsymbol{v}$ is defined as:

$$P = (x_{P1}, x_{P2}, ..., x_{Pn}); \quad T = (x_{T1}, x_{T2}, ..., x_{Tn})$$

$$\boldsymbol{v} = \overrightarrow{PT} = (x_{T1} - x_{P1}, x_{T2} - x_{P2}, ..., x_{Tn} - x_{Pn})$$

The next step is to calculate the dot product of these two vectors: $\boldsymbol{n}$ and $\boldsymbol{v}$:

$$\boldsymbol{n} \circ \boldsymbol{v} = |\boldsymbol{n}|\,|\boldsymbol{v}| \cos \alpha$$

To decide whether the point T is lying on the correct side of the condition we should consider the value of the dot product in the following way:

1. If the value is greater than 0, the point T is considered to be on the correct side of the condition.
2. If the value is equal to 0, the point T is assumed to be on the correct side of the condition.
3. If the value is less than 0, the point T is not on the correct side of the condition.

In this moment we can limit the bound for the angle θ in such a way $\theta \in [0, \pi)$ and for each θ consider also the second case when the correct side is the opposite one.

4   Description of the Algorithm

The purpose of the algorithm is to find the best oblique decision rules for each decision class of the input data taking into account several defined constraints. In general, the are two basic steps of the algorithm:

1. Create a parameter grid using a determined step for each parameter.
2. The growth of the new created rule depends on checking all conditions defined with the grid nodes.

It is possible to constrain a number of rules defining the maximal number of rules which describe each class. Successive rules should be generated as long as there are still training objects which do not support any rule and the constraint is still not achieved. For each decision rule successive oblique conditions are obtained using a hill climbing method. Below, the description of generating the single oblique decision rule is shown:

1. For each cell of parameter grid create a condition and calculate its quality for the given training set using one of possible quality measures.
2. Save only the first best condition (with the highest quality).
3. Reduce the training set (just for the time of generating next condition) by rejecting all training objects which do not cover previously found conditions.
4. Find a successive condition with the first highest quality using the reduced training set.
5. A new condition should be added to the rule only if the extended rule is better than the rule generated in the previous iteration and the constraint (maximal number of descriptors for each rule) is not achieved. Otherwise, the new condition must be rejected and the search of the next conditions for this rule is stopped.
6. Continue searching successive conditions after reducing the training set by rejecting all objects which do not recognise the current rule. The addition of conditions should be stopped when the rule consists of the determined maximal number of conditions or the quality of the oblique decision rule with added condition is not improved (such a found condition is excluded).

After the rule is generated we remove all covered positive objects from the training set and in the case when the maximal number of rules per decision class is not achieved we start to generate the new rule.

5   Experiments and Results

First experiments were done for three synthetic datasets, prepared exactly for the task of searching oblique decision rules: two two-dimensional (2D and double2D) and one three-dimensional (3D). Simple visualisation of these datasets is shown on the Fig. 3. Each dataset contains 1000 objects that belong to two classes. Two-dimensional datasets are almost balanced (562:438 and 534:466) but the third dataset has the proportion of classes size 835:165. First two-dimensional dataset looks like the square divided into two classes by its diagonal. The second two-dimensional dataset may be described as follows: one class is in two opposite corners and the second class is the rest. Three-dimensional dataset are unbalanced because only the one corner belongs to the smaller class. For this datasets the limitation of the maximal number of the rules per decision class and the maximal number of conditions per decision rule is given in the table with the results. As the quality measure the average of the rule precision and coverage was used.

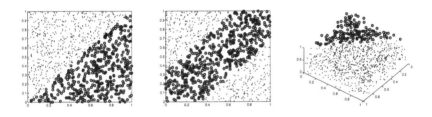

Fig. 3. Visualisation of the synthetic datasets: 2D (left); double2D (center); 3D (right)

For the further experiments several datasets from UCI repository were taken into consideration: iris, balance scale, ecoli, breast wisconsin [6]. Also the Ripley's synth.tr data were used [15]. For every experiment the limitation of number of rules per decision class and the number of conditions per single rule for the ORG algorithm was the same: at most two rules built from at most two conditions. The quality measure remained the same as for the previous datasets.

Results of ORG are compared with PART algorithm [7] obtained with the WEKA software. The WEKA implementation of PART algorithm does not give the information about the error standard deviation in the 10-CV model so it can not be compared with the ORG results.

6   Conclusions and Further Works

In this short article the intuitive and kind of exhausting way of oblique decision rules generating was presented. This algorithm, called ORG, is based on the limitation for parameters of oblique condition. In this approach it is possible to constrain the number of obtained rules (per single decision class) and also the shape of rules (with the definition of maximal number of oblique conditions).

Table 1. Results on synthetic datasets

dataset	avg. accuracy PART	ORG	std dev. PART	ORG	avg. rules number PART	ORG	avg. elem. cond. number PART	ORG	ORG params/class max number of: rules	conditions
2D	95.5	96.0	–	1.5	10	2	18	3	2	2
double 2D	93.8	84.3	–	3.1	14	3	23	6	2	2
3D	94.8	98.2	–	1.2	13	2	22	2	1	1

Table 2. Results on popular benchmark datasets

dataset	avg. accuracy PART	ORG	std dev. PART	ORG	avg. rules number PART	ORG	avg. elem. cond. number PART	ORG
iris	94	94	–	4.6	2	3.1	3	5.2
balance scale	84	92	–	2.4	46	6	126	12
Ripley	85	81	–	8.4	4	2	6	4
breast wisconsin	94	97	–	1.7	10	3	18	6.1
ecoli	84	76	–	8.1	12	10	33	19

We may see, on the basis of the results for the synthetic datasets, that ORG may be successfully applied for datasets that contain various oblique dependencies. It may be observed, in comparison with PART results, in the decrease (on average: five times) of the average number of decision rules for every decision class. In the case of popular benchmark datasets the decrease of the number of rules per decision class may be also observed.

On the basis of these observations our further works will focus on finding the best conditions in the strategy with taking into consideration also the length of the condition. It should be also worth being examined whether the calculation of oblique condition parameters limitations should be analyzed more often than only in the beginning of dataset analysis.

Acknowledgements. This work was supported by the European Community from the European Social Fund.

The research and the participation of the second author is supported by National Science Centre (decision DEC-2011/01/D/ST6/07007)

References

1. An, A., Cercone, N.: Rule quality measures for rule induction systems - description and evaluation. Computational Intelligence 17, 409–424 (2001)
2. Bazan, J., Szczuka, M., Wróblewski, J.: A New Version of Rough Set Exploration System. In: Alpigini, J.J., Peters, J.F., Skowron, A., Zhong, N. (eds.) RSCTC 2002. LNCS (LNAI), vol. 2475, pp. 397–404. Springer, Heidelberg (2002)
3. Bennett, K.P., Blue, J.A.: A support vector machine approach to decision trees. In: Proceedings of the IJCNN 1998, pp. 2396–2401 (1997)
4. Bloedorn, E., Michalski, R.S.: Data-Driven Constructive Induction. IEEE Intelli. Syst. 13(2), 30–37 (1998)

5. Cantu-Paz, E., Kamath, C.: Using evolutionary algorithms to induce oblique decision trees. In: Proc. of Genet. and Evol. Comput. Conf., pp. 1053–1060 (2000)
6. Frank, A., Asuncion, A.: UCI Machine Learning Repository (2010), http://archive.ics.uci.edu/ml
7. Frank, E., Witten, I.H.: Generating Accurate Rule Sets Without Global Optimization. In: Proc. of the 15th Int. Conf. on Mach. Learn., pp. 144–151 (1998)
8. Greco, S., Matarazzo, B., Słowiński, R.: Rough sets theory for multi-criteria decision analysis. Eur. J. of Oper. Res. 129(1), 1–47 (2001)
9. Kim, H., Loh, W.-Y.: Classification trees with bivariate linear discriminant node models. J. of Comput. and Graph. Stat. 12, 512–530 (2003)
10. Latkowski, R., Mikołajczyk, M.: Data decomposition and decision rule joining for classification of data with missing values. In: Peters, J.F., Skowron, A., Grzymała-Busse, J.W., Kostek, B.z., Świniarski, R.W., Szczuka, M.S. (eds.) Transactions on Rough Sets I. LNCS, vol. 3100, pp. 299–320. Springer, Heidelberg (2004)
11. Mikołajczyk, M.: Reducing Number of Decision Rules by Joining. In: Alpigini, J.J., Peters, J.F., Skowron, A., Zhong, N. (eds.) RSCTC 2002. LNCS (LNAI), vol. 2475, pp. 425–432. Springer, Heidelberg (2002)
12. Murthy, S.K., Kasif, S., Salzberg, S.: A system for induction of oblique decision trees. J. of Artif. Intell. Res. 2, 1–32 (1994)
13. Pindur, R., Sasmuga, R., Stefanowski, J.: Hyperplane Aggregation of Dominance Decision Rules. Fundam. Inf. 61(2), 117–137 (2004)
14. Raś, Z.W., Daradzińska, A., Liu, X.: System ADReD for discovering rules based on hyperplanes. Eng. App. of Artif. Intell. 17(4), 401–406 (2004)
15. Ripley, B.D.: Pattern Recognition and Neural Networks. Cambridge University Press (1996)
16. Sikora, M.: An algorithm for generalization of decision rules by joining. Found. on Comp. and Decis. Sci. 30(3), 227–239 (2005)
17. Ślęzak, D., Wróblewski, J.: Classification Algorithms Based on Linear Combinations of Features. In: Żytkow, J.M., Rauch, J. (eds.) PKDD 1999. LNCS (LNAI), vol. 1704, pp. 548–553. Springer, Heidelberg (1999)

Mini-models – Local Regression Models for the Function Approximation Learning

Marcin Pluciński

Faculty of Computer Science and Information Systems,
West Pomeranian University of Technology,
Żołnierska 49, 71-062 Szczecin, Poland
mplucinski@wi.zut.edu.pl

Abstract. Mini-models are local regression models which can be used for the function approximation learning. In the paper, there are presented mini-models based on hyper-spheres and researches were made for linear and nonlinear models with no limitations for the problem input space dimension. Learning of the approximation function based on mini-models is very fast and it proved to have a good accuracy. Mini-models have also very advantageous extrapolation properties. It results from a fact, that they take into account not only samples target values, but also a tendency in the neighbourhood of the question point.

Keywords: Mini-model, local regression, k-nearest neighbours method, function approximation.

1 Introduction

Learning of function approximators with an application of so called memory-based learning methods is very often attractive approach in comparison with creating of global models based on a parametric representation. In some situations (for example: small number of samples), building of global models can be difficult and memory-based methods become then one of possible solutions for the approximation task.

Memory-based methods are very well explored and described in many bibliography positions. The most important here is the k-nearest neighbors method (kNN), which is described in many versions [2,3,6], but still is the subject of new researches [4,5]. Another approaches can be methods based on locally weighted learning [1,2] which use different ways of a samples weighting. Methods widely applied in this category are probabilistic neural networks and generalised regression networks [9,10].

The concept of mini-models was introduced by prof. Andrzej Piegat. In papers [7,8] there were described local regression models based on simplexes. Described models were linear and a research work was made only for problems in a 1 and 2-dimensional input space.

In this paper, there are presented mini-models based on hyper-spheres and researches were made for linear and nonlinear models with no limitations for the problem input space dimension.

L. Rutkowski et al. (Eds.): ICAISC 2012, Part II, LNCS 7268, pp. 160–167, 2012.

2   Linear and Nonlinear Mini-Models

The main idea of mini-models is similar to the kNN method. During calculations of an answer for a question point $\mathbf{X}^*$ only k nearest (in a meaning of an applied metric – here Euclidean metric) samples are taken into account. In the classic kNN method the model answer is calculated as a mean value of target function values or a weighted mean value. In such case, weight values usually depend on a distance $\delta(\mathbf{X}^*, \mathbf{X})$ between the question point $\mathbf{X}^*$ and analysed neighbors $\mathbf{X}$, for example:

$$w_{\mathbf{X}^*;\mathbf{X}} = \frac{1}{1 + m \cdot (\delta(\mathbf{X}^*, \mathbf{X})/k)^2} \,, \tag{1}$$

where: the m parameter is taken empirically.

The mini-model is a local regression and the answer for the question point $\mathbf{X}^*$ is calculated on a base of a local model created for k-nearest neighbors. The mini-model is always created in time of answer calculations.

In the simplest case the linear mini-model can be applied, and then the answer is calculated on the base of the linear regression:

$$f(\mathbf{X}^*) = \mathbf{W}^T \cdot \mathbf{X}^* \,, \tag{2}$$

where: $\mathbf{W}$ – the vector of linear mini-model coefficients found for k-neighbors.

In papers [7,8] there are described mini-models created for sectors of the input space that have a triangle shape (in a 2-dimensional input space) or a simplex shape in a multi-dimensional input space. Such sector will be called a mini-model base. In this paper, mini-models will be created for a circular base in a 2-dimensional input space or a spherical (hiper-spherical) base in a 3 or multi-dimensional input space.

The mini-model base has a center in the question point $\mathbf{X}^*$ and its radius is defined by a distance between the point $\mathbf{X}^*$ and the most distant point from k neighbors, Fig. 1.

Nonlinear mini-models have better possibilities of fitting to the samples. An answer of such model is a sum of a linear mini-model and an additional nonlinear component:

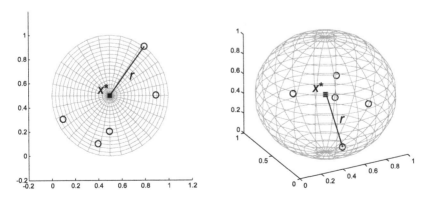

Fig. 1. The mini-model base for a 2 and 3-dimensional input space

$$f(\mathbf{X}^*) = \mathbf{W}^T \cdot \mathbf{X}^* + f_N(\mathbf{X}^*) . \tag{3}$$

As the mini-model is usually created for a small number k of nearest neighbors, the nonlinear function f_N should have a possibility of changing its shape thanks to as small number of coefficients as possible (because $n+1$ coefficients must be tuned in the vector $\mathbf{W}$).

Among many inspected functions, very advantageous properties has the function:

$$f_N(\mathbf{X}) = w_N \cdot \sin\left[\frac{\pi}{2} - ||\mathbf{X} - \mathbf{X}^*||\frac{\pi}{r}\right] , \tag{4}$$

where: r is the radius of the mini-model base. In such created function we have only one coefficient w_N to learn, Fig. 2. During learning we must find such a w_N value to obtain the best fit of the mini-model to k neighbors. Exemplary linear and nonlinear mini-models in a 1 and 2-dimensional input space are presented in Fig. 3 and Fig. 4.

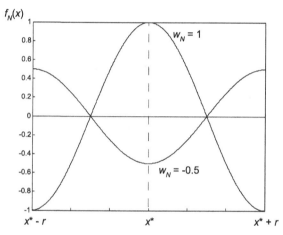

Fig. 2. Exemplary shapes of the mini-model nonlinear component for $w_N = 1$ and $w_N = -0.5$

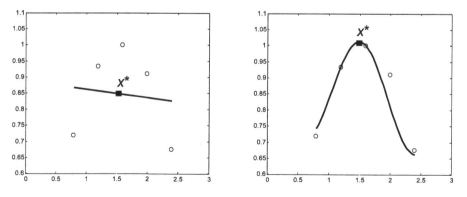

Fig. 3. Exemplary linear and nonlinear mini-model in a 1-dimensional input space

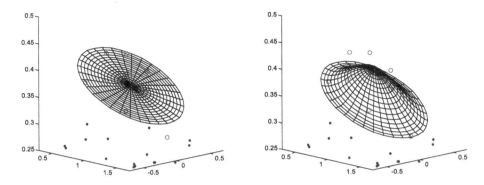

Fig. 4. Exemplary linear and nonlinear mini-model in a 2-dimensional input space

3   Experiments

For better visualisation of mini-models work, first experiments were realised for data with a 1 and 2-dimensional input space. Fig. 5 presents characteristics of models created with an application of linear and nonlinear mini-models. For comparison, there are also presented characteristics of models created by kNN methods.

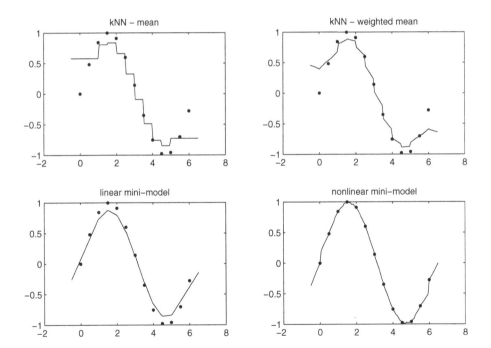

Fig. 5. Characteristics of approximators created for data with a 1-dimensional input space by kNN methods, linear and nonlinear mini-models

Mini-models have a very good extrapolation property what is presented in Fig. 6. As before, there are presented characteristics of models created with an application of kNN methods and mini-models. First of all, an attention should be paid for a behaviour of mini-models in places where there are no samples (information gaps) and outside of the samples input domain. Mini-models give answers that are much more consistent with a common sense and a shape of their characteristic lines is more smooth.

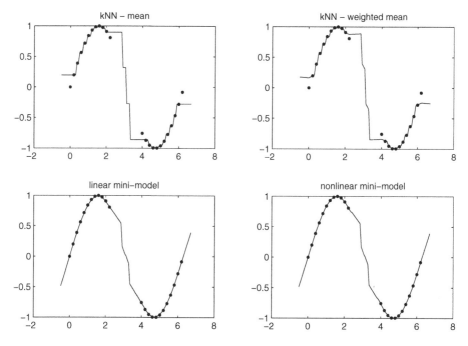

Fig. 6. Characteristics of models created for data with the information gap

Fig. 7 presents surfaces created for samples with a 2-dimensional input space. Both mini-models from Fig. 5 and Fig. 7 have better accuracy than the kNN method and values of model real errors are given in the Table 1.

In the next part of experiments, there was calculated a real accuracy of function approximators based on mini-models, Table 1. The research work was performed on data created by the author and data from popular web repositories. Data were normalised due to different ranges of its inputs.

The real error was calculated with an application of the leave one out crossvalidation method. Mini-models are compared with kNN method and in each case calculation results are presented for an optimal number of neighbors (giving the lowest real error). Additionally, for comparison purpose, there is also given an approximation accuracy for a generalised regression network (GRN) also with a neuron width optimally tuned.

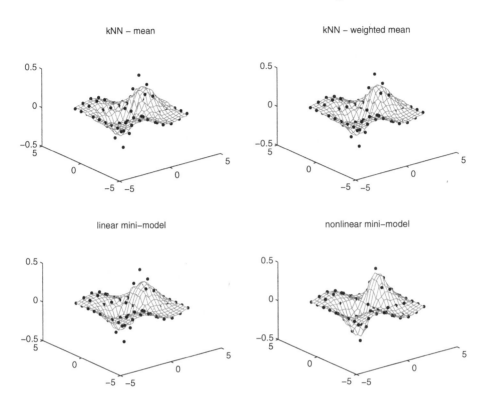

Fig. 7. Characteristics of approximators created for data with a 2-dimensional input space by kNN methods, linear and nonlinear mini-models

Table 1. The real error of function approximators

data	inputs number	mean kNN	weighted mean kNN	linear mini-model	nonlinear mini-model	GRN
$\sin(x)$ with 0.5 sampling step (Fig. 5)	1	0.166	0.161	0.095	0.086	0.142
$\sin(x)$ with 0.2 sampling step	1	0.031	0.030	0.013	0.008	0.025
$\frac{\sin(x_1)*\cos(x_2)}{x_1^2+x_2^2+1}$ with 0.25 sampling step (Fig. 7)	2	0.0281	0.0277	0.0228	0.0259	0.0254
$\frac{\sin(x_1)*\cos(x_2)}{x_1^2+x_2^2+1}$ with 0.1 sampling step	2	0.0058	0.0058	0.0049	0.0055	0.0052
bodyfat	14	2.236	2.211	0.472	0.475	2.671
cpu	6	29.507	28.937	27.305	27.826	28.771
diabetes_numeric	2	0.474	0.481	0.475	0.487	0.471
housing	13	2.771	2.685	2.311	2.293	2.506

4 Conclusions

First of all, the approximation function based on mini-models proved to have a good accuracy, Table 1. The accuracy is particularly great for data without noise. In the case of noised data, mini-models have the accuracy comparable or slightly worse than kNN methods.

Learning of the approximator is very fast – it is enough to memorise learning data and the proper mini-model is created only in time of calculating an answer for the question point $\mathbf{X}^*$. Mini-models creating is not computationally complex because they are build on the base of a small number of samples (k nearest neighbors). The linear mini-model is a linear regression found for k neighbors and the nonlinear one has only one additional coefficient to compute.

Mini-models have very advantageous extrapolation properties. It results from a fact, that they take into account not only samples target values, but also a tendency in the neighbourhood of the question point. Using information about this tendency cause better modeling in places where there is no data (information gaps and outside of the input space domain). Information gaps are very characteristic property of multi-dimensional data with a small number of samples.

A weakness of mini-models in comparison with the kNN method is a necessity of taking into account a greater number of neighbors k during building the linear mini-model. A minimal number of neighbors is equal here $n + 1$, where n is a size of an input space.

References

1. Atkeson, C.G., Moore, A.W., Schaal, S.A.: Locally weighted learning. Artificial Intelligence Review 11, 11–73 (1997)
2. Cichosz, P.: Learning systems. WNT Publishing House, Warsaw (2000) (in polish)
3. Hand, D., Mannila, H., Smyth, P.: Principles of data mining. The MIT Press (2001)
4. Kordos, M., Blachnik, M., Strzempa, D.: Do We Need Whatever More Than k-NN? In: Rutkowski, L., Scherer, R., Tadeusiewicz, R., Zadeh, L.A., Zurada, J.M. (eds.) ICAISC 2010. LNCS, vol. 6113, pp. 414–421. Springer, Heidelberg (2010)
5. Korzeń, M., Klęsk, P.: Sets of approximating functions with finite Vapnik-Czervonenkis dimension for nearest-neighbors algorithm. Pattern Recognition Letters 32, 1882–1893 (2011)
6. Moore, A.W., Atkeson, C.G., Schaal, S.: Memory-based learning for control. Technical Report CMU-RI-TR-95-18, Carnegie-Mellon University, Robotics Institute (1995)
7. Piegat, A., Wąsikowska, B., Korzeń, M.: Application of the self-learning, 3-point mini-model for modeling of unemployment rate in Poland. Studia Informatica, University of Szczecin (2010) (in Polish)
8. Piegat, A., Wąsikowska, B., Korzeń, M.: Differences between the method of mini-models and the k-nearest neighbors on example of modeling of unemployment rate in Poland. In: Proceedings of 9th Conference on Information Systems in Management, pp. 34–43. WULS Press, Warsaw (2011)

9. Plucinski, M.: Application of data with missing attributes in the probability RBF neural network learning and classification. In: Sołdek, J., Drobiazgiewicz, L. (eds.) Artificial Intelligence and Security in Computing Systems: 9th International Conference ACS 2002: Proceedings, pp. 63–72. Kluwer Academic Publishers, Boston (2003)
10. Wasserman, P.D.: Advanced methods in neural computing. Van Nostrand Reinhold, New York (1993)

A Cluster Validity Index for Hard Clustering

Artur Starczewski

Department of Computer Engineering, Częstochowa University of Technology,
Al. Armii Krajowej 36, 42-200 Częstochowa, Poland
starcz@kik.pcz.czest.pl
http://kik.pcz.pl

Abstract. This paper describes a new cluster validity index for the
well-separable clusters in data sets. The validity indices are necessary
for many clustering algorithms to assign the naturally existing clusters
correctly. In the presented method, to determine the optimal number of
clusters in data sets, the new cluster validity index has been used. It
has been applied to the *complete link* hierarchical clustering algorithm.
The basis to define the new cluster validity index is founding of the large
increments of intercluster and intracluster distances, when the clustering
algorithm is performed. The maximum value of the index determines
the optimal number of clusters in the given set simultaneously. Obtained
results confirm very good performances of the proposed approach.

1 Introduction

Clustering a data set is also called unsupervised learning or unsupervised classification. It makes a split of the data elements into the homogeneous subsets
(named clusters), inside which elements are more similar to each other, while
they are more different in other groups. The number of clusters, which should
be created in a data set is a very important parameter. For lots of algorithms,
this parameter must be given *a priori*. Then, the *cluster validity indices* are used,
so the perfect partition of a data set can be realized. A lots of cluster validity
indices are based on the analysis of two distances: intercluster and intracluster
distances. They make it possible to determine two major properties of clusters,
their separability and compactness [2,5]. The Euclidean distance between elements of different clusters is the most often used separability measure. To define
the compact measure, variance is used mostly. The cluster validity index is most
often a ratio of intercluster and intracluster distance or vice versa. It can be also
the sum of these distances. Then, relatively to the type of the *validity index*, the
best partition of a data set corresponds to the maximum or the minimum index
value. The analysis of proprieties of different types of validity indices have been
described in [6]. The indices for crisp clustering includes e.g., *Dunn's index* [3],
Davies–Bouldin index [1], *PBM index* [11], *RS index* [5], *SIL index* [13].

   In this paper, assignation of the optimal number of clusters in a data set is
analysed and a new cluster validity index to determine the number of clusters in
a data set is proposed. The paper is organized as follows. Section 2 describes the

L. Rutkowski et al. (Eds.): ICAISC 2012, Part II, LNCS 7268, pp. 168–174, 2012.
© Springer-Verlag Berlin Heidelberg 2012

new cluster validity index, which is named $S-index$, and basic dependencies that refer to compactness and separability of clusters. Sections 3 presents a method, which uses the new validity index. Section 4 illustrates the experimental results on artificial and real data sets. Finally, there are conclusions in Section 5.

2   The New Cluster Validity Index

For the optimal partition of a data set, the new cluster validity $S - index$ is proposed. In this index, increments of interclaster and intraclaster distances are calculated. For this purpose, the *complete link* hierarchical algorithm is used [12]. Let $C^{(k)} = \{C_1^{(k)}, C_2^{(k)}, ..., C_m^k\}$ be a set of m-clusters, which creates a k-partition of the data set $X = \{x_1, x_2, ..., x_n\}$. Instead, $C_j^{(k)}$, where $j = 1, .., m$ denotes a cluster in the k-partition of the data set and $\mathbf{v}_j^{(k)}$ is its prototype vector. Clusters separability in the k-partition of X can be represented as below:

$$S^k = \min_{i \neq j} \left\{ d\left(C_i^{(k)}, C_j^{(k)}\right) \right\} \tag{1}$$

where $i, j = 1, ..., m$, whereas $d\left(C_i^{(k)}, C_j^{(k)}\right)$ marks a measure of the distance between ith and jth cluster. We look for such k-partition of data X, where formula Eq.(1) will have a maximal value and all obtained clusters will represent homogeneous groups, that is:

$$S_o = \max_{1 \leq k \leq n} \left\{ S^k \right\} \tag{2}$$

where S_o denotes the clusters separability for the optimal partition of data X. Let us denote o as the optimal number of clusters in the set X. For the number of clusters $m > o$, the separability value of clusters is relatively not large. It results from the fact that clusters are determined in naturally existing groups of set X, so the intercluster distance Eq.(1) is not large respectively. Instead, when $m = o$ the separability value increases steeply. That is so, because the data set includes well-separable clusters and the distance between them is proportionally larger. Further, when $m < o$ the large value of intercluster distance remains unchanged so much, because clusters are already considerably distant and every next merger of two clusters will not change this situation. The second important property is the compactness of clusters. The most often used the compactness measure is variance. It measures the closeness of cluster elements. Low variance values denote compact clusters, while the large value is an indicator of the elements being scattered. For a single cluster in data set X, the variance can be expressed as follows :

$$\sigma_j^{(k)} = \frac{1}{|C_j|} \sum_{\mathbf{x} \in C_j} (\mathbf{x} - \mathbf{v}_j)^2 \tag{3}$$

where $|C_j|$ is the number of elements in the jth cluster, and $\mathbf{v}_j$ is its centre:

$$\mathbf{v}_j = \frac{1}{|C_j|} \sum_{x \in C_j} \mathbf{x}_j \tag{4}$$

The clusters compactness of the k-partition of X can be expressed as follows:

$$\sigma^{(k)} = \max_{1 \leq j \leq m} \left\{ \sigma_j^{(k)} \right\} . \tag{5}$$

Of course, we look for such the k-partition of X, where the value of the clusters compactness Eq.(5) is the smallest and obtained clusters will represent the naturally existing clusters in the data set, that is:

$$\sigma_o = \min_{1 \leq k \leq n} \left\{ \sigma^k \right\} \tag{6}$$

where σ_o denotes the cluster compactness for the optimal partition of data X. Unlike to the separability Eq.(1), when the number of cluster equals optimal $m = o$, the compactness does not increase sharply. That is so, because the clusters are still quite compact, so the variance value is not large. However, when $m < o$, then the value Eq.(5) increases sharply, so the clusters compactness is low.

The proposed cluster validity index uses increments of interclaster and intracluster distances and it can be expressed as follows:

$$V_k = \max_{1 \leq j \leq m} \left\{ m \left(S_{\max} - S^{(k)} \right) \left(\frac{\Delta \sigma^{(k)} \Delta S^{(k-1)}}{\sigma^{(k)} S^{(k-1)}} \right) \right\} \tag{7}$$

In the formula Eq.(7), the increment of the value of the clusters compactness, which refers to the k partition, can be expressed as follows:

$$\Delta \sigma^{(k)} = \sigma^{(k)} - \sigma^{(k-1)} \tag{8}$$

Then, the increment of the value of the clusters separability, which refers to the $k - 1$ partition, can be represented as below:

$$\Delta S^{(k-1)} = S^{(k-1)} - S^{(k-2)} \tag{9}$$

For the number of clusters $m = o - 1$, the value of the index Eq.(7) increases sharply. The phenomenon is caused by increments of the value of the clusters compactness in the k partition and the clusters separability in the $k - 1$ partition (formulated in the numerator), which are large. However, for $m < o - 1$ the value of the index decreases, because the value of the numerator in Eq.(7) does not change so much. Since, the distances between clusters can be very different in following iterations of the clustering algorithm when $m < o - 1$, the increments of the numerator values can be quite large again. Thus, it is necessary to introduce an additional component in the formula, which is expressed as follows:

$$m \left(S_{\max} - S^{(k)} \right) \tag{10}$$

where S_{max} marks the maximal distance between elements belonging to the data set. In order to get the number of clusters equal to optimal $m = o$ the value m has to be increased $m + 1$. In the next section, the method which uses the novel cluster validity index is proposed.

3   Determination of Number of Clusters

This proposed $S - index$ has been applied to the *complete link* agglomerative hierarchical algorithm. The algorithm starts with a number of clusters $m = n$, where n denotes the number of elements in a data set. Instead, it is finished when $m = 1$. After each updating of the number of clusters, the cluster validity index is being calculated and its value is recorded in a table. Once the hierarchical algorithm is finished, the maximum value can be read out from the table. The value allows to determine the optimal number of clusters, which equals $m + 1$ (see Section 2). The presented method determines the number of cluster precisely. Below, the results obtained for a different number of clusters are presented.

4   Experimental Results

Experiments have been performed on both artificial and real data sets. The machine learning toolkit Weka 3.6 [19] has been used to generate artificial data sets. The generated data sets are 2-dimensional and multidimensional with a different number of clusters. The real data sets, i.e. the *Iris*, the *Wine* and the *Glass Identification* are from UCI machine learning repository [8]. The detailed description of those sets is described in Table 1. The number of clusters is different and clusters are located in various distances from each other, some of them are quite close. The obtained results are presented in Table 2, which include the key parameter for the correct qualification of elements of sets to clusters, that is, the number of clusters. The determination of the number of clusters in the data sets is realized by means of the *S-index*, *PBM-index* and *SIL-index* using *complete link* agglomerative hierarchical algorithm (see Section 3). For example, in Figure1 are presented the values of the validity indices obtained for different partitions of the data sets, i.e. A and C. For *S-index*, the number of clusters is increased by one (see Section 2). In those figures the axis x means the number of clusters, while the axis y is the value of the validity indices. Note, that the maximal index value assigns the optimal partition of data A and B (that is 3 and 8) simultaneously. Comparison

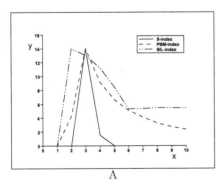
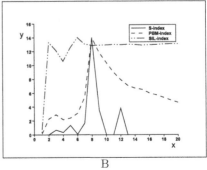

A   B

Fig. 1. Values of the validity indices y depending on the number of clusters x in A and B data sets

Table 1. Detailed information of the data sets

Data set	Clusters	Number of attributes	Total number of instances
A	3	2	134
B	8	2	300
C	15	2	429
D	7	5	229
E	12	5	395
F	3	10	177
G	6	10	207
H	10	10	294
Iris	3	4	150
Wine	3	13	178
Glass	7	10	214

Table 2. Comparision of the number of clusters obtained by means of the *S-index*, *PBM-index* and *SIL-index* using *complete link* agglomerative hierarchical algorithm

Data sets	Actual number of clusters	Number of clusters obtained		
		S-index	*PBM-index*	*SIL-index*
A	3	3	3	2
B	8	8	8	6
C	15	15	15	14
D	7	7	6	7
E	12	12	12	12
F	3	3	3	3
G	6	6	6	6
H	10	10	10	10
Iris	3	3	3	2
Wine	3	4	10	2
Glass	7	6	2	2

of the number of clusters identified by *S-index*, *PBM-index* and *SIL-index* using *complete link* agglomerative hierarchical algorithm is presented in Table 2. As it has been mentioned earlier, the number of clusters is the key parameter to perform data clustering correctly. It can be seen, despite the large number of clusters and high dimensionality of the sets, the new $S-index$ defined in Section 2 has assigned the optimal number of clusters in sets correctly. However, for the real data sets, i.e. *Wine* and the *Glass* results are not correct, but they are more accurate than the results obtained by other indexes.

5   Conclusions

All the presented results confirm the very good performance of the *S-index*. The number of clusters is assigned correctly for clusters of different sizes and distances from each other. The hierarchical algorithm also has influence on determination of the optimal number of clusters in sets. In the described method, *complete link* algorithm has been used. Other versions of hierarchical algorithms e.g., *single* or *average link* [9] have other properties, which can have influence on values of the validity indexes. When the number of clusters is determined, a clustering algorithm e.g., the *k-means* [4] can be used to enable exact assignation of elements membership to clusters in a data set. The test sets have not included data noise. When the data noise is in sets, additional methods which removing it have to be applied. To sum up, the performed experiments confirm the high effectiveness of the new cluster validity index. The idea of this paper can be applied to designing various neuro-fuzzy structures [7,10,14,15,16,17,18].

References

1. Davies, D.L., Bouldin, D.W.: A cluster separation measure. IEEE Trans. Pattern Anal. Mach. Intell. 1(4), 224–227 (1979)
2. Duda, R.O., Hart, P.E., Stork, D.G.: Pattern Classification. Wiley, New York (2002)
3. Dunn, J.C.: A fuzzy relative of the ISODATA process and its use in detecting compact well-separated clusters. J. Cybernet. 3(3), 32–57 (1973)
4. Faber, V.: Clustering and the continuous k-means algorithm. Los Alamos Science 22, 138–144 (1994)
5. Halkidi, M., Batistakis, Y., Vazirgiannis, M.: Clustering validity checking methods: Part II. ACM SIGMOD Record 31(3) (2002)
6. Kim, M., Ramakrishna, R.S.: New indices for cluster validity assessment. Pattern Recognition Letters 26, 2353–2363 (2005)
7. Korytkowski, M., Scherer, R., Rutkowski, L.: On Combining Backpropagation with Boosting. In: International Joint Conference on Neural Networks, IEEE World Congress on Computational Intelligence, Vancouver, BC, Canada, pp. 1274–1277 (2006)
8. Mertez, C.J., Murphy, P.M.: UCI repository of machine learning databases, http://www.ics.uci.edu/pub/machine-learning-databases
9. Murtagh, F.: A survey of recent advances in hierarchical clustering algorithms. The Computer Journal 26(4), 354–359 (1983)
10. Nowicki, R.: Rough Sets in the Neuro-Fuzzy Architectures Based on Non-monotonic Fuzzy Implications. In: Rutkowski, L., Siekmann, J.H., Tadeusiewicz, R., Zadeh, L.A. (eds.) ICAISC 2004. LNCS (LNAI), vol. 3070, pp. 518–525. Springer, Heidelberg (2004)
11. Pakhira, M.K., Bandyopadhyay, S., Maulik, U.: Validity index for crisp and fuzzy clusters. Pattern Recognition 37(3), 487–501 (2004)
12. Rohlf, F.: Single link clustering algorithms. In: Krishnaiah, P., Kanal, L. (eds.) Handbook of Statistics, Amsterdam, North-Holland, vol. 2, pp. 267–284 (1982)
13. Rousseeuw, P.J.: Silhouettes: a graphical aid to the interpretation and validation of cluster analysis. J. Comput. Appl. Math. 20, 53–65 (1987)
14. Rutkowski, L., Cpałka, K.: A general approach to neuro - fuzzy systems. In: Proceedings of the 10th IEEE International Conference on Fuzzy Systems, Melbourne, December 2-5, vol. 3, pp. 1428–1431 (2001)
15. Rutkowski, L., Cpałka, K.: A neuro-fuzzy controller with a compromise fuzzy reasoning. Control and Cybernetics 31(2), 297–308 (2002)

16. Scherer, R.: Neuro-fuzzy Systems with Relation Matrix. In: Rutkowski, L., Scherer, R., Tadeusiewicz, R., Zadeh, L.A., Zurada, J.M. (eds.) ICAISC 2010, Part I. LNCS (LNAI), vol. 6113, pp. 210–215. Springer, Heidelberg (2010)
17. Starczewski, J., Rutkowski, L.: Interval type 2 neuro-fuzzy systems based on interval consequents. In: Rutkowski, L., Kacprzyk, J. (eds.) Neural Networks and Soft Computing, pp. 570–577. Physica-Verlag, Springer-Verlag Company, Heidelberg, New York (2003)
18. Starczewski, J.T., Rutkowski, L.: Connectionist Structures of Type 2 Fuzzy Inference Systems. In: Wyrzykowski, R., Dongarra, J., Paprzycki, M., Waśniewski, J. (eds.) PPAM 2001. LNCS, vol. 2328, pp. 634–642. Springer, Heidelberg (2002)
19. Weka 3: Data Mining Software in Java, University of Waikato, New Zealand, http://www.cs.waikato.ac.nz/ml/weka

A New Hierarchical Clustering Algorithm

Artur Starczewski

Department of Computer Engineering, Częstochowa University of Technology,
Al. Armii Krajowej 36, 42-200 Częstochowa, Poland
starcz@kik.pcz.czest.pl
http://kik.pcz.pl

Abstract. In this paper a new hierarchical clustering technique is presented. This approach is similar to two popular hierarchical clustering algorithms, i.e. *single-link* and *complete-link*. These hierarchical methods play an important role in clustering data and allow to create well-separable clusters, whenever the clusters exist. The proposed method has been used to clustering artificial and real data sets. Obtained results confirm very good performances of the method.

1 Introduction

Nowadays, a large number of clustering algorithms exist and these algorithms can be divided into two basic groups, hard (crisp clustering) and fuzzy (soft clustering). Hard clustering algorithms make partitions of the data which are separable, i.e. each element of the set belongs to one cluster only. Further on, the algorithms can be classified under two categories, partitional and hierarchical [3]. Partitional clustering algorithms create a one-level partitioning of the data [17,19]. Hierarchical algorithms create multi-levels partitioning [4,1,16]. Among popular hierarchical methods one can mention, i.e. *single-link* [10], *complete-link*, *average-link* [2], which belong to agglomerative hierarchical clustering. The methods start with clusters, which contain only one element and the number of the clusters equals the number of elements in the data set. Then, the nearest pair of clusters is merged according to some similarity criteria. This process is repeated until all elements of data set are in one cluster. Other approach represents the so-called divisive hierarchical clustering. This approach starts with a single cluster, where all elements of a data set are located, and next the large cluster is split into smaller ones. Then, the split is repeated until the number of the clusters equals the number of elements of the data set. Both approaches have the same drawbacks, i.e. if points of data set have been grouped incorrectly at any early step, they can not be corrected and the different similarity measures can lead to different results.

In this paper a new agglomerative hierarchical method is proposed. Section 2 describes the theoretical basics of some popular hierarchical methods. Sections 3 presents the new approach to hierarchical clustering. In Section 4, the experimental results on artificial and real data sets are illustrated. Finally, there are conclusions in Section 5.

L. Rutkowski et al. (Eds.): ICAISC 2012, Part II, LNCS 7268, pp. 175–180, 2012.

2   The Popular Agglomerative Hierarchical Methods

As it has been mentioned earlier, these three agglomerative hierarchical methods are popular and can be implemented to different applications. Usually, they are not used to large sets, since the memory space and CPUs time are $O(n^2)$ and $O(n^3)$ respectively [7,20]. The next sections describe the methods in details.

2.1   The Single-Link Clustering Method

This algorithm is one of the simplest hierarchical clustering method. It is also known as the nearest neighbour method, the minimum method or the connect-edness method. It is not constrained to shape cluster, so it has an ability to detect irregular clusters. Unfortunately, while creating clusters the method has *the chaining tendency*. Let c_1, c_2 and c_3 be three clusters in a data set. Thus, the distance $Dist(c_1, (c_2, c_3))$ can be represented as shown below:

$$\min\left\{dist\left(c_1, c_2\right), dist\left(c_1, c_3\right)\right\} \tag{1}$$

where, $dist(c_1, c_2)$ and $dist(c_1, c_3)$ can be defined as:

$$dist\left(c_1, c_2\right) = \min_{\mathbf{x}\in c_1, \mathbf{y}\in c_2} d\left(\mathbf{x}, \mathbf{y}\right) \tag{2}$$

$$dist\left(c_1, c_3\right) = \min_{\mathbf{x}\in c_1, \mathbf{z}\in c_3} d\left(\mathbf{x}, \mathbf{z}\right) \tag{3}$$

Any two clusters in the data set should be nonempty, nonoverlapping and the Euclidean distance is the most often used similarity measure.

2.2   The Complete-Link Clustering Method

The method is not similar to *single-link*, since to measure the similarity between to clusters the farthest neighbour distance is used. It can be deployed to create compact clusters with some equal diameters. Let c_1, c_2 and c_3 be three clusters in a data set. Thus, the Eq.(1) represents the $Dist(c_1, (c_2, c_3))$, whereas the $dist(c_1, c_2)$ and the $dist(c_1, c_3)$ can be defined as:

$$dist\left(c_1, c_2\right) = \max_{\mathbf{x}\in c_1, \mathbf{y}\in c_2} d\left(\mathbf{x}, \mathbf{y}\right) \tag{4}$$

$$dist\left(c_1, c_3\right) = \max_{\mathbf{x}\in c_1, \mathbf{z}\in c_3} d\left(\mathbf{x}, \mathbf{z}\right) \tag{5}$$

Any two clusters in data set should be nonempty, nonoverlapping and the distance function to compute the dissimilarity matrix is also used (e.g. the Euclidean distance).

2.3   The Average-Link Method

In this method, the distance between two clusters is determined as the average of all distances between all pairs of data points from the clusters. This algorithm has a tendency to create clusters with the same variance. Let c_1, c_2 and c_3 be three clusters in a data set. Thus, the Eq.(1) represents the $Dist(c_1, (c_2, c_3))$, whereas the $dist(c_1, c_2)$ and the $dist(c_1, c_3)$ can be expressed as follows:

$$dist\,(c_1, c_2) = \frac{1}{|c_1|\,|c_2|} \sum_{\mathbf{x} \in c_1, \mathbf{y} \in c_2} dist\,(\mathbf{x}, \mathbf{y}) \tag{6}$$

$$dist\,(c_1, c_3) = \frac{1}{|c_1|\,|c_3|} \sum_{\mathbf{x} \in c_1, \mathbf{z} \in c_3} dist\,(\mathbf{x}, \mathbf{z}) \tag{7}$$

The clusters should be nonempty and nonoverlapping and the dissimilarity matrix is also created.

3   The New Agglomerative Hierarchical Method

This proposed method integrates properties of two algorithms, i.e. *single-link* and *complete-link*. As it has been mentioned earlier, each of the methods is characterized by different properties. For example, the *single-link* algorithm has the chaining tendency while creating clusters, but it has also an ability to detect irregular clusters. Instead, the *complete-link* forms compact clusters with some equal diameters. It is advisable to create such an algorithm that somehow integrates these desirable properties and forms irregular, compact clusters and does not have *the chaining* tendency. The key issue is a choice of a method for calculating distances between clusters. Let c_1, c_2 and c_3 be three clusters in data set. The Eq.(1) represents the $Dist(c_1, (c_2, c_3))$. Then, the $dist(c_1, c_2)$ is defined as shown below:

$$0.5 \left(\max_{\mathbf{x} \in c_1, \mathbf{y} \in c_2} d\,(\mathbf{x}, \mathbf{y}) - \min_{\mathbf{x} \in c_1, \mathbf{y} \in c_2} d\,(\mathbf{x}, \mathbf{y}) \right) + \min_{\mathbf{x} \in c_1, \mathbf{y} \in c_2} d\,(\mathbf{x}, \mathbf{y}) \tag{8}$$

and the $dist(c_1, c_3)$ is

$$0.5 \left(\max_{\mathbf{x} \in c_1, \mathbf{y} \in c_3} d\,(\mathbf{x}, \mathbf{y}) - \min_{\mathbf{x} \in c_1, \mathbf{y} \in c_3} d\,(\mathbf{x}, \mathbf{y}) \right) + \min_{\mathbf{x} \in c_1, \mathbf{y} \in c_3} d\,(\mathbf{x}, \mathbf{y}) \tag{9}$$

Any two clusters in the data set should be nonempty and nonoverlapping and the Euclidean distance can be used. For n clusters, the distance $Dist(c_1, (c_2, ..., c_n))$ is given below:

$$\min \left\{ dist\,(c_1, c_2)\,, ..., dist\,(c_1, c_n) \right\} \tag{10}$$

where, the distances $dist(c_1, c_1), ..., dist(c_1, c_n)$ of the expression Eq.(10) are defined in the same way as earlier in Eq.(8) or Eq.(9). The clustering results for artificial and real data are described below.

4   Experimental Results

The different experiments have been performed on both artificial and real data sets. The machine learning toolkit Weka 3.6 [18] has been used to generate artificial data sets. The presented artificial sets are 2-dimensional and multidimensional with a different number of clusters. The real data sets are the two well known machine learning problems from the UCI database [6], i.e. *the Iris data* and the *Wine* data. The sets are used in an unsupervised manner, this means that the information about the classes is not available to the clustering algorithm. The detailed description of the sets is described in Table 1. The shape of the data sets is so fixed in order to the distances among clusters were different. For example, in the Figure 1 the artificial sets S1 and S2 are presented. As we can see, the data set S1 consists of three clusters, while the set S2 includes five clusters. Clusters are located at various distances from each other, some of them are quite close. Data points create different shapes and can be variously identified. The *new hierarchical method* described in Section 3 and the three popular methods (see Section 2) have been used to test the artificial and the real data sets. Of course, the starting number of clusters is equal to the number of points in the data set. The obtained results for the hierarchical algorithms are presented in Table 2. For comparing the results provided by the hierarchical algorithms, the Rand Index [9] is used. This index takes values in $[0, 1]$, where the value 1

Table 1. Detailed information of the data sets

Data set	Clusters	Number of attributes	Total number of instances
S1	3	2	107
S2	5	2	194
S3	11	2	283
S4	8	5	228
S5	13	5	334
Iris	3	4	150
Wine	3	13	178

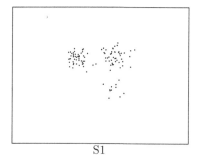
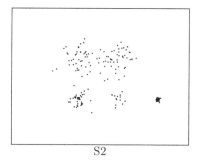

S1   S2

Fig. 1. Graphic representation of the artificial data sets S1 and S2

Table 2. Comparision of the hierarchical clustering algorithms

Data sets	Values of the *Rand-index* obtained for clustering algorithms			
	New method	*Average-link*	*Complete-link*	*Single-link*
S1	**0.967**	0.6	0.967	0.967
S2	**0.981**	0.981	0.981	0.88
S3	**0.955**	0.975	0.936	0.905
S4	**0.986**	0.309	0.993	0.473
S5	**0.993**	0.217	0.984	0.416
Iris	**0.95**	0.886	0.837	0.777
Wine	**0.662**	0.626	0.714	0.363

indicates the perfect partition of a data set, whereas values close to 0 correspond to the bad membership of elements of the data set to clusters. So, one can see that the obtained results for *single-link* are worse in comparison to results of the other methods. The other approaches e.g., *average-link, the complete-link* and *the new method* have correct results in most cases. However, *the complete-link* assigns points of the sets S1, S2, S4 and *the Wine* to individual clusters very well. Note, that *the new method* has the best results and almost all values of the *Rand Index* are close to 1. The experiments for artificial and real data prove that the performance of *the new hierarchical method* is very good.

5   Conclusions

All the presented results confirm the very good effectiveness of *the new hierarchical method* described in Section 3. In the case of the artificial data sets, despite the fact that the points have different distances from each other and form variety of shapes, they are assigned to clusters correctly. Other versions of hierarchical algorithms e.g., *single-link, complete-link* and *average-link* have other properties and the obtained results are often worse as compared with the results obtained with *the new hierarchical method*. For the real data sets is similarly. In most experiments, when *the new method* is applied, a number of wrongly assigned points to clusters is the smallest. Of course, when the test sets include data noise, additional methods which remove it have to be applied. To sum up, all the results confirm the good performance of *the new method*, which is very promising. The results of this paper can be used to designing various neuro-fuzzy systems [5,8,11,12,13,14,15].

References

1. Guha, S., Rastogi, R., Shim, K.: ROCK: a robust clustering algorithm for categorical attributes. In: Proceedings of 15th International Conference on Data Engineering, pp. 512–521 (1999)
2. Jain, A., Dubes, R.: Algorithms for clustering data. Prentice-Hall, Englewood Cliffs (1988)

3. Jain, A.K., Murty, M.N., Flynn, P.J.: Data clustering: A review. ACM Comput. Surveys 31(3), 264–323 (1999)
4. Karypis, G., Han, E.H., Kumar, V.: CHAMELEON: a hierarchical clustering algorithm using dynamic modeling. IEEE Comput. 32(8), 68–75 (1999)
5. Korytkowski, M., Rutkowski, L., Scherer, R.: From Ensemble of Fuzzy Classifiers to Single Fuzzy Rule Base Classifier. In: Rutkowski, L., Tadeusiewicz, R., Zadeh, L.A., Zurada, J.M. (eds.) ICAISC 2008. LNCS (LNAI), vol. 5097, pp. 265–272. Springer, Heidelberg (2008)
6. Mertez, C.J., Murphy, P.M.: UCI repository of machine learning databases, http://www.ics.uci.edu/pub/machine-learning-databases
7. Murtagh, F.: A survey of recent advantces in hierarchical clustering algorithms. The Computer Journal 26(4), 354–359 (1983)
8. Nowicki, R.: Rough Sets in the Neuro-Fuzzy Architectures Based on Monotonic Fuzzy Implications. In: Rutkowski, L., Siekmann, J.H., Tadeusiewicz, R., Zadeh, L.A. (eds.) ICAISC 2004. LNCS (LNAI), vol. 3070, pp. 510–517. Springer, Heidelberg (2004)
9. Rand, W.: Objective criteria for the evaluation of clustering methods. J. Am. Stat. Assoc. 66(336), 846–850 (1971)
10. Rohlf, F.: Single link clustering algorithms. In: Krishnaiah, P., Kanal, L. (eds.) Handbook of Statistics, Amsterdam, North-Holland, vol. 2, pp. 267–284 (1982)
11. Rutkowski, L., Cpałka, K.: A general approach to neuro - fuzzy systems. In: Proceedings of the 10th IEEE International Conference on Fuzzy Systems, Melbourne, December 2-5, vol. 3, pp. 1428–1431 (2001)
12. Rutkowski, L., Cpałka, K.: A neuro-fuzzy controller with a compromise fuzzy reasoning. Control and Cybernetics 31(2), 297–308 (2002)
13. Scherer, R.: Neuro-fuzzy Systems with Relation Matrix. In: Rutkowski, L., Scherer, R., Tadeusiewicz, R., Zadeh, L.A., Zurada, J.M. (eds.) ICAISC 2010, Part I. LNCS (LNAI), vol. 6113, pp. 210–215. Springer, Heidelberg (2010)
14. Starczewski, J., Rutkowski, L.: Interval type 2 neuro-fuzzy systems based on interval consequents. In: Rutkowski, L., Kacprzyk, J. (eds.) Neural Networks and Soft Computing, pp. 570–577. Physica-Verlag, Springer-Verlag Company, Heidelberg, New York (2003)
15. Starczewski, J.T., Rutkowski, L.: Connectionist Structures of Type 2 Fuzzy Inference Systems. In: Wyrzykowski, R., Dongarra, J., Paprzycki, M., Waśniewski, J. (eds.) PPAM 2001. LNCS, vol. 2328, pp. 634–642. Springer, Heidelberg (2002)
16. Vijaya, P.A., Narasimha Murty, M., Subramanian, D.K.: Efficient bottom-up hybrid hierarchical clustering techniques for protein sequence classification. Pattern Recognition 39, 2344–2355 (2006)
17. Vrahatics, M.N., Boutsinas, B., Alevizos, P., Pavlides, G.: The new k-windows algorithm for improving the k-Means clustering algorithm. J. of Complexity 18, 375–391 (2002)
18. Weka 3: Data Mining Software in Java, University of Waikato, New Zealand, http://www.cs.waikato.ac.nz/ml/weka
19. Wong, C.C., Chen, C.C., Su, M.C.: A novel algorithm for data clustering. Pattern Recognition 34, 425–442 (2001)
20. Zait, M., Messatfa, H.: A comparative study of clustering methods. Future Generation Computer Systems 13(2-3), 149–159 (1997)

An Application of the Self-Organizing Map to Multiple View Unsupervised Learning

Tomasz Gałkowski and Artur Starczewski

Department of Computer Engineering, Częstochowa University of Technology,
Al. Armii Krajowej 36, 42-200 Częstochowa, Poland
tomasz.galkowski@kik.pcz.pl, starcz@kik.pcz.czest.pl

Abstract. In various data mining applications performing the task of extracting information from large databases is serious problem, which occurs in many fields e.g.: bioinformatics, commercial behaviour of Internet users, social networks analysis, management and investigation of various databases in static or dynamic states. In recent years many techniques discovering hidden structures in the data set like clustering and projection of data from high-dimensional spaces have been developed. In this paper, we propose a model for multiple view unsupervised clustering based on Kohonen self-organizing-map algorithm. The results of simulations in two dimensional space using three views of training sets having different statistical properties have been presented.

1 Introduction

Lots of techniques discovering hidden structures in the data set base on variations of correlation analysis, see e.g. [20]. The phenomenon of multidimensionality has an unpleasant feature because of the memory space and CPUs time. Therefore, techniques leading to reduction of dimensionality of data sets [11] or reduction of attributes in the rough sets [10] are used by many researchers. In many important data mining applications, the same instances have multiple representations from different spaces (so called views). Different representations often could have different statistical properties, and the answer on question how to learn a consensus pattern from multiple representations is an impressive challenge. For example, suppose that the following thesis is true: similar groups of web surfers probably should buy similar products in internet shops. The analysis of such similarity is a difficult multi-space problem. One of possible way of solving this problem is to classify users through their behavior in the internet. It means that they visit similar web pages, click similar links, etc. The characteristics of visited web-pages can be used as description of this behavioral user model. But multi-view approach arises from the fact that the web pages can have following multiple representations [4]:

- the term vector corresponding to words occurring in the pages themselves,
- the graph of hyper-links between the pages, and
- the term vectors corresponding to words contained in anchor text of links pointing to the pages.

L. Rutkowski et al. (Eds.): ICAISC 2012, Part II, LNCS 7268, pp. 181–187, 2012.

Solving the problem of clustering of web-users someone may prepare an appropriate offer for the possible customer expectation. Note that the view in each space could have different measure. There is the question is the multi-view approach better than clustering in one-dimension? Does a consensus pattern trained basing on multiple representations is more accurate and robust than patterns based on a single view? In recent years such as above and similar questions inspired many researchers to find satisfactory solutions relating tasks like multi-view clustering [4] and intelligent data analysis [21]. The area of interests with respect to initial knowledge could be pointed and developed as supervised, semi-supervised and unsupervised methods. In this paper, we propose a model for multiple view unsupervised clustering based on Kohonen self-organizing-map algorithm. The semi-supervised case of multiple view learning was introduced in [3] by Blum and Mitchell. In their work the co-training method of training a classifier from two representations with unlabeled and labeled instances was investigated. During the first phase of the co-training approach one learner is trained on each view of the labeled instances and in the second one each learner iteratively predicts unlabeled instances with the highest confidence. Newly labeled examples from one learner may give the other learner new information to improve its model. In [7] authors extend the idea of co-training to explicitly measure the degree of agreement between the rules in different views. A number of papers have extended the original co-training idea [5], [9], [13], [16]. One may find a limited work on named multiple view clustering [2], [17], [22]. Known approaches are focused on the simple case of two views with strong assumptions. Authors in [2] proposed an algorithm for the multiple view data clustering based on two independent views, which can be extended to entirely unsupervised case. In [17] and [22] authors investigate a spectral clustering algorithms using the minimizing-disagreement rule and the normalized cut from a single view to multiple views, respectively. There are several works known on related topics such as: ensemble clustering [8], [19] which combines different clusters for a single view data and/or multi-type clustering [18] using attribute information for clustering process. Bo Long (et all) in [4] described two directions in multi-view unsupervised learning: designing of centralized algorithms and solving problems by distributed approaches. The first class of methods is using the multiple representations simultaneously to mine hidden patterns from the data. The main problem in this approach results from the fact that different representations could have different formulations (numbers and graphs), and also could have very different statistical properties (e.g. various distributions). One may find the reviews of investigated in literature methods in [1], [12]. The aim of the distributed approaches is to learn hidden patterns individually from each representation of a multiple view data and then learn the optimal hidden patterns from those previously learnt patterns. In article [4] authors accent some advantages of distributed framework comparing to the centralized one. Let us cite this feature on which our work is based, too: "an algorithm which learns an optimal pattern from multiple patterns can be used for various types of multiple view data, since it does not work on the data directly".

In this paper a new approach to multiple view unsupervised learning is proposed. Section 2 describes the main scope of the work. In Section 3, the experimental results on artificial data sets are illustrated. Finally, there are conclusions in Section 4.

2   Main Scope of the Work and Used Tools

Long et all in [15] proposed two possible ways for finding solution of clustering task: Multiple View Clustering and Multiple View of Spectral Embedding algorithms. Both of them base on special mapping functions and finding optimum of criteria of type:

$$\min_{B,P} \sum_{i=1}^{m} w_i \left\| A^{(i)} - BP^{(i)} \right\|^2 \tag{1}$$

or

$$\min_{B,P} \sum_{i=1}^{m} w_i GI \left(A^{(i)} || BP^{(i)} \right) \tag{2}$$

where $A^{(i)}$ is a pattern matrix, B is an optimal pattern matrix, $P^{(i)}$ is a mapping matrix (in linear function space), $||.||$ denotes Frobenius norm and GI is a generalized I-divergence function (see [15] for details). To solve minimization problem described by above equations is very difficult in real applications. Authors proposed their solutions under several simplifying assumptions, with constraints and limitations.

Our paper is placed in the direction of using unsupervised clustering of the data in distributed framework. We propose the method based on Kohonen Self-Organizing-Map (SOM) [14]. The training sets (views) in simulation study have different probability distributions (see Table 1). At first we use Kohonen SOM for clustering of the data. In the final phase c-means algorithm is used to find the optimal representation for the previously learnt classes. The well known from literature [14] Kohonen SOM is a type of neural network which classifies the input vectors regarding their natural similarity. The main algorithm may be used in unsupervised mode - then it is leading to natural clustering algorithm discovering internal structure of the data. The vectors of the input space (so called feature space) are projected to the network at input layer and the classes are formed on the output layer basing of similarities and differences of inputs. The Figure 1 shows the base structure of the network.

Algorithm:

1. Initialize weights of the map nodes (for instance: random or uniform)
2. Pass input vector to the input nodes
3. Calculate the Euclidean distance between input vector and all nodes, finding the smallest distance output node (named: winner node).
4. Update weights of the winning node and its neighbor by the formulas:

$$w_{n+1}(k,j) = w_n(k,j) + \xi(n)[x(j) - w_n(k,j)] \tag{3}$$

for the input weights of winner node, and

$$w_{n+1}(m,j) = w_n(m,j) + d(m,n,k)\xi(n)[x(j) - w_n(k,j)] \tag{4}$$

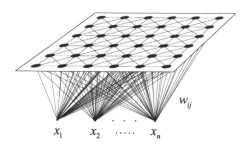

Fig. 1. The base structure of the Kohonen SOM network

for the neighbor nodes inside the area around the winner of radius defined by function $d(m, n, k)$ (decreasing function of the number of iteration);

where n - number of iteration, k - number of winning node, $j - j'th$ coordinate of the vector, $\xi(n)$ - decreasing function of modification weights depending on number of iteration, $x(j)$ input pattern vector $j'th$ coordinate.

5. Repeat above steps until a measure of convergence (e.g. recursive mean square error method RMS) reaches assumed limit level.

The self-organizing-map performs in natural manner human brain method of organizing information. The outcome of the algorithm is a low-dimensional (e.g. two-dimensional) representation of the input space of the training samples, called a map. SOM reduces the dimensionality of the input space preserving its topological properties.

The clustering results for artificial data sets are described below.

3   Experimental Results

The different experiments have been performed on artificial data sets. The presented artificial set is 2-dimensional and consist of three views. The views contain random variables, which are generated from popular distributions viz., the first view is from the normal distribution (see Figure 2), the second is from the chisquare distribution (see Figure 3) and the next is from the Poisson distribution (see Figure 4). The detailed description of the data sets is described in Table 1. As we can see, the views consists of three clusters and the clusters are located at various distances from each other, some of them are quite close. The *new approach* described in Section 2 have been tested using the data sets. The Kohonen maps received for the individual views are presented in Figures 2, 3 and 4.

Table 1. Detailed information of the data sets

Data set	Clusters	Number of attributes	Distribution	Total number of instances
View 1	3	2	Normal	600
View 2	3	2	Chisquare	600
View 3	3	2	Poisson	600

The final map of neurons is a logical product of the matrices, which represent the activity of neurons in different views. Values of active neurons are equal to one, the remaining values of neurons are zero. The final map and the neurones, which defines the consensus pattern are shown in Figure 5. The clustering $c - means$ algorithm is used to obtain the consensus pattern.

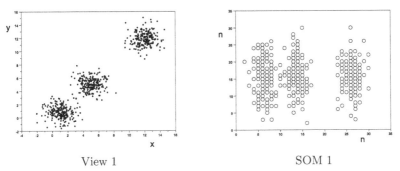

View 1   SOM 1

Fig. 2. Graphic representation of the View 1 (the normal distribution) and the Kohonen map SOM1 for View 1

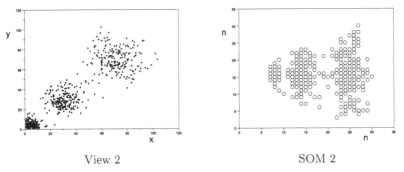

View 2   SOM 2

Fig. 3. Graphic representation of the View 2 (the chisquare distribution) and the Kohonen map SOM2 for View 2

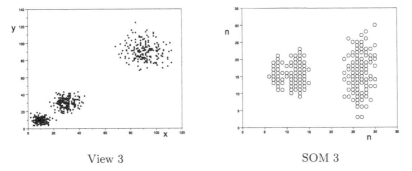

View 3   SOM 3

Fig. 4. Graphic representation of the View 3 (the Poisson distribution) and the Kohonen map SOM3 for the View 3

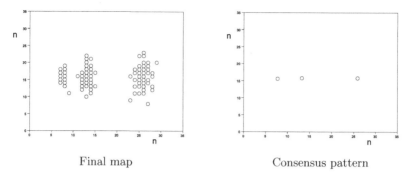

Final map   Consensus pattern

Fig. 5. Graphic representation of the final map of neurons and the consensus pattern (three neurons from Kohonen map)

4   Conclusions

In this paper, we propose the Kohonen SOM based method for multiple view unsupervised learning. Our algorithm is applicable to various types of multiple view data sets. The evaluation of the numerical experiments for synthetic data sets is presented. The simulations demonstrate the effectiveness and great potential of the proposed approach. In the future research we will develop various variants (see e.g. [6]) of algorithms (3) and (4) for multiple view unsupervised learning.

References

1. Berkhin, P.: Survey of clustering data mining techniques. Technical report, Accrue Software, San Jose, CA (2002)
2. Bickel, S., Scheffer, T.: Multi-view clustering. In: ICDM 2004, pp. 19–26 (2004)
3. Blum, A., Mitchell, T.: Combining labeled and unlabeled data with co-training. In: COLT 1998, pp. 92–100 (1998)
4. Long, B., Yu, P.S., Zhang, Z.: A General Model for Multiple View Unsupervised Learning. In: Proceedings of the 2008 SIAM International Conference on Data Mining, pp. 822–833 (2008)
5. Brefeld, U., Scheffer, T.: Co-em support vector learning. In: ICML 2004, p. 16 (2004)
6. Cierniak, R., Rutkowski, L.: On image compression by competitive neural networks and optimal linear predictors. Signal Processing: Image Communication - a Eurasip Journal 15(6), 559–565 (2000)
7. Collins, M., Singer, Y.: Unsupervised models for named entity classification (1999)
8. Fern, X.Z., Brodley, C.E.: Solving cluster ensemble problems by bipartite graph partitioning. In: ICML 2004 (2004)
9. Ghani, R.: Combining labeled and unlabeled data for text classification with a large number of categories. In: ICDM 2001, pp. 597–598 (2001)
10. Hedar, A.R., Wang, J., Fukushima, M.: Tabu search for attribute reduction in rough set theory. Soft Computing 12, 909–918 (2008)

11. Herawan, T., Ghazali, R., Deris, M.M.: Soft Set Theoretic Approach for Dimensionality Reduction. International Journal of Database Theory and Application 3(2) (June 2010)
12. Jain, A.K., Murty, M.N., Flynn, P.J.: Data cluster-ing: a review. ACM Computing Surveys 31(3), 264–323 (1999)
13. Karypis, G., Kumar, V.: A fast and high quality mul-tilevel scheme for partitioning irregular graphs. SIAM J. Sci. Comput. 20(1), 359–392 (1998)
14. Kohonen, T.: The Self-Organizing Map. Proceedings of The IEEE 78(9) (September 1990)
15. Long, B., Yu, P.S., Zhang, Z.: A General Model for Multiple View Unsupervised Learning. In: Proceedings of the 2008 SIAM International Conference on Data Mining, pp. 822–833 (2008)
16. Nigam, K., Ghani, R.: Analyzing the effectiveness and applicability of co-training. In: CIKM 2000, pp. 86-93 (2000)
17. Sa, V.R.: Spectral clustering with two views. In: ICML Workshop on Learning with Multiple Views (2005)
18. Taskar, B., Segal, E., Koller, D.: Probabilistic classification and clustering in relational data. In: Proceeding of IJCAI 2001 (2001)
19. Topchy, A., Jain, A.K., Punch, W.: Combining multiple weak clusterings. In: Proceedings of the Third IEEE International Conference on Data Mining, p. 331 (2003)
20. Wang, Y., Gongxuan, Z., Qian, J.-B.: ApproxCCA: An approximate correlation analysis algorithm for multidimensional data streams. Knowledge-Based Systems 24, 952–962 (2011)
21. Chen, Y., Yao, Y.: A multiview approach for intelligent data analysis based on data operators. Information Sciences 178, 1–20 (2008)
22. Zhou, D., Burge, C.J.C.: Spectral clustering and transductive learning with multiple views. In: ICML 2007, pp. 1159–1166 (2007)

Graphical Models as Surrogates
for Complex Ground Motion Models

Kristin Vogel, Carsten Riggelsen, Nicolas Kuehn, and Frank Scherbaum

University of Potsdam, Institute of Earth and Environmental Science,
Karl-Liebknecht-Str. 24/25, 14476 Golm-Potsdam, Germany
{kvog,riggelsen,nico,fs}@geo.uni-potsdam.de

Abstract. In Probabilistic Seismic Hazard Analysis, which has become the basis of decision making on the design of high risk facilities, one estimates the probability that ground motion caused by earthquakes exceeds a certain level at a certain site within a certain time interval. One of the most critical aspects in this context is the model for the conditional probability of ground motion given earthquake magnitude, source-site-distance and potentially additional parameters. These models are usually regression functions, including terms modelling interaction effects derived from expert knowledge. We show that the framework of Directed Graphical Models is an attractive alternative to the standard regression approach. We investigate Bayesian Networks, modelling the problem in a true multivariate way, and we look into Naive Bayes and Tree-Augmented Naive Bayes, where the target node coincides with the dependent variable in standard ground motion regression. Our approach gives rise to distribution-free learning when necessary, and we experiment with and introduce different discretization schemes to apply standard learning and inference algorithms to our problem at hand.

1 Introduction

In the context of Probabilistic Seismic Hazard Analysis (PSHA) strong ground motion at a particular site, caused by an earthquake, is modelled by physical relationships between various parameters, usually dictated by physical principles. This requires accurate knowledge of the source process, of the properties of the propagation medium as well as of the subsurface under the site. In regions of well recorded seismicity the most popular modelling approach is to fit a regression function to the observed data, where the functional form is determined by expert knowledge. In regions, where we lack a sufficient amount of data, it is popular to fit the regression function to a data set generated by a so-called *stochastic model* [1], which distorts the shape of a random time series according to physical principles to obtain a time series with properties that match ground-motion characteristics. The stochastic model does not have nice analytical properties nor does it come in a form amenable for easy analytical handling and evaluation. In order to determine the ground motion the stochastic model is simulated, posing a time-consuming and computationally expensive challenge. Instead of using a stochastic model directly, a surrogate model, which describes the stochastic model in a more abstract sense (e.g. regression), is often used in PSHA.

L. Rutkowski et al. (Eds.): ICAISC 2012, Part II, LNCS 7268, pp. 188–195, 2012.
© Springer-Verlag Berlin Heidelberg 2012

In this paper we show how *Directed Graphical Models* (DGM) may be seen as a viable alternative to the classical regression approach. Graphical models have proven to be a "all-round" pre/descriptive probabilistic framework for many problems. The transparent nature of the graphical models is attractive from a domain perspective allowing for a better understanding and gives direct insight into the relationships and workings of a system. A possible application of DGMs for PSHA is already described in [7].

In the following sections we give a short introduction into the ground motion domain and into DGMs. How the DGMs are learned for discrete variables is explained in Sect. 4. Discretization methods and how we deal with a continuous target variable are given in Sect. 5. In Sect. 6 we apply DGMs to a dataset simulated by a stochastic model and we end with the conclusions.

2 Ground Motion Models

Formally speaking, in ground motion modelling we want to estimate the conditional probability of a ground motion parameter Y such as (horizontal) peak ground acceleration (PGA) or spectral acceleration (PSA) given earthquake and site related predictor variables, $\mathbf{X}$. In the regression approach the ground motion parameter is usually assumed to be log-normally distributed, $\ln Y = f(\mathbf{X}) + \epsilon$, with $\epsilon \sim \mathcal{N}(0, \sigma^2)$.

Which predictor variables are used is a matter of choice; in thus sequel we have at our disposal, $\mathbf{X} = \{M, R, SD, Q_0, \kappa_0, V_S 30\}$. The moment magnitude of the earthquake (M) and distance between source and site (R) traditionally have special status in PSHA, however, we treat them no differently than the other variables: Stress released during the earthquake (SD), attenuation of seismic wave amplitudes in deep layers (Q_0) and near the surface (κ_0), Average shear-wave velocity in the upper 30 m ($V_S 30$). [1]

Seismological expert knowledge determines the functional form of the regressions function; in our case a reasonable form for a regression function is the following, which is based on the description of the Fourier spectrum of seismic ground motion [1],

$$f(\mathbf{X}) = a_0 + a_1 M + a_2 M \cdot \ln SD + (a_3 + a_4 M) \ln \sqrt{a_5^2 + R^2} \qquad (1)$$
$$+ a_6 \kappa R + a_7 V_S 30 + a_8 \ln SD$$

with $\kappa = \kappa_0 + t^*$, $t^* = \frac{R}{Q_0 V_{sq}}$ and $V_{sq} = 3.5 \frac{km}{s}$, where a_i is fitted to data simulated from the stochastic model.

3 Directed Graphical Models

DGM's describe a joint probability distribution of a set of variables, $\mathbf{X}$, decomposing it into a product of (local) conditional probability distributions $P(\mathbf{X}|DAG, \boldsymbol{\theta}) = \prod_i P(X_i|\mathbf{X}_{Pa(i)}) = \prod_i \theta_{X_i|\mathbf{X}_{Pa(i)}}$ according to a directed acyclic graph (DAG), with vertices X_i and edges pointing from the parent set, $\mathbf{X}_{Pa(i)}$, to X_i, encoding the conditional independences. The local conditional probability distributions, $P(X_i|\mathbf{X}_{Pa(i)})$

---

[1] In the next sections we will sometimes include Y in $\mathbf{X}$; it will be clear from the context when this is the case.

may be defined according to our prior knowledge, e.g., as Gaussians where the mean and the variance could be associated with corresponding vertices in the DAG. However often we want to make no such explicit assumptions, that is, we want to be able to model a wide range of distributions, because no prior knowledge may be available. By adhering to categorical distributions we may approximate (by "histograms") any continuous distribution asymptotically; this would be called *distribution-free learning*. E.g. if estimated from observations, the parameters could be the maximum likelihood estimates, $\hat{\theta}_{x_i|\mathbf{x}_{Pa(i)}} = \frac{n(x_i, \mathbf{x}_{Pa(i)})}{n(\mathbf{x}_{Pa(i)})}$ using the statistics $n(\cdot)$, the counts of a particular configuration from data. More about discretization follows in Sect. 5.

In contrast to classical regression, DGMs treat all random quantities, including co-variates, as random variables. This is not only reasonable, since the measure of the covariates is often defective, but also allows to infer in "all directions" and calculate any conditional distributions of interest. Furthermore DGMs offer a different perspective on how variables (including co-variates) relate, since no assumptions about the functional form for physical relationships between the variables have to be given. On the other hand, expert knowledge can be included by the usage of informative priors, both on structure and parameters. For a more detailed description of DGMs see [3].

4 Learning Approaches for Discrete Variables

In the sections to come we assume that we have at our disposal an i.i.d. sample, **d**, with n records (for now assume discretized data); this will in our case be the simulated data from the stochastic model, from which we want to learn. We investigate DGMs admitting to different decompositions/factorizations of the joint distribution, that is, the restrictions that are imposed by the DAG: Bayesian Networks (BNs), Naive Bayes (NBs) and Tree Augmented Naive Bayes (TANs).

4.1 Bayesian Networks

In contrast to the regression approach, for BNs we do not need to make any assumptions about any (functional or (in)dependence) relationship of the involved variables *a priori*. When learned from data, we automatically get a concise surrogate model. By inspecting the learned BN structure we may get an intuition about the workings of the underlying data generating system (the stochastic model) from an (in)dependence perspective. The BN at the same time enables for computing any marginal/conditional of interest.

BN learning involves traversing the space of BNs looking for the one yielding the highest score. As scoring function we use the Bayesian MAP scoring, introduced in [10], assuming a joint uniform prior $P(DAG, \Theta) = P(\Theta|DAG)P(DAG)$, with $P(\Theta|DAG)$ a uniform product Dirichlet distribution (with restricted hyper-parameters α guaranteeing DAG scoring equivalence), and $P(DAG)$ uniform over BN structures too. This yields the MAP scoring metric which needs to be maximized,

$$S(DAG|\mathbf{d}) = \prod_i \prod_{\mathbf{x}_{Pa(i)}} \prod_{x_i} \hat{\theta}_{x_i|\mathbf{x}_{Pa(i)}}^{n(x_i, \mathbf{x}_{Pa(i)}) + \alpha(x_i, \mathbf{x}_{Pa(i)}) - 1} \times \text{regularization term.}$$

To traverse the (simulated) space of essential graphs we use a hill-climber algorithm, applying the Repeated Covered Arc Reversal operator [2], where arc addition and removal are the basic operations. Without going into detail, we note that the thus obtained structure also dictates the parameter estimates of θ as the maximum likelihood (see previous section), but now based on $\alpha(\cdot) + n(\cdot) - 1$.

4.2 Naive Bayes

In the BN approach, the structure is learned, and all variables are treated equally; there is no dedicated "output" node. In the context of our surrogate mode there is however a variable of interest, Y. The network structure in Naive Bayes (NBs) is simple and fixed: The target variable Y, often referred to as class variable, is the only parent of each attribute X_i. Even though the assumed independence between the attributes is most likely violated, NBs usually perform well (competitive with or better than BNs) in classification tasks [5]. Obviously, in contrast to the BNs, with NBs we lack the ability to gain insight into the relationships between the variables via inspection.

The (local) conditional distributions may be the usual maximum likelihood estimates; however, we use the smoothed maximum likelihood estimator given in [5] instead, $\hat{\theta}_{x_i|\mathbf{x}_{Pa(i)}} = \alpha \frac{n(x_i, \mathbf{x}_{Pa(i)})}{n(\mathbf{x}_{Pa(i)})} + (1 - \alpha) \frac{n(x_i)}{n}$ with $\alpha = \frac{n(\mathbf{x}_{Pa(i)})}{n(\mathbf{x}_{Pa(i)})+5}$.

4.3 Tree Augmented Naive Bayes

Tree Augmented Naive Bayes (TANs) are an extension of the NBs. They allow each attribute to have one more parent in addition to the target variable. This relaxes the independence assumption for the attributes made in NB, but maintains the computational simplicity. In a TAN construction we start off with the NB structure. To determine on the presence or absence of connections between the attributes, we use a score based on entropy, $\mathsf{Ent_d}(\mathbf{X}) = -\sum_{\mathbf{x}} \frac{n(\mathbf{x})}{n} \log_2 \frac{n(\mathbf{x})}{n}$. Entropy measures the amount of information, needed to specify $\mathbf{X}$ in the dataset $\mathbf{d}$ with n records. We determine for each pair, $(X_i, X_j)_{i \neq j}$, the *explaining away residual* (EAR) [9],

$$\mathsf{EAR}(X_i, X_j | Y) = \mathsf{Ent_d}(X_i, Y) + \mathsf{Ent_d}(X_j, Y) - \mathsf{Ent_d}(X_i, X_j, Y) - \mathsf{Ent_d}(Y)$$
$$- \mathsf{Ent_d}(X_i) - \mathsf{Ent_d}(X_j) + \mathsf{Ent_d}(X_i, X_j),$$

which is high for pairs which are mutually informative conditioned on Y and at the same time not mutually informative unconditionally. In an undirected *maximum spanning tree* the weights of the edges are associated with the EAR, all edges with negative weights are deleted and for the remaining tree(s) we choose a root node and set the direction of the edges pointing away from the root. These are the edges, which are added to the NB, ultimately yielding the TAN. The estimation of θ is done as described for NBs.

5 Discretization

For a distribution-free learning, we need to discretize the continuous variables of our data set. A discretization splits the range of $\mathbf{X}$ into (multidimensional) intervals and merges all real values of one interval into one state of a discrete variable, $\mathbf{X}'$. The number of intervals and their boundaries have to be chosen carefully, since essential information about the distributions and dependencies of the variables may be lost otherwise.

5.1 Bayesian Network

For BN's, where we are mainly interested in learning the dependency structure, we discretize all variables simultaneously, using a *multivariate discretization*, which takes the interaction between all connected variables into account. We use a method developed in [8], assuming that the observed data, were generated in two steps. In the first step an interval is selected by drawing from $P(\mathbf{X}'|DAG)$. Afterwards we draw $\mathbf{X}$ from a uniform distribution over the selected interval, $P(\mathbf{X}|\mathbf{X}') = \prod_i P(X_i|X_i')$. According to [8] we now seek a discretization $\mathbf{d}'$ of $\mathbf{d}$, which maximizes for a given structure $P(\mathbf{d}'|DAG)P(\mathbf{d}|\mathbf{d}')$; here $P(\mathbf{d}'|DAG)$ is the so-called *marginal likelihood*.

The optimal discretization depends on the BN structure and has to be adjusted dynamically as the structure changes. We do this in an iterative way, similar to [6], first learning the discretization for an initial network, which in turn is used to learn a new BN with the MAP-scoring function. The discretization and the BN-learning steps are repeated until we reach a local maximum of the MAP-score. Starting with different initial networks can lead to different results. We use the structure of a TAN to start with, but ideally different initial GMs should be tested.

5.2 Naive Bayes and Tree Augmented Naive Bayes

The above mentioned approach is not ideal for the NB and TAN approach. Here our attention is on the estimation of the target variable, and we discretize only the attributes, while the continuous target is approximated with a kernel density estimator.

Our method is based on the approach developed in [4], which is widely used for the discretization of continuous attributes in classification tasks *with a discrete class variable* Y. The discretization of each attribute X_i depends on Y, but is independent of the other attributes. It splits the total dataset $\mathbf{d}$ into subsets $\cup_{k=1}^{K} \mathbf{d}_k = \mathbf{d}$, where $\mathbf{d}_k$ includes all records, for which X_i falls into the k-th interval. We aim to choose interval boundaries that lead to a small *Minimum Description Length* (MDL). The MDL can be expressed as $\sum_k \frac{n_k}{n} \text{Ent}_{\mathbf{d}_k}(Y) + cost$, where n_k is the number of records in $\mathbf{d}_k$, $\text{Ent}_{\mathbf{d}_k}(Y)$ is the *class entropy* based on the dataset $\mathbf{d}_k$ and $cost$ is a regularization term restricting the number of intervals.

The above method is only valid for a discrete target variable, but our target is $Y = \ln PGA$, i.e., continuous. To apply the class entropy, we replace the continuous Y with a discrete approximation Y', whose states, $y_1', ..., y_{n_Y}'$, correspond to the interval midpoints, we get by splitting the range of Y into n_Y equidistant intervals of width Δ_Y. We choose a large number n_Y (e.g. $n_Y = 512$) to allow a precise approximation of Y. In order to estimate $\text{Ent}_{\mathbf{d}_k}(Y)$ reliably, we now use a Gaussian kernel density estimator, $\hat{P}_{Y,\mathbf{d}}$, with a bandwidth according to Silverman's "rule of thumb" [11] and set, $\hat{P}(y_i') = \Delta_Y \cdot \hat{P}_{Y,\mathbf{d}}(y = y_i')$. The class entropy $\text{Ent}_{\mathbf{d}_k}(Y) \approx -\sum_{i=1}^{n_Y} \hat{P}(y_i') \log_2 \hat{P}(y_i')$ can now be used for the discretization of the attributes as described above.

The very fine discretization allows a precise estimation of Y, while its prediction would be limited to a couple of states, if we use a coarse discretization as we would get by applying the method described in Sect. 5.1. Anyhow a coarse discretization is often more effective to capture the essentials of the joint distribution.

5.3 Adopted Parameter Estimation

Working with a continuous variable or rather a discrete one with lots of states Y', also requires a transformed parameter estimation for the graphical model. Using the statistics $n(\cdot)$, would lead to weak maximum likelihood estimates $\hat{\theta}_{X_i|\mathbf{X}_{Pa(i)}}$ whenever $Y' \in \mathbf{X}_{Pa(i)}$, since they are based on only a few observations. Hence, in case of $Y' \in \mathbf{X}_{Pa(i)}$, we rewrite,

$$P(X_i|\mathbf{X}_{Pa(i)}) = \frac{P(X_i, \mathbf{X}_{Pa(i)})}{\sum_{x_i} P(x_i, \mathbf{X}_{Pa(i)})} = \frac{P(Y'|X_i, \mathbf{X}_{Pa(i)-Y'}) P(X_i, \mathbf{X}_{Pa(i)-Y'})}{\sum_{x_i} P(Y'|x_i, \mathbf{X}_{Pa(i)-Y'}) P(x_i, \mathbf{X}_{Pa(i)-Y'})},$$

with $\mathbf{X}_{Pa(i)-Y'} = \mathbf{X}_{Pa(i)} \setminus Y'$. Here $P(Y'|\mathbf{z})$ is again estimated with a kernel density estimator, $\hat{P}_{Y,\mathbf{d_z}}$, based on $\mathbf{d_z}$, which are all records matching $\mathbf{z}$ in $\mathbf{d}$. Thus we get $\hat{P}(y_i'|\mathbf{z}) = \Delta_Y \cdot \hat{P}_{Y,\mathbf{d_z}}(y = y_i')$. The Gaussian kernel of the density estimator is smoothed by multiplying it with a symmetric $n_Y \times n_Y$-weight-matrix. The matrix entries are choosen in order to keep the mean squared error of the target variable prediction small.

6 Application Experiment

We generate $\mathbf{d}$ from the stochastic model [1], with $n = 10.000$ records. The predictor variables are either uniform or exponentially distributed within a particular interval: $M \sim \mathcal{U}_{[5,7.5]}$, $R \sim \mathrm{Exp}_{[1km, 200km]}$, $SD \sim \mathrm{Exp}_{[0bar,300bar]}$, $Q_0 \sim \mathrm{Exp}_{[0s^{-1},5000s^{-1}]}$, $\kappa_0 \sim \mathrm{Exp}_{[0s,0.1s]}$, $V_S30 \sim \mathcal{U}_{[600\,m/s,2800\,m/s]}$ and the PGA is generated by the stochastic model. In the development of the GMs, we use $\ln PGA$ instead of PGA, as we also use $Y = \ln PGA$ in the regression model. The learned GMs are illustrated in Fig. 1.

The BN structure gives insight into the data generating process. We already know, the learned direct independences between the attributes hold (no arcs), due to data construction. However, we observe conditionally induced dependences, which are reflected in the *v-connections*, e.g., $R \rightarrow \ln PGA \leftarrow SD$. The dependency between Q_0 and $\ln PGA$ is weak in our dataset and does not induce a conditional dependency to another co-variate. The influence of V_S30 may be ignored; apparantly this variable is not essential in establishing $\ln PGA$.

An evaluation of the learned models may be done in terms of the performance of the $\ln PGA$ prediction. However, the BN has not been learned to perform well in terms of predicting $\ln PGA$ well; the BN captures the joint of all variables such that the performance is well "overall" for all variables. It is therefore somewhat unfair to judge the BN based just on the performance of one single variable. On the other hand, the TAN only captures the model structure in the sense that it yields the best performance of predicting $\ln PGA$. The performance test in terms of $\ln PGA$ prediction is done

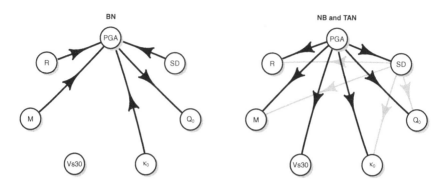

Fig. 1. left: BN learned using MAP scoring metric; right: TAN learned with EAR, where the black edges show the NB and the gray ones the extension to TAN

using a 5-fold cross validation and measured using mean squared errors (MSE); see Table 1.

For the prediction of $\ln PGA$ with the BN, we use the network structure and discretization of the covariates learned by applying the MAP scoring metric and the discretization method described in Sect. 5.1, but we ignore the discretization learned for $\ln PGA$. Instead, to allow a more precise prediction, we discretize $\ln PGA$ into $n_Y = 512$ equidistant intervals, as it is also done for NB and TAN (see Sect. 5.2) and recalculate the parameters of the affected variables as described in Sect. 5.3.

The prediction results of the GMs are quite well compared to the regression, using Eq. 1. There is only one case (4th dataset, BN) in which the GM performs worse than the regression model. In this case the algorithm failed to learn the connection to Q_0. The TAN and NB perform almost the same; the added flexibility of TANs, including the interaction effects of some predictor variables, does not seem to result in improvements in terms of MSE.

Table 1. Mean squared errors of a 5-fold cross validation on a synthetic dataset using 8000 records for learning and a test set of 2000 records

	1.	2.	3.	4.	5.	Avg.
BN	0.569	0.598	0.583	0.759	0.579	0.617
NB	0.488	0.489	0.566	0.592	0.473	0.522
TAN	0.509	0.525	0.566	0.597	0.494	0.538
Regression	0.666	0.679	0.688	0.681	0.650	0.673

7   Conclusion

We presented an alternative to regression models for the construction of surrogates for ground motion models. Three GMs (BN, NB and TAN) were investigated along with schemes for discretization. On average they all perform better than the regression model in terms of predicting $\ln PGA$. Moreover, the entirely data-driven approach of learning the BN enables for a correct interpretation of the (in)dependences between the variables, as opposed to imposed algebraic interaction effects of the regression model. The advantages of GMs can help to tackle typical problems in PSHA. For instance are variables as κ_0 and Q_0 usually unknown and therefore not included in regression models. GMs offer the possibility to work with a distribution function instead of a precise value. This allows to deal with the uncertainty of these parameters in a more accurate way as in done in the general regression approach.

An obvious extension to NBs and TANs is to learn the entire Markov blanket of Y; this approach would yield an unrestricted *Bayesian Network classifier*. Hence, for vertex Y learn the parent set, children set and children's parent sets. Evaluation/model-selection would in that case rely on cross-validation of the predictive performance of Y (no direct scoring metric required).

References

1. Boore, D.M.: Simulation of ground motion using the stochastic method. Pure and Applied Geophysics 160, 635–676 (2003)
2. Castelo, R., Kocka, T.: On inclusion-driven learning of Bayesian networks. The Journal of Machine Learning Research 4, 527–574 (2003)
3. Edwards, D.: Introduction to graphical modelling. Springer (2000)
4. Fayyad, U.M., Irani, K.B.: Multi-interval discretization of continuous-valued attributes for classification learning (1993)
5. Friedman, N., Goldszmidt, M.: Building Classifiers using Bayesian Networks. In: AAAI 1996, pp. 1277–1284 (1996)
6. Friedman, N., Goldszmidt, M.: Discretizing Continuous Attributes While Learning Bayesian Networks. In: Proc. ICML (1996)
7. Kuehn, N., Riggelsen, C., Scherbaum, F.: Facilitating Probabilistic Seismic Hazard Analysis Using Bayesian Networks. In: Seventh Annual Workshop on Bayes Applications (in Conjunction with UAI/COLT/ICML 2009) (2009)
8. Monti, S., Cooper, G.: A multivariate discretization method for learning Bayesian networks from mixed data. In: Uncertainty in Artificial Intelligence (UAI), pp. 404–413 (1998)
9. Pernkopf, F., Bilmes, J.: Discriminative versus generative parameter and structure learning of Bayesian network classifiers. In: Proceedings of the 22nd International Conference on Machine Learning (2005)
10. Riggelsen, C.: Learning Bayesian Networks: A MAP Criterion for Joint Selection of Model Structure and Parameter. In: 2008 Eighth IEEE International Conference on Data Mining, pp. 522–529 (December 2008)
11. Silverman, B.: Density estimation for statistics and data analysis, vol. 26. Chapman & Hall/CRC (1986)

Text Classifiers for Automatic Articles Categorization

Mateusz Westa, Julian Szymański, and Henryk Krawczyk

Department of Computer Systems Architecture,
Faculty of Electronics, Telecommunications and Informatics,
Gdańsk University of Technology, Poland
{mateusz.westa,julian.szymanski,henryk.krawczyk}@eti.pg.gda.pl

Abstract. The article concerns the problem of automatic classification of textual content. We present selected methods for generation of documents representation and we evaluate them in classification tasks. The experiments have been performed on Wikipedia articles classified automatically to their categories made by Wikipedia editors.

Keywords: documents categorization, documents classification, document representation, n-Gram, Ranking Method, Naive Bayes Classifier, k-NN.

1 Introduction

Classification of text collections into specific subject groups is one of the methods for automatic document categorization. The task of assigning a document into a category according to its thematic issues finds many applications eg.: in spam filtering or language identification.

As a text for the computer is only a set of characters without any meaningful (semantic) information it is essential to prepare a content of documents in computationalable form. In this article we focus on the problem of documents representation and their evaluation in classification task.

Creating document representation involves a selection of document features and then associate weights that define their descriptiveness. We describe three methods of documents representation based on: words (terms), n-words (phrases) and n-grams (letters frequency distributions). The representations we evaluate with application in three classifiers: Ranking Method, Naive Bayes and k-Nearest Neighbors. The results of the experiments allow us to select the most suitable representation method.

2 Document Representations

Acquiring from the text features that form documents characteristics requires to perform text preprocessing. This task significantly reduces the dimensionality of features set as well as allows to eliminate a noise. Also it leads to decrease of the classification time as well as learning and test phase. The elimination of unnecessary words and characters also improves classification quality due to the fact that the classifier uses only the most characteristic features (eg. specific vocabulary for a given area of science) rather than those that occur in most documents (eg. common words, stop words or honorifics). Also the words are brought into their basic form with the use of stemmers and lemmatizers.

L. Rutkowski et al. (Eds.): ICAISC 2012, Part II, LNCS 7268, pp. 196–204, 2012.

2.1 Words

The most intuitive method for representation of a document is to use words that appear in it. This approach is simple to implement, but it has some drawbacks. One disadvantage results from the fact that certain words tend to recur in many documents even from a very different thematic areas. This problem becomes even greater for the analysis of short texts, where the probability of common words dominance over words that are characteristic for the document subject is high. In addition, certain words appear in phraseological compounds and analyzed as a single word can significantly change their meaning. This leads to false detection of similarities between the differing thematic documents [8]. Another problem is incorrect spelling and typing errors that may occur in the documents. In conjunction with the occurrence of words in various forms, it may consequently lead to abnormal distribution of frequency characteristics, which easily propagates into decrease of classification quality.

2.2 N-Words

N-word is considered to be n consecutive words. Application of N-word representation solves one problem of words representation. By analyzing interchanging words the context of their occurrence is created, which allows to detect phrases occurring in the text. In this approach it is necessary to determine the value of parameter n determining the length of the frame used to generate n-word chunks. In our experiments we perform a series of tests aiming to find a n value that produces the most accurate classification results.

One of drawbacks is caused by existence of words that may appear in many different phraseological compounds. Therefore, the weight of that word may be underestimated what would negatively affect the accuracy of classification. Situation is even worse because one mistake in the word is propagated to the whole n-word chunk.

2.3 N-Grams

The idea behind n-grams is very similar to the previously described n-words. The method instead of whole words use fixed n-letter chunks [15]. Let's assume that the n-gram is n characters in succession. The approach based on n-grams generation fulfill Zipf law [13], which states as follows:

> *"The n-th most common word in a human language text occurs with a frequency inversely proportional to n."*

It shows that in every language there is a group of words that significantly dominates in the number of occurrence count over other words. As in the case of n-words, during the generation of the representation with n-grams there must be selected an appropriate value for n which allows to generate a representative set of features. Finding the proper n value was a goal of one of our experiments described in section 5.1.

One of the main advantages of n-gram representation is reduction of negative influence of misspellings in the text as well as of different words inflections. This is due to a much smaller propagation of errors only in individual n-grams rather than in the whole word or phrase. Also this method can be applied in rough, no preprocessed text. In addition, the method works well even for short texts due to the generation of large features dictionaries, sufficient to construct good classifiers with them.

2.4 Features Weighting

Once we obtain the features that are to be used to represent document set we need to relate them with documents. As we mentioned before features are not equally important to describe documents. Below we present two main methods that allow to introduce value of the descriptives of the particular feature to a document.

Boolean. Boolean method is the simplest way for weighing features that appear in represented documents. It assigns to representation vectors weight values 0 or 1. These values indicate whether the feature from the dictionary (obtained from a whole document set) occurs in the analyzed document or not.

This weighting type is very fast and efficient in computations. However its ease while applied to words, when it describes whether a given word appears in a document or not, may lead to over-simplifying representation. Thus it may lead to errors in classification process. It is caused mainly by the assumption that a single occurrence of features indicates that the document is closely related to the subject indicated with this feature, which sometimes is false. In addition, a weight value 1 is assigned regardless of the number of occurrence of a feature, which means that features which occur repeatedly in the text are treated identically as the features that appeared in it only once, sometimes even accidentally.

Weighting with Frequency. One of the most popular approaches for determining weights of document features is the usage of the number of their occurrences in the document. This frequency consists of summing up the number of occurrences of all features in the document and creates ranking based on the calculated frequency.

This weighting promotes terms that appear in the document frequently. Application of the TF for the document needs only to analyze its contents, without reference to any other documents in the collection. This guarantees high performance of this approach, even with limited memory size. Relying only on the number of occurrences of features in the document is sometimes sufficient for creating the correct representation of the document, but very often it happens that, despite the multiple use of a feature (eg. a word) in the document, it carries no information about the subject content of the processed text. In extreme cases, because of such features, misclassification may occur.

It should be stressed here it is not the only method, but the most popular one, that is reported to obtain good results. The other ones such as IDF, TF*IDF and BM25 [14] are subjects of our interest and further we plan to investigate their influence on classification task.

Features (terms) and weights w that associate them with the documents allows to represent the collection of the documents as points in feature space called Vector Space Model (VSM) [17]. Document similarity is there easily computed using distance measures such as eg.: cosine or euclidean measures [7].

VSM limitation is the lack of analysis of the order of occurrence of words in the document. Thus this approach is called BOW (**B**ag **of W**ords). The impact of this problem can be reduced by applying the method which binds several features in one - for words such example is the n-word. A much bigger problem is multidimensionality of vectors generated for large text collections. It can cause a large demand for memory and processing time and lead to a very small degree of similarity between vectors.

3 Document Classification

The process of classification of documents consists of calculating distance measures between the document representation and the representations of categories [1]. This measure indicates how likely it is that the document belongs to the category. A final decision is taken based on the thematic proximity created with distance measures. Below we describe three classifiers: Ranking Method, Naive Bayes and k-NN classifier we used for testing representation methods.

3.1 Ranking Method

This is one of the simplest methods of document classification [3]. To represent a class it uses the calculated features weights and creates with them ranking lists, sorted from largest to smallest values indicating their descriptiveness for a class. Features rankings are created for all categories and for documents that are to be classified. The process of classification is based on comparing the distance between document and category. The distance typically is the summation of differences between the occurrences of a given features positions in the rankings of the document and category. Distances calculated in this way are called the *out-of-place* measure and they are sorted in ascending order. The classification decision is the category with the lowest distance. Major advantages of this approach are its simplicity and speed, the drawback – possibly not very good quality of returned results highly dependent on ranking comparing methods.

3.2 k-NN Classifier

Classification using k-Nearest Neighbor (k-NN) [11] is based on the assignment document to a category whose representatives are most numerous among its k nearest neighbors. The proximity of the documents can be determined in various ways, most common is used Euclidean distance. This measure we used in our test presented further. The disadvantages of this method are distortions caused by unbalanced datasets when large groups of object prevail small classes [9]. One of the methods of its improving is working on prototypes that represent original data [4]. The main advantage of k-NN classifier is good accuracy of the results achieved with very simple approach.

3.3 Naive Bayes Classifier

Naive Bayes [5] is a probabilistic approach to classification based on the assumption of the independence of features occurring in documents. This assumption is obviously not true as in language there are many phraseological compounds where strong dependence between consecutive words is found. However, this simplification does not influence significantly the quality of results and allows to obtain good classifications.

For classification of text documents using Bayes classifier it is assumed that the document belongs to one class. Then probabilities of document features w in all categories C are calculated using the formula (1).

$$p(C|w_1, w_2, ...w_n) = log(p(C_i)) + \sum_{j=1}^{n} log(p(w_j|C_i)) \tag{1}$$

The probability $p(C_i)$ is calculated according to the formula (2)

$$p(C_i) = \frac{|C_i|}{\sum_{j=1}^{m} |C_j|} \tag{2}$$

where $|C_i|$ is the number of texts that belong to the class, and m is the number of all classes.

The probability $p(w_j/C)$ is calculated according to the formula (3)

$$p(w_j|C) = \frac{|(w_j, C)| + 1}{|C|} \tag{3}$$

where $|C|$ is the number of texts belonging to the class C and $|(w_j, C)|$ is the number of documents belonging to class C, in which a given feature was found.

The document is classified to the category for which the calculated probability value is the highest among all others. Naive Bayesian classifier is known to has high classification accuracy and good processing speed which is confirmed by a very good test results presented in the [10] [9].

4   Test Data and Evaluation Methodology

Our experiments were performed using data generated from MATRIX'u application. The application allows to prepare Wikipedia content[1] in computationable form. Among many functionalities it allows to select Wikipedia categories that narrow a set of articles and generate for them a set of characteristic features, selected according to chosen text representation method. In experiments presented here we use representations described in section 2, but application allows to use other approaches: based on references between articles, suffix trees and common substrings [6], information content computed by compression [2]. The application is available to download on-line[2] and free for academic use.

Using before mentioned application we generate four *data packages* each representing different aspects of classification within category hierarchies. Each of the data package contains 10 independent *data sets* so aggregated results obtained for each of the data package is more reliable. Each of data sets have been constructed from *300 articles* from Wikipedia that belong to 10 categories. If the category was too small we add articles from its subcategories.

---

[1] http://dumps.wikimedia.org/
[2] http://lab527.eti.pg.gda.pl/CompWiki/

Each of the data packages contains different cases of complexity of classification:

- The first data package contains general categories (from the highest level of the hierarchy structure). This package would show how classifiers are able to distinguish classes that are significantly different.
- The second consists of thematically different categories from second level of category tree structure. It allows to examine whether the distant thematic categories translate into increasing quality of the classification results and evaluate ability to differentiate horizontal similarity of the categories.
- The third and the fourth data packages contain categories linked thematically. The classes have been constructed from the categories belonging to the same one upper category. The third package includes categories connected with biology and the fourth with social sciences. Test cases will show whether category theme puts any impact on classification results.

The aim of constructing the packages in this way was to examine classifiers sensitivity to changing similarity between categories.

To evaluate classification in each dataset we use cross-validation technique and its the most common variation - so-called k-fold validation. Its main objective is to partition the data into test and learn sets, which in subsequent iterations of testing process have to be changed in such way that each element forming part of evaluation at least once belongs to a testing and learning set.

5   Results

Tests were performed on three classifiers: Naive Bayesian Classifier, Ranking Method and k-NN Classifier. The classification accuracy has been evaluated using 10-fold cross-validation. Before we tested classification accuracy we performed experiments aimed at selecting the values of n for the n-word and n-grams representations. Similar experiments have been performed to evaluate values of k for k-NN classifier.

5.1   Selection of Parameter n

To select values of n for which n-word and n-grams representations give the best results we have performed series of classification tests for different n values. In Tables 1 we present results of classification quality. The values are arithmetic means of the results obtained within each of data packages achieved for tested successive values of n. What can be seen from the results the best parameter n for n-words is $n \in <1; 3>$ and for n-grams is $n \in <2; 5>$. We use these values in later experiments.

5.2   Selection k Parameter for k-NN Classifier

For selecting the value of k for which k-NN classifier achieves the best results we perform tests for different values of k and for three different representations. On the basis of the results that are presented in the table 2 we determine the usage $k=3$ gives the best performance.

Table 1. Evaluation of classification performance in the function of parameter n for n-grams and n-words

n value	n-words		n-grams									
	1-2	1-3	2	2-3	2-4	2-5	3	3-4	3-5	4	4-5	5
Package 1	74,42	**74,93**	68,00	43,30	75,42	**78,63**	43,30	75,20	78,53	72,42	78,30	76,85
Package 2	86,43	**86,88**	71,42	57,22	85,92	**88,57**	57,32	85,27	88,25	83,95	87,93	86,97
Package 3	**81,25**	81,12	69,43	56,43	80,55	81,92	56,58	80,68	82,08	79,78	82,08	**82,33**
Package 4	**46,92**	46,72	**60,47**	31,55	47,60	53,83	31,50	47,03	53,33	43,40	52,77	48,77

Table 2. Evaluation of k-NN classification performance in the function of parameter k

k value	1	2	3	4	5	10	15
Words	26,00	38,22	49,63	49,30	50,70	51,20	50,42
N-words <1; 3>	32,23	44,07	52,23	50,63	50,97	52,00	51,83
N-grams <2; 5>	48,17	65,73	**67,53**	65,47	63,23	56,07	48,80

5.3   Results of Classification Quality

The obtained results for classifiers have been shown in Table 3. What can be seen the best results have been achieved by the Naive Bayesian classifier generally regardless of the representation of features. Slightly poorer results got ranking method and k-NN classifier. Another observation is slight decrease (by about 1-3%) of classification quality after using stemming process for creating words features. This may be due to "blurring" distributions of words specific to the document as a result of stemming.

Table 3. Classification quality estimated by 10-fold cross-validation for packages [%]

	Package 1	Package 2	Package 3	Package 4	Average
Ranking Method + Words	76,20	87,17	82,63	47,40	73,35
Ranking Method + Stemmed Words	73,33	85,33	81,47	44,60	71,18
Ranking Method + N-words <1; 3>	76,80	85,73	80,47	45,57	72,14
Ranking Method + N-grams <2; 5>	78,20	**88,57**	81,90	53,37	75,51
Naive Bayes + Words	75,80	87,13	**82,93**	47,03	73,23
Naive Bayes + Stemmed Words	73,70	84,97	82,03	44,83	71,38
Naive Bayes + N-words <1; 3>	73,07	88,03	81,77	47,87	72,68
Naive Bayes + N-grams <2; 5>	**79,07**	**88,57**	81,93	**54,30**	**75,97**
k-NN + Words	51,97	76,40	70,23	47,23	61,46
k-NN + Stemmed Words	47,30	70,93	68,83	43,23	57,58
k-NN + N-words <1; 3>	52,23	76,03	69,57	46,40	61,06
k-NN + N-grams <2; 5>	67,53	74,47	62,03	49,07	63,28

Results confirmed the expected high classification accuracy for the second data package. This package includes categories that are significantly different from each other because they belong to distant thematic areas. Evident is also increasing difficulty of correct classifications for the categories of similar topics that were included in the package 3 and the package 4.

The table 3 shows the average global values of classification quality (for all data packages) achieved using particular representations. It can be seen that the best classification results were obtained by the Naive Bayesian method using N-grams <2; 5>. Slightly weaker results were obtained for the Naive Bayesian Classifier combinated with Words and Ranking Method with N-grams. The weakest classifier, regardless the method of representation of features, has proved to be a 3-NN classifier.

6   Discussion and Future Work

As a result of our evaluation three classifiers have been implemented as web services on KASKADA platform[3]. Services are used now as a part of anty-plagiarism system run on GALERA[4] – one of the most powerful super–computers in Central Europe. The text classification is used here in initial stage to narrow the number of necessary comparisons and use only to the articles that fall into the same category.

The obtained results show that the use of n-gram representation leads to achieve better classification results than using other types (word, n-word). Additionally it was observed that the processes of stemming or lematization has no positive effect on results of the classification of documents.

The processing time of the collections of the data is considerable. Now we perform classifications of documents into 2000 categories. Effective computation on such a large data collections requires the reduction of representations space. We plan to apply the mentioned earlier PCA method for dimension reduction but effective calculation of eigenvectors and eigenvalues for spaces over 20.000 dimensions requires parallelization of computations. We are now in the initial stage of implementation and in a few months we plan to extend our approach to classification with filtering based on dimensionality reduction.

Another idea to improvement of text representations is to introduce more background knowledge and capture some semantics. Our approach is to map words into network of senses. In our case we use Wordnet synsets [12]. First results of creating representations based on synsets are promising – for now we achieved 65% of succesfoul desambiguations [16].

Proposed in the article simple classifiers are used as initial (rough) classifiers in KASKADA platform. We plan to implement the second layer with more complex and computionally expensive SVM approach. As it is very effective binary classifier, and introducing multi-label and multi-class classifications require use of additional tricks that make it suitable only for narrowed domain of a few classes.

The presented approach for Wikipedia articles representation is a basis for our long term goal in SYNAT project. We plan here to build large scale text classifier which using Wikipedia Categories will be able to categorize web search results.

Acknowledgment. This work has been supported by the National Center for Research and Development (NCBiR) under research Grant No. SP/I/1/77065/1 SYNAT:

---

[3] http://mayday-dev.task.gda.pl:48080/mayday.uc/
[4] http://www.task.gda.pl/kdm/sprzet/Galera

"Establishment of the universal, open, hosting and communication, repository platform for network resources of knowledge to be used by science, education and open knowledge society".

References

1. Aas, K., Eikvil, L.: Text Categorisation: A Survey. Raport NR 941 (1999)
2. Bennett, C., Li, M., Ma, B.: Chain Letters and Evolutionary Histories. Scientific American 288(6), 76–81 (2003)
3. Cavnar, W.B., Trenkle, J.M.: N-Gram-Based Text Categorization
4. Duch, W., Blachnik, M., Wieczorek, T.: Probabilistic Distance Measures for Prototype-Based Rules (in polish). In: Proc. of the 12 International Conference on Neural Information Processing, ICONIP, Citeseer, pp. 445–450 (2005)
5. Eyheramendy, S., Lewis, D., Madigan, D.: On the Naive Bayes Model for Text Categorization (2003)
6. Grossi, R., Vitter, J.: Compressed Suffix Arrays and Suffix Trees with Applications to Text Indexing and String Matching. In: Proceedings of the Thirty-Second Annual ACM Symposium on Theory of Computing, pp. 397–406. ACM (2000)
7. Korenius, T., Laurikkala, J., Juhola, M.: On Principal Component Analysis, Cosine and Euclidean Measures in Information Retrieval (in polish). Information Sciences 177(22), 4893–4905 (2007)
8. Kosmulski, M.: Representation of Text Documents in The Vector Space Model (in polish), 14–25, 34–41 (2005)
9. Łazewski, Ł., Pikuła, M., Siemion, A., Szklarzewski, M., Pindelski, S.: The Classification of Text Documents (in polish), 17–26, 62–66
10. Leahy, P.: n-Gram-Based Text Attribution
11. Li, Y., Jain, A.: Classification of Text Documents. The Computer Journal 41(8), 537 (1998)
12. Miller, G.A., Beckitch, R., Fellbaum, C., Gross, D., Miller, K.: Introduction to WordNet: An On-line Lexical Database. Cognitive Science Laboratory. Princeton University Press (1993)
13. Newman, M.: Power laws, Pareto Distributions and Zipf's Law. Arxiv Preprint cond-mat/0412004 (2004)
14. Robertson, S., Zaragoza, H., Taylor, M.: Simple BM25 Extension to Multiple Weighted Fields. In: Proceedings of the Thirteenth ACM International Conference on Information and Knowledge Management, pp. 42–49. ACM (2004)
15. Steffen, J.: N-gram Language Modeling for Robust Multi-Lingual Document Classification. In: The 4th International Conference on Language Resources and Evaluation (LREC 2004). German Research Center for Artificial Intelligence (2004)
16. Szymański, J., Mizgier, A., Szopiński, M., Lubomski, P.: Disambiguation Words Meaning Using WordNet Dictionary (in polish). Scientific Publishers PG TI 2008 18, 89–195 (2008)
17. Wong, S.K.M., Ziarko, W., Wong, P.N.: Generalized Vector Spaces Model in Information Retrieval. In: SIGIR 1985, pp. 18–25. ACM Press, New York (1985)

Part II

Hardware Implementation

Structure Searching for Adaptive Spring Networks for Shape Programming in 3D

Maja Czoków and Tomasz Schreiber*

Faculty of Mathematics and Computer Science,
Nicolaus Copernicus University,
Toruń, Poland
maja@mat.umk.pl

Abstract. In this paper we propose a heuristic algorithm for construction an optimal spring network architecture aimed at obtaining desired mechanical behaviour in response to physical input (control) stimuli. The part of the algorithm that searches for a network structure is based on random graph walks. To ensure desired mechanical behaviour of the graph, physical parameters of the spring network are adjusted by an appropriate gradient descent learning algorithm. In addition, we discuss numerical results of the network search procedure.

1 Introduction

Design processes in engineering are commonly supported by computers, which make their cycles faster, more accurate and less expensive. For example software implementations of the spring systems are widely used for modelling large scale elastic properties of physical systems [5,8], disordered media in material sciences [6,11], self-organisation and system design in material and architectural sciences [7,9] and in many other contexts.

In this paper we propose a stochastic algorithm for searching an optimal spring network architecture for given physical input and output displacements. We also present numerical analysis, concerning dependence between architecture resources and its efficiency. These results enable us to select proper resources in order to construct relatively small networks, capable of producing expected physical behaviour. Structure simplicity is important in the context of increasing revenue of production of a real-world objects, devices etc.

In our previous work [4] we advocated use of complex spring networks as adaptive systems for *shape programming*. Note that, the algorithm described in [4] uses assigned system structure, quite the opposite in this paper we present structure searching procedure for given input – output relations. The principal task for such systems, embedded in a physical space $\mathbb{R}^2$, is to assume a

---

* An Associate Professor at Faculty of Mathematics and Computer Science, NCU, a bright young scientist carrying researches in mathematics, computer science and physics, prematurely died in December 2010.

L. Rutkowski et al. (Eds.): ICAISC 2012, Part II, LNCS 7268, pp. 207–215, 2012.

required shape (physical locations of network nodes, regarded as output) in response to suitable physical stimuli (displacements of control nodes, regarded as input). In our previous work we also showed how such systems can be implemented and, most importantly, we developed a suitable learning algorithm, of a gradient-descent type, where the physical spring parameters (rest length, elastic constants) are iteratively adjusted to accomplish the shape programming task specified by a collection of training examples. While, in [4] emphasis was laid on $\mathbb{R}^2$, the extension to $\mathbb{R}^3$ is natural and effectuated in our model/application. To the best of our knowledge our work [4], was the first one to propose the use of adaptive spring systems as learning mechanical devices capable of assuming desired relation between input and output nodes.

The work is organised as follows: in Sect. 2 we briefly reiterate the formal model of the spring system and its dynamics described in [4]. The stochastic algorithm for generating an optimal spring network architecture for shape control problems is shown in Sect. 3. Results analysis is provided in Sect. 4. Finally, we give concluding remarks in Sect. 5.

2   Formal Definition of the Spring System

Formally, we represent a spring system as an undirected rigid [10] graph $\mathcal{G} := (\mathcal{V}, \mathcal{E})$ with vertex/node set $\mathcal{V} \subset \mathbb{R}^3$ partitioned into

- Set $\mathcal{V}_{\text{in}}$ of control nodes. These are nodes, whose position is determined by external intervention, such as user interaction and thus is regarded as system's *input*.
- Set $\mathcal{V}_{\text{out}}$ of observed nodes, whose positions are regarded as system's *output*.
- Set $\mathcal{V}_{\text{fixed}}$ of immobilised nodes, whose positions are kept fixed in the course of system's evolution.
- The remaining set $\mathcal{V}_*$ of auxiliary movable nodes, usually constituting the vast majority of system's vertices.

The coordinates of a vertex $v \in \mathcal{V}$ are denoted by $(x_v^{(1)}, x_v^{(2)}, x_v^{(3)})$. $\mathcal{E}$ is edge/spring set. With each edge $e = \{u, v\} \in \mathcal{E}$, $u, v \in \mathcal{V}$ we associate its equilibrium (rest) length $\ell_0[e]$ and we write $\ell[e]$ for its actual length (the Euclidean distance between vertices u and v). Moreover, the spring constant $k[e] \geq 0$ is ascribed to each edge $e \in \mathcal{E}$, determining the elastic properties of the spring represented by the edge e. The energy (Hamiltonian) of a spring system configuration $\bar{x}_{\mathcal{V}} := ((x_v^{(1)}, x_v^{(2)}, x_v^{(3)})_{v \in \mathcal{V}})$ is given by the usual formula [3]

$$\mathcal{H}(\bar{x}_{\mathcal{V}}) := \frac{1}{2} \sum_{e \in \mathcal{E}} k[e] \left(\ell[e] - \ell_0[e]\right)^2 . \tag{1}$$

The system configuration $\bar{x}_{\mathcal{V}}$ is said to be a *ground state (equilibrium point)* if $\mathcal{H}$ has a global minimum in $\bar{x}_{\mathcal{V}}$. To determine the equilibrium of the spring system (1) we can move nodes belonging to the sets $\mathcal{V}_{\text{out}}$ and $\mathcal{V}_*$ only [4]. We usually require that the set of control nodes be rich enough to uniquely determine the equilibrium $G[\bar{x}_\mathcal{V}]$, which allows us to write $G[\bar{x}_\mathcal{V}] = G[\bar{x}_{\mathcal{V}_{in}}]$, see ibidem.

Let as recall the basic notions of spring system shape learning problem with fixed system structure. We are given spring system graph $\mathcal{G} := (\mathcal{V}, \mathcal{E})$ where the sets $\mathcal{V}$ and $\mathcal{E}$ are predefined. In addition, we are given a set $(E^{(i)})_{i=1}^N$ of *training examples*, each example $E^{(i)} := (\bar{y}_{\mathcal{V}_{in}}^{(i)}, \bar{y}_{\mathcal{V}_{out}}^{(i)})$ consisting of

1. input part $\bar{y}_{\mathcal{V}_{in}}^{(i)}$ specifying the locations of input nodes,
2. and output part $\bar{y}_{\mathcal{V}_{out}}^{(i)}$ specifying the desired locations of output nodes.

The shape learning problem with a fixed structure $\mathcal{G} = (\mathcal{V}, \mathcal{E})$ is to find parameters $k[e]$ and $\ell_0[e]$, $e \in \mathcal{E}$ so that the positions $\bar{x}_{\mathcal{V}_{out}}[G[\bar{y}_{\mathcal{V}_{in}}^{(i)}]]$ of output vertices in equilibrium $G[\bar{y}_{\mathcal{V}_{in}}^{(i)}]$, reached upon setting $\bar{x}_{\mathcal{V}_{in}} := \bar{y}_{\mathcal{V}_{in}}^{(i)}$, are as close as possible to the desired output locations part $\bar{y}_{\mathcal{V}_{out}}^{(i)}$. In order to evaluate a quality of the solution we adapt a mean squared error function $\Phi^{(i)}$ for each training $E^{(i)}$ example. The learning algorithm of adaptation of the parameters $k[e]$ and $\ell_0[e]$ was put forward and discussed in our previous work [4].

A foregone conclusion pointed out in [4] and the main focus of this work is to extend the learning problem to more general case when a structure of the spring network is not known. Formally, we are given only the training examples $E^{(i)} = (\bar{y}_{\mathcal{V}_{in}}^{(i)}, \bar{y}_{\mathcal{V}_{out}}^{(i)})$, however the structure of the network $\mathcal{G} = (\mathcal{V}, \mathcal{E})$ is no longer provided. Instead, finding of the structural graph $\mathcal{G}$ along with spring elastic constants $k[e]$ and spring rest lengths $\ell_0[e]$ is our explicit target. The set of input nodes $\mathcal{V}_{in}$ and observed nodes $\mathcal{V}_{out}$ are predefined by the set of the training examples $(E^{(i)})_i^N$. The goal is to find set of auxiliary nodes $\mathcal{V}_*$, fixed nodes $\mathcal{V}_{fixed}$ and set of edges $\mathcal{E}$, for which parameters adjusting will achieve low error

$$\Phi = \sum_i^N \Phi^{(i)} := \sum_i^N \sum_{v \in \mathcal{V}_{out}} \text{dist}\left(y_v^{(i)}, x_v\left[G\left[\bar{y}_{\mathcal{V}_{in}}^{(i)}\right]\right]\right)^2 . \tag{2}$$

Since the system is embedded in euclidean space $\mathbb{R}^3$, the distances are unitless (dimensionless) and so is the error function. Of course, if there is requirement to relate our spring systems to real-world objects, any appropriate physical metric system can be used.

3   Structure Searching for a Set of Training Examples

In this section we propose the algorithm for generating an optimal spring network architecture for shape control problems formulated earlier.

As mentioned above $\mathcal{G} := (\mathcal{V}, \mathcal{E})$ is rigid, it means that there exists a minimally rigid subgraph $\mathcal{G}' := (\mathcal{V}, \mathcal{E}') \subseteq \mathcal{G}$. Since $\mathcal{G}'$ is minimally rigid, there holds $|\mathcal{E}'| = 3|\mathcal{V}| - 6$ (removing an edge yields losing rigidity by graph), for more details see [1] and [2]. Our algorithm is based on the Henneberg construction method, which is an inductive approach that creates minimally rigid graph in d (in our case 3) dimensional space. This inductive construction starts from the complete graph with 4 nodes K_4 at the first step and then it adds a new node with 3 edges to the existing graph, for more details see [1]. One must keep in mind, that 3 noncollinear *immobilised* nodes are required to prevent the system from rotating, translating or combining of them. The greater number of *immobilised* nodes in the system is the less edges are required to obtain a rigid graph. For simplification it is not taken into account in our algorithm, since additional edges and fixed points can enhance system's stability.

The generation of the graph is performed on the set of the training examples $(E^{(i)})_{i=1}^N$ according to the following scheme:

1. Find the mean value m of all input and output locations specified in $(E^{(i)})_{i=1}^N$

$$
m := \frac{1}{N\left(|\mathcal{V}_{\text{in}}| + |\mathcal{V}_{\text{out}}|\right)} \sum_{i=1}^N \left(\sum_{v \in \mathcal{V}_{\text{in}}} y_v^{(i)} + \sum_{v \in \mathcal{V}_{\text{out}}} y_v^{(i)} \right) . \tag{3}
$$

2. Randomly pick 4 different nodes uniformly distributed in the ball centred at the point m, and with the diameter equals to maximal distance between point m and any location described in $(E^{(i)})_{i=1}^N$.
3. Add the random nodes to the set $\mathcal{V}_*$, link each pair of these nodes with an edge.
4. Add *aux_const* subsequent graph nodes to the set $\mathcal{V}_*$ always requiring that the new node is connect to *edge_const* ≥ 3 already existing ones.
5. Fix *fixed_const* nodes; as a result of this operation *fixed_const* nodes are moved from the set $\mathcal{V}_*$ to the set $\mathcal{V}_{\text{fixed}}$.
6. Sequentially add input nodes to the set $\mathcal{V}_{\text{in}}$. The number of this nodes is determined by the set of training example. Each new node is connected to *edge_const* ≥ 3 already existing ones belonging to the set $\mathcal{V}_*$ and the respective location specified in $\bar{y}_{\mathcal{V}_{\text{in}}}^{(1)}$ is ascribed to it. In order to eliminate the rigid motions of the graph $\mathcal{G}$ it has to be satisfied *fixed_const* $+ |\mathcal{V}_{\text{in}}| \geq 3$.
7. Sequentially add output nodes to the set $\mathcal{V}_{\text{out}}$. The number of this nodes is determined by the set of training example. Each new node is connected to *edge_const* ≥ 3 already existing ones belonging to the set $\mathcal{V}_* \cup \mathcal{V}_{\text{in}}$ and the respective location specified in $\bar{y}_{\mathcal{V}_{\text{out}}}^{(1)}$ is ascribed to it.
8. Perform the adaptation of parameters $k[e]$, $\ell_0[e]$, $e \in \mathcal{E}$ according to the gradient descent algorithm in order to minimise the value of the error function Φ.
9. Return the obtained structure.

It is advisable to reiterate the algorithm many times and pick the spring system structure with the lowest error Φ. This seems reasonable due to the stochastic dynamics of the points 2–7 of the algorithm.

When adding a new node, each of existing vertices has the same chance to be connected with it. There can also be other method of choosing neighbours of the new node, for example the new node can be connected to the nearest.

One must however note, that this can bring about instabilities when used on examples whose inputs are non-uniformly distributed. It is clear, that for more complicated tasks the algorithm has to use more resources (edges, nodes) and consistently in order to obtain proper stability more nodes have to be fixed.

It is worth emphasising, that both input and output nodes are added to the graph at the end phase of the building scheme. This maximises probability that they have distinct neighbours.

4   Implementation and Example Applications

The learning algorithm for spring systems as introduced in Sect. 3 has been implemented in the programming language D [12]. In this section we present numerical results returned by our software implementation.

For visualisation purposes we consider a system with three training examples $(E^{(i)})_{i=1}^{3}$ as depicted in Fig. 1. In our implementation springs are visualised by lines, when its actual length is equal to ℓ_0 it has grey colour, during stretching its colour is gradually becoming lighter, in turn during compression its colour is gradually becoming darker. Nodes, which can be moved to determine the equilibrium of the spring system (auxiliary nodes $v \in \mathcal{V}_*$ and output nodes $v \in \mathcal{V}_{\text{out}}$) are plotted in grey. Additionally, from each output node comes out grey dotted line ended with arrow, which points out respective location specified by output part for current example. Nodes, which can not be moved to determine the equilibrium of the spring system (fixed nodes $v \in \mathcal{V}_{fixed}$ and input nodes $v \in \mathcal{V}_{\text{in}}$) are plotted in black. Additionally, from each input node comes out black dotted line ended with arrow, which points out respective location specified by input part for current example.

In Fig. 1 we present the system in a pre-learning state and after the learning process in its respective equilibria $(G[\bar{y}_{\mathcal{V}_{\text{in}}}^{(i)}])_{i=1}^{3}$. This system possesses 3 input nodes and 3 output nodes. The structure of the network (the remaining nodes and edges) was generated by our constructing algorithm.

We tested our structure searching algorithm on a system with three training examples $(E^{(i)})_{i=1}^{3}$ as described above. During the constructing phase 2 nodes are frozen. For this example initial error is of the order $\Phi = 10^4$. For each pair $(|\mathcal{V}|, edge\_const)$ the structure generating algorithm is run 31 times and first obtained architecture is returned. Figures 2 and 3 present plots of the resulting solution error Φ vs number of auxiliary vertices $|\mathcal{V}_*|$ for various parameters $edge\_const$. Fig. 2 for 1 and Fig. 3 for the mean value of 5 lowest errors Φ obtained for each pair $(|\mathcal{V}|, edge\_const)$ in 31 independent simulations. The values of error for the remaining results are not taken into account, because they can be extremely large and obscure substantial information. This anomalies are caused by sticking in large value local minimum (with high potential barriers impassable for algorithm dynamics) of error function portrait by the algorithm during adjusting parameters ℓ_0 and k. Tests imply that number of auxiliary nodes $\mathcal{V}_*$ has low impact on learning capability of system, at least for small number of input/output nodes. Additionally, only for larger values of parameter $edge\_const$

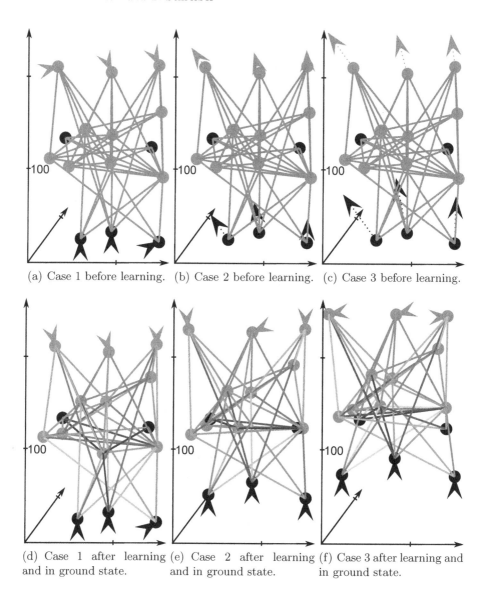

(a) Case 1 before learning. (b) Case 2 before learning. (c) Case 3 before learning.

(d) Case 1 after learning and in ground state. (e) Case 2 after learning and in ground state. (f) Case 3 after learning and in ground state.

Fig. 1. Training example $E^{(3)}$ before learning (in the upper row) and respective example after learning in equilibria $G[\bar{y}_{\mathcal{V}_{in}}^{(3)}]$ (in the bottom row)

and to some extent increasing $|\mathcal{V}_*|$ enhances learning capability of system. Instead, the value of the parameter $edge\_const$ (proportional to average degree of nodes belonging to $\mathcal{V}$) has a large impact on error Φ of returned solution. As it can be seen in Fig. 2, an increase of value of the parameter $edge\_const$ from 3 to 5 significantly improves learning ability of constructed systems. For $edge\_const = 5$ and $edge\_const = 6$ obtained structures learn in the similar way, therefore, average degree of node, which improves a learning ability, is saturated

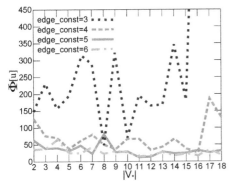

Fig. 2. A plot of error Φ vs number of auxiliary vertices $|\mathcal{V}_*|$, for various parameters *edge_const* for best result in 31 independent simulations

Fig. 3. A plot of error Φ vs number of auxiliary vertices $|\mathcal{V}_*|$, for various parameters *edge_const* for mean value of 5 best results in 31 independent simulations

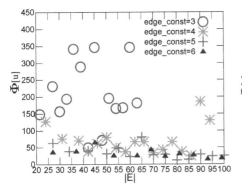

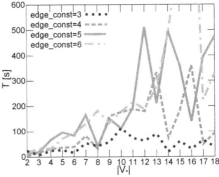

Fig. 4. A plot of error vs number of edges $|\mathcal{E}|$, for various parameters *edge_const* for best result in 31 independent simulations

Fig. 5. A plot of executing time vs number of auxiliary vertices $|\mathcal{V}_*|$, for various parameters *edge_const* for best result in 31 independent simulations

for *edge_const* = 5. It is worth emphasising that for two systems with similar number of edges the one with higher parameter *edge_const* (consequently with lower number of auxiliary nodes) yields significantly lower values of error Φ, which can be seen in Fig. 4. The time necessary to yield the error, depicted in Fig. 2, by respective network is presented in Fig. 5. The computer architecture used to make all tests was Intel Core Duo (clock speed 2 GHz) and 4 GB RAM. Clearly the more resources (auxiliary nodes and edges) the network has, the longer it takes to learn it according to algorithm described in Sect. 3 in [4].

5   Conclusions

In this paper we have proposed the algorithm searching an optimal structure for learning 3D extension shape-control tasks described in [4]. We have also presented numerical analysis showing dependence between value of algorithm parameters ($|\mathcal{V}_*|$, $edge\_const$) and it efficacy. The most interesting remark is that sequential increasing parameter $edge\_const$ up to 5 significantly improves the ability of finding network, able to learn given learning example at the expense of the learning time. Also, it would be interesting to look at the portrait energy in dependence on other more elaborated graph statistics such as average connectivity, degree distribution etc. The applications of the algorithms studying defects in different materials are subject of our ongoing work. The constructing algorithm presented in this work can be developed in different directions according to defined particular materials or scientific problem. We also plan to use the architecture, found by the constructing algorithm, to search network for much more complicated shape-programming problems by bottom-up oriented structure searching algorithm. This approach is justified by our other tests.

References

1. Anderson, B.D.O., Belhumeur, P.N., Morse, A.S., Eren, T.: A Framework for Maintaining Formations Based on Rigidity. In: Proc. of the IFAC World Congress, Barcelona, Spain (2002)
2. Anderson, B.D.O., Fidan, B., Hendrickx, J.M., Yu, C.: Rigidity and Persistence for Ensuring Shape Maintenance of Multiagent Meta Formations. Asian Journal of Control (Special Issue on Collective Behavior and Control of Multi-Agent Systems) 10(2), 131–143 (2008)
3. Connelly, R.: Rigidity and energy. Inventiones Mathematicae 66, 11–33 (1982)
4. Czoków, M., Schreiber, T.: Adaptive Spring Systems for Shape Programming. In: Rutkowski, L., Scherer, R., Tadeusiewicz, R., Zadeh, L.A., Zurada, J.M. (eds.) ICAISC 2010, Part II. LNCS (LNAI), vol. 6114, pp. 420–427. Springer, Heidelberg (2010)
5. Gusev, A.A.: Finite Element Mapping for Spring Network Representations of the Mechanics of Solids. Phys. Rev. Lett. 93, 034302 (2004)
6. Jagota, A., Bennison, S.J.: Spring–Network and Finite–Element Models for Elasticity and Fracture. In: Bardhan, K.K., Chakrabarti, B.K., Hansen, A. (eds.) Proceedings of a Workshop on Breakdown and Non-Linearity in Soft Condensed Matter, Saha Institute for Nuclear Physics, Calcutta, India, December 1-9, 1993. Spring-Verlag Lecture Notes in Physics, vol. 437, pp. 186–201. Springer, Heidelberg (1994)
7. Kanellos, A.: Topological Self-Organisation: Using a particle-spring system simulation to generate structural space-filling lattices. Masters thesis, UCL (University College London) (2007)
8. Kellomäki, M., Aström, J., Timonen, J.: Rigidity and Dynamics of Random Spring Networks. Phys. Rev. Lett. 77, 2730 (1996)
9. Kilian, A., Ochsendorf, J.: Particle–Spring Systems for Structural Form Finding. Journal of the International Association for Shell and Spatial Structures: IASS 46 (2005)

10. Olfati-Saber, R., Murray, R.M.: Graph Rigidity and Distributed Formation Stabilization of Multi-Vehicle Systems. In: Proc. of the 41st IEEE Conf. on Decision and Control, Las Vegas, Nevada (2002)
11. Ostoja–Starzewski, M.: Lattice Models in Micromechanics. Appl. Mech. Rev. 55, 35–60 (2002)
12. http://digitalmars.com/d/

Implementation of Fuzzy Logic Controller in FPGA Circuit for Guiding Electric Wheelchair

Marek Poplawski and Michal Bialko

Department of Electronics and Computer Science,
Koszalin University of Technology, Sniadeckich 2 Street,
75-453 Koszalin, Poland
{marpop,mibia}@ie.tu.koszalin.pl

Abstract. This paper describes an implementation of fuzzy logic control system for guiding a wheelchair. For this purpose, a dedicated architecture of fuzzy logic controller was elaborated in FPGA circuit. Input and output linguistic variables and corresponding fuzzy sets were defined and based on those, a fuzzy rule address was formed. The proposed fuzzy system drives two permanent magnet DC motors of the wheelchair.

1 Introduction

An objective of this work is a presentation of practical implementation of a digital fuzzy logic controller, for electric steering of the wheelchair for unable persons [1,2,3]. For this purpose, a dedicated architecture of the fuzzy logic controller was elaborated [4]. The electric wheelchair is driven by two permanent magnet DC motors M0 and M1 (fig.1), which are supplied from battery [5]. Steering of the wheelchair is based on differential control of electric motors driving rear wheels of the wheelchair, allowing driving the wheelchair in left/ right and onward/ back directions. The task of the fuzzy system (fig. 1) is a generation of output signals (y0,y1), which are driving electric motors (M0,M1) based on input signals (left/ right - l/r, front/ back - f/b), created by joystick JOY manipulated by the wheelchair operator; additionally a feedback signal (Δv) is used to cancel a difference of rotations of electric motors, while driving straight on [6,7].

The knowledge, based on which the steering signals are generated is included in rules and terms of linguistic variables, written down in the memory of the fuzzy system [8]. The proposed fuzzy system is based on classical Mamdani model in which one can distinguish the blocks: fuzzification, inference and defuzzification. In hardware realization of fuzzy systems only 2^n rules from L^n rules existing in the rule base are activated (where L - number of input fuzzy sets, n - number of input linguistic variables) [9,10]. An aplication of techniques of addressing in fuzzy systems allows to process only active rules; also, elimination of verification the activation degree of all fuzzy rules allows to accelerate inference process [11,12]. In the proposed system a techniques of addressing is applied, and is implemented in FPGA hardware [13].

L. Rutkowski et al. (Eds.): ICAISC 2012, Part II, LNCS 7268, pp. 216–222, 2012.

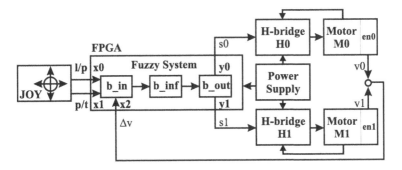

Fig. 1. General block diagram of fuzzy logic system for guiding a wheelchair

2   Propossed Fuzzy Logic System

The digital fuzzy system assigned for steering electric wheelchair was simulated and realized in FPGA circuit Spartan III XC3S1000 [14]. This system has 3 independent inputs and 2 outputs, and is composed of 3 internal blocks: fuzzification (b_in), inference (b_inf) and defuzzification (b_out). The terms of input linguistic variables (fig. 2 and 3a) are described by 256 samples, with 8 bit resolution. The distribution and shapes of fuzzy sets (fig. 2 and 3a) allow to activate one or two fuzzy rules for one discrete (sharp) value of the input variable. The source of steering signal of the system is a joystick JOY (fig. 2). The deflection of the joystick are directly proportional to the value of signal l/r (or f/b). The neutral state of the joystick correspond to 2,5[V] and is coded as a state "ZE".

Utilization of the feedback signal Δv, proportional to the difference of wheel rotations allows to correct the wheel speed during driving straight on, what increases the quality of steering of the wheelchair. The signal of the wheel speed difference - Δv marked as the input linguistic variable x2 is supplied to the input of fuzzy system. The fuzzy terms of x2= Δv are shown in figure 3a.

In proposed system the control of driving motor speed is based on pulse width modulation (PWM) [15]; the value of aspect ratio of modulated signal is determined by defuzzificated output values (y0,y1). The output variables are

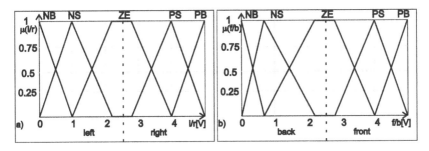

Fig. 2. Fuzzy-sets of the input linguistic variable a) l/r and b) f/b (N- negativ, ZE - zero, P - positiv, B - big, S - small)

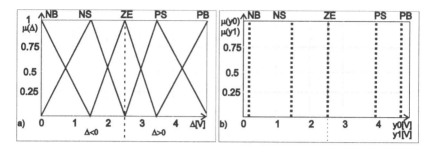

Fig. 3. Terms of linguistic variables a) input value x2 corresponding to error signal Δv, b) output values y0,y1 corresponding to rotation speed of driving motors (N- negativ, ZE - zero, P - positiv, B - big, S - small)

represented by five singletons (fig. 3b). A fuzzy rule base was created based on relations between input and output variables, which was written in the system's memory as a look-up table. A single pair of rules (Ra,Rb) controling two electric motors consists of three simple premises connected by conjunction operator AND, and has the form.

$$Ra := If\ x0 = A0\ AND\ x1 = A1\ AND\ x2 = A2\ then\ Y0 = B0 \qquad (1)$$

$$Rb := If\ x0 = A0\ AND\ x1 = A1\ AND\ x2 = A2\ then\ Y1 = B1 \qquad (2)$$

where: x0,x1,x2 - input linguistic variable, which corresponding to input signals: p/t, l/p, Δv; A0,A1,A2 - terms of linguistic variable xi (i=0,1,2);y0,y1 - output linguistic variable, which corresponding to output signals p0 and p1, B0,B1 - terms of linguistic variable yi (i =0,1).

A possible number of rules describing this system equals to $2 * 5^3 = 250$ rules or 125 pair of rules, but only $2 * 8$ are activated for each inference process. A part of the rule table board, corresponding to output signals y0,y1 driving motors M0/M1, is presented in Tab. 1 (assuming that input value of linguistic variable x2, Δv = "ZE"). At sides of the rule table the increases of values of input linguistic variables are shown (neutral value marked as the zero ZE), and in the interior of the table output steering signals y0/y1 for motors M0/M1 are given.

In the proposed fuzzy system the fuzzification process is performed by reading out the values of membership function of activated sets and also codes of

Table 1. The part of the look-up rule table of the fuzzy system for signal Δ v = "ZE" (N- negativ, ZE - zero, P - positiv, B - big, S - small)

f-b	l-r	Negativ right		Zero	Positiv right	
		NB	NS	ZE	PS	PB
Positiv	PB	NS/PB	NS/PB	PB/PB	PB/PB	PB/PB
front	PS	NS/PB	ZE/PB	PS/PS	PB/ZE	PB/PB
Zero	ZE	ZE/PB	ZE/PS	ZE/ZE	PS/ZE	PB/ZE
Negativ	NS	ZE/ NB	ZE/NS	NS/NS	NS/ZE	NS/ZE
back	NB	ZE/NB	ZE/NS	NB/NB	ZE/NS	NB/ZE

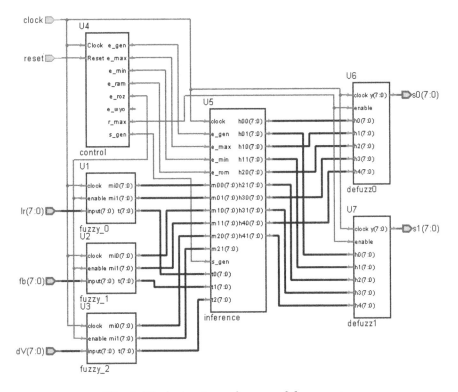

Fig. 4. Block structure of proposed fuzzy system

theses sets from system's memory. The input block (b_in) is divided into three independent fuzzy channels composed of blocks "fuzzy_x" (where x=0,1,2), as is shown in Fig. 4. An appearance of the high state on the input "enable" of fuzzy_x blocks begins the fuzzification process. A sharp value of the input signal "input(7:0)" indicates the address of memory, which corresponds to the appropriate discreet sample of the point of the rule activation stored in the memory of the block "fuzzy_x". This discreet sample contains two 8-bit values of the points of the rule activation ($\check{I}0$, $\check{I}1$) and two 3 - bit codes of fuzzy sets (T0,T1). In the memory of the block "fuzzy_x" altogether 256 of such samples describing the input linguistic variables are stored. Reading a 3 - byte values of the samples $\mu1$, $\mu2$,T from the memory and transferring them to the output mi0, mi1 and t of the block "fuzzy_x" finishes operations of fuzzyfication. Next, these data are transferred to the inference block (b_inf).

The inference block shown in fig. 5 was realized in five types of architecture such as: a) serial inference - fig. 5a, b) serial inference with technique of addressing mode - fig. 5b, c) serial inference with pipelining and with technique of addressing mode fig. 5c, d) two channel serial inference with pipelining and with technique of addressing mode - fig. 5d, e) parallel inference with technique of addressing mode - fig. 5e. Proposed architectures allow to limit the speed of fuzzy inference processing.

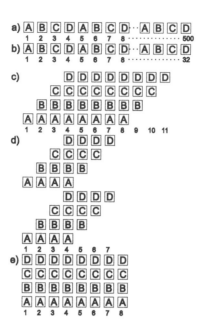

Fig. 5. Collection of the proposed inference architectures, example for system with 2^n inputs, where n=3, A - generation of address, B - reading fuzzy rule from memory, C- MIN operation, D - MAX operation

A high state of the steering line "e_gen" coming from the block "control" begins the inference process; the 3 - bit codes of active fuzzy sets are introduced through 8-bit inputs, in the range tx(2:0) and tx(6:4) (where x=0,1,2) and corresponding to them values of membership functions through inputs mix0, mix1 (where x=0,1,2) are also introduced. The task of the block "inference" is appropriate connection of values Ĩ1, Ĩ2 and T to the outputs of the subblock "memory" of block "inference" based on individual 3 - bit code with weights b2,b1,b0 written in the memory. These weights corresponded to input linguistic variables x2,x1,x0; in particular the value of the weight '0' corresponds to connection of the value '0' and the T0 code, and '1' corresponds to connection of the value '1' and the T1 code. Based on the values of weights b2, b1, b0 in the range tx(2:0) tx(2:0), tx(5:3) and tx(8:6) (where x=0,1,2) a sequential linking of codes of active fuzzy sets is performed; in this way a 9 - bit address of the conclusion is created. Table 2 shows the values of weights - b2, b1, b0, based on which the codes of input fuzzy sets in the range tx(2:0) and tx(6:4) (where x=0,1,2) are read out from input of the subblock "address_generatorx" (where x=0-7) of the block "inference" and the values of membership functions from input mix0, mix1 (where x=0,1,2) are also read.

A creation of the address of the conclusion is initiated by the steering signal coming from the block "control" (fig. 4). The "inference" block contains the conclusion codes of fuzzy rules stored at precisely determined addresses, which values correspond to premises of activated rules. During the reading of

Table 2. The values of state in block "inference", where examples values of input linguistic variable: x0 - (T0=100, μ0=6;T1=011, μ1=94), x1 - (T0=000, μ0=84; T1=001, μ1=16), x2 - (T0=010, μ0=100; T1=011, μ1=0)

b2	b1	b0	μ2	μ1	μ0	Read codes			Address
0	0	0	100	84	6	010	000	100	010000100
0	0	1	100	16	94	010	000	011	010000011
0	1	0	100	84	6	010	001	100	010001100
0	1	1	100	16	94	010	001	011	010001011
1	0	0	0	84	6	011	000	100	011000100
1	0	1	0	16	94	011	000	011	011000011
1	1	0	0	84	6	011	001	100	011001100
1	1	1	0	16	94	011	001	011	011001011

indicated codes of rule conclusions, the block "control" initiates an operation "MIN"; which gives as the result the lowest value of the membership function. In proposed fuzzy system for each of initial output fuzzy sets, the block MAX is assigned. The tasks of this block is a choice of the highest value of activated output fuzzy set. In proposed realization, as a defuzzification process the CoGS (Center of Gravity for Singletons) was used; this operation is performed parallelly for two output channels in "defuzzx" (where x=0,1) blocks giving the values of y0 and y1. Next this result is transferred into the block controlling the drive of the wheelchair motors M0 and M1.

3   Conclusions

Proposed digital parallel fuzzy system was described in the language of the equipment description VHDL, and was simulated in the Activ- Hdl environment of the Aldec company. For this purpose in the first step of testing the values of the membership functions of the fuzzy sets as well as the table of rules were written down in the memory of the system. Next the test values of input linguistic variables x0, x1, x2 were introduced. In the second step of testing, the proposed fuzzy system was programed in FPGA circuit Spartans 3. Results of measurements confirmed correct operation of the system.

In table 3, a collection of number of clock cycles in inference block is shown. Using the techniques of addressing in the inference process and application parallel processing, allows for very quick selection of only active rules from the whole rule base; for example, for whole number of 125 rules only 8 rules are active in one "inference". The fastest method (Tab 3, method e) of inference process, allows to calculate the degree of rule activations during only 4 clock cycles. Used addressing techniques requires writing downing rule conclusions in strictly determined addresses in the system memory; however this demand increases the time nessery to create the rule base at the time of constructing of fuzzy system.

Table 3. Number of clock cycles in inference block for diffrent types of architectures a,b,c,d,e of propossed fuzzy system, where: n - number of inputs, A - number of fuzzy rules, B - activated rules in inference process, L - number of fuzzy sets

L=5	n=2	n=3	n=4	n=5	n=6	n=7
A	25	125	625	3125	15625	78125
B	4	8	16	32	64	128
a	100	500	2500	12500	62500	78125
b	16	32	64	128	256	512
c	7	11	19	35	67	131
d	5	7	14	19	35	67
e	4	4	4	4	4	4

References

1. Pires, G., Nunes, U.: A Wheelchair Steered through Voice Commands and Assisted by a Reactive Fuzzy-Logic Controller. Journal of Intelligent and Robotic Systems 34, 301–314 (2002)
2. Martin, P., Mazo, M., Fernandez, I., Lazaro, J.L., Rodriguez, F.J., Gardel, A.: Multifunctional and autonomous, high performance architecture: application to a wheelchair for disabled people that integrates different control and guidance strategies. Microprocessors and Microsystems 23 (1999)
3. Poplawski, M., Bialko, M.: Implementation of parallel fuzzy logic controller in FPGA circuit for guiding electric wheelchair. In: Conference on Human System Interactions - IEEE Xplore, Kraków (2008)
4. Reznik, L.: Fuzzy Controllers Handbook. Elsevier (1997)
5. Kalus M., Skoczkowski T.: Sterowanie napedami asynchronicznymi i pradu stalego, Gliwice (2003) (in polish)
6. Yager, R.R., Filev, D.P.: Essentials of Fuzzy Modeling and Control. John Wiley and Sons, New York (1994)
7. Piegat, A.: Modelowanie i sterowanie rozmyte, Exit (1998) (in polish)
8. Patyra, M.J., Grantner, J.L.: Hardware implementaions of digital fuzzy logic controller. Elesiver Information Science 113, 19–54 (1999)
9. Patyra, M.J., Grantner, J.L.: Digital fuzzy logic controller: design and implementaions. IEEE Transactions on Fuzzy Systems 4 (1996)
10. Gabrielli, A., Gandolfi, E., Falchieri, D.: Very fast rate 2 input fuzzy processor for high energy physics. Fuzzy Sets and Systems 132, 261–272 (2002)
11. Guo, S., Peters, L.: A high-speed fuzzy co-processor implemented in analogue digital technique. Computers and Electrical Engineering 24 (1998)
12. Barriga, A., Sanchez-Solano, S., Brox, P., Cabrera, A., Baturone, I.: Modelling and implementation of fuzzy systems based on VHDL. International Journal of Approximate Reasoning 41 (2006)
13. Xilinx DS099 Spartan-3, Complete data sheet
14. Whale3 DC servo drive - data sheet

Real-Time On-Line-Learning Support Vector Machine Based on a Fully-Parallel Analog VLSI Processor

Renyuan Zhang and Tadashi Shibata

Department of Electrical Engineering and Information Systems,
The University of Tokyo,
7-3-1 Hongo, Bunkyo-ku, Tokyo 113-8656, Japan
tyoninen@if.t.u-tokyo.ac.jp, shibata@ee.t.u-tokyo.ac.jp

Abstract. An analog VLSI implementation of on-line learning Support Vector Machine (SVM) has been developed for the classification of high-dimensional pattern vectors. A fully-parallel self-learning circuitry employing analog high-dimensional Gaussian-generation circuits was used as an SVM processor. This SVM processor achieves a high learning speed (one clock cycle at $10MHz$) within compact chip area. Based on this SVM processor, an on-line learning system has been developed with the consideration of limited hardware resource. According to circuit simulation results, the image patterns from an actual database were all classified into correct classes by the proposed system. The ineffective samples are successfully identified in real-time and updated by on-line learning patterns.

Keywords: on-line-learning, Support Vector Machine, fully-parallel, high-dimensional.

1 Introduction

Support Vector Machine is one of the most powerful classification algorithms applied in the pattern recognition problems [1]. Recently, some attempts were made to implement the SVM algorithm directly by VLSI circuits [2,3]. Since the learning function was not implemented on-chip in these works, off-chip learning sessions are needed to activate the system. To implement the on-chip learnable SVM, several digital VLSI architectures have been developed with linear or quadratic function kernels [4,5,6].

It is found that, SVMs with Gaussian function kernels have an enhanced capacity in classifying linearly non-separable patterns [7], especially when the number of dimensions is very high. On the other hand, the Gaussian function is computationally expensive when it is implemented by digital VLSI circuits. In order to improve the classification speed, an analog on-chip learnable SVM has been reported [8] to classify four vectors with two dimensions. However, this approach employing traditional analog Gaussian-generation circuits can be hardly implemented in high dimensional pattern classification due to intolerably increased errors. Furthermore, the previously presented digital and analog SVM processors have very

L. Rutkowski et al. (Eds.): ICAISC 2012, Part II, LNCS 7268, pp. 223–230, 2012.

limited capacities on the amounts of learning samples due to the limited hardware resource. Since a remarkable part of hardware is inactive, the hardware-efficiency is not high for the traditional VLSI implementations of SVMs.

One reasonable solution to enhance the capacity is applying on-line learning strategy in SVMs, which was originally developed by software programs [9,10]. Several works have implemented the on-line learning SVMs into the real-time applications such as the object tracking problems [11,12] using software. However, since on-line learning results in a large number of SVM learning operations, the real-time applications usually require the high learning speed, which is difficult to realize using software or traditional VLSI processors. In addition, these on-line learning strategies always increase the number of learning samples. As a result, they are hardly implemented by VLSI circuits with the consideration of limited hardware resource.

The purpose of this work is to propose a hardware-efficient on-line leaning SVM system for the classification of high-dimensional pattern vectors. A fully-parallel analog circuitry employing compact Gaussian-generation circuits [13] is used as SVM processor. The learning process autonomously proceeds without any clock-based control and self-converged within a single clock cycle of system (at $10MHz$). In addition, the SVM learning processor achieves high learning speed within compact chip size by computing vector Euclidean distances and exponential functions separably. Based on this SVM processor, a hardware-efficient on-line learning strategy has been proposed with limited hardware resource. The performances of the proposed SVM processor and on-line learning system were verified by circuit simulation results. The image patterns from an actual database were used as initial learning samples and test patterns. All the test patterns were classified into correct classes, and the ineffective samples were updated by the test patterns along with on-line learning.

2   Hardware-Efficient On-Line Learning Strategy

In the real-time applications of on-line learning SVMs, the number of learning samples is usually very large and unpredictable. As a result, the traditional on-line incrementally learning strategies [9,10] can be hardly implemented by VLSI circuits since the hardware resource is strictly limited. Fortunately, in SVM theory some of the learning samples (non-support vectors) are ineffective, which can be removed from sample space. A hardware-efficient on-line learning strategy with constant number of learning samples is proposed in this work. In order to reduce the loss of accuracy, the effectiveness of each sample is evaluated and only the most ineffective sample is replaced by an on-line pattern. In this manner, the learning sample space can be expanded within compact chip area.

2.1   SVM Algorithm Used in This Work

A hardware-friendly SVM algorithm [8] is used to classify n-dimensional vectors $\mathbb{X}$s with the form of $\mathbb{X} = (x_1, x_2, \cdots, x_n)$. A set of learning samples $(\mathbb{X}_i, y_i)_{1 \leq i \leq N}$

is needed, where N is the number of learning samples and $y_i \in \{-1, 1\}$ is the class label of the i-th sample $\mathbb{X}_i$. Receiving a vector $\mathbb{X}$, the decision function to classify this vector can be given as

$$f(\mathbb{X}) = sign[\sum_{i=1}^{N} \alpha_i y_i G(\mathbb{X}, \mathbb{X}_i) + b], \qquad (1)$$

where $G(\mathbb{X}, \mathbb{X}_i)$ is the Gaussian kernel function: $G(\mathbb{X}, \mathbb{X}_i) = exp(-\gamma(\mathbb{X} - \mathbb{X}_i)^2)$. Since the bias b has negligible effect on the performance in this case [8], it is set as 0 in both learning and classifying modes. The updating rule to obtain α_is is shown by

$$\alpha_i \leftarrow \min(C, \max(0, 1 - y_i \sum_{j(\neq i)} \alpha_j y_j G(\mathbb{X}_i, \mathbb{X}_j))). \qquad (2)$$

where C is a regularization parameter.

2.2   On-Line Learning Strategy

The strategy of proposed on-line learning SVM with a constant number of samples is illustrated in Fig. 1. The SVM learning proceeds as soon as one on-line pattern is received. The function used to identify the most ineffective pattern is given by

$$\min_i \sum_{j(y_j \neq y_i)} \alpha_j G(\mathbb{X}_i, \mathbb{X}_j). \qquad (3)$$

The process of this on-line learning strategy is shown as follows:

1. Initial SVM learning according to a small set of samples as it is shown in Fig. 1(a);
2. Classifying the new-received on-line pattern;
3. Evaluating the effectiveness of previous samples and replacing the most inefficient one by new-received pattern as it is shown in Fig. 1(b);

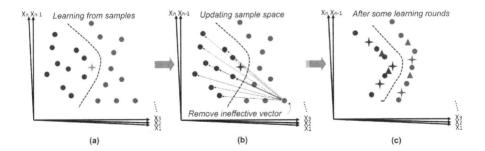

Fig. 1. Proposed on-line learning strategy: (a) initial learning according to a small set of samples; (b) on-line pattern is classified and the most ineffective pattern is identified; (c) only effective patterns (support vectors) remain after sufficient on-line learning operations

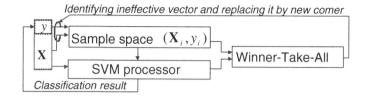

Fig. 2. Architecture of proposed on-line learning SVM system

4. SVM learning according to the updated samples;
5. Receiving new on-line pattern and repeating 2, 3, and 4.

After sufficient on-line learning operations, all the inefficient samples are replaced by significant on-line patterns as shown in Fig. 1(c).

3   Hardware Implementation

3.1   System Architecture

The architecture of proposed on-line learning SVM system is illustrated in Fig.2. This system is composed of an analog on-chip learnable SVM processor and a Winner-Take-All (WTA) circuit with N candidates. According to the learning samples $(\mathbb{X}_i, y_i)_{1 \leq i \leq N}$, on-line pattern $\mathbb{X}$ is classified by the SVM processor. As soon as the most ineffective sample is identified by WTA circuit, $\mathbb{X}$ replaces this sample along with classification result y.

3.2   Circuit Organization of SVM Processor

The fully-parallel learning SVM processor is designed as shown in Fig. 3. N vectors (learning samples) in the form of digital data are used as input, which are converted into analog signals by a set of on-chip DACs. N sets of Euclidean distance calculation circuits were constructed in block I to compute the distances between the vector $\mathbb{X}_i$ and all other samples in parallel. The class label y_i is reflected by the switches connected to the row buses. Each cell in block II contains a capacitor (as an analog memory) and an exponential generation circuit, which generates the final output as Gaussian function in the current mode. The Euclidean distance values are stored in array II row by row as voltages. As a result, a fully-parallel array of Gaussian kernels has been implemented in such a small area even for the high dimensionality. The circuits of α adjuster are current mirror based adders/subtracters. Collecting all the currents on the row bus, the α adjusters realize the function represented in Eq.2. During the learning process, the α values in block III are fed-back to block II and the learning process proceeds autonomously in a fully-parallel manner. Therefore, the training process can be accomplished only in single clock cycle.

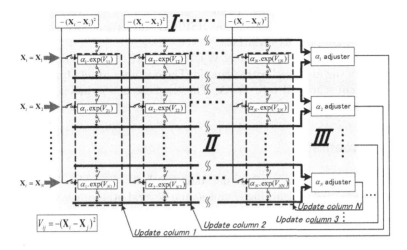

Fig. 3. Organization of fully-parallel learning SVM processor

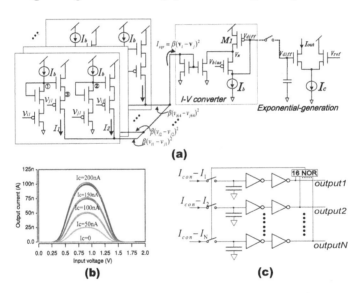

Fig. 4. (a) Schematic of analog Gaussian-generation circuit with 64-dimensional inputs; (b) function feature obtained by HSPICE simulation and (c) schematic of Winner-Take-All circuit

An analog Gaussian-generation circuit with 64 dimensions was developed as it is shown in Fig. 4(a), where I_b is a sufficiently small bias current. Receiving two vectors $\mathbb{X}_i = \{v_{i1}, v_{i2}, \cdots, v_{i64}\}$ and $\mathbb{X}_j = \{v_{j1}, v_{j2}, \cdots, v_{j64}\}$, the output current I_{out} is given by: $I_{out} \approx \frac{I_c}{2} e^{-\gamma |\mathbb{X}_i - \mathbb{X}_j|^2}$, where $\gamma = \frac{K_n}{(V_{dd} - V_{bias} - |V_{thp}|)(\sqrt{K_p} + \sqrt{K_n})^2}$ and V_{ref} is set as $\frac{V_{dd} + V_{bias} - |V_{thp}|}{2}$. The peak-height value of the obtained Gaussian function feature can be scaled by I_c, which reflects the α values in the SVM algorithm. According to the circuit simulation, Fig. 4(b) shows the obtained Gaussian function feature by HSPICE simulation with the consideration of fabrication process variations.

Figure 4(c) shows the schematic of WTA circuit with 16 candidates, which is used to identify the most ineffective sample. The output currents from Gaussian-generation circuits are fed into WTA. The smallest one is indexed by a high voltage pulse.

4   Experiments

Images in two classes from an actual database COIL-20 (Columbia Object Image Library [15]) are used as learning samples, and several other images are used as test patterns. The class labels are represented by a high voltage signal (class "a") and a low voltage signal (class "b"). All the images are converted into 64-dimensional vectors employing the PPED method (Projected Principle Edge Distribution[14]) before experiments.

4.1   Verification of Fully-Parallel Learning SVM Processor

The SVM processor is designed for 16 samples learning in a CMOS $0.18\mu m$ technology. The Nanosim simulation results are given in Fig. 5 with a DAC clock frequency of $10MHz$. The learning process is accomplished within one clock cycle ($100ns$). All the test patterns are classified into their respective classes correctly.

4.2   Verification of On-Line Learning System

Receiving the on-line learning patterns, the inefficient ones of previous learning samples are indexed by high voltage signals as shown in Fig. 6(a). According

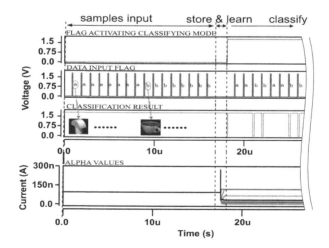

Fig. 5. Circuit simulation results of SVM processor

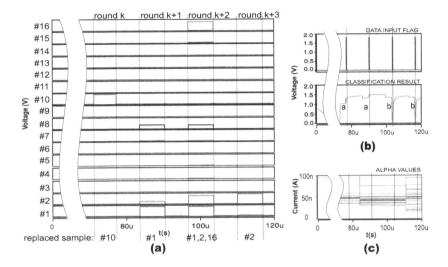

Fig. 6. Circuit simulation results of the proposed on-line learning SVM system by Nanosim (a) identification labels to search the most ineffective sample; (b) on-line classification results and (c) α values during the on-line learning operations

Table 1. Performance comparisons

	[3]	[8]	This work
Learning Parallelism	Off-chip	Row-parallel	Fully-parallel
Kernel Function	Quadratic	Gaussian	Gaussian
No. of Kernels	720	12	18.8*
Input Vector	Analog current	Digital (8bits)	Digital (8bits)
No. of Samples	720	12	On-line
No. of Dimensions	14	2	$1 \sim 64$
Learning Time	N/A	$12 \times l \times 60ns^{\sharp}$	$100ns$
Classification speed	40 vectors/s	8.7×10^5 vectors/s	10^6 vectors/s

* The number of kernels is calculated from the viewpoint of chip area.

$\sharp$ l is the number of iterations for convergence.

to the database, all the on-line classification results in Fig. 6(b) are correct. The α values are self-adjusted while every on-line learning pattern is input as shown in Fig. 6(c). Comparisons between the proposed SVM system and some other works are given in Tab. 1.

5   Conclusions

An on-line learning SVM system has been presented in this paper for the application of high-dimensional patterns recognition. Employing an analog fully-parallel SVM processor, each learning operation takes only $100ns$ implemented by a compact circuitry. With the consideration of limited hardware resource, an hardware-efficient on-line learning strategy has been proposed. According to circuit simulation results, the proposed system classified all the test patterns correctly and realized the on-line learning successfully.

References

1. Vapnik, V.: The Nature of Statistical Learning Theory. Springer, New York (1995)
2. Genov, R., Cauwenberghs, G.: Kerneltron: Support Vector Machine in Silicon. IEEE Transactions on Neural Networks 14, 1426–1434 (2003)
3. Chakrabartty, S., Cauwenberghs, G.: Sub-Microwatt Analog VLSI Trainable Pattern Classifier. IEEE J. Solid-State Circuits 42, 1169–1179 (2007)
4. Anguita, D., Ridella, S., Rovetta, S.: Circuital implementation of support vector machines. IEEE Electron Letters 34, 1596–1597 (1999)
5. Xia, Y., Wang, J.: A One-Layer Recurrent Neural Network for Support Vector Machine Learning. IEEE Transactions on Systems, Man, and Cybernetics, Part B 34, 1261–1269 (2004)
6. Perfetti, R., Ricci, E.: Analog Neural Network for Support Vector Machine Learning. IEEE Transactions Neural Networks 17, 1085–1091 (2006)
7. Schoelkopf, B., Sung, K., Burges, C., Girosi, F., Niyogi, P., Poggio, T., Vapnik, V.: Comparing Support Vector Machines with Gaussian Kernels to Radial Basis Function Classifiers. IEEE Transactions Signal Processing 45, 2758–2765 (1997)
8. Kang, K., Shibata, T.: An On-Chip-Trainable Gaussian-Kernel Analog Support Vector Machine. IEEE Transactions Circuits and Systems 45, 1513–1524 (2010)
9. Cauwenberghs, G., Poggio, T.: Incremental and Decremental Support Vector Machine Learning. In: Advances in Neural Information Processing Systems, vol. 13 (2001)
10. Matthews, L., Ishikawa, T., Baker, S.: The Template Update Problem. IEEE Transactions Pattern Analysis and Machine Intelligence 26, 810–815 (2004)
11. Tian, M., Zhang, W., Liu, F.: On-Line Ensemble SVM for Robust Object Tracking. In: Yagi, Y., Kang, S.B., Kweon, I.S., Zha, H. (eds.) ACCV 2007, Part I. LNCS, vol. 4843, pp. 355–364. Springer, Heidelberg (2007)
12. Tang, F., Brennan, S., Zhao, Q., Tao, H.: Co-Tracking Using Semi-Supervised Support Vector Machines. In: IEEE 11th International Conference on Computer Vision, pp. 1–8 (2007)
13. Zhang, R., Shibata, T.: A Fully-Parallel Self-Learning Analog Support Vector Machine Employing Compact Gaussian-Generation Circuits. In: International Conference on Solid State Devices and Materials (SSDM), Nagoya, pp. 174–175 (2011)
14. Yagi, M., Shibata, T.: An Image Representation Algorithm Compatible with Neural-Associative-Processor-Based Hardware Recognition Systems. IEEE Transactions Neural Networks 14, 1144–1161 (2003)
15. Columbia Object Image Library, http://www.cs.columbia.edu/

Part III

Bioinformatics, Biometrics and Medical Applications

COID-FDCM: The Fuzzy Maintained Dendritic Cell Classification Method

Zeineb Chelly, Abir Smiti, and Zied Elouedi

LARODEC, University of Tunis,
Higher Institute of Management of Tunis,
41 Street of liberty, Bouchoucha, 2000 Bardo, Tunisia
zeinebchelly@yahoo.fr, smiti.abir@gmail.com, zied.elouedi@gmx.fr

Abstract. The Dendritic Cell Algorithm (DCA) is an immune-inspired classification algorithm based on the behavior of natural dendritic cells (DC). A major problem with DCA is that it is sensitive to the data order. This limitation is due to the existence of noisy or redundant data and to the crisp separation between the DC semi-mature context and the DC mature context. This paper proposes a novel immune-inspired alleviated model of the DCA grounded in fuzzy set theory and a maintenance database method. Our new model focuses on smoothing the crisp separation between the two DCs' contexts using fuzzy set theory. A maintenance database approach is used as well to guarantee the quality of the DCA database. Experiments are provided to show that our method performs much better than the standard DCA in terms of classification accuracy.

Keywords: dendritic cells, fuzzy set theory, fuzzy c-means clustering, DBSCAN clustering method, outliers.

1   Introduction

The dendritic cell algorithm (DCA) [1] is a bio-inspired algorithm as abstract model of dendritic cell behavior. The DCA aims to perform anomaly detection by correlating a series of informative signals inducing a signal database with a sequence of repeating abstract identifiers. The DCA is used as a classifier for a static machine learning data set [1]. Nevertheless, the DCA suffers from some shortcomings as it is sensitive to the data order [2].

The first reason of this drawback is related to the DCA signal database which contains disagreeable objects such as noisy, inconsistent or redundant instances. This situation may occur due to several reasons like the existence of many sources of anomaly detection that makes the DCA reach of inconsistencies. Therefore, it affects negatively its classification results. To handle this drawback, maintaining the DCA signal database, as a first step, becomes necessary. Hence, the first objective of our paper is to use a maintenance policy.

Based on our first objective, we choose to apply the maintaining method named Clustering, Outliers and Internal cases Detection (COID) [4] for the DCA

L. Rutkowski et al. (Eds.): ICAISC 2012, Part II, LNCS 7268, pp. 233–241, 2012.

signal database. COID is originally applied in Case Based Reasoning technique and it seems appropriate to DCA since it is characterized by its capability of removing noisy and redundant instances as well its ability to improve the classification accuracy and offering a reasonable execution time.

Another drawback of DCA is the crisp separation between normality (semimature) and abnormality (mature). In fact, if the difference value between these two DCs' context is small, then the context of the DC will be hard to be defined. Thus, it could change the decision of the context affectation. Not considering this case, has a negative effect on classification accuracy when the class of data instances changes over time. So, the second objective of this work is to smooth this abrupt separation, since we can neither identify a clear boundary between the two contexts nor quantify exactly what is meant by "semi-mature" or "mature". This will be handled by the use of fuzzy set theory. Furthermore, we aim at generating automatically the extents and midpoints of the membership functions which describe the variables of our model using fuzzy c-means clustering. Hence, we can avoid negative influence on the results when an ordinary user introduces such parameters. Thus, we propose in this paper a novel immune-inspired alleviated model of the DCA named COID-Fuzzy Dendritic Cell Method (COID-FDCM). Our fuzzy classification approach is grounded in fuzzy set theory, a fuzzy clustering technique and a maintenance database method. The purpose of our contribution is to improve the classification accuracy. In addition, we aim to show that our method does not depend on the class transitions neither demand any intervention from the user to determine the parameters of the system.

This paper is structured as follows: in Section 2, we introduce the dendritic cell algorithm. Section 3 describes our fuzzy maintained dendritic cell method in detail, the experimental setup and results are given in Section 4.

2   The Dendritic Cell Algorithm

The dendritic cell algorithm was first introduced in [1] and has been subject to various modifications [5] [6]. Before explaining the function of the algorithm, we introduce in brief the biological principles used by the DCA.

2.1   Introducing Dendritic Cells

Dendritic cells are types of antigen-presenting cells. They are sensitive to the concentration of signals (PAMPs, danger and safe) collected from their neighborhood. Hence, resulting in three different maturity levels. The first maturation state of a DC is the immature state (iDCs). iDCs differ either to a full or partial maturation state. It depends on the combination of the various signals received. Under the reception of safe signals (SS), iDCs migrate to the semi-mature state (smDCs) and they cause antigens tolerance. iDCs migrate to the mature state (mDCs) if they are more exposed to danger signals (DS) and to pathogenic associated molecular patterns (PAMPs) than SS. They present the collected antigens in a dangerous context.

2.2 Abstract View of the Dendritic Cell Algorithm

The DCA combines several signals and antigen to fix the context of each object (DC). The input signals of the system are pre-categorized as "danger", "PAMP" and "safe". In biology, PAMPs definitely indicate an anomalous situation. DS are indicators of abnormality but with lower value of confidence than PAMPs. SS are indicators of normality generating a tolerance to the collected antigen. These signals are processed by the algorithm in order to get three output signals: costimulation signal (Csm), mature signal (Mat) and semi-mature signal (Semi). A migration threshold is incorporated into the DCA in order to determine the lifespan of a DC. As soon as the Csm exceeds the migration threshold; the DC ceases to sample signals and antigens. The DCs differentiation direction is determined by the comparison between cumulative Semi and cumulative Mat. If the cumulative Semi is greater than the cumulative Mat, then the DC goes to semi-mature context, which implies that the antigen data was collected under normal conditions. Otherwise, it goes to mature context, signifying a potentially anomalous data item. The nature of the response is determined by measuring the number of DCs that are fully mature and is represented by the mature context antigen value (MCAV). MCAV is used to assess the degree of anomaly of a given antigen. The closer the MCAV is to 1, the greater the probability that the antigen is anomalous. By applying thresholds at various levels, analysis can be performed to assess the anomaly detection capabilities of the algorithm. Those antigens whose MCAV are greater than the anomalous threshold are classified into the anomalous category, while the others are classified into the normal one.

3 COID-FDCM: The Fuzzy Maintained Dendritic Cell Method

According to [2], the DCA suffers from some shortcomings as it is sensitive to the data order. Once the context changes multiple times in a quick succession (data are randomized between the classes), the percent of classification accuracy of the DCA decreases notably. This is due to an environment characterized by a crisp evaluation in its context assessment phase as well as to the existence of redundant and noisy instances in the DCA signal database. Hence, in this paper, we propose a new model of the standard DCA named COID-Fuzzy Dendritic Cell Method (COID-FDCM). Our method takes into account the fact of alleviating the crisp assessment task and maintaining the DCA signal database by eliminating its "useless" objects. Our COID-FDCM steps are described in the following Subsections.

3.1 Maintaining the Signal Database

As stated previously, the DCA signal database contains disagreeable objects especially noisy and redundant instances, in the sense that it affects negatively the quality of the DCA classification results. To guarantee the DCA's performance, the maintenance of the signal database becomes essentially. Thus, we apply the Clustering, Outliers and Internal cases Detection maintenance approach (COID) [4] as a first step in our new COID-FDCM. For that, COID defines two important types of objects which should not be eliminated from the signal database:

Outlier: an isolated instance, no other object can replace it or be similar to it.

Internal instance: is one object from a group of similar objects. Each instance from this group provides similar coverage to the other instances of the same group. Deleting any member of this group has no effect on the system's performance since the remaining objects offer the same value. Thus, we can keep one instance from each group of similar objects. Based on this idea, the COID method reduces the original signal database by keeping only these two types of instances and eliminates the rest. The COID maintaining method steps are itemized as follows:

For the clustering method, COID adopts the Density-Based Spatial Clustering of Applications with Noise (DBSCAN) [7] since it can detect the noisy instances. Hence, the improvement of classification accuracy could be achieved.

For the selection of the internal instances, COID calculates the Euclidean distance between the cluster's center and each instance from the same cluster and selects objects which have the smallest distance.

For the outliers detection, COID applies the Interquartile Range IQR and the Mahalanobis distance as they are robust statistical methods.

Consequently, the result of applying the maintaining COID method is the generation of a new reduced signal database lacking noisy and redundant objects while preserving nearly the same performance of the original DCA signal data set. Hence, our COID-FDCM can treat the new signal database easily and it guaranties better classification results.

3.2   Fuzzy System Inputs-Output Variables

Once the signal database is maintained using COID policy, the DCA processes these signals to get the semi-mature and the mature signals values. In order to describe each of these two object contexts, we use linguistic variables [8]. Two inputs (one for each context) and one output are defined. The semi-mature context and the mature context denoted respectively C_s and C_m are considered as the input variables to the fuzzy system. The final state "maturity" of a DC (object), S_{mat}, is chosen as the output variable. All the system's inputs and output are defined using fuzzy set theory.

$$C_s = \{\mu_{C_s}(c_{s_j})/c_{s_j} \in X_{C_s}\} \ ; \ C_m = \{\mu_{C_m}(c_{m_j})/c_{m_j} \in X_{C_m}\}$$

$$S_{mat} = \{S_{mat}(s_{mat_j})/s_{mat_j} \in X_{S_{mat}}\}$$

where c_{s_j}, c_{m_j} and s_{mat_j} are, respectively, the elements of the discrete universe of discourse X_{C_s}, X_{C_m} and $X_{S_{mat}}$. μ_{C_s}, μ_{C_m} and $\mu_{S_{mat}}$ are, respectively, the corresponding membership functions.

3.3   Linguistic Variables

The basic tools of fuzzy set theory are linguistic variables. The term set $T(S_{mat})$ interpreting S_{mat} which is a linguistic variable that constitutes the final state of maturity of a DC, could be: $T(S_{mat}) = \{Semi - mature, Mature\}$.

Each term in $T(S_{mat})$ is characterized by a fuzzy subset in a universe of discourse $X_{S_{mat}}$. Semi-mature might be interpreted as an object (data instance) collected under safe circumstances, reflecting a normal behavior and Mature as an object collected under dangerous circumstances, reflecting an anomalous behavior. Similarly, the input variables C_s and C_m are interpreted as linguistic variables with: $T(Q) = \{Low, Medium, High\}$, where $Q = C_s$ and C_m respectively.

3.4   Fuzzy and Membership Functions Construction

In order to specify the range of each linguistic variable and based on the maintained signal database, we have run the DCA and we have recorded both semimature and mature values which reflect the (Semi) and (Mat) outputs generated by the DCA. Then, we picked up the minimum and maximum values of each of the two generated values to fix the borders of the range which are:

$$min(range(S_{mat})) = min(min(range[C_m]), min(range[C_s]))$$

$$max(range(S_{mat})) = max(max(range[C_m]), max(range[C_s]))$$

It seems important now to fix the extents and midpoints of each membership function. In fact, involving ordinary users to determine these parameters influences negatively the results since the user is not an expert in the domain. Hence, these parameters have to be automatically generated by our system. For this, our choice can be focused on the use of the fuzzy c-means clustering algorithm (FCM) [9]. To the recorded list of (Mat) and (Semi) values, we apply FCM. It helps to build a fuzzy inference system by creating membership functions to represent the fuzzy qualities of each cluster. Each cluster reflects a membership function. The number of clusters is relative to the number of the membership functions of each variable (inputs and output). The output of this phase is a list of cluster centers and several membership grades for each data point (object). Thus, the extents and midpoints of the membership functions which describe the system's variables are automatically determined.

3.5   The Fuzzy Rule Sets Description

A knowledge base, comprising rules, is built to support the fuzzy inference. The different rules of the fuzzy system are extracted from the information reflecting the effect of each input signal on the state of a dendritic cell which is:

Safe Signals: in increase in value is a probable indicator of normality. High values of the safe signal can cancel out the effects of both PAMPs and DS.

Danger Signals: in increase in value is a probable indicator of damage, but there is less certainty than with a PAMP signal.

PAMPs: in increase in value is a definite indicator of anomaly.

Inflammation: has the effect of amplifying the other three categories of input signals, but is not sufficient to cause any effect on DCs when used in isolation.

From the list above, we can generate the following set of rules where all the mentioned signals are taken into account implicitly in the fuzzy system.

1. If (C_m is Low) and (C_s is Low) then (S_{mat} is Mature)
2. If (C_m is Low) and (C_s is Medium) then (S_{mat} is Semi-mature)
3. If (C_m is Low) and (C_s is High) then (S_{mat} is Semi-mature)
4. If (C_m is Medium) and (C_s is Low) then (S_{mat} is Mature)
5. If (C_m is Medium) and (C_s is Medium) then (S_{mat} is Semi-mature)
6. If (C_m is Medium) and (C_s is High) then (S_{mat} is Semi-mature)
7. If (C_m is High) and (C_s is Low) then (S_{mat} is Mature)
8. If (C_m is High) and (C_s is Medium) then (S_{mat} is Mature)
9. If (C_m is High) and (C_s is High) then (S_{mat} is Mature)

Let us consider Rule (2) as an example: if the C_m input is set to its first membership function "Low" and the second input C_s to its second membership function "Medium", then the "Semi-mature" context of the output S_{mat} is assigned. This could be explained by the effect of the high values of SS (which lead to the semi-mature context) that cancel out the effects of both PAMPs and DS (which lead to the mature context). The same reasoning is affected to the rest of the rules.

3.6   The Fuzzy Context Assessment

Our COID-FDCM is based on the "Mamdani" composition method and the "centroid" defuzzification mechanism. Once the inputs are fuzzified and the output (centroid value) is generated, the cell context has to be fixed by comparing the output value to the middle of the S_{mat} range. In fact, if the centroid value generated is greater than the middle of the output range then the final context of the object is "Mature" indicating that the collected antigen may be anomalous; else the antigen collected is likely to be normal.

4   Experiments

4.1   Experimental Setup

For the evaluation of our COID-FDCM, different experiments are performed using two-class data sets from [10] described in Table 1.

Data items with the largest standard deviation form the DS. To generate concentrations for SS and PAMPs, the attribute with the next greatest standard deviation is chosen. Antigen is represented as the identification number of a data item within the database. The threshold for classification which is applied to the MCAVs is set to 0.54, 0.76, 0.52, 0.12, 0.78, 0.4, 0.12, 0.4 and 0.3 for

Table 1. Description of databases

Database	Ref	♯ instances	♯ attributes
Mammographic Mass	MM	961	6
Pima Indians Diabetes	PID	768	8
Blood Transfusion Service Center	BTSC	748	5
Ionosphere	IONO	351	34
Liver Disorders	LD	345	7
Haberman's Survival	HS	306	4
Statlog (Heart)	STAT	270	13
Connectionist Bench	CB	208	60

the databases respectively. Items below the threshold are classified as class 1 (normal) and above as class 2 (anomaly). As for the parameter of the FCM clustering techniques, m is set to 2.

In [2] it was shown that the DCA is sensitive to the data order producing unsatisfying classification results when applied to a randomized database unlike when applied to an ordered data set. Hence, with our new COID-FDCM, our experimentations are based on randomizing the data more and more between the classes and to notice the effect of this randomization on our new COID-FDCM. We try to show that the performance of our COID-FDCM does neither depend on such transitions nor on ordered data sets contrary to the DCA. To achieve this, three different data orders are used. Experiment one uses a one-step data order i.e. all class one items are processed followed by all class two items. In experiment two, data are partitioned into three sections, resulting in a two-step data order. The data comprising class one is split into two sections and the class two data is embedded between the class one partitions. Experiment three consists of data randomized between class one and class two. For the evaluation of our COID-FDCM, we will consider the PCC as a principal criterion which is the mean percentage of correct classification over stratified ten fold cross validation.

4.2   Results and Discussion

In this Section, we try to show the effectiveness of our COID-FDCM. For that, our COID-FDCM experimental results will be compared to the standard DCA which is the non-fuzzy case. We will also compare our method to the Fuzzy Dendritic Cell Method (FDCM) [5] which is the first work based on fuzzy set theory where the parameters of the system were defined by ordinary users. Hence, presenting some limitations which we try to overcome using our COID-FDCM.

Previous examinations with DCA, in [1], show that the misclassifications occur exclusively at the transition boundaries. This problem was partially solved in [5] with FDCM via the new fuzzy context assessment phase. However, FDCM gives unsatisfying classification results in case of ordered contexts, which could be explained by involving the ordinary user in the determination of the system's parameters. Note that both DCA and FDCM use the original signal database which contains noisy and redundant instances. To handle the drawbacks of DCA and FDCM, we developed our COID-FDCM which is based on generating automatically the parameters of the fuzzy inference system, on smoothing the crisp evaluation of the DC's contexts assessment phase and on maintaining the DCA signal database. Our new COID-FDCM gives better classification results in both ordered and disordered contexts when compared to the DCA and FDCM, which is confirmed by the results presented in Table 2.

Table 2. Experimental measures PCC (%)

	DCA			FDCM			COID-FDCM		
	1-Step	2-Step	Random	1-Step	2-Step	Random	1-Step	2-Step	Random
MM	97.19	86.88	64.51	91.25	97.19	97.5	98.28	99.68	99.53
PID	96.48	93.48	89.84	95.31	95.43	96.87	99.59	99.79	99.79
BTSC	94.38	78.87	77.4	97.19	96.92	99.59	98.2	99.23	99.48
IONO	94.58	78.63	66.09	78.34	85.75	97.15	97.29	97.29	98.19
LD	96.23	76.52	62.6	66.08	81.44	96.52	97.01	99	99.05
HS	95.75	79.73	27.45	27.77	90.84	99.01	98.67	99.33	99.33
STAT	93.33	84.81	62.96	75.92	87.03	95.55	99.33	99.33	99.33
CB	92.3	86.53	75	80.76	91.34	96.63	98.24	98.24	99.12

From Table 2, it is clearly noticed that our COID-FDCM has given good results in terms of classification accuracy (PCC). In fact, by randomizing the data between classes (two-step and random experiments), the PCCs of our COID-FDCM are better than those given by DCA and FDCM. This remark also includes the case of an ordered database. For instance, by applying our COID-FDCM to the Connectionist Bench (CB) database and with the randomization of the database, the PCC increases from 98,24% to 99,12%. In case of an ordered database, the PCC takes a value of 98,24%. Whereas, when applying the DCA to the same database, the PCC decreases from 86,53% to 75% and in case of ordered contexts it takes a value of 92,3%. This high value is explained by the appropriate use of this algorithm only in case of ordered databases. From these results, we can conclude that our COID-FDCM produces better classification results than DCA in both cases: ordered and disordered contexts. Indeed, by applying the FDCM to the same database, the PCC varies from 91,34% to 96,63% and in case of an ordered contexts it takes a value of 80,67%. This low value is explained by the use of arbitrary midpoints and extents for the system's membership functions since they are given by an ordinary user. Again, we can easily remark that COID-FDCM generates better results than those of the FDCM in case of disordered contexts as well as in case of an ordered database.

These encouraging COID-FDCM classification results are explained by the appropriate use of the COID maintaining method for the original DCA signal database. The fact of applying this policy induces a small signal database without redundant or noisy objects. Eliminating this kind of instances avoids the use of "wrong" and "useless" data which guaranties a maintained signal database for our method. Moreover, reducing the size of the original DCA signal database decreases the execution time of our COID-FDCM comparing it to DCA and FDCM one since they are applied to the entire database (including the noisy data). In addition, our COID-FDCM is an interesting classification method able to smooth the crisp separation between the two DCs' contexts using fuzzy set theory. As a result, our COID-FDCM generates better classification results than those of the standard DCA and FDCM.

5   Conclusion and Future Works

In this paper, we have developed a modified version of the standard dendritic cell method. Our method aims at maintaining the signal database, smoothing the crisp separation between the two contexts and generating automatically the parameters of the system leading to better results in terms of classification accuracy. As future work, we intend to further explore this new instantiation of our COID-FDCM by introducing weighting methods in order to check the reliability of our classification technique.

References

1. Greensmith, J., Aickelin, U., Cayzer, S.: Introducing Dendritic Cells as a Novel Immune-Inspired Algorithm for Anomaly Detection. In: Jacob, C., Pilat, M.L., Bentley, P.J., Timmis, J.I. (eds.) ICARIS 2005. LNCS, vol. 3627, pp. 153–167. Springer, Heidelberg (2005)
2. Aickelin, U., Greensmith, J.: The Deterministic Dendritic Cell Algorithm. In: 7th International Conference on Artificial Immune Systems, Phuket, Thailand, pp. 291–302 (2008)
3. Smiti, A., Elouedi, Z.: Overview of Maintenance for Case based Reasoning Systems. International Journal of Computer Applications. Foundation of Computer Science 32(2), 49–56 (2011)
4. Smiti, A., Elouedi, Z.: COID: Maintaining Case Method Based on Clustering, Outliers and Internal Detection. In: Lee, R., Ma, J., Bacon, L., Du, W., Petridis, M. (eds.) SNPD 2010. SCI, vol. 295, pp. 39–52. Springer, Heidelberg (2010)
5. Chelly, Z., Elouedi, Z.: FDCM: A Fuzzy Dendritic Cell Method. In: 9th Internatinal Conference of Artificial Immune Systems, Edinburgh, U.K, pp. 102–115 (2010)
6. Chelly, Z., Elouedi, Z.: Further Exploration of the Fuzzy Dendritic Cell Method. In: 10th International Conference of Artificial Immune Systems, Cambridge, U.K, pp. 419–432 (2011)
7. Sander, J., Ester, M., Kriegel, H.P., Xu, X.: Density-Based Clustering in Spatial Databases The Algorithm GDBSCAN and Its Applications. Data Mining, Knowledge Discovery 2, 169–194 (1998)
8. Zadeh, L.: The Concept of a Linguistic Variable and its Application to Approximate Reasoning. Information Sciences 8, 199–251 (1975)
9. Bezdek, J.: Pattern Recognition with Fuzzy Objective Function Algorithms. Plenum Press, New York (1981)
10. UCI machine learning repository, http://archive.ics.uci.edu

Multilayer Neural Networks with Receptive Fields as a Model for the Neuron Reconstruction Problem

Wojciech Czarnecki

Department of Computer Linguistics and Artificial Intelligence,
Faculty of Mathematics and Computer Science,
Adam Mickiewicz University, Poznan, Poland

Abstract. The developed model consists of a multilayer neural network with receptive fields used to estimate the local direction of the neuron on a fragment of microscopy image. It can be used in a wide range of classical neuron reconstruction methods (manual, semi-automatic, local automatic or global automatic), some of which are also outlined in this paper. The model is trained on an automatically generated training set extracted from a provided example image stack and corresponding reconstruction file. During the experiments the model was tested in simple statistical tests and in real applications, and achieved good results. The main advantage of the proposed approach is its simplicity for the end-user, one who might have little or no mathematical/computer science background, as it does not require any manual configuration of constants.

Keywords: artificial neural network, receptive fields, computer vision, neuron reconstruction.

1 Introduction

Understanding how the brain works is one of the greatest challenges of modern science [1]. The development of computational methods for the study of neural anatomy is of particular importance in this field [2]. The neuron reconstruction problem, i.e. retrieving a three-dimensional spatial structure graph of the neural cells imaged using various types of light microscopy, has been investigated since the 1980s [3]. A number of studies have been carried out, e.g. some concerning local automatic tracing methods, where a structure template (e.g. cylinders) is matched to the image data during the iterative greedy process [4]. Others represent a global approach to the problem, where after the seeding step, a minimum spanning tree search with some custom metric is executed [5]. Evers et al. [6] also proposed an approach based on the geodesic active contour model. There are also many semi-automatic algorithms, such as the efficient 3D tracing and editing method by Peng et al. [7]. To our knowledge, there have been no studies regarding the possible applications of fully machine learning-based models.

L. Rutkowski et al. (Eds.): ICAISC 2012, Part II, LNCS 7268, pp. 242–250, 2012.

2   Motivation

Artificial intelligence methods are being successfully used in many fields of biology, from gene detection [8], through protein secondary structure prediction [9], to the analysis of microarrays [10]. They are also becoming more common in general computer vision as well as in biologically related applications [11] [12]. The choice of a neural network with receptive fields as the underlying model for the neuron reconstruction problem is motivated by the successful application of similar methods to image segmentation problems [13] [15], the fact that it is a simplified model of the human visual system, and that for a neurobiologist, i.e. the end-user of this kind of system, such an approach means that there is no required mathematical or computer science knowledge needed to use it, as the whole configuration of the model is executed automatically.

3   Model

The general idea is to create a feedforward neural network based model which, for a given two-dimensional matrix of voxel intensities (being its range of sight, located in the three-dimensional space, rotated in some direction $d \in \mathbb{R}^3$), can estimate if the neuron in this point is rotated in d. For a better analogy to actual sight, this *vision field* is also shifted in the direction $-d$ (so it sees more of what is 'ahead' than 'behind' it, as this data is more important for making a correct estimation).

3.1   Vision Field

Let us denote for some fixed $p \in \mathbb{N}$ (called the *size of the vision field*):

$$V_{XY} = \{-p, -p+1, ..., 0, ..., p-1, p\} \times \{-p, -p+1, ..., 0, ..., p-1, p\} \times \{0\} \quad (1)$$

where XY corresponds to an XY slice of the 3D intensity array. Similarly, one can define V_{XZ}, V_{YZ} and any other type of field. The vision field of type t, centered in point $q \in \mathbb{R}^3$, rotated in the direction d can now be defined as the translation and rotation of V_f (for some fixed $v \in \mathbb{R}$ - *size of the shift*).

$$F_{t,q,d} = \left\{ q + x' + \frac{d}{\|d\|_2} v : x' \in R_d(V_t) \right\} \quad (2)$$

where $R_d(V_t)$ is a set of points from V_t, rotated in the spherical coordinate system of angles between vector d and $(1, 0, 0)$. Naturally, there is an infinite number of possible rotations of the two-dimensional plane in the direction of a given vector. Selecting this particular one is motivated by the fact that it ensures the biggest projection on the XY plane, which has the best resolution in the input data (and as such is the most reliable source of information). The input data is a three-dimensional array I of voxel intensities, and most of the points of the vision fields defined in Equation 2 have non-integer coordinates, so some interpolation of the image function is required. The simplest possibility is to define f as a weighted sum of the values of the closest points with integer coordinates.

$$f(x) = \frac{\sum_{y \in BB(x)} I(y) \cdot max(1 - \|y - x\|_2, 0)}{\sum_{y \in BB(x)} max(1 - \|y - x\|_2, 0)} \tag{3}$$

where $BB(x)$ is a set of eight points with integer coordinates forming a unit bounding box of x. More advanced methods are also possible, but as this function is called many times during an algorithm's execution, it should be computationally easy. Figure 1 shows sample f function values for some vision fields.

Fig. 1. Sample f function values of some XY vision fields, visualized as 31x31 px 8bit images ($p = 15$, $v = 5$)

3.2   Neural Network Estimator

The neural network estimator is composed of artificial neural networks (ANNs) that accept as their input a matrix of voxel intensity and output a value in the $[0, 1]$ range. This value shows if the image from a vision field, placed in point $x \in \mathbb{R}^3$, rotated in the direction d, represents a correctly rotated part of the neuron. The vision fields were defined as a set of points for simplicity but, naturally, we can treat them as two-dimensional matrices. The main element of this model is a four-layer feedforward neural network (Fig. 2), which is trained on the automatically generated training set and extracted from the provided example image stack and corresponding reconstruction file (Sec. 3.3). The weight sharing technique is not used, so that the network can develop different feature detectors in each receptive field (similar to the Phung et al. [13] approach). Every neuron, except for the output one, uses the hyperbolic tangent activation function, so it can provide both inhibitory and excitatory signals [14], while the output node activation is a simple sigmoid function. Bias neurons are also used in all layers.

The neural network estimator can be composed of many actual ANNs trained on various orientations of the vision fields. This helps to easily build more accurate models. Let us denote:

$$NNE(x, d) = \frac{\sum_{t \in T} NN_t(F_{t,x,d})}{|T|} \tag{4}$$

where T is a set of all the used field types (e.g. $T = \{XY, XZ\}$), and $NN_t(F_{t,x,d})$ is the output of the neural network indexed with t on the vision field $F_{t,x,d}$ values of function f (Eq. 3).

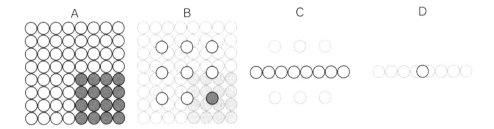

Fig. 2. Neural network topology. A - input layer, with each neuron connected to the corresponding point in the vision field, B - hidden receptive layer, where each neuron is connected only to its square shaped receptive field (gray neurons) in the input layer, C - hidden layer, fully connected with the previous one, D - output layer, also fully connected.

3.3   Learning

To train this model, only an image stack and corresponding manual reconstruction are needed. The depth first search algorithm executed on the reconstruction tree can extract (on each point of this graph) all the required vision fields. The only problem then is to find the expected output for this input according to the given data. A good heuristic for this task should:

- be absolute, i.e. its results have to be comparable whichever tracing position is considered
- prefer locally best fitted directions
- not use information from the image stack
- consider difficulties deriving from the bifurcation points
- take into account the diameter of the neuron in the current location
- be bounded, as it will be used as the desired output of the neural network.

For this purpose, the heuristic S defined in Equations 5, 6 and 7 is given. First, $dist_q(d, x)$ is defined, which measures the distance of point x from the half-line between the origin and direction d (with respect to the neuron diameter $diam_q$ in point q).

$$
dist_q(d, x) = \begin{cases} 0, & \text{for} \quad \|x\|_2 \leq diam_q \\ \|x - d(x^T d)\|_2, & \text{for} \quad \|x\|_2 > diam_q \text{ and } x^T d \geq 0 \\ \|x\|_2, & \text{for} \quad \|x\|_2 > diam_q \text{ and } x^T d < 0 \end{cases} \tag{5}
$$

To prefer locally best fitted directions, the *small score function* is defined as a weighted mean of *dist* values.

$$
s_q(d, \{x_i\}_{i \in \{1,..,k\}}) = 1 - \frac{2}{k(k+1)} \sum_{i=1}^{k} (k - i + 1) \frac{min\{dist_q(d, x_i - q), maxdist\}}{maxdist},
$$
$$
\tag{6}
$$

where *maxdist* is the maximum value of *dist* worth considering in our applications. As it is a simple cut-off, its exact value is not crucial and can be set in the (1,p] range.

S is defined as a search through all possible paths starting in the considered point for the best (in the sense of s value) fit.

$$S(d, q) = max_{X \in T_q^p} \frac{max_{x \in X} max\{0, (x - q)^T d\}}{p} s_q(d, X) \tag{7}$$

where T_q^p is a set of paths in the reconstruction tree T from q to some leaf, with all nodes removed that are more distant from q than the size of the vision field - p. Sample S function values with corresponding f function values of some vision fields extracted during the learning phase are given in Figure 3.

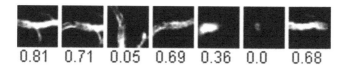

0.81   0.71   0.05   0.69   0.36   0.0   0.68

Fig. 3. Example f function values of vision fields with corresponding S values

4   Experiments and Results

After simple tests the model parameters were set to 20 hidden neurons, 31x31 vision fields, and 4x4 receptive fields with 2 pixel overlapping. The network was trained using the backpropagation algorithm (learning rate set to 0.02, momentum set to 0.7). The early stopping method was used to find the best training stop moment [16]. Confocal microscopy images of the olfactory bulb of Drosophila, retrieved from the DIADEM Challenge [17] competition, were used during the experiments. One image (with a corresponding gold standard reconstruction) was used to construct the training set (3000 samples) and validation set (750 samples), and the rest of the images were used for testing. Tests were also run on images from the Stanford FlyBrain Database containing images from the same type of microscopy and brain region as the training data (unfortunately without corresponding reconstructions).

In most cases the DIADEM metric [18] was used to compare the results of the algorithm to the correct, manual reconstructions. During the statistical tests some other metrics were also used:

- SE - mean amount of incorrectly ordered triples (max, mid, low) by NNE, generated during validation of set extraction,
- ME - mean squared error on the validating set,
- MA - mean angle (in radians) between the correct direction (according to the heuristic S) and the one with the highest response of NNE among all possible directions (tested using one whole reconstruction file).

4.1 Learning Phase Tests

The first step of the experiments was to test the learning phase of the model and to find some of the remaining parameters. As mentioned before in Section 3.2, NNE can use many different vision fields and neural networks for them. In Table 1 one can find the sample results of testing three different settings. After this phase all of the following experiments were performed using NNE composed of two vision fields (XY, XZ) trained on a single (XY) field, as this achieved the best results (mostly because of the low resolution among the Z-axis, which caused a low quality of the XZ training vectors). These were all executed on the testing set of images (different than those used for the training).

Table 1. The 'trained' column contains vision fields on which the neural network(s) was/were trained. In the second experiment both vision fields were evaluated using a network trained on the XY field.

id	trained	used	SE	ME	MA
1.	XY	XY	0.0048	0.0096	0.289
2.	XY	XY, XZ	0.0032	0.0077	0.258
3.	XY, XZ	XY, XZ	0.0048	0.0104	0.290

4.2 Evaluation Tests

The simple greedy local tracing algorithm was implemented to test the model's usefulness in local automatic approaches. At each step the algorithm sets NNE in every direction (from the precomputed set of possible directions) and records its output. It moves in the direction d_{max} of the highest value.

It bifurcates if and only if there is a non-empty set of other directions (candidates) with a value of at least 0.7 of the d_{max} value. It chooses the direction d_{bif} from this set by searching through the shortest paths on the unit sphere between those directions and d_{max} and selecting the point which has the lowest value on its path (see Figure 4 for more details).

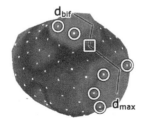

Fig. 4. A visualization of the NNE values (color and distance from the 'sphere' center is proportional to the network output) of all possible directions (white squares) - the directions in white circles are the 'candidates' for the bifurcation point and the direction in the white square is the one with the lowest value among all the shortest paths between d_{max} and the candidates.

Table 2. Results of greedy local tracing in comparison to free NeuronStudio software and the DIADEM Challenge finalists' algorithm [19]

	NeuronStudio	NNE	Eugene Myers Team
score	0.80	0.82	0.97

The best achieved result during the tests was 0.82 (Fig. 5), which is comparable to the NeuronStudio results, but far behind one of the DIADEM challenge finalists' algorithms - that of the Eugene Myers Team (Table 2). The results for the rest of the testing set were between 0.4 and 0.7 (mostly because of the weak bifurcation condition, but when it was user manually helped, by running it from the bifurcation points, the score increased to 0.7-0.9).

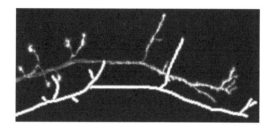

Fig. 5. Fragment of the XY projection of the best reconstruction achieved using the local greedy algorithm. The reconstruction is shifted for better visualization.

In applications where the user traces a neuron by continuously selecting some (possibly distant) points of the cell, the trained NNE can trace the dendrite using Dijkstra's algorithm with the distance between two spatially adjacent voxels a and b defined as follows:

$$d(a,b) = \left(1 - \frac{NNE(a, b-a) + NNE(b, a-b)}{2}\right) \|a - b\|_2 \tag{8}$$

Tests of this type of approach (Fig. 6) resulted in reconstructions of the DIADEM metric between 0.8 and 0.95, with a mean score of 0.89.

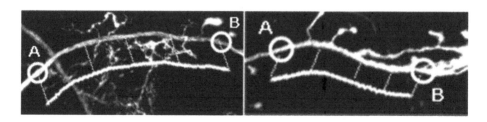

Fig. 6. Fragment of the XY projection of semi-automated tracing between point A and B selected by the user. Reconstruction is shifted for better visualization.

A similar approach can be used in global automatic methods, where after the seeding part (preprocessing of the image to find voxels that are definitely parts of the neuron), the minimum spanning tree algorithm (e.g. Kruskal's or Prim's algorithm) is executed according to the distance function defined in Equation 8.

5   Conclusion

The model proposed in this paper is the first approach to using machine learning methods directly to the neuron reconstruction problem. The achieved results, wide range of possible applications (from manual reconstruction systems, where it can serve as a reconstruction assistant, suggesting the best tracing direction or simply visualizing the network output for all possible directions, to local and global automatic systems) and intuitive configuration (as every neurobiologist dealing with the reconstruction problem already has some manual reconstructions that can be used to train this model), all show that it can be a valuable alternative to the models currently being used.

Future plans include tuning the model's structure (e.g. introducing both inhibitory and excitatory receptive fields, similarly to those in Fernandes et al. [20]), improving the heuristic used for learning set extraction and a more complex method of network training (e.g. reinforcement learning with the agent moving along the neuron structure instead of simple batch learning).

References

1. Roysam, B., Shain, W., Ascoli, G.A.: The central role of neuroinformatics in the national academy of engineering's grandest challenge: reverse engineer the brain. Neuroinformatics 7, 1–5 (2009)
2. Ascoli, G.A.: Computational Neuroanatomy: Principles and Methods. Humana Press, New Jersey (2002)
3. Capowski, J.J.: An automatic neuron reconstruction system. Journal of Neuroscience Methods 8, 353–364 (1983)
4. Al-Kofahi, K.A., Lasek, S., Szarowski, D.H., Pace, C.J., Nagy, G., Turner, J.N., Roysam, B.: Rapid automated three-dimensional tracing of neurons from confocal image stacks. IEEE Trans. Informat. Technol. Biomed. 6, 171–187 (2002)
5. Peng, H., Ruan, Z., Atasoy, D., Sternson, S.: Automatic reconstruction of 3D neuron structures using a graph-augmented deformable model. Bioinformatics 26, 138–146 (2010)
6. Evers, J.F., Schmitt, S., Sibila, M., Duch, C.: Progress in functional neuroanatomy: Precise automatic geometric reconstruction of neuronal morphology from confocal image stacks. Journal of Neurophysiology 93, 2331–2342 (2005)
7. Peng, H., Ruan, Z., Long, F., Simpson, J.H., Myers, E.W.: V3D enables real-time 3D visualization and quantitative analysis of large-scale biological image data sets. Nature Biotechnology 28(4), 348–353 (2010)
8. Burge, C.B.: Modeling dependencies in pre-mRNA splicing signals. Computational Methods in Molecular Biology, 127–163 (1998)
9. Jones, D.T.: Protein secondary structure prediction based on position-specific scoring matrices. Journal of Molecular Biology 292(2), 195–202 (1999)

10. Brown, M.P.S., Grundy, W.N., Lin, D., Cristianini, N., Sugnet, C.W., Furey, T.S., Ares, M., Haussler, D.: Knowledge-based analysis of microarray gene expression data by using support vector machines. Proceedings of the National Academy of Sciences of the United States of America 97(1), 262–267 (2000)

11. Turaga, S.C., Murray, J.F., Jain, V., Roth, F., Helmstaedter, M., Briggman, K., Denk, W., Seung, H.S.: Convolutional networks can learn to generate affinity graphs for image segmentation. Neural Computation 22(2), 511–538 (2010)

12. Kreshuk, A., Straehle, C.N., Sommer, C., Koethe, U., Cantoni, M., Knott, G., Hamprecht, F.A.: Automated detection and segmentation of synaptic contacts in nearly isotropic serial electron microscopy images. PLoS ONE 6 (2011)

13. Phung, S.L., Bouzerdoum, A.: A pyramidal neural network for visual pattern recognition. IEEE Transactions on Neural Networks 18(2), 329–343 (2007)

14. Haykin, S.: Neural Networks and Learning Machines. Prentice Hall (2008)

15. Egmont-Petersen, M.: Image processing with neural networks - a review. Pattern Recognition 35, 2279–2301 (2002)

16. Sarle, W.S.: Stopped Training and Other Remedies for Overfitting. In: Proceedings of the 27th Symposium on the Interface of Computing Science and Statistics, pp. 352–360 (1995)

17. Brown, K.M., Barrionuevo, G., Canty, A.J., De Paola, V., Hirsch, J.A., Jefferis, G.S.X.E., Lu, J., Snippe, M., Sugihara, I., Ascoli, G.A.: The diadem data sets: Representative light microscopy images of neuronal morphology to advance automation of digital reconstructions. Neuroinformatics 9(2-3), 143–157 (2011)

18. Gillette, T., Brown, K., Ascoli, G.A.: The diadem metric: Comparing multiple reconstructions of the same neuron. Neuroinformatics 9, 233–245 (2011)

19. Zhao, T., Xie, J., Amat, F., Clack, N., Ahammad, P., Peng, H., Long, F., et al.: Automated Reconstruction of Neuronal Morphology Based on Local Geometrical and Global Structural Models. Neuroinformatics 9(2-3), 247–261 (2011)

20. Fernandes, B.J.T., Cavalcanti, G.D.C., Ren, T.I.: Nonclassical receptive field inhibition applied to image segmentation. Neural Network World 19, 21–36 (2009)

Human Gait Recognition Based on Signals from Two Force Plates

Marcin Derlatka

Bialystok University of Technology,
Wiejska Street 45C, 15-351 Bialystok, Poland
mder@pb.edu.pl

Abstract. This paper presents a practical approach to person recognition by gait. The biometric system is based on ground reaction forces and positions of the center of pressure generated during the subject gait and the single-output multilayer neural network. The article discusses both the identification and the verification problems as well as influence of the security level on the quality of the proposed biometric system. The achieved results (almost 96% of correct recognition) show that human gait is a biometric measure which enables efficient authorization in a simple way.

Keywords: biometrics, human gait, force plate, neural networks.

1 Introduction

The biometrics can be regarded as a pattern recognition system based on individuals physical or behavioral features which allow to distinguish individuals. Using the most commonly biometrics authentication methods have the significant advantage over traditional authentication techniques based on, for instance, the knowledge of passwords or the possession of a special card. The biometric patterns are unique for each individual and cannot be lost, stolen or forgotten. This is the reason why biometrics systems are recently increasingly popular. The physiological biometrics is based on a measurable characteristics of some part of human body like fingerprints, retina, iris. The behavioral biometrics manages data which are the result of performing common human activity, for example: speech, handwriting or gait.

Among the above given biometrics methods the special attention should be paid to human gait. Gait is a very complex human activity. It is a symmetrical and repetitive phenomenon in its normal form. The movement of each limb is partitioned for the support phase - when the foot is in contact with the ground and the swing phase when the foot is lifted and moved forward. The human gait is developed during child growth. It is assumed that the human gait pattern is evaluated till the child is seven years old and next stay almost unchanged till his death. The human gait is the result of synergistic activity of: bones, muscles and nervous systems. The cooperation of those three systems makes the human movement unique for every person.[8]

L. Rutkowski et al. (Eds.): ICAISC 2012, Part II, LNCS 7268, pp. 251–258, 2012.
© Springer-Verlag Berlin Heidelberg 2012

In contrast to other biometrics authentication methods, human gait has the following advantages:

- the person does not need to interact with any measurement system in an unnatural way; it is sufficient that the subject passes through a pathway equipped, in this case, with force plates;
- trails can be done only by a living person;
- the verified subject does not need to be aware of being submitted to the authentication procedure.

Gait is not actually new biometrics. Nowadays the most popular approach used in authentication people by the way they walk is based on a video analysis. In this case, a set of parameters is calculated from a sequence of images[1]. The problems with using video data in biometrics systems are: changes of the lighting and the clothing of the investigated person. The other popular approach is based on the signals describing how the plantar of the human foot acting on the surface. In work [6] the authors used two one-sized insoles which were fastened to the ground for measuring foot's center pressure during the special planned excersises executed by the subject. In [4] footprints of the individuals have been used for human recognition. In this unique approach the authors achieved up to 85% of correct recognition. A different approach has been proposed in[5]. The authors used the vertical component of the ground reaction force (GRF) and the nearest neighbour classification for subject recognition. They used ten parameters such as: the mean and standard deviation of the profile, the length of the profile (number of samples), the area under the profile and finally the coordinates of two maximum points and the minimum point to describe each of the GRF profiles. In the previous author's work [2] the biometric system which made the authentication task based on GRF signals by means of set single-output multilayer neural network has been described. The results pointed to that there is a need to use two force plates to achieve better quality of the biometrics system.

2   Recognition of Human Gait

There are two main tasks to be performed by the biometric system. They are: verification and identification. The system in the identification mode should return the name or the number of the investigated subject. In the verification mode the user introduces himself and enters his biometrics patterns. The system should check if the presented pattern does belong to the user.

2.1   Ground Reaction Force and Trajectories of Center of Pressure

In the biomechanical approach, the ground reaction force (GRF) is the force which is acting on the body as a response to its weight and inertia during the contact of the human plantar with the surface. The all three components of GRF are used in the presented work. They are: anterior/posterior F_x, vertical F_y and medial/lateral F_z components of GRF. The common profiles of the GRF components are presented in Fig. 1 (a-c).

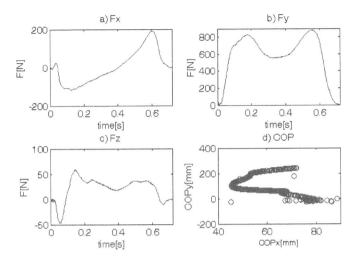

Fig. 1. Analyzed signals: components of GRF in: a) anterior/posterior, b) vertical, c) medial/lateral direction, d) trajectory of COP during the support phase of the left lower limb

The anterior/posterior component has two main phases. The value of F_x is negative in the first phase. It is a result of the deceleration of the investigated lower limb, in this case the force direction is opposite in direction of walking. The minimum of the deceleration phase is most often reached a moment before the maximum of the limb-loading phase in the vertical component of GRF. The value of F_x is positive in the second phase, respectively. The maximum of the acceleration phase is reached when the toe-off phase starts.

There are three extremes in Fig. 1b. They correspond to: the maximum of the limb-loading phase, the minimum of the limb-unloading phase and the maximum of the propulsion phase (a moment before the toe off). It is not difficult to point to the same extremes for the medial/lateral component of GRF as for the vertical GRF.

A force plate could measure the center of pressure (COP), too. The COP is the point of location of the vertical component of GRF. The point is given as coordinates where the origin of coordinates is determined before the experiment. The work presented took into consideration the trajectory of COP during the support phase of the subject. In [3] COP has been used as a good index to calculate the balance of individuals.

2.2   Vector of Features

The force plates record the all three components of GRF and the coordinates of COP position. This gives ten vectors of the measure values depended on time as a result of the investigation. The measured data can be presented as a matrix which is representation of one token:

$$\mathbf{P} = \begin{bmatrix} \mathrm{p}_1^1 & \mathrm{p}_1^2 & \cdots & \mathrm{p}_1^i & \cdots & \mathrm{p}_1^{10} \\ \mathrm{p}_2^1 & \mathrm{p}_2^2 & \cdots & \mathrm{p}_2^i & \cdots & \mathrm{p}_2^{10} \\ \vdots & \vdots & & \vdots & & \vdots \\ \mathrm{p}_N^1 & \mathrm{p}_N^2 & \cdots & \mathrm{p}_N^i & \cdots & \mathrm{p}_N^{10} \end{bmatrix} \qquad (1)$$

where: i= 3,4,5 consists of the three components of the GRF for the left lower limb; i=8,9,10 - components of the GRF for the right lower limb; i=1,2 and i=6,7 trajectories of COPs measured by the forces plates for the left and the right lower limb respectively; N - number of samples.

Here, in contrast to the approach used in biomechanics, the GRF is not normalized, because the value of GRF corresponds to body weight of the investigated subject, so it could be useful in distinguishing individuals. It was also proved experimentally in [9] where normalization of GRF drastically reduced the quality of the biometrics system. In the presented work the following parameters are extracted for representation of the support phase of a single step:

- duration of the support phase separately for the left lower limb and the right one;
- relatively duration of the single support phase separately for the left lower limb and the right one;
- mean of the each GRF profiles;
- standard deviation of the each GRF profiles;
- eigenvalues and eigenvectors of the covariance matrix created based on token P (only parameters indicated by i=3,4,5,8,9,10);
- the coefficients of a polynomial of 9th degree that fits the F_j=f(time) best in a least-squares sense: $a_{j,9}, a_{j,8}, ..., a_{j,1}, a_{j,0}$, where $j \in \{x_L, y_L, z_L, x_R, y_R, z_R\}$; L - left leg, R - right leg;
- the coefficients of a polynomial of 9th degree that fits the COP_{x_L}=f(COP_{y_L}) and COP_{x_R}=f(COP_{y_R})best in a least-squares sense $b_9, b_8, ..., b_1$ except b_0, because b_0 don't indicate the shape, but only position of heel strike during trials.

As a conclusion, each token is converted into an input vector used by the neural network in the biometric system.

2.3   Applying of the Neural Networks

The classical multilayer neural network with one hidden layer and one output neuron is implemented. Each neuron has a sigmoid activation function. The neural network is learned with Rprop algorithm with the same learning parameters as many times as the users are presented in the database. The network is learned to recognize only one user at time (Fig. 2). It is achieved by changing the network output desirable value in the training set. The neural network is learned to get the output equal 1 for the considered user and to get output equal 0 for other users. The neural network is initialized with the same weight's values before the

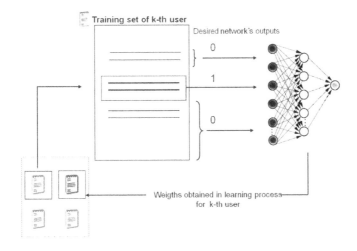

Fig. 2. The process of learning the single user gait

learning process for each user. The weights of the neural networks are written into the proper file associated with the considered user after training.

In the verification mode the neural network weights are read from the file associated with the claim user. The user's gait is transformed according to the way described in subsection 2.2 and the input vector is presented into the network's input. The response value is compared with the assumed security level $(0.1 \div 0.9)$. The positive verification is accepted only if the network response is greater than the security level.

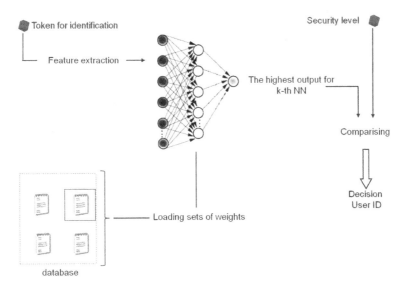

Fig. 3. Scheme of identification process

In the identification mode, as well as in the verification the user's gait is transformed into the network's input vector. Subsequently, the network response for every weights vector stored in the database is checked up. The system chooses this user's ID for which the neural network response is the greatest. If the chosen response of the neural network is greater than the assumed threshold the decision about the recognition of a user is positive. Otherwise the system treats the subject as unrecognized (Fig. 3).

3 Results

3.1 Measurements and Experimental Population

The measurements were made in the Bialystok University of Technology on a group of 54 students (39 men and 15 women) by means of the two Kistler force plates. The subjects who took part in the investigations were at age 20.7 ± 1.15, body weight 75.39 ± 15.17 and body height 177.2 ± 8.22. The number of volunteers is rather big comparing to others work in the biometrics systems using gait[7]. Moreover, the recruiting the volunteers from students make the database more homogeneous (that is harder for correct classification) than in real life.

The subjects filled the special questionnaire before investigations. The questions were connected to the health history of the subjects and their emotional and physical state. Twenty nine subjects had not experienced injuries or abnormalities affecting their gait. Eleven volunteers reported a sprain of ankle (four students in two legs) in the past. Five person had the broken leg in the past(a tibia or a hallux)and six students reported a posture's defect (scoliosis, kyphosis). Only one volunteer has flat foot. A few volunteers reported two or more deficiencies which existed together. Among the volunteers was one subject who walked in an unnatural way holding his elbow by the second hand. The two Kistler force plates were hidden on the pathway and recorded data with frequency 1kHz. The volunteers made several trails (10 ÷ 16) with comfortable self-selected velocity in their own shoes hitting at the plate with the left and the right leg, so almost 800 gait cycles have been recorded. 457 tokens from 49 users were used to build the learning set. 336 tokens from all 54 users were treated as the testing set. Five subjects (55 trials) who were represented only in the testing set were used for checking the biometric system's ability to stop intruders both in the identification and the verification tasks. Among the intruders only one reported a sprain of ankle injury which took place 5 years before the investigation. Moreover he was emotional person with rather unstable and small repeatability gait. The rest of intruders did not rise any health problem which can influence their gait.

3.2 Recognition Accuracy

The results of the identification and verification of the subject depending on the security level are presented in Table 1. The presented values were calculated on base of the data from the testing set.

Table 1. The results of the identification and verification of the users and intruders

security level	identification			verification	
	users		intruders	users	intruders
	false rejected	false accepted	false accepted	false rejected	false accepted
0.1	1.42%	1.42%	80.0%	1.42%	2.37%
0.2	2.49%	0.71%	49.1%	2.49%	1.22%
0.3	2.49%	0.71%	29.1%	2.49%	0.59%
0.4	2.49%	0.36%	20.0%	2.49%	0.41%
0.5	2.49%	0.36%	7.27%	2.49%	0.15%
0.6	2.49%	0.36%	5.45%	2.49%	0.11%
0.7	3.20%	0.36%	3.64%	3.20%	0.07%
0.8	4.27%	0%	1.82%	4.27%	0.03%
0.9	12.1%	0%	0%	12.1%	0%

Choosing the optimal value of the security level one should remember that projecting of the biometrics system is the compromise between false rejected rate and false accepted rate. Moreover, it should be taken into consideration the value of false accepted intruders, too. In the author's previous work [2] the security level has been estimated as equal 0.8. This value gives more than 95.5% correct recognised user's cycles both in the identification and the verification modes and 0% false accepted gait cycles (see Table 1).

One third of bad recognised gait cycles belong to one person. The neural network's output for him was close to zero in many his cycles. It means that the presented biometrics system regards that the gait cycles from testing set are too much different than the strides included in training set. At first look, the security level equal 0.8 gives almost 2% chances for intruders in the identification mode. In fact, bad recognized was only one cycle. The more detailed analysis of this case show that there are some similarities between user and this particular intruder. They are the same gender. They have almost the same body masses and body weights. None of them didn't report any injuries in the past. Moreover they prescribed in the questionnaire their physical and emotional state in the exactly the same words. The presented biometrics system has no special problems with authentication subjects who reported any injuries in the past. The quality of the system is similar like in case of healthy volunteers.

To sum up, the general recognition accuracy is really high especially comparing to works where GRF profiles have been used. In work [7] where the resuls of some authors have been presented the best results achieved 94% of correct recognised subjects.

4 Conclusions

The presented biometric system based on the signals derived from two force plates shows that the human gait is a biometric measure which enables efficient authorization in a simple way. It works in the way invisible to the subjects.

It can be successfully applied in both indoor or outdoor conditions without any changes and, what is the most important, it works with high efficiency. The author is aware of some limitations of the presented results, of course. First of all, the presented system is hard flexible. It is necessary to rebuild each of the training sets and to retrain each of the neural networks in the case of addition at least one more authorized user to the database. Second there is a need to investigate how some of the external factors like shoes or loading influence for the quality of the system. These limitations will be dealt with in future works.

Acknowledgments. This paper is supported by grant S/WM/1/12 from the Bialystok University of Technology.

References

1. Balista, J.A., Soriano, M.N., Saloma, C.A.: Compact Time-independent Pattern Representation of Entire Human Gait Cycle for Tracking of Gait Irregularities. Pattern Recognition Letters 31, 20–27 (2010)
2. Derlatka, M.: Biometric System for Person Recognition Using Gait. In: Kryszkiewicz, M., Rybinski, H., Skowron, A., Raś, Z.W. (eds.) ISMIS 2011. LNCS (LNAI), vol. 6804, pp. 565–574. Springer, Heidelberg (2011)
3. Karlsson, A., Frykberg, G.: Correlations Between Force Plate Measures for Assessment of Balance. Clin. Biomech. 15(5), 365–369 (2000)
4. Nakajima, K., Mizukami, Y., Tanaka, K., Tamura, T.: Footprint-Based Personal Recognition. IEEE Transactions on Biomedical Engineering 47(11), 1534–1537 (2000)
5. Orr, R.J., Abowd, G.D.: The Smart Floor: a Mechanism for Natural User Identification and Tracking. In: Proc. of Conference on Human Factors in Computing Systems (2000)
6. Porwik, P., Zygula, J., Doroz, R., Proksa, R.: Biometric Recognition System Based on the Motion of the Human Body Gravity Centre Analysis. Journal of Medical Informatics and Technologies 15, 61–69 (2010)
7. Rodriguez, V.R., Manson, J., Evans, N.: Assessment of a Footstep Biometric Verification System Handbook of Remote Biometrics. In: Tistarelli, et al. (eds.) Advances in Pattern Recognition, London, pp. 313–327 (2009)
8. Winter, D.A.: Biomechanics and Motor Control of Human Movement, 4th edn. John Wiley & Sons inc. (2009)
9. Yao, Z., et al.: A Novel Biometric Recognition System Based on Ground Reaction Force Measurements of Continuous Gait. Human System Interactions. In: 3rd Conf. on Digital Object Identifier, Rzeszow Poland, pp. 452-458 (2010)

Prediction of Radical Hysterectomy Complications for Cervical Cancer Using Computational Intelligence Methods

Jacek Kluska[1], Maciej Kusy[1], and Bogdan Obrzut[2]

[1] Faculty of Electrical and Computer Engineering, Rzeszow University of Technology,
35-959 Rzeszow, W. Pola 2, Poland
{jacklu,mkusy}@prz.edu.pl
[2] Department of Obstetrics and Gynecology, Pro-Familia Hospital in Rzeszow,
Faculty of Medicine, University of Rzeszow, 35-205 Rzeszow,
Warszawska 26a, Poland
b.obrzut@interia.pl

Abstract. In this work, eleven classifiers were tested in the prediction of intra- and post-operative complications in women with cervical cancer. For the real data set the normalization of the input variables was applied, the feature selection was performed and the original data set was binarized. The simulation showed the best model satisfying the quality criteria such as: the average value and the standard deviation of the error, the area under ROC curve, sensitivity and specificity. The results can be useful in clinical practice.

Keywords: machine learning classifiers, cervical cancer, cross validation, complications prediction, diagnostic accuracy.

1 Introduction

Computational intelligence methods, in medical domain, are mostly used in diagnosis support, survival prognosis and prediction of treatment complications [4], [5], [13], [16], [24]. The methods of complication predictions among patients with cervical cancer, which is the third most commonly diagnosed carcinoma and the fourth leading cause of cancer death in females worldwide [11], have not been elaborated so far though.

Carcinoma of the uterine cervix grows locally and may extend in continuity to the adjacent tissues, spread to regional lymph nodes and later metastasize to distant organs. Spread of the disease is most often clinically staged by the International Federation of Gynecology and Obstetrics (FIGO) [17].

In early tumor stages, the surgical methods are preferred. Patients with cervical cancer FIGO 0-IA1 should be treated with conisation or simple hysterectomy. For more advanced disease (FIGO IA2-IIB), in many medical centers, radical hysterectomy with pelvic lymphadenectomy remains the therapy of choice [23]. This operation is one of the most extensive surgical procedures in gynecological oncology and is burdened with significant risk of severe complications, e.g.: injuries of large blood vessels and related organs or pulmonary embolism [15].

L. Rutkowski et al. (Eds.): ICAISC 2012, Part II, LNCS 7268, pp. 259–267, 2012.

The complications resulting from the radical hysterectomy may cause an additional stress of a patient, postpone the adjuvant therapy and significantly increase hospital costs. Thus, the identification of patients with high risk of intra- and post-operative complications is of a great importance, since the chemoradiation would be probably more safe and equally effective therapeutic option for them.

The aim of this contribution is to evaluate the efficacy of artificial intelligence methods in the prediction of radical hysterectomy complications in women with cervical cancer FIGO IA2-IIB. The real data consisting of 107 patients with 10 attributes obtained from the Clinical Department of Obstetrics and Gynecology of Rzeszow State Hospital in Poland was investigated.

The paper is organized as follows. In Section 2, the data set description and the binbarization method of predictors are presented. Section 3 describes how the input data is partitioned into training and testing subsets. Section 4 highlights the algorithms used for classification purposes. In Section 5, the simulation results are presented. Finally, Section 6 summarizes the work.

2   Data Set Description and Binarization of Predictors

Each data record from the original data set consists of 10 predictor variables: age (x_1 [y]), height (x_2 [cm]), weight (x_3 [kg]), body mass index (BMI, x_4 [kg / m^2]), comorbidities ($x_5 \in \{no, yes\}$), previous operations ($x_6 \in \{no, yes\}$), hormonal status ($x_7 \in \{premenopausal, postmenopausal\}$), histology of tumor ($x_8 \in \{plano, other\}$), histologic grade ($x_9 \in \{G1, G2, G3\}$), FIGO stage ($x_{10} \in \{IA2, IB1, IB2, IIA, IIB\}$) [17]. The output variable is $y \in \{no, yes\}$, where yes means occurrence of intra- or post-operative complications, and $y = no$ − means vice-versa.

In this work we use both original and normalized data set. There are many ways of normalization of the input variables, but we consider a specific type of coding called "binarization" what is briefly described below.

The input variables x_1, x_2 and x_3 (age, height, weight, respectively) are from the finite sets containing real numbers, i.e. $x_k \in X_k = \{r_{k,1}, \ldots, r_{k,q}\}$, ($k = 1, 2, 3$). First, for every variable x_k we make a partition of the whole set X_k into three subsets: $X_{1,k}$, $X_{2,k}$, and $X_{3,k}$, so that $\bigcup_{i=1,2,3} X_{i,k} = X_k$ and $X_{i,k} \cap X_{j,k} = \emptyset$ for $i \neq j$. Next, we compute a mean value m_k and the standard deviation σ_k for each set X_k. The subset $X_{1,k}$ contains "low" values from the set X_k, i.e. $x_k \leqslant m_k - \sigma_k$. The subset $X_{2,k}$ contains all the "middle" values from the set X_k, ($m_k - \sigma_k < x_k < m_k + \sigma_k$), and the subset $X_{3,k}$ contains all the "high" values from the set X_k, ($x_k \geqslant m_k + \sigma_k$). For the input variable x_1 (age) from the set $X_1 = \{29, \ldots, 73\}$ we obtain $X_{1,1} = \{29, \ldots, 39\}$, $X_{2,1} = \{40, \ldots, 58\}$, $X_{3,1} = \{59, \ldots, 73\}$. On the basis of such a subseting we determine data binarization as follows. We introduce the binary values $b_i \in \{0, 1\}$ so that any subset of the input variables x_1, x_2 and x_3 is unambiguously identified by new variable b_i, e.g. $b_1 = 1$ iff $x_1 \in X_{1,1}$, $b_2 = 1$ iff $x_1 \in X_{2,1}$, $b_3 = 1$ iff $x_1 \in X_{3,1}$, $b_4 = 1$ iff $x_2 \in X_{1,2}$ and so on. In this way $b_1 + b_2 + b_3 = 1$, $b_4 + b_5 + b_6 = 1$, $b_7 + b_8 + b_9 = 1$

where $b_i \in \{0, 1\}$. Thus, for x_1, x_2 and x_3 we have 9 binary variables $b_1 \ldots b_9$. In case of x_4 variable (BMI) we have the following classification according to WHO: $x_4 \in [17, 18.5)$ – underweight: mild thinness $\Rightarrow b_{10} = 1$, $x_4 \in [18.5, 25)$ – normal range $\Rightarrow b_{11} = 1$, $x_4 \in [25, 30)$ – overweight: severe thinness $\Rightarrow b_{12} = 1$, $x_4 \in [30, 35)$ – obese class I $\Rightarrow b_{13} = 1$, $x_4 \in [35, 40)$ – obese class II $\Rightarrow b_{14} = 1$, and $x_4 \geq 40$ – obese class III $\Rightarrow b_{15} = 1$. For coding $x_5 \ldots x_8$ inputs we use $b_{16} \ldots b_{19}$ binary values. In case of $x_9 \in \{G1, G2, G3\}$, we assume that $b_{19+i} = 1$ iff $x_9 = Gi$, $(i = 1, 2, 3)$. The variable x_{10} denotes FIGO staging of cervical cancer and it is coded as follows: $x_{10} = IA2 \Rightarrow b_{23} = 1$, $x_{10} = IB1 \Rightarrow b_{24} = 1$, $x_{10} = IB2 \Rightarrow b_{25} = 1$, $x_{10} = IIA \Rightarrow b_{26} = 1$, and finally $x_{10} = IIB \Rightarrow b_{27} = 1$. In case of variables $x_1 - x_3$, such a type of the binarization has natural and simple clinical interpretation. In case of the remaining variables, it is consistent with the categorization according to WHO and FIGO.

3   Data Partition for Training and Testing

Cross-validation is a statistical method of evaluating and comparing learning algorithms by dividing data into two segments: one used to train a model and the other used to validate the model. Usually, we divide the training data containing n samples into v equal-sized groups and conduct v separate operations. Each group is omitted in turn from the data, the model is fitted to the remaining $(v - 1)$ groups and the predictions are obtained for the omitted group [19]. The number of individuals in each omitted group is $k = n/v$, so the method of assessment is called *leave-k-out*. There are $h = n! / (v! (k!)^v)$ ways of dividing the training set into v groups each of size k, and different partitions may yield very different performance assessments [12]. For $n = 100$, the number of ways of dividing the training set into $v = 10$ groups each of size $k = 10$, exceeds 10^{98}. Thus, considering all possible training sets is computationally intractable in practice. Usually a random data partition is assumed by the value of $v = 10$. Nevertheless, the question of choosing v remains widely open [1].

We consider the partition of $n = 107$ samples into 6 training and testing parts, which are taken randomly. The percentage of testing data are 50%, 40%, 30%, 20%, 10% and 5%, i.e. $2 \leqslant v \leqslant 18$, what is in accordance with [1].

4   Algorithms Used in Analysis

In the research we use eleven classification algorithms: k-nearest neighbor (kNN), classification and regression trees (CART), C5, logistic regression (Log. Reg.), bayesian network (BN), support vector machine (SVM), multilayer perceptron (MLP), k-means clustering (k-Means), probabilistic neural network (PNN), linear discriminant analysis (LDA) and radial basis function neural network (RBF), which are well described in the literature, e.g. [28]. Therefore only the models: CART, C5, Log. Reg., BN, SVM, MLP, and k-Means, are shortly characterized in the following subsections. Because of limited paper space, the results for only these algorithms will be given in Section 5.

4.1   Classification and Regression Trees

Classification and regression trees (CART) were originally described in [3]. Decision trees are represented by a set of questions which splits the training sample into smaller and smaller parts. CART algorithm searches for all possible variables and all possible values in order to find the best split – the question that splits the data into two parts, i.e. until the some stopping criterion is satisfied. The process is then repeated for each of the resulting data fragments. Roughly speaking, CART methodology consists of construction of maximum tree, choice of the right tree size, and classification of new data using constructed tree.

4.2   C5 Algorithm

C5 (or See5) is an algorithm used to generate a decision tree developed by Quinlan [18]. It is a successor to C4.5 which, in turn, is an extension of Quinlan's earlier ID3 algorithm. C4.5 first grows an initial tree using the divide-and-conquer algorithm [28]. This tree is pruned to avoid overfitting. C4.5 generates classifiers expressed as decision trees, but it can also construct classifiers in ruleset form. In comparison to C4.5, C5 is faster, more memory efficient, produces considerably smaller decision trees, supports for boosting, and can automatically winnow the attributes to remove those that may be unhelpful. More details are available at http://rulequest.com/see5-comparison.html.

4.3   Logistic Regression

Logistic regression (Log. Reg.) works by building an equation that relates the input field values to the probabilities associated with each of the output field category. Once the model is generated, it can be used to estimate probabilities for new data. For each record, a probability of membership is computed for each output category. The target category with the highest probability is assigned as the predicted output value for that record. Since in our data set the target variable has two distinct categories, a binomial model was created.

4.4   Bayesian Network Classifier

Bayesian network (BN) is a graphical model that provides probabilistic relationship for some variables. It can only accommodate discrete values. Therefore, in our work, numeric predictors are discretized into 5 equal-width bins before the BN model was built. Two different methods for building Bayesian network models were used: tree augmented naïve Bayes (TAN classifier [7]) and Markov blanket estimation [6]. Tree augmented naïve Bayes efficiently creates a simple Bayesian network model. The Markov blanket identifies all the variables in the network that are needed to predict the target variable.

4.5   Support Vector Machine

Support vector machine (SVM) is a classification algorithm which constructs an optimal separating hyperplane for the input vectors $\mathbf{x}_i$, with associated class label $y_i = \pm 1$, $(i = 1, \ldots, l)$. Two types of SVM algorithms were considered in the work: C-SVM model [27] and ν-SVM model [21].

4.6   Multilayer Perceptron

Multilayer perceptron (MLP) is the feedforward neural network [20]. In case of both original and binarized data set, the error functions of the MLPs were *sum squared error* or *cross entropy*. The model was composed of one or two hidden layers activated by the transfer functions from the set {*linear, hyperbolic tangent, logistic, exponential*}. The same set of transfer functions was applied for the output neurons, when the *sum squared error* function was calculated. For the *cross entropy* error function, the output neurons were of the *softmax* type. The number of neural network outputs was 2, whereas the number of inputs was 25 for the original data and 54 for the binarized data set (see Section 2). The number of hidden layer neurons was optimized in order to minimize the network error. Three MLP training algorithms were used: *Broyden-Fletcher-Goldfarb-Shanno* [2], *scaled conjugate gradient* [14] and traditional *gradient descent* algorithm.

4.7   k-Means Clustering

The k-Means method (k-Means) is a clustering algorithm used to group records based on similarity of values for a set of input fields [9]. The basic idea is to try to discover k clusters, such that the records within each cluster are similar to each other and distinct from records in other clusters. The grouping process relies on the iterative minimization of the sum of squared distances computed between input data and the cluster center. An initial set of clusters is defined, and the cluster centers are repeatedly updated until no modification of their coordinate values is obtained. The problem of k selection was resolved by carrying out an extensive number of experiments with different parameter values.

5   Simulation Results

In order to conduct data classification we used algorithms implemented in the following software: IBM SPSS Modeler 14.1 (kNN, CART, C5, Log. Reg., BN, SVM) [10], Statistica 9.1 Data Miner (MLP) [25] and DTREG (k-Means, PNN, LDA, RBF) [22]. After hundreds of thousands simulations we computed: the test error (*Error*), the area under ROC [8] curve (*AUC*), sensitivity (*Sen*) and specificity (*Spe*). These indices were obtained on the independent data subsets extracted from the entire data set. The subsets covered 5%, 10%, 20%, 30%, 40%, and 50% of the input patterns excluded from the training process. It was necessary to average the results. For all the classifiers, *Error*, *AUC*, *Sen* and

Spe indicators were computed for different parameters of the particular models. For example, in case of MLP network, four activation functions was applied, and the number of hidden layers and neurons was changed. For SVM model, two types of the algorithm (C, ν) and various kernel functions along with their parameters were regarded.

As shown in Table 1 - Table 4, MLP is the best classifier in respect of both minimum test error value and the highest area under ROC curve.

Table 1. Classifiers' ranking with respect to the test error for original data

Algorithm	Error [%]	Algorithm	σ_{Error} [%]	Algorithm	$(Error + \sigma_{Error})$ [%]
MLP	18.775	BN	3.966	MLP	30.593
C5	29.925	Log. Reg.	4.063	C5	35.963
k-Means	32.959	C5	6.038	SVM	39.995
SVM	33.805	SVM	6.190	CART	42.711
CART	36.433	CART	6.278	k-Means	43.990
BN	40.633	k-Means	11.031	BN	44.599
Log. Reg.	40.807	MLP	11.818	Log. Reg.	44.870

Table 2. Classifiers' ranking with respect to the test error for binarized data

Algorithm	Error [%]	Algorithm	σ_{Error} [%]	Algorithm	$(Error + \sigma_{Error})$ [%]
MLP	17.217	Log. Reg.	2.995	MLP	30.635
k-Means	27.780	BN	3.403	k-Means	42.339
C5	32.793	CART	4.888	Log. Reg.	42.552
SVM	34.508	SVM	10.692	BN	42.825
CART	38.377	MLP	13.418	CART	43.265
BN	39.422	k-Means	14.559	SVM	45.200
Log. Reg.	39.557	C5	16.245	C5	49.038

Table 3. Classifiers' ranking with respect to the area under ROC curve for original data

Algorithm	AUC	Algorithm	σ_{AUC}	Algorithm	$AUC - \sigma_{AUC}$
MLP	0.75600	BN	0.05021	MLP	0.62837
C5	0.70967	Log. Reg.	0.05239	C5	0.58258
k-Means	0.68280	CART	0.12424	BN	0.52212
SVM	0.64117	C5	0.12709	CART	0.51659
CART	0.64083	MLP	0.12763	Log. Reg.	0.50861
BN	0.57233	SVM	0.13345	SVM	0.50772
Log. Reg.	0.56100	k-Means	0.19929	k-Means	0.48351

The authors considered necessary to calculate the average values of quality indices ($Error$, AUC) and their standard deviations (σ_{Error}, σ_{AUC}). Suppose that the final criterion of the model selection are the quantities $Error + \sigma_{Error}$ and $AUC - \sigma_{AUC}$, then one may admit that the averages $Error + \sigma_{Error}$ and $AUC - \sigma_{AUC}$ determine the utility thresholds of the classifier. In such a case, in original data classification, there are successively four models: MLP, C5, SVM,

Table 4. Classifiers' ranking with respect to the area under ROC curve for binarized data

Algorithm	AUC		Algorithm	σ_{AUC}		Algorithm	$AUC - \sigma_{AUC}$
MLP	0.76450		Log. Reg.	0.02743		MLP	0.58041
BN	0.75317		CART	0.09114		SVM	0.56796
k-Means	0.71528		SVM	0.09304		BN	0.56192
C5	0.69117		C5	0.15966		k-Means	0.55399
SVM	0.66100		k-Means	0.16129		CART	0.55303
CART	0.64417		MLP	0.18409		C5	0.53151
Log. Reg.	0.53733		BN	0.19125		Log. Reg.	0.50991

Table 5. Classifiers' ranking with respect to sensitivity (Sen) and specificity (Spe) determined for original and binarized data

Original data					Binarized data			
Algorithm	Sen [%]		Algorithm	Spe [%]		Algorithm	Sen [%]		Algorithm	Spe [%]

Algorithm	Sen [%]	Algorithm	Spe [%]	Algorithm	Sen [%]	Algorithm	Spe [%]
MLP	84.991	MLP	79.805	MLP	90.011	MLP	81.352
C5	77.544	CART	72.321	k-Means	73.604	CART	71.469
k-Means	71.918	BN	69.947	SVM	71.449	k-Means	71.019
SVM	68.563	C5	67.710	C5	68.814	BN	67.667
Log. Reg.	59.173	Log. Reg.	65.471	BN	62.506	Log. Reg.	67.629
CART	53.542	SVM	64.443	Log. Reg.	50.036	C5	65.488
BN	45.240	k-Means	63.565	CART	48.542	SVM	60.488

CART below $Error + \sigma_{Error}$ threshold. When classifying binarized data, there are five classifiers: MLP, kNN, k-Means, Log. Reg. and BN below this threshold. We can similarly proceed with computing the utility thresholds for the area under ROC curve parameter, providing four classifiers (MLP, C5, kNN and BN) and seven classifiers (MLP, SVM, BN, k-Means, CART, C5, kNN) in the classification of original and binarized data, respectively (the results for kNN were not included).

In the classification of original data, regardless the criterion of the model selection, C5 was the second best algorithm. It is worth to notice that this model, in addition to the classification outcome, provides the set of rules. By applying the binarization, these rules are easily interpretable.

Analyzing the outcomes in Table 3 and Table 4 one can observe that the binarization of the features of the input vectors increased the AUC value by the margin of 24% for BN model.

In Table 5 the average values of the diagnostic accuracy parameters, sensitivity (Sen) and specificity (Spe), are solely placed. The standard deviations, positive and negative predictive values, and the utility thresholds were not included because of limited paper space.

6 Conclusions

In this work, the classifiers: MLP, C5, kNN, k-Means, SVM, CART, RBF, BN, Log. Reg., PNN and LDA were tested for intra- and post-operative complications in women with cervical cancer. The real data set consisted of 107 vectors, where each record was described by 10 attributes: 3 continuous and 7 categorical. For original data the normalization of the input variables was applied and the feature selection was performed. Additionally, the original data set was binarized.

The models were compared for both original and binarized data. The purpose of the simulation was to provide the ranking of the classifiers and to show the best model satisfying the quality criteria such as: the average value and the standard deviation of the error, the area under ROC curve, sensitivity and specificity. All the quality indices were averaged solely for the data unseen for classifiers during the training process. The simulation results for ensemble classifiers were not included in the article. According to the quality indices, the results for these models were much worse though.

In each case, for original and binarized data classification, taking all criteria (generalization error, area under ROC curve, sensitivity and specificity) and standard deviations for quality indices into account, MLP network turned out to be the best classifier. For this model the lowest average test error was found (17.22%). In authors' opinion achieving better result is very difficult, if possible at all.

According to the best knowledge of the authors, there have been no related works on the prediction of intra- and post-operative complications for cervical cancer. The subject of the research is very important from the medical point of view and the present results can be useful in clinical practice [15]. The authors aim to predict the cases of severe, moderate and mild intra- and post-operative complications in patients with cervical cancer and to extract easily interpretable decision rules.

Acknowledgments. This work was supported in part by the National Science Centre (Poland) under Grant No. NN 514 705540. The authors appreciate SPSS Polska Sp. z o.o. Krakow, Poland, for providing the evaluation copy of IBM SPSS Modeler.

References

1. Arlot, S.: A survey of cross-validation procedures for model selection. Statistics Surveys 4, 40–79 (2010)
2. Bishop, C.M.: Pattern Recognition and Machine Learning. Springer (2006)
3. Breiman, L., Friedman, J.H., Olshen, R.A., Stone, C.J.: Classification and regression trees. Wadsworth, Belmont (1984)
4. Chen, H., Wang, X., Ma, D., Ma, B.: Neural network-based computer-aided diagnosis in distinguishing malignant from benign solitary pulmonary nodules by computed tomography. Chin. Med. J. 120, 1211–1215 (2007)
5. Chien, C.-W., Lee, Y.-C., Ma, T., et al.: The application of artificial neural networks and decision tree model in predicting post-operative complication for gastric cancer patients. Hepato-Gastroenterology 55, 1140–1145 (2008)
6. Deng, H., Davila, S., Runger, G., Tuv, E.: Learning Markov blankets for continuous or discrete networks via feature selection. In: Proc. ECML-SUEMA 2010, pp. 97–108 (2010)

7. Friedman, N., Geiger, D., Goldszmidt, M.: Bayesian network classifiers. Machine Learning 29, 131–163 (1997)
8. Hanley, J.A., McNeil, B.J.: The Meaning and Use of the Area under a Receiver Operating Characteristic (ROC) Curve. Radiology 143, 29–36 (1982)
9. Hartigan, J.A., Wong, M.A.: A k-means clustering algorithm. Journal of the Royal Statistical Society - Series C (Applied Statistics) 1, 100–108 (1979)
10. IBM SPSS Modeler 14.1 Algorithms Guide. IBM Corporation (2011)
11. Jemal, A., Bray, F., Center, M.M., Ferlay, J., et al.: Global cancer statistics. CA Cancer J. Clin. 61, 69–90 (2011)
12. Jonathan, P., Krzanowski, W.J., McCarthy, W.V.: On the use of cross-validation to assess performance in multivariate prediction. Statistics and Computing 10, 209–229 (2000)
13. Kusy, M.: System for Cancer Diagnosis Based on Support Vector Machines and Neural Networks. PhD Thesis, Warsaw (2008)
14. Moller, M.: A Scaled Conjugate Gradient Algorithm for Fast Supervised Learning. Neural Networks 6, 525–533 (1993)
15. Obrzut, B.: The extent of surgery and its impact on FIGO IA2-IIB cervical cancer treatment outcomes (in polish). OWN XVIII, Poznan (2008)
16. Ochi, T., Murase, K., Fujii, T., Kawamura, M., Ikezoe, J.: Survival prediction using artificial neural networks in patients with uterine cervical cancer treated by radiation therapy alone. Int. J. Clin. Oncol. 7, 292–300 (2002)
17. Pecorelli, S., Zigliani, L., Odicino, F.: Revised FIGO staging for carcinoma of the cervix. Int. J. Gynecol. & Obstet. 105, 107–108 (2009)
18. Quinlan, J.R.: C4.5: Programs for machine learning. Morgan Kaufmann Publishers, San Mateo (1993)
19. Refaeilzadeh, P., Tang, L., Liu, H.: Cross-Validation. Encyclopedia of Database Systems, 532–538 (2009)
20. Rumelhart, D., McClelland, J.: Parallel Distributed Processing. MIT Press, Cambridge (1986)
21. Schölkopf, B., Smola, A.J., Williamson, R.C., Bartlett, P.L.: New support vector algorithms. Neural Computation 12, 1207–1245 (2000)
22. Sherrod, P.H.: DTREG predictive modeling software (2011), www.dtreg.com
23. Schneider, A., Kohler, C.: In: Gross, G., Tyring, S.K. (eds.) Sexually Transmitted Infections and Sexually Transmitted Diseases, pp. 477–488. Springer, Heidelberg (2011)
24. Śmietański, J., Tadeusiewicz, R., Łuczyńska, E.: Texture Analysis in Perfusion Images of Prostate Cancer–A Case Study. Int. J. AMCS 20, 149–156 (2010)
25. StatSoft, Inc. Electronic Statistics Textbook. Tulsa, OK: StatSoft (2011), www.statsoft.com/textbook/
26. Tan, T.Z., Queka, C., See Ng, G., Razvi, K.: Ovarian cancer diagnosis with complementary learning fuzzy neural network. AI in Medicine 43, 207–222 (2008)
27. Vapnik, V.: The Nature of Statistical Learning Theory. Springer, New York (1995)
28. Wu, X., Kumar, V., Quinlan, J.R., et al.: Top 10 algorithms in data mining. Knowledge Information Systems 14, 1–37 (2008)

Improved Fuzzy Entropy Algorithm for X-Ray Pictures Preprocessing

Mariusz Korkosz[1], Marzena Bielecka[2], Andrzej Bielecki[3], Marek Skomorowski[3], Wadim Wojciechowski[4], and Tomasz Wójtowicz[3]

[1] Division of Rheumatology, Departement of Internal Medicine and Gerontology,
Jagiellonian University Hospital,
Śniadeckich 10, 31-531 Cracow, Poland
mariuszk@mp.pl
[2] Department of Geoinformatics and Applied Computer Science,
Faculty of Geology, Geophysics and Environmental Protection,
AGH University of Science and Technology,
Mickiewicza 30, 30-059 Cracow, Poland
bielecka@agh.edu.pl
[3] Institute of Computer Science,
Faculty of Mathematics and Computer Science,
Jagiellonian University,
Łojasiewicza 6, 30-348 Cracow, Poland
{bielecki,skomorowski,tomasz.wojtowicz}@ii.uj.edu.pl
[4] Department of Radiology, Jagiellonian University Hospital,
Kopernika 19, 31-531 Cracow, Poland
wadim@mp.pl

Abstract. The fuzzy entropy algorithm was designed for preprocessing of photos taken in the visible spectrum of light. However it did not produce satisfying results when it is directly applied to X-ray pictures. In this paper we present significant improvements of this approach and apply it to hand radiographs. The noise elimination and the bone contourisation is the task which is studied in this paper. Not only is the algorithm modified but also it is combined with using of median and minimum filters. The presented approach allows us to obtain satisfying noise elimination and clear bone contourisation.

1 Introduction

X-ray pictures are one of the most important diagnostic tools in contemporary medicine - see, for instance, [7,9,13,22]. Despite competition from computer tomography and magnetic resonance, X-ray pictures remain popular due to low cost and simplicity. The application of computer power in the field of automatic or semi-automatic processing makes X-ray imaging even more attractive. However such approach requires good preprocessing of the medical image [1,21,25].

In the field of rheumatology there are several diseases, of both inflammatory and non-inflammatory nature, detectable on X-ray pictures, especially in palm region [22]. Numerical processing have been proposed on various levels, beginning

L. Rutkowski et al. (Eds.): ICAISC 2012, Part II, LNCS 7268, pp. 268–275, 2012.

from preprocessing [1,8,12,26,27]. Then, recognition of interesting features like contour or joints detection [4,8,11,14], and detection of pathological changes in joint spaces and bone contours are done [2,3,5,6,17,18,20]. Further research employs pattern recognition and image understanding [16,23,24] in order to create computer-aided medical diagnostic system [15].

Processing of X-ray pictures is more difficult than pictures taken in visible spectrum for various reasons which have been discussed in the paper [25] and are also a subject of this paper. High noise level, low contrast between soft tissue and background and high variability in the level of gray due to differences in tissue thickness between finger area and wrist area are the main issues associated with X-ray pictures.

On the level of preprocessing, important goal is to extract the hand itself from raw image. Low contrast between soft tissue and background and high variability in luminance cause problems with binarisation whereas high noise level causes failing of direct application of visible spectrum pictures preprocessing algorithm to X-ray images.

A certain algorithm, called *fuzzy entropy direction feature image edge detection*, designed for visible spectrum images (see [10,19]), is the starting point of our studies. The adaptation of this algorithm to X-ray pictures processing is presented in this paper.

The algorithm, called shortly *fuzzy entropy* is a multi-stage algorithm consisting of four steps. In the previous paper [25] only its first step was analyzed. This issue and the whole algorithm is briefly described in Section 2. In the paper [25], the aspect of noise filtering is also discussed. It is shown there that if this algorithm is used to X-ray images processing, it must be supported by external noise filter. The filtering must be done even twice, between steps of fuzzy entropy algorithm. This problem is discussed in Section 3 whereas in Section 4 the fourth step of fuzzy entropy algorithm is discussed in the aspect of possible algorithm improvements. The last Section is a final conclusion.

2   Fuzzy Entropy

The fuzzy entropy algorithm, consisting of four steps, is introduced in the paper [10]. The entropy calculation is its first step. For each pixel of image the value of entropy, depending on the level of gray of this pixel and its neighbourhood , is calculated. Let p be the pixel and $N(p)$ be its neighborhood, and let $\#N(p)$ denotes the number of elements in the set $N(p)$. The entropy value of p is given as

$$E(p) = \frac{1}{\#N(p)} \sum_{v \in N(p)} H(U(v,p)), \qquad (1)$$

where

$$U(v,p) = \frac{1}{1 + |\lambda(v) - \lambda(p)|}, \qquad (2)$$

and

$$H(x) = -x \cdot log_2 x - (1-x) \cdot log_2(1-x). \qquad (3)$$

The symbol $\lambda()$ denotes the level of gray of a given pixel. Let us observe that the function U returns 1 when both analyzed pixels are identical whereas the function H is incomputable for arguments equal to 0 and 1.

It has been proposed to replace the function H with a less troublesome one. In the paper [25] various aspects of such replacements are discussed. It was finally decided that a polynomial, $4 \cdot x \cdot (1 - x)$ is the best replacement. First of all, there are no points in the function domain for which the function value can not be calculated. Secondly, computations are less time-consuming which is crucial according to the huge number of pixels in a radiograph.

In the second step of the algorithm the direction of possible edge around each pixel is calculated. For each pixel 3×3 neighborhood possibility of creation of the fragment of the edge is analyzed. The outlined edge must satisfy three following conditions:

1. the edge goes through center pixel,
2. the edge starts on any border pixel and goes straight or turns maximally of 45 degrees,
3. the edge is undirected.

This produces twelve possible edge contours on the 3×3 mask, four straight and eight bent. In this step all twelve possibilities are examined in such a way that entropy values, calculated in the first step of the algorithm, are summed along the supposed edge. Then the largest sum is taken and direction on which it was calculated is assumed to be an edge.

The third step of the algorithm, named *Non-Maxima Supression*, is aimed to reduce a certain type of noise. However, it does not remove properly the noise associated with X-ray pictures, and because of that other solutions of filtering have been proposed in Section 3. The last step is binarisation, discussed with details in Section 4.

3   Noise

As it has been already mentioned in Section 1, X-ray pictures have high level of noise. This noise causes a problem to the fuzzy entropy algorithm. Due to the fact that the algorithm is sensitive to weak edges, the noise can be treated as such edges - see Fig.1.

In the paper [25] two noise filtering algorithms have been proposed - the median filter (4) and the minimum filter (5). For given image pixel p there is his 3×3 neighborhood $N(p)$ such that $p \in N(p)$:

$$\lambda(p) = median\{\lambda(v) : v \in N(p)\}, \tag{4}$$

$$\lambda(p) = min\{\lambda(v) : v \in N(p)\}. \tag{5}$$

It has been proved that the best results can be received when filtering is applied twice - first before the step 1 of fuzzy entropy algorithm, and second after the step 1 and before steps 2,3,4, hence the fuzzy entropy algorithm must be stopped after step 1 and be restarted once again.

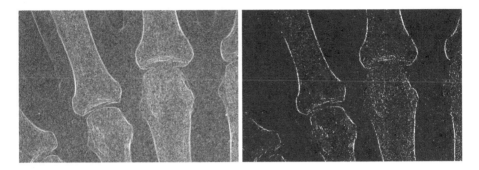

Fig. 1. Pure fuzzy entropy algorithm applied without filtering. The left picture presents the result after step 1. Noise is very much visible, what results in poor overall contrast. The right picture presents the final result. It is noticeable that the algorithm has done its best, yet the effect is not acceptable for further calculation.

From all execution possibilities, the following seem to produce interesting results (digits 1-4 indicate algorithm steps 1-4):

– median–1–2–3–4 (see Fig.2)
– median–1–median–2–3–4 (see Fig.3)
– median–1–minimum–2–3–4 (see Fig.4)

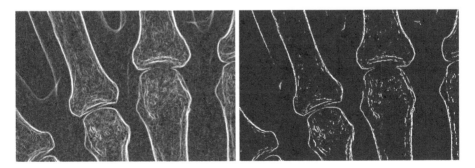

Fig. 2. Median filter applied only once, before step 1. Result after step 1. (left) and final result (right).

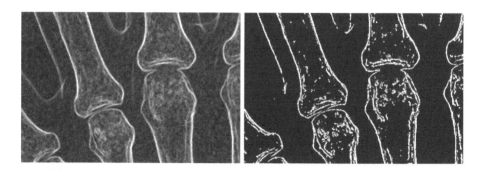

Fig. 3. Median filter applied twice - before and after step 1. Result after second median filtering on the left. Note the image is more blurry than corresponding image in Fig.2. On the right final result. Note that important features appear stronger than in Fig.2.

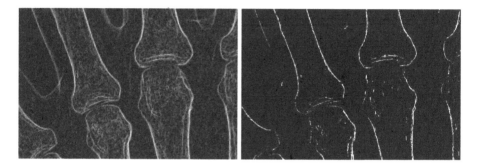

Fig. 4. Median filter applied before and minimum filter applied after step 1. The left picture presents the result of minimum filter applied after step 1. The right picture presents the final result. It does not look much useful because the median filter has "eaten" too much, yet in Section 4 this problem is discussed in details.

4 Binarisation

Another interesting aspect is adaptive threshold control situated in the step 4 of fuzzy entropy algorithm. The threshold value T determines whether a pixel will be finally black or white, what depends whether its level of gray is below or above the threshold, which is calculated in the following way:

$$T = J + k \cdot \sigma, \tag{6}$$

J is an arithmetic mean of all pixels' value, σ is a variance, and k is a special tuning value, the "expert's knob". The authors of [10] propose the usage of k for noise suppression. However,this works well with visible-spectrum images and poorly with X-ray images. The problem is, that the contrast between anatomical features and noise is too small to sort it out in such a simple way. For this reason this other means of filtering are proposed in this paper - see Section 3.

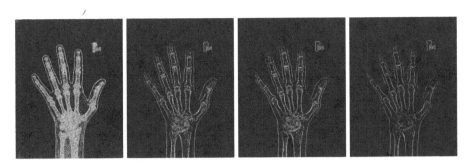

Fig. 5. Four different values of k in process where median filter was applied twice. From left: 0.5, 1.1, 2.1, 3.0.

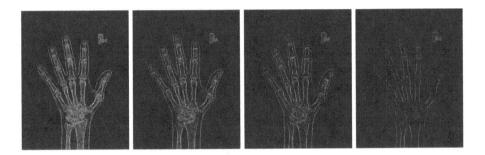

Fig. 6. Four different values of k : 0.5, 0.8, 1.1, 2.1 in process where median and then minimum filter were applied

Nevertheless the ability to tweak the value of k may help the filtering from step 3 to achieve optimal result. Let us observe that in Fig.5 tests show that optimal value of k is in a wide range from 1.0 to 2.0. If $k = 0.5$ white bones in the picture are in fact of black-white mosaic and the background noise is not well visible. If $k = 3.0$ then certain anatomical features around fingers disappeared, which means that the value of k is too high. In the case presented in Fig.6 the optimum value is in narrow range around the value of 0.8. The picture obtained for $k = 2.1$ is absolutely unacceptable as a result.

5   Conclusion

It has been shown that the algorithm designed for visible spectrum images can be adapted for X-ray images preprocessing. One important achievement is that various combination of filters, combined with setting of k value in the proposed algorithm, produces results useful but differing one from another. Therefore this algorithm can be utilized to produce results which will be useful in various context for higher-level algorithms which refer to medical image recognition and understanding. These topics are outside of scope of this paper, but their effectiveness is intrinsically depended on results of preprocessing.

References

1. Bielecki, A., Korkosz, M., Zieliński, B.: Hand radiographs preprocessing, image representation in the finger regions and joint space width measurements for image interpretation. Pattern Recognition 41, 3786–3798 (2008)
2. Bielecka, M., Skomorowski, M., Zieliński, B.: A Fuzzy Shape Descriptor and Inference by Fuzzy Relaxation with Application to Description of Bones Contours at Hand Radiographs. In: Kolehmainen, M., Toivanen, P., Beliczynski, B. (eds.) ICANNGA 2009. LNCS, vol. 5495, pp. 469–478. Springer, Heidelberg (2009)
3. Bielecka, M., Bielecki, A., Korkosz, M., Skomorowski, M., Wojciechowski, W., Zieliński, B.: Application of Shape Description Methodology to Hand Radiographs Interpretation. In: Bolc, L., Tadeusiewicz, R., Chmielewski, L.J., Wojciechowski, K. (eds.) ICCVG 2010. LNCS, vol. 6374, pp. 11–18. Springer, Heidelberg (2010)
4. Bielecki, A., Korkosz, M., Wojciechowski, W., Zieliński, B.: Identifying the Borders of the Upper and Lower Metacarpophalangeal Joint Surfaces on Hand Radiographs. In: Rutkowski, L., Scherer, R., Tadeusiewicz, R., Zadeh, L.A., Zurada, J.M. (eds.) ICAISC 2010. LNCS, vol. 6113, pp. 589–596. Springer, Heidelberg (2010)
5. Bielecka, M., Bielecki, A., Korkosz, M., Skomorowski, M., Wojciechowski, W., Zieliński, B.: Modified Jakubowski Shape Transducer for Detecting Osteophytes and Erosions in Finger Joints. In: Dobnikar, A., Lotrič, U., Šter, B. (eds.) ICANNGA 2011, Part II. LNCS, vol. 6594, pp. 147–155. Springer, Heidelberg (2011)
6. Bottcher, J., et al.: Digital X-ray radiogrammetry combined with semiautomated analysis of joint space widths as a new diagnostic approach in rheumatoid arthritis: a cross-sectional and longitudal study. Arthritis and Rheumatism 52, 3850–3859 (2006)
7. Choi, S., Lee, Y., Hong, S., Lee, G., Kang, S., Park, J., Park, J., Park, H.: Evaluation of inflammatory change and bone erosion using a murine type II collagen-induced arthritis model. Rheumatology International 31, 595–603 (2011)
8. Choi, S., Lee, G.J., Hong, S.J., Park, K.H., Urtnasan, T., Park, H.K.: Development of a joint space width measurement method based on radiographic hand images. Computers in Biology and Medicine 41, 987–998 (2011)
9. Choi, S., Su-Jin Chae, S., Kang, S., Cheong, Y., Hong, S., Park, H.: Non-invasive screening of progressive joint defects in the type II collagen - induced arthritis animal model using radiographic paw images. Inflammation Research 60, 447–456 (2011)
10. Chun, H., Jun, L., Junwei, H.: Image edge detection method based on the direction feature of fuzzy entropy. In: Proc. 6th International Conference on Natural Computation, pp. 3581–3584 (2010)
11. Davis, L., Theobald, B.J., Toms, A., Bagnall, A.: On the Extraction and Classification of Hand Outlines. In: Yin, H., Wang, W., Rayward-Smith, V. (eds.) IDEAL 2011. LNCS, vol. 6936, pp. 92–99. Springer, Heidelberg (2011)
12. He, X.Q., Ran, L.K., Tan, P.C., Jin, J.: Hand radiographs preprocessing and improved k-cosine algorithm in location method for phalangeal key points. Journal of Clinical Rehabilitative Tissue Engineering Research 15, 4817–4820 (2011)
13. Jantan, S., Hussain, A., Mustafa, M.M.: Distal radius bone age estimation based on fuzzy model. In: Proceedings of Conference on Biomedical Engineering and Sciences, IECBES, pp. 427–432 (2010)
14. Kaufmann, J., Slump, C.H., Bernelot Moens, H.J.: Segmentation of hand radiographs by using multi-level connected active appearance models. In: Proceedings of the SPIE, vol. 5747, pp. 1571–1581 (2005)

15. Klooster, R., Hendrics, E.A., Watt, I., Kloppenburg, M., Reiber, J.H.C., Stoel, B.C.: Automatic quantification of osteoarthritis in hand radiographs: validation of a new method to measure joint space width. Osteoarthritis and Cartilage 16, 18–25 (2008)
16. Ogiela, M.R., Tadeusiewicz, R., Ogiela, L.: Image languages in intelligent radiological palm diagnostics. Pattern Recognition 39, 2157–2165 (2006)
17. Pfeil, A., et al.: Computer-aided joint space analysis of the metacarpal-phalangeal and proximal-interphalangeal finger joint: normative age-related and gender-specific data. Skeletal Radiology 36, 853–864 (2007)
18. Pfeil, A., et al.: Normative Reference Values of Joint Space Width Estimated by Computer-aided Joint Space Analysis (CAJSA): The Distal Interphalangeal Joint. Journal of Digital Imaging 21(suplement 1), 104–112 (2008)
19. Qi, B., Tang, L., Zhang, J.: Research on measurement of hydrophobocity of insulators. Proceedings of the CSEE 26, 120–124 (2008)
20. Sharp, J., Gardner, J., Bennett, E.: Computer-based methods for measuring joint space and estimating erosion volume in the finger and wrist joints of patients with rheumatoid arthritis. Arthritis and Rheumatism 43, 1378–1386 (2000)
21. Szostek, K., Gronkowska-Serafin, J., Piórkowski, A.: Problems of corneal endothelial image binarization. Schedae Informaticae 20, 211–218 (2011)
22. Staniszewska-Varga J., Szymańska-Jagiełło W., Luft S., Korkosz M.: Rheumatic diseases atlas. Medycyna Praktyczna, Kraków (2003) (in Polish)
23. Tadeusiewicz, R., Ogiela, M.R.: Medical image understanding technology. STUDFUZZ. Springer, Heidelberg (2004)
24. Tadeusiewicz, R., Ogiela, M.R.: Picture languages in automatic radiological palm interpretation. International Journal of Applied Mathematics and Computer Science 15, 305–312 (2005)
25. Wójtowicz, T.: An improvement in fuzzy entropy edge detection for X-ray imaging. Schedae Informaticae 20, 159–166 (2011)
26. Zieliński, B.: A fully automated algorithm dedicated to computing metacarpophalangeal and interphalangeal joint cavity widths. Schedae Informaticae 16, 47–67 (2007)
27. Zieliński, B.: Hand radiograph analysis and joint space location improvement for image interpretation. Schede Informaticae 17/18, 45–61 (2009)

Influence of Facial Asymmetry
on Human Recognition

Damian Kurach and Danuta Rutkowska

Department of Computer Engineering,
Al. Armii Krajowej 36, 42-200 Czestochowa, Poland
{dkurach,drutko}@kik.pcz.pl

Abstract. In this paper, two types of holistic asymmetry representations are introduced: a) asymmetry of facial silhouette *AFS*, b) asymmetry of facial elements *AFE*. These asymmetry types in combination with the maintaining aspect ratio facial normalization [3], to the best of our knowledge have not been yet proposed in literature by other authors. To investigate quantitative influence of such approach, classification based on the *PCA* and the *Mahalanobis distance* is studied. Performed observations confirm existence of correlation between facial asymmetry and classification rate. The experiment results to demonstrate the proposed approach efficiency and accuracy are provided.

Keywords: facial asymmetry, face recognition, classification, *PCA*.

1   Introduction

The facial asymmetry was investigated in such science fields like biology, psychology [1], social science [14], medicine [10], [19], etc. Researchers examined influence of asymmetry on the attractiveness [4], [15], the relation with diseases, dependency with brain hemisphere functionality [8], [12] and so on.

Most often the facial asymmetry is considered as a significant characteristic in face recognition [2]. In [5], [6], [9] the usage of holistic representation of facial asymmetry as a factor enhancing facial recognition rate (as well as the identification of emotions) was proposed. The authors [6] for the first time were concerning asymmetry as biometrics. In addition, they defined two quantitative measures of asymmetry: D-face (Density Difference) and S-face (Edge Orientation Similarity) defined as:

$$D(x, y) = I(x, y) - I'(x, y) \ , \tag{1}$$

$$S(x, y) = cos(\varphi_{Ie(x,y), Ie'(x,y)}) \ , \tag{2}$$

where I – a given normalized face density image with a coordinate system defined on the face with X axis perpendicular to the face midline and Y axis coincides with the face midline;
I' – its vertically reflected (w.r.t. axis Y) image;
I_e , I_e' – their respective edged images.

L. Rutkowski et al. (Eds.): ICAISC 2012, Part II, LNCS 7268, pp. 276–283, 2012.

The D-face is a measure of luminance difference of the original image and its mirror image relative to the vertical axis. The S-face represents the edge orientation difference after edge detection on the original image and its mirror image.

The authors [6] prepared some experiments, in combination with the available methods (principal component analysis PCA, linear discriminant analysis LDA) which confirmed the usefulness of these measures in both classification and facial expressions recognition tasks. This study used a set of frontal face images of 55 persons taken under controlled conditions. Each face image was normalized by scaling the distance between characteristic points on human faces (horizontally – inner eye corners, and vertically – center between the eye corners and the philtrum). After that, facial images were cropped into 128x128 squared images with face midline.

The issues concerning this method are:

- density images are strongly influenced by the light conditions on images – different light sources will provide different density image even for this same face
- normalization based on the scaling distances (between the eyes corners and the philtrum) removed features like the real size and proportions of face; individual proportions are distorted – hence the natural differences between faces of people are fuzzed.

The paper is organized as follows. In Section 2, we present the process of face normalization with maintaining aspect ratio. In Section 3, the new concept of asymmetry representations are introduced. In Section 4, learning and testing procedures are described and the datasets are established. In Section 5, the results are provided.

2   Image and Face Normalization

First step of image normalization is the face location on the image. It is made by skin color detection. The transformation's formula is the following combination of normalized RGB model color and component $I2$ from $I1I2I3$ color model:

$$S1 = (RB)(GI) and S2 = \frac{255}{max(RB) - min(RB)}(RB - min(RB)) , \qquad (3)$$

where

$RB = |\frac{R}{R+G+B} - \frac{B}{R+G+B}|$,

$GI = 0.299R + 0.587G + 0.144B,$

$S1, S2$ – skin color masks,

R, G, B – components of RGB color model.

Second step is finding eyes position. It is obtained by calculation of directional changes in the intensity of image (image gradient). Significant improvement of the classical approaches was introduced in [16]:

$$\arg\max_c \frac{1}{N} \sum_{i=1}^{N} w_c (d_i^T g_i)^2 \ , \tag{4}$$

where

$w_c = I^*(c_x, c_y)$– pixel value of processed input image at (c_x, c_y),

d_i – displacement vectors,

g_i– gradient vectors.

Based on changes of region average pixel intensity the exact points on the edge of iris are determined (Fig. 1). After that the iris size is calculated. This is a significant part because the size of the iris is considered as constant ($10 \pm 0,56mm$) [2] and become the normalization unit. Since we have the unit, all face images are normalized by scaling to the same size of iris with maintaining aspect ratio. It allows to keep real facial proportions.

3   Asymmetry Representation

The facial asymmetry is represented by composite images. The asymmetry image composites are based on the vertical axis that split the face into two parts. We call it *vertical asymmetry axis* or *face midline*. This axis is investigated in [3], [13]. However, before applying these methods, the eye corners must be found. In both cases the procedure is similar. The points on upper and lower eyelids are estimated, then based on the founded points, two functions are approximated for each eyelid. The intersection points of those functions are assumed as the inner and outer eye corners (Fig. 1).

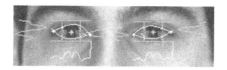

Fig. 1. The result of the iris size and the eyes corners extraction

The main difference in presented approaches is that in [3] the classical gradient optimization method was used. This not always guarantee finding the global optimum. The solution was described in [13], where the problem was successfully solved by an evolutionary algorithm. Figure 2 shows comparison of those two methods regarding the case of asymmetrical face.

We consider two kinds of composites. The first composite is the image representing the asymmetry of facial elements. The *AFE* is built by use of transparency to generate a weighted average of original and mirrored facial image. The process of image mirroring and the process of combining those two images is precisely executed based on the vertical axis. The second type of composite consists of two images. Those images are representing the asymmetry of facial

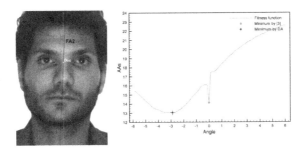

Fig. 2. The comparison of the vertical asymmetry axis finding [13]

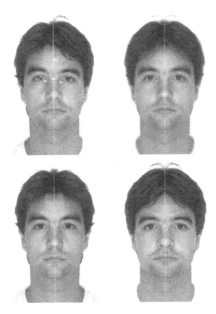

Fig. 3. From top left: original image, *AFE* composite, *AFSR* and *AFSL* composites

silhouette. The *AFSL* is combined of left face side on image and mirrored left side by vertical axis. The *AFSR* is combined image of right face side on image and mirrored right side respectively. The original face image and all composites are shown in Fig. 3.

4   Method of Examination

In this section, learning and testing procedures are described. The brief description of main *PCA* algorithm [17], [18] steps is presented. The overview of database is made. The types of experiment are designed and the datasets are proposed.

4.1   Learning and Testing Procedures

The basic *PCA* algorithm steps [11] as the learning procedure can be as follows:

Step 1. *Data preparation*
In this step, the training set Γ_i of the faces is prepared for processing.

Step 2. *The mean subtraction*
Firstly, the average face is calculated (matrix Ψ):

$$\Psi = \frac{1}{M} \sum_{i=1}^{M} \Gamma_i \ , \tag{5}$$

where M – the number of images in the training set, then subtracted from the original faces Γ_i:

$$\Phi_i = \Gamma_i - \Psi \ . \tag{6}$$

Step 3. *The eigenvectors and eigenface calculation*
By means of *PCA* one can transform each original image of the training set into a corresponding eigenface. To avoid a huge amount of calculation, the reduction, according to [17], from the number of pixels (N^2 x N^2) to the number of images in the training set (M) is performed. The covariance matrix C has a dimensionality of (N^2 x N^2), that is N^2 eigenfaces and eigenvalues. The formula of the covariance matrix C is given only for explanation of A:

$$C = \frac{1}{M} \sum_{n=1}^{M} \Phi_n \Phi_n^T = AA^T \ , \tag{7}$$

$$L = A^T A, \quad L_{n,m} = \Phi_m^T \Phi_n \ , \tag{8}$$

$$u_l = \sum_{k-1}^{M} v_{lk} \Phi_k, \quad l = 1, \ldots, M, \tag{9}$$

where L is a M x M matrix, v are M eigenvectors of L and u are eigenfaces.

Step 4. *The principal components selection*
Eigenfaces represent face differences. The first few are showing most dominant features of faces. Since last ones are not contributing much to the image, the subset of M eigenfaces can be used. The amount of eigenfaces is reduced to the most dominant ones without losing/effecting the image quality. Each face of dataset can be represented as the combination of eigenface images and the vector of weights. The weights calculation formula is as follows:

$$w_l = u_l^T \Phi_k \ . \tag{10}$$

The testing procedure is similar to the training one and can be summarized only by two steps:

Step 1. *The image into eigenface components transformation*
In this step the same *PCA* calculations as before can be applied to find the eigenfaces and weights vector representation of input image.

Step 2. *The testing faces classification*
For classification the *Mahalanobis distance* is used:

$$d(x,y) = \sqrt{(x-y)^T C^{-1}(x-y)} \; , \tag{11}$$

where C is the covariance between the variables involved.

This means that the weight vector of testing face is taken and the distances with the weight vectors associated with each of the training images are calculated. The lowest distance value indicates which face (or class of faces) is recognized. To make sure that the face belongs to the database, the threshold value is used.

4.2   Dataset

The AR-Face database [7] is used to investigate the relationship between facial asymmetry and recognition rate. It contains color images of 126 people (70 men and 56 women). The pictures show the frontal view of faces with different facial expressions, illumination conditions and occlusions. The pictures were taken in two sessions, separated by two weeks. All images are available as *RGB RAW* files of 768x576 pixels and 24 bits of depth.

We have examined seven types of datasets:

- training on neutral expression – no facial expression on image (Dataset1)
- training on *AFE* of neutral expression (Dataset2)
- training on *AFSL* and *AFSR* of neutral expression ((Dataset3))
- training on neutral expression + *AFE* (Dataset4)
- training on neutral expression + *AFSL* and *AFSR* (Dataset5)
- training on *AFE* + *AFSL* and *AFSR* (Dataset6)
- training on neutral expression + *AFE* + *AFSL* and *AFSR* (Dataset7)

The training was performed on images from first session respectively to the examined types of datasets. The testing process was performed in each case on the neutral images from the second session.

All face images in the dataset are after applied procedures of:

- finding facial axis
- image rotating to make the face axis vertical (if needed)
- image scaling to the giving iris size (face normalization)
- image cropping based on vertical axis to make them all the same size

5   Results

When using the AFE faces, classification rate is $91,9\%$ and it is close to the rate of neutral faces $90,7\%$. Similar results were obtained using only AFS $(92,6\%)$. Combination of both the AFE and AFS increased the classification rate to $92,9\%$. Better results are obtained for neutral $+ AFE$ $(93,3\%)$ and neutral $+ AFS$ $(93,8\%)$. The best accuracy occurs when all types are combined and it is equal $94,9\%$.

Table 1. Classification error

Dataset	Dataset1	Dataset2	Dataset3	Dataset4	Dataset5	Dataset6	Dataset7
Error %	9.3	8.1	7.4	6.7	6.2	7.1	5.1

6   Conclusion and Final Remarks

In this paper, the facial asymmetry influence on the recognition rate was studied. We proposed two types of holistic facial asymmetry. They have been applied to a classification system and proved significant meaning for face recognition. By use of AFE we achieved comparable accuracy as using AFS. Combination of AFE and AFS enhanced classification rate.

Obtained results show the advantages of proposed approach. Moreover, the results confirm that there is a close relation between facial asymmetry and face recognition effectiveness.

The presented method can be successfully used for human face recognition based on images of frontal face view taken under controlled conditions.

The examples of asymmetry types and the process of normalization given in Sections 2 and 3 do not exhaust all the possibilities of this method. Future work will focus on evaluation and exploration of improved techniques for classification. The support vector machine and/or neural network solutions may be applied since such classifiers are successfully employed to problems concerning faces without asymmetry. Additionally, new potential datasets could be developed to better examine the asymmetry influence. Finally, we plan to investigate and design a system for face recognition based only on eye regions and the approach demonstrated in this paper.

References

1. Borod, J.C., Koff, E., White, B.: Facial asymmetry in posed and spontaneous expressions of emotion. Brain and Cognition 2, 165–175 (1983)
2. Kompanets, L.: Biometrics of Asymmetrical Face. In: Zhang, D., Jain, A.K. (eds.) ICBA 2004. LNCS, vol. 3072, pp. 67–73. Springer, Heidelberg (2004)
3. Kompanets, L., Kurach, D.: On Facial Frontal Vertical Axes Projections and Area Facial Asymmetry Measure. Intern. J. of Computing, Multimedia and Intelligent Techniques 3(1), 61–88 (2007)

4. Kowner, R.: Facial asymmetry and attractiveness judgement in developmental perspective. Journal of Experimental Psychology: Human Perception and Performance 22, 662–675 (1996)
5. Liu, Y., Schmidt, K., Cohn, J., Mitra, S.: Facial asymmetry quantification for expression invariant human identification. In: AFGR 2002, pp. 198–204 (2002)
6. Liu, Y., Weaver, R., Schmidt, K., Serban, N., Cohn, J.: Facial asymmetry: A new biometric. CMU-RI-TR (2001)
7. Martinez, A.M., Benavente, R.: The AR face database. CVC Technical report#24 (1998)
8. Milczarski, P., Kompanets, L., Kurach, D.: An Approach to Brain Thinker Type Recognition Based on Facial Asymmetry. In: Rutkowski, L., Scherer, R., Tadeusiewicz, R., Zadeh, L.A., Zurada, J.M. (eds.) ICAISC 2010, Part I. LNCS (LNAI), vol. 6113, pp. 643–650. Springer, Heidelberg (2010)
9. Mitra, S., Liu, Y.: Local facial asymmetry for expression classification. In: Proc. IEEE Conference on Computer Vision and Pattern Recognition, pp. 889–894 (2004)
10. O'Grady, K., Antonyshyn, O.: Facial Asymmetry: Three-Dimensional Analysis Using Laser Surface Scanning. Plastic & Reconstructive Surgery 104, 928–937 (1999)
11. Pissarenko, D.: Eigenface-based facial recognition,
   `http://openbio.sourceforge.net/resources/eigenfaces/eigenfaces.pdf`
12. Rutkowska, D.: An Expert System for Human Personality Characteristics Recognition. In: Rutkowski, L., Scherer, R., Tadeusiewicz, R., Zadeh, L.A., Zurada, J.M. (eds.) ICAISC 2010, Part I. LNCS (LNAI), vol. 6113, pp. 665–672. Springer,7 Heidelberg (2010)
13. Rutkowska, D., Kurach, D.: A Genetic Algorithm for a Facial Vertical Axis Determination, Selected Topics in Computer Science Applications, pp. 164–175. Academic Publishing House EXIT, Warsaw (2011)
14. Shackelford, T.K., Larsen, R.J.: Facial asymmetry as an indicator of psychological, emotional, and physiological distress. Journal of Personality and Social Psychology 72, 456–466 (1997)
15. Swaddle, J.P., Cuthill, I.C.: Asymmetry and Human Facial Attractiveness: Symmetry not Always be Beautiful. In: Proceedings: Biological Sciences, pp. 111–116 (May 1995)
16. Timm, F., Barth, E.: Accurate Eye Centre Localisation by Means of Gradients. In: Proceedings of the Int. Conference on Computer Theory and Applications (VISAPP), Algarve, Portugal, pp. 125–130 (2011)
17. Turk, M., Pentland, A.: Eigenfaces for recognition. Journal of Cognitive Neuroscience 3(1), 71–86 (1991)
18. Turk, M., Pentland, A.: Face recognition using eigenfaces. In: Proc. IEEE Conference on Computer Vision and Pattern Recognition, pp. 586–591 (1991)
19. Yu, Z., Mu, X., Feng, S., Han, J., Chang, T.: Flip-Registration procedure of Three-dimensional laser surfacescanning images on quantitative evaluation of facial asymmetries. The Journal of Craniofacial Surgery 20, 157–160 (2009)

Feature Selection Based on Activation of Signaling Pathways Applied for Classification of Samples in Microarray Studies

Henryk Maciejewski

Institute of Computer Engineering, Control and Robotics,
Wroclaw University of Technology,
ul. Wybrzeze Wyspianskiego 27, 50-370 Wroclaw, Poland
`Henryk.Maciejewski@pwr.wroc.pl`

Abstract. This paper presents a new method of deriving features for sample classification based on massive throughput data such as microarray gene expression studies. The number of features in these studies is much bigger than the number of samples thus strong reduction of dimensionality is essential. Standard approaches attempt to select subsets of features (genes) realizing highest association with the target, and they tend to produce unstable and non-reproducible feature sets. The purpose of this work is to improve feature selection by using prior biological knowledge of potential relationships between features, available e.g., in signaling pathways databases. We first identify most activated pathways and then derive pathway-based features based on expression of the up- and down-regulated genes in the pathway. We demonstrate performance of this approach using real microarray data.

Keywords: Classification, feature selection, gene-set analysis, signaling pathways.

1 Introduction - Formulation of the Problem

Massive throughput experiments such as gene expression microarray studies have recently posed one of the most challenging tasks for bioinformatics which is building prognostic or diagnostic classifiers based on data from such assays. The task is considered challenging or even ill-formulated mainly due to the fact that the number of samples n is usually much smaller than the number of features (gene expressions), p (a $n \ll p$ problem). Many approaches to class prediction based on such high-dimensionality data have been developed, e.g., [2],[7]. These methods generally attempt to identify sets of prognostic genes (features) in a data-driven manner, ie., by focusing on features with high association with the target, but without taking into account domain knowledge about relationships between the genes (features). Such information about sets of related genes is available e.g. in signaling pathway databases (Biocarta, KEGG) or in the Gene Ontology database. This information is typically used by biologists to improve

L. Rutkowski et al. (Eds.): ICAISC 2012, Part II, LNCS 7268, pp. 284–292, 2012.

interpretability of massive throughput results, but has not been so far used with class prediction based on massive throughput studies.

One of the most clear limitations of current approaches to class prediction based on massive throughput data is related to instability and poor reproducibility of feature sets derived from such data, [14],[13],[8],[9]. It is often observed that sets of prognostic (most informative) features identified by one group show little overlap with results obtained by another group. This issue was investigated in [4], leading to a conclusion that generation of stable (robust) feature sets from massive throughput data would require thousands of samples. However, current microarray studies are able to afford up to hundred(s) of samples. Hence instability of features seems inevitable with massive throughput data, which clearly implies instability of classifiers, as shown e.g. in [9].

In our previous works [10],[11], we proposed and examined an enhanced procedure of feature selection which uses information about a priori specified sets of functionally related genes (e.g., KEGG signaling pathways). We built classifiers using genes-members of the most strongly activated pathways as predictors. We showed that these feature sets prove more stable than features generated from purely data-driven procedures and that they can bring improvement in class prediction. However, a drawback of the method investigated in [10],[11] is the fact that we still use individual genes (members of pathways) as predictors. This can lead to substantial number of features if we increase the number of pathways considered as important for class prediction. The main incentive of this paper is to propose an improved method of pathway-based feature selection which aggregates the pathway activation into a small number of features. In this way samples could be classified based on the *level of activation* of consecutive pathways (or a priori defined gene sets) rather than expression of individual genes.

In the following section we present a generic framework of the procedure to generate per-sample aggregate features which represent activation of pathways. We also discuss specific methods of gene set analysis used in this procedure. Next we describe an algorithm used to evaluate predictive performance of the derived features. Finally, we illustrate performance of this method by a numerical study based on two real microarray datasets.

2   Feature Selection Based on Gene Sets

The purpose of the proposed method is to derive features for class prediction from a priori specified collection of gene sets ordered by some measure of associated with the target variable. The method will be presented using the following notation. Let us denote the results of a massive throughput study as the matrix $X_{p,n}$ with columns related to the n samples (e.g., patients) tested and with p rows related to gene expressions. The target variable is denoted as Y, where Y_i, $i = 1, 2, \ldots, n$, represents the class label of the sample i (e.g., disease vs control group). Is should be noted that although it is often the case in microarray studies, Y does not have to be a binary variable or even a qualitative variable, ie., multi-class or quantitative targets can be used. We also denote the collection of a priori specified gene sets as $\mathbf{S} = \{S_1, S_2, \ldots, S_d\}$. The sets comprise groups of related genes, e.g., genes in a signaling pathway (these sets are defined in the KEGG or Biocarta database), or genes with common gene ontology terms (as specified in the GO database).

The proposed method of feature selection works in the following steps.

1. First, calculate the class comparison score for all the p genes; we denote this by $z_1, z_2, \ldots, z_p$. For instance, for the binary target Y, the score $z_i, i = 1, \ldots, p$, can be calculated as the t-statistic used to compare the groups $\{X_{i,j} : Y_j = 1\}$ against $\{X_{i,j} : Y_j = 0\}$. Note that the sign of z scores determines whether a particular gene is up- or down-regulated between the groups compared.

2. Next, calculate the measure of association of the gene sets in $\mathbf{S}$ with the target, referred to as the gene-set scores and denote the scores by $s_i, i = 1, \ldots, d$. Gene set scores can be calculated using numerous methods, e.g., gene set enrichment analysis (GSEA, [13]), gene set analysis (GSA, [5]), or the global test (GT, [3]) algorithm. The next step is to order the gene sets by decreasing association with the target: $S_{(1)}, S_{(2)}, \ldots, S_{(d)}$. For instance, if s_i are calculated as the p-value of the GT or similar test (with the null hypothesis assuming no association between the gene set and the target), elements in $\mathbf{S}$ should be ordered by increasing p-value of the test.

3. For each of the samples j, a gene set S_i will contribute two features derived as the average expression of the genes in S_i realizing positive z scores and the average expression of the genes in S_i realizing negative z scores. More specifically, the features are defined as:

$$v_{i,j}^+ = \frac{1}{N_i} \sum_{\substack{k \in S_i \\ z_k \geq 0}} X_{k,j} \quad \text{and} \quad v_{i,j}^- = \frac{1}{N_i} \sum_{\substack{k \in S_i \\ z_k < 0}} X_{k,j} \tag{1}$$

where N_i is the number of genes in S_i. If the set of genes with positive or negative scores is empty, the corresponding feature assumes the value of 0.

4. Represent each of the samples by the features calculated as in (1) based on the collection of top nPW gene sets: $S_{(1)}, S_{(2)}, \ldots, S_{(nPW)}, nPW \leq d$, where nPW is a parameter of the method (we analyze sensitivity of this parameter in the following numerical study).

The measures defined in (1) are inspired by the max-mean statistic proposed in [3] and used by the authors as a gene-set ranking statistic in their GSA algorithm. More specifically, the max-mean statistic for the gene-set S_i is defined as the maximum of the two averages obtained from positive z gene scores and from negative z gene scores calculated for genes in the set S_i. The 'winning' average score (ie., the one bigger in absolute value) is then used by the GSA algorithm to identify most strongly activated pathways. Using the max-mean statistic roughly means that if up-regulated genes dominate in the the gene set over down-regulated genes, then activation of the pathway is represented by mean score the up-regulated genes.

Although the formulation of gene-set based features (1) is inspired by these ideas, we represent activation of a pathway in a sample by taking both up- and down-regulated genes into account, and not just the winning group. Besides, our method is open in terms of selection of the gene set ranking method. In principle any gene set analysis method can be used (an excellent overview of different approaches in given in [14]). In the numerical study we focus on the GT and GSA methods which represent conceptually different ways of testing activation of pathways:

- the GT method tests the null hypothesis assuming that no genes in the gene set are associated with the target. Small p-value of this test indicates pathway (gene-set) activation.
- the GSA method tests the hypothesis that genes in the gene-set are at most as often differentially expressed as the genes not in the gene set, ie., it essentially compares the gene set to its complement. The method calculates the max-mean statistic and the associated p-value.

These methods belong the class of *self-contained* and *competitive* gene set analysis methods, respectively [6]. In the following numerical study we investigate performance of these methods in terms of quality of features generated according to (1).

3   Numerical Study

In this numerical study we build classifiers based on two microarray datasets. The first analysis is is based on a subset of the ALL data, published in [1], and representing B-cell leukemia patients. The classifier is supposed to distinguish between leukemia and control samples (dataset includes 79 samples, 37 leukemia and 42 control, designated in the original data as 'BCR/ABL' and 'NEG', respectively). We preprocess the data by logging and removing genes with very low variability across samples (technically, IQR below 0.5 or signal below 100 in more than 75% of samples were used as the condition to filter genes out). This reduced the number of features from original 12625 to 2391.

The second analysis is based on the chronic lymphocytic leukemia data (available in the CLL Bioconductor package). The data contains 14 samples related to progressive disease and 8 samples related to stable disease. Data preprocessing was done as in the ALL analysis.

In the study we use the KEGG pathway database as the collection of gene sets **S**, with the number of pathways $d = 210$.

3.1   Algorithm to Estimate Predictive Performance

An important problem related to class prediction based on massive throughput data ($n \ll p$ case) is proper estimation of classification error expected for new data. Since the number of samples is small, the error is usually estimated with data-reuse techniques. Here we will use leave-one-out (LOO) cross-validation. It is very important that for fair estimation of the error *internal* cross-validation is used [12], where features are selected repeatedly in the consecutive iterations of cross validation (an alternative version, *external* CV, selects features once, based on all samples). The procedure used to estimate classification error is summarized below.

1. Leave out sample i, $i = 1, 2, \ldots, n$ for model testing, ie., remove column i from X and element i from vector Y and denote the remaining matrix and vector as X^i and Y^i.
2. Based on (X^i, Y^i) calculate the gene set based features using the method proposed in the previous section; the training data represented in this new feature space is denoted as X^i_{pw}.
3. Based on the training data (X^i_{pw}, Y^i) fit a predictive model f and classify the sample Y_i as $\hat{Y}_i = f(Y_i)$.
4. Repeat steps 1 through 3 for $i = 1, 2, \ldots, n$.
5. Calculate the expected misclassification rate as $error = \sum_{i=1}^{n} I(\hat{Y}_i \neq Y_i)$.

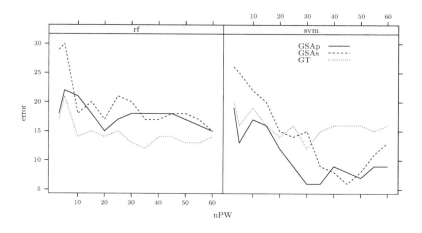

Fig. 1. ALL data: prediction error for different methods of pathway ranking (GT or GSA with ranks based on pathway scores or p-values), different number of pathways used to generate features (nPW) and different classifiers (random forests and SVM)

3.2   Results

The overall performance of classifiers for the ALL data is summarized in Fig. 1, with different methods of gene set analysis and different number of pathways used to generate features. We used the GT or GSA algorithm for pathway ranking with GSA ranks based either on gene set scores (GSAs) or p-values (GSAp). Similar results for the CLL data are presented in Fig. 4. These results can be compared with Figs. 2 and 5 where performance of classifiers with standard feature selection is summarized, based on collection of the most differentially expressed genes.

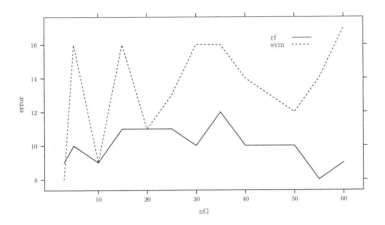

Fig. 2. ALL data: prediction error for features based on nG most differentially expressed genes, for random forests and SVM

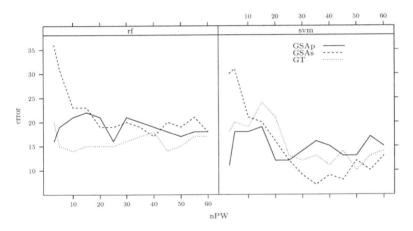

Fig. 3. ALL data: prediction error for max-mean features. See caption of Fig. 1 for explanation of symbols.

Generally pathway based features realize slightly smaller prediction error for both data sets. Secondly, we observe better stability of pathway based classifiers with performance generally improving with growing number of pathways. This can be contrasted with the ragged shape in Fig. 2, which illustrates instability of classifiers. We also observed that, consistently with [11], pathway-based sets of features generated in subsequent iterations of cross validation are more stable than the sets of most differentially expressed genes in generated in subsequent iterations (results not shown). This suggests that despite slight changes in the data pathway based features seem more reproducible. Comparing different classifiers, we observe that with pathway-based features SVM generally outperforms random forests.

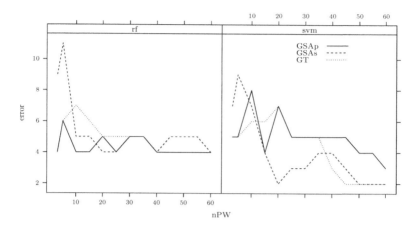

Fig. 4. Prediction error for CLL data. See caption of Fig. 1 for explanation of symbols.

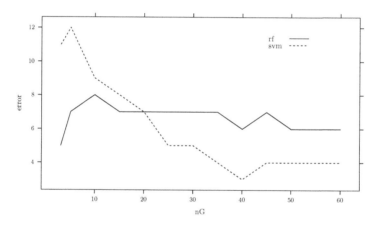

Fig. 5. CLL data: prediction error for features based on nG most differentially expressed genes, for random forests and SVM classifiers

The purpose of additional analyses summarized in Figs. 3 and 6 is to verify suggestion made by authors of the GSA algorithm [3], that features could be generated in a manner similar in spirit to the max-mean statistic. Ie., if up-regulated genes dominate in a gene set, then their average may be used as a pathway based feature. We repeated previous analyses using a simplified version of the proposed feature selection procedure, where a pathway is represented by just one feature equal $max\left(|v_{i,j}^{+}|, |v_{i,j}^{-}|\right)$, ignoring the minority-based other. Results in Figs. 3 and 6 indicate that this simplification leads to deteriorated performance. Hence it seems worth representing a pathway by terms corresponding to both up- and down-regulated genes, irrespective of which dominates in the pathway.

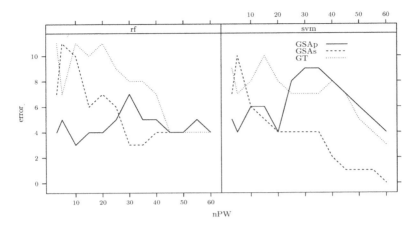

Fig. 6. CLL data: prediction error for max-mean features. See caption of Fig. 1 for explanation of symbols.

4   Conclusions

In this work a method was presented that allows to generate features for class prediction based on the collection of activated pathways (gene sets). This method can be regarded as an implementation of the idea that a difficult task of feature selection / dimensionality reduction in massive throughput data can be made more feasible by incorporating a priori domain knowledge about sets of related features. We proposed a method of feature generation based on such sets and we analyzed predictive performance of these features based on real microarray data. These analyses lead to the overall conclusion that the proposed approach can bring improvement in both performance of classifiers as well as in stability and reproducibility of prognostic or diagnostic feature sets. This result seems not obvious, taking into account that individual features in active pathways generally show lower association with target as compared with standard features. It is also interesting to observe that the GSA method of gene set analysis (a competitive approach) tends to produce at least not worse features than the global test. The latter, a self contained method, directly analyzes association of sets with the target and as such might be expected to generate better features for prediction of the target. However, our study does not support this hypothesis. The reason for this is worth further investigation. In this work we also showed that in order to produce good features pathways (gene sets) should be represented by both up- and down-regulated features, and not just by the majority group as done in the GSA algorithm. Results shown in this work also suggest that the method deserves further analysis and more comprehensive evaluation based on both simulation are additional real datasets.

This work was sponsored by the grant MNiSzW N516 510239.

References

1. Chiaretti, S., Li, X., Gentleman, R., et al.: Gene expression profile of adult T-cell acute lymphocytic leukemia identifies distinct subsets of patients with different response to therapy and survical. Blood 103, 2771–2778 (2004)
2. Dudoit, S., Fridlyand, J., Speed, P.: Comparison of discriminant methods for classification of tumors using gene expression data. JASA 192, 77–87 (2005)
3. Efron, B., Tibshirani, R.: On testing the significance of sets of genes. Ann. Appl. Stat. 1(1), 107–129 (2007)
4. Ein-Dor, L., Zuk, O., Domany, E.: Thousands of samples are needed to generate a robust gene list for predicting outcome in cancer. Proc. Natl. Acad. Sci. USA 103(15), 5923–5928 (2006)
5. Goemann, J.J., et al.: A global test for groups of genes: testing association with a clinical outcome. Bioinformatics 20(1), 93–99 (2004)
6. Goeman, J.J., Buehlmann, P.: Analyzing gene expression data in terms on gene sets: methodological issues. Bioinformatics 23(8), 980–987 (2007)
7. Lin, Y.H., et al.: Multiple gene expression classifiers from different array platforms predict poor prognosis of colorectal cancer. Clin. Cancer Res. 13, 498–507 (2007)
8. Maciejewski, H.: Quality of Feature Selection Based on Microarray Gene Expression Data. In: Bubak, M., van Albada, G.D., Dongarra, J., Sloot, P.M.A. (eds.) ICCS 2008, Part III. LNCS, vol. 5103, pp. 140–147. Springer, Heidelberg (2008)
9. Maciejewski, H., Twaróg, P.: Model Instability in Microarray Gene Expression Class Prediction Studies. In: Moreno-Díaz, R., Pichler, F., Quesada-Arencibia, A. (eds.) EUROCAST 2009. LNCS, vol. 5717, pp. 745–752. Springer, Heidelberg (2009)
10. Maciejewski, H.: Class Prediction in Microarray Studies Based on Activation of Pathways. In: Corchado, E., Kurzyński, M., Woźniak, M. (eds.) HAIS 2011, Part I. LNCS (LNAI), vol. 6678, pp. 321–328. Springer, Heidelberg (2011)
11. Maciejewski, H.: Competitive and self-contained gene set analysis methods applied for class prediction. In: Proc. of the Federated Conference on Computer Science and Information Systems. IEEE Computer Society Press (2011)
12. Markowetz, F., Spang, R.: Molecular diagnosis. Classification, Model Selection and Performance Evaluation, Methods Inf. Med. 44, 438–443 (2005)
13. Subramanian, A., et al.: Gene set enrichment analysis: A knowledge-based approach for interpreting genome-wide expression profiles. Proc. Natl. Acad. Sci. USA 102(43), 15545–15550 (2005)
14. Wu, M.C., Lin, X.: Prior biological knowledge-based approaches for the analysi of genome-wide expression profiling using gene sets and pathways. Statistical Methods in Medical Research 18, 577–593 (2009)

Feasibility of Error-Related Potential Detection as Novelty Detection Problem in P300 Mind Spelling

Nikolay V. Manyakov, Adrien Combaz, Nikolay Chumerin, Arne Robben,
Marijn van Vliet, and Marc M. Van Hulle

Laboratory for Neuro- and Psychofysiology, KU Leuven,
Herestraat 49, bus 1021, 3000 Leuven, Belgium
{NikolayV.Manyakov,Adrien.Combaz,Nikolay.Chumerin,Arne.Robben,
Marijn.vanVliet,Marc.VanHulle}@med.kuleuven.be

Abstract. In this paper, we report on the feasibility of the Error-Related Potential (ErrP) integration in a particular type of Brain-Computer Interface (BCI) called the P300 Mind Speller. With the latter, the subject can type text only by means of his/her brain activity without having to rely on speech or muscular activity. Hereto, electroencephalography (EEG) signals are recorded from the subject's scalp. But, as with any BCI paradigm, decoding mistakes occur, and when they do, an EEG potential is evoked, known as the Error-Related Potential (ErrP), locked to the subject's realization of the mistake. When the BCI would be able to also detect the ErrP, the last typed character could be automatically corrected. However, since the P300 Mind Speller is optimized to correctly operate in the first place, we have much less ErrP's than responses to correctly typed characters. In fact, exactly because it is supposed to be a rare phenomenon, we advocate that ErrP detection can be treated as a novelty detection problem. We consider in this paper different one-class classification algorithms based on novelty detection together with a correction algorithm for the P300 Mind Speller.

1 Introduction

A *brain-computer interface* (BCI) is a device that records and decodes brain activity automatically, allowing the subject to interact with the world via computers, robots, actuators, and so on, bypassing the need for speech or muscular activity. BCIs can significantly improve the quality of life of patients suffering from amyotrophic lateral sclerosis, stroke, brain/spinal cord injury, cerebral palsy, muscular dystrophy, etc [1,2]. Brain-computer interfaces are either invasive [3,4,5,6] or noninvasive [2,7,8,9,10,11]. The latter ones based on *electroencephalograms* (EEG) recorded from the subject's scalp have recently enjoyed an increasing visibility since they do not require any surgical procedure, and can therefore be more easily tested on human subjects. Several noninvasive BCI paradigms have been described in the literature, but the one we concentrate

L. Rutkowski et al. (Eds.): ICAISC 2012, Part II, LNCS 7268, pp. 293–301, 2012.

on relies on *event-related potentials* (ERPs, a stereotyped electrophysiological response to an internal or external stimulus [12]).

One of the most explored ERP components is the P300. It can be detected while a subject is shown two types of events with one occurring much less frequently than the other ("rare event"). The rare event elicits an ERP consisting of an enhanced positive-going signal component with a latency of about 300 ms after stimulus onset [12]. In order to detect ERPs, single trial recordings are usually not sufficient, and recordings over several trials need to be averaged: the recorded signal is a superposition of the activity related to the stimulus and all other ongoing brain activity together with noise. By averaging, the activity that is time-locked to a known event (*e.g.*, the onset of the attended stimulus) is extracted as an ERP, whereas the activity that is not related to the stimulus onset is expected to be averaged out. The stronger the ERP signal, the fewer trials are needed, and *vice versa*. There has been a growing interest in the ERP detection problem, as witnessed by the increased availability of BCIs that rely on it. A notorious example is the P300 Mind Speller [9,10], with which subjects are able to type words on a computer screen.

But, as with any BCI system, mistakes occur, slowing down the typing speed, since they need to be corrected, for example, by selecting the *backspace* option followed by a re-typing of the character the subject had in mind. Thus, such a procedure requires two additional P300 Mind Speller rounds. To overcome this problem, two different methods can be considered. In the first case, the subject is allowed to continue typing, thus, without attempting any corrective action, after which the mistyped "word" is corrected by matching it to the closest one (according to some metric) from an adapted dictionary [13]. But this method is prone to disambiguities (when two or more words from the dictionary have the same distance to the mistyped one) and, more importantly, it can lead to new mistakes since it assumes that the number of types characters of the "word" is correct. Indeed, an error can be made not only in the middle of the word, but also at the end: when instead of selecting the *end of input* or the *space* symbol, another character becomes selected. In another class of methods, as is investigated in this paper, one tries to use the Error-Related Potential (ErrP), which is the ERP evoked when the subject "realizes" the error made by the BCI system [11,14]. When performing ErrP detection, one could avoid the selection of a corrective option (such as *backspace*) by the subject, or one could even impute the correct character (thus, the one the subject originally had in mind) with the use of a smart correction algorithm. With the latter, the correction could be done automatically, without any intervention from the subject. While the concept looks attractive, there is not much proof of the feasibility of ErrP detection and its possible gain in P300 speller performance. This is due to the fact that ErrP detection algorithms also make mistakes, since we need to perform single trial decoding of the ErrP, thus, with a low signal-to-noise ratio, and that these mistakes occur not only for incorrectly detected ErrP's (false positives), which consequently require corrective actions from the subject (selecting *backspace* and re-typing), but also for wrongly classified non-ErrP responses (false negatives), which leads to the replacing of a correctly typed character by another. All these call for tedious corrective actions by the subject. In summary, an acceptable trade-off need to be found between false negatives and false positives.

Another problem is due to the fact that a properly tuned P300 system should not have a large amount of mistakes in the first place. Thus, for training an ErrP detector, we have a large amount of non-ErrP responses, but a small amount of ErrP responses. This motivated us to consider it as novelty detection algorithm where the ErrP responses are treated as outliers in a one-class classification problem.

In this paper, we test different one-class classifiers for ErrP detection on three subjects and discuss its potential for optimizing the P300 Mind Speller. We investigate ErrP detection *per se* in search of a trade-off between false negatives and false positives to boost the P300 Mind Speller's performance. In addition, we also discuss one possible correction procedure that automatically replaces wrongly typed characters. A possible gain in performance from the latter is also assessed.

2 Methods

2.1 P300 Mind Speller

We have used (see [2,15] from more details) visual stimulation paradigm based on a matrix of 6×6 characters (see Fig. 1), where '_' corresponds to *space* and '¶' to the *end of input* indicator. Each experiment started with a training stage where the subject was asked to type 8 characters, so that the corresponding recordings could be labeled, followed by a testing phase where the subject could type anything (s)he has in mind (free spelling mode). During both stages, columns and rows of the matrix were intensified (see Figure 1) in a random manner. The duration of the intensification was fixed to 100 ms, followed by 100 ms of no intensification. Each column and each row flashed only once during one trial, so each trial consisted of 12 stimulus presentations. For typing one character, recordings from m such trials were averaged, to increase the signal-to-noise ratio.

During both the training and testing stages, the subject was asked to count the number of times the desired character was intensified, which led to P300 responses connected to these events. Thus, each trial includes 2 responses with P300 components (intensification of a row and column with the desired character) and 10 non-P300 responses (locked to the intensification of other rows and columns). Furthermore, we have a repetition of m such trials for each character to be typed. These averaged recordings are used for tuning a classifier to discriminate between the P300 vs. non-P300 cases given the available labels. During the test phase, the averaged ERP responses from each row and column are subjected to the previously trained classifier, and the distances to border separating the P300 and non-P300 classes in feature space are estimated. After that, each character on the typing matrix receives a score in terms of the sum of

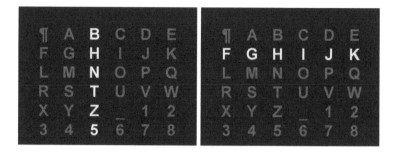

Fig. 1. Typing matrix of the P300 Mind Speller. The intensification of the third column (left panel) and of the second row (right panel) are shown.

the aforementioned distances from the row and column containing this character. The character with the highest score is communicated as the output of the classification procedure.

2.2 EEG Experiment and Preprocessing

The EEG recordings were performed with a prototype of a miniature wireless EEG system developed by *imec*[1] around their ultra-low power 8-channel EEG amplifier chip [16]. Signals are sampled at a rate $f_s^{\mathrm{EEG}} = 1000$ Hz with a resolution of 12 bits/sample. We have used an electrode cap with large filling holes and sockets for active Ag/AgCl electrodes (ActiCap, Brain Products). The eight electrodes were placed primarily on the parietal cortex, namely at positions Fz, FCz, Cz, CP1, CP2, P3, Pz and P4, according to the international 10–20 system. The reference and ground electrodes were placed on the left and right mastoids, respectively.

Three subjects (one male and two females, age range 24–27 years) participated in the experiment. Each of the subjects participated in 6-7 typing sessions during which 659, 963 and 758 characters were typed in total. In order to provoke more errors (and, thus, more ErrP responses) the number of intensifications m during the test phase was decreased (down to 5, 4 or even 3 intensifications, depending on how accurately the subjects were typing), leading to a total number of 171 (26%), 114 (12%) and 121 (16%) mistakes, respectively. To avoid a deterioration of the ErrP signal caused by an overlap with a subsequent P300 ERP, we introduced a 2 second interval between the presentation of the feedback (*i.e.*, showing the character as it is deduced by the P300 Mind Speller) and the start of the next character. These 2 second segments containing ErrP's where taken out from the EEG recordings, after being filtered in the range between 0.5 and 30 Hz with a zero-phase 4th order Butterworth filter and downsampling to 250 Hz. For classification, we considered only Fz, FCz, Cz responses, for which the ErrP was reported to be more prominent [14].

---

[1] http://www.imec.be

2.3 One-Class Classification

One-class classification is a particular type of classification, where the training set mainly consists of examples from one class (targets) and only some or even no examples from the second class (outliers). In our case, the target class describes non-ErrP responses, while the outliers are the ErrPs as they are only sparsely represented in the training set. We consider in this paper one-class classification algorithms [17] based on three main approaches: density-, boundary-, and reconstruction methods. Density methods (Gaussian model, Mixture of Gaussians, Parzen density estimator) try to estimate the density function (by adjusting the parameters of some predefined distributions or by non-parametric methods) of the training examples. By setting up a threshold on these densities, new data can be classified into targets and outliers. But the construction of the density function is a more demanding task than deriving a boundary "around" the target class. This influenced the appearance of boundary methods, which construct a "shell" around the target data but with the additional constraint to arrive at a minimal volume solution. Here we account for the such boundary methods as k-centers [18] and k-nearest neighbor [17]. The reconstruction methods make use of data modeling, where it is assumed that a more compact representation of the target data can be constructed. Thus, the transformation of the target data to such a representation and back is expected to have a smaller reconstruction error for the target examples (since we model them), than for the outliers. As a consequence, it allows us to discriminate between these two classes. Here, we consider principal component analysis (PCA) [17] and the auto-encoders neural network (NN) [19]. An algorithmic implementation of some one-class classification methods can be found in [20].

3 Results

For our analysis, we split the recorded data into two parts (training and test sets), and we intentionally use the first part of the data (according to the date of appearance in the dataset) for training (25%, 50% or 75% of all data), while retaining the rest of the data for testing, since we wanted to follow the natural order of our recording sessions. Since for our one-class classifiers it is desirable to keep the dimension of feature space low, we considered n ($n = 3, 6, 9$) features for classification, where those disjoint features where selected as the best ones, from the training set, based on the Student t-test. The trained classifiers were applied to the test data and a ROC (receiver operating characteristic) curve was generated, showing the performance of classifiers for the different threshold values. But since our requirements of ErrP detection are different from pure classification, we modified the way to present the results. For considering an ErrP decoder in the context of a P300 Mind Speller, we have to increase the speed of typing by correcting mistakes with the use of ErrP detection, while we also have to avoid erroneous "correction" of correctly typed symbols (false negatives). Thus, we have to minimize the ratio of the sum of false negatives and false positives given all trials (*i.e.*, the 1-accuracy, called here mistake rate). Figure 2 (a,c,e)

Table 1. Gain in performance (in percent) of P300 Mind Speller after incorporating ErrP detection (I) and ErrP detection with correction (II), for different one-class classifiers, subjects, and data splitting strategies

Strategy	method	Subject 1			Subject 2			Subject 3		
		25 %	50%	75%	25 %	50%	75%	25 %	50%	75%
I	Gaussian	3.005	5.327	12.295	0	1.179	1.415	0.418	0.019	0
	Mixture of Gaussians	7.103	12.704	17.213	1.726	2.830	1.415	0.627	0.019	0
	Parzen	1.092	2.459	9.836	0.157	0.235	0	0.209	0	0
	k-nearest neighbor	1.092	2.049	8.196	0	0	0	0.209	0	0
	k-centers	2.185	7.786	9.836	0.627	0.471	0	0	0	0
	PCA	3.278	6.147	11.475	1.569	2.358	4.245	0.224	0.418	0
	auto-encoder NN	3.825	3.688	13.114	0.314	0	0	0.627	0	0
II	Gaussian	3.005	5.327	12.295	0	1.179	1.415	0.418	0.019	0
	Mixture of Gaussians	7.103	12.704	17.213	1.726	2.830	1.415	0.627	0.019	0
	Parzen	1.092	2.459	9.836	0.157	0.235	0	0.209	0	0
	k-nearest neighbor	1.092	2.049	8.196	0	0	0	0.209	0	0
	k-centers	2.185	7.787	9.836	0.628	0.472	0	0	0	0
	PCA	3.279	6.147	11.475	1.570	2.358	4.245	0.224	0.418	0
	auto-encoder NN	3.825	3.688	13.114	0.314	0	0	0.628	0	0

shows this mistake rate (in percent) for different classifier thresholds (presented here in terms of the number of possible threshold positions in the ROC curve, so as to obtain a unified representation of the results of the different classifiers), for the investigated one-class classification methods, together with the mistake rate (red horizontal line) in the case of only P300 detection (thus, no ErrP detection). Here, the best results among all numbers n features considered for each classifier, as well as the best value for k (for the k-nearest neighbor and k-centers methods), the best number of Gaussians in the Mixture of Gaussians method, and the best number of components in the PCA method, all of which were optimized through cross-validation. Table 1 (I) shows the maximal gain in performance (in percent with respect to the case where no ErrP detector was incorporated) for each subject and for all data splitting strategies considered (25%, 50% or 75% of the recorded data as the training set). But we have to remember that, despite mistakes are identified, we still need to re-type the character.

To potentially speed up mind typing even more, we can include a correction algorithm in addition to mistake detection. Here, for example, we can take the second character in our ranking (see Sec. 2.1) when a mistake is detected. In this case, the correction will be done automatically, and the typing procedure will become faster. The results of the described procedure are presented in Fig. 2 (b,d,f) for some subjects and data splittings, while Table 1 (II) represents the maximal gain in accuracy with such a procedure for all subjects, methods and data splittings.

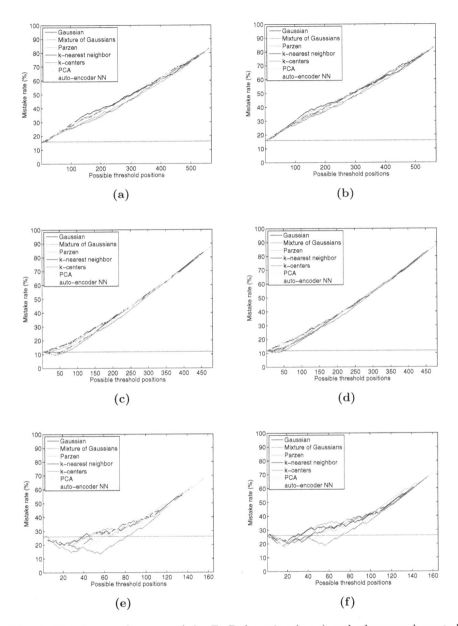

Fig. 2. Mistake rate (in percent) for ErrP detection (a,c,e) and when supplemented with error correction (b,d,f). Red horizontal line indicates the mistake rate, when no ErrP detection is applied. The results are shown for subject 3 with 25% of data in the training set (a,b), subject 2 with 50% of data (c,d) and subject 3 with 75% of data (e,f).

4 Discussion and Conclusion

The results show that for two of our three subjects we can benefit from error correction based on ErrP detection using one-class classification. While for the second subject the benefit is moderate, the first subject can gain up to 11.6% when error correction is implemented. The results indicate that, in general, Mixture of Gaussians produce the most best results. While the results look promising, we should remember that we still have to select the best threshold based on training data, which could be viewed as a difficult task. Another problem can be with the feature selection procedure. In this paper, we used a t-test to find the time points with a good separability between target and outlier classes. But in real applications we have to be aware that the outlier class could be small, thus, probably, other feature selection methods considering information only from the target class could be investigated.

In summary, the results of this work show the benefit of incorporating the ErrP in the P300 Mind Speller when using classifiers that account for the majority of the responses to correctly typed characters.

Acknowledgments. NVM is supported by the research grant GOA 10/019, NC is supported by IST-2007-217077, AC and AR are supported by IWT doctoral grants, MvV is supported by IUAP P6/29, MMVH is supported by PFV/10/008, CREA/07/027, G.0588.09, IUAP P6/29, GOA 10/019, IST-2007-217077.

References

1. Mak, J.N., Wolpaw, J.R.: Clinical applications of brain-computer interfaces: current state and future prospects. IEEE Reviews in Biomedical Engineering 2, 187–199 (2009)
2. Manyakov, N.V., Chumerin, N., Combaz, A., Van Hulle, M.M.: Comparison of classification methods for P300 Brain-Computer Interface on disabled subjects. Computational Intelligence and Neuroscience 2011, Article ID 519868, 1–12 (2011)
3. Lebedev, M.A., Nicolelis, M.A.L.: Brain-Machine Interface: Past, Present and Future. Trends in Neurosc. 29(9), 536–546 (2005)
4. Manyakov, N.V., Van Hulle, M.M.: Decoding Grating Orientation from Micro-electrode Array Recordings in Monkey Cortical Area V4. International Journal of Neural Systems 20(2), 95–108 (2010)
5. Manyakov, N.V., Vogels, R., Van Hulle, M.M.: Decoding Stimulus-Reward Pairing from Local Field Potentials Recorded from Monkey Visual Cortex. IEEE Transactions on Neural Networks 21(12), 1892–1902 (2010)
6. Velliste, M., Perel, S., Spalding, M.C., Whitford, A.S., Schwartz, A.B.: Cortical Control of a Prosthetic Arm for Self-Feeding. Nature 453, 1098–1101 (2008)
7. Birbaumer, N., Kübler, A., Ghanayim, N., Hinterberger, T., Perelmouter, J., Kaiser, J., Iversen, I., Kotchoubey, B., Neumann, N., Flor, H.: The Thought Translation Device (TTD) for Completely Paralyzed Patients. IEEE Transactions on Rehabilitation Egineering 8(2), 190–193 (2000)
8. Blankertz, B., Dornhege, G., Krauledat, M., Müller, K.-R., Curio, G.: The Non-Invasive Berlin Brain-Computer Interface: Fast Acquisition of Effective Performance in Untrained Subjects. Neuroimage 37(2), 539–550 (2007)

9. Farwell, L.A., Donchin, E.: Talking o the top of your head: toward a mental prosthesis utilizing event-related brain potentials. Electroencephalography and Clinical Neurophysiology 70(6), 510–523 (1988)

10. Combaz, A., Manyakov, N.V., Chumerin, N., Suykens, J.A.K., Van Hulle, M.M.: Feature Extraction and Classification of EEG Signals for Rapid P300 Mind Spelling. In: Proc. International Conference on Machine Learning and Applications, pp. 386–391 (2009)

11. Combaz, A., Chumerin, N., Manyakov, N.V., Robben, A., Suykens, J.A.K., Van Hulle, M.M.: Towards the detection of Error-Related Potentials and its integration in the context of a P300 Speller Brain-Computer Interface. Neurocomputing 80, 73–82 (2012)

12. Luck, S.: An Introduction to the Event-Related Potential Technique. MIT Press, Cambridge (2005)

13. Ahi, S.T., Kambara, H., Koike, Y.: A dictionary driven P300 speller with modified interface. IEEE Transaction on Neural Systems and Rehabilitation Engineering 19(1), 6–14 (2011)

14. Combaz, A., Chumerin, N., Manyakov, N.V., Robben, A., Suykens, J.A.K., Van Hulle, M.M.: Error-related Potential recorded by EEG in the context of a P300 Mind Speller Brain-Computer Interface. In: Proc. IEEE International Workshop on Machine Learning for Signal Processing, pp. 65–70 (2010)

15. Chumerin, N., Manyakov, N.V., Combaz, A., Suykens, J.A.K., Yazicioglu, R.F., Torfs, T., Merken, P., Neves, H.P., Van Hoof, C., Van Hulle, M.M.: P300 Detection Based on Feature Extraction in On-line Brain-Computer Interface. In: Mertsching, B., Hund, M., Aziz, Z. (eds.) KI 2009. LNCS (LNAI), vol. 5803, pp. 339–346. Springer, Heidelberg (2009)

16. Yazicioglu, R.F., Torfs, T., Merken, P., Penders, J., Leonov, V., Puers, R., Gyselinckx, B., Van Hoof, C.: Ultra-low-power biopotential interfaces and their applications in wearable and implantable systems. Microel J. 40(9), 1313–1321 (2009)

17. Tax, D.M.J.: One-class classification, PhD thesis, p. 202 (2001)

18. Ypma, A., Duin, R.: Support objects for domain approximation. In: ICANN 1998, pp. 2–4 (1998)

19. Japkowicz, N., Myers, C., Gluck, M.: A novelty detection approach to classification. In: Proceedings of the Fourteenth International Joint Conference on Artificial Intelligence, pp. 518–523 (1995)

20. Tax, D.M.J.: DDtools, the Data Description Toolbox for Matlab, ver. 1.9.0 (2011)

Class-Adaptive Denoising for EEG Data Classification

Ignas Martišius and Robertas Damaševičius

Software Engineering Department, Kaunas University of Technology,
Studentų 50-415, Kaunas, Lithuania
ignas.martisius@inbox.com, robertas.damasevicius@ktu.lt

Abstract. Brain-computer interface (BCI) systems use electro-encephalogram (EEG) data to control external electronic devices. The main task of BCI systems is to differentiate the classes of mental tasks from the EEG data. The EEG data is inherently complex and difficult to analyze due to interference by eye and muscle movements as well as electrical grid noise. In this paper we analyze shrinkage functions for signal filtering and propose a class-adaptive method for EEG data denoising. The results are evaluated using a Support Vector Machine.

Keywords: Brain-Computer Interface, EEG, denoising, shrinkage function, Support Vector Machine.

1   Introduction

The majority of BCI systems work by reading and interpreting cortically evoked electro-potentials across the scalp via an electro-encephalogram (EEG). The EEG data is inherently complex and difficult to analyze. Oscillatory activity in the EEG is classified into different frequency bands or rhythms: delta (0.5 – 3.5 Hz), theta (4 – 8 Hz), alpha-1 (8 – 10.5 Hz), alpha-2 (10.5 – 13 Hz), beta-1 (13 – 21 Hz), beta-2 (20 – 32 Hz) and gamma (36 – 44 Hz). Because EEG signals are non-stationary, nonlinear and interfered by eye movements and muscle noises, it is difficult to differentiate the classes of mental tasks from raw EEG data [1]. Different features can be extracted from the EEG data such as: time domain features related to changes in the amplitude of neurophysiologic signals, frequency domain features related to changes in oscillatory activity, and spatial domain features extracted from several electrodes [2].

BCI systems require correct classification of signals interpreted from the brain for useful operation. After acquiring the EEG data, pre-processing (filtering/denoising), feature extraction and dimensionality reduction is performed, before machine learning algorithms can be applied to learn from a training dataset how to classify the signals into classes, where each class corresponds to a specific action of the user. Usually, raw EEG data is pre-processed using digital signal processing (DSP) methods such as Fourier analysis or wavelet transform for denoising. Then classification methods are used to detect classes in denoised data.

The novelty of the paper is the proposed Class-Adaptive denoising method to select optimal parameter value(s) of a standard shrinkage function by maximizing class distance between frequency domain components of the positive and negative data

L. Rutkowski et al. (Eds.): ICAISC 2012, Part II, LNCS 7268, pp. 302–309, 2012.
© Springer-Verlag Berlin Heidelberg 2012

classes. The denoised data is classified using Support Vector Machine (SVM) and quality of classification is evaluated using standard accuracy metrics (F-measure, Area Under Curve, Average Precision).

The structure of the paper is as follows. Section 2 discusses related works. Section 3 presents analysis of the shrinkage function domain. Section 4 proposes the Class-Adaptive (CA) shrinkage method. Section 5 presents a case study. Finally, Section 6 presents conclusions and outlines future work.

2   Related Works

Numerous authors consider application of noise reduction methods for the BCI systems. RIA [3] is a noise reduction scheme based on applying the thresholding denoising to each signal and averaging the denoised signals. This procedure produces good denoising, since it can benefit from the statistical characteristics of randomness.

The denoised results can be further improved, if the thresholds at each frequency scale are chosen optimally. Such subband-adaptive denoising is used by modern wavelet-based denoising algorithms such as SureShrink [4] and BayesShrink [5]. Optimization of the class-to-class distance for two-class discrimination using Fisher distance is described by Aldjem [6]. Mu *et al.* [7] also use Fisher distance in feature selection algorithm and apply it for classification of EEG data.

3   Analysis of the Shrinkage Function Domain

There are many types of shrinkage function proposed in the signal denoising domain. For our analysis, here we classify shrinkage functions depending upon the dimensionality of their parameter space as: single-parameter, two-parameter, three-parameter and multi-parameter shrinkage functions. Dimensionality of the parameter space is important for the selection of an optimization method to find best parameter values. Below we provide a short description and analysis of some of these functions.

3.1   Single Parameter Shrinkage Functions

Donoho and Johnston [8] propose hard (Eq. 1) and soft (Eq. 2) shrinkage functions:

$$\hat{y} = \begin{cases} 0, & |y| \le \lambda \\ y, & |y| > \lambda \end{cases}, \tag{1}$$

$$\hat{y} = \begin{cases} 0, & |y| \le \lambda \\ y - \lambda, & y > \lambda \\ y + \lambda, & y < -\lambda \end{cases}. \tag{2}$$

here y is the noisy value, $\hat{y}$ is the shrinked value, and λ is universal threshold [8].

Norouzzadeh and Jampour [9] propose the following shrinkage function:

$$\hat{y} = y - \frac{\lambda^2 y}{y^8 + \lambda^2} \, . \tag{3}$$

Poornachandra and Kumaravel [10] propose a hyper trim shrinkage function:

$$\hat{y} = \begin{cases} 0, & |y| \le \lambda \\ \text{sgn}(y) \cdot \sqrt{y^2 - \lambda^2}, & |y| > \lambda \end{cases} . \tag{4}$$

3.2   Two-Parameter Shrinkage Functions

Poornachandra and Kumaravel [10] also propose a hyper shrinkage function:

$$\hat{y} = \begin{cases} 0, & |y| \le \lambda \\ \tanh(\rho \cdot y), & |y| > \lambda \end{cases} . \tag{5}$$

Another two-parameter shrinkage function is proposed by Mrazek *et al.* [11]:

$$\hat{y} = y \cdot \left(1 - 2 \cdot 10^{-\frac{2y^2}{\lambda_1^2}} + 10^{-\frac{2y^2}{\lambda_2^2}} \right) . \tag{6}$$

here ρ, λ_1 and λ_2 are the parameters of the functions.

3.3   Three-Parameter Shrinkage Functions

Yang and Wei [12] propose a generalization of soft, firm and Yasser shrinkage function:

$$\hat{y} = \begin{cases} 0, & |y| \le \lambda_L \\ \text{sgn}(y) \cdot \left[\dfrac{|y - \lambda_L|^{\lambda} \cdot \lambda_H}{|\lambda_H - \lambda_L|^{\lambda}} \right], & \lambda_L < |y| \le \lambda_H \, , \\ y, & |y| > \lambda_H \end{cases} \tag{7}$$

here γ, λ_L and λ_H are the parameters of the functions.

Atto *et al.* [13] propose the smooth sigmoid based shrinkage function:

$$\hat{y} = \frac{\text{sgn}(y) \cdot (|y| - t)_+}{1 + e^{-\tau(|y| - \lambda)}} \, , \tag{8}$$

here t, τ, λ are the parameters of the function.

3.4   Multi-parameter Shrinkage Functions

Poornachandra and Kumaravel [14] propose a sub-band dependent adaptive shrinkage function that generalizes the hard and soft shrinkage functions:

$$
\hat{y} = \begin{cases} \rho\left[\dfrac{1-\lambda_j^{-2\lambda_j y}}{1+\lambda_j^{-2\lambda_j y}}\right], & |y| \geq \lambda_j \\ 0, & |y| < \lambda_j \end{cases} \tag{9}
$$

here λ_j are function parameters for each sub-band j.

3.5   Evaluation

The soft (Eq. 1), hard (Eq. 2) and various variants of firm shrinkage (such as Eq. 7) are commonly used for denoising, so based on other author's results [9, 13, 15] we can provide the following evaluation of the shrinkage functions. The signal denoised using soft shrinkage tends to have a bigger bias due to the shrinkage of large coefficients, while the discontinuities of the hard shrinkage function produce a bigger variance. Firm shrinkage is less sensitive than hard shrinkage to small fluctuations and less biased than soft shrinkage, however it is more computationally expensive. Hard shrinkage is discontinuous and is not differentiable. Soft shrinkage is continuous, but does not have first order derivation. Sigmoid based shrinkage is smooth (i.e., induces small variability among data with close values), it produces strong attenuation is imposed for small data and weak attenuation for large data.

4   Signal Denoising Using Shrinkage Functions

4.1   General Denoising Scheme Using Shrinkage Function

Signal denoising by thresholding is based on the observation that a limited numbers of the DSP transform coefficients in the lower bands are sufficient to reconstruct the original signal. The key steps of signal denoising using DSP transforms are the selection of shrinkage function and its parameter(s). The goal of the shrinkage function is to remove noise so that separability of positive class and negative class in a binary classification problem is increased.

Assume that the observed data $X(t) = S(t) + N(t)$ contains the true signal $S(t)$ corrupted with additive noise $N(t)$ in time t. Let $T(\cdot)$ and $T^{-1}(\cdot)$ be the forward and inverse transform operators. Let $H(Y,\varLambda)$ be the denoising operator with a set of parameters $\varLambda = (\lambda_1, \lambda_2 ..., \lambda_k)$. Then the denoising algorithm is defined as follows:

1) Compute the DSP transform for a noisy signal $X(t)$: $Y = T(X)$;
2) Perform frequency shrinkage in the frequency domain: $\hat{Y} = H(Y,\varLambda)$;

3) Compute the inverse DSP transform to obtain a denoised signal $\hat{S}(t)$ as an estimate of $S(t)$: $\hat{S} = T^{-1}(\hat{Y})$.

Steps 1-3 can be generalized into a single equation as follows:

$$\hat{S} = T^{-1}(H(T(X),\Lambda)) . \tag{10}$$

4.2   Proposed Class-Adaptive Shrinkage Method

The scheme described in subsection 4.1 might not work well in case where signal $S(t)$ and noise $N(t)$ have many different components as is the case with the EEG data. Also the selection of the shrinkage function and its parameters is problematic due to a large number of shrinkage functions proposed in the literature (see Section 3) and large variability in signal data. Therefore, some adaptivity must be introduced when selecting shrinkage function and its parameters. Below, we provide a description of the proposed Class-Adaptive (CA) shrinkage method.

Let P and Q be the positive and negative classes of data. Let $D(X_P, X_Q)$ be a distance function between datasets X_P and X_Q belonging to P and Q, respectively. We improve the denoising algorithm described in subsection 4.1 by optimizing shrinkage function parameters for each frequency component f of X_P and X_Q, while the aim function is described as follows:

$$\Psi(X_P, X_Q) = \max_{\Lambda} \, D(H(T(X_P),\Lambda), H(T(X_Q),\Lambda)), \tag{11}$$

here D is a distance metric between classes.

To calculate a distance between data classes, several distance metrics can be used. We use Fisher distance and Hellinger distance. The Fisher distance [16] between two data classes is calculated as follows:

$$F = \frac{(\mu_1 - \mu_2)^2}{\sigma_1^2 + \sigma_2^2} , \tag{12}$$

here μ and σ are the mean and the standard deviation of the class they correspond to.

The squared Hellinger distance [17] between two data classes with normal distributions is calculated as follows:

$$H^2 = 1 - \sqrt{\frac{2\sigma_1\sigma_2}{\sigma_1^2 + \sigma_1^2}} e^{-\frac{1}{4}\frac{(\mu_1 - \mu_2)^2}{\sigma_1^2 + \sigma_2^2}} . \tag{13}$$

The proposed CA shrinkage algorithm is as follows:

1) Convert the time domain signals to frequency domain signals using a standard DSP transform.

2) For each frequency f :
   a. maximize distance between frequency components of positive class and negative class with respect to a set of shrinkage function parameters Λ;
   b. retain Λ for maximal distance as Λ_{max} .
3) Perform shrinkage of the DSP transform coefficients using Λ_{max} .
4) Convert the shrinked frequency domain signal to the time domain using an inverse DSP transform.

5   Case Study

For our experiments, Data set Ia (Tübingen, ‹self-regulation of SCPs›, subject 1) [18] from the BBCI competition datasets (http://bbci.de/competition/) was used. The datasets were taken from a healthy subject, who was asked to move a cursor up and down on a computer screen, while his EEG data were taken. During the recording, the subject received visual feedback of his slow cortical potentials (SCPs). The dataset consists of 135 trials belonging to class 0 and 133 trials belonging to class 1. Each trial consists of 896 samples from each of 6 channels.

The dataset was randomly partitioned into 5 parts, and 5-fold cross-validation was used to evaluate the classification results. On each channel data, a FFT was applied and the shrinkage function parameters were optimized to obtain maximal distance between positive and negative classes. The optimization was performed using Nelder-Mead (downhill simplex) optimization method [19] (implemented in Perl's Amoeba package). The classification was performed using Support Vector Machine (SVM) [20], a binary classification algorithm based on structural risk minimization. We used the SVMPerf [21] implementation of SVM (available at http://svmlight.joachims.org/) with linear kernel. To evaluate the precision of classification, we used the *F-measure*, *Area Under Curve* (AUC), and *Average Precision* (Avg. Prec.) metrics. The results of experiments are given in Table 1 (using Fisher distance) and Table 2 (using Helliger distance).

Table 1. Experimental results using Fisher distance

CA shrinkage function	Parameter No.	F-measure	AUC	Avg. Prec.
Not applied	-	80.36	90.06	91.45
Hard	1	83.84	91.53	92.60
Soft	1	78.18	88.60	89.97
Norouzzadeh	1	79.16	87.76	90.07
Hyperbolic	1	81.42	88.60	91.26
Hyper	2	85.37	90.87	91.44
Mrazek	2	74.65	87.23	89.71
Yang	**3**	**88.79**	**94.45**	**94.64**
Atto	**3**	**88.16**	**94.38**	**94.67**

Table 2. Experimental results using Helliger distance

CA shrinkage function	Parameter No.	F-measure	AUC	Avg. Prec.
Not applied	-	80.36	90.06	91.45
Hard	1	76.20	84.87	85.68
Soft	1	65.46	72.59	73.87
Norouzzadeh	1	52.29	56.98	56.63
Hyperbolic	1	76.50	83.69	85.37
Hyper	2	77.25	85.19	85.76
Mrazek	2	75.90	86.60	88.33
Yang	3	76.51	84.14	83.68
Atto	3	75.03	83.35	82.92

The achieved results are in line with the best results achieved by other authors while using the BCI competition Ia dataset (e.g., Mench *et al.* [21] report 88.7% correct classification rate using Thomson multitaper method).

6   Conclusions and Future Work

In this paper, we have proposed the Class-Adaptive (CA) denoising method for processing of the EEG signal data. The method uses Fisher (or Helliger) distance metric to evaluate distances between shrinked frequency components of time-frequency representations of signal data belonging to positive and negative dataset classes. To achieve maximal separation between positive and negative classes, distance metric values are maximized using Nelder-Mead (downhill simplex) optimization method. The optimized shrinkage function is used for EEG data denoising. The denoised data are classified using Support Vector Machine with linear kernel and the results are evaluated using standard classification evaluation metrics (F-measure, AUC, Average Precision). The experimental results show that CA denoising can improve the classification results as compared with the case were no signal denoising is used. Best denoising is achieved using three-parameter shrinkage functions (proposed by Yang, Wei [12] and Atto [13]) with their parameter values optimized for each frequency component of the frequency domain representation of the EEG signal, while soft denoising has failed due to large bias of the denoised signal. The Fisher distance metric generally allows achieving better results than the Helliger distance metric. In fact, denoising using Helliger distance has failed to produce better results even when compared with original (noisy) data.

Future work will focus on the extension of the proposed methods for other class distance metrics and shrinkage functions (sigmoid based shrinkage functions look especially promising). Other optimization methods such as evolutionary algorithms and particle swarm optimization will be considered, too.

References

1. Guo, L., Wu, Y., Zhao, L., Cao, T., Yan, W., Shen, X.: Classification of Mental Task From EEG Signals Using Immune Feature Weighted Support Vector Machines. IEEE Trans. on Magnetics 47(5), 866–869 (2011)

2. Hoffmann, U., Vesin, J.M., Ebrahimi, T.: Recent advances in brain-computer interfaces. In: Proc. of IEEE 9th Workshop on Multimedia Signal Processing, MMSP 2007, vol. 17 (2007)

3. Yang, Y., Wei, Y.: Random interpolation average for signal denoising. Signal Process 4(6), 708–719 (2010)

4. Donoho, D.L.: De-noising by soft-thresholding. IEEE Trans. Inf. Theory 41(3), 613–627 (1995)

5. Chang, S.G., Yu, B., Vetterli, M.: Adaptive wavelet thresholding for image denoising and compression. IEEE Trans. Image Proc. (9), 1532–1546 (2000)

6. Aladjem, M.E.: Two-Class Pattern Discrimination via Recursive Optimization of Patrick-Fisher Distance. In: Proc. of the 13th Int. Conf. on Pattern Recognition, ICPR 1996, Washington, DC, USA, vol. 2, p. 60 (1996)

7. Mu, Z., Xiao, D., Hu, J.: Classification of Motor Imagery EEG Signals Based on STFTs. In: Proc. of 2nd Int. Congress on Image and Signal Processing, CISP 2009, pp. 17–19 (2009)

8. Donoho, D.L., Johnston, I.M.: Ideal spatial adaptive via wavelet shrinkage. Biometrika (81), 425–455 (1994)

9. Norouzzadeh, Y., Jampour, M.: A novel curvelet thresholding function for additive gaussian noise removal. Int. Journal of Computer Theory and Engineering (3-4) (2011)

10. Poornachandra, S., Kumaravel, N.: Hyper-trim shrinkage for denoising of ECG signal. Digital Signal Processing (15), 317–327 (2005)

11. Mrazek, P., Weickert, J., Steidl, G.: Diffusion-inspired shrinkage functions and stability results for wavelet denoising. Int. J. Comput. Vision 64(2-3), 171–186 (2005)

12. Yang, Y., Wei, Y.: New Threshold and Shrinkage Function for ECG Signal Denoising Based on Wavelet Transform. In: Proc. of 3rd Int. Conf. on Bioinformatics and Biomedical Engineering, ICBBE 2009, pp. 1–4 (2009)

13. Atto, A.M., Pastor, D., Mercier, G.: Smooth Sigmoid Wavelet Shrinkage For Non-Parametric Estimation. In: IEEE Int. Conf. on Acoustics, Speech, and Signal Processing, ICASSP 2008, Las Vegas, Nevada, USA, pp. 3265–3268 (2008)

14. Poornachandra, S., Kumaravel, N.: Subband-adaptive shrinkage for denoising of ECG signals. EURASIP J. Appl. Signal Process., 42–42 (2006)

15. Gao, H.-Y.: Wavelet shrinkage denoising using the non-negative garrote. J. Comput. Graph. Statist. (7-4), 469–488 (1998)

16. Ince, N.F., Arica, S., Tewfik, A.: Classification of single trial motor imagery EEG recordings with subject adapted nondyadi arbitrary time-frequency tilings. J. Neural Eng. (3), 235–244 (2006)

17. Yang, G.L., Lucien, L.-C.: Asymptotics in Statistics: Some Basic Concepts. Springer, Berlin (2000)

18. Birbaumer, N., Flor, H., Ghanayim, N., Hinterberger, T., Iverson, I., Taub, E., Kotchoubey, B., Kübler, A., Perelmouter, J.: A brain-controlled spelling device for the completely paralyzed. Nature 398, 297–298 (1999)

19. Nelder, J.A., Mead, R.: A Simplex Method for Function Minimization. Computer Journal 7(4), 308–313 (1965)

20. Vapnik, V.: Statistical Learning Theory. Wiley-Interscience, New York (1998)

21. Joachims, T.: A Support Vector Method for Multivariate Performance Measures. In: Proc. of 22nd Int. Conf. on Machine Learning, ICML 2005, pp. 377–384 (2005)

22. Mensh, B.D., Werfel, J., Seung, H.S.: BCI Competition 2003 - Data set Ia: combining gamma-band power with slow cortical potentials to improve single-trial classification of electroencephalographic signals. IEEE Trans. Biomed. Eng. 51, 1052–1056 (2004)

Analysis and Classification of EEG Data: An Evaluation of Methods

Krzysztof Patan[1] and Grzegorz Rutkowski[2,*]

[1] Institute of Control and Computation Engineering, University of Zielona Góra
[2] Faculty of Electrical Engineering, Computer Science and Telecommunication,
University of Zielona Góra

Abstract. Analysis and interpretation of electroencephalogram signals have found a wide spectrum of applications in clinical diagnosis. In spite of the outstanding experience of specialists, the analysis of biomedical data encounters many difficulties. Problems are associated with both technical aspects and nonstationary character of EEG sequences. Hardware and software solutions in this area are subjected to the continuous improvement due to the technological development. A very promising tool in analysis and interpretation of EEG signals are artificial neural networks. The paper presents the application of artificial neural networks along with the discrete wavelet transform to the analysis and classification of neurological disorders based on recorded EEG signals.

1 Introduction

ElectroEncephaloGraphy (EEG) is one of the non-invasive measurement techniques of the human brain dynamics. This technique allows for the direct measurement of the electrical potential of the neuronal activity in a given time resolution. The EEG recording is therefore generated by the electrical activity of nerve cells on the surface of the cerebral cortex. Analysis of similar-epilepsy signals and epilepsy itself is a very important element in clinical diagnosis due to the search for the causal tendency of the brain to create unexpected discharges of electricity. Interpretation of these signals renders it possible an early treatment and the appropriate choice and proper adjustment of drug therapy for individual cases.

Recently, it has been observed a significant interest in the application of artificial intelligence methods to the biomedical signals analysis. The majority of works in the field of electroencephalography using artificial neural networks are based on the recognition of characteristic graphoelements. Neural networks are able to extract the significant information contained in EEG signals and solve problems such as identification of the characteristic EEG patterns [1,5,6] or recognizing patterns based on spectral EEG topography [3]. Neural networks are also used to artefact recognition, where inputs to the classifier are proposed in the form of selected parameters of the wave [10].

---

* Ph.D. student.

L. Rutkowski et al. (Eds.): ICAISC 2012, Part II, LNCS 7268, pp. 310–317, 2012.

In the present study the classification of EEG data recorded using a four channel equipment is presented. To extract attributes of EEG signals, the discrete wavelet transform is applied. The final stage of classification is carried out using different methods including the discriminant analysis, nearest neighbour classifier, naive Bayes and neural network based solutions.

2   EEG Signal Preprocessing

Recorded EEG signals are often used to assist the diagnosis of various neurological abnormalities. One of the frequently observed dysfunctions is epileptic seizure, which has a character of sudden discharges which cause sudden increase of the signal amplitude. The nature of such "epileptic behaviour" is defined as periodical spontaneous electrical discharges on the surface of the cortex, which disrupt the nervous system. This type of discharge may occur locally in the brain or can be observed on multiple channels simultaneously, depending on the degree of a particular dysfunction. Such electrical discharges can appear as a result of damages in the brain structure, hormonal fluctuations, sudden changes in the intensity of the perception of the severity of different types of external stimuli and undesirable physiological conditions. Early diagnosis and careful analysis of EEG records may help take a proper decision concerning suitable treatment, adjusting pharmacology and performing individual therapy.

In the current study EEG data downloaded from the site `ftp://sigftp.cs.tut.fi/pub/eeg-data` has been used. This data was recorded in the system configured according to the banana arrangement: F8-C4, F7-C3, T6-O2, T5-O1. There were four measurement channels. The low-pass filter was set to $70Hz$. Figure 1 presents an example of EEG recording taken in the banana arrangement. On the record it is clearly observable a change in the behavior of the signal starting at 1200th sample. This is an example of the seizure.

In order to carry out disorder classification, EEG sequences should be preprocessed first. The sequence recorded in each channel has been cut into a number of subsequences of the length equal to 200 samples. To each subsequence, the suitable label from the set {`'seizure'`,`'healty'`} has been assigned. Thus, a set of preprocessed EEG sequences was formed for further processing.

3   Wavelet Transform

Fourier Transform uses sinusoidal signals, which have the infinite support (the range within which the function values differ from zero). Therefore, the Fourier method cannot be used to analysis of nonstationary signals or signals with transient characteristics. One of possible solutions in that case is to use Wavelet Transform. Wavelet analysis uses time windows of the varying size depending on the frequency. The fundamental element of the wavelet analysis is the base function called a wavelet. The wavelet is a wave-like oscillation with the amplitude starting at zero, increasing, and then decreasing back to zero. Continuous

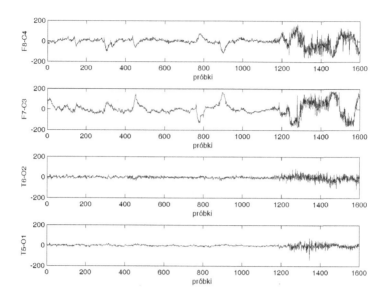

Fig. 1. Example of recorded EEG signal

Wavelet Transform (CWT) is defined as follows:

$$CWT(a,b) = \frac{1}{\sqrt{a}} \int_{-\infty}^{\infty} \Psi\left(\frac{t-b}{a}\right) x(t)dt \tag{1}$$

where Ψ is the base function, a represents the scale parameter, b is the shift parameter, and $x(t)$ is analysed signal. The common approach to perform Discrete Wavelet Transform (DWT) is to use the dyadic scheme to sample the base function. A particularly important property of DWT is the multiresolution signal decomposition [7,8]. At each stage, the signal S is defined as a sum of approximation and detail representations. At the next stage, the approximation representation from the upper stage A_{i-1} is defined again as a sum of approximation A_i and detail representations D_i. The illustration of multiresolution representation of the signal is shown in Fig. 2. In this way, the signal S can be represented with the arbitrary accuracy using approximation and detail coefficients using suitable number of representation stages. For the situation portrayed in Fig. 2 the signal S can be reconstructed using coefficients D_1, D_2, D_3 and A_3. In this paper multiresolution signal decomposition is used to extract the features of EEG signals. The results of feature extraction are presented later in the paper, in the section reporting experiments.

4   Classification

To extract attributes of the EEG signal DWT has been applied. Unfortunately, the multiresolution signal decomposition on the subsequence of the length of

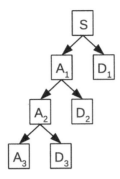

Fig. 2. Multiresolution signal decomposition

200 samples gives hundreds of coefficients. Moreover, data was recorded in four channel setting. As a result, the number of parameters describing the signal is huge. In the paper the attributes of the signal were calculated using simple statistics. For each stage of multiresolution representation indicators in the form of the mean value and standard deviation were calculated [9]. For example, taking into account the representation of the signal up to 3rd stage, it gives 32 attributes (4 channels × 4 sets of coefficients × 2 indicators). Based on attributes prepared in this way the classification is carried indicating seizures (the output equal to one) or normal conditions (the output equal to zero). The block scheme of proposed recognition system is presented in Fig. 3. To carry out classification, different methods were tried. They are briefly portrayed in the following sections.

Fig. 3. Block scheme of recognition system

4.1 Naive Bayes

Naive Bayes is a simple probabilistic classifier based on Bayes' theorem [2]. Naive Bayes assumes that the presence of a class feature is unrelated to the presence of any other feature. This classifier can be effectively trained using supervised learning. In practical applications classifier parameters are estimated using the maximum likelihood. The advantage of the naive Bayes classifier is that it requires a small amount of training data to estimate parameters required for classification.

4.2 K Nearest Neigbours

K nearest neighbours algorithm is a method for classifying patterns based on the closest training examples in the feature space [2]. This algorithm is the simplest method among all machine learning algorithms. The pattern is classified by a majority vote of its neighbours, with the pattern being assigned to the class most common amongst its k nearest neighbours. If $k = 1$, then the pattern is simply assigned to the class of its nearest neighbour.

The training phase of the algorithm consists of storing the attributes and class labels of the training samples. In the classification phase, k is the user-defined constant, and an input vector is classified by assigning the label which is the most frequent among the k training samples nearest to that query point. Usually the Euclidean distance is used as the distance metric.

4.3   Support Vector Machines

Support Vector Machine invented by Vapnik is a concept related to supervised learning methods which are able to analyse and recognize patterns, widely used for classification and regression [4]. Support vector machine constructs a hyperplane or set of hyperplanes in a high dimensional space. Good separation is achieved by the hyperplane that has the largest distance to the nearest training data points of any class. SVM belongs to the family of generalized linear classifiers and can be interpreted as an extension of the perceptron network. It minimizes the empirical classification error and simultaneously maximizes the geometric margin, so it is also known as the maximum margin classifier.

The original classifier proposed by Vapnik was the linear one. However, using a nonlinear kernel function it is possible to obtain a nonlinear classifier. Common kernels include: polynomial, gaussian radial basis function or hyperbolic tangent.

4.4   Multilayer Perceptron

The most popular neural structure is the multilayer feedforward network commonly referred as a multilayer perceptron [4]. Typically, the network consists of an input layer, one or more hidden layers with processing elements, and an output layer. Multilayer perceptrons have been applied successfully to solve different problems by training them in a supevised manner. Artificial neural networks are an excellent mathematical tool for dealing with nonlinear problems. They have an important property according to which any continuous nonlinear relation can be approximated with an arbitrary accuracy using a neural network with a suitable architecture and weight parameters. The multilayer perceptrons are widely and frequently used in classification. For a given problem the neural classifier should map a relation between attributes and labels of possible classes. This mapping is determined during training procedure carried out using training samples.

5   Results

As it was stated in Section 2, in the first stage of experiment, EEG sequences were split into a number of subsequences with the length of 200 samples each. To each subsequence a suitable label from the set {'seizure','healthy'} has been assigned. Finally, the set of 163 patterns was obtained, containing 120 patterns representing normal behaviours and 43 representing seizures.

5.1 Feature Extraction

In order to perform classification, each sequence should be represented by a set of features called attributes. Attributes should be selected in such a way to fully represent the subsequence. Attributes make it possible to discriminate sequences one from another and to estimate the level of similarity between them. Taking into account that the EEG signal has the nonstationary character to extract features DWT was applied. In this study, each sequence was represented using 3-th level of multi-resolution representation using Daubechies 3 (db3) wavelet. As it was mentioned in Section 4, the attributes of the signal were calculated using the mean value and standard deviation of wavelet coefficients. As a result, for each subsequence, 32 attributes (4 channels × 4 sets of coefficients × 2 indicators) were extracted.

5.2 Discriminant Analysis

While the attributes have been determined one need to check whether the patterns belonging to different classes are separated. To carry out this, Linear Discriminant Analysis (LDA) has been used [2]. LDA is trying to find a linear combination of features which separate classes. The obtained combination can be used as a linear classifier or for dimensionality reduction before classification. Results of LDA are presented in the first row of Table 1. This clearly shows that classes are not linearly separated. Nonlinear projection methods combined with disriminant analysis using the quadratic boundary were also checked. The authors tested two projection methods Multidimensional Scalling (MDS) and Sammon's mapping. Results of discriminant analysis using MDS are presented in Fig. 4(a) while using Sammon's projection in Fig. 4(b). In the case of MDS the misclassification rate was 7.36% and for the Sammon's mapping 14.11%.

5.3 Classification

During the classification stage different classifiers were tested: Naive Bayes (NB), k Nearest Neighbours (kNN) with a different number of neighbours, Support Vector Machines (SVM) with different kernels, and MultiLayer Perceptron (MLP) with a different number of hidden neurons. The classification process using each classifier was repeated 1000 times, calculating the best misclassification rate Q_{min}, the worst one Q_{max} and average Q_{av} (mean value over 1000 tests). At each run the entire set of samples was divided into the train set containing 40% of samples, and the testing one containing the rest of patterns. The classification results are shown in Table 1, where the best rates are marked with the bold face. The best results were achieved for both the Bayes classifier and for kNN with

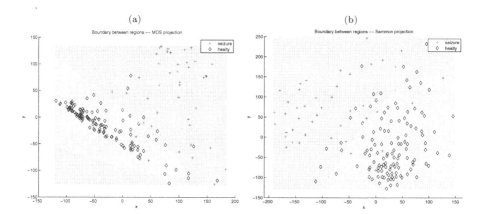

Fig. 4. Visualisation of the pattern distribution achieved using MDS (a), and Sammon's mapping (b)

5 neighbours. For more complex classifier such as SVM and MLP the misclassification rate was a little bit worse. In the case of SVM the best kernel was in the form of the polynomial. In the case of MLP 3 or 5 hidden neurons are quite enough to achieve a relatively good misclassification rate.

Table 1. Classification results

		misclassification rate [%]		
		Q_{min}	Q_{max}	Q_{av}
LDA		5.15	40.21	17.22
kNN	NN	3.09	26.8	13.48
	5 neighbours	**2.06**	**18.56**	10.83
NB		**2.06**	23.71	**8.89**
SVM	linear	5.15	30.93	14.46
	quadratric	6.19	35.05	17.49
	polynomial	4.12	32.99	14.76
MLP	3 neurons	4.12	32.99	15.97
	5 neurons	4.12	42.27	15.47
	9 neurons	5.15	45.36	15.14

6 Conclusions

This study presents the analysis and classification of biomedical data using different techniques including the classical methods like the naive Bayes and nearest neighbours classifiers as well as artificial intelligence methods including the support vector machine and multilayer perceptron. In spite of the fact that the classical methods achieved better results in contrast to neural networks, it should be kept in mind that the database used in experiments was of a small size (only 163 examples). Moreover, this data was recorded using four channel setting, while in most cases data is recorded using, e.g. sixteen channels. Our future research will be focused on the classification of EEG data recorded at the Ward of Neurology and Strokes of Provincial Hospital of Zielona Góra, which is more complete database of neurological disorders acquired using 16 channels equipment.

References

1. Bankman, I.N., Sigilliti, V.G., Wise, R.A., Smith, P.L.: Feature-based detection of the k-complex wave in the human electro-encephalogram using neural networks. IEEE Transactions on Biomedical Engineering 39(12), 1305–1310 (1992)
2. Duda, R.O., Hart, P.E., Stork, D.H.: Pattern Classification, 2nd edn. Wiley Interscience (2000)
3. Emiliani, G.M.M., Frietman, E.E.E.: Automatic classification of EEGs with neural networks. Microelectronic Systems Integration 1(1), 41–62 (1994)
4. Haykin, S.: Neural Networks. A Comprehensive Foundation, 2nd edn. Prentice-Hall, New Jersey (1999)
5. Huuponen, E., Varri, A., Himanen, S.L., Hasan, J., Lehtokangas, M., Saarinen, J.: Autoassociative MLP in sleep spindle detection. Journal of Medical Systems 24(3), 183–193 (2000)
6. James, C.J., Jones, R.D., Bones, P.J., Carroll, G.J.: Detection of epileptiform discharges in the EEG by a hybrid system comprising mimetic, self-organized artificial neural network, and fuzzy logic stages. Clinical Neurophysiology 12, 2049–2063 (1999)
7. Mallat, S.: A theory for multiresolution signal decomposition: The wavelet representation. IEEE Trans. Pattern Anal. Mach. Intell. 11(7), 674–693 (1989)
8. Mustafa, G., Chen, F., Huang, Z.: Ternary wavelets and their applications to signal compression. International Journal of Applied Mathematics and Computer Science 14(2), 233–240 (2004)
9. Rutkowski, G.: Artificial neural networks in the classification of EEG signals. In: Proceedings of XIII International Workshop OWD 2011, Krynica, Poland, October 22–25 (2011)
10. Übeyli, E.D.: Combined neural network model employing wavelet coefficients for EEG signals classification. Digital Signal Processing 19, 297–308 (2009)

Surrogate Measures of Thickness in the Regime of Limited Image Resolution: Part 1: Fuzzy Distance Transform*

Rafał Petryniak and Zbisław Tabor

Cracow University of Technology,
Al. Jana Pawa II 37, 31-864 Cracow, Poland
rpetryniak@gmail.com, ztabor@pk.edu.pl

Abstract. In the present study the performance of the fuzzy distance transform-based method of computing surrogate measure of thickness from gray-level images is analyzed for a set of 25 μCT images of trabecular bone. Analytical formulas derived in this study identify the limitations of the fuzzy distance transform-based approach to thickness measurement.

1 Introduction

Quantitative description of complex structures is one of the challenges of image analysis. In many cases it can be assumed that satisfactory precision of the measurements can be achieved at the cost of improved resolution of analyzed images. It is not however the case of biological tissues, which must be analyzed *in vivo*. The fundamental limitations of the *in vivo* resolution follow at least from the finite time of measurements and/or acceptable dose of ionizing radiation. Trabecular (or cancellous) bone is an important example of a system of particular interest in medicine, that must be examined under *in vivo* conditions.

Trabecular bone is a highly porous structure, constituting interior parts of bones like vertebral bodies, with porosity ranging from 40% to even 95%. Several structural parameters have been proposed to quantitatively characterize the properties of trabecular bone. Standard histomorphometry involves computing volume fraction (BV/TV) and metric indices: trabecular thickness (Tb.Th), trabecular number (Tb.N), and trabecular separation (Tb.Sp). The standard methods to compute metric indices are applicable only to binary images [5,1]. Clinical images of trabecular bone cannot be easily binarized because the spatial resolution of clinical imaging devices is not good enough to depict individual trabeculae. The consequence is that the methods of calculating trabecular parameters, developed for high-resolution binary data should not be directly applied to images acquired by clinical CT or MRI scanners. The published results [4,3,7] indicate that the correlation of the "apparent" thickness (thickness measured

---

* The paper is supported by project funded from 2009–2012 resources for science as a research project.

L. Rutkowski et al. (Eds.): ICAISC 2012, Part II, LNCS 7268, pp. 318–326, 2012.

for low-resolution images) and the reference thickness (thickness measured for high-resolution images) is not very good.

A few alternative approaches have been proposed to estimate trabecular thickness directly from gray-level images. An approach based on wavelet transform was reported in the study of Krug et al. [2] but no correlation between the wavelet-based and the gold-standard methods of thickness measurement was found. In the study of Wald et al. [9] spatial autocorrelation function was used to derive trabecular thickness. In the study of Saha and Wehrli [6], a fuzzy distance transform was proposed as a method to asses thickness of trabeculae. The results concerning correlation between the proposed measures and reference measurements of trabecular thickness are however lacking in these studies.

In the present study a method based on the gray-weighted distance transform [8] is used to compute surrogate measure of thickness from gray-level images. Analytical formulas derived in this study identify conditions necessary for the equality of the surrogate measure of thickness and real thickness of model objects. Based on a set of 25 μCT images it is shown that the reference thickness values are very well correlated with the surrogate measure of thickness.

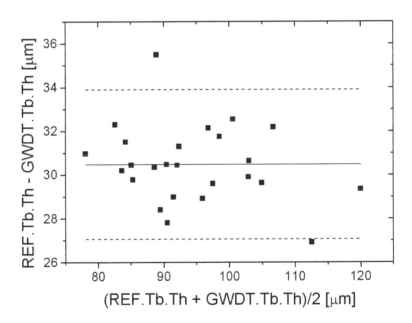

Fig. 1. Bland-Altman plot, comparing REF.Tb.Th with a surrogate measure of thickness GWDT.Tb.Th. All numbers were calculated for μCT images. The values of the bias are marked with the solid lines. The 95% limits of agreement are marked with dashed lines.

2   Materials and Methods

2.1   Materials

3D μCT images of distal radius trabecular bone were obtained from 15 individuals. The samples were scanned with a μCT-20 scanner (Scanco Medical, Br uttisellen, Switzerland) with an isotropic voxel size of 34μm. The 3D μCT images were filtered with a 3D Gaussian filter and binarized, using a global threshold. The craniocaudal direction was identified with the z-axis of each sample. Then a total of 25 volumes with size of 200x200x200 voxels were selected from all μCT images and analyzed. Further details concerning the sample preparation and image acquisition protocols are described in the previous study of Laib et al. [3].

2.2   Methods

Image preprocessing: The surrogate measurements of thickness were applied to μCT images and artificially corrupted images. In the latter case corrupted images Im_C were generated, based on the following equation:

$$Im_C = B(D \bigotimes Im + \eta) \tag{1}$$

According to that model, the operator D resamples a binary image Im at voxel sizes corresponding to integer multiples (2 to 5) of the parent resolution by means of box averaging. Next i.i.d. Gaussian noise η of varying intensity (zero mean and standard deviation from 10 to 30) is added to the data and finally the corrupted images are convolved with an anisotropic 3D Gaussian blurring kernel B. The kernel widths σ_x, σ_y and σ_z of the kernel were equal to 100μm, 100μm and 240μm. The corrupted images were written to files (16 bits per a voxel, signed integer data) and further analyzed. For comparison purpose the reference values REF.Tb.Th of thickness were calculated based on binary μCT images. BoneJ plugin (bonej.org) for ImageJ (rsbweb.nih.gov/ij) was used to compute REF.Tb.Th.

The computation of the gray-weighed distance transform (GWDT) requires binary masks (fuzzy set support) on input. Thus, before computing GWDT for corrupted gray-level images, these images were thresholded. The threshold was calculated individually for each corrupted image according to the two-phase mixture model. First, porosity *App.BV/TV* of a 3D sample was computed, based on the mean intensity I of the 3D image, known intensity I_B (equal to 255) of pure bone and known intensity I_M (equal to 0) of pure marrow phase. Assuming two-phase model, *App.BV/TV* is equal to:

$$App.BVTV = \frac{I_B - I}{I_B - I_M} \tag{2}$$

The threshold is equal to such gray-level intensity Th, that the fraction of all image voxels which have gray-level intensities less or equal to Th is not larger than $App.BV/TV$. In practice, neither I_B nor I_M are known exactly. To account for this uncertainty and to test the threshold dependence of GWDT, a buffer value Th_{BUFF} is introduced such that the final threshold Th_F is equal to $Th - Th_{BUFF}$. To compute the surrogate GWDT-based measure of thickness, GWDT values were averaged over the skeletons of the binary masks. To find the skeletons of the binary masks, an ImageJ (http://rsb.info.nih.gov/ij/) plugin Skeletonize3D was used.

Gray-weighted distance transform of a 1D rectangular signal: Consider a 1D rectangular signal $Ob(x)$ given by the following formula:

$$Ob(x) = \begin{cases} 1, & -x_c \leqslant x \leqslant x_c \\ 0, & x > x_c, x < -x_c \end{cases} \tag{3}$$

Neglecting for now the noise and the resolution decrease one has:

$$Im(x) = \int_{-\infty}^{\infty} B(x - y)Ob(y)dy \tag{4}$$

Obviously, the point $x = 0$ is the medial axis of the object defined in Eq. (4). Let R denote some user-defined cut-off. Then the gray-weighted distance transform $GWDT(Im)(x)$ of the image Im is defined as follows:

$$GWDT(Im)(x) = \begin{cases} 0, & x < -R, x > R \\ \int_{-R}^{x} Im(y)dy, & -R \leqslant x \leqslant 0 \\ \int_{x}^{R} Im(y)dy, & 0 \leqslant x \leqslant R \end{cases} \tag{5}$$

It immediately follows from the above equations that in the case of even blurring kernel ($B(-x) = B(x)$) and in the limit $R \to \infty$ the value of gray-weighted distance transform at $x = 0$ is equal to x_c. The latter constraint cannot be met in practice. However, it can be shown that for any finite R, $GWDT(Im)(0)$ can be used as an estimate of object thickness only provided that the size of the support of the blurring kernel B is smaller than $|Rx_c|$. Ideally, R should be large but in practice it is limited by the typical separation of objects present within the field of view.

Gray-weighted distance transform of a 2D rectangular signal: Consider a 2D rectangular signal $Ob(x, y)$ equal to 1 for $-a \leqslant x \leqslant a, -b \leqslant y \leqslant b$ and zero otherwise. Assuming imaging process analogous to the one defined in Eq. (4) and a 2D isotropic Gaussian blurring kernel width width equal to σ, it immediately follows that:

$$GWDT(Im)(0,0) = min\left(a \cdot erf\left(\frac{b}{\sigma\sqrt{2}}\right), b \cdot erf\left(\frac{a}{\sigma\sqrt{2}}\right) \right) \tag{6}$$

Clearly, if the size of the blurring kernel is small, compared to the structure size, GWDT can be successfully used to estimate an objects thickness. In a case of a generic rectangular 2D signal a single measurement of $GWDT(Im)(0,0)$ is however not sufficient to determine an objects thickness and, consequently, there is no unique relation between GWDT and thickness. In that case at least two independent measurements of line integrals together with the knowledge of the point spread function of the imaging system are necessary to better estimate an objects thickness. However, if it can be assumed that the dimensions a and b of the object are not independent, i.e. $b = f(a)$, where $f()$ is some monotonic function, then $GWDT(Im)(0,0)$ is a nonlinear and monotonic function of an objects thickness. Consequently, although $GWDT(Im)(0,0)$ cannot be used in that case as an estimate of an objects thickness, it can nevertheless be a surrogate measure of an objects thickness in the sense that there exists positive correlation between an objects thickness and GWDT measured at the medial axis of the object.

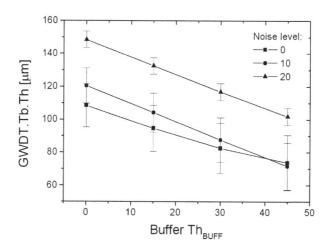

Fig. 2. GWDT.Tb.Th plotted vs. the buffer value Th_{BUFF} for different levels of noise. Error bars represent the standard deviation of GWDT.Tb.Th.

Implementation of the Gray-Weighted Distance Transform: Before computing GWDT, the gray-level intensities of the degraded images were divided by 255. Then, the known intensity I_B (equal to 255) of pure bone was equal to 1, the known intensity I_M (equal to 0) of pure marrow phase was equal to 0 and all other intensities were float numbers, possibly lower than zero (in the presence of noise). The GWDT algorithm requires at the input a gray-level image and a binary mask (with 0 corresponding to background and 1 corresponding to the structure of interest). At the output a GWDT image is obtained. The implementation of the gray-weighted distance transform is described in detail elsewhere ([8]). To obtain surrogate GWDT-based measure of thickness, GWDT values were averaged over the skeletons of the binary masks. After multiplying the average by the factor of 2, the surrogate measure of thickness was obtained, referred to as the GWDT thickness GWDT.Tb.Th.

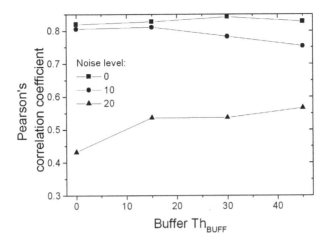

Fig. 3. The values of the Pearsons coefficient of correlation between GWDT.Tb.Th and REF.Tb.Th plotted vs. the buffer value Th_{BUFF} for different levels of noise.

3 Results

The mean (standard deviation) values of REF.Tb.Th and GWDT.Tb.Th calculated for original high-resolution μCT images were equal to 110 (10)μm and 79 (10)μm. The values of Pearsons coefficient of correlation between REF.Tb.Th and GWDT.Tb.Th were equal to 0.99. The slope of REF.Tb.Th vs. GWDT.Tb.Th plot was equal to 1.03±0.04, what suggests that the difference between the two measures corresponds to some shift only. This conjecture is further supported by the BlandAltman plot, shown in Fig. 1. Next, it was tested how image degradation factors influence the precision of the estimation of GWDT.Tb.Th. First, it was checked how the threshold buffer Th_{BUFF} influences the measurement of GWDT.Tb.Th. The values of GWDT.Tb.Th are plotted vs. the buffer Th_{BUFF} in Fig. 2 for different values of noise. It follows from the figure that GWDT.Tb.Th decreases linearly with increasing Th_{BUFF}. The decrease of GWDT.Tb.Th can be explained, if it is noted that thinner trabeculae influence GWDT.Tb.Th value only if Th_{BUFF} is sufficiently high. The Pearsons coefficient of correlation between GWDT.Tb.Th and REF.Tb.Th depends on Th_{BUFF} only marginally (Fig. 3). The values of GWDT.Tb.Th are plotted vs. the voxel size in Fig. 4 for different values of noise. GWDT.Tb.Th underestimates REF.Tb.Th, like GWDT.Tb.Th calculated for original, high-resolution images. GWDT.Tb.Th calculated for degraded images is however quite close to GWDT.Tb.Th calculated for high-resolution data, except for the largest voxel size. The values of the Pearsons coefficient of correlation between GWDT.Tb.Th and REF.Tb.Th are plotted vs. the voxel size in Fig. 5 for different values of noise. In the calculations Th_{BUFF}=15 was used.

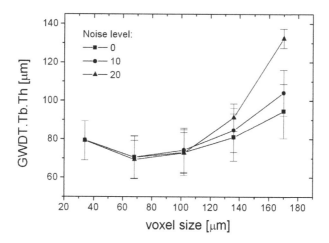

Fig. 4. GWDT.Tb.Th plotted vs. the voxel size for different levels of noise. Error bars represent the standard deviation of GWDT.Tb.Th

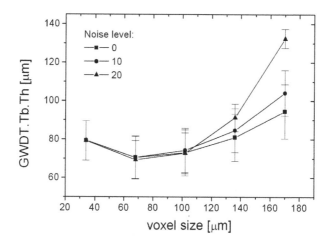

Fig. 5. The values of the Pearsons coefficient of correlation between GWDT.Tb.Th and REF.Tb.Th plotted vs. the voxel size for different levels of noise.

4   Discussion

In the present study the performance of a method of estimating a surrogate measure of thickness has been considered. The term "surrogate" is used here to indicate that the values of GWDT.Tb.Th, although different from the reference thickness values, are correlated with REF.Tb.Th. The surrogate character of GWDT.Tb.Th has been demonstrated on Bland-Altman plots, suggesting that the difference between GWDT.Tb.Th and REF.Tb.Th corresponds to a shift. An important contribution of the present paper is that analytical arguments have been provided to justify the use of GWDT.Tb.Th as the surrogate measure of thickness. The conditions necessary for the equality of GWDT.Tb.Th and the real thickness have been identified. It has been shown that the equality of the surrogate and reference measures of thickness holds if 3D images of plate-like objects (or 2D images of linear objects) are analyzed and the separation of objects is sufficiently large. Importantly, this equality is true independently of the size of the blurring kernel. If the size of the blurring kernel is small compared to the object thickness then the methods described in the present paper can be used to assess thickness of objects with other shapes.

Concluding, it is possible to derive surrogate measures of thickness from low-resolution data even if the voxel size is of the order of typical structure size. For some classes of objects (e.g. well separated planar objects in 3D) thickness can be in principle derived precisely even if the size of the blurring kernel is larger than the structure size.

Acknowledgement. The authors thank Sharmila Majumdar, Andrew Burghardt, Andres Laib and Ahi Issever for providing them with μCT images of distal radius trabecular bone.

References

1. Hildebrand, T., Ruegsegger, P.: A new method for the model-independent assessment of thickness in three-dimensional images. J. Microsc. 185(1), 67–75 (1997)
2. Krug, R., Carballido-Gamio, J., Burghardt, A.J., Haase, S., Sedat, J.W., Moss, W.C., Majumdar, S.: Wavelet-based characterization of vertebral trabecular bone structure from magnetic resonance images at 3 T compared with micro-computed tomographic measurements. Magnetic Resonance Imaging 25(3), 392–398 (2007)
3. Laib, A., Beuf, O., Issever, A., Newitt, D.C., Majumdar, S.: Direct measures of trabecu-lar bone architecture from MR images. Adv. Exp. Med. Biol. 496, 37–46 (2001)
4. Majumdar, S., Kothari, M., Augat, P., Newitt, D.C., Link, T.M., Lin, J.C., Lang, T., Lu, Y., Genant, H.K.: High-resolution magnetic resonance imaging: three-dimensional trabecular bone ar-chitecture and biomechanical properties. Bone 22(5), 445–454 (1998)
5. Parfitt, A.M., Mathews, C.H.E., Villanueva, A.R., Kleerekoper, M., Frame, B., Rao, D.S.: Relation-ships between surface, volume, and thickness of iliac trabecular bone in aging and in osteoporosis. Implications for the microanatomic and cellular mechanisms of bone loss. J. Clin. Invest. 72(4), 701–716 (1983)
6. Saha, P.K., Wehrli, F.W.: Measurement of trabecular bone thickness in the limited resolution regime of in vivo MRI by fuzzy distance transform. IEEE Trans. Med. Imaging 23(1), 53–62 (2004)

7. Sell, C.A., Masi, J.N., Burghardt, A., Newitt, D., Link, T.M., Majumdar, S.: Quantification of trabecular bone structure using magnetic resonance imaging at 3 Tesla-calibration studies using microcomputed tomography as a stan-dard of reference. Calcif. Tissue Int. 76(5), 355–364 (2005)
8. Toriwaki, J., Yoshida, H.: Fundamentals of Three-Dimensional Digital Image Processing. Springer, Heidelberg (2009)
9. Wald, M.J., Vasilic, B., Saha, P.K., Wehrli, F.W.: Spatial autocorrelation and mean intercept length analysis of trabecular bone anisotropy ap-plied to in vivo magnetic resonance imaging. Med. Phys. 34(3), 1110–1120 (2007)

eBi – The Algorithm for Exact Biclustering

Magdalena Stawarz and Marcin Michalak

Silesian University of Technology, ul. Akademicka 16, 44-100 Gliwice, Poland
{Magdalena.Stawarz,Marcin.Michalak}@polsl.pl

Abstract. This article presents an algorithm for finding exact and over-lapping biclusters, all covered by the same discrete value. It can be very useful to analyse data where the key task is finding which objects (elements in rows) across subset of attributes (elements in columns) have the same value in case of discrete data or belong to this same discrete state in case of continuous data.

Keywords: machine learning, biclustering.

1 Introduction

Clustering data is the problem of machine learning that is usually understood as joining objects into groups on the basis of their features. From the early 70's [4] the new approach of clustering has been developing as the twodimensional clustering called also biclustering. In the case of biclustering we try to group cells from the given matrix due to their values, but the aim of grouping is to point the subset of rows and subset of columns whose intersection determines similar cells. This task may be reduced to the problem of typical clustering when we treat cells as normal objects without considering their matrix coordinates together.

Nowadays, the most popular data considered to be biclustered come from the bioinformatical domain [3,6,9] but also from text mining [2] and collaborative filtering [7].

In this paper we show the new algorithm of exact biclustering (eBi). In the present form it is dedicated only for data with discrete values. The main advantage of this algorithm is that it assures two kinds of exactness: every cell with currently considered value belongs to at least one bicluster and from the other hand every bicluster contains cells with the same discrete value. The eBi definition is based on feature and co-feature notions, developed as the way of not recognising rows from columns and vice versa. This approach was used first time successfully in our previous work with the BicDM algorithm – the algorithm for biclustering discrete matrices [5].

2 Exact Biclustering Algorithm

Let us consider the binary matrix M with r rows and c columns. From the biclustering point of view it may be rotated by 90 degrees without any loss

L. Rutkowski et al. (Eds.): ICAISC 2012, Part II, LNCS 7268, pp. 327–334, 2012.

of information. That means that rows and columns may be named alternately. In our previous work ([5]) we introduced two notions that are useful in this situation: feature and co-feature. If we assume that a row is a feature then every column is a co-feature and the other way round. The set of all features is $\mathcal{F}$, the set of all co-features is denoted with asterisk: $\mathcal{F}^*$. Single features are marked with small letter f and co-features similarly – with small letter with an asterisk f^*. For the given matrix M, $M\{f, f^*\}$ is the value in the cell with indexes f and f^* but it depends on the previous assumptions whether $M\{f, f^*\} = M(f, f^*)$ or $M\{f, f^*\} = M(f^*, f)$. The advantage of generalization rows and columns is presented in the Fig. 1.

	c_1	c_2	c_3
r_1	1	2	3
r_2	4	5	6

Original table

	f_1^*	f_2^*	f_3^*
f_1	1	2	3
f_2	4	5	6

Rows as features

	f_1	f_2	f_3
f_1^*	1	2	3
f_2^*	4	5	6

Rows as co-features

Fig. 1. Illustration of features and co-features

2.1 Biclustering Indiscernibility Relation

Let us define the following biclustering indiscernibility relation $IND \subseteq \mathcal{F} \times \mathcal{F}$:

$$\forall f, g \in \mathcal{F} \quad (f, g) \in IND_{\mathcal{X}^*}^v \iff \forall t \in \mathcal{X}^* \quad M\{t, f\} = M\{t, g\} = v$$

where $\mathcal{X}^* \subseteq \mathcal{F}*$, $v \in V$ and V is the set of values from the matrix M.

For each two features f, g we may define the set $\mathcal{X}^*(f, g)$ in such a way that it is the largest subset of $\mathcal{F}^*$ in the sense of the inclusion that $(f, g) \in IND_{\mathcal{X}}^v$. On the basis of the matrix M we may define indiscernibility matrix for features $IN_{card(\mathcal{F}) \times card(\mathcal{F})}$:

$$IN(f, g) = \mathcal{X}^*(f, g)$$

It is worth to mention that indiscernibility matrix for features stores subsets of co-features in its cells.

Notions of IND and IN have its equivalents IND^* and IN^* which definition differs in such a way that features replace co-features (and vice versa):

$$\forall f^*, g^* \in \mathcal{F}^* \quad (f^*, g^*) \in IND_{\mathcal{X}}^{*v} \iff \forall t \in \mathcal{X} \quad M\{t, f^*\} = M\{t, g^*\} = v$$

$$IN_{card(\mathcal{F}^*) \times card(\mathcal{F}^*)}^* : IN^*(f^*, g^*) = \mathcal{X}(f^*, g^*)$$

$\mathcal{X}(f^*, g^*)$ is of course the largest subset of $\mathcal{F}$ in the sense of the inclusion that $(f^*, g^*) \in IND_{\mathcal{X}}^{*v}$.

2.2 Halfbiclusters

We see that the both of matrices IN and IN^* groups co-features and features with respect to the fact of having the same discrete value in the matrix M. Now let us define halfbicluster as the largest in the sense of inclusion subset

Table 1. Matrix M and its matrix IN

(a) Matrix M.

	f_1^*	f_2^*	f_3^*	f_4^*	f_5^*
f_1	1	1	1	0	0
f_2	1	1	1	1	0
f_3	0	0	1	1	0
f_4	0	0	1	1	1
f_5	0	0	0	1	1

(b) Indiscernibility matrix IN for the matrix M.

	f_1	f_2	f_3	f_4	f_5
f_1	$\{f_1^*,f_2^*,f_3^*\}$	$\{f_1^*,f_2^*,f_3^*\}$	$\{f_3^*\}$	$\{f_3^*\}$	$\emptyset$
f_2	$\{f_1^*,f_2^*,f_3^*\}$	$\{f_1^*,f_2^*,f_3^*,f_4^*\}$	$\{f_3^*,f_4^*\}$	$\{f_3^*,f_4^*\}$	$\{f_4^*\}$
f_3	$\{f_3^*\}$	$\{f_3^*,f_4^*\}$	$\{f_3^*,f_4^*\}$	$\{f_3^*,f_4^*\}$	$\{f_4^*\}$
f_4	$\{f_3^*\}$	$\{f_3^*,f_4^*\}$	$\{f_3^*,f_4^*\}$	$\{f_3^*,f_4^*,f_5^*\}$	$\{f_4^*,f_5^*\}$
f_5	$\emptyset$	$\{f_4^*\}$	$\{f_4^*\}$	$\{f_4^*,f_5^*\}$	$\{f_4^*,f_5^*\}$

of features (co-features) that makes it possible to not discern two co-features (features) from each other. With this definition each cell of IN^* (IN) becomes one halfbicluster. The set of all halfbiclusters will be denoted as H^* (H). Now it is very important to stress that matrix IN generates the set H^* and the matrix IN^* generates the set H.

For every feature (co-feature) halfbicluster a subset of one of the other type halfbicluster (co-feature or feature respectively) may be generated. Let there be a given halfbicluster $h^* \in H^*$. Then, as it is the subset of co-features, it determines a submatrix from the IN^*. The intersection of cells in this submatrix is the corresponding set for the given halfbicluster.

2.3 eBi – Exact Biclustering Algorithm

eBi algorithm may be performed in two ways, starting from the matrix IN or IN^*, but some steps are common.

Table 2. eBi algorithm

step	starting from IN	starting from IN^*
1.	Generate matrices IN and IN^*.	
2.	Generate set of halfbiclusters	
	H^*	H
	For each	
3.	$h^* \in H^*$	$h \in H$
	generate its corresponding set	
4.	For every halfbicluster from step 2. build exact bicluster as the ordered pair of halfbicluster and its corresponding set.	

Results of these two ways will differ. It is caused by the fact that for most of halfbiclusters their corresponding sets are halfbiclusters of another type. However nothing limits us to perform eBi in both ways and as the final result use the sum of sets of biclusters.

3 Exactness of the Algorithm

The exactness of this algorithm may be considered in two levels: every bicluster points cells with the same value and every considered value $v \in V$ belongs to at least one bicluster. The proof of the first kind of exactness is very simple: let us start from the one of halfbiclusters $h^* \in H*$. Its presence in the matrix IN points that there exist some features that do not differ from each other on co-features belonging to this halfbicluster. Which features? The ones on which these co-features do not differ from each other – as we know it from the cells in the submatrix of the IN^*. That is why the product of halfbicluster and its corresponding set gives matrix M cells with the same value.

Now let us assume that in the matrix M exists a cell $M(f, f^*) = v$ which does not belong to any bicluster: $\exists_{(f,f^*)} : \forall_{h^* \in H^*} f^* \notin h^*$. In the matrix IN on the intersection of f−th row and f−th column we obtain the set of co-features on which f−th feature does not differs from itself. t comes from the assumption we have that at least the co-feature f^* belongs to this set. As the set in $IN(f, f)$ contains at least f^* we may say that exists at least one halfbicluster h^* from H^* that $f^* \in h^*$. This ends the proof that every cell of M with the value v is covered with at least one bicluster.

4   Other Biclustering Algorithms

To compare eBi with other existing methods of biclustering we selected two of them called Cheng & Church's Algorithm (CC) and Order Preserving Submatrix Algorithm (OPSM). In our previous work [5] we used also algorithm called xmotif [10], but it can not be applied for dataset with more than 64 columns, so this time it was excluded from the comparison. To obtain biclusters found by CC and OPSM algorithms we used a tool called BicAT [11], where they were already implemented. All parameters were left on default values, except the number of output biclusters in case of CC, which was set on 10, 40, 70 and 100. Brief descriptions of compared methods are presented below. More detailed information can be found in [11,12].

Order Preserving Submatrix Algorithm

Authors of this algorithm defined bicluster as submatrix (subset of rows under subset of columns) of dataset, which is order preserving. This condition is satisfy if it is possible to arrange columns belonging to biclusters in ascending order. Bicluster is called as order-preserving submatrix (OPSM). This algorithm was designed for finding among dataset large and statisticaly significant biclusters satisfying strict OPSM requirements, based on own probabilistic model to simulate real data, in which OPSMs are latent among otherwise random matrix. Based on the same data set, algorithm allows to find more than one biclusters, also when they overlap. Heuristic approach was used to solve the NP-hard problem of finding OPSM [1].

Cheng and Church's Algorithm

In this method [3] bicluster is defined as a subset of dataset for which mean squared residue score (MSRS) is below some treshold determined by user. To solve the problem of finding the largest biclusters among matrix, two step strategy has been proposed. In the first phase columns and rows are deleted from the data, in the second step those removed columns and rows are insterted into dataset, until the MSRS is below defined level. Algorithm founds the biclusters based on various random seeds in an repetitive search way, where previously found biclusters are hidden by random values.

5   Experiments and Results

We compared eBi with other algorithms on artificial data containing three discrete levels of expression and a background in the 100x100 matrix. The dataset is shown on the Fig. 2: the background is white and expression levels are black (#0 – 1415 cells), grey (#77 – 1327 cells, three areas) and light grey (#237 – 2148 cells, banana shape). It is worth to notice that expression level areas do not have sharp edges and some parts of banana shape area are surrounded by the grey cells.

Fig. 2. Synthetic data

Evaluation of biclusters is performed on the basis of the following notions and measures: bicluster area is the total number of cells covered with this bicluster; bicluster weight is the number of correctly biclustered cells (number of cells with the value v); bicluster accuracy is the fraction of bicluster weight and area; bicluster coverage is the fraction of bicluster and whole matrix weights.

Results from the CC algorithm are in the Table 3. For every assumed number of biclusters the number of biclusters describing each discrete value is presented in the column total number. For every discrete value v the average value of bicluster accuracy (avg. acc.) and coverage (avg. cov.) are given. The column sum. cov. means the summarized coverages of all biclusters. If its value is higher than one it is possible that all considered values are covered by biclusters and there are some overlapping or redundant biclusters. The last column total cov. means the total coverage of considered cells with the set of biclusters. The value lower than one points that there are some cells that do not belong to any bicluster.

Table 3. Biclusters from CC algorithm

$v-$ value	total number	avg. acc.	avg. cov.	sum. cov.	total cov.
#0	10	0.00	0.00	0.00	0.00
#77	10	0.38	0.06	0.17	0.17
#237	10	0.32	0.06	0.55	0.55
#0	9	0.25	0.01	0.13	0.10
#77	22	0.34	0.02	0.50	0.46
#237	37	0.31	0.02	0.79	0.73
#0	20	0.29	0.02	0.41	0.35
#77	37	0.30	0.02	0.72	0.59
#237	60	0.32	0.02	0.94	0.79
#0	23	0.27	0.02	0.42	0.36
#77	50	0.30	0.02	0.80	0.61
#237	86	0.33	0.01	1.07	0.82

In the Table 4. analogical results of application the OSPM algorithm are presented.

Table 4. OSPM results

$v-$ value	total number	avg. acc.	avg. cov.	sum. cov.	total cov.
#0	27	0.15	0.17	3.41	0.43
#77	33	0.12	0.09	3.07	0.48
#237	40	0.21	0.07	2.76	0.28

In our experiments we assumed that rows are features and columns are co-features. The next table (Table 5.) contains results of the eBi algorithm. Because of the algorithm double exactness columns avg. acc. and total cov. are missing (values are equal 1). The additional column strategy has the following meaning: f – biclusters were generated from the matrix IN, f^* – biclusters were generated from the matrix IN^*, f, f^* – the set of biclusters is the sum of sets from strategy f and f^*.

Table 5. eBi results before postprocessing

$v-$value	strategy	total number	avg. cov	sum. cov.
#0	f^*	881	0.09	80.21
#0	f	570	0.09	51.16
#0	ff^*	1451	0.09	131.4
#77	f^*	328	0.07	24.49
#77	f	335	0.07	24.64
#77	ff^*	663	0.07	49.13
#237	f^*	1332	0.07	95.91
#237	f	954	0.07	67.02
#237	ff^*	2286	0.07	162.9

As we may observe (Table 5.) each strategy (f, f^*, ff^*) generates a big number of biclusters that are redundant (total coverage is 1 and the summarized coverage is a few dozens higher) the filtration strategy should be used to limit the set of biclusters. This approach is almost the same as the one presented in [5] with only one modification. In the previous paper the Michalski WS quality measure [8] was used as the most simple one that takes into consideration both accuracy and coverage of biclusters. As all eBi biclusters are accurate there is no need to use the accuracy component what means that the quality measure simplifies to the bicluster coverage. The results of postprocessing (filtering) eBi biclusters are in the Table 6.

Table 6. eBi results after postprocessing

$v-$value	strategy	total number	avg cov	sum. cov
#0	f^*	119	0.09	10.7
#0	f	141	0.10	14.3
#0	ff^*	66	0.02	1.02
#77	f^*	147	0.08	11.2
#77	f	140	0.08	11.2
#77	ff^*	146	0.02	1.72
#237	f^*	240	0.08	18.3
#237	f	257	0.06	15.9
#237	ff^*	235	0.01	2.42

We may observe that the filtration of biclusters gives very good results especially when we filter the sum of biclusters from the both f and f^* strategies. The best result we obtained for the biclustering of values #0 where there are only 66 biclusters that cover all considered values and only 2% of them overlaps (statistically 2% of cells belong to two biclusters). What may be also interesting, for other two values (#77 and #237) strategy ff^* gives the comparable number of biclusters but with almost ten times less biclusters overlapping.

6   Conclusions and Further Works

In this article the new algorithm for discrete values biclustering is presented. The greatest advantage of eBi is its exactness which provides that all derived biclusters will contain strictly the same value and that each occurrence of the considered value will be part of at least one bicluster.

Our next goal, very important from the analysis of real bioinformatical data point of view, is to develop methods of continuous values discretisation which will satisfy two conditions of exactness defined with the discrete eBi. It may be also interesting to perform the further analysis of small exact bicluster which will give bigger ones without breaking the exactness rule.

eBi was presented as the algorithm for finding biclusters among discrete matrix, although its usage is not limited only to the analysis of this kind of data. It seems to be very promising to use this method for biclustering microarray genes expression profiles which are continuous values. Based on observation that from biological point of view the most important information coming from the genes expression level is whether it is upregulated, downregulated or regularly expressed. Rely on simply statistics we can assign each expression of genes to one of these three states. In matrix, which is filled with three discrete values eBi can indicate all groups of genes across subset of samples that behave in similar way.

Summarizing, these methods can be widely used in the analysis of a data where belonging each cell from the dataset to one of some discrete states is much more informative than its exact numerical value.

Acknowledgements. This work was supported by the European Community from the European Social Fund.

References

1. Ben-Dor, A., Chor, B., Karp, R., Yakhini, Z.: Discovering Local Structure in Gene Expression Data: The Order-Preserving Sub-Matrix Problem. J. of Comput. Biol. 10(3-4), 373–384 (2003)
2. Chang, F.C., Huang, H.C.: A refactoring method for cache-efficient swarm intelligence algorithms Inf. Sci. (2010) (in press), (corrected proof), doi: 10.1016/j.ins.2010.02.025
3. Cheng, Y., Church, G.M.: Biclustering of expression data. In: Proc of the 8th Int. Conf. on Intell. Syst. for Mol. Biol., pp. 93–103 (2000)
4. Hartigan, J.A.: Direct Clustering of a Data Matrix. J. Am. Stat. Assoc. 67(337), 123–129 (1972)
5. Michalak, M., Stawarz, M.: Generating and Postprocessing of Biclusters from Discrete Value Matrices. In: Jedrzejowicz, P., Nguyen, N.T., Hoang, K. (eds.) ICCCI 2011, Part I. LNCS, vol. 6922, pp. 103–112. Springer, Heidelberg (2011)
6. Pensa, R., Boulicaut, J.F.: Constrained Co-clustering of Gene Expression Data. In: Proc. SIAM Int. Conf. on Data Min., SDM 2008, pp. 25–36 (2008)
7. Sayoud, H., Ouamour, S.: Speaker Clustering of Stereo Audio Documents Based on Sequential Gathering Process. J. of Inf. Hiding. and Multimed. Signal Process. 4, 344–360 (2010)
8. Sikora, M.: Filtering of decision rules using rules quality function. Stud. Inform. 4(46), 5–21 (2001)
9. Yang, E., Foteinou, P.T., King, K.R., Yarmush, M.L., Androulakis, I.P.: A Novel Non-overlapping biclustering Algorithm for Network Generation Using Living Cell Array Data. Bioinforma. 17(23), 2306–2313 (2007)
10. Murali, T.M., Kasif, S.: Extracting Conserved Gene Expression Motifs from Gene Expression Data. In: Pacific Symposium on Biocomputing, pp. 77–88 (2003)
11. Madeira, S.C., Oliveira, A.L.: Biclustering Algorithms for Biological Data Analysis: A Survey. IEEE/ACM Trans. on Comput. Biol. and Bioinforma. 1, 24–45 (2004)
12. Prelić, A., Bleuler, S., Zimmermann, P., Wille, A., Bühlmann, P., Gruissem, W., Hennig, L., Thiele, L., Zitzler, E.: A systematic comparison and evaluation of biclustering methods for gene expression data. Bioinformatics 22, 1122–1129 (2006)

Application of Neural Networks in Assessing Changes around Implant after Total Hip Arthroplasty

Arkadiusz Szarek[1], Marcin Korytkowski[2,3], Leszek Rutkowski[2,4],
Rafał Scherer[2], and Janusz Szyprowski[5]

[1] Institute of Metal Working and Forming, Quality Engineering and Bioengineering
Częstochowa University of Technology
http://iop.pcz.pl/

[2] Department of Computer Engineering, Częstochowa University of Technology
al. Armii Krajowej 36, 42-200 Częstochowa, Poland
http://kik.pcz.pl

[3] Olsztyn Academy of Computer Science and Management
ul. Artyleryjska 3c, 10-165 Olsztyn, Poland
http://www.owsiiz.edu.pl/

[4] SWSPiZ Academy of Management, Institute of Information Technology,
ul. Sienkiewicza 9, 90-113 Łódź, Poland
http://www.swspiz.pl/

[5] Orthopedics and Traumatic Surgery Department of NMP Voivodship Specialist Hospital in
Częstochowa. 42-200 Częstochowa, Bialska 104/118
szarek@iop.pcz.pl, marcin.korytkowski@kik.pcz.pl,
lrutko@kik.pcz.czest.pl, rafal@ieee.org

Abstract. Bone and joint diseases afflict more and more younger people. This is
due to the work habits, quality and intensity of life, diet and individual factors.
Hip arthroplasty is a surgery to remove the pain and to allow the patient to return
to normal functioning in society. Endoprosthesoplasty brings the desired effect,
but the life span of contemporary endoprosthesis is still not satisfactory. Clinical studies have shown that the introduction of the implant to the bone causes a
number of changes within the bone – implant contact. The correct prediction of
changes around the implant allows to plan the surgery and to identify hazardous
areas where bone decalcification and loss of primary stability in implant can
occur.

1 Introduction

The demand for a variety of prostheses, resulting from increasingly higher number of
injuries and osteoarticular pathologies which are a consequence of ageing society, stim-
ulates the necessity for improvement of materials used for implants [5]. Reconstruction
surgery allows for repairing the tissues damaged as a result of an injury or pathological
changes, which makes it possible to regain the lost functions [13]. An essential problem is proper diagnosing of tissue structure and identification of functional deficiency.
Achievement of these aims necessitates the use of proper diagnostic methods, precision and experience of the surgeons [15]. Due to its functions, hip joint is one of the
most frequently used load–bearing joint [2], which leads to occurrence of degenerative

L. Rutkowski et al. (Eds.): ICAISC 2012, Part II, LNCS 7268, pp. 335–340, 2012.
© Springer-Verlag Berlin Heidelberg 2012

changes [8]. Human race has always sought methods of reconstruction of damaged tissues and organs and the scientists have focused on these activities for over a hundred years. The only method of treatment in the case of serious problems was to remove the damaged organ. However, it improved life comfort only to an insignificant degree. The situation changed when progress in both medical science and material engineering allowed for collection and transplantation of living tissues and implantation of synthetic or natural biomaterials in order to restore the functions of defected or even removed organs [14].

We use neural networks which are one of methods constituting the soft computing concept. There are other soft computing methods [4][7][9][10][11][12][16] but neural networks are the best choice for nonlinear regression problem as we deal with in the paper. Some methods [6] have inherent ability to handle missing data but in our case we had complete vectors with patient evaluation data.

2   Research Method

Retrospective control examination of patients with implanted stem was carried out among 109 women and men. The oldest woman at the moment of surgery was 86 years old, whereas the youngest one was 43 (age average 71 years). Among women, the most frequent hip joint replacement concerned the right leg (61.1% of the cases with 38.9% cases for the left leg). In the case of two women, two-sided hip joint replacement was carried out. In the group of men, average age of the patients on the day of operation was 68 years (the oldest men was 83 years old whereas the youngest one was 47 years old). In the studied group of males, right hip joint replacement was carried out in 64.5% of the cases: hip joint replacement for the left leg was carried out in 35.5% cases. In one patient, the surgery was carried out in both legs.

Average age of the patients was 70 years. Indications for hip joint replacement in the analysed group of patients are presented in chart 1. In the case of 134 persons, side surgical access was used, whereas 19 cases concerned rear surgical access. In order

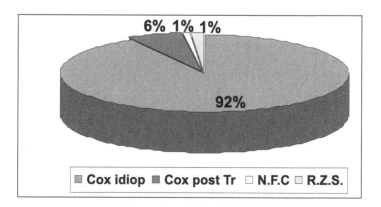

Fig. 1. Dysfunction of hip joint as a reason for hip joint replacement

to determine the effect of implantation of stem on femur remodelling, a representative group of 153 persons after implantation of stems with observation period from 12 to 66 months (average observation time of 58 months) was selected.

Based on RTG images the assessment of heterotopic ossifications and determination of bone decalcification which proves occurrence of bone defects. Patchy ossification in soft tissues, qualified under classification of Broker as I0 was observed in 18% of the patients (example RTG image see Fig. 1a). Exostosis (calcifications) from proximal part of femur or pelvis, not connected with the opposite side, a break over 1 [cm] was confirmed in 7% of person after 2hip joint replacement (example RTG image see Fig. 1b).

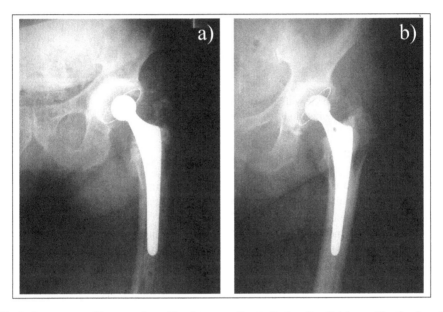

Fig. 2. Assessment of heterotopic ossification according to Broker. 2a - Patchy ossification in soft tissue, 2b - Exostosis (calcifications) from proximal part of femur.

Based on RTG images of the bone with implanted stem, the zones of bone decalcification were defined. Figure 2 present radiograms of hip joint with implanted stem. In the case of Fig. 2a and 2b, visible decalcifications of the bone in Gruen zone VI and VII can be observed. The RTG image presented in Fig. 2a presents decalcification in the acetabula in the area of De Lee zone III (central part of pelvis). Radiogram 2c presents the bone with decalcifications in the area of Gruen zone I and VII. Changes in the whole area of acetabulum can also be observed (De Lee zone I, II and III). Bone calcification which can be observed in RTG images might confirm that implantation of the stem causes changes in loading of femur, particularly in the area of contact of bone–implant (bone – cement – implant), where bone stiffness occurs. It should be emphasized that changes are insignificant in the adopted period of time, which makes prediction for stem life in the body satisfactory.

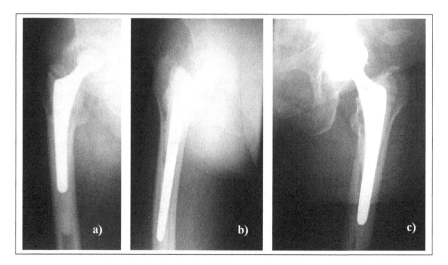

Fig. 3. RTG images of the bone with implanted stem, 2 a)b) decalcifications of the bone in Gruen zone VI and VII, 2c) decalcifications in the area of Gruen zone I and VII

3   Experimental Results

The presented results reveal that hip joint replacement brings desirable effects in a considerable majority of the cases. This is confirmed by the results obtained during analysis and assessment of the data according to the set criteria.

To learn a neural network to forecast and assess changes in bone around the implant, 153 patients histories from Orthopedics and Traumatic Surgery Department of NMP Voivodship Specialist Hospital in Częstochowa were used. Rated factors affecting bone strength parameters such as age and sex of patients, the cause of qualifications for arthroplasty (traumatic and degenerative) together with an indication for implantation of the waiting period (illness behavior) and the life of the prosthesis by the patient. Additionally, analyzed the factors that may affect the state of the bone around the implant after the implant prosthesis. These factors were introduced in three groups: The first group - motility of patients - the functionality of the limb during gait, her mobility with regard to physical activity. The second group - the biomechanical parameters affecting the load arm during basic activities such as limb length, the stability of the prosthesis in the bone, the shape of bones, etc. The data in the third group were obtained after evaluation of X-ray images of the type of implanted prosthesis and method of attachment in bone. X-ray studies allowed us to determine the changes around the implant (Gruen zones) characteristic for the type of prosthesis and ossification outside the bones (Brook's classification). The above data allowed to teach the neural network forecasting changes in the femur in various stages of use of selected types of prosthetics and evaluation of the bone in the area of contact around the stem. We used the LevenbergMarquardt algorithm [3] to train multilayer nonlinear feedforward artificial neural network [1]. The network had five neurons in the first hidden layer, five neurons in the second hidden layer and one neuron in the output layer. The network had several dozens inputs and one output denoting artificial hip assessment from 1 to 10. We obtained 100% accuracy. The neural network was able to reflect accurately the assessment made by orthopaedists.

4 Conclusions

We used a multilayer perceptron trained to assess changes around changes around implant after total hip arthroplasty. We used several dozens inputs and one output to numerically determine level of changes in femur. The neural network was trained by the Levenberg–Marquardt algorithm. The algorithm is able to find a local minimum of a nonlinear function over a space of parameters of the function. In the case of neural networks the parameters are weights which store the knowledge obtained during learning. During learning the weights are changed to fit the network to the learning data. Using moderately sized neural network we achieved maximal accuracy, thus the artificial neural network was able to imitate the assessments made by orthopaedists.

Acknowledgments. This work was supported by the Foundation for Polish Science – TEAM project 2010-2014.

References

1. Bishop, C.M.: Neural Networks for Pattern Recognition. Oxford University Press, Inc., New York (1995)
2. Canalis, E.: Regulation of Bone Remodeling: Primer on the Metabolic Bone Diseases and Disorders of Mineral Metabolism, An Official Publication of The American Society for Bone and Mineral Research. Amer. Society for Bone & Mineral, 33-31 (2009)
3. Hagan, M.T., Menhaj, M.B.: Training feed forward network with the Marquardt algorithm. IEEE Trans. on Neural Net. 5(6), 989–993 (1994)
4. Jankowski, N., Grąbczewski, K.: Universal Meta-Learning Architecture and Algorithms. In: Jankowski, N., Duch, W., Grąbczewski, K. (eds.) Meta-Learning in Computational Intelligence. SCI, vol. 358, pp. 1–76. Springer, Heidelberg (2011)
5. Marciniak, J.: Biomaterials. Silesian University of Technology Press, Gliwice (2002)
6. Nowicki, R., Rutkowski, L.: Rough-Neuro-Fuzzy System for Classification. In: Proceedings of Fuzzy Systems and Knowledge Discovery, Singapore, pp. 463–466 (2002)
7. Nowicki, R., Rutkowski, L.: Soft Techniques for Bayesian Classification. In: Rutkowski, L., Kacprzyk, J. (eds.) Neural Networks and Soft Computing. AISC, pp. 537–544. Springer Physica-Verlag (2003)
8. Pauwels, F.: Biomechanics of the Locomotor Apparatus, Berlin (1976)
9. Rutkowski, L., Cpałka, K.: A general approach to neuro - fuzzy systems. In: Proceedings of the 10th IEEE International Conference on Fuzzy Systems, Melbourne, December 2-5, vol. 3, pp. 1428–1431 (2001)
10. Rutkowski, L., Cpałka, K.: A neuro-fuzzy controller with a compromise fuzzy reasoning. Control and Cybernetics 31(2), 297–308 (2002)
11. Starczewski, J., Rutkowski, L.: Connectionist Structures of Type 2 Fuzzy Inference Systems. In: Wyrzykowski, R., Dongarra, J., Paprzycki, M., Waśniewski, J. (eds.) PPAM 2001. LNCS, vol. 2328, pp. 634–642. Springer, Heidelberg (2002)

12. Starczewski, J., Rutkowski, L.: Interval type 2 neuro-fuzzy systems based on interval consequents. In: Rutkowski, L., Kacprzyk, J. (eds.) Neural Networks and Soft Computing, pp. 570–577. Physica-Verlag, Springer-Verlag Company, Heidelberg, New York (2003)
13. Szarek, A.: Hip Joint Replacement in Biomechanical and Clinical Approach. Rusnauckniga, Belgorod (2010)
14. Szarek, A.: Chosen aspects of biomaterials, Publishing house Education and Science s.r.o. - Rusnauckniga, Praga-Belgorod (2011)
15. Williams, D.F.: Definitions in biomaterials. Elsevier, Amsterdam (1987)
16. Zalasiński, M., Cpałka, K.: A new method of on-line signature verification using a flexible fuzzy one-class classifier, pp. 38–53. Academic Publishing House EXIT (2011)

Forecasting Wear of Head and Acetabulum in Hip Joint Implant

Arkadiusz Szarek[1], Marcin Korytkowski[2,3], Leszek Rutkowski[2,4], Rafał Scherer[2], and Janusz Szyprowski[5]

[1] Institute of Metal Working and Forming, Quality Engineering and Bioengineering, Częstochowa University of Technology
http://iop.pcz.pl/

[2] Department of Computer Engineering, Częstochowa University of Technology, al. Armii Krajowej 36, 42-200 Częstochowa, Poland
http://kik.pcz.pl

[3] Olsztyn Academy of Computer Science and Management, ul. Artyleryjska 3c, 10-165 Olsztyn, Poland
http://www.owsiiz.edu.pl/

[4] SWSPiZ Academy of Management in Łódź, Institute of Information Technology, ul. Sienkiewicza 9, 90-113 Łódź, Poland
http://www.swspiz.pl/

[5] Orthopedics and Traumatic Surgery Department of NMP Voivodship Specialist Hospital in Częstochowa. 42-200 Częstochowa, Bialska 104/118
szarek@iop.pcz.pl, marcin.korytkowski@kik.pcz.pl, lrutko@kik.pcz.czest.pl, rafal@ieee.org

Abstract. Total hip joint replacement is a multi-aspect issue, where life span of the implant system in human body depends on numerous factors. One of the main reasons for having a hip replacement is loosening or wear of the associated components in artificial joint. The rate of wear depends mainly on the type of materials working together in the artificial joint, the burden resulting from the patient's body weight, intensity of use, limb functionality, age of the patient's and individual factors. The analysis of all factors leading to the joint wear and articulation expensiveness will allow for the appropriate selection of an head–acetabulum system which provide long-lasting and trouble-free operation. We use neuro–fuzzy systems to machine–learn the data to predict automatically the wear of elements in the artificial hip joint.

1 Introduction

Restoration of the pathologically changed or damaged in an accident, apart from removing hip pain, should ensure normal mobility and functionality of the hip joint. The human hip joint carries a large load and its mobility should allow the patient normal activities resulting from the daily duties [10]. Low friction occurring in human joints burdened with the normal and tangential force can be explained by the creation of a lubricant wedge formed by the synovial fluid that fully separates the contacting surfaces of bones, covered with elastic tissue of femoral cartilage [11]. Hip replacement

L. Rutkowski et al. (Eds.): ICAISC 2012, Part II, LNCS 7268, pp. 341–346, 2012.

is accompanied by a change of elements working in an artificial joint. Originally elements working together in the hip joint were made of metal, but due to rapid wear more new materials are being introduced to improve the life of the friction node[3]. Currently in the reconstruction of the hip joint, we can distinguish many kinds of friction pairs, differing in both strength parameters, tribological parameters as well as energy absorption. The main factor determining the type of head–acetabular system, apart from its life span, is the price of artificial joint components [9]. Reconstruction of the bone around the friction node should provide strong fixation of the acetabulum with pelvic bone, however, the resulting ossification should not restrict joint mobility [8]. Proper selection of artificial joint components should guarantee full comfort of the patient, maximally long life of elements in the body and the minimal cost of articulation. In addition, the wear of the elements should be small enough so they do not transfer wear products into the patient.

2   Materials and Methods

Prediction of the head and acetabulum wear in artificial hip joints was carried out on the base of the disease history of the 220 patients of Orthopedics and Traumatic Surgery Department of NMP Voivodship Specialist Hospital in Czestochowa. The criterion for selection of artificial joint components has been structured in three groups. In the first group, the pelvic bone changes seen on X-Ray (DeLee zone) were rated. The parameters evaluated in this criterion were determined in the way of mounting acetabulum in the bone. The first method (press fit) is pocketing the acetabulum with a larger size than prepared bone lodge (oversized component). The second method (exact fit) is equivalent to fitting the acetabulum of the size of milled box (on-line fit). The initial stabilization of the acetabulum takes place by micromechanical anchoring by the elastic and plastic deformations of trabeculae. Evaluation of clinical material helped to systematize the mechanism of late loosening of bearings such as the resorption process starting from the edge of the acetabulum, or the formation of the intermediate connective membrane at the border of cement - bone. On the basis of radiographic evaluation, we obtained also patches ossification in the soft tissues and bone decalcification were defined, showing the formation of bone defects. Second factor affecting the intensity of the friction is the set of parameters such as age, sex, body weight of patients, and the functionality of the limb: the possibility of walking and physical activity. In addition, range of mobility was analyzed by assessing the joint angular values: flexion, abduction, external rotation in extension, adduction, and straightening the limb. In the third group the type material of the head and the acetabulum, their respective configurations, their life-span and friction were analyzed. To predict the wear intensity we used common in orthopedics configurations of the following materials:

1. head
    - CoCr – standard finish
    - CoCr – increased smoothness (also for metal / metal),
    - Aumina + zircon.

2. inserts
 - plain UHMWPE,
 - partially cross–linked UHMWPE,
 - HXLPE highly crosslinked,
 - HXLPE + Vit E,
 - Metal / metal,
 - Alumina + zirconia,

All diagnostic procedures and measurements were carried out in accordance with the criteria commonly used in medicine [1][2][5][6]. The above data allowed to teach the neural network prediction of changes in the tribological parameters of the various stages of use of selected elements of the head and the acetabulum. In addition, evaluated changes of the factors of the bone–tissue in the pelvic area (DeLee zone) and ossification in the soft tissue and joint mobility allow for precise prediction and adaptation of the selected type of articulation to individual patient needs.

3   Numerical Simulations

We used Mamdani-type neuro-fuzzy systems [4][7][12] to learn obtained data described in the previous section. At the beginning of this section we describe the neuro fuzzy systems. We consider multi-input-single-output fuzzy system mapping $\mathbf{X} \to Y$, where $\mathbf{X} \subset R^n$ and $Y \subset R$. Theoretically, the system is composed of a fuzzifier, a fuzzy rule base, a fuzzy inference engine and a defuzzifier. The fuzzifier performs a mapping from the observed crisp input space $\mathbf{X} \subset R^n$ to a fuzzy set defined in X. The most commonly used fuzzifier is the singleton fuzzifier which maps $\bar{\mathbf{x}} = [\bar{x}_1, \ldots, \bar{x}_n] \in X$ into a fuzzy set $A' \subseteq X$ characterized by the membership function

$$\mu_{A'}(x) = \begin{cases} 1 \text{ if } x = \bar{x} \\ 0 \text{ if } x \neq \bar{x} \end{cases} \tag{1}$$

Equation (1) means that, in fact, we get rid of the fuzzifier. The knowledge of the system is stored in the fuzzy rule base which consists of a collection of N fuzzy IF-THEN rules in the form

$$R^{(k)} : \begin{cases} \text{IF} \quad x_1 \text{ is } A_1^k \text{ } AND \\ \qquad x_2 \text{ is } A_2^k \text{ } AND \ldots \\ \qquad x_n \text{ is } A_n^k \\ THEN \text{ } y \text{ is } B^k \end{cases} \tag{2}$$

or

$$R^{(k)}: \text{IF } \mathbf{x} \text{ is } A^k \text{ THEN } y \text{ is } B^k \tag{3}$$

where $\mathbf{x} = [x_1, \ldots, x_n] \in \mathbf{X}$, $y \in Y$, $A^k = A_1^k \times A_2^k \times \ldots \times A_n^k$, $A_1^k, A_2^k, \ldots, A_n^k$ are fuzzy sets characterized by membership functions $\mu_{A_i^k}(x_i)$, $i = 1, \ldots, n$, $k = 1, \ldots, N$, whereas B^k are fuzzy sets characterized by membership functions $\mu_{B^k}(y)$, $k = 1, \ldots, N$. The firing strength of the k-th rule, $k = 1, \ldots, N$, is defined by

$$\tau_k(\bar{\mathbf{x}}) = \overset{n}{\underset{i=1}{T}} \left\{ \mu_{A_i^k}(\bar{x}_i) \right\} = \mu_{A^k}(\bar{\mathbf{x}}) \tag{4}$$

The defuzzification is realized by the following formula

$$\overline{y} = \frac{\sum_{r=1}^{N} \overline{y}^r \cdot \mu_{\overline{B}^r}(\overline{y}^r)}{\sum_{r=1}^{N} \mu_{\overline{B}^r}(\overline{y}^r)}. \tag{5}$$

The membership functions of fuzzy sets $\overline{B}^r$, $r = 1, 2, \ldots, N$, are defined using the following formula:

$$\mu_{\overline{B}^r}(y) = \sup_{\mathbf{x} \in \mathbf{X}} \left\{ \mu_{A^r}(\mathbf{x}) \overset{T}{*} \mu_{A^r \to B^r}(\mathbf{x}, y) \right\}. \tag{6}$$

With singleton type fuzzification, the formula takes the form

$$\mu_{\overline{B}^r}(y) = \mu_{A^r \to B^r}(\overline{\mathbf{x}}, y) = T(\mu_{A^r}(\overline{\mathbf{x}}), \mu_{B^r}(y)). \tag{7}$$

Since

$$\mu_{A^r}(\overline{\mathbf{x}}) = \overset{n}{\underset{i=1}{T}}(\mu_{A_i^r}(\overline{x}_i)), \tag{8}$$

we have

$$\mu_{\overline{B}^r}(y) = \mu_{A^r \to B^r}(\overline{\mathbf{x}}, y) = T\left[\overset{n}{\underset{i=1}{T}}(\mu_{A_i^r}(\overline{x}_i)), \mu_{B^r}(y)\right], \tag{9}$$

where T is any t-norm. Because

$$\mu_{B^r}(\overline{y}^r) = 1 \tag{10}$$

and

$$T(a, 1) = a, \tag{11}$$

we obtain the following formula

$$\mu_{\overline{B}^r}(\overline{y}^r) = \overset{n}{\underset{i=1}{T}}(\mu_{A_i^r}(\overline{x}_i)). \tag{12}$$

Finally we obtain

$$\overline{y} = \frac{\sum_{r=1}^{N} \overline{y}^r \cdot T_{i=1}^n(\mu_{A_i^r}(\overline{x}_i))}{\sum_{r=1}^{N} T_{i=1}^n(\mu_{A_i^r}(\overline{x}_i))}. \tag{13}$$

Input linguistic variables are described by means of Gaussian membership functions, that is

$$\mu_{A_i^r}(x_i) = \exp\left[-\left(\frac{x_i - \overline{x}_i^r}{\sigma_i^r}\right)^2\right], \tag{14}$$

If we apply the Larsen (product) rule of inference, we will get the following formula

$$\overline{y} = \frac{\sum_{r=1}^{N} \overline{y}^r \left(\prod_{i=1}^n \exp\left[-\left(\frac{\overline{x}_i - \overline{x}_i^r}{\sigma_i^r}\right)^2\right]\right)}{\sum_{r=1}^{N} \left(\prod_{i=1}^n \exp\left[-\left(\frac{\overline{x}_i - \overline{x}_i^r}{\sigma_i^r}\right)^2\right]\right)}. \tag{15}$$

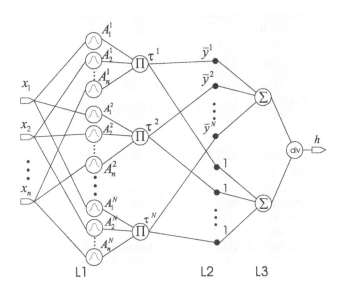

Fig. 1. Single Mamdani neuro-fuzzy system

The output of the single Mamdani neuro-fuzzy system, shown in Fig. 1, is defined

$$h = \frac{\sum_{r=1}^{N} \bar{y}^r \cdot \tau^r}{\sum_{r=1}^{N} \tau^r} \,, \tag{16}$$

where $\tau^r = \underset{i=1}{\overset{n}{T}} \left(\mu_{A_i^r} (\bar{x}_i) \right)$ is the activity level of the rule $r = 1, ..., N$. Structure depicted by (16) is shown in Fig. 1. We used several dozen inputs and one output. The system was trained by the backpropagation gradient learning. The neuro–fuzzy system achieved 96% accuracy.

4   Conclusions

Total hip joint replacement is a multi-aspect issue, where life span of the implant system in human body depends on numerous factors. The rate of wear depends mainly on the type of materials working together in the artificial joint, the burden resulting from the patient's body weight, intensity of use, limb functionality, age of the patient's and individual factors. The analysis of all factors leading to the joint wear and articulation expensiveness will allow for the appropriate selection of an head–acetabulum system which provide long-lasting and trouble-free operation. We used neuro–fuzzy systems to machine–learn the data to predict automatically the wear of elements in the artificial hip joint. All system parameters were determined by the backpropagation algorithm.

Thanks to neuro-fuzzy systems, apart from purely data-driven designing, we can use some expert knowledge in the form of fuzzy rules. The system was able to predict accurately the wear of the artificial hip joint.

Acknowledgments. This work was supported by the Foundation for Polish Science – TEAM project 2010-2014.

References

1. Bergner, M., Bobbit, R.A., Carter, W.B., et al.: The sickness impact profile: development and final revision of a health status measure. Medical Care 19, 787–805 (1981)
2. Harris, W.H.: Traumatic arthritis of the hip after dislocation and acetabular fractures: treatment by mold arthroplasty. An end-result study using a new method of result evaluation. Journal Bone Joint Surg. Am. 51, 737–755 (1969)
3. Hwang, D.S., Kim, Y.-M., Lee, C.H.: Alumina Femoral Head Fracture in Uncemented Total Hip Arthroplasty With a Ceramic Sandwich Cup. The Journal of Arthroplasty 22(3), 468–471 (2007)
4. Jang, R.J.-S., Sun, C.-T., Mizutani, E.: Neuro-Fuzzy and Soft Computing. In: A Computational Approach to Learning and Machine Intelligence. Prentice Hall, Upper Saddle River (1997)
5. Johnston, R.C., et al.: Clinical and radiographic evaluation of total hip replacement. A standard system of terminology for reporting results. Journal Bone Joint Surg. Am. 72, 161–168 (1990)
6. Merle d'Aubigone, R., Postel, M.: Functional results of hip arthroplasty with acrylic prosthese. Journal Bone Joint Surg. Br. 36-A, 451–457 (1954)
7. Nowicki, R.: Nonlinear modelling and classification based on the MICOG defuzzification. Nonlinear Analysis 71, e1033–e1047 (2009), doi:10.1016/j.na.2009.01.125
8. Nowin, S.C., Hegedus, D.H.: Bone remodeling I: theory of adaptive elasticity. Journal of Elasticity 6(3), 313–326 (1976)
9. Szarek, A.: Hip Joint Replacement in Biomechanical and Clinical Approach. Rusnauckniga. Belgorod (2010)
10. Szarek, A.: Chosen aspects of biomaterials, Publishing house Education and Science s.r.o. - Rusnauckniga, Praga-Belgorod (2011)
11. Ungethüm, M., Winkler-Gniewek, W.: Trybologie In der Medizin. Tribologia und Schmierungstechnik (5), 268–277 (1990)
12. Rutkowski, L.: Flexible Neuro Fuzzy Systems. Kluwer Academic Publishers (2004)

Fingerprint Recognition
Based on Minutes Groups
Using Directing Attention Algorithms

Michał Szczepanik and Ireneusz Jóźwiak

Wrocaw University of Technology, Institute of Informatics,
Wybrzeze Wyspianskiego 27, 50-370 Wroclaw, Poland
{michal.szczepanik,ireneusz.jozwiak}@pwr.wroc.pl
http://www.ii.pwr.wroc.pl

Abstract. In this paper author presents new solutions for fingerprint recognition based on minutes groups. They compered existing fingerprint recognition algorithm and test their ineffectiveness in the event of changes in the structure of a fingerprint as a result of physical damage. Authors proposed a new algorithm based on distribution groups minutiae using selective attention algorithms. Fingerprint analysis, which takes account of frequent damage to the imprint. The proposed algorithm can be applied in new smart phones which restrict unauthorized access to sensitive data or other users resources.

Keywords: biometric, fingerprint, minutes group, directing attention algorithms, identification system, image processing.

1 Introduction

Fingerprints are the most widely used biometric feature for person identification and verification in the field of biometric identification [2]. The most popular automatic fingerprint identification systems (AFIS) are based on a comparison of minute details of ridgehalley structures of fingerprints [1][3]. There are more than thirty different types of local characteristic points descriptions have been identified [10]. Among them, ridge endings and ridge bifurcations, which are usually called minutiae, are the two most prominent structures used to fingerprint recognition. The effectiveness of fingerprint recognition algorithms depends mainly on the quality of input digital fin-gerprint images [8][9] . Because of image that and other infraclass variations in cap-ture devices, and the limitations of AFIS, and matching algorithms, realistically, a genuine individual could be mistakenly recognized as an imposter.

The security level is determined by the parameter False Acceptance Rate (FAR) [3], is a pattern likely to qualify for the class, even though he belongs to another. In the biometric system: the probability of granting access to the system despite the absence of applied access level.

The level of usability is determined by the parameter False Rejection Rate (FRR) [3], the probability of ineligibility pattern to the class, although it should be.

L. Rutkowski et al. (Eds.): ICAISC 2012, Part II, LNCS 7268, pp. 347–354, 2012.

In the bio-metric system: the probability of denial of access to the system despite having access level.

Both FRR and FAR are indicated in corresponding areas given the selected threshold, and can be computed as follows:

$$FAR(T) = \int_{th}^{1} p_i(x)dx \qquad (1)$$

$$FRR(T) = \int_{0}^{th} p_i(x)dx \; . \qquad (2)$$

2   Fingerprint Recognition Systems in Intelligent Gateways

Intelligent gateway is used to identify or to authorize employees in enterprises. Con-stitute a security restricting access to only certain personnel resources, or serves as a time record system, it is important that the level of security and usability was high enough so as not to constitute obstacles to the work. Existing algorithms for finger-print recognition, although using them for years, are not immune to changes in physi-cal structure of fingerprints. Occurrence of damage to the footprint significantly re-duces the level of utility workers often causing frustration and reluctance to use them. The problem of fingerprint matching is a complex process, even in laboratory con-ditions, therefore, used in the intelligent gateway algorithm should be insensitive to certain natural changes in physical structure of fingerprints, which can include:

- ☐ incomplete fingerprint - a few imprints may partially overlap

- ☐ scanned fingerprint can be rotated (rotation)

- ☐ part of the fingerprint can be blurred or unreadable (a finger partially applied to the AFIS device)

- ☐ even when collecting fingerprint proper elastic deformations can occur

- ☐ finger with the fingerprint may be injured (injury)

3   The Most Commonly Used Algorithms to Solve the Problem

AFIS are usually used one of the algorithms:

- ☐ Elastic minutiae matching [4]

- ☐ Minutiae Adjacency Graph [6]

- ☐ Delaunay Triangulation [5]

- ☐ Pattern-Based Templates [7]

3.1   Pattern-Based Templates Algorithm - PBTA

Algorithm based on the patterns of the original image stored fingerprint pattern. After scanning a fingerprint search the fingerprint core, then used the basic graphic trans-formations such as scaling and rotation, the image is compared with the model. Such a procedure makes the algorithm practically to damage. Due to the storage of the original picture impression there is a high risk that this image can be read from the memory card reader or a database.

3.2   Elastic Minutiae Matching - EMM

Elastic minutiae matching adjustment model nonlinear transformation in two stages. Firstly, local matching determines which points on the fingerprint may match. It is based on the characteristics of local similarity. Without this step solution to the prob-lem would require more degrees of freedom. Then the global fit is carried out which uses fragments corresponding to the designation of a global transformation. Corre-sponding points are calculated using the method permissible squares minimization of errors that must be chosen carefully, because the distance between corresponding points on the elastic registration are rather small.

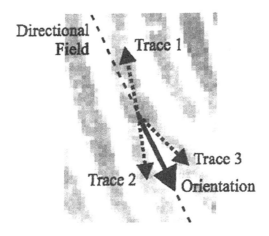

Fig. 1. Orientation for bifurcation type of minutiae [3]

Each minutiae is described by 3 or 4 parameters (x, y, T, Θ), where x and y are coordinates of the minutiae, T is an optional parameter specifying the type, e.g. beginning/ending, bifurcation, and determines the orientation Θ of the minutiae. The cor-rect orientation is selected by following all lines of the test point by some distance. For the point of beginning/end of line orientation course edge, and for the bifurcation lines fork has at that point (Fig. 1 shows it).

The local neighborhood matching is created by the next two characteristic points which are the closest to the analyzed minutiae, then search similar points dependences in the recording pattern (original fingerprint). After that, it creates a global transformation of the image. Depending on the distortion using one of the methods: Threshold based on the threshold of r_0, which defines permissible difference in distance between minutiaes in original and the analyzed fingerprint The transformation of Thin-Plate Spline (TPS)

3.3 Minutiae Adjacency Graph - MAG

The algorithm starts its operation by creating a graph connecting the stars of neigh-boring minutiae. Like in the previous algorithm, minutiae is described by 3 or 4 parameters $v = (x, y, T, \Theta)$, where x and y are the coordinate, T is an optional parameter specifying the type and Θ which determines orientation of minutiae. In addition, defined edges connecting the two points representing the minutiae of each edge is defined as follows $e = (u, v, rad, r_c, \Theta)$, where u, v are nodes (minutiaes) initial and marginal, rad it is Euclidean distance between minutiaes, r_c determines the distance by the number of ridges (fingerprint) between minutiaes, and Θ is the angle between the edge and the axis x.

The next step is the graph connecting the only neighbors, nodes are considered neigh-bors if the distance between them is less than dmax. This method is highly resistant to multiple injuries, mainly cuts, because they generate additional minutiae that com-pletely disrupt the structure of the graph.

The algorithm is based on triangulation connects neighboring minutiae thus creating triangles, unfortunately, just as minutiae adjacency graph algorithm is not resistant to injury of physical fingerprint.

4   The Proposed Solution Based on Minutiaes Groups Matching - MGM

The proposed solution, in contrast to those known from the literature not only analysis minutiaes as a points but also as minutiaes group. This analysis of the fingerprint image is much more resistant to damage, because if they has damages, the group can only slightly (about 1 or 2) change the number of characteristic points contained therein.

4.1 Detection of the Fingerprint and Significant Damage

Image analysis begins with the search for the imprint area including the exclusion of areas containing significant damage. Fingerprint image is described in shades of gray scale that defines the area of forced application fingerprint to the reader:

$$I_{fp}(i,j) = <1, 255> \tag{3}$$

Image is subjected to single-threshold binarization in which the parameter tg exclude from the analysis poorly read fingerprint areas:

$$B_{fp}(i,j) = \begin{cases} 1 \, for \, I_f p(i,j) \geqslant t_g \\ 1 \, for \, I_f p(i,j) < t_g \end{cases} \tag{4}$$

The last step is the imposition of a mask based on binarized image. Mask for the area of the square (X, Y), whose size is 2.5 wide edges, determines by two parameters plo which is a limitation that excludes areas with too small number of pixels describing the image, and phi excludes blurred areas, such as moist.

$$F_f p(X, Y) = \begin{cases} I_f p(X, Y) \, for \, \sum\limits_{i \in X} \sum\limits_{j \in Y} Bfp(i,j) \geqslant p_{lo} \wedge \sum\limits_{i \in X} \sum\limits_{j \in Y} Bfp(i,j) \leqslant p_{hi} \\ 0 \, otherwise \end{cases}$$

$$\tag{5}$$

After applying the mask image obtained without significant damage which would distort the analysis of the fingerprint (Fig. 2 presents all steps) . Created mask is also used in a neural network that determines the least damaged areas of the fingerprint.

Fig. 2. Steps of detection fingerprints damage process (Source: own work)

4.2   Leveling Damage and Find Minutiaes

Leveling of damage is carried out by calculating the variance of points and the analysis of brightness. Based on these two parameters is calculated the frequency of furrows. After applying Gabor filter [10]to highlight the pits and valleys, it use segmentation, in accordance with its size 2.5 width of segment furrow, the image is redrawn. After that process fingerprints are continuous and lint. In contrast to the literature algorithm does not require additional transformations to find the minutiae, such as converting all the width of 1px furrows. It does not require information about the orientation of minutiaes, it only requires the data about its position. Therefore, the resulting image is used to find the edge - the minutiae are located at the intersection of the edge of the furrows.

4.3   Fingerprints Comparison

Minutiaes image is divided into segments, each segment corresponding minutiaes group is described by parameters (x, y, nom), where x and y are the coordinates, and nom determines the number of minutiaes in the group. Additionally, in one imple-mentation uses an additional parameter specifying the probabilities of damage in a given segment which is estimated by neural network. Based on the distribution of areas rejected by the mask described by the formula. The last step is to create a matrix of Euclidean distances between the groups. When comparing the use of two parameters: dx - the distance, the difference between groups in the pattern and fingerprint test px - the threshold probability of damage (determined by whether the group is under consideration in the analysis). When comparing the groups are divided according to the weight that defines the number of minutiaes in the group and selective attention (SA) algorithms [8] which based on probabilities of damage in group segment. This provides quick verification of whether the analyzed fingerprint is consistent with the pattern (Fig. 3 shows it).

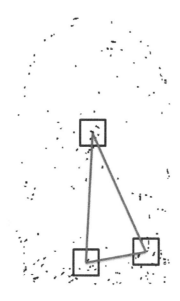

Fig. 3. Steps of detection fingerprints damage process (Source: own work)

5   The Results

The developed algorithm was compared with other algorithms described above using the fingerprint database 220 different fingerprints of 8 samples each. The database contained 12% of the fingerprints of damage (25-30% of the surface), which were mostly cuts and burns, the most frequently encountered in daily life damage.

Table 1. The result of experiment for the most popular algoritm and proposed solutions

	FAR	FRR
The most popular algorithms:		
MAG	1.58%	0.95%
EMM	2.35%	2.65%
PBTA	0.35%	8.52%
Proposed solutions:		
MGM64	8.45%	0.10%
MGM32	3.10%	0.10%
MGM32_SA	0.30%	0.10%

As expected, the algorithm based on the patterns is the most sensitive to damage and did not recognize most of the damaged finger. The existing algorithms for the best turned out to be based on graph matching. In the case of the proposed algorithm is a very important segment size, when it amounts to five furrows (MGM64) algo-rithm does not provide the required level of security. After reducing the size of the group in half and use the parameter of the likelihood of damage in a given segment (MGM32_SA) it was found most effective.

6   Conclusions

The proposed solution can be used in factories and other enterprises in which workers are exposed to damaging fingerprints. The use of smart goals much easier to verify the working time of employees does not require them to hold, no additional cards are easily lost. The system can also be applied to protect access to important data or premises to which some employees should not have access.

References

1. Grzeszyk, C.: Forensic fingerprint examination marks (in polish). Wydawnictwo Centrum Szkolenia Policji, Legionowo (1992)
2. Wayman, J.L., Jain, A.K., Maltoni, D., Maio, D.: Biometric Systems. Technology, Design and Performance Evaluation, 1st edn. Springer (2005)
3. Maltoni, D., Maio, D., Jain, A.K., Prabhakar, S.: Handbook of Fingerprint Recognition, 2nd edn. Springer (2009)
4. Chikkerur, S., Cartwright, A.N., Govindaraju, V.: K-plet and Coupled BFS: A Graph Based Fingerprint Representation and Matching Algorithm. In: Zhang, D., Jain, A.K. (eds.) ICB 2005. LNCS, vol. 3832, pp. 309–315. Springer, Heidelberg (2005)
5. Bebis, G., Deaconu, T., Georgiopoulos, M.: Fingerprint Identification Using Delaunay Triangulation. In: IEEE ICIIS, pp. 452–459 (1999)
6. He, Y., Ou, Z.: Fingerprint matching algorithm based on local minutiae adjacency graph. Journal of Harbin Institute of Technology 10(05), 95–103 (2005)

7. Ross, A., Dass, S.C., Jain, A.K.: A deformable model for fingerprint matching. Pattern Recognition 38(1), 95–103 (2005)
8. Huk, M., Szczepanik, M.: Multiple classifier error probability for multi-class problems. Maintenance and Reliability 3, 12–17 (2011)
9. Szczepanik, M., Szewczyk, R.: Fingerprint identification algorithm (in polish). In: KNS, Wrocaw, vol. 1, pp. 131–136 (2008)
10. Hong, L., Wan, Y., Jain, A.K.: Fingerprint image enhancement: Algorithm and performance evaluation. IEEE Transactions on Pattern Analysis and Machine Intelligence, 777–789 (1998)
11. Blonski, G.: Hardware Hacking cheating biometric security. Hakin9 9(07), 33–43 (2007)

Surrogate Measures of Thickness in the Regime of Limited Image Resolution: Part 2: Granulometry*

Zbisław Tabor and Rafał Petryniak

Cracow University of Technology,
Al. Jana Pawa II 37, 31-864 Cracow, Poland
ztabor@pk.edu.pl, rpetryniak@gmail.com

Abstract. In the present study a granulometry-based method of computing surrogate measure of thickness from gray-level images is introduced. Using Bland-Altman analysis it is demonstrated for a set of 25 μCT images that the difference between surrogate and reference measures of thickness corresponds to some non-zero bias. Analytical formulas derived in this study identify conditions necessary for the equality of surrogate measures of thickness and real thickness. The performance of the proposed method in the presence of image degradation factors (resolution decrease and noise) is tested.

1 Introduction

Trabecular bone is a highly porous structure, constituting interior parts of bones like vertebral bodies. Trabecular thickness is one of the parameters used to characterize trabecular structure. The procedure of trabecular thickness measurement is well defined for binary images. Images of trabecular bone, when acquired in laboratory experiments by clinical devices like CT or MRI scanners, are however coded with multiple gray levels. Such images cannot be easily binarized because the spatial resolution offered nowadays by clinical imaging devices is not good enough to depict individual trabeculae. In the present study a novel method of computing surrogate measure of thickness from gray-level images is introduced. The proposed method is based on the notion of granulometry [2]. Analytical formulas derived in this study identify conditions necessary for the equality of the surrogate granulometric measure of thickness and the real thickness of model objects in a continuous space. Implementation of the proposed method in the case of a discrete space is provided. Based on a set of 25 μCT images it is shown that the reference thickness values are well correlated with the surrogate measure of thickness.

---

* The paper is supported by project funded from 2009–2012 resources for science as a research project.

L. Rutkowski et al. (Eds.): ICAISC 2012, Part II, LNCS 7268, pp. 355–361, 2012.

2   Materials and Methods

2.1   Materials

3D μCT images of distal radius trabecular bone were obtained from 15 individuals. The samples were scanned with a μCT-20 scanner (Scanco Medical, Br uttisellen, Switzerland) with an isotropic voxel size of 34μm. The 3D μCT images were filtered with a 3D Gaussian filter and binarized, using a global threshold. The craniocaudal direction was identified with the z-axis of each sample. Then a total of 25 volumes with size of 200x200x200 voxels were selected from all μCT images and analyzed. Further details concerning the sample preparation and image acquisition protocols are described in the previous study of Laib et al. [1].

2.2   Methods

Image Preprocessing: The surrogate measurements of thickness were performed on original μCT images and on artificially corrupted images. In the latter case corrupted images Im_C were generated, based on the following equation:

$$Im_C = B(D \bigotimes Im + \eta) \qquad (1)$$

According to that model, the operator D resamples a binary μCT image Im (in which 0 corresponds to marrow and 255 to bone) at voxel sizes corresponding to integer multiples (2 to 5) of the parent resolution by means of box averaging. Given the voxel size of the original μCT images equal to 34μm, the voxel size of the resampled images is in the range from 68μm to 170μm. Note that the voxel size of images acquired by clinical devices spans similar range (form around 80μm for HR-pQCT to around 150μm for HR-CT). Next i.i.d. Gaussian noise η of varying intensity (zero mean and standard deviation from 10 to 30) is added to the data and finally the corrupted images are convolved with an anisotropic 3D Gaussian blurring kernel B. The kernel widths σ_x, σ_y and σ_z of the kernel were equal to 100μm, 100μm and 240μm. The corrupted images were written to files (16 bits per a voxel, signed integer data) and further analyzed. For comparison purpose the reference values REF.Tb.Th of thickness were calculated based on binary μCT images. BoneJ plugin (bonej.org) for ImageJ (rsbweb.nih.gov/ij) was used to compute REF.Tb.Th.

Granulometry of a 1D Rectangular Signal: In a variety of image analysis problems, one is interested in extracting the size distribution of the "objects" or "structures" present in an image. Meaningful size distributions are formally characterized within the framework of mathematical morphology by the concept of granulometry [2]. A granulometry is a family of openings $\Phi = (\Phi_\lambda)_{\lambda \geqslant 0}$ satisfying the following requirement:

$$\forall \lambda \geqslant 0, \mu \geqslant 0 : \lambda \geqslant \mu \Rightarrow \Phi_\lambda \subseteq \Phi_\mu \qquad (2)$$

Granulometric analysis of an image Im with granulometry Φ involves mapping each size λ to some measure $m(\Phi_\lambda(Im))$ of the opened image $\Phi_\lambda(Im)$. In a discrete case the family of openings is indexed on an integer parameter n rather than a real-valued λ. The measure $m(Im)$ of a discrete image Im is usually the sum of voxel values for both binary and grayscale images. Then, the granulometric analysis of Im with Φ results in a granulometric curve or granulometric pattern spectrum $PS_\Phi(Im)(n)$ [2]:

$$\forall n > 0, PS_\Phi(Im)(n) = m(\Phi_{n-1}(Im)) - m(\Phi_n(Im)) \tag{3}$$

In practice the most useful granulometries are based on openings with simple convex structuring elements like line segments, squares or hexagons. Usefulness of the concept of the granulometric pattern spectrum in the case of binary images can be illustrated by basic examples. Unfortunately, basic numerical experiments show that granulometric pattern spectrum cannot be directly used to estimate thickness distribution from gray-level images. Below it is shown how thickness information can be extracted from granulometry. Consider a 1D rectangular signal $Ob(x)$ equal to 1 for x in the range from $-x_c$ to x_c and zero otherwise. Neglecting for now the noise and the resolution decrease one has:

$$Im(x) = \int_{-\infty}^{\infty} B(x - y)Ob(y)dy \tag{4}$$

The profile of $Im(x)$ after opening it with a ball structuring element of size r is drawn in Fig. 1 with squares. After some basic manipulations it can be shown that:

$$PS_\Phi(Im)(r) = 2r(B(r - x_c) - B(r + x_c)) \tag{5}$$

If the size of the blurring kernel B is small, compared to the object size x_c, the second term on the right hand side of Eq. (5) can be neglected and a mean structure thickness can be easily reproduced from the granulometric pattern spectrum. If the size of B is large compared to x_c, Eq. (5) can still be used to estimate x_c, provided that an appropriate model is fitted to the granulometric pattern spectrum.

Granulometry of a 2D Rectangular Signal: An approximate formula for the granulometric pattern spectrum of a 2D rectangular signal can be found under an assumption that the length a of an object is larger than its width b and variations of image intensity in the regions corresponding to the corners of the object can be neglected. Then, the measure $m(\Phi_r(Im))$ is approximately equal to:

$$m(\Phi_r(Im)) = 4 \cdot (a - r) \cdot \left(r \cdot Im(r) + \int_r^{\infty} Im(z)dz \right) \tag{6}$$

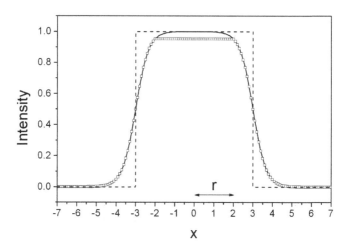

Fig. 1. A rectangular 1D object (dashed line), its image (solid line) - the result of convolution of the object and a Gaussian blurring kernel, and the image after opening with a kernel with radius r (squares)

Clearly, the expression for the granulometric pattern spectrum becomes more complicated than in the case of 1D object and involves higher powers of r and integrals of the blurring kernel B. Moreover, openings with generic structuring elements can be prohibitively expensive in 3D. For these reasons only 1D granulometries were implemented in the present study. Then a surrogate measure of thickness can be obtained as the result of fitting Eq. (5) to the granulometric pattern spectrum.

Implementation of the Granulometry: The following procedure was used to estimate the granulometric pattern spectrum. First, the analyzed gray-level image Im was eroded by linear structuring elements oriented along the three axes of the 3D frame of reference resulting in three images $\epsilon_x Im$, $\epsilon_y Im$ and $\epsilon_z Im$. An eroded image ϵIm was defined as the pixel-wise minimum over $\epsilon_x Im$, $\epsilon_y Im$ and $\epsilon_z Im$. Next, ϵIm was dilated using analogous procedure and the opened image $\Phi(Im)$ was obtained. The following model was fitted to the ratio of the granulometric pattern spectrum and the size n of the opening kernel:

$$\frac{PS_\Phi(Im)(n)}{n} = K \cdot \left(exp\left(-\frac{(n - x_c)^2}{2\sigma^2} \right) - exp\left(-\frac{(n + x_c)^2}{2\sigma^2} \right) \right) \qquad (7)$$

where K, σ and x_c are some parameters, to be found. Prior to the model fitting, the values of the granulometric pattern spectrum were normalized so that the area under the experimentally found curve on the left hand side of Eq. (7) was equal to 1. Then, the value of K became a parameter dependent on σ and x_c. The value of x_c estimated from the model defined in Eq. (7) is referred to as the granulometric thickness GR.Tb.Th. Of course, Eq. (7) can be used in the analysis of gray level data only, because in the case of binary images blurring operator B is not defined. As an estimate of GR.Tb.Th in the case of binary data a weighted average of n is used. The weight corresponding to an opening kernel size n is equal to the granulometric pattern spectrum value:

$$GR.Tb.Th = \frac{\sum\limits_{n} n \cdot PS_{\Phi}(Im)(n)}{\sum\limits_{n} PS_{\Phi}(Im)(n)} \qquad (8)$$

3   Results

The mean (standard deviation) values of REF.Tb.Th and GR.Tb.Th, calculated for original high-resolution μCT images were equal to 110 (10)μm and 90 (9)μm, respectively. The Pearsons coefficient of correlation between REF.Tb.Th and GR.Tb.Th was equal to 0.87. The slope of REF.Tb.Th vs. GR.Tb.Th plot was equal to 0.93$\pm$0.11, what suggests that the difference between the two measures corresponds to some shift only. The BlandAltman plot, demonstrating the difference between REF.Tb.Th and GR.Tb.Th in the function of the mean value of REF.Tb.Th and GR.Tb.Th is shown in Fig. 2.

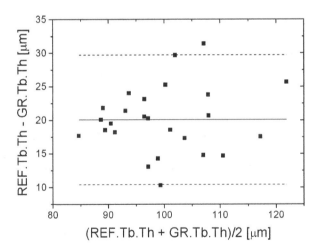

Fig. 2. Bland-Altman plot, comparing REF.Tb.Th with a surrogate measure of thickness GR.Tb.Th. All numbers were calculated for μCT images. The values of the bias are marked with the solid lines. The 95% limits of agreement are marked with dashed lines.

The values of GR.Tb.Th are plotted vs. the voxel size in Fig. 3 for different values of noise. GR.Tb.Th overestimates REF.Tb.Th. GR.Tb.Th calculated for degraded images is not stable. It appears however that the values of the Pearsons coefficient of correlation between GR.Tb.Th and REF.Tb.Th are not strongly dependent on noise (Fig. 4).

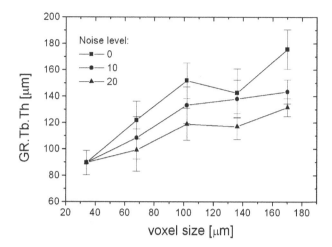

Fig. 3. GR.Tb.Th plotted vs. the voxel size for different levels of noise. Error bars represent the standard deviation of GR.Tb.Th.

4   Discussion

In the present study a method of computing surrogate granulometric measure of thickness has been introduced. The term "surrogate" is used here to indicate that the values of GR.Tb.Th, although different from the reference thickness values, correlate well with REF.Tb.Th. The surrogate character of GR.Tb.Th has been demonstrated on Bland-Altman plots, suggesting that the difference between GR.Tb.Th and REF.Tb.Th corresponds to a shift. The conditions necessary for equality of GR.Tb.Th and the real thickness have been identified.

Computation of GR.Tb.Th does not require any initial preprocessing. However, to calculate GR.Tb.Th from the granulometric pattern spectrum some assumptions about the blurring introduced by the imaging device are necessary. In this study the shape of the blurring kernel was known because it was explicitly chosen at the stage of the degraded images processing. Moreover, to obtain the best fit results, parameter σ in Eq. (7) was fixed in our computations and set close to the with of the Gaussian blurring kernel. Then, in the course of the fitting procedure only parameters K and x_c in Eq. (7) were adjusted to minimize the fitting error. Although it is certainly a limitation of the method, the point spread function of real imaging devices is often measured and then the shape of the blurring kernel can be determined experimentally. Importantly, the shape of the point spread function is the feature dependent only on the imaging device, not on the object under study and thus the procedure of GR.Tb.Th can be standardized. Moreover, it was found that the coefficient of correlation between GR.Tb.Th and REF.Tb.Th does not depend strongly on the specific choice of σ. The coefficient of correlation between GR.Tb.Th and REF.Tb.Th was robust with respect to noise and it is an argument, besides simplicity of implementation, for using that parameter as a surrogate measure of thickness in low-quality data.

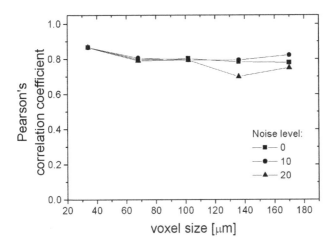

Fig. 4. The values of the Pearsons coefficient of correlation between GR.Tb.Th and REF.Tb.Th plotted vs. the voxel size for different levels of noise

It should be also noted that granulometry is a standard procedure to assess objects size distribution in various fields of science e.g. materials engineering.

Concluding, it is possible to derive surrogate measures of thickness from low-resolution data even if the voxel size is of the order of typical structure size. For some classes of objects (e.g. well separated planar objects in 3D) thickness can be in principle derived precisely even if the blurring is higher than the structure size.

Acknowledgement. The authors thank Sharmila Majumdar, Andrew Burghardt, Andres Laib and Ahi Issever for providing them with μCT images of distal radius trabecular bone.

References

1. Laib, A., Beuf, O., Issever, A., Newitt, D.C., Majumdar, S.: Direct measures of trabecu-lar bone architecture from MR images. Adv. Exp. Med. Biol. 496, 37–46 (2001)
2. Maragos, P.: Pattern spectrum and multiscale shape representation. IEEE Transactions on Pattern Analysis and Machine Intelligence 11(7), 701–716 (1989)

Novel Algorithm
for the On-Line Signature Verification

Marcin Zalasiński and Krzysztof Cpałka

Czestochowa University of Technology,
Department of Computer Engineering, Poland
{marcin.zalasinski,krzysztof.cpalka}@kik.pcz.pl

Abstract. On-line signature is a biometric attribute used in a identity
verification process. One of the most effective methods of signature verification is the method based on partitioning of signature trajectories.
In this paper a concept of new approach to identity verification based
on partitioning of trajectories is presented. In this approach signature is
partitioned into subspaces which are weighted by weights of importance.
The weights are used in classification process. Partitions associated with
high values of weight have greater importance in classification process
than partitions associated with low weight values. The algorithm was
tested with use of public on-line signature database SVC 2004.

1   Introduction

Biometrics is the science of recognizing the identity of a person based on some
kind of unique personal attributes. Biometrics, which uses the soft-computing
technologies (see e.g. [9],[10],[11]), is called Soft-Biometrics.

On-line (dynamic) signature is a behavioral biometric attribute, which is commonly acceptable in society, e.g. in offices or banks. This is very important, because this kind of identity verification is not controversial and may be used in
many areas of life (see [3]).

Identity verification problem based on signature trajectories partitioning was
considered in literature (see e.g. [5],[7],[8]). In our paper a concept of a new
approach to identity verification based on partitioning of signature trajectories
is presented. In this approach signature is also partitioned into four subspaces
which are weighted by weights of importance. These weights are used in classification process. Partitions with high weight values have greater importance
level in classification process than partitions with low weight values. Moreover,
in our paper we propose a classifier based on the t-conorm with the weights of
arguments (see e.g. [12],[13]).

This paper is organized into five sections. In Section 2 the description of
approach to signature trajectories partitioning is given. In Section 3 the new
approach to signature trajectories partitioning is presented. Simulation results
are presented in Section 4. Conclusions are drawn in Section 5.

L. Rutkowski et al. (Eds.): ICAISC 2012, Part II, LNCS 7268, pp. 362–367, 2012.
© Springer-Verlag Berlin Heidelberg 2012

2   Signature Verification Based on Trajectories Partitioning

Identity verification based on dynamic signature is more effective than verification based on image of signature (see e.g. [4]), because dynamic features of signature (e.g. pressure and velocity) are unique for each signer. One of the method of increase classification effectiveness is division of velocity and pressure signals into two parts and selection for each signer a part which contains the most discriminative trajectories features (see [5]). Selection of the most stable partition used in verification and classification phase is performed on the basis of templates generated from training signatures of signer. The result of classification phase is decision if test signature is genuine or forgery.

The main part of considered in [5] algorithm may be described in the following steps:

- **Step 1. Partitioning of Signatures.** In this step trajectories of signature are partitioned on the basis of two dynamic features - velocity and pressure.
- **Step 2. Template Generation.** In this step templates for each partition are generated.
- **Step 3. Calculation of Signatures Similarity in Each Partition.** In this phase similarity of user signature for each partition is calculated. Partition with the best similarity score is used in verification phase. This partition is called *stable partition*.
- **Step 4. Classification.** In this step signature is classified as genuine or forgery. Classification process is performed on the basis of distance between template and sample signature in stable partition.

More details of above algorithm are presented in [5],[15].

3   The New Approach to Signature Verification Based on Trajectories Partitioning

In this paper we propose a new method of signature verification based on trajectories partitioning. Main advantages of our method are listed below:

- In our method all partitions are considered in the training and classification phase because it is assumed, that all partitions may contain some important information about signer.
- In the classification process weights of importance are used. Weights are calculated individually for each signer, for each signature partition. High value of weight means, that partition correlated with this weight has high value of importance level in the classification phase.
- In the classification phase a classifier based on the t-conorm with the weights of arguments is proposed. This classifier uses weights of importance during classification process.
- Weights of importance are associated with the inputs. The conception of use of weights in triangular norms and fuzzy rules is described in [1],[2],[11]-[13].

3.1   A New Concept of Weights of Signature Partitions

New approach to signature verification based on trajectories partitioning assumes use of weights of importance. Weights of importance are correlated with each generated partition, not only with the stable one (see [5]). Weights of importance are calculated on the basis of mean distance between signatures and template and on the basis of similarity in distances between signatures and template. High value of weight means that partition correlated with this weight has high value of importance level.

First step to compute weights of importance is calculation of mean distances between signatures and template in partitions. Mean distance between signatures of the i-th signer and template of the i-th signer in the p-th partition based on signal s (*velocity* or *pressure*) ($\bar{d}_{p,i}^{\{s\}}$, $p = \{0,1\}$, $i = 1,2,\ldots,I$) is calculated by the formula:

$$\bar{d}_{p,i}^{\{s\}} = \frac{1}{J} \sum_{j=1}^{J} d_{p,i,j}^{\{s\}}. \tag{1}$$

In the next step standard deviation of distances in each partition should be calculated. Standard deviation of signatures of the i-th user from the p-th partition based on signal s (*velocity* or *pressure*) ($\sigma_{p,i}^{\{s\}}$, $p = \{0,1\}$, $i = 1,2,\ldots,I$) is calculated using the following equation:

$$\sigma_{p,i}^{\{s\}} = \sqrt{\frac{1}{J-1} \sum_{j=1}^{J} \left(\bar{d}_{p,i}^{\{s\}} - d_{p,i,j}^{\{s\}} \right)^2}. \tag{2}$$

In the next step weights of importance are calculated. Weight of the p-th partition of the i-th user based on signal s (*velocity* or *pressure*) ($w_{p,i}^{'\{s\}}$, $p = \{0,1\}$, $i = 1,2,\ldots,I$) is calculated by the following formula:

$$w_{p,i}^{'\{s\}} = \bar{d}_{p,i}^{\{s\}} \sigma_{p,i}^{\{s\}}. \tag{3}$$

After that, weights should be normalized. Weight of the p-th partition of the i-th user based on signal s (*velocity* or *pressure*) ($w_{p,i}^{\{s\}}$, $p = \{0,1\}$, $i = 1,2,\ldots,I$) is normalized by the following equation:

$$w_{p,i}^{\{s\}} = 1 - \frac{0.9 \cdot w_{p,i}^{'\{s\}}}{\max\left\{ w_{0,i}^{'\{s\}}, w_{1,i}^{'\{s\}} \right\}}. \tag{4}$$

Use of coefficient 0.9 in formula (4) causes that partition with the lowest value of weight of importance is also used in classification process.

3.2   A Concept of New Approach to Classification of the Signatures

In this section a concept of new approach to classification of signatures is presented. The classification process is described as follows:

- **Step 1.** Partitioning of signatures. The step is performed analogously to the step presented in the algorithm in Section 2.
- **Step 2.** Template generation. The step is performed analogously to the step presented in the algorithm in Section 2.
- **Step 3.** Computation of the weights of importance. High value of the weight means, that partition correlated with the weight has high value of importance level and signatures which belong to the partition are more important in classification process. Details of computation of the weights are presented in Section 3.1.
- **Step 4.** Selection of location of decision boundary, which is located between genuine signatures and forgery signatures. During this process genuine signatures of the other users are considered as forged signatures. For this purpose value of parameter $c_{p,i}^{\{s\}}$, $p = \{0,1\}$, $i = 1, 2, \ldots, I$, $s = \{v, z\}$, is determined (see [5]). Value of the parameter must be determined in such a way, that $\hat{d}lrn_{p,i}^{\{s\}}$ is equal to $\hat{d}for_{p,i}^{\{s\}}$. The dependence is shown in Fig. 1a. This step is performed during training phase. Result of this step are parameters $c_{p,i}^{\{s\}}$, $p = \{0,1\}$, $i = 1, 2, \ldots, I$, $s = \{v, z\}$, determined individually for the user and used during test phase.
- **Step 5.** Determination of the value $dlrnmax_{p,i}^{\{s\}}$, $p = \{0,1\}$, $i = 1, 2, \ldots, I$, $s = \{v, z\}$, between classification boundary and the most distant point, which represents genuine signature. This is presented in Fig. 1b. The determined values have an impact on spacing of fuzzy sets, which represent values assumed by the four linguistic variables "the truth of the user signature from p partition of s signal" ($p = \{0,1\}$, $s = \{v, z\}$). This step is performed during training phase. Result of this step are parameters $dlrnmax_{p,i}^{\{s\}}$, $p = \{0,1\}$, $i = 1, 2, \ldots, I$, $s = \{v, z\}$, determined individually for the user.
- **Step 6.** Signature verification. It is assumed, that the signature can be considered as a genuine one, if

$$y_i\left(dtst_{0,i}^{\{v\}}, dtst_{1,i}^{\{v\}}, dtst_{0,i}^{\{z\}}, dtst_{1,i}^{\{z\}}; w_{0,i}^{\{v\}}, w_{1,i}^{\{v\}}, w_{0,i}^{\{z\}}, w_{1,i}^{\{z\}}\right) > cth_i, \quad (5)$$

where

$$y_i\left(dtst_{0,i}^{\{v\}}, dtst_{1,i}^{\{v\}}, dtst_{0,i}^{\{z\}}, dtst_{1,i}^{\{z\}}; w_{0,i}^{\{v\}}, w_{1,i}^{\{v\}}, w_{0,i}^{\{z\}}, w_{1,i}^{\{z\}}\right) =$$
$$S^*\left\{\begin{array}{c} \mu_{A_1}\left(dtst_{0,i}^{\{v\}}\right), \mu_{A_2}\left(dtst_{1,i}^{\{v\}}\right), \mu_{A_3}\left(dtst_{0,i}^{\{z\}}\right), \mu_{A_4}\left(dtst_{1,i}^{\{z\}}\right); \\ w_{0,i}^{\{v\}}, w_{1,i}^{\{v\}}, w_{0,i}^{\{z\}}, w_{1,i}^{\{z\}} \end{array}\right\}. \quad (6)$$

In the equation (6) the following symbols mean:
- $S^*\{\cdot\}$ - t-conorm with the weights of arguments, proposed in [13].
- $dtst_{0,i}^{\{v\}}$ - distance between the test signature trajectory of the i-th signer and decision boundary in the 0 partition generated on the basis of velocity v. Distances $dtst_{1,i}^{\{v\}}$, $dtst_{0,i}^{\{z\}}$, $dtst_{1,i}^{\{z\}}$ are described analogously.

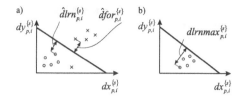

Fig. 1. Illustration of selection of: (a)location of decision boundary, (b)the $dlrnmax_{p,i}^{\{s\}}$ value. Genuine training signatures of the user are described as circles, genuine training signatures of other users are described as crosses.

- $w_{0,i}^{\{v\}}$ - weight of the 0 partition of the i-th user based on velocity v. Weights $w_{1,i}^{\{v\}}$, $w_{0,i}^{\{z\}}$, $w_{1,i}^{\{z\}}$ are described analogously.
- $cth_i \in [0,1]$ - coefficient determined experimentally during training phase for each user to eliminate disproportion between FAR and FRR error (see [14]).

Result of this step is parameter $cth_i \in [0,1]$, computed individually for the i-th user, $i = 1, 2, \ldots, I$, which are used during verification process in the test phase.

4   Simulation Results

Our simulation was performed with use of public database SVC 2004 (see [14]). The database contains 40 signers and for each signer 20 genuine and 20 forgery signatures. Our test was performed five times for all signers. During training phase 5 genuine signatures (numbers 1-10) of each signer were used. During test phase 10 genuine signatures (numbers 11-20) and 20 forgery signatures (numbers 21-40) of each signer were used. The test was performed by the authorial testing environment implemeted in C# language. Method presented in [5] was also implemented to compare the results. Results of simulation are presented in Table 1 as values of FAR (False Acceptance Rate) and FRR (False Rejection Rate), which are commonly use in biometrics (see e.g. [6]).

Table 1. Results of simulation performed by our system

Method	Average FAR value	Average FRR value
Method presented in [5]	17.30 %	21.35 %
Our method	**15.53 %**	**16.80 %**

5   Conclusions

In this paper a conception of the new approach to identity verification based on partitioning signatures trajectories is presented. Proposed approach assumes partitioning signature and calculation weights of each partition. Calculated weights are used in classification process. Weight of importance contains information about reliability of partition of signature. Classification of signatures is performed by classifier based on t-conorm with the weights of arguments. Results of simulation confirm, that presented approach increases effectiveness of identity verification with use of on-line signature.

Acknowledgment. The project was financed by the National Science Center on the basis of the decision number DEC-2011/01/N/ST6/06964.

References

1. Cpałka, K.: A New Method for Design and Reduction of Neuro-Fuzzy Classification Systems. IEEE Transactions on Neural Networks 20(4), 701–714 (2009)
2. Cpałka, K.: On evolutionary designing and learning of flexible neuro-fuzzy structures for nonlinear classification. Nonlinear Analysis series A: Theory, Methods & Applications, vol. 71. Elsevier (2009)
3. Fabregas, J., Faundez-Zanuy, M.: On-line signature verification system with failure to enroll management. Pattern Recognition 42 (2009)
4. Faundez-Zanuy, M.: On-line signature recognition based on VQ-DTW. Pattern Recognition 40 (2007)
5. Ibrahim, M.T., Khan, M.A., Alimgeer, K.S., Khan, M.K., Taj, I.A., Guan, L.: Velocity and pressure-based partitions of horizontal and vertical trajectories for on-line signature verification. Pattern Recognition 43 (2010)
6. Jain, A.K., Ross, A.: Introduction to Biometrics. In: Jain, A.K., Flynn, P., Ross, A.A. (eds.) Handbook of Biometrics. Springer (2008)
7. Khan, M.K., Khan, M.A., Khan, M.A.U., Lee, S.: Signature verification using velocity-based directional filter bank. In: IEEE Asia Pacific Conference on Circuitsand Systems, APCCAS, pp. 231–234 (2006)
8. Khan, M.A.U., Khan, M.K., Khan, M.A.: Velocity-image model for online signature verification. IEEETrans. Image Process 15 (2006)
9. Korytkowski, M., Rutkowski, L., Scherer, R.: From Ensemble of Fuzzy Classifiers to Single Fuzzy Rule Base Classifier. In: Rutkowski, L., Tadeusiewicz, R., Zadeh, L.A., Zurada, J.M. (eds.) ICAISC 2008. LNCS (LNAI), vol. 5097, pp. 265–272. Springer, Heidelberg (2008)
10. Nowicki, R.: Nonlinear modelling and classification based on the MICOG defuzzification. Journal of Nonlinear Analysis, Series A: Theory, Methods & Applications 71, e1033–e1047 (2009)
11. Rutkowski, L.: Computational intelligence. Springer (2007)
12. Rutkowski, L., Cpałka, K.: Designing and learning of adjustable quasi triangular norms with applications to neuro-fuzzy systems. IIEEE Trans. Fuzzy Syst. 13(1), 140–151 (2005)
13. Rutkowski, L., Cpałka, K.: Flexible neuro-fuzzy systems. IEEE Trans. Neural Networks 14(3), 554–574 (2003)
14. Yeung, D.-Y., Chang, H., Xiong, Y., George, S.E., Kashi, R.S., Matsumoto, T., Rigoll, G.: SVC2004: First International Signature Verification Competition. In: Zhang, D., Jain, A.K. (eds.) ICBA 2004. LNCS, vol. 3072, pp. 16–22. Springer, Heidelberg (2004)
15. Zalasiński, M., Cpałka, K.: A new method of on-line signature verification using a flexible fuzzy one-class classifier. In: Selected Topics in Computer Science Applications, EXIT, pp. 38–53 (2011)

Part IV

Concurrent Parallel Processing

Concept of Nonlinear Orthogonal Filter of Volterra-Wiener Class Realization Using Multiprocessor Platform

Pawel Biernacki

University of Technology Wroclaw, Janiszewskiego 7/9, 50-350 Wroclaw, Poland
pawel.biernacki@pwr.wroc.pl
http://zts.ita.pwr.wroc.pl

Abstract. The article presents the concept of realization of nonlinear orthogonal parametrization filter of Volterra-Wiener class using multi-processor platform. Examined two variants of solutions: working off-line and on-line. Parallelism of calculations can allow for faster working or change filters parameters during operations.

1 Introduction

In many applications the Volterra-Wiener filter is attractive because it is a straightforward generalization of the linear system description and the behaviour of many physical systems can be described with a Volterra filter [2,7].

The discrete-time invariant Volterra filter with memory length N and order of nonlinearity M, is defined by [6]:

$$\hat{y}_0 = \sum_{i_1=0}^{N} {}^x\rho^{i_1} x_0^{i_1} + \sum_{i_1=0}^{N} \sum_{i_2=i_1}^{N} {}^x\rho^{i_1,i_2} x_0^{i_1,i_2} + \dots$$

$$\dots + \sum_{i_1=0}^{N} \sum_{i_2=i_1}^{N} \dots \sum_{i_M=i_{M-1}}^{N} {}^x\rho^{i_1,\dots,i_M} x_0^{i_1,\dots,i_M} \tag{1}$$

where

$$\begin{aligned}
{}^x\rho^{i_1} &= (x_0, r_0^{i_1}) \\
{}^x\rho^{i_1,i_2} &= (x_0, r_0^{i_1,i_2}) \\
&\dots \\
{}^x\rho^{i_1,\dots,i_M} &= (x_0, r_0^{i_1,\dots,i_M})
\end{aligned} \tag{2}$$

are the generalized (multi-dimensional) Fourier [2](i.e. Schur-type) coefficients. The coefficients (2) can be interpreted as the orthogonal representation of the y_0 signal in the multidimensional space.

It is easy to see that the parameters that represent the complexity of the filter are: filter order N (memory of the filter) and the degree of nonlinearity of the filter M. Increasing any one of them involves a rapid increase in computational effort needed to estimate y_0.

L. Rutkowski et al. (Eds.): ICAISC 2012, Part II, LNCS 7268, pp. 371–377, 2012.

Considering nonstationary case for filter input, the number of rotors (elementary sections) in the decorelation block of the filter is expressed by the formula:

$$L_{N,M} = \sum_{m=1}^{M} \frac{(N+m-1)!}{m!(N-1)!} \tag{3}$$

Figure 1 shows how rapidly rising value of the expression (3) with the change of N or M.

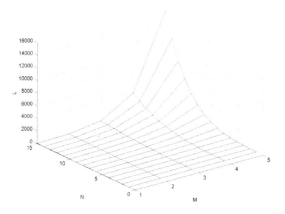

Fig. 1. Number of elementary sections $L_{N,M}$ of the filter

Implementation of the filter using many computational units at once (parallel computing) could allow to:

– the filter to work faster,
– reduction of computing power for single unit,
– expansion of the filter with new rotors (improved estimation of filter output).

2   Proposed Solution

The structure of the nonlinear orthogonal Volterra-Wiener class filter is shown in figure 2. Where the parametrization block which is the most expensive computationally is shown in figure 3.

The filter can work in off-line mode or in on-line mode. In the first case, at one point in time on all inputs of the filter the corresponding x signal appears. Every elementary section (rotor) is used only ones during filtering. Such filter action is used by the signal parameterization procedure, signal extraction parameters procedure, batch operations [3,4].

Figure 4 demonstrates how to split the calculations performed by the filter into two streams (dual-processor structure, processors P1 and P2).

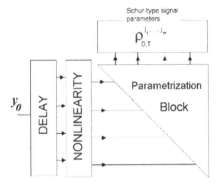

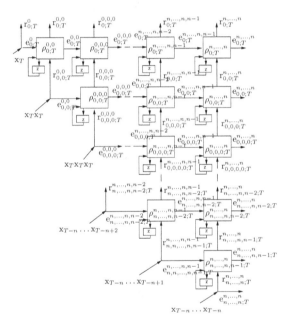

Fig. 2. Volterra-Wiener filter structure

Fig. 3. Parametrization block of order n

The filtration process is divided into two stages. The first of these calculations are performed in the areas of P1.1 (the first processor, the first moment) and P2.1 (the second processor, the first moment). In the second stage the operations are performed in the areas of P1.2 and P2.2. Calculations of rotors lying at the interface between P1.2 and P2.2 fields are carried out by both processors. Assuming the same computing power of both units provides a synchronization of calculations and there is no need of supervision results in the appearance of the corresponding rotors outputs.

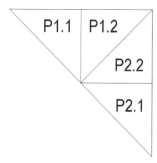

Fig. 4. Dual-processor structure of the filter (off-line mode)

Obviously increase the number of processors (above two) action speeds up the filter. Figures 5 and 6 show the possible sequence of calculations for versions 4 and 5 processors.

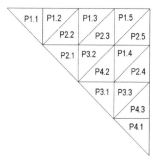

Fig. 5. 4-processor structure of the filter (off-line mode)

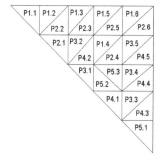

Fig. 6. 5-processor structure of the filter (off-line mode)

You can see that the increase in the number of processors causes some of them are not used at certain stages of the calculations. This follows from the structure of the filter and how to pass the signal through it.

In order to evaluate the effectiveness of multiprocessing solutions the efficiency measure was defined

$$Ef = \frac{speed_up}{cost} \tag{4}$$

where $speed_up$ is a profit of the acceleration calculations for a multiprocessor version in relation to the single-processor solution and $cost$ is an investment needed to increase the computing power (the number of processing units used). Figure 7 shows the variation in the Ef measure in the function of adding another processor to the processing system.

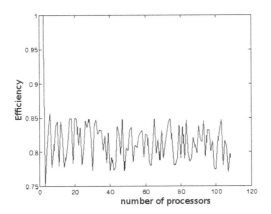

Fig. 7. Efficiency for off-line filter mode

The most effective is a dual-processor version. Further enhancing the computing power accelerates the action of the filter, but system costs are increasing.

3   On-Line Filter Mode Solution

In the case of the filter is working in real time (eg., echo elimination, noise reduction) [2,5,6] only part of the rotors must be activated to calculate the output when a new filter input sample appears. This is illustrated in figure 8.

'Old results' (calculated in the previous moments) are used as the inputs for needed rotors ('working part'). Multiprocessor solution in this case will consist of cascaded structure of the processors which using 'pipeling' method calculate the output signal (see figure 9).

Efficiency (4) of this solution is constant. Adding another processor results in a proportionate increase in the speed of the filter.

Fig. 8. Active and non-active areas of the filter working in on-line mode

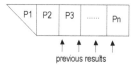

Fig. 9. Multiprocessor sulution for filter on-line mode

4   Some Experiments

The proposed parallel realization of Volterra-Wiener filter was implemented in C language on PC computer. The OpenMP platform [8] which is an Application Program Interface (API) that may be used to explicitly direct multi-threaded, shared memory parallelism was employed. Intel i7 processor with 8 cores was used as a platform for simulations. Off-line filter mode was considered. Figure 10 shows the filter operation time for single processor realization. Only one core was employed.

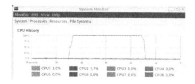

Fig. 10. Computing timing for single processor filter implementation

Figure 11 shows the time of the filter operation for the case when all the 8 cores performed the calculations. Computations acceleration is not linear. This follows from the structure of the filter and how to pass the signal through it (see above).

Another interesting and inexpensive multiprocessor hardware platform are multi-core graphics cards [9]. Graphics Processing Units (GPUs) are high-performance many-core processors capable of very high computation and data

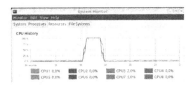

Fig. 11. Computing timing for multiprocessor (8 cores) filter implementation

throughput. GPUs are general-purpose parallel processors with support for accessible programming interfaces and industry-standard languages such as C. Using popular NVIDIA CUDA architecture [10] presented parallel realization of the Volterra-Wiener filter can be performed more efficiently.

5   Conclusion

Multiprocessor systems are becoming increasingly popular today. Their cost is still decreasing, which encourages their use, where high speed processing is needed. Skillful selection the number of computing units and the division of tasks are a key to achieving high performance processing system. The article proposes an efficient way to implement the orthogonal Volterra-Wiener class filter in the multiprocessor structure. Filters operate on-line and off-line were analyzed. It was proposed division of the filter for performing parallel parts. The formula for efficiency measure allows the selection of number of processing units by designers and those responsible for the cost of the Volterra-Wiener filter class system.

References

1. Rabiner, L.: Fundamentals of Speech Recognition. Prentice Hall PTR (1993)
2. Lee, D.T.L., Morf, M., Friedlander, B.: Recursive Least-Squares Ladder Estimation Algorithms. IEEE Trans. on CAS 28, 467–481 (1981)
3. Schetzen, S.: The Voltera & Wiener Theories of nonlinear systems. John Wiley & Sons, New York (1980)
4. Haitsma, J., Kalker, T., Oostveen, J.: Robust audio hashing for content identification. In: Proc. of the Content-Based Multimedia Indexing, Firenze, Italy (September 2001)
5. Biernacki, P.: Orthogonal Schur-type solution of the nonlinear echo-cancelling problem. In: IEEE ICECS 2007, Piscataway, NJ (2007)
6. Biernacki, P., Zarzycki, J.: Multidimensional Nonlinear Noise-Cancelling Filters of the Volterra-Wiener Class. In: Proc. 2-Nd Int. Workshop on Multidimensional (nD) Systems (NDS-2000), pp. 255–261. Inst. of Control and Comp. Eng. TU of Zielona Gora Press, Czocha Castle (2000)
7. Nowak, R.D., Van Veen, B.D.: Random and Pseudorandom Inputs for Volterra Filter Identification. IEEE Trans. on Signal Processing 42(8) (1994)
8. http://www.openmp.org
9. http://www.gpgpu.org
10. http://www.nvidia.com/object/cuda_home_new.html

Fast Parallel Cost Function Calculation
for the Flow Shop Scheduling Problem*

Wojciech Bożejko[1], Mariusz Uchroński[1,2], and Mieczysław Wodecki[3]

[1] Institute of Computer Engineering, Control and Robotics,
Wrocław University of Technology,
Janiszewskiego 11-17, 50-372 Wrocław, Poland
wojciech.bozejko@pwr.wroc.pl
[2] Wrocław Centre of Networking and Supercomputing,
Wyb. Wyspańskiego 27, 50-370 Wrocław, Poland
mariusz.uchronski@pwr.wroc.pl
[3] Institute of Computer Science, University of Wrocław,
Joliot-Curie 15, 50-383 Wrocław, Poland
mwd@ii.uni.wroc.pl

Abstract. In this paper we are proposing a methodology of the fast determination of the objective function for the flow shop scheduling problem in a parallel computing environment. Parallel Random Access Machine (PRAM) model is applied for the theoretical analysis of algorithm's efficiency. The presented method needs a fine-grained parallelization, therefore the proposed approach is especially devoted to parallel computing systems with fast shared memory, such as GPUs.

1 Introduction

We can see the process of jobs flowing through machines (processors) in many practical problems of scheduling: in computer systems as well as in production systems. Thus, the flow shop scheduling problem represents a wide class of possible applications, depending on the cost function definition. For each of them, a corresponding discrete model has to be constructed and analyzed. Some of them (e.g. with the makespan criterion and with total weighted tardiness cost function) have got a special elimination-criteria (so-called *block properties*) which speed up the calculation significantly, especially in the multithread computing environment.

1.1 Formulation of the Problem

The problem has been introduced as follows. There are n jobs from a set $\mathcal{J} = \{1, 2, \ldots, n\}$ to be processed in a production system having m machines, indexed by $1, 2, \ldots, m$, organized in the line (sequential structure). A single job reflects one final product (or sub product) manufacturing. Each job is performed in m

---

* The work was supported by MNiSW Poland, within the grant No. N N514 23223.

L. Rutkowski et al. (Eds.): ICAISC 2012, Part II, LNCS 7268, pp. 378–386, 2012.

subsequent stages, in a way common to all the tasks. The stage i is performed by a machine i, $i = 1, 2, \ldots, m$. Each job $j \in \mathcal{J}$ is split into a sequence of m operations $O_{1j}, O_{2j}, \ldots, O_{mj}$ performed on machines. The operation O_{ij} reflects processing of job j on machine i with processing time $p_{ij} > 0$. Once started the job cannot be interrupted. Each machine can execute at most one job at a time, each job can be processed on at most one machine at a time.

The sequence of loading jobs into a system is represented by a permutation $\pi = (\pi(1), \ldots, \pi(n))$ of elements of the set $\mathcal{J}$. The optimization problem is to find the optimal sequence π^* so that

$$C_{\max}(\pi^*) = \min_{\pi \in \Phi_n} C_{\max}(\pi) \tag{1}$$

where $C_{\max}(\pi)$ is the makespan for a permutation π and Φ_n is the set of all permutations of elements of the set $\mathcal{J}$. Denoted by C_{ij} the completion time of job j on machine i we obtain $C_{\max}(\pi) = C_{m,\pi(n)}$. The values C_{ij} can be found by using either the recursive formula

$$C_{i\pi(j)} = \max\{C_{i-1,\pi(j)}, C_{i,\pi(j-1)}\} + p_{i\pi(j)}, \tag{2}$$

$i = 1, 2, \ldots, m$, $j = 1, 2, \ldots, n$, with initial conditions $C_{i\pi(0)} = 0$, $i = 1, 2, \ldots, m$, $C_{0\pi(j)} = 0$, $j = 1, 2, \ldots, n$, or a non-recursive one

$$C_{i\pi(j)} = \max_{1 = j_0 \leq j_1 \leq \ldots \leq j_i = j} \sum_{s=1}^{i} \sum_{k=j_{i-1}}^{j_i} p_{s\pi(k)}. \tag{3}$$

Computational complexity of (2) is $O(mn)$, whereas for (3) it is

$$O(\binom{j+i-2}{i-1}(j+i-1)) = O(\frac{(n+m)^{n-1}}{(n-1)!}). \tag{4}$$

The former formula has been commonly used in practice. It should be noticed that the problem of transforming sequential algorithm for scheduling problems into parallel one is nontrivial because of the strongly sequential character of computations carried out using (2) and other known scheduling algorithms.

Garey et al. [8] showed that the flow shop problem with makespan criterion $C_{\max}$ is strongly NP-hard for $m \geq 3$ machines. Various serial and parallel local search methods are available. Tabu search algorithms were proposed by Taillard [12], Reeves [11], Nowicki and Smutnicki [10], Grabowski and Wodecki [9]. Bożejko and Wodecki [3] applied this method in the parallel path-relinking method used to solve the flow shop scheduling problem. Bożejko and Wodecki also proposed a parallel scatter search [4] for this problem. Bożejko and Pempera [5] presented a parallel tabu search algorithm for the permutation flow shop problem of minimizing the criterion of the sum of job completion times. Bożejko and Wodecki [6] proposed applying multi-moves in parallel genetic algorithm for the flow shop problem. The theoretical properties of these multi-moves were considered by Bożejko and Wodecki in the paper [7]. A survey of single-walk parallelization methods of the cost function calculation and neighborhood searching for the flow shop problem can be found in Bożejko [1].

1.2   Models

The values C_{ij} from equations (2) and (3) can also be determined by means of a graph model of the flow shop problem. For a given sequence of job execution $\pi \in \Phi_n$ we create a graph $G(\pi) = (M \times J, F^0 \cup F^*)$, where $M = \{1, 2, \ldots, m\}$, $J = \{1, 2, \ldots, n\}$.

$$F^0 = \bigcup_{s=1}^{m-1} \bigcup_{t=1}^{n} \{((s,t), (s+1,t))\} \tag{5}$$

is a set of technological arcs (vertical) and

$$F^* = \bigcup_{s=1}^{m} \bigcup_{t=1}^{n-1} \{((s,t), (s,t+1))\} \tag{6}$$

is a set of sequencing arcs (horizontal).

Arcs of the graph $G(\pi)$ have no weights but each vertex (s,t) has a weight $p_{s\pi(t)}$. A time C_{ij} of finishing a job $\pi(j)$, $j = 1, 2, \ldots, n$ on machine i, $i = 1, 2, \ldots, m$ equals the length of the longest path from vertex $(1,1)$ to vertex (i,j) including the weight of the last one. A sample 'mesh' graph $G(\pi)$ is shown in Fig. 1. The mesh is always the same, vertices weights depend on the π. For the flow shop problem with $C_{\max}$ cost function the value of the criterion function for a fixed sequence π equals the length of the critical path in the graph $G(\pi)$. For the flow shop problem with the C_{sum} criterion the value of the criterion function is the sum of lengths of the longest paths which begin from vertex $(1,1)$ and ends on vertices $(m,1), (m,2), \ldots, (m,n)$.

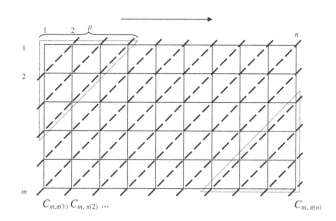

Fig. 1. Scheme of a fast parallel cost function calculation in the flow shop

The graph $G(\pi)$ is also strongly connected with formulas (2) and (3) of completion times C_{ij} calculation. By using formula (2), it is enough to generate consecutive vertices, as dashed lines show (see Fig. 1) taking in the vertex (i,j), connected with the C_{ij}, a greater value from the left vertex, $C_{i,j-1}$, and from the upper one, $C_{i-1,j}$, and adding p_{ij} to it. Such a procedure generates the longest path in the graph $G(\pi)$ in time $O(nm)$. Formula (3) can also be presented as the longest path generation algorithm but its conception is based on the all horizontal sub-paths generation and its computational complexity is exponential.

2 Parallel Cost Function Determination

The recurrent formula (2) is applied to determination times of jobs completion C_{ij} on particular machines. With the use of a single processor, the calculations time T_s of the $C_{i\pi(j)}$ value (according to (2)) is $O(nm)$.

There is a method of times of jobs finishing determination $C_{i\pi(j)}$ ($i = 1, 2, \ldots, m$, $j = 1, 2, \ldots, n$) on the p ($p < m$) -processors CREW PRAM (a theoretical parallel calculations model) in the paper [2]. Without the loss of generality let us assume that $\pi = (1, 2, \ldots, n)$. Calculations of $C_{i,j}$ by using (2) have been clustered. Cluster k contains values C_{ij} such that $i + j - 1 = k$, $k = 1, 2, \ldots, n+m-1$ and requires at most m processors. Clusters are processed in an order $k = 1, 2, \ldots, n + m - 1$. The cluster k is processed in parallel on at most m processors. The sequence of calculations is shown in Fig. 2 on the background of a grid graph commonly used for the flow shop problem. Values linked by dashed lines constitute a single cluster. The value of C_{max} criterion is simple $C_{m,n}$. To calculate $C_{sum} = \sum_{j=1}^{n} C_{m,j}$ we need to add n values $C_{m,j}$, which can be performed sequentially in n iterations or in parallel by using m processors with the complexity $O(n/m + \log m)$. In this case, the calculation time is

$$T_p = \frac{nm}{p} + n + m - 1. \tag{7}$$

As we can see, calculations are made in groups of p processors and there are many situations, in which some part of processors from a group has an *idle time* (iterations 1, 2, 3, 6, 8, 10, 12, 14, 16, 18, 20, 21, 22 in Fig. 2). Therefore, the speedup equals

$$s_p = \frac{T_s}{T_p} = \frac{nm}{\frac{nm}{p} + n + m - 1}. \tag{8}$$

In this case a limiting value of the speedup is

$$\lim_{n \to \infty} s_p = \lim_{n \to \infty} \frac{T_s}{T_p} = \lim_{n \to \infty} \frac{nm}{\frac{nm}{p} + n + m - 1} = \frac{mp}{m + p} = \frac{p}{1 + \frac{p}{m}}. \tag{9}$$

Here we are proposing the new method of calculation of jobs finishing times, in which we fully take advantage of multiprocessor environment by reducing processors idle times. The idea is shown in Fig. 3.

Therefore, in the beginning, the following elements are determined: $C_{1,\pi(1)}$, $C_{1,\pi(2)}, C_{2,\pi(1)}, C_{1,\pi(3)}, C_{2,\pi(2)}, C_{3,\pi(1)}, \ldots, C_{p,\pi(p)}$, $p < m$. These elements create a "triangle" with the width p in the Fig. 1, and their number is $\frac{p(p+1)}{2}$. The time

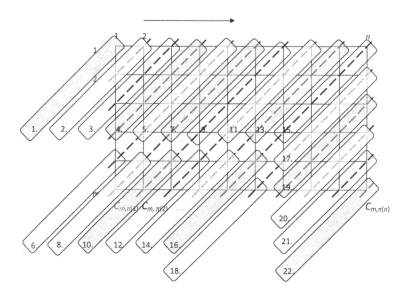

Fig. 2. Scheme of a classic parallel cost function calculation in the flow shop

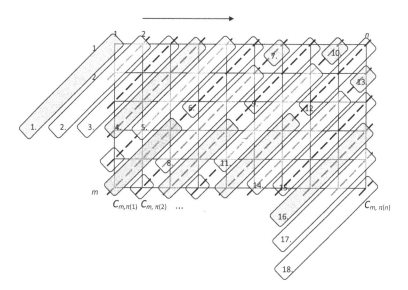

Fig. 3. Scheme of a fast parallel cost function calculation in the flow shop

of its calculation (on the p-processors CREW PRAM)) is p (but there are some idle times, as in iterations 1,2,3 in the Fig. 3). It is obvious, that the number of the symmetric lower right "triangle" is also $\frac{p(p+1)}{2}$. Because the number of all $C_{i,\pi(j)}$, $i = 1, 2, \ldots, n$, $j = 1, 2, \ldots, m$ is nm, so there is $nm - 2\frac{p(p+1)}{2} = nm - p(p+1)$ elements out of both "triangles". We do not generate idle times inside the region between "triangles" because if a group of processors calculates elements on the bottom of the graph, including the lowest element $C_{m,\pi(k)}$, for some k, then the rest of the processors, which normally have an idle time, calculates elements $C_{1,\pi(k+m-1)}$, $C_{2,\pi(k+m-3)}$, etc.

The time of calculations of the region between "triangles", in accordance with the scheme presented in Fig. 3, is $\frac{nm-p(p+1)}{p}$ on p-processors CREW PRAM. Therefore, the total calculations time, including "triangles", is

$$T_p^\circ = \frac{p(p+1)}{2} + \frac{nm - p(p+1)}{p} + \frac{p(p+1)}{2} = p(p+1) + \frac{nm - p(p+1)}{p} \quad (10)$$

and consequently the speedup equals

$$s_p^\circ = \frac{T_s}{T_p^\circ} = \frac{nm}{p(p+1) + \frac{nm-p(p+1)}{p}}. \quad (11)$$

However, the limiting value of this speedup is

$$\lim_{n\to\infty} s_p^\circ = \lim_{n\to\infty} \frac{T_s}{T_p^\circ} = \lim_{n\to\infty} \frac{nm}{p(p+1) + \frac{nm-p(p+1)}{p}} = \quad (12)$$

$$= \lim_{n\to\infty} \frac{nm}{p^2(p+1) + nm - p(p+1)} = p. \quad (13)$$

Thus, we have obtained a much better limiting speedup comparing to the method taken from the paper [2].

3   Experimental Results

The parallel algorithm of calculating goal function in permutation flow shop problem was coded in C(CUDA) for GPU, ran on the 1792-processors nVidia Tesla S2050 GPU and tested on the benchmark problems of Taillard [12]. The GPU was installed on the server based on Intel Core i7 3.33GHz processor working under 64-bit Ubuntu 10.04 operating system. The algorithm considered uses $m - 1$ GPU processors for calculating a makespan. Its sequential version is obtained by assigning $p = 1$ and is also executed on GPU. The sequential algorithm, using one GPU processor, was coded with the aim of determining the speedup value of the parallel algorithm. Table 1 shows computational times for the sequential and parallel algorithm as well as a speedup. The value of a relative speedup s can be found by the following expression $s = \frac{t_s}{t_p}$, where t_s - the computational time of sequential algorithm executed on the single GPU processor,

t_p - the computational time of parallel algorithm executed on p GPU processors. As we can notice the highest average speedup values were obtained for the problem instances with bigger number of jobs n and bigger number of machines m, because in these cases the influence of "triangles" regions (described in the Section 2) on the total parallel computations is the lowest, from the theoretical point of view.

Table 1. Experimental results for Taillard's instances

$n \times m$	p	$t_p[ms]$	$t_s[ms]$	speedup s
20×5	4	0.0237	0.0665	2.7998
20×10	9	0.0293	0.1461	4.9792
20×20	19	0.0463	0.3694	7.9685
50×5	4	0.0539	0.1583	2.9336
50×10	9	0.0676	0.3356	4.9642
50×20	19	0.1039	0.7460	7.1753
100×5	4	0.1033	0.3157	3.0548
100×10	9	0.1243	0.6460	5.1939
100×20	19	0.1844	1.3762	7.4627
200×10	9	0.2387	1.2717	5.3267
200×20	19	0.3445	2.6378	7.6555
500×20	19	0.8248	6.3980	7.7567

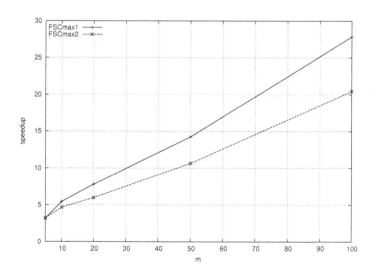

Fig. 4. Speedup comparison

The proposed parallel algorithm has been compared with another parallel algorithm for calculating makespan in permutation flow shop from [2]. Fig. 4 shows a speedup obtained by a parallel algorithm from [2] – FSCmax2 and a speedup obtained by a proposed algorithm – FSCmax1. Compared algorithms were tested on the test instances with a big number of jobs ($m = 500$) and a different number of machines ($m = 10, 20, 50, 100$). For both algorithms the speedup value increases with the number of machines. For the FSCmax1 algorithm the speedup is bigger than the speedup for FSCmax2 algorithm.

4   Conclusions

The method proposed in this paper can be used for computations' acceleration in metaheuristics solving the flow shop scheduling problem. The calculation time of goal function in algorithms which solve the job shop problem take even over 90% of the whole algorithm computation time, so the use of parallel algorithm for goal function calculation might result in significant decreasing of algorithm execution time for solving the flow shop problem. The theoretical results proposed here were fully confirmed by the conducted computational experiments.

References

1. Bożejko, W.: A new class of parallel scheduling algorithms. Monographs series. Wroclaw University of Technology Publishing House (2010)
2. Bożejko, W., Smutnicki, C., Uchroński, M.: Parallel Calculating of the Goal Function in Metaheuristics Using GPU. In: Allen, G., Nabrzyski, J., Seidel, E., van Albada, G.D., Dongarra, J., Sloot, P.M.A. (eds.) ICCS 2009, Part I. LNCS, vol. 5544, pp. 1014–1023. Springer, Heidelberg (2009)
3. Bożejko, W., Wodecki, M.: Parallel Path-Relinking Method for the Flow Shop Scheduling Problem. In: Bubak, M., van Albada, G.D., Dongarra, J., Sloot, P.M.A. (eds.) ICCS 2008, Part I. LNCS, vol. 5101, pp. 264–273. Springer, Heidelberg (2008)
4. Bożejko, W., Wodecki, M.: Parallel Scatter Search Algorithm for the Flow Shop Sequencing Problem. In: Wyrzykowski, R., Dongarra, J., Karczewski, K., Wasniewski, J. (eds.) PPAM 2007. LNCS, vol. 4967, pp. 180–188. Springer, Heidelberg (2008)
5. Bożejko, W., Pempera, J.: Parallel Tabu Search Algorithm for the Permutation Flow Shop Problem with Criterion of Minimizing Sum of Job Completion Times. In: Conference on Human System Interaction HSI 2008. IEEE Computer Society (2008) 1-4244-1543-8/08/(c)2008 IEEE
6. Bożejko, W., Wodecki, M.: Applying Multi-Moves in Parallel Genetic Algorithm for the Flow Shop Problem. In: Computation in Modern Science and Engineering: Proceedings of the International Conference on Computational Methods in Science and Engineering 2007 (ICCMSE 2007): Volume 2, Part B. AIP Conference Proceedings, vol. 963, pp. 1162–1165 (2007)
7. Bożejko, W., Wodecki, M.: On the theoretical properties of swap multimoves. Operations Research Letters 35(2), 227–231 (2007)
8. Garey, M.R., Johnson, D.S., Seti, R.: The complexity of flowshop and jobshop scheduling. Mathematics of Operations Research 1, 117–129 (1976)

9. Grabowski, J., Wodecki, M.: A very fast tabu search algorithm for the permutation flow shop problem with makespan criterion. Computers & Operations Research 31, 1891–1909 (2004)

10. Nowicki, E., Smutnicki, C.: A fast tabu search algorithm for the permutation flow shop problem. European Journal of Operational Research 91, 160–175 (1996)

11. Reeves, C.: Improving the Efficiency of Tabu Search for Machine Sequencing Problems. Journal of Operational Research Society 44(4), 375–382 (1993)

12. Taillard, E.: Some efficient heuristic methods for the flow shop sequencing problem. European Journal of Operational Research 47(1), 65–74 (1990)

Solving the Flexible Job Shop Problem on GPU

Wojciech Bożejko[1], Mariusz Uchroński[1,2], and Mieczysław Wodecki[3]

[1] Institute of Computer Engineering, Control and Robotics,
Wrocław University of Technology,
Janiszewskiego 11-17, 50-372 Wrocław, Poland
wojciech.bozejko@pwr.wroc.pl
[2] Wrocław Centre of Networking and Supercomputing,
Wyb. Wyspańskiego 27, 50-370 Wrocław, Poland
mariusz.uchronski@pwr.wroc.pl
[3] Institute of Computer Science, University of Wrocław,
Joliot-Curie 15, 50-383 Wrocław, Poland
mwd@ii.uni.wroc.pl

Abstract. In this work we examine a model of flexible job shop problem in which for a given operation there is a possibility of a choice of the machine on which this operation will be carried out. This problem is a generalization of the classic job shop problem. We present a tabu search algorithm in which "a golf neighborhood" was applied. Because it is a huge neighborhood, the concurrent programming tools based on GPU platform were thus used to its searching. The computational results indicate that by acceleration of computations with the utilization of GPU one obtains very good values of a speedup. Computational experiments executed on benchmark instances show the efficiency of this approach.

1   Introduction

There is a set of tasks and machines of various types given. A flexible job shop problem (FJS problem in short) consists in assigning tasks to adequate machines and determining an optimal sequence of its execution. Machines of the same type, that is executing only one type of operation, create production nests. Tasks' operations must be executed on adequate machines in a fixed order called a production itinerary. For each operation there is created a nest in which this operation will be carried out. Thus, the times of execution of operations are given.

FJS problem consists in assigning operations to machines and defining the sequence of their execution in order to minimize the time of finishing tasks' completion ($C_{\max}$). The problem presented in this work also belongs to the strongly NP -hard class.

Although the exact algorithms based on a disjunctive graph representation of the solution have been developed (see Adrabiński and Wodecki [1], Pinedo [8]), they are not effective for instances with more than 20 jobs and 10 machines. From metaheuristic algorithms, Nowicki and Smutnicki [7] proposed a tabu search approach using block properties for the special case of the considered problem.

L. Rutkowski et al. (Eds.): ICAISC 2012, Part II, LNCS 7268, pp. 387–394, 2012.

2 Flexible Job Shop Problem

A flexible job shop problem (FJSP), also called a general job shop problem with parallel machines, can be formulated as follows. Let $\mathcal{J} = \{1, 2, \ldots, n\}$ be a set of jobs which have to be executed on machines from the set $\mathcal{M} = \{1, 2, \ldots, m\}$. There exists a partition of the set of machines into types, i.e. subsets of machines with the same functional properties. A job constitutes a sequence of some operations. Each operation has to be executed on an adequate type of machine (nest) within a fixed time. The problem consists in allocating the jobs to machines of an adequate type and scheduling of jobs execution determination on each machine to minimize a total jobs' finishing time ($C_{\max}$).

Let $\mathcal{O} = \{1, 2, \ldots, o\}$ be the set of all operations. This set can be partitioned into sequences which correspond to jobs where the job $j \in \mathcal{J}$ is a sequence of o_j operations which have to be executed in an order on dedicated machines.

The set of machines $\mathcal{M} = \{1, 2, \ldots, m\}$ can be partitioned into q subsets of the same type (*nests*) where i-th type $\mathcal{M}^i$. An operation $v \in \mathcal{O}$ has to be executed on the machines type $\mu(v)$, i.e. on one of the machines from the set (nest) $\mathcal{M}^{\mu(v)}$ in the time $p_{v,j}$ where $j \in \mathcal{M}^{\mu(v)}$. Let

$$\mathcal{O}^k = \{v \in \mathcal{O}: \ \mu(v) = k\}$$

be a set of operations executed in the k-th nest ($k = 1, 2, \ldots, q$). A sequence of operations sets being a partition of $\mathcal{O}$ (pair-disjoint)

$$\mathcal{Q} = [\mathcal{Q}^1, \mathcal{Q}^2, \ldots, \mathcal{Q}^m],$$

we call an *assignment of operations from the set $\mathcal{O}$ to machines from the set $\mathcal{M}$*.

For an assignment of operation $\mathcal{Q}$, let $\pi(\mathcal{Q}) = (\pi_1(\mathcal{Q}), \pi_2(\mathcal{Q}), \ldots, \pi_m(\mathcal{Q}))$ where $\pi_i(\mathcal{Q})$ is a permutation of operations executed on a machine M_i. Any feasible solution of the FJSP is a pair $(\mathcal{Q}, \pi(\mathcal{Q}))$ where $\mathcal{Q}$ is an assignment of operations to machines and $\pi(Q)$ is a permutations concatenation determining the operations execution sequence which are assigned to each machine (see [3]).

3 Solution Method

There is an exponential number of possible jobs to machines assignments, due to the number of operations. Each feasible assignment generates a NP-hard problem (job shop) whose solution consists in determining an optimal jobs execution order on machines. One has to solve an exponential number of NP-hard problems.

Therefore, we will apply an approximate algorithm based on the tabu search method. The main element of this approach is a neighborhood – subsets of all feasible solutions set, generated from the current solution by transformations called *moves*. By searching a neighborhood we choose an element with the lowest cost function value, which we take as a new current solution in the next iteration of the algorithm. It is possible to generate another solution from the fixed solutiont by executing a move which consists in:

1. moving (transferring) an operation from one machine into another machine in the same nest (of the same type), or
2. changing operations execution order on machines.

Let $\Theta = (\mathcal{Q}, \pi(\mathcal{Q}))$ be a feasible solution, where $\mathcal{Q} = [\mathcal{Q}^1, \mathcal{Q}^2, \ldots, \mathcal{Q}^m]$ is an assignment of operations to machines, ϱ_i is a number of operations executed on a machine M_i (i.e. $\pi(\mathcal{Q}) = (\pi_1(\mathcal{Q}), \pi_2(\mathcal{Q}), \ldots, \pi_m(\mathcal{Q}))$ is a concatenation of m permutations). A permutation $\pi_i(\mathcal{Q})$ determines an order of operations from the set $\mathcal{Q}^i$ which have to be executed on the machine M_i.

3.1   Transfer Type Moves

By $t^i_j(k, l)$ we define a *transfer* type move (*t-move*) which consist in moving of an operation from the position k in a permutation π_i into position l in a permutation $\pi_j(k)$. Execution of the move $t^i_j(k, l)$ generates from $\Theta = (\mathcal{Q}, \pi)$ a new solution $\Theta' = (\mathcal{Q}', \pi')$. Its computational complexity is $O(n)$.

If τ is a *t-move*, then we define a solution generated from Θ by execution of the τ move by $\tau(\Theta)$. It is possible that the solution $\tau(\Theta)$ is not feasible.

Let Θ be a feasible solution. The set

$$T^i_j(\Theta) = \{t^i_j(k, l) : \ k \in Q^i \text{ and } l \in Q^j\}$$

includes all *t-moves* which transfers operations from a machine M_i into a machine M_j and

$$T(\Theta) = \sum_{i,j}^m T^i_j(\Theta)$$

includes all *t-moves* for the solution Θ. The number of elements of this set has an upper bound $O(qm^2o^2)$.

3.2   Insert Type Moves

In order to simplify the problem, let us assume that a permutation $\pi = (\pi(1), \pi(2), \ldots, \pi(t))$ determines an operations' execution order on a machine.

Insert type move i^k_l (*i-move*) is moving an element $\pi(k)$ into the position l, generating a permutation $i^k_l(\pi) = \pi^k_l$. The number of all such moves (for a determined machines) is $t(t-1)$. For a fixed feasible solution Θ, let $\mathcal{I}_k(\Theta)$ be a set of all *i-moves* for the machine $M_k \in \mathcal{M}$ and let

$$I(\Theta) = \sum_{k=1}^m \mathcal{I}_k(\Theta)$$

be a set of all *i-moves* on all machines.

3.3   Graph Models

Any feasible solution $\Theta = (\mathcal{Q}, \pi(\mathcal{Q}))$ determining the operations' execution sequence on each machine) of the FJSP can be presented as a directed graph with weighted vertices $G(\Theta) = (V, \mathcal{R} \cup \mathcal{E}(\Theta))$ where V is a set of vertices and a $\mathcal{R} \cup \mathcal{E}(\Theta)$ is a set of arcs, with:

1) $V = \mathcal{O} \cup \{s, c\}$, where s and c are additional operations which represent 'start' and 'finish', respectively. A vertex $v \in V$ possesses two attributes:
   - $\lambda(v)$ – a number of machines on which an operation v has to be executed,
   - $p_{v,\lambda(v)}$ – a weight of vertex which equals the time of operation $v \in \mathcal{O}$ execution on the assigned machine $\lambda(v)$ ($p_s = p_c = 0$).

2) A set $\mathcal{R}$ includes arcs which connect successive operations of the job, arcs from vertex s to the first operation of each job and arcs from the last operation of each job to vertex c.

3) Arcs from the set $\mathcal{E}(\Theta)$ connect operations executed on the same machine.

Arcs from the set $\mathcal{R}$ determine the operations execution sequence inside jobs and arcs from the set $\mathcal{E}(\pi)$ the operations execution sequence on each machine.

Remark 1. *A pair $\Theta = (\mathcal{Q}, \pi(\mathcal{Q}))$ is a feasible solution for the FJSP if and only if the graph $G(\Theta)$ does not include cycles.*

3.4   Golf Neighborhood

A transfer type move is like a long shot in golf: it moves an operation into other machines. In turn, an insert type move makes only a little modification of operation sequence on machines. An inspiration to these researches was a paper of Bożejko and Wodecki [2] which considered multimoves.

Let Θ be a feasible solution and let $\mathcal{T}(\Theta)$ be a set of all *t-moves*. We consider the move $t_j^i(k, l) \in \mathcal{T}(\Theta)$. It transfers an operation from the position k-th on the machine M_i into a position l-th on the machine M_j. This move generates the solution $\Theta' = t_j^i(k, l)(\Theta)$. The set $\mathcal{I}(\Theta')$ includes all *i-moves* connected with a solution Θ' and $\mathcal{I}_j(\Theta')$ – *i-moves* defined on operations executed on the machine M_j. Let $i_t^s \in \mathcal{I}_j(\Theta')$ be an *i-move*. Its execution generates a new solution $\Theta'' = i_t^s(\Theta')$. The transformation which generates a solution Θ'' from the Θ we call an *it-multimove*. It constitutes a product of the *t-move* $t_j^i(k, l)$ and *i-move* i_t^s. We will denote this move shortly as $i_t^s \circ t_j^i(k, l)$. Therefore $\Theta'' = i_t^s \circ t_j^i(k, l)(\Theta)$.

By $\mathcal{I} \circ \mathcal{T}(\Theta)$ we denote a set of all *it-multimoves* determined for a solution Θ. *The golf neighborhood Θ is the set*

$$\mathcal{N}(\Theta) = \{\lambda(\Theta) : \ \lambda \in \mathcal{I} \circ \mathcal{T}(\Theta)\}. \tag{1}$$

In the paper Bożejko et al. [3] a so-called elimination criterion was proved. It allows to eliminate all *i-moves* and *t-moves*, which generate unfeasible solutions. Moreover, multimoves are generating solutions, for which the cost function value is not less than $C_{\max}(\Theta)$ are also eliminated. Such a determined golf neighborhood will be applied to the tabu search algorithm.

3.5   Neighborhood Determination

Execution of a *t-move* can lead to a non-feasible solution, i.e., a graph connected with this solution can have a cycle. Therefore, checking feasibility equals checking if a graph has a cycle.

Let $\Theta = (\mathcal{Q}, \pi)$ be a feasible solution. We consider two machines M_i and M_j from the same nest. A permutation π_i determines a processing order of operations from the set $\mathcal{Q}^i$ on the machine M_i and π_j – a processing order of operations from the set $\mathcal{Q}^j$. For an operation $\pi_i(k) \in \mathcal{Q}^i$ we define two parameters connected with paths in the graph $G(\Theta)$. The first parameter is

$$
\eta_j(k) = \begin{cases} 1, \text{ if there is no path } C(\pi_j(v), \pi_i(k)) \; \forall\, v = 1, 2, \ldots, \varrho_j, \\ 1 + \max_{1 \le v \le \varrho_j} \{\text{there is a path } C(\pi_j(v), \pi_i(k))\}, \text{ otherwise.} \end{cases} \tag{2}
$$

Thus, there is no path to the operation (vertex) $\pi_i(k)$ from any of the operations placed in the permutation π_j in positions $\eta_j(k)$, $\eta_j(k) + 1, \ldots, \varrho_j$.

The second parameter is

$$
\rho_j(k) = \begin{cases} 1 + \varrho_j, \text{ if there is no path } C(\pi_j(v), \pi_i(k)) \; \forall\, v = 1, 2, \ldots, \varrho_j, \\ 1 + \min_{\eta_j(k) \le v \le \varrho_j} \{\text{there is a path } C(\pi_i(k), \pi_j(v))\}, \text{ otherwise.} \end{cases} \tag{3}
$$

From the definition formulated above it follows that in the graph there is no path from a vertex $\pi_i(k)$ to any operation placed in positions $\eta_j(k), \eta_j(k)+1, \ldots, \rho_j(k)$ in the permutation π_j.

Theorems for characterizing a *t-moves* whose execution generates an unfeasible solutions can be found in our previous work [3]. The structure of assumptions allows an easy implementation in the parallel computing environment, such as GPUs. Basically, in order to check solution feasibility the information about the longest paths between all vertexes in graph connected with flexible job shop problem solution are needed. Calculating the longest paths between all vertexes in graph (Floyd–Warshall algorithm) with sequential algorithm takes the time $O(o^3)$. Parallel algorithm using o^2 processors calculate the longest paths between all vertexes in graph with the time $O(o)$. This algorithm can be easily implemented in the parallel computation environment such as GPU.

4   Computational Experiments

Proposed algorithm for the flexible job shop problem was coded in C++ and C(CUDA) and run on HP workstation with CPU and NVIDIA GTX480 GPU. Algorithms were tested on the set of benchmark problem instances taken from Brandimarte [5]. Table 1 shows computational times for parallelized part of golf neighborhood determination procedure. Particular columns in Table 1 denote:

- p - number of GPU threads,
- t_s - computational time for sequential algorithm on CPU,
- t_p - computational time for parallel algorithm on GPU,
- s - speedup. A measured speedup increases with a number of processors (in all cases it is greater than one) but still quite small in comparison with a number of used GPU processors. There are two reasons for a relative small speedup in considered parallel GPU algorithm. Firstly, it is connected with the time needed for transferring data between CPU and GPU. This is a well known bottleneck of GPU computations. The second reason is an unoptimized access to the GPU memory during computation for this particular implementation.

Table 1. Speedup for parallelized part of algorithm

problem	p	$t_s[ms]$	$t_p[ms]$	s
Mk01	55	5.98876	4.32949	1.38325
Mk02	58	7.09983	4.46129	1.59143
Mk03	150	154.99	15.8564	9.7746
Mk04	90	29.8697	7.68228	3.88813
Mk05	106	51.3419	9.52336	5.39115
Mk06	150	150.047	16.5776	9.05119
Mk07	100	43.043	8.79722	4.8928
Mk08	225	517.379	25.3213	20.4326
Mk09	240	628.237	27.3808	22.9444
Mk10	240	637.619	27.6397	23.069

A parallel speedup of the algorithm is a measure of the success of the parallelization process. All algorithms contain some parts that can be parallelized and some parts which cannot undergo this process. The time spent in the parallelized parts of the algorithm is reduced by using increasing number of processors, but the sequential parts remain the same. Finally, the execution time of the algorithm is dominated by the time taken to compute the sequential part, which is an upper limit of the expected speedup. This effect is known as Amdahl's law and can be formulated as [6] $s = \frac{1}{(f_{par}/p+(1+f_{par}))}$ where f_{par} is parallel fraction of the code and p is the number of processors.

We compare a theoretical speedup (calculated with Amdahl's law) of proposed tabu search algorithm with an experimentally measured speedup. Table 2 shows our results. Particular columns in Table 2 denote:

- f_{par} - parallel fraction of the metaheuristic,
- s_t - theoretical speedup calculated with Amdahl's law,
- s_e - speedup measured experimentally.

For small values of the parallel fraction of the code (Mk02, Mk04 and Mk06) the difference between theoretical and experimentally measured speedup is small.

Table 2. Tabu search algorithm speedup

problem	p	f_{par}	$t_s[s]$	$t_p[s]$	s_t	s_e
Mk01	55	0.70098	0.85433	0.71478	3.20757	1.19523
Mk02	58	0.20656	3.43712	3.09198	1.25471	1.11162
Mk03	150	0.90118	17.1986	3.23384	9.53945	5.31832
Mk04	90	0.32281	9.25294	7.65297	1.46892	1.20907
Mk05	106	0.88954	5.77173	1.59326	8.4139	3.62259
Mk06	150	0.02064	247.16	254.661	1.02093	0.97054
Mk07	100	0.80061	5.37627	1.97047	4.82169	2.72842
Mk08	225	0.97586	53.0176	3.78734	35.1208	13.9986
Mk09	240	0.84383	74.4503	14.4714	6.26241	5.14465
Mk10	240	0.78271	81.4627	20.2549	4.53415	4.02188

5 GPU Implementation Details

In our tabu search algorithm for flexible job shop problem we adopt Floyd-Warshall algorithm for computing the longest path between each pair of nodes in a graph. The main idea of the algorithm is as follows. Find the longest path

```
1   extern "C" void FindPathsOnGPU(const int &o, int *graph)
2   {
3     int *graphDev;
4     const int dataSize = (o+1)*(o+1)*sizeof(int);
5     const int size=(int)(log((double)o)/log(2.0));
6     dim3 threads(o+1);
7     dim3 blocks(o+1);
8     cudaMalloc( (void**) &graphDev, dataSize);
9     cudaMemcpy( graphDev, graph, dataSize, cudaMemcpyHostToDevice);
10    for (int iter=1; iter <= size+1; ++iter)
11    {
12      for(int k=0; k<=o; ++k)
13      {
14        PathsKernel<<<blocks, threads>>>(o, graphDev, k);
15        cudaThreadSynchronize();
16      }
17    }
18    cudaMemcpy( graph, graphDev, dataSize, cudaMemcpyDeviceToHost);
19    cudaFree(graphDev);
20  }
```

Fig. 1. CUDA implementation of computing the longest path in a graph

```
1   __global__ void PathsKernel(const int o, int *graph, const int i)
2   {
3     int x = threadIdx.x;
4     int y = blockIdx.x;
5     int k = i;
6     int yXwidth = y * (o+1);
7
8     int dYtoX = graph[yXwidth + x];
9     int dYtoK = graph[yXwidth + k];
10    int dKtoX = graph[k*(o+1) + x];
11
12    int indirectDistance = dYtoK + dKtoX;
13    int max = 0;
14    int tmp = 0;
15
16    if(dYtoK !=0 and dKtoX !=0)
17    {
18      tmp = indirectDistance;
19      if(max < tmp)
20        max = tmp;
21    }
22    if(dYtoX < max)
23    {
24      graph[yXwidth + x] = max;
25    }
26  }
```

Fig. 2. CUDA kernel

between node v_i and v_j containing the node v_k. It consist of a sub-path from v_i to v_k and a sub-path v_k to v_j. This idea can be formulated as follows: $d_{ij}^{(k)} = \max\{d_{ij}^{(k-1)}, d_{ik}^{(k-1)} + d_{kj}^{(k-1)}\}$ where $d_{ij}^{(k)}$ is the longest path from v_i to v_j such that all intermediate nodes on the path are in set $v_1, \ldots, v_k$. Figure 1 shows CUDA implementation of of computing the longest path between each pair of nodes. The CUDA kernel (Figure 2) is invoked o times, where o is the number of nodes in the graph. At the k-th iteration, the kernel computes two values for every pair of nodes in the graph. The direct distance between them and the indirect distance through node v_k. The larger of the two distances is written back to the distance matrix. The final distance matrix reflects the lengths of the longest paths between each pair of nodes. The inputs of the CUDA kernel are the number of the graph nodes, path distance matrix and the iteration (step) number.

6   Conclusions

We present the tabu search based algorithm with the golf neighborhood for the flexible job shop problem. In the golf neighborhood generation procedure parallel GPU acceleration has been applied, which allows to obtain an absolute speedup (in comparison to CPU) for each tested algorithm bigger than 1, and in extreme cases even the 14th times bigger.

Acknowledgement. The work was partially supported by the Polish Ministry of Science and Higher Education, grant N N514 232237.

References

1. Adrabiński, A., Wodecki, M.: An algorithm for solving the machine sequencing problem with parallel machines. Applicationes Mathematicae XVI 3, 513–541 (1979)
2. Bożejko, W., Wodecki, M.: On the theoretical properties of swap multimoves. Operations Research Letters 35(2), 227–231 (2007)
3. Bożejko, W., Uchroński, M., Wodecki, M.: Parallel hybrid metaheuristics for the flexible job shop problem. Computers and Industrial Engineering 59, 323–333 (2010)
4. Bożejko, W., Uchroński, M., Wodecki, M.: The new golf neighborhood for the flexible job shop problem. Procedia Computer Science 1, 289–296 (2010)
5. Brandimarte, P.: Routing and scheduling in a flexible job shop by tabu search. Annals of Operations Research 41, 157–183 (1993)
6. Chapman, B., Jost, G., van der Pas, R.: Using OpenMP Portable Shared Memory Parallel Programming. The MIT Press (2007)
7. Nowicki, E., Smutnicki, C.: The flow shop with parallel machines: A tabu search approach. European Journal of Operational Research 106, 226–253 (1998)
8. Pinedo, M.: Scheduling: theory, algorithms and systems. Prentice-Hall, Englewood Cliffs (2002)

Automatic Privatization for Parallel Execution of Loops

Palkowski Marek

Faculty of Computer Science, West Pomeranian University of Technology,
70210, Zolnierska 49, Szczecin, Poland
mpalkowski@wi.zut.edu.pl
http://kio.wi.zut.edu.pl/

Abstract. Privatization of data is an important technique that has been used by compilers to parallelize loops by eliminating storage-related dependences. The code can be executed on multi-processors machines in reduced period of time. In this paper, we present an approach to automatic privatization of variables involved in data dependences that permits for extracting loop parallelism. The input of the algorithm is a set of relation dependences, the output is a parallel loop when appropriate. The scope of the applicability of the approach is illustrated by means of the NAS Parallel Benchmark suite. Received results are compared with those produced by the tool Pluto. Future work is outlined.

Keywords: automatic privatization, fine- and coarse-grained parallelism, loop parallelization, NAS Parallel Benchmark.

1 Introduction

The lack of automated tools permitting for exposing parallelism for multicore and multiprocessor systems decreases the productivity of programmers and increases the time and cost of producing the parallel program. Because most computations are contained in program loops, automatic extraction of parallelism from loops is extremely important, allowing us to produce parallel code from existing sequential applications and to create multiple threads that can be easily scheduled to achieve high program performance.

Different techniques have been developed to extract coarse-grained parallelism that is represented with synchronization-free slices of computations available in loops, for example, those presented in papers [1,2]. Unfortunately, these techniques very often fail to parallelize complex loops exposing hundreds storage-related dependence relations. Hence, potential parallelism is left unexploited in some cases.

In this paper, we demonstrate the automatic privatization of variables in loops that permits for extracting fine- and coarse-grained parallelism. The variables can stand for scalars or arrays. Proposed algorithms reduce loop dependences and find parallelism when appropriate. Furthermore, privatization may extend applicability of other loop transformations.

L. Rutkowski et al. (Eds.): ICAISC 2012, Part II, LNCS 7268, pp. 395–403, 2012.

There are many techniques of privatization using theory of graphs or solving systems of equations [3,12,13]. In this paper, a loop dependences analysis obtained from the Petit tool [4], is used. The dependences are presented in the form of relations. Proposed algorithms are applicable to the arbitrarily nested parameterized loop. Cases of loops, which cannot be successfully parallelized by the automatic parallelizer - Pluto [6], are analysed. Experimental results are presented exposing speed-up and efficiency of parallel programs generated in the OpenMP standard [5] by the tool implementing the proposed approach.

2   Background

In this paper, we deal with affine loop nests where, for given loop indices, lower and upper bounds as well as array subscripts and conditionals are affine functions of surrounding loop indices and possibly of structure parameters, and the loop steps are known constants.

Dependence analysis is required for the correct loop parallelization. Two statement instances I and J are *dependent* if both access the same memory location and if at least one access is a write. I and J are called the *source* and *destination* of a dependence, respectively, provided that I is lexicographically smaller than J ($I \prec J$, i.e., I is executed before J).

There are three types of data dependence: flow dependence, anti-dependence, and output dependence [3,9].

- flow dependence (or true dependence) - data dependence from an assignment to a use of a variable.
- anti dependence - data dependence from a use of a variable to a later reassignment of that variable.
- output dependence - data dependence from an assignment of a variable to a later reassignment of that variable.

Our approach requires an exact dependence analysis which detects a dependence if and only if it actually exists. To describe and implement our algorithm, the dependence analysis proposed by Pugh and Wonnacott [10] and the tool Petit [4], were chosen. Petit provides the data about loop dependences: a type, relations, distance and direction vectors and numbers of code lines representing dependence sources and destinations.

A dependence relation is a tuple relation of the form [*input list*]→[*output list*]: *formula*, where *input list* and *output list* are the lists of variables and/or expressions used to describe input and output tuples and *formula* describes the constraints imposed upon *input list* and *output list* and it is a Presburger formula built of constraints represented with algebraic expressions and using logical and existential operators.

Privatization is a technique that allows each concurrent thread to allocate a variable in its private storage such that each thread access a distinct instance of a variable. Since deleting loop-carried dependences can convert sequential loops into parallel loops, privatization is an important transformation in increasing coarse-grained parallelism.

Definition 1. A scalar variable x defined within a loop is said to be privatizable with respect to that loop if and only if every path from the beginning of the loop body to a use of x within that body must pass through a definition of x before reaching that use [3].

As an example, consider the simple example:

```
for(i=1; i<=N; i++)
{
s1:   t = A[i];
s2:   A[i] = B[i];
s3:   B[i] = t;
}
```

Dependences calculated with Petit are as follows:

```
flow      s1: t   -->   s3: t
output    s1: t   -->   s1: t
anti      s3: t   -->   s1: t
```

Because of the loop carried dependences, the loop is not parallelizable as it is currently formulated. Fortunately, all of the carried dependences are due to assignments and uses of the scalar variable t. All of these carried dependences go away if each iteration has its own copy of the variable t.

In the next section, algorithms for automatic privatization of variables in loops using the dependence analysis implemented in the Petit tool, are presented.

3   Automatic Privatization of Loop Variables

This section presents algorithms which realize scalar variables privatization using the analysis of loop dependences implemented in Petit. The main idea is checking whether a variable in the loop body is initialized before a use. For this purpose, *anti* dependences are examined. The variable cannot be privatized if there exists any *anti* dependence source refers to that variable and represents the smallest number of a line of the loop code. Otherwise, the variable can be privatized and corresponded dependences can be removed. The approach can be used also for array variables, when each item of an array (found with the Petit dependence analysis) is treated as a single item of memory, like a scalar variable. Parallel code is achieved when the output set of dependence relations is empty. Otherwise, other techniques of loop parallelization must be considered.

The proposed approach can be used prior applying other loop transformation, e.g. [11]. This will permit for receiving of a reduced set of dependence relations. Below the privatization algorithm is presented. Let us analyse the following example:

Algorithm 1. Finding synchronization-free parallelism using privatization in loops

---

Input : Set of loop-carried dependence relations, S; set of originating dependences variables, V

Output : Modified set S of dependence relations, parallel code if S is empty

  1 **for each** variable X in set V **do**

      1.1 $y = \text{MIN}(\text{NumLines}(X, S))$
      1.2 **for each** dependence relation R in set S **do**
          if $\text{Type}(R) = anti$ **and** $R(\text{sour}) = X$ **and** $R(\text{dest}) = X$ **and** $\text{LinSour}(R) \leq y$ **then**
          $\text{Private}(X) = \text{FALSE}$, goto 1.
          else
          $\text{Private}(X) = \text{True}$
          Remove all the relation dependences satisfying the condition:
          $R(\text{sour}) = X$ **and** $R(\text{dest}) = X$
          end if
          end for

    end for
  2 **if** $S = \varnothing$ **then** privatize all index variables and parallelize the outermost loop
      else use other technique, e.g. [1,2,11].
    end if

NumLines(X, S): the set of numbers of lines in code, where variable X originates a source or destination described by all dependence relations in set S

R(sour / dest): the variable, which refers to a source/destination of a dependence is described by relation R

Type(R): the kind of a dependence relation R (*flow/anti/output*)

LineSour(R): the number of a line in code which refers to the source of a dependence R

```
0: # parallel for private(ntemp, iel, j, i) //Added by Algorithm 1
1: for iel=1 to N1 do
2:   ntemp=lx1*lx1*lx1*(iel-1)  //s1
3:   for j=1 to N2 do
4:     for i=1 to N3 do
5:       idel(i,j,1,iel)=ntemp+(i-1)*lx1 + (j-1)*lx1*lx1+lx1 //s2
6:       idel(i,j,2,iel)=ntemp+(i-1)*lx1 + (j-1)*lx1*lx1+1   //s3
7:     endfor
8:   endfor
9: endfor
```

Applying the presented algorithm results in the following outcome.
input:
Set S:
flow 2: ntemp $\rightarrow$ 5: ntemp

flow 2: ntemp → 6: ntemp
anti 5: ntemp ↛ 2: ntemp
anti 6: ntemp ↛ 2: ntemp
output 2: ntemp → 2: ntemp
Set V = ntemp

   1 For *ntemp* do
     1.1 NumLines(*ntemp*, S) = 2,5,6, y = 2
     1.2 All *anti* dependences: LinSour(R) = 5,6; condition LinSour(R) $\leq y$ is
        not satisfied.
       Private(*ntemp*) = True
   2 $S = \varnothing$. The outermost nested loop can be parallelized. The Private variables:
    ntemp and the index variables: *iel, j, i*.

To extend the applicability of automatic privatization, Algorithm 2 is proposed
below. It analyses individual nests of a loop to apply Algorithm 1. The cost of
this solution is introducing additional points of synchronization. Algorithm 2
produces fine-grained parallelism. It is used when Algorithm 1 fails to parallelize
the outermost loop.

Algorithm 2. Finding fine-grained parallelism using privatization in inner loops

---

   Input : Set of dependence relations S, code of the input loop
   Output : Parallel code of the input loop

For outermost loop L:
   1 Find new set of dependence relations $S' \in S$, which describe sources and desti-
     nations within the body of loop L
   2 Parallelize loop L with Algorithm 1 and the set of dependences S'
   3 **If** Algorithm 1 is not able to produce parallel code for loop L **then**
     for each loop L' in the body of L **do**
       $L = L'$ and go to step 1
     end for
    end if

---

4   Experiments

The presented technique was implemented in a tool by means of the Petit anal-
yser. The input code of a loop is transformed by inserting OpenMP pragmas.
The NAS Parallel Benchmark (NPB 3.2) [14] were subject of experiments.

   The loops of the benchmark suite are a small set of programs designed to
help evaluate performance of parallel supercomputers. The test suite, which is
derived from computational fluid dynamics (CFD) applications, consists of five
kernels and three pseudo-applications [14].

From 431 loops of the NAS benchmark suite, Petit was able to analyse 257 loops, and dependences were found in 133 loops. For these loops, the presented approach is able to extract parallelism for 59 loops. Algorithm 1 transforms 42 loops and produces coarse-grained parallel code without any synchronization points. Algorithm 2 transforms 17 loops by parallelizing inner loops and produces fine-grained parallelism.

To check the performance of parallel code, speed-up and efficiency were studied. Speed-up is the ratio of sequential time and parallel time, $S=T(1)/T(P)$, where P is the number of processors. Efficiency, $E=S/P$, tells us about the usage of available processors by parallel code. Four loops from the benchmark suite were examined: $BT\_rhs.f2p\_3$, $LU\_erhs.f2p\_3$, $LU\_jacld.f2p\_1$, $SP\_rhs.f2p\_4$. Three of them were transformed by Algorithm 1. The coarse-grained parallel code includes synchronization-free slices. The loop $LU\_erhs.f2p\_3$ was transformed using Algorithm 2 to fine-grained parallel code.

The first three columns of Table 1 presents the names, numbers of dependences, and numbers of code lines of these loops. The next columns include the used algorithm, the times of parallelization (in seconds) and the numbers of synchronization points. Table 2 shows speed-up and efficiency for 2, 4, and 8 processors. The experiments were carried with the workstation Intel Xeon Quad Core, 1.6 Ghz, 8 CPU (2 quad core CPU with cache 4 MB), 2 GB RAM, Fedora Linux.

Table 1. The characteristic of the examined NAS loops

Loop	Number of dependences	Number of lines of code	Algorithm	Time of parallelizing	Synchr. points
BT_rhs.f2p_3	702	59	1	0.406	0
LU_erhs.f2p_3	640	76	2	0.640	(N3-N2)*(N1-1)
LU_jacld.f2p_1	2594	154	1	0.766	0
SP_rhs.f2p_4	507	63	1	0.265	0

5   Related Work

Different techniques and compilers based on the polyhedral models [7,15] have been developed to extract coarse-grained parallelism available in loops. The affine transformation framework, considered in papers [1,2] unifies a large number of previously proposed loop transformations. However, affine transformations do not exploit all parallelism with synchronization-free slices in some cases of loops [11].

Pluto [6,8] is an automatic parallelization tool based on the polyhedral model. Pluto transforms C programs from source to source for coarse-grained parallelism and data locality simultaneously. The core transformation framework mainly works by finding affine transformations for efficient tiling and fusion, but not limited to those.

Table 2. Time, speed-up, and efficiency

Loop	Parameters	1 CPU	2 CPUs			4 CPUs			8 CPUs		
		times	times	S	E	times	S	E	times	S	E
BT_rhs.f2p_3	N1,N2,N3,N4,N5=100	3.166	1.754	1.805	0.903	0.878	3.606	0.901	0.555	5.705	0.713
	N1,N2,N3,N4,N5=150	12.922	7.074	1.827	0.913	3.772	3.426	0.856	2.062	6.267	0.783
	N1,N2,N3,N4,N5=200	26.005	14.728	1.766	0.883	6.648	3.912	0.978	4.695	5.539	0.692
LU_erhs.f2p_3	N1,N3=32; N4,N6,N8,N10,N11=1000; N2,N5,N7,N9=1	2.231	1.333	1.674	0.837	0.987	2.260	0.565	0.936	2.384	0.298
	N1,N3=48; N4,N6,N8,N10,N11=2000; N2,N5,N7,N9=1	15.053	7.722	1.949	0.975	4.204	3.581	0.895	3.621	4.157	0.520
	N1,N3=64; N4,N6,N8,N10,N11=3000; N2,N5,N7,N9=1	79.114	42.002	1.884	0.942	29.009	2.727	0.682	18.410	4.297	0.537
LU_jacld.f2p_1	N1,N3=1; N2,N4=1000	10.663	6.040	1.765	0.883	3.207	3.325	0.831	1.896	5.624	0.703
	N1,N3=1; N2,N4=1000	24.853	13.486	1.843	0.921	6.981	3.560	0.890	4.304	5.774	0.722
	N1,N3=1; N2,N4=1000	45.077	24.639	1.829	0.915	12.287	3.669	0.917	7.053	6.391	0.799
SP_rhs.f2p_4	N1,N2,N3,N4,N5, N6,N7,N8,N9=75	1.648	0.833	1.978	0.989	0.478	3.448	0.862	0.330	4.994	0.624
	N1,N2,N3,N4,N5, N6,N7,N8,N9=100	3.417	1.788	1.911	0.956	0.860	3.973	0.993	0.486	7.031	0.879
	N1,N2,N3,N4,N5, N6,N7,N8,N9=125	7.790	3.901	1.997	0.998	2.216	3.515	0.879	1.186	6.568	0.821

However, Pluto does not offer scalar or array privatization techniques [6]. The tool is able only to parallelize three of 59 NAS loops (transformed by the presented approach in this paper). All of the other loops, parallelized by the Pluto compiler, can be also transformed by the Iteration Space Slicing Framework, presented in paper [11].

6   Conclusion

The proposed approach can be used to extend the spectrum of loops transformed by the Iteration Space Slicing (ISS) solution [11]. The presented algorithms reduce loop dependences and find parallelism for those cases of the NAS benchmark suite which cannot be analysed automatically by other compilers. The technique is able to transform the loops with large number of statements and dependence relations in a short time.

An impact of variable privatization on extracting synchronization-free slices presented in [11] will be studied in the future. The implementation of the approach can be found at the website: `http://code.google.com/p/auto-priv/`.

References

1. Lim, A., Lam, M., Cheong, G.: An affine partitioning algorithm to maximize parallelism and minimize communication. In: ICS 1999, pp. 228–237. ACM Press (1999)
2. Feautrier, P.: Some efficient solutions to the affine scheduling problem, part I and II, one and multidimensional time. International Journal of Parallel Programming 21, 313-348 and 389-420 (1992)
3. Allen, R., Kennedy, K.: Optimizing compilers for modern architectures: A Dependence based Approach. Morgan Kaufmann Publish., Inc. (2001)
4. Kelly, W., Pugh, W., Maslov, V., Rosser, E., Shpeisman, T., Wonnacott, D.: New User Interface for Petit and Other Extensions. User Guide (1996)
5. OpenMP Specification 3.0 (2008), `http://www.openmp.org`
6. PLUTO - An automatic parallelizer and locality optimizer for multicores, `http://pluto-compiler.sourceforge.net`
7. Bondhugula, U., Baskaran, M., Krishnamoorthy, S., Ramanujam, J., Rountev, A., Sadayappan, P.: Automatic Transformations for Communication-Minimized Parallelization and Locality Optimization in the Polyhedral Model. In: Hendren, L. (ed.) CC 2008. LNCS, vol. 4959, pp. 132–146. Springer, Heidelberg (2008)
8. Bondhugula, U., Hartono, A., Ramanujan, J., Sadayappan, P.: A practical automatic polyhedral parallelizer and locality optimizer. In: ACM SIGPLAN Programming Languages Design and Implementation, PLDI 2008 (2008)
9. Moldovan, D.: Parallel Processing: From Applications to Systems. Morgan Kaufmann Publishers, Inc. (1993)
10. Pugh, W., Wonnacott, D.: An Exact Method for Analysis of Value-Based Array Data Dependences. In: Banerjee, U., Gelernter, D., Nicolau, A., Padua, D.A. (eds.) LCPC 1993. LNCS, vol. 768, pp. 546–566. Springer, Heidelberg (1994)
11. Beletska, A., Bielecki, W., Cohen, A., Palkowski, M., Siedlecki, K.: Coarse-grained loop parallelization: Iteration space slicing vs affine transformations. Parallel Computing 37, 479–497 (2011)

12. Gupta, M.: On Privatization of Variables for Data-Parallel Execution. In: Proceedings of the 11th International Parallel Processing Symposium (1997)
13. Padua, D., Peng, T.: Automatic Array Privatization. In: Proc. 6th Workshop on languages and compilers for Parallel Computing (1993)
14. The NAS benchmark suite, http://www.nas.nasa.gov
15. Griebl, M.: Automatic Parallelization of Loop Programs for Distributed Memory Architectures, habilitation thesis, Department of Mathematics and Informatics, University of Passau (2004)

Efficient Parallel Computation of the Stochastic MV-PURE Estimator by the Hybrid Steepest Descent Method

Tomasz Piotrowski[1] and Isao Yamada[2]

[1] Dept. of Informatics, Nicolaus Copernicus University,
Grudziądzka 5, 87-100 Toruń, Poland
tpiotrowski@is.umk.pl
[2] Dept. of Communications and Integrated Systems,
Tokyo Institute of Technology,
Tokyo 152-8550, Japan
isao@sp.ss.titech.ac.jp

Abstract. In this paper we consider the problem of efficient computation of the stochastic MV-PURE estimator which is a reduced-rank estimator designed for robust linear estimation in ill-conditioned inverse problems. Our motivation for this result stems from the fact that the reduced-rank estimation by the stochastic MV-PURE estimator, while avoiding the problem of regularization parameter selection appearing in a common regularization technique used in inverse problems and machine learning, presents computational challenge due to nonconvexity induced by the rank constraint. To combat this problem, we propose a recursive scheme for computation of the general form of the stochastic MV-PURE estimator which does not require any matrix inversion and utilize the inherently parallel hybrid steepest descent method. We verify efficiency of the proposed scheme in numerical simulations.

Keywords: stochastic MV-PURE estimator, reduced-rank approach, parallel processing, subspace extraction, hybrid steepest descent method.

1 Introduction

The correspondence between ill-conditioned inverse problems and machine learning is viewed mostly via the commonly used in both fields regularization technique [1–3] introduced originally by Tikhonov [4]. Nevertheless, many problems common to both of these fields such as data compression and robust estimation may be solved using another robust reduced-rank technique [5–7], which is closely related to matrix nearness problems (see e.g. [8–10] and references therein). In particular, the reduced-rank approach enables one to avoid the problem of a suitable choice of certain form and value of the regularization parameter [11–13].

However, at the heart of the reduced-rank approach lies the non-convex rank constraint, which frequently renders efficient computation of the reduced-rank solution difficult. The challenge is then to reformulate the original (non-convex) reduced-rank problem into one that can be solved using efficient methods such as convex optimization algorithms [14].

L. Rutkowski et al. (Eds.): ICAISC 2012, Part II, LNCS 7268, pp. 404–412, 2012.
© Springer-Verlag Berlin Heidelberg 2012

This paper shows an example of this approach, as we demonstrate how a certain difficult multi-layered reduced-rank problem considered in the ill-conditioned inverse problems settings can be solved using powerful convex optimization algorithms. Namely, we focus on the optimization problem leading to the recently introduced linear stochastic MV-PURE estimator [15, 16], a robust reduced-rank estimator for stochastic linear model in the inverse problems case. The stochastic MV-PURE estimator builds on the previously introduced linear *minimum-variance pseudo-unbiased reduced-rank estimator* (MV-PURE) [12, 13] for deterministic ill-conditioned inverse problems, and is a solution to a hierarchical non-convex optimization problem for which to date no efficient computation scheme exists. To circumvent this difficulty, we show that the stochastic MV-PURE estimator can be cast as a solution to a subspace extraction problem followed by a linearly constrained convex quadratic optimization. Such reformulation enables us to employ a variety of efficient algorithms for computation of the stochastic MV-PURE estimator, and in this paper we demonstrate an application of this result, where we employ the method proposed in [17] to obtain the desired subspace estimate in the first stage of the optimization problem, and the hybrid steepest descent method [18–20] in the second stage, which due to its inherent parallelism enables computationally efficient implementation of the proposed method. We provide numerical simulations verifying efficiency of the proposed scheme.

A preliminary results leading to results of this paper were presented in part in [21].

2 Preliminaries

The stochastic MV-PURE estimator has been derived as a robust linear estimator for the stochastic linear model:

$$\mathbf{y} = H\mathbf{x} + \mathbf{n}, \tag{1}$$

where $\mathbf{y}, \mathbf{x}, \mathbf{n}$ are observed random vector, random vector to be estimated, and additive noise, respectively, and $H \in \mathbb{R}^{n \times m}$ is a known matrix of rank m. We assume that $\mathbf{x}$ and $\mathbf{n}$ have zero mean and are uncorrelated: $R_{\mathbf{xn}} = 0$.

It can be easily verified that any two random vectors $\mathbf{x} \in \mathbb{R}^m, \mathbf{y} \in \mathbb{R}^n$, for which $R_{\mathbf{x}}, R_{\mathbf{y}}, R_{\mathbf{yx}}$ are known, where $rk(R_{\mathbf{yx}}) = m$ [by $rk(X)$ we denote rank of a matrix X], and for which the joint covariance matrix is positive definite, can be cast into model (1) by setting $H = R_{\mathbf{yx}}R_{\mathbf{x}}^{-1}$ and $\mathbf{n} = \mathbf{y} - R_{\mathbf{yx}}R_{\mathbf{x}}^{-1}\mathbf{x}$, see [22]. Thus, model (1) is general enough to accomodate a variety of scenarios e.g. in signal processing, machine learning, inverse problems in medicine and economics, to name just a few.

We focus on the problem of linear estimation of $\mathbf{x}$ given $\mathbf{y}$, under the mean square error (MSE) criterion. Thus, we seek to find a fixed matrix $W \in \mathbb{R}^{m \times n}$, called here an estimator, for which the estimate of $\mathbf{x}$ given by:

$$\widehat{\mathbf{x}} = W\mathbf{y}, \tag{2}$$

is optimal with respect to a certain measure related to the mean square error of $\widehat{\mathbf{x}}$:

$$J(W) = tr\left[\mathrm{E}[(\widehat{\mathbf{x}} - \mathbf{x})(\widehat{\mathbf{x}} - \mathbf{x})^t]\right] = tr[WR_{\mathbf{y}}W^t] - 2tr[WR_{\mathbf{yx}}] + tr[R_{\mathbf{x}}]. \tag{3}$$

We note that in machine learning applications with Gaussian priors on $\mathbf{x}$ and $\mathbf{n}$, the globally optimum solution $W_{MMSE} = R_{\mathbf{xy}}R_{\mathbf{y}}^{-1}$ of the inverse problem (2) for model (1) under mean square error criterion (3) results in $\hat{\mathbf{x}}_{MMSE} = W_{MMSE}\mathbf{y}$ recognized as the mean of the posterior distribution in Bayesian linear estimation, see e.g. [23, Chapter 2.], which is equivalent in this case to the maximum a posteriori (MAP) estimate.[1] However, the $\hat{\mathbf{x}}_{MMSE}$ estimate is inherently sensitive to imperfectly known models, and this inadequacy is amplified by high noise levels and ill-conditioning of H [15, 16], in which case its MSE can be significantly larger than that of the theoretically suboptimal solutions. This situation would occur in the settings considered in this paragraph (interpreting rows of H as training samples) if the samples are noisy (which would result in imperfectly known H), possibly collinear (which would result in ill-conditioned H), and if the level of observation noise $\mathbf{n}$ is high.

The stochastic MV-PURE estimator has been designed to overcome this sensitivity of the W_{MMSE} estimator. More precisely, the stochastic MV-PURE estimator has been introduced as a solution of a hierarchical non-convex optimization problem related to the mean square error (3), in order to achieve smallest distortion among reduced-rank estimators. Namely, the stochastic MV-PURE estimator is defined as a solution of the following problem, for a given rank constraint $r \leq m$:

$$\begin{cases} \text{minimize} \quad J(W_r) \\ \text{subject to } W_r \in \bigcap_{\iota \in \mathfrak{J}} \mathcal{P}_r^\iota, \end{cases} \tag{4}$$

where

$$\mathcal{P}_r^\iota = \arg \min_{W_r \in \mathcal{X}_r^{m \times n}} \| W_r H - I_m \|_\iota^2, \ \iota \in \mathfrak{J}, \tag{5}$$

where $\mathcal{X}_r^{m \times n} := \{W_r \in \mathbb{R}^{m \times n} : rk(W_r) \leq r \leq m\}$, and where $\mathfrak{J}$ is the index set of all unitarily invariant norms.[2]

The following Theorem, cited from [15], provides a closed algebraic form of the stochastic MV-PURE estimator.

Theorem 1 ([15]). *1. Let us set rank constraint $r < m$ and let us set:*

$$K = \left(H^t R_{\mathbf{y}}^{-1} H\right)^{-1} - 2R_{\mathbf{x}}. \tag{6}$$

Moreover, let the symmetric matrix K be given with an eigenvalue decomposition $EVD(K) = E\Delta E^t$, with eigenvalues organized in nondecreasing order:

$$\delta_1 \leq \delta_2 \leq \cdots \leq \delta_m.$$

Then $W_{MV-PURE}^r \in \mathbb{R}^{m \times n}$ is a solution to problem (4) if and only if $W_{MV-PURE}^r$ is of the following form:

$$W_{MV-PURE}^r = E_r E_r^t (H^t R_{\mathbf{y}}^{-1} H)^{-1} H^t R_{\mathbf{y}}^{-1}, \tag{7}$$

---

[1] However, it shall be emphasised that we do not assume below any special form of the model matrix H, nor we assume that either $\mathbf{x}$ of $\mathbf{n}$ are Gaussian.

[2] Matrix norm ι is unitarily invariant if it satisfies $\| UXV \|_\iota = \| X \|_\iota$ for all orthogonal $U \in \mathbb{R}^{m \times m}$, $V \in \mathbb{R}^{n \times n}$ and all $X \in \mathbb{R}^{m \times n}$ [24, p. 203]. The Frobenius, spectral, and trace (nuclear) norms are examples of unitarily invariant norms.

where $E = (e_1, \ldots, e_m)$ with $E_r = (e_1, \ldots, e_r)$ for $r < m$. If $\delta_r \neq \delta_{r+1}$, the solution is unique. Moreover, we have:

$$J(W_{MV-PURE}^r) = \sum_{i=1}^{r} \delta_i + tr[R_x]. \tag{8}$$

2. For no rank constraint imposed, i.e., when $r = m$, the solution to problem (4) is uniquely given by $W_{MV-PURE}^m = (H^t R_y^{-1} H)^{-1} H^t R_y^{-1}$, with:

$$J(W_{MV-PURE}^m) = \sum_{i=1}^{m} \delta_i + tr[R_x]. \tag{9}$$

In particular, it should be noted that for no rank constraint (when $r = m$) the optimization problem (4) is essentially equivalent to the optimization problem which produces as the solution in the deterministic case the well-known *best linear unbiased estimator* (BLUE) [22].

As a solution to problem (4), the stochastic MV-PURE estimator is gifted with inherent robustness to model mismatches and ill-conditioning of the inverse problem (2), as derived by theoretical considerations and confirmed by numerical simulations in [15, 16].[3] However, as can be seen from the form (7) of the stochastic MV-PURE estimator given in Theorem 1, it requires in particular computation of the nested inverses of certain matrices, which is computationally expensive and numerically unstable if the matrix to be inverted is ill-conditioned [25]. To overcome these limitations, in the following section we propose a recursive computation scheme for the stochastic MV-PURE estimator.

3   Recursive Computation Scheme

Let us set rank constraint $r < m$. From the closed algebraic form of the stochastic MV-PURE estimator given in Theorem 1 it is seen that for a given rank constraint $r < m$ the estimate $\hat{x} = E_r E_r^t (H^t R_y^{-1} H)^{-1} H^t R_y^{-1} y$ of x is formed by projecting the estimate $(H^t R_y^{-1} H)^{-1} H^t R_y^{-1} y$ obtained by the BLUE estimator onto the minor subspace spanned by the r minor eigenvectors of K (6), by the projection matrix $E_r E_r^t$ in (7). This observation suggests that we may cast the stochastic MV-PURE estimator as a solution of the following equality-constrained minimization problem [11, p.120]:

$$\begin{cases} \text{minimize} \ \ tr[W R_y W^t] \\ \text{subject to} \ \ WH = E_r E_r^t. \end{cases} \tag{10}$$

Problem (10) is a standard linearly constrained convex quadratic optimization problem, coupled with a subspace extraction needed to estimate the projection matrix $E_r E_r^t$. Thus, denoting at $k-th$ iteration by $X_r^k \in \mathbb{R}^{r \times m}$ an estimate of r minor components of K, we should derive an algorithm which at $k-th$ iteration

---

[3] For further insight into the MV-PURE estimation, see the original papers [12, 13], where the deterministic version of the MV-PURE estimator was developed.

step performs first an update of an estimate of $(X_r^k)^t X_r^k$ converging to $E_r E_r^t$, followed by an update of an estimate of the solution to (10), given at $k - th$ iteration as an estimate of a solution to:

$$\begin{cases} \text{minimize} \quad tr[W R_{\mathbf{y}} W^t] \\ \text{subject to } WH = (X_r^k)^t X_r^k. \end{cases} \tag{11}$$

Such an algorithm is presented below. Moreover, we note that subspace tracking methods (see e.g. [17, 26]) give us a possibility of estimating minor subspace of time-varying K (6) from a finite sample estimate of $K = \left(H^t R_{\mathbf{y}}^{-1} H\right)^{-1} - 2R_{\mathbf{x}}$ (e.g., when H is slowly time-varying), which in turn open up the possibility to derive a scheme for estimation of a non-stationary random processes by the stochastic MV-PURE estimator. Such an important extension will be the subject of future research.

Here, we present a parallel method for estimation of a wide-sense stationary process $\mathbf{x}(k)$ by the stochastic MV-PURE estimator in the linear model (1) (of the form $\mathbf{y}(k) = H\mathbf{x}(k) + \mathbf{n}(k)$, where k denotes the time step of realization of random vectors under consideration). We assume that the matrix K which projection matrix $E_r E_r^t$ shall be extracted (where $EVD(K) = E\Delta E^t$) is known a priori, as for wide-sense stationary processes it is measurable off-line.

The extraction of a minor subspace of K spanned by E_r is performed by the method proposed in [17]. Since matrix K (6) is only symmetric, we equivalently extract a minor subspace of a positive definite matrix:

$$K' := K + tr[R_{\mathbf{x}}]I_m \succ 0. \tag{12}$$

Positive definiteness of K' can be shown using [24, p.181].

The resulting equality-constrained convex optimization is performed by the hybrid steepest descent method (HSDM) [18–20]. Due to its inherent parallelism, we are able to design a method which computes in parallel each row of the solution with low computational cost.

We note that for the i-th row of the solution to (11) we have m linear constraints of the form

$$C_{i,j}^k = \left\{ x \in \mathbb{R}^n : \ x H_j = [(X_r^k)^t X_r^k]_{i,j} \right\}, \ j = 1, \ldots, m, \ i = 1, \ldots, m, \tag{13}$$

where H_j is the j-th column of H, $j = 1, \ldots, m$, and $(X_r^k)^t X_r^k$ is an estimate of $E_r E_r^t$ at k-th step obtained by the minor components extraction method as [17]:

$$X_r^{k+1} = X_r^k - \beta * [X_r^k (X_r^k)^t X_r^k K' - X_r^k K' (X_r^k)^t X_r^k], \tag{14}$$

where the factor β was set to $\beta = 10^{-3}$ in our simulations.

In order to accomodate multiple constraints (13) [essentially a system of m linear equations with n unknowns for each row of the solution to (11) where $m \leq n$] we use the form of the HSDM method as given in [18, Corollary 3.6]. For i-th row, we use the orthogonal projector $P_{i,j}$ onto the j-th constraining hyperplane of the form (see e.g. [27, p.141]):

$$P_{i,j}(W_r^k)_i = (W_r^k)_i - \frac{(W_r^k)_i H_j - [(X_r^k)^t X_r^k]_{i,j}}{\| H_j \|^2} H_j^t, \ j = 1, \ldots, m, \ i = 1, \ldots, m, \tag{15}$$

where $(W_r^k)_i$ is an estimate of i-th row at k-th iteration step of the solution to (11). We note that linear combination of orthogonal projectors (15) which are firmly nonexpansive is also firmly nonexpansive:

$$T(W_r^k)_i = \sum_{j=1}^{m} w_j P_{i,j}(W_r^k)_i, \tag{16}$$

provided $\sum_{j=1}^{m} w_j = 1$ for nonnegative weights w_j [18]. In our simulations we simply set $w = 1/m$. We note further that due to positive definiteness of $R_\mathbf{y}$, the derivative of the (iteration-invariant) cost function in (11) is α-monotone and $\| R_\mathbf{y} \|_2$-Lipschitzian, where $\alpha > 0$ is any constant satisfying $x^t R_\mathbf{y} x \geq \alpha \| x \|^2$ for any $x \in \mathbb{R}^n$ [18]. Thus, by choosing $\mu \in (0, \frac{2\alpha}{\|R_\mathbf{y}\|_2^2})$, an update of i-th row of an estimate $(W_r^k)_i$ at k-th iteration step is given in view of [18, Corollary 3.6] by:

$$(W_r^{k+1})_i = T(W_r^k)_i - 2\lambda_{k+1}\mu T(W_r^k)_i R_\mathbf{y}, \tag{17}$$

where λ_k is any sequence satisfying $\lim_{k\to\infty} \lambda_k = 0$, $\sum_{k=1}^{\infty} \lambda_k = +\infty$, $\sum_{k=1}^{\infty} |\lambda_k - \lambda_{k+1}| < +\infty$. In our simulations we set $\mu = 5 * 10^{-6}$ and $\lambda_k = 1/k$.

Since the initial point for iteration of the HSDM method can be arbitrary, we set $W_r^1 = 0 \in \mathbb{R}^{m \times n}$ in our simulations. For initialization of the minor subspace extraction algorithm we follow the recommendation given in [17, p.387] and set $X_r^1 = I_{r,m} \in \mathbb{R}^{r \times m}$.

Thus, the recursive method works as follows:
Initialization: set $r < m, k = 1, X_r^1 = I_{r,m} \in \mathbb{R}^{r \times m}, W_r^1 = 0 \in \mathbb{R}^{m \times n}$;
Iteration steps:

1. Compute $X_r^{k+1} :=$ estimate of r minor components of K at time $k + 1$ by:

$$X_r^{k+1} = X_r^k - \beta * [X_r^k(X_r^k)^t X_r^k K' - X_r^k K'(X_r^k)^t X_r^k]; \tag{18}$$

2. Compute $T(W_r^k)_i = (1/m) \sum_{j=1}^{m} P_{i,j}(W_r^k)_i$, where $P_{i,j}$ projects orthogonally the i-th row of W_r^k onto the j-th constraint hyperplane defined by $\{x \in \mathbb{R}^n : xH_j = [(X_r^k)^t X_r^k]_{i,j}\}$, $j = 1, \ldots, m$, $i = 1, \ldots, m$, where $H = (H_1, \ldots, H_m)$, and is of the form:

$$P_{i,j}(W_r^k)_i = (W_r^k)_i - \frac{(W_r^k)_i H_j - [(X_r^k)^t X_r^k]_{i,j}}{\| H_j \|^2} H_j^t,$$

$$j = 1, \ldots, m, \ i = 1, \ldots, m; \tag{19}$$

3. Compute $W_r^{k+1} :=$ estimate of $W_{MV-PURE}^r$ at time $k + 1$ by:

$$(W_r^{k+1})_i = T(W_r^k)_i - 2\lambda_{k+1}\mu T(W_r^k)_i R_\mathbf{y}, \ i = 1, \ldots, m. \tag{20}$$

It is seen that the proposed scheme requires no matrix inversion, and that it inherently enables parallel computation. In particular, the orthogonal projectors $P_{i,j}$ (19) onto the constraining hyperplanes can be computed with very little computational effort. Moreover, it is seen that the proposed scheme is specially suitable for large rank reductions where $r \ll m$, as in such a case the above algorithm can be implemented using only $O(mn)$ flops at each iteration. This complexity corresponds to the result obtained for the related *reduced rank Wiener filter* in [28].

In particular, algorithm (18) generates at each step an estimate X_r^k such that $(X_r^k)^t X_r^k$ converges to $E_r E_r^t$ in (11). On the other hand, the hybrid steepest descent method is guaranteed to converge to a unique minimizer of (10) if the fixed point set of the firmly nonexpansive mapping T computed in Step 2 is given by $\{x_i \in \mathbb{R}^n : x_i H = (E_r E_r^t)_i\}$ for $i = 1, \ldots, m$, where $(E_r E_r^t)_i$ denotes the $i-th$ row of $E_r E_r^t$, which will happen (up to steady state error of the subspace tracking algorithm) after algorithm (18) converges. Taking into account a notable robustness of the hybrid steepest descent method (see e.g. [19, Section 4.]), future research will also aim at defining precise conditions of the convergence of the proposed scheme based on the results provided in [18–20], for a given selection of the subspace tracking algorithm.

We motivate further the use of the above scheme by demonstrating the following simple numerical simulations, which give an average performance of the proposed method. In model (1), we consider randomly generated $R_{\mathbf{x}} \succ 0$, H having iid. Gaussian entries of unity variance, and a white noise case $R_{\mathbf{n}} = I_n$. The parameters are set to $\beta = 10^{-3}$ in (18), $\lambda_k = 1/k$ and $\mu = 5 * 10^{-6}$ in (20). The size of the model is $m = 50, n = 200$. The rank constraint was set to $r = 10$.

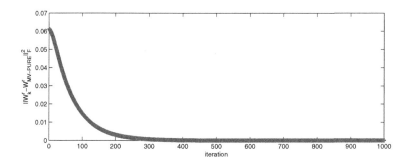

Fig. 1. The proposed scheme generates a converging rapidly estimate of the stochastic MV-PURE estimator

We note that in the simulations shown in Figure 1 an estimate (20) of the stochastic MV-PURE estimator converged after approximately 250 iterations. This indicates in particular that an estimate (18) of r minor components of K converged in this case in less than 250 iterations.

Finally, we would like to remark that the proposed scheme can be also used to compute iteratively the (deterministic) MV-PURE estimator introduced in [12, 13] if no linear constraints have been imposed on the deterministic vector of parameters. This can be immediately verified using Theorem 3 in [13] and the discussion of the results of Corollary 1 in [15], by setting $R_{\mathbf{x}} = I_m$ in the above scheme.

4 Conclusions

As the first step for establishing numerically efficient method of using the stochastic MV-PURE estimator, we have proposed a parallel computational method for recursive computation of the stochastic MV-PURE estimator applicable to estimation of wide-sense stationary random processes. The proposed method requires no matrix inversion and only quadratic number of flops in the data size at each iteration. The future research will be devoted to extend the proposed scheme to estimation of non-stationary random processes, and establishing convergence properties of the generalized scheme.

Acknowledgement. The authors would like to thank anonymous reviewers for their constructive comments.

References

1. Poggio, T., Girosi, F.: Networks for Approximation and Learning. Proceedings of the IEEE 78(9), 1481–1497 (1990)
2. Evgeniou, T., Pontil, M., Poggio, T.: Regularization Networks and Support Vector Machines. Advances in Computational Mathematics 13(1), 1–50 (2000)
3. De Vito, E., Rosasco, L., Caponetto, A., De Giovannini, U., Odone, F.: Learning from Examples as an Inverse Problem. Journal of Machine Learning Research 6, 883–904 (2005)
4. Tikhonov, A.N.: Solution of Incorrectly Formulated Problems and the Regularization Method. Soviet Math. Doktl. 5, 1035–1038 (1963)
5. Marquardt, D.W.: Generalized Inverses, Ridge Regression, Biased Linear Estimation, and Nonlinear Estimation. Technometrics 12, 591–612 (1970)
6. Scharf, L.L., Thomas, J.K.: Wiener Filters in Canonical Coordinates for Transform Coding, Filtering, and Quantizing. IEEE Transactions on Signal Processing 46(3), 647–654 (1998)
7. Yamashita, Y., Ogawa, H.: Relative Karhunen-Loeve Transform. IEEE Transactions on Signal Processing 44(2), 371–378 (1996)
8. Kulis, B., Sustik, M., Dhillon, I.: Learning Low-Rank Kernel Matrices. In: ICML 2006, pp. 505–512 (2006)
9. Smola, A.J., Schölkopf, B.: Sparse Greedy Matrix Approximation for Machine Learning. In: ICML 2000, pp. 911–918 (2000)
10. Bach, F.R., Jordan, M.I.: Predictive Low-Rank Decomposition for Kernel Methods. In: ICML 2005, pp. 33–40 (2005)
11. Ben-Israel, A., Greville, T.N.E.: Generalized Inverses: Theory and Applications, 2nd edn. Springer, New York (2003)
12. Yamada, I., Elbadraoui, J.: Minimum-Variance Pseudo-Unbiased Low-Rank Estimator for Ill-Conditioned Inverse Problems. In: IEEE ICASSP 2006, pp. 325–328 (2006)
13. Piotrowski, T., Yamada, I.: MV-PURE Estimator: Minimum-Variance Pseudo-Unbiased Reduced-Rank Estimator for Linearly Constrained Ill-Conditioned Inverse Problems. IEEE Transactions on Signal Processing 56(8), 3408–3423 (2008)
14. Boyd, S., Vandenberghe, L.: Convex Optimization. Cambridge University Press, New York (2004)
15. Piotrowski, T., Cavalcante, R.L.G., Yamada, I.: Stochastic MV-PURE Estimator: Robust Reduced-Rank Estimator for Stochastic Linear Model. IEEE Transactions on Signal Processing 57(4), 1293–1303 (2009)

16. Piotrowski, T., Yamada, I.: Why the Stochastic MV-PURE Estimator Excels in Highly Noisy Situations? In: IEEE ICASSP 2009, pp. 3081–3084 (2009)
17. Chen, T., Amari, S., Lin, Q.: A Unified Algorithm for Principal and Minor Components Extraction. Neural Networks 11, 385–390 (1998)
18. Yamada, I.: Hybrid Steepest Descent Method for Variational Inequality Problem Over the Intersection of Fixed Point Sets of Nonexpansive Mappings. In: Butnariu, D., Censor, Y., Reich, S. (eds.) Inherently Parallel Algorithm for Feasibility and Optimization and Their Applications, pp. 473–504. Elsevier (2001)
19. Yamada, I., Ogura, N., Shirakawa, N.: A Numerically Robust Hybrid Steepest Descent Method for the Convexly Constrained Generalized Inverse Problems. In: Nashed, Z., Scherzer, O. (eds.) Inverse Problems, Image Analysis and Medical Imaging, vol. 313, pp. 269–305. American Mathematical Society, Contemporary Mathematics (2002)
20. Yamada, I., Yukawa, M., Yamagishi, M.: Minimizing the Moreau Envelope of Non-smooth Convex Functions over the Fixed Point Set of Certain Quasi-Nonexpansive Mappings. In: Bauschke, H.H., Burachik, R.S., Combettes, P.L., Elser, V., Luke, D.R., Wolkowicz, H. (eds.) Fixed-Point Algorithms for Inverse Problems in Science and Engineering. Springer Optimization and Its Applications, vol. 49, pp. 345–390 (2011)
21. Piotrowski, T., Yamada, I.: Convex Formulation of the Stochastic MV-PURE Estimator and Its Relation to the Reduced Rank Wiener Filter. In: IEEE ICSES 2008, pp. 397–400 (2008)
22. Kailath, T., Sayed, A.H., Hassibi, B.: Linear Estimation. Prentice Hall, New Jersey (2000)
23. Rasmussen, C.E., Williams, C.K.I.: Gaussian Processes for Machine Learning. The MIT Press, Cambridge (2006)
24. Horn, R.A., Johnson, C.R.: Matrix Analysis. Cambridge University Press, New York (1985)
25. Golub, G.H., Van Loan, C.F.: Matrix Computations. The Johns Hopkins University Press, Baltimore (1996)
26. Badeau, R., Richard, G., David, B.: Fast and Stable YAST Algorithm for Principal and Minor Subspace Tracking. IEEE Transactions on Signal Processing 57(4), 3437–3446 (2008)
27. Stark, H., Yang, Y.: Vector Space Projections: A Numerical Approach to Signal and Image Processing, Neural Nets, and Optics. John Wiley & Sons, New York (1998)
28. Hua, Y., Nikpour, M.: Computing the Reduced-Rank Wiener Filter by IQMD. IEEE Signal Processing Letters 6(9), 240–242 (1999)

Part V

Agent Systems, Robotics and Control

Distributed Computing in Sensor Networks Using Multi-agent Systems and Code Morphing

Stefan Bosse[1,3], Florian Pantke[2,3], and Frank Kirchner[1,3]

[1] University of Bremen, Department of Computer Science, Robotics, Germany
[2] TZI Centre for Computing and Communication Technologies
[3] University of Bremen, ISIS Sensorial Materials Scientific Centre, Germany

Abstract. We propose and show a parallel and distributed runtime environment for multi-agent systems that provides spatial agent migration ability by employing code morphing. The focus of the application scenario lies on sensor networks and low-power, resource-aware single System-On-Chip designs. An agent approach provides stronger autonomy than a traditional object or remote-procedure-call based approach. Agents can decide for themselves which actions are performed, and they are capable of reacting on the environment and other agents with flexible behaviour. Data processing nodes exchange code rather than data to transfer information. A part of the state of an agent is preserved within its own program code, which also implements the agent's migration functionality. The practicability of the approach is shown using a simple distributed Sobel filter as an example.

1 Introduction and Overview

Recently emerging trends in engineering and microsystem applications such as the development of sensorial materials pose a growing demand for autonomous networks of miniaturized smart sensors and actuators embedded in technical structures [8]. With increasing miniaturization and sensor-actuator density, decentralized network and data processing architectures are preferred or required. We propose and show a spatial distributed and execution-parallel runtime environment for multi-agent systems providing migration mobility using a code morphing approach in which computing nodes exchange code rather than data to transfer information, basically similar to work discussed in [2]. The advantage of this distributed computation model is the computational independence of each node and the eliminated necessity for nodes to comply with previously defined common data types and structures as well as message formats. Computing nodes perform local computations by executing code and cooperate by distributing modified code to execute a global task. Multi-agent systems providing migration mobility using code morphing can help to reduce the communication cost in a distributed system [5]. The distributed programming model of mobile agents has the advantage of simplification and reduction of synchronization constraints owing to the autonomy of agents. Traditionally, mobile agents are executed on generic

L. Rutkowski et al. (Eds.): ICAISC 2012, Part II, LNCS 7268, pp. 415–423, 2012.
© Springer-Verlag Berlin Heidelberg 2012

computer architectures [6][7], which usually cannot easily be reduced to single-chip systems as they are required, for example, in sensorial materials with high sensor node densities. We present a hardware architecture for mesh networks of data processing nodes, which can be organized, for example, in a two-dimensional grid topology with each node having connections to its up to four direct neighbours. An example of such a network with dimensions 2 x 2 is illustrated in figure 1. A fault-tolerant message-based communication system SLIP is used to transfer messages (containing code) between nodes using smart delta-distance-vector routing [4]. The network topology can be irregular or incomplete, depending on design choices or failures. Smart routing is used to deliver messages on alternative routes around partially connected or defective areas. For the data processing architecture used for the execution of code and code morphing, a multi-parallel stack-based multi-stack, zero-operand FORTH machine was chosen leading to small programs, low system complexity, and high system performance [9]. The architecture design focuses on low-power and resource-aware single System-On-Chip (SoC) design on RT level, though both hardware and software implementations were created. Though the FORTH programming language is high level, it can be directly mapped to and executed on the machine level.

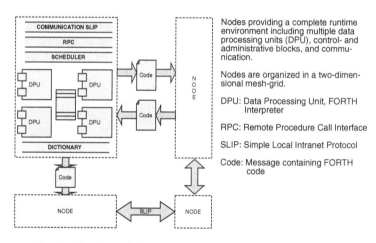

Fig. 1. Distributed data processing framework with four nodes

A complete runtime unit consists of a communication system with a smart routing protocol stack, one or more FORTH processing units with a code morphing engine, resource management, code relocation and dictionary management, and a scheduler managing program execution and distribution, which are normally part of an operating system which does not exist here.

2   Implementing Migrating Agents with FORTH Using Code Morphing

FORTH is an interpreted language whose source code is extremely compact. Furthermore, FORTH is extensible, that is new language constructs can be defined on the fly by its users [3]. A FORTH program contains built-in core instructions directly executed by the FORTH processing unit and user-defined high-level word and object definitions that are added to and looked up from a dictionary data structure. This dictionary plays a central role in the implementation of distributed systems and mobile agents. Words can be added, updated, and removed (forgotten), controlled by the FORTH program itself (already considered in [3]). User-defined words are composed of a sequence of words. FORTH maintains two push-down stacks, providing communication between FORTH words (expressed with reverse polish notation, RPN). Most instructions interact directly with the data stack SS, the second stack is known as the return stack RS and is used to hold return addresses enabling nesting. Literal values are treated as special words pushing the respective value on the data stack. FORTH provides common arithmetic data manipulation instructions and high-level control constructs like loops and branches. A FORTH program can be sent to and executed on any node in the network. For mobile agents, not only code may migrate from node to node but also state information of the agent, at least a subset of the process state has to be transferred with the agent. On the one hand, the process state of a stack-based FORTH program and execution environment consists of the data values stored on the data stack (and in an additional random-access data segment), on the other hand, of the control state defined by the program counter and the values on the return stack. A program capable of modifying its own code can store a subset of its process state by modifying code, applied to both data and control instructions. A program can fork a modified (or unmodified) replica of itself for execution on a different processing unit (locally parallel or globally distributed). This feature enables migration of dynamic agents holding locally processed information and a subset of execution state in their code. The simple FORTH instruction format is an appropriate starting point for code morphing, the ability of a program to modify itself or make a modified copy, mostly as a result of a previously performed computation. Calculation results and a subset of the processing state can be stored directly in the program code which changes the program behaviour. The standard FORTH core instruction set was extended and adapted for the implementation of agent migration in mesh networks with two-dimensional grid topology. Table 1 gives a summary of the new words provided for code morphing. These instructions can be used to modify the program behaviour and enable the preservation of the current program execution state. In our system, a FORTH program is contained in a contiguous memory fragment, called a frame. A frame can be transferred to and executed on remote nodes and processing units. Modification of the program code is always performed in a shadow frame environment, which can be identical with the execution frame. This is the default case used for in-place code modification. One or more different frames can be allocated and used for out-of-place modification, required if the execution frame is used beyond code morphing. All code morphing instructions operate on the shadow frame. Both the execution and the shadow frames have their own code pointer. The STOC command is used to store the data that is part of an agent's process state for migration. The TOC and COPYC instructions can be used to indirectly save the control state of the agent as they enable reassembly and modification of code fragments depending on the current data and control state.

Table 1. FORTH extensions providing program code morphing

Word	Description
c!	SETC: Sets frame of shadow environment for code morphing. RESET sets code pointer of shadow frame to the beginning of shadow frame.
>>c	COPYC: Switches to morphing state: Transfers code from program frame between markers m1 and m2 into shadow frame (including markers). Only marker and STOC commands are interpreted.
>c	TOC: Copies next word from program frame into shadow frame.
s>c	STOC: Pops n data value(s) from stack and stores values as word literals in shadow frame.
<m>	MARKER: Sets a marker position anywhere in a program frame.
<m>@	GETMARKER: Gets a marker (maps symbolic names to unique numbers).
<m>!	SETMARKER: Sets shadow code pointer after marker in shadow frame. Marker is searched in shadow frame, thus either in-place of execution frame or in a new created/copied shadow frame (containing already code and marker). Can be used to edit a partial range of shadow frame code using STOC and TOC instructions.

Table 2. Some FORTH extensions providing 1. dictionary modification and object creation, and 2. multi-processing support and frame distribution

Instruction	Description
VARIABLE x ARRAY [n,m] x VARIABLE* x	Creates a new variable or array and allocates memory. The first two definitions create public objects and they are added to the dictionary. The star definitions create private objects.
OBJECT MUTEX x OBJECT FRAME f	Creates (allocates) a new IPC or frame object. The object is added to the dictionary. Other supported IPC object types: SEMA, EVENT, TIMER.
IMPORT VARIABLE x IMPORT OBJECT x	Imports a variable or object from the dictionary. If not found, then the program execution terminates (return status 0).
dx dy fork	Sends contents of shadow frame for execution to node relative to actual node. If dx=0 and dy=0, then the shadow frame is executed locally and concurrently on a different FORTH processing unit. The fork instruction returns the frame sequence or processing unit number.
id join	Waits for termination of a forked frame or the reception and execution of a reply program frame.
$status$ return	Finishes execution of a program. If status is zero, no reply is generated. If status is equal to -1, an empty reply is generated. Finally, if status is equal 1, the contents of the shadow frame are sent back to the original sender of the execution frame.

Table 2 explains several FORTH extensions which can be used for the modification of the dictionary and for the creation of objects. These instructions allow mobil agents to create (allocate) and import memory, word, and interprocess communication (IPC) objects. Finally, FORTH instructions required for program frame execution and distribution are shown. The contents of a shadow frame are always sent to and executed on a different or remote processor.

3   Runtime Environment and Data Processing Architecture

The principal system architecture of one **FORTH processing unit** (PU) part of the node runtime environment is shown in figure 2. A FORTH processing unit executes instructions from a node-shared code segment CS. The code segment is partitioned into frames. The next instruction to be executed is pointed by a program counter PC. A FORTH program containing top-level instructions and word definitions belongs to one particular frame, thus the code segment can hold various programs (and word definitions). The actually executed program is referenced by a frame pointer FRAME. In addition to the frame to be executed (the execution frame) there is a shadow frame environment with its own set of program and frame pointers, PC'' and FRAME''. This shadow frame, which is initially identical to the execution frame, is used for code morphing. Local data manipulation performed by the program uses a data stack SS and return stack RS, known from traditional FORTH architectures. Data manipulation with random-access behaviour is possible and operates on a separate data segment DS shared by all PUs of the same network node. There is a third stack ES used for exception handling.

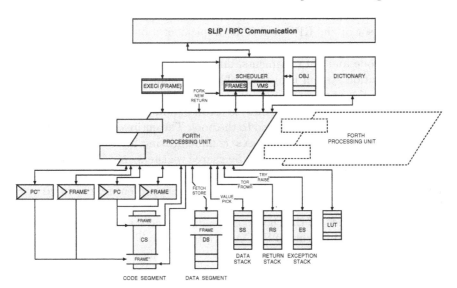

Fig. 2. Runtime architecture consisting of FORTH data processing units, shared memory and objects, dictionary, scheduler, and communication

A FORTH processing unit initially waits for a frame to be executed. During program execution, the FORTH processing unit interacts with the scheduler to perform program forking, frame propagation, program termination, object creation (allocation), and object modification. The set of objects consists of the inter-process communication objects and frames. There are private and public (node-visible) variables and arrays. All program frames have access to public variables by looking up references stored in the dictionary. Program word, memory variable, and object relocation are carried out by using a frame-bounded **lookup table LUT**. The **scheduler** is the bridge between a set of locally parallel executing FORTH processing units, and the communication system, a remote procedure call (RPC) interface layered above SLIP. The RPC processing unit receives messages (packets) from the protocol stack and transforms them into program frames, finally passed to the scheduler. The scheduler takes a free FORTH processor from the processor pool (queue) **VMS** and schedules execution of the frame. During program execution, the scheduler can be used to send a program frame to a different node, passed to the RPC processing unit. All program processing units share a common dictionary, code, and data segment. There is a pool of objects **OBJ** (memory, IPC, frames), managed by the scheduler and a garbage collector.

3.1   From High-Level Modelling to a Hard- and Software Implementation of a Node

The runtime environment is modelled on behavioural level using a high-level multi-process programming language with atomic-guarded actions and interprocess-communication (communicating sequential processes)[1]. Mostly, processes communicate with each other by using queues, for example, the FORTH processor or the RPC and SLIP implementation processes. The architecture and implementation model can be matched to different word and data sizes, sizes of code and data segments, and the number of FORTH processors. The communication system is also scalable and adaptable to different environments. Because the implementation of the FORTH runtime system is static, a pool of objects (memory, IPC, frames) is created, and during runtime those objects are allocated from and returned to the pool. The entire design is partitioned into 43 concurrently executed processes, communicating by using 24 queues, 13 mutex, 8 semaphores, 52 RAM blocks, 59 shared registers, and 11 timers. All architecture parts of the node, including communication, FORTH processing units, scheduler, dictionary and relocation support, are mapped entirely to **hardware** multi-RT level and a single SoC design using the ConPro compiler [1]. The resource demand depends on the choice of design parameters and is between 1M - 3M equivalent gates (in terms of FPGA architectures). The same multi-process programming model and source code used for the synthesis of the hardware implementation can also be compiled into **software** with the ConPro compiler. The software model has the same function as the hardware model. A special FORTH compiler transforms source code into machine instructions.

4   Distributed Sobel Filter: An Example

This section gives an example of how the described runtime environment can be used. We proof the approach with a FORTH implementation of a distributed Sobel operator. Originally applied in image processing and computer vision, this edge detection filter can also be of use for crack detection in the aforementioned application scenario of sensorial materials. It is assumed that each network node can read data from one local sensor, that is, an accumulated central view of the structural state does not exist. A Sobel kernel S is used for a neighbourhood operation on the original image composed of sensor data, for example, a 4x4 matrix A, and each matrix entry represents a node in the sensor network. There are two different operators S, each for a different direction sensitivity (x/y), shown in Eq. 1. The output image G results from a convolution operation. The FORTH program implementing an agent moving and migrating through the area of interest is shown in Fig. 3. Initially, a master agent is sent to the upper left corner node, sampling data and performing a partial image convolution. Each node calculation carries out sum terms of $g_{i,j}$ elements containing only the local sensor data $a_{x,y}$, updating $g_{i,j}$ with pseudo-code shown in Eq. 2 (assuming array index numbers within range 1...N).

$$S^x = \begin{bmatrix} 1 & 0 & -1 \\ 2 & 0 & -2 \\ 1 & 0 & -1 \end{bmatrix}, \quad S^y = \begin{bmatrix} 1 & 2 & 1 \\ 0 & 0 & 0 \\ -1 & -2 & -1 \end{bmatrix}, \quad \begin{aligned} G^x &= S^x \bullet A, \\ G^y &= S^y \bullet A. \end{aligned} \quad (1)$$

$$\forall (i,j) \in \{x-1, x, x+1\} \times \{y-1, y, y+1\} \ DO$$
$$g_{i,j} \leftarrow g_{i,j} + s_{2-i+x, 2-j+y} \cdot a_{x,y} \quad (2)$$

The results are stored in the agent program code using code morphing and finally the agent travels to the next node, and so forth. If the last node has been visited, then the agent is sent to the first initial node and initiates a reply to be sent to the original node requesting the filtered image data. The FORTH program consists of five words (private, indicated by the star after the definition command). In lines 9 to 15, arrays a and g are defined, either private or public depending on the location of the agent. Public arrays are required for the processing of the final result and creation of a reply agent performed by the master agent at the origin node (1,1). In line 16, the Sobel s matrix is defined and initialized with (constant) values (line 17). The >>[] operator copies values taken from the stack to the respective array. The main word execution sequence is defined in lines 113-116. First, a new data value is sampled from the node s AD converter by calling the word sample. The value is saved in the image array a and variable data. The [a] operator calculates the memory address required for the matrix access. After data sampling, the Sobel computation is performed by calling the word sobel. Two nested loops (lines 25 to 37) compute sum terms of elements of array g containing only the actual sampled image value a[x,y]. The x and y positions are stored in their respective variables. The migrate code distinguishes different cases regarding the agent's current location. When code morphing is performed, the modified program frame is dispatched to the next node. Once all nodes have been visited, the agent sends back a reply agent to the requesting node. This transmits the final result of the distributed computation (line 94). The program is compiled to a machine program consisting of 599 words. The final reply code requires only 103 words. The size of the program code (determining the communication cost) of the migrating agent performing the computations can be reduced by using a two-level agent system. The arrays a, g, and s, and the definitions for the words **sample**, **sobel**, and **update**, which remain untouched by code morphing the entire time, are distributed and permanently stored using a distribution agent before the computation agent is started.

```
1   VARIABLE* x
2   VARIABLE* y
3   VARIABLE* dir
4   VARIABLE* data        4 CONSTANT N
5   <x> 1 x !
6   <y> 1 y !
7   <dir> 1 dir !
8   IMPORT WORD getdata
9   x @ 1 = y @ 1 = and if
10    ARRAY [N,N] a    ( original sensor data )
11    ARRAY [N,N] g    ( convoluted data      )
12  else
13    ARRAY* [N,N] a   ( original sensor data )
14    ARRAY* [N,N] g   ( convoluted data      )
15  then
16  ARRAY* [3,3] s     ( sobel operator )
17  1 0 -1 -2 0 -2 1 0 -1   s >>[]
18  ( a11,a12,a13,a14,a21,....,a44 )
19  <matrix_start>
20    <matrix_a>  0 0 0 0 0 0 0 0 0 0 0 0 0 0 0 0   a >>[]
21    <matrix_g>  0 0 0 0 0 0 0 0 0 0 0 0 0 0 0 0   g >>[]
22  <matrix_end>
23
24  :* sobel              ( note: lowest array index is 0 )
25    x @ x @ 2 - do      ( pos. x-1..x+1 => array x-2..x )
26      I a!              ( save index i in register a   )
27      y @ y @ 2 - do    ( pos. y-1..y+1 => array y-2..y )
28        I b!            ( save index j in register b   )
29        a@ 0 >= and a@ < N and b@ 0 >= and b@ < N and if
30          a@ b@ [g] @   ( fetch g[i,j]     )
31          1 a@ - x @ +  ( 2-i+x  => 1-i+x )
32          1 b@ - y @ +  ( 2-j+y  => 1-j+y )
33          [s] @ data @ * ( s[i',j']*a[x,y] )
34          + a@ b@ [g] !  ( store g[i,j]    )
35        then
36      loop
37    loop
38  ;
39  :* sample
40    getdata  dup
41    x @ 1 - y @ 1 - [a] !
42    data !  ( save sampled data for local computation )
43  ;
44  :* update
45  (
46      transfer data of array to stack and then
47      convert values to word literals in program code
48  )
49    N 1- 0 do
50      I a!
51      N 1- 0 do
52        I b!
53        a@ b@ [g] @
54      loop
55    loop
56    <matrix_g>! N N * s>c
57    N 1- 0 do
58      I a!
59      N 1- 0 do
60        I b!
61        a@ b@ [a] @
62      loop
63    loop
64    <matrix_a>! N N * s>c
65  ;
```

```
66  :* reply
67    RESET c!
68    <reply_header_start>@ <reply_header_end>@ >>c
69    <matrix_start>@ <matrix_end>@ >>c
70    <reply_start>@ <reply_end>@ >>c
71  ;
72  :* migrate
73  (
74      migrate to next node depending on (x,y,dir) settings
75  )
76    dir @ 1 = if
77      x @ 4 = if
78        y @ 1 + <y>! 1 s>c    ( update y counter          )
79        <dir>! -1 1 s>c       ( revert propagation direction )
80        0 1 fork
81      else
82        x @ 1 + <x>! 1 s>c    ( update x counter, goto right )
83        1 0 fork
84      then
85    else
86      x @ 1 = y @ N <> and if
87        y @ 1 + <y>! 1 s>c    ( update y counter          )
88        <dir>! 1 1 s>c        ( revert propagation direction )
89        0 1 fork
90      else
91        y @ N = if
92          ( create reply and go back to origin )
93          reply
94          0 -4 fork
95        else
96          x @ 1 - <x>! 1 s>c  ( update x counter, goto left )
97          -1 0 fork
98        then
99      then
100   then
101   x @ 1 = y @ 1 = and if
102     ( master agent, wait for reply )
103     OBJECT EVENT sobel_await
104     sobel_await #await
105     ( propagate reply to original sender of agent )
106     update reply
107     forget a forget g    ( cleanup dictionary        )
108     1 return
109   else
110     0 return
111   then
112  ;
113  sample
114  sobel
115  update
116  migrate
117
118  ( not reached )
119  <reply_header_start>
120    IMPORT ARRAY [N,N] a
121    IMPORT ARRAY [N,N] g
122    IMPORT OBJECT sobel_await
123  <reply_header_end>
124  <reply_start>
125    sobel_await #wakeup
126    0 return
127  <reply_end>
```

Fig. 3. FORTH implementation of the Sobel filter agent. Note: only the x-sensitive Sobel operator is shown here.

5   Summary, Conclusion, and Outlook

This paper introduced a hardware architecture and runtime environment specifically designed towards the implementation of mobile agents by using dynamic code morphing under the constraints of low-power consumption and high component miniaturization. It uses a modified and extended version of FORTH as the programming language for agent programs. The runtime environment is modelled on the behavioural level using a multi-process-oriented programming language and can be embedded in a single-SoC hardware design. A functional equivalent piece of software can be synthesized and executed on a generic desktop computer. To show the viability of the presented distributed and parallel computing approach, a filtering algorithm was borrowed from the field of image processing and applied in the application scenario of sensorial materials. In the given example, multiple mobile agents move through a network of sensor nodes, jointly executing a spatially distributed data processing task. Calculation results and a subset of the agent's execution state are preserved within the agent's program code during migration to different network nodes. The size of the migrating code can be significantly reduced in size by decoupling functions that remain unaffected by code morphing during operation from the migrating agent program and distributing them in the data processing network beforehand. Synchronous inter-agent communication can be carried out by using reply agents sent back to a parent agent waiting for the reception and execution of the reply. Future work will be the development and practical evaluation of sophisticated distributed load and defect detection algorithms on this architecture for use in sensorial materials.

References

1. Bosse, S.: Hardware-Software-Co-Design of Parallel and Distributed Systems Using a unique Behavioural Programming and Multi-Process Model with High-Level Synthesis. In: Proceedings of the SPIE Microtechnologies 2011 Conference, Prague, Session EMT 102 VLSI Circuits and Systems, April 18-20 (2011)
2. Iftode, L., Borcea, C., Kang, P.: Cooperative Computing in Sensor Networks. In: Ilyas, M. (ed.) Handbook of Sensor Networks: Compact Wireless and Wired Sensing Systems. CRC Press, Boca Raton (2004)
3. Rather, E.D., Colburn, D.R., Moore, C.H.: The evolution of Forth. In: Proceedings SIGPLAN Not., vol. 28(3) (March 1993)
4. Bosse, S., Lehmhus, D.: Smart Communication in a Wired Sensor- and Actuator-Network of a Modular Robot Actuator System using a Hop-Protocol with Delta-Routin. In: Proceedings of Smart Systems Integration Conference, Como, Italy, March 23-24 (2010)
5. Kent, A., Williams, J.G. (eds.): Mobile Agents. Encyclopedia for Computer Science and Technology. M.Dekker Inc., New York (1998)
6. Peine, H., Stolpmann, T.: The Architecture of the Ara Platform for Mobile Agent. In: Rothermel, K., Popescu-Zeletin, R. (eds.) MA 1997. LNCS, vol. 1219, pp. 50–61. Springer, Heidelberg (1997)
7. Wang, A.I., Soerensen, C.F., Indal, E.: A Mobile Agent Architecture for Heterogeneous Devices. Wireless and Optical Communications (2003)
8. Pantke, F., Bosse, S., Lehmhus, D., Lawo, M.: An Artificial Intelligence Approach Towards Sensorial Materials. In: Future Computing Conference (2011)
9. Koopmann, P.: Stack Computers: the new wave (1989)

Multi-agent System for Parallel Road Network Hierarchization

Łukasz Chomątek and Aneta Poniszewska-Marańda

Institute of Information Technology, Technical University of Lodz, Poland
lukasz.chomatek@p.lodz.pl, anetap@ics.p.lodz.pl

Abstract. The paper describes the proposal of solving the path finding problem with the use of multi-agent system. Efficient vehicle routing is a very significant task nowadays, as the number of vehicles on the roads is growing rapidly. The idea of multi-agent system includes cooperation between autonomous software agents to complete a certain task.

1 Introduction

Nowadays, the increasing number of vehicles on the roads provoke more and more road problems - road accidents, traffic jams. From other side, the road network is more and more complex and complicated and it is more and more difficult to find sometime the right way in the tangle of motorways. Such situation caused the increase of popularity of GPS devices that the drivers can install in their cars. Internet sites, where it is possible to compute efficient route from one point to another are also popular, because they are not only maps but also can fulfill some needs of the user. The user's needs can be divided into some groups:

- saving of time - user of the system only needs to know the destination address and in some cases he needs to enter the start point as well because the path is computed automatically by the system,
- finding some information - system can show the way to the nearest restaurant, gas station or shop,
- informing about the situation on the road, e.g. traffic jams, speed cameras, road works, accidents.

Both mentioned websites and GPS devices have to execute large numbers of queries about the route between points on the map. The website is a service dedicated for the large number of users and GPS device has to reflect dynamically changing road conditions (i.e. driver was supposed to turn left on the crossroads but went straight and now the system must compute a detour). Large number of queries can only be handled when either users' requests can be processed in a longer time or by use of very efficient path finding algorithms.

Finding optimal route can be solved either by deterministic [1,2] or stochastic [9] methods. The most efficient algorithms for solving Single Source Shortest Path (SSSP) are hierarchical approaches [1]. They are usually based on the fact that some road segments can be marked as having higher importance than

L. Rutkowski et al. (Eds.): ICAISC 2012, Part II, LNCS 7268, pp. 424–432, 2012.

others. What is more, road network can be preprocessed by removing some nodes and introduce some shortcuts instead (i.e. there is only one connection from one node to another, so all nodes between them can be substituted by a direct link for this nodes).

The paper describes the proposition of solving the path finding problem with the use of multi-agent system. The idea of multi-agent system includes cooperation between autonomous software agents to complete a certain task. For solution of SSSP problem based on road network hierarchy, the agents can be divided into some groups: graph constructing agents, agents interacting with the system user and miscellaneous agents. The second significant term in the domain of multi-agent systems is the environment, in which the agents are located. In the case of road traffic it is very well defined and contains hardly any subjective factors. It includes vehicles, roads, road signs, signals and some important places which are usually named points of interest (POI). Road environment is dynamic, due to the fact that hardly any part of it remains unchanged for a long time.

2   Approaches of Hierarchical Single Source Shortest Path

Typical algorithms designed for solving SSSP problems do not use any preprocessing of the graph. Preprocessing phase can take a long time, so that such algorithms can be easily applied, when there is a little number of queries about the shortest path. Most popular SSSP solving algorithms are Dijkstra's algorithm, Bellman-Ford algorithm and A* algorithm.

Hierarchical algorithms include some kind of preprocessing of the graph in order to shorten the time required to process a single query. It is notably important when number of queries is very high and sometime can be expended before deployment of the system. The algorithm of Hierarchical Path Views proposed in the literature [4,5] was based on the following ideas:

- base road network was split into some fragments - places of split were chosen by its geographical coordinates,
- connections which are outside generated fragments belong to higher hierarchy level,
- division and level transfer is an iterative process.

The result of such a division are the matrices containing the shortest path lengths for each segment and each level. After the division phase, to perform a query, A* algorithm was used. In [4] the concept of "reach" value for each vertex was introduced. It was calculated as a number of long distance paths between some points including this vertex. When a query is sent to the system, vertices with low "reach" value are not considered.

Base for other branch of hierarchical algorithms for solving SSSP problem was Highway Hierarchies algorithm proposed in [1,2]. Dijkstra's algorithm is used in the preprocessing phase to calculate the neighborhood for each vertex. Next, the vertices that fulfill some criteria are moved to the higher hierarchy level. When this phase is done, the higher hierarchy level is preprocessed that allows to generate shortcuts between certain vertices. Number of hierarchy levels and size of the neighborhood are parameters of the algorithm. Proper choose of them influences on the amount of time needed to process a single query. To improve performance of the queries, the use of A* algorithm instead of Dijkstra's search is proposed.

Some parts of construction phase of Highway Hierarchies algorithm can be performed concurrently. We decided to try performing division of road network graph, so that Highway Hierarchies algorithm can be performed on a single part of this graph. After completion of the algorithm on each part, all subgraphs should be merged to obtain a final Highway Hierarchies graph. Obviously, processing of all subgraphs is believed to be faster than processing of whole graph.

3   Architecture of Proposed Multi-agent System

The standards of architecture for multi-agent systems were described by FIPA organization [7]. Due to this specification, multi-agent system consists of some number of Agent Platforms that were as a parts of the system and they can be used to host the agents. Each Agent Platform consists of three parts to handle the management of agents:

- Message Transport System (MTS) that is supposed to be used by the agents for communication,
- Agent Management System (AMS) that represents catalog of existing agents,
- Directory Facilitator (DF) that stores the information about the services provided by the agents.

The analysis of modern programming techniques shows that some practices can be applied in newly designed multi-agents systems:

- use Service Oriented Architecture (SOA) to simplify and improve the possibilities of agent communication,
- make Directory Facilitator the mandatory part of multi-agent system,
- try to apply the enterprise design patterns such as dependency injection to coordinate the communication of agents on a single machine,
- simplify the architecture using the Windows Communication Foundation (WCF) [6,7].

The introduction of web services allowed the developers to connect the applications based on different software and hardware platforms, for example Java and .NET Framework. The Web Services use a specific protocol to expose a schema of transferred data and allow the clients to make the synchronous calls of exposed methods [3].

The service oriented architecture is used in the process of creation of the multi-agent systems. It gives the system more elastic and moreover the interaction between the agents is simpler and its safety is on the upper level. Figure 1 presents the skeleton of proposed architecture of the multi-agent system based on service oriented architecture. An agent uses the service directories: *Directory*

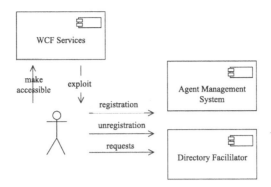

Fig. 1. System components from the agent's point of view

Facilitator and *Agent Management System*, he makes accessible certain services and he profits by the services offered by other agents [3].

Important thing in such a system is the applicated communication model, as agents need to get information about other agents from DF component. What is more, agents need to have the possibility to communicate asynchronously. Asynchronous communication is important, because calculations on the road graph are distributed between many agents.

In general, all agents exposes at least on service, and all of the services offered by the agent are registered in Directory Facilitator component. In most cases, general communication model (Fig. 2), based on [6] is used for the communication. In this way agent B exposes a service X, and agent A wants to communicate with the agent that exposes X. Note, that agent A does not know, that agent B offers such a service. At first, agent B registers the service X in the Directory Facilitator component, denoted as F. Then, agent A asks the DF about agents that offers the service X and receives the reply. Now agent A knows agent B, so that they can communicate. In this model, to make the communication possible, three auxiliary actions are needed, but agent A can hold information about agent B for further communication. This model can be applied both for synchronous and asynchronous communication, as we do not specify, whether agent A needs to wait for the `tell(X)`.

4   Multi-agent System for Distributed Highway Hierarchies Algorithm

Application of multi-agent system for building Highway Hierarchies graph was proposed in [8]. Two main assumptions were made for proposed application of multi-agent system for building Highway Hierarchies graph:

- system must be able to take into account the user's preferences (i.e. route should be the shortest, traveling time should be lowest) and environmental conditions (i.e. weather, time of a day),
- computations should be done concurrently, where it is possible to be done.

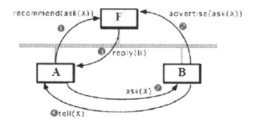

Fig. 2. General Communication Model

To complete the first of these assumptions, weights of the road segments must be assigned using different criteria, such as length, average traveling time, speed limits, etc. It was decided to introduce some number of reactive agents that collect the data from different road segments. This type of agents can work in two different ways, depending on the data structure which is used to store the road network technology. The first way is associated with the nodes as it is easy to get information about edges connected to the node. Second way is related to edges. If list of edges in the graph is directly provided, it can be divided into some parts and each part can be analyzed by a single agent.

In our system both graph nodes and edges are kept in the separate lists. However references are duplicated and it simplifies the way of access to the needed data and allows the simple and complex weight assignment rules.

Regardless of the chosen solution, this process can be performed in parallel, what means sharing work for several agents. Depending on the selection criteria by which individual weights are calculated, work on each road section may perform one or more agents (each can calculate the weight using different method). If the weight of the segment is calculated on the basis of several criteria, use of a coordinating agent for the weights assignment process can be considered. The coordinating agent can calculate weight in accordance with certain rules (e.g. use the weighted average of values calculated by agents). Coordinating agent may have some adaptive abilities, depending on application of the system [8].

Concurrent computation can be also applied in the other parts of Highway Hierarchies graphs creation process. Obviously, calculation of neighborhood N_H^l for each vertex is independent of each other. The only nuisance is that for each vertex, different queue of vertices intended to be visited must be kept. Any number of agents can be used to calculate such a neighborhood. Depending on the developer choice, these agents cooperate directly with agents responsible for assigning weights to graph edges or with the coordinating agent.

The responses to user's queries for the system should take into account his preferences regarding the itinerary and the current conditions on the road. It might be necessary to create several Highway Hierarchies graphs, which will be used to obtain a system response depending on certain factors. Different graphs can be prepared for example for the city center during peak hours and at night. To implement this assumption, the introduction of a special type of agent can be considered. Such an agent will redirect the user query to the appropriate

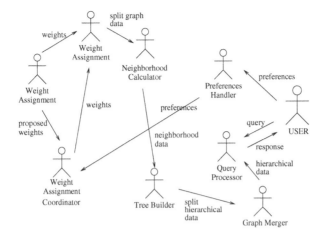

Fig. 3. Types of agents in Highway Hierarchies algorithm

Highway Hierarchies graph. Relay agent may assist in work of coordinating agent by suggesting the criteria by which the weight of the edge should be calculated [8]. Proposed architecture of multi-agent system is shown on figure 3.

One of the simplest agents are *Weight Assignment Agents*. Their task is to calculate proper weight for the road segment, that they are responsible for. As it was mentioned, weights can be based on different criteria. In our tests, these were the length of the road segment, speed limit on the segment and average traveling time. As *Weight Assignment Agents* perform their calculations when they are asked by *Weight Assignment Coordinator Agent*, they are supposed to be understood as reactive agents. There can be many agents of this type in the system. Responsibility of each agent is specified, when the map is loaded into the system. In our case, simple division of the road network is made: as number of road segments is known from the map, each *Weight Assignment Agent* takes the same number of segments.

Weight Assignment Coordinator Agent is a single agent that is supposed to handle User's criteria. User can specify, whether he want to arrive as fast as possible to the destination or don't want to drive on roads with low speed limit. All of the preferences influence the final hierarchical division of the road network. *Weight Assignment Coordinator* collects weights from *Weight Assignment Agents* and builds a final weight according to User's preferences. After that, weight are sent to the *Neighborhood Calculator Agents*. This agent is the proactive agent. When it receives request from the *Preferences Handler Agent*, it collects data from *Weight Assignment Agents* and provides data for *Neighborhood Calculator Agent*. Agent is autonomous, as the method of combining weights is not specified by rules provided by other agent.

Preferences Handler Agent is another reactive agent. When User changes his constraints about route, the agent send the data to *Weight Assignment Coordinator*. We decided to put one *Preferences Handler* into the system, as its work is limited to send some data to other agent from time to time. When some number of Users work with the system, this agent can hold preferences of all of them.

Another agent which interacts with the user, is the *Query Processor Agent*. Its task is to collect data from User and show him a path between specified points. It interacts with *Tree Builder Agent*, from which it collects data to process the query. However it seems that this agent is reactive, as it only processes some queries, it can be also considered as a proactive agent, because the algorithm used for finding the path is owned by this agent. It means that *Query Processor Agent* decides which algorithm to choose and what data to get from *Tree Builder*.

To perform the initial phase of the Highway Hierarchies algorithm, two additional types of agents are needed. The first one is *Neighborhood Calculator Agent*. This agent receives data either from *Weight Assignment Agents*, when only single criterion is considered, or from *Weight Assignment Coordinator Agent*, when weight of the road segment is calculated using different criteria. This is a social agent, as it decides with what agents to cooperate and has an autonomy to choose the method of finding the neighborhood. As this work must be performed for each node in the road graph, many agents of this type can appear in the system. Finally, *Tree Builder agent* is needed to merge data provided by *Neighborhood Calculator Agents*. However one *Tree Builder Agent* is sufficient for the correct results of the basic hierarchical algorithm, in some cases more *Tree Builder Agents* should be used. This will be discussed later. *Tree Builders* are proactive agents as they have an autonomy to choose proper *Neighborhood Calculator agents*, which they want to communicate with, as well as the method of building Highway Hierarchies graph. Communication between agents in the system is realized using one of the models mentioned in the previous section. Proposed weights for the *Weight Assignment Coordinator* are sent using a simplified model, as this agent does not need to know, what agents are actually responsible for each weight. Communication between *Neighborhood Calculators* and *Weight Assignment Coordinator* is more complex. In this case, when many agents are supposed to calculate the neighborhoods, general model performs better. This is caused by the fact that there will be many acts of communication between this agents as new query should be made for each node. The same situation happens when weights are send directly from *Weight Assignment Agents*. Communication between *Tree Builder* and *Neighborhood Calculators* uses simplified model. This model was chosen, as communication act between *Tree Builder* and *Neighborhood Calculators* is made only once for each node. Communication between *Query Processor* and *Tree Builder* is made using general model. User interacts directly with *Query Processor Agent* and *Preferences Handler*. Preferences data are sent to *Weight Assignment Coordinator Agent* by general communication model. This model is also used to process User's queries in the system.

The tests revealed that for diverse criteria the calculated hierarchies differ very much. The results obtained for three proposed criteria: speed limits, traveling time and road length, shown that these hierarchies graphs have at each level only a few common edges with other hierarchies graphs. Moreover, expected

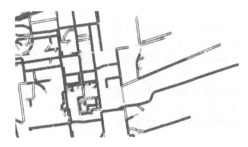

Fig. 4. Example of Hierarchical Division for neighborhood of Technical University of Lodz HH(3,5)

Fig. 5. HH algorithm performed for a subgraph HH(3,5)

convergence between dominating user's preference and number of common edges with the hierarchies graph for this criterion was observed.

Algorithm described above was implemented using C# 4.0 language in Windows environment. Tests were run on different maps both for single and split road network graph. In general, road segments on the top hierarchy levels in the full graph are on high hierarchy level in a part of the graph too, overall number on the highest hierarchy level is smaller for the subgraphs. It is caused by the fact that when the number of edges is smaller, promotion to the higher hierarchy level is harder. The tests performed for both maps shown that the time needed to execute the calculations depends in slight degree on the number of edges in the subgraph.

In general, road segments on the top hierarchy levels in the full graph are on high hierarchy level in a part of the graph too, overall number on the highest hierarchy level is smaller for the subgraphs. It is caused by the fact that when the number of edges is smaller, promotion to the higher hierarchy level is harder.

The tests performed for both maps shown that the time needed to execute the calculations depends in slight degree on the number of edges in the subgraph. In case of real road map, both subgraphs contain after a division the exact number of vertices. However, the first part contains significantly more edges. The time needed to compute the hierarchy levels for both parts were almost identical.

The second graph was an artificial road mesh, where after a division the number of edges was the same in the both parts. Performed tests shown that the time of computing for both subgraphs was also the same in this case.

In the next step, Highway Hierarchies was run for the subgraphs with identical parameters. Obtained results for subgraphs show that when a division is made, number of edges on each level differs from number of these edges when the whole graph is taken into account in Highway Hierarchies. For real road network, such a difference was up to 70%. It was caused by the fact that large number of edges was included in the first subgraph. This difference for the artificial road network was smaller then in the real network.

5   Conclusions

Performing the hierarchical division of road network on the split of the road graph can improve the construction phase processing time due to the lower computational complexity. Number of edges on certain levels in subgraphs can differ very much from these from division of whole graph. Adjusting hierarchical algorithm parameters can improve results of divisions of subgraphs. Multi-agent system can be utilized to solve this problem, what allows to compute most parts of the algorithm in parallel. Architecture of presented system is extensible. There is a possibility to implement new agents for different graph split methods.

References

1. Sanders, P., Schultes, D.: Engineering Highway Hierarchies. In: Azar, Y., Erlebach, T. (eds.) ESA 2006. LNCS, vol. 4168, pp. 804–816. Springer, Heidelberg (2006)
2. Sanders, P., Schultes, D.: Highway Hierarchies Hasten Exact Shortest Path Queries. In: Brodal, G.S., Leonardi, S. (eds.) ESA 2005. LNCS, vol. 3669, pp. 568–579. Springer, Heidelberg (2005)
3. Chomatek, L., Poniszewska-Marańda, A.: Modern Approach for Building of Multi-Agent Systems. In: Rauch, J., Raś, Z.W., Berka, P., Elomaa, T. (eds.) ISMIS 2009. LNCS (LNAI), vol. 5722, pp. 351–360. Springer, Heidelberg (2009)
4. Nannicini, G., Baptiste, P., Barbier, G., Krob, D., Liberti, L.: Fast paths in large-scale dynamic road networks. Computational Optimization and Applications 45(1), 143–158 (2008)
5. Eppstein, D., Goodrich, M., Trott, L.: Going off-road: transversal complexity in road networks. In: Proc. of 17th ACM SIGSPATIAL, pp. 23–32 (2009)
6. Vasters, C.: Introduction to Building WCF Services. MSDN Library (2005)
7. FIPA, Abstract Architecture Specification (2002)
8. Chomatek, L.: Multi-agent approach for building highway hierarchies graph. In: Proc. of 31th Intern. Conference Information Systems, Architecture and Technology (2010)
9. Koszelew, J., Piwonsk, A.: A New Evolutionary Algorithm for Routes Generation with Optimal Time of Realization in Public Transport Network. JACS 18 (2010)

Hybrid Position/Force Control
of the SCORBOT-ER 4pc Manipulator
with Neural Compensation of Nonlinearities

Piotr Gierlak

Rzeszow University of Technology,
Department of Applied Mechanics and Robotics
8 Powstańców Warszawy St., 35-959 Rzeszów, Poland
pgierlak@prz.edu.pl

Abstract. The problem of the manipulator hybrid position/force control is not trivial because the manipulator is a nonlinear object, whose parameters may be unknown, variable and the working conditions are changeable. The neural control system enables the manipulator to behave correctly, even if the mathematical model of the control object is unknown. In this paper, the hybrid position/force controller with a neural compensation of nonlinearities for the SCORBOT-ER 4pc robotic manipulator is presented. The presented control law and adaptive law guarantee practical stability of the closed-loop system in the sense of Lyapunov. The results of a numerical simulation are presented.

Keywords: Neural Networks, Robotic Manipulator, Tracking Control, Force Control.

1 Introduction

Robotic manipulators are devices which find different applications in many domains of the economy. The requirements in relation to precision of motion and autonomy of manipulators are increasing as well as the tasks performed by them are more and more complex. In contemporary industrial applications it is desired for the manipulator to exert specified forces and move along a prescribed path. Manipulators are objects with nonlinear and uncertain dynamics, with unknown and variable parameters (masses, mass moments of inertia, friction coefficients), which operate in changeable conditions. Control of such complex systems is very problematic. The control system has to generate such control signals that will guarantee the execution of movement along a path with a suitable force and with desired precision in spite of the changeable operating conditions.

In the control systems of industrial manipulators, the computed torque method [1,2] for non-linearity compensation is used. However, these approaches require precise knowledge about the mathematical model (the structure of motion equations with coefficients) of the control object. Moreover, in such an approach, parameters in the compensator have nominal values so the control

L. Rutkowski et al. (Eds.): ICAISC 2012, Part II, LNCS 7268, pp. 433–441, 2012.
© Springer-Verlag Berlin Heidelberg 2012

system acts without taking into account the changeable operating conditions. In the literature exists many variation of algorithms, in which parameters of the mathematical model of manipulator are adapted [1,2]. However these approaches do not eliminate the problem with structural uncertainty of the model.

In connection with the present difficulties, neural control techniques were developed [3,4,5,6]. In these methods the mathematical model is unnecessary. These techniques are used in hybrid position/force controller. In works [7,8] such controllers have been presented. But in the first of the works only force normal to the contact surface is taking into account, and in the second work some assumption is hard to satisfy in practical applications, namely some stiffness matrix which characterizes features of environment and allows to calculate contact forces, must be known.

In previous author's paper only position controllers have been considered. In present paper hybrid position/force neural controller is shown. This approach takes into account all forces/moments which acts on the end-effector. These forces/moments are measured by sensor located in the end-effector.

2   Description of the SCORBOT-ER 4pc Robotic Manipulator

The SCORBOT-ER 4pc robotic manipulator is presented in Fig. 1. It is driven by direct-current motors with gears and optical encoders. The manipulator has 5 rotational kinematic pairs: the arm of the manipulator has 3 degrees of freedom whereas the gripper has 2 degrees.

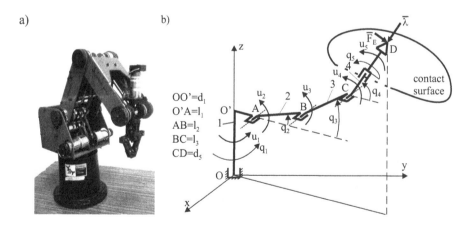

Fig. 1. a) SCORBOT-ER 4pc robotic manipulator, b) scheme

The transformation from joint space to Cartesian space is given by the following equation

$$y = k(q) \,, \tag{1}$$

where $q \in R^n$ is a vector of generalized coordinates (angles of rotation of links), $k(q)$ is a kinematics function, $y \in R^m$ is a vector of a position/orientation of the end-effector (point D). Dynamical equations of motion of the analysed model are in the following form [7], [9]:

$$M(q)\ddot{q} + C(q,\dot{q})\dot{q} + F(\dot{q}) + G(q) + \tau_d(t) = u + J_h^T(q)\lambda + \tau_F , \qquad (2)$$

where $M(q) \in R^{nxn}$ is an inertia matrix, $C(q,\dot{q}) \in R^n$ is a vector of centrifugal and Coriolis forces/moments, $F(\dot{q}) \in R^n$ is a friction vector, $G(q) \in R^n$ is a gravity vector, $\tau_d(t) \in R^n$ is a vector of disturbances bounded by $\|\tau_d\| < b$, $b > 0$, $u \in R^n$ is a control input vector, $J_h(q) \in R^{m_1 xn}$ is a Jacobian matrix associated with the contact surface geometry, $\lambda \in R^{m_1}$ is a vector of constraining forces exerted normally on the contact surface (Lagrange multiplier), $\tau_F \in R^n$ is a vector of forces/moments in joints, which come from forces/moments $F_E \in R^m$ applied to the end-effector (except the constraining forces). The vector τ_F is given by

$$\tau_F = J^{bT}(q)F_E , \qquad (3)$$

where $J^b(q) \in R^{mxn}$ is a geometric Jacobian in body [2]. The Jacobian matrix $J_h(q)$ can be calculated in the following way

$$J_h(q) = \frac{\partial h(q)}{\partial q} , \qquad (4)$$

where $h(q) = 0$ is an equation of the holonomic constraint, which describes the contact surface. This equation reduces the number of degrees of freedom to $n_1 = n - m_1$, so the analysed system can be described by the reduced position variable $\theta_1 \in R^{n_1}$ [7]. The remainder of variables depend on θ_1 in the following way

$$\theta_2 = \gamma(\theta_1) , \qquad (5)$$

where $\theta_2 \in R^{m_1}$, and γ arise from the holonomic constraint. The vector of generalized coordinates may be written as $q = [\theta_1^T \theta_2^T]^T$. Let define the extended Jacobian [7]

$$L(\theta_1) = \begin{bmatrix} I_{n_1} \\ \frac{\partial \gamma}{\partial \theta_1} \end{bmatrix} , \qquad (6)$$

where $I_{n_1} \in R^{n_1 xn_1}$ is an identity matrix. This allows to write the relations:

$$\dot{q} = L(\theta_1)\dot{\theta}_1 , \qquad (7)$$

$$\ddot{q} = L(\theta_1)\ddot{\theta}_1 + \dot{L}(\theta_1)\dot{\theta}_1 , \qquad (8)$$

and write a reduced order dynamics in terms of θ_1, as:

$$M(\theta_1)L(\theta_1)\ddot{\theta}_1 + V_1(\theta_1,\dot{\theta}_1)\dot{\theta}_1 + F(\dot{\theta}_1) + G(\theta_1) + \tau_d(t) = u + J_h^T(\theta_1)\lambda + J^{bT}(\theta_1)F_E , \qquad (9)$$

where $V_1(\theta_1,\dot{\theta}_1) = M(\theta_1)\dot{L}(\theta_1) + C(\theta_1,\dot{\theta}_1)L(\theta_1)$. Pre-multiplying eq. (9) by $L^T(\theta_1)$ and taking into account that $J_h(\theta_1)L(\theta_1) = 0$, the reduced order dynamics is given by:

$$\overline{M}\ddot{\theta}_1 + \overline{V}_1\dot{\theta}_1 + \overline{F} + \overline{G} + \overline{\tau}_d = L^T u , \qquad (10)$$

where $\overline{M} = L^T M L$, $\overline{V}_1 = L^T V_1$, $\overline{F} = L^T F$, $\overline{G} = L^T G$, $\overline{\tau}_d = L^T [\tau_d - J^{bT} F_E]$.

3   Neural Network Hybrid Control

The aim of a hybrid position/force control is to follow a desired trajectory of motion $\theta_{1d} \in R^{n_1}$, and exert desired contact force $\lambda_d \in R^{m_1}$ normally to the surface. By defining a motion error e_θ, a filtered motion error s, a force error $\tilde{\lambda}$ and an auxiliary signal v_1 as:

$$e_\theta = \theta_{1d} - \theta_1 \,, \tag{11}$$

$$s = \dot{e}_\theta + \Lambda e_\theta \,, \tag{12}$$

$$\tilde{\lambda} = \lambda_d - \lambda \,, \tag{13}$$

$$v_1 = \dot{\theta}_{1d} + \Lambda e_\theta \,, \tag{14}$$

where Λ is a positive diagonal design matrix, the dynamic equation (10) may be written in terms of the filtered motion error as

$$\overline{M}\dot{s} = -\overline{V}_1 s + L^T f(x) + L^T \left[\tau_d - J^{bT} F_E \right] - L^T u \,, \tag{15}$$

with a nonlinear function

$$f(x) = ML\dot{v}_1 + V_1 v_1 + F + G \,, \tag{16}$$

where $x = \begin{bmatrix} e_\theta^T & \dot{e}_\theta^T & \theta_{1d}^T v & \dot{\theta}_{1d}^T & \ddot{\theta}_{1d}^T \end{bmatrix}^T$. The mathematical structure of hybrid position/force controller has a form of [7]

$$u = \hat{f}(x) + K_D L s - J_h^T \left[\lambda_d + K_F \tilde{\lambda} \right] - \nu \,, \tag{17}$$

where K_D and K_F are positive definite matrixes of position and force gain, ν is a robustifying term, $\hat{f}(x)$ approximates the function (16). This function may be approximated by the neural network. In this work a typical feedforward neural network (Fig. 2b) with one hidden layer is assumed. The hidden layer with sigmoidal neurons, is connected with an input layer by weights collected in a matrix D, and with an output layer by weights collected in a matrix W. The input weights are randomly chosen and constant, but the output weights initially are equal zero, and will be tuned during adaptation process. Such neural network is linear in the weights, and has the following description [3,4]:

$$f(x) = W^T \varphi(x) + \varepsilon \,, \tag{18}$$

with output from hidden layer $\varphi(x) = S(D^T x)$, where x is an input vector, $S(.)$ is a vector of neuron activation functions, ε is an estimation error bounded by $\|\varepsilon\| < \varepsilon_N$, $\varepsilon_N = const > 0$. The matrix W is unknown, so an estimation $\hat{W}$ is used, and a mathematical description of a real neural network, which approximates function $f(x)$ is given by

$$\hat{f}(x) = \hat{W}^T \varphi(x) \,. \tag{19}$$

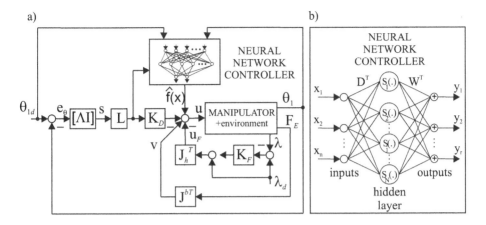

Fig. 2. a) scheme of closed-loop system, b) neural network

Substituting equations (18), (18) and (19) into (15), we obtained a description of the closed-loop system (Fig. 2a) in terms of the filtered motion error

$$\overline{M}\dot{s} = -L^T K_D L s - \overline{V}_1 s + L^T \tilde{W}^T \varphi(x) + L^T \left[\tau_d + \varepsilon - J^{bT} F_E + \nu \right] , \qquad (20)$$

where $\tilde{W} = W - \hat{W}$ is an error of weight estimation.

In order to derive an adaptation law of the weights and the robustifying term ν, the Lyapunov stability theory is applied. Define a Lyapunov function candidate, which is a quadratic form of the filtered motion error and the weight estimation error [4]

$$V = 1/2 s^T \overline{M} s + 1/2 tr \left(\tilde{W}^T \Gamma_W^{-1} \tilde{W} \right) , \qquad (21)$$

where Γ_W is a diagonal design matrix, $tr(.)$ denotes trace of matrix. The time derivative of the function V along the solutions to (20) is

$$\dot{V} = -s^T L^T K_D L s + tr \left[\tilde{W}^T \left(\varphi(x) s^T L^T + \Gamma_W^{-1} \dot{\tilde{W}} \right) \right] + \\ + s^T L^T \left[\tau_d + \varepsilon - J^{bT} F_E + \nu \right] , \qquad (22)$$

where a skew symmetric matrix property of $\dot{\overline{M}} - 2\overline{V}_1$ was used. Defining an adaptive law of the weight estimation as [7]

$$\dot{\hat{W}} = \Gamma_W \varphi(x) s^T L^T - k \Gamma_W ||L s|| \hat{W} , \qquad (23)$$

with $k > 0$, and choosing robustifying term in the form

$$\nu = J^{bT} F_E , \qquad (24)$$

function (22) may be written as

$$\dot{V} = -s^T L^T K_D L s + k ||L s|| tr \left(\tilde{W}^T \hat{W} \right) + s^T L^T \left[\tau_d + \varepsilon \right] . \qquad (25)$$

Function $\dot{V} \leq 0$ if at least one of two the following conditions will be satisfied

$$\psi_s = \{s : ||Ls|| > (b + \varepsilon_N + kW_{max}^2/4)/K_{Dmin} = b_s\}, \qquad (26)$$

$$\psi_W = \{\tilde{W} : ||\tilde{W}||_F > W_{max}/2 + \sqrt{(b + \varepsilon_N)/k + W_{max}^2/4} = b_W\}, \qquad (27)$$

where K_{Dmin} is the minimum singular value of K_D, $||W||_F \leq W_{max}$, $||.||_F$ denotes Frobenius norm. This result means, that the function $\dot{V}$ is negative outside a compact set defined by (26) and (27). According to a standard Lyapunov theorem extension [10], both $||Ls||$ and $||\tilde{W}||_F$ are uniformly ultimately bounded to sets ψ_s and ψ_W with practical limits b_s and b_W. Adaptive law (23) guarantees that weight estimates will be bound without persistency of the excitation condition. In order to prove, that force error $\tilde{\lambda}$ is bounded, we write equation (9) in terms of the filtered motion error, taking into account (17), (18), (19) and (24). After conversion, we obtained

$$J_h^T [K_F + I] \tilde{\lambda} = ML\dot{s} + V_1 s + K_D Ls - \tilde{W}^T \varphi(x) - \varepsilon - \tau_d = B\left(s, \dot{s}, x, \tilde{W}\right), \quad (28)$$

where all quantities on the right hand side are bounded. Pre-multiplying eq. (28) by J_h and computing the force error, we obtain:

$$\tilde{\lambda} = [K_F + I]^{-1}[J_h J_h^T]^{-1} J_h B\left(s, \dot{s}, x, \tilde{W}\right), \qquad (29)$$

where $J_h J_h^T$ is nonsingular. This result means, that the force error is bounded and may be decreased by increasing the force gain K_F.

4   Results of the Simulation

In order to confirm the behaviour of the proposed hybrid control system, a simulation was performed. We assumed, that the contact surface was flat, rough and parallel to xy plane. The end-effector was normal to the contact surface, moved on that surface on a desired circular path (Fig. 3a) and exerted prescribed force (Fig. 3b). The desired trajectory in a joint space (Fig. 3c) was obtained by solving the inverse kinematics problem.

Problem of nonlinearities compensation have been decomposed on five simple tasks. For control of each link, a separate neural network with a single output was used. Neural networks have correspondingly 11, 10, 10, 12 and 4 inputs. Neural networks for links 1-4 had 15 neurons, and for link 5 had 9 neurons in the hidden layer. The input weights are randomly chosen from range $< -0.5, 0.5 >$. The design matrixes were chosen as: $\lambda = diag\{1,1,1,1\}$, $K_D = diag\{1,1,1,1,1\}$, $\Gamma_W = 4I$, where I is an identity matrix with suitable dimension, and moreover $K_F = 3$, $k = 0.1$.

In relation to the controller, only the results for the second link are presented in this paper. At the beginning of the movement, the compensatory signal $\hat{f}_2(x_2)$ (Fig. 4b) generated by the compensator was not accurate, because the initial weight estimates were set to zero. The signal u_{PD2} (Fig. 4b) generated by the

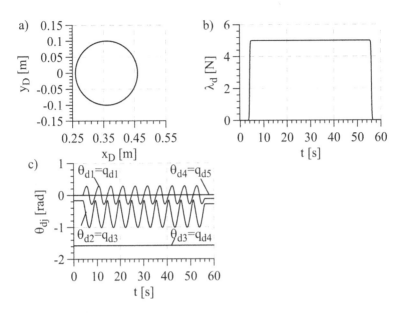

Fig. 3. a) the desired patch of the end-effector, b) the desired force, c) the desired trajectory in a joint space

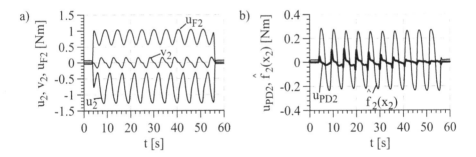

Fig. 4. Control inputs for the second link: a) u_2 - the total control signal, v_2 - the robustifying term, u_{F2} - the second element of the term $J_h^T \left[\lambda_d + K_F \tilde{\lambda} \right]$, b) u_{PD2} - the second element of the PD term $K_D Ls$, $\hat{f}_2(x_2)$ - the compensatory signal

PD controller takes majority meaning at the beginning, and then the influence of the PD signal decreases during the movement, because the weight estimates adaptation, and the meaning of the compensatory signal increases. The signal u_{F2} (Fig. 4a), which results from "force" control, take an important part in the total control signal u_2 (Fig. 4a). The robustifying term ν_2 (Fig. 4a) is associated with the presence of a dry friction force $T = \mu\lambda$ (Fig. 5a), where $\mu = 0.2$ is a friction coefficient. The force error (Fig. 5b) was bounded.

Sometimes, the friction forces are neglected in theoretical considerations, and in practical applications are treated as disturbances. But in such approaches control quality is worse.

In the initial movement phase motion errors have the highest values, so $\|Ls\|$ (Fig. 6a) has the highest values. Afterwards, it is decreased during the adaptation of weight estimates (Fig. 6b). In accordance with the theory presented in the paper, the weight estimates were bounded.

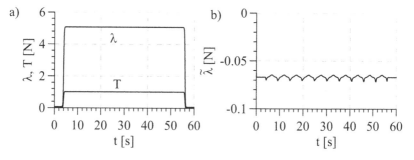

Fig. 5. a) exerted force λ normal and $T = \mu\lambda$ tangential to the contact surface, b) the force error $\tilde{\lambda}$

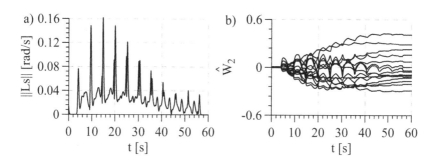

Fig. 6. a) $\|Ls\|$, b) the weight estimates of neural network associated with the second link

5   Conclusion

All signals in the control system were bounded, so control system was stable. Moreover, the motion errors decreased during movement. For numerical evaluation of the hybrid control system quality, we used a root mean square of errors, defined as: $\varepsilon_s = \sqrt{1/n\Sigma_{k=1}^{n}||Ls||_k^2} = 0.0363[rad/s]$ and $\varepsilon_\lambda = \sqrt{1/n\Sigma_{k=1}^{n}\tilde{\lambda}_k^2} = 0.0667[N]$, where k is an index of sample, n is a number of sample. In order to comparison neural hybrid controller with other control technique, adaptive hybrid controller was tested in the same work conditions. Such controller is based on the mathematical model of the manipulator. For testing of the adaptive controller in case of modelling errors, model of dry friction in joints is omit in the controller structure. In this case we obtain $\varepsilon_s = 0.0439[rad/s]$ and $\varepsilon_\lambda = 0.0671[N]$. These indices show, that the neural hybrid controller is better than the adaptive hybrid controller if the model of control object is not well known.

Acknowledgments. This research was realized within a framework of research project No. U-8313/DS/M.

Apparatus/equipment purchased in the project No POPW.01.03.00-18-012/ 09 from the structural funds, the Development of Eastern Poland Operational Programme co-financed by the European Union, the European Regional Development Fund.

References

1. Canudas de Wit, C., Siciliano, B., Bastin, G.: Theory of Robot Control. Springer, London (1996)
2. Tchon, K., Mazur, A., Duleba, I., Hossa, R., Muszynski, R.: Manipulators and mobile robots: models, movenent planning and control. AOW PLJ, Warsaw (2000) (in polish)
3. Gierlak, P., Zylski, W.: Tracking control of manipulator. In: Methods and Models in Automation and Robotics, vol. 14, part 1 (2009), `ifac-papersonline.net`
4. Lewis, F.L., Liu, K., Yesildirek, A.: Neural-Net Robot Controller with Guaranteed Tracking Performance. IEEE Trans. Neural Networks 6, 703–715 (1995)
5. Zalzala, A.M.S., Morris, A.S.: Neural networks for robotic control. Ellis Horwood (1996)
6. Zylski, W., Gierlak, P.: Verification of Multilayer Neural-Net Controller in Manipulator Tracking Control. Trans. Tech Publications. Solid State Phenomena 164, 99–104 (2010)
7. Lewis, F.L., Jagannathan, S., Yesildirek, A.: Control of Robot Manipulators and Nonlinear Systems. Taylor & Francis, London (1999)
8. Kumar, N., Panwar, V., Sukavanam, N., Sharma, S.P., Borm, J.-H.: Neural Network Based Hybrid Force/Position Control for Robot Manipulators. IJPEM 12(3), 419–426 (2011)
9. Sabanowic, A., Ohnishi, K.: Motion control system. IEEE Press, Singapore (2011)
10. Narendra, K.S., Annaswamy, A.M.: A new adaptive law for robust adaptation without persistant excitation. IEEE Trans. Automat. Contr. AC-32(2), 134–145 (1987)

Opportunistic Motivated Learning Agents

James Graham[1], Janusz A. Starzyk[1,2], and Daniel Jachyra[2]

[1] School of Electrical Engineering and Computer Science, Ohio University,
Athens, OH, USA
{jg193404,starzykj}@ohio.edu
[2] University of Information Technology and Management, Rzeszow, Poland
djachyra@wsiz.rzeszow.pl

Abstract. This paper presents an extension of the Motivated Learning model that includes environment masking, and opportunistic behavior of the motivated learning agent. Environment masking improves an agent's ability to learn by helping to filter out distractions, and the addition of a more complex environment increases the simulation's realism. If conditions call for it opportunistic behavior allows an agent to deviate from the dominant task to perform a less important but rewarding action. Numerical simulations were performed using Matlab and the implementation of a graphical simulation based on the OGRE engine is in progress. Simulation results show good performance and numerical stability of the attained solution.

Keywords: Motivated learning, cognitive agents, reinforcement learning, goal creation.

1 Introduction

In this paper we expand on our previous Motivated Learning (ML) work and show how it can yield an opportunistic learning system. The goal of this paper is to discuss the changes made to the algorithm presented in [2, 9] and to indicate how they yield a more complex and efficient system.

Motivated Learning is defined as an extension of reinforcement learning that uses intrinsic motivations as a way to build a motivated agent. These motivations are internal to the agent and are derived from various "pain" signals. "Pain" signals represent an underlying need, drive, or irritation. These signals can originate from internal states of the agent (memories and/or other internal drives) or external environmental states such as basic needs for sustenance and shelter.

This previously proposed system [2] is self-organizing and controls an agent's behavior via competition between the dynamically changing needs of the system. In some respects, ML can be seen as an extension of reinforcement learning, in that it receives its reinforcement from the environment for its primitive objectives (i.e. its most basic needs). Upon this initial structure a more complex systems of goals and values can be built to establish complex internal motivations for advanced stages of development. This includes the creation of abstract concepts and needs and the creation of internal rewards for satisfying these needs.

L. Rutkowski et al. (Eds.): ICAISC 2012, Part II, LNCS 7268, pp. 442–449, 2012.

However, unlike reinforcement learning, motivated learning, does not suffer from the "credit assignment" problem [6, 7]. Reinforcement learning typically spreads the value of a reward to earlier actions via a temporal difference mechanism; however, this often leads to credit assignment to actions that had no relation to the reward. In contrast, the ML approach, while not necessarily immune is much more resistant to this problem due to the focus on motivations and the creation of abstract needs. The abstract pains/needs serve to "break-up" the reward chain to the "primitive" needs (or basic reward in RL) and improve an agent's overall learning ability.

Motivated learning also has some similarities and uses some elements of BDI (belief-desire-intention) agents. The work by Rao and Georgeff [3] is one of the first papers to consider how an actual BDI agent might be implemented and serves as a bridge between BDI theory and actual practice. Others such as Dastani et al. [4] and Wooldridge [5] deal more with individual aspects of BDI such as the deliberative processes and the open-mindedness of an agent.

The presented ML model can be related to a BDI model in several respects. ML has belief in the sense that it observes the environment and extracts rules and state information to create its own internal "representation" of the state of the world around it. The ML agent's beliefs link its perceptions to semantic knowledge about the environment as coded through the system of perceptions, pain centers, goals, and planned actions. Desires in BDI agents correspond to motivations as expressed by the pain centers in ML. The pains (or needs) compete for attention and are not handled unless one of them dominates or passes some threshold. And lastly, intentions are represented in the ML agent as the selected (or preferred) method for implementing a goal chosen by the agent. The most notable difference between BDI and ML agents is that BDI agents have their actions predetermined by their designers, while ML agents create their own as they learn to exist within their environment. BDI agents lack the ability to define more complex abstract motivations as is typically performed by ML agents.

In our earlier work [2], we presented a basic implementation of a goal creation system and the motivated learning idea. In this paper, several enhancements of ML are implemented, ranging from enhancements to the environment and the ability to attempt and track multiple tasks. Our current work is modified to accommodate the computational model of a cognitive machine [1]. We discuss the effects these enhancements have had on the ML algorithm. Finally, we discuss ongoing work and present our future plans.

2   Design of the Motivated Learning System

Motivated Learning uses a neural network to weigh its options and create goals. Goals are created not only in response to externally set motivations (primitive pains) but also in response to needs determined at the various levels of abstract goals created by the machine during the learning process. As the machine learns, it develops associations between its percepts and builds representations of discovered abstract concepts. Initially these representations relate directly to its perception of the environment, however, over time, and with experience, the machine will begin to perceive increasingly complex relationships and behaviors.

In order to satisfy an agent's motivation, a mechanism is needed to select which goals, or actions, to pursue. This mechanism needs to be able to process existing motivations and build new ones. Signals representing various abstract pains will compete against each other with input from the environment and other parts of the agent's architecture. Additionally, as the machine effects the environment, the changes in the environment affect the machine. These changes will be perceived by the agent and influence its cognitive process. It is possible, however, to partially block outside influence in instances where it is "desirable" for the machine to focus on some internal mental task. For instance an agent may need to spend time performing mental analysis of various possible scenarios, steps, and combinations of actions needed to perform the task.

Once the agent determines the dominant need/pain it will attempt to choose a goal or action to remedy the pain. To do so, it uses a winner-take-all (WTA) neural-network (NN) based approach, whereby bias weights and goal weights are decreased or increased based on the success or failure of a particular action. In the case of bias weights, they act on the previously mentioned pain biases, and increase when the resource associated with a specific pain is shown to be of relevance. However, they decrease gradually when a resource (or pain) is unused. Goal weights increase when a pain is decreased by the completions of the action associated with the goal. They decrease when the pain is unaffected, or worse, increased by the goal implementation. For a more detailed overview of the basic internal structures behind a ML agent refer to [2].

2.1   Expanded Environment and Masking

Presented in [2] environment for testing the ML agent consisted of only 6 sensors and 6 motor commands allowing for a total of 36 possible goals/actions.

While this environmental set-up is an appropriate first step, it is too simple to properly evaluate the efficacy of the model. Therefore, a significantly more complex environment has been implemented (see Figure 1) that utilizes 17 sensors and 26 motor commands for a total of 442 different possible goals/actions. This leads to a much longer search time for the correct actions.

In the basic simulation, there is only a single primitive pain, while in the more complex simulation, depicted in Figure 1, there are three primitive pains with six resources and 8 motor commands directly associated with them. Thus, at the very beginning of the expanded environment, the agent has a greater number of choices to process than in the basic simulation. To improve its learning in such environment we developed goal "masking".

The idea behind the use of masking is to block certain sensors and motor commands so that the agent does not perceive them until a certain time or environmental state is attained. The "masked" environment, combined with the masking of motor commands, emulates guided learning. The agent is not directly told what to do, it is guided and accelerates its learning by limiting available options.

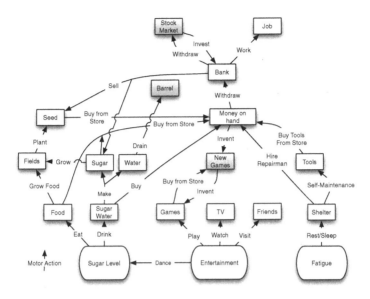

Fig. 1. Expanded Environment

Currently environments are focused on resource consumption. However, work is currently being undertaken to expand into areas such as location, motion, on/off options, and so on.

2.2   Resource Utilization and Multi-cycle Task/Goals

At the beginning of a simulation, the agent does not know which resources relieve what pains, nor does it know how the use of one resource impacts another one. Exploring a common situation such as dealing with "hunger" presents a good example of resource utilization. In this example, hunger is the pain, and the associated resource can be represented as blood sugar. When hungry the machine eats, but it does not know how much food it needs to consume to alleviate its hunger pain. As the simulation progresses, the machine will gradually be able to estimate the relationship between food and blood sugar level by evaluating the hunger pain. It does this by calculating the ratio of expected/desired pain reduction vs. actual pain reduction and determines the amount of resource needed by comparing it to what was used previously and its effects on the pain. Refining the ratio estimation will continue every time the hunger pain is above threshold. Additionally, because pain is a logarithmic function of resource utilization and because w_{BP} changes with time affecting the pain value, the ratio will continue to change over time.

Goals are defined in our system as a need, or in BDI terms, a desire to reduce a specific pain. A task is an action selected by the machine in the hope that it will reduce the dominant pain. In a real world, it will not always be possible to complete a task or action in one cognitive cycle. Therefore, the system has been modified to allow for the effort required to perform the actions selected. In the current implementation, effort requirements are based solely on the amount of time needed to perform the selected motor action. The implementation takes into account the quantity of resource consumed to determine how long it takes to complete an action (to reduce pain below threshold) and travel time in cases where movement is needed. However, the rate at which pains change is not necessarily constant and depends on the task.

2.3   Opportunistic Behavior

The following describes an opportunistic task selection system, whereby the agent can decide to pause in execution of its current task to perform another task. In order to select another task, there needs to be sufficient difference in the required effort or change in the pain levels for the deviation from the original task to be worthwhile. In order to decide the value of a task (action value), the level of the pain that initiated the task, time needed to complete the task (shorter is better), and how useful is the task, are taken into account:

$$Action\,Value = \frac{1}{1+\Delta t}\left(P + \sum \Delta P_e\right). \qquad (1)$$

The amount of time needed to perform the action is represented by Δt, P is the pain considered for reduction, and ΔP_e represents the predicted changes in the pain levels. The agent computes "Action Values" in conjunction with w_{PG} weights generating a "Task Value" for all possible actions. It then operates on the winning action. If an ongoing action is interrupted, the agent can resume it where it was left off. The biological and algorithmic reasoning for "opportunistic behavior" has the potential to be fairly complex. However, we take a relatively simple approach by attempting to evaluate the "worth" or a task in progress against that of other potential tasks.

3   Simulation of Motivated Learning in Virtual Environments

Virtual environments are excellent developmental platforms for embodied intelligence concepts. Many robotics projects such as the iCub [8] make use of simulated environments. The iCub project is an open hardware and software platform for developmental robotics. Of course, it is not practical for most people to purchase the iCub hardware (over $200,000 for a complete robot), meaning many have to rely on a virtual environment, the iCub Simulator, which is included in the free software package.

The initial versions of the Motivated Learning software [9] used a very simple simulated environment to demonstrate its advantages over RL; however, this is inadequate for testing of more complex behaviors and systems.

This is why we are working on integrating our agent with NeoAxis [10]. NeoAxis provides a graphical game engine with many existing assets and the ability to add more as needed. It is designed to be easily modifiable by users, and is provided as a free SDK for non-commercial use. The NeoAxis engine itself is based on OGRE (Object-oriented Graphics Rendering Engine) [11]. Figure 2 shows an image from one of the demo maps included in the NeoAxis SDK.

Fig. 2. NeoAxis graphics example

To embed the ML agent into NeoAxis we decided to modify the game's AI and integrate the agent into the decision making part of the code. Additionally, a new class of environmental objects referred to as "Resources" was created to simplify the transition. Integrating the ML agent required providing information from the environment to the agent and receiving and interpreting the agent's responses.

3.1   Simulation and Discussion of Results

While at the time of writing integration with NeoAxis is under development, the ML agent described in Section 2 is fully operational.

Figures 3 and 4 depict the results from the simulation in a more complex environment shown on Figure 1. Figure 3 shows resource utilization for simulated environment over a period of 30,000 iterations. The figure displays the results in 2000 iteration increments, or to clarify from zero to 2000, from 6000 to 8000, from 12,000 to 14,000, and so on. Figure 4 displays iterations in the same manner as Figure 3. Notice in Figure 4 how the pains stabilize at relatively low levels. And while there is at least one instance where the pains spike to greater levels, once the machine learns how to handle them they stabilize once more.

3.2   Impact of Opportunistic Behavior on Results

In section 2.3 several changes to the original motivated learning algorithm were discussed including, an expanded environment model, masking of sensors and motors, quantitative rather than probability based resource availability, actions requiring multiple cycles, and opportunistic behavior.

One can observe how increasing the complexity of the environment changes the simulation dynamics. The most obvious effect is that the simulation requires longer time to run in a more complex environment. From Figure 4, it is apparent that only a fraction of the available resources have been utilized in 30,000 iterations. This is partially an effect of masking, since many resources are not available until the system reaches a higher level of development.

The effect of masking sensory inputs and motor commands should be clear. With higher "level" sensors and motor commands masked until the agent needs them, the agent will have fewer options to select from, and thus will be able to learn how to navigate the environment more quickly. Masking can either be done manually (via setting the masks to be enabled or disabled at specific times) or "automatically" by probing the agent's internal weights to see if it has learned a desired concept and introduce the sensors/motors it would need for the next learning level. Automatic masking has the most favorable impact on improving the learning speed.

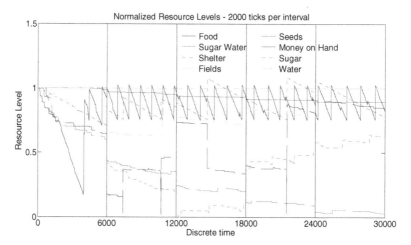

Fig. 3. Resource Usage

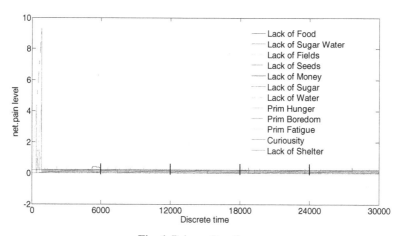

Fig. 4. Pain vs. Iterations

Resource consumption is tied in with the environment model. Early versions of the environment model were probability based, however, in the recent version the environment contains measurable quantities of each resource. As such, it became important to the agent to be able to determine how much of each resource to use (and how it affects another resource). This change did not affect the performance of the agent in a significant way, however it helped to integrate the agent with a more realistic environment such as the NeoAxis.

The use of multi-cycle tasks was another significant change for the agent. It has the effect of significantly increasing the amount of time required for simulation. It also paves the way for a more realistic implementation of the agent. As has been mentioned, tasks can easily take variable amounts of time. The use of variable task times has also allowed for the implementation of more complex opportunistic behavior.

4   Conclusions

In this paper we presented Opportunistic Motivated Learning model. Also discussed was our effort to integrate the ML agent with simulated environments using NeoAxis graphics engine. As confirmed by the simulation results our model can surpass other reinforcement learning based models [2]. With the planned additions to the motivated learning model, combined with an effective cognitive model discussed in [1, 12] we hope to design a machine capable of cognition. Simulation results showed good performance and numerical stability of opportunistic ML. In the future we would like to implement our model not only in various simulated environments but also in real robots.

References

1. Starzyk, J.A., Prasad, D.K.: A Computational Model of Machine Consciousness. International Journal of Machine Consciousness (2011) (to appear)
2. Starzyk, J.A., Graham, J.T., Raif, P., Tan, A.-H.: Motivated Learning for Autonomous Robots Development. Cognitive Science Research (2011) (to appear)
3. Rao, A.S., Georgeff, M.P.: BDI Agents: From Theory to Practice. In: Lesser, V. (ed.) Proceedings of the 1st International Conference on Multi-Agent Systems (ICMAS), pp. 312–319. MIT Press (1995)
4. Dastani, M., Dignum, F., Meyer, J.-J.: Autonomy, and Agent Deliberation. In: Proc. of the 1st International Workshop on Computational Autonomy (Autonomy 2003) (2003)
5. Wooldridge, M.: Reasoning about Rational Agents. In: Intelligent Robots and Autonomous Agents. The MIT Press, Cambridge (2000)
6. Sutton, R.S.: Temporal Credit Assignment in Reinforcement Learning. PhD thesis, University of Massachusetts, Amherst, MA (1984)
7. Fu, W.-T., Anderson, J.R.: Solving the Credit Assignment Problem: Explicit and Implicit Learning with Internal and External State Information. In: Proceedings of the 28th Annual Conference of the Cognitive Science Society. LEA, Hillsdale (2006)
8. iCub, RobotCub – An Open Framework for Research in Embodied Cognition (2004), http://www.robotcub.org/
9. Starzyk, J.A.: Motivation in Embodied Intelligence. In: Frontiers in Robotics, Automation and Control, pp. 83–110. I-Tech Education and Publishing (October 2008)
10. NeoAxis – all-purpose, modern 3D graphics engine for 3D simulations, visualizations and games, http://www.neoaxis.com/
11. OGRE – Open Source 3D Graphics Engine, http://www.ogre3d.org
12. Starzyk, J.A.: Mental Saccades in Control of Cognitive Process. In: Int. Joint Conf. on Neural Networks, San Jose, CA, July 31-August 5 (2011)

Neural Dynamic Programming
in Reactive Navigation of Wheeled Mobile Robot

Zenon Hendzel and Marcin Szuster

Rzeszow University of Technology,
Department of Applied Mechanics and Robotics,
8 Powstancow Warszawy St., 35-959 Rzeszow, Poland
{zenhen,mszuster}@prz.edu.pl

Abstract. In the article a new approach to a reactive navigation of a wheeled mobile robot (WMR), using a neural dynamic programming algorithm (NPD), is presented. A proposed discrete hierarchical control system consists of a trajectory generator and a tracking control system. In the trajectory generator we used a sensor-based approach to path design for the WMR in an unknown 2-D environment with static obstacles. The main part of the navigator is an action dependant heuristic dynamic programming algorithm (ADHDP), that generates control signals used to design a collision-free trajectory, that makes reaching a goal possible. ADHDP is the discrete algorithm of actor-critic architecture, that works on-line and does not require a preliminary learning or a controlled system knowledge. The tracking control system realises the generated trajectory, it consists of dual-heuristic dynamic programming (DHP) structure, PD controller and the supervisory term derived from the Lyapunov stability theorem. Computer simulations have been conducted to illustrate the performance of the algorithm.

Keywords: Neural Dynamic Programming, Reactive Navigation, Wheeled Mobile Robot.

1 Introduction

The development of the autonomous mobile robotics in recent years allowed to increase the area of its applications, but still one of the most challenging problems is to generate the collision-free trajectory in order to reach the destination. There are many different approaches to the path-planning problem, e. g. [1], [3], [8], [9], [10], two most popular are global and local methods. In the model based algorithms the path planing problem is solved in a global way, but knowledge about the environment is required [9]. The local methods use sensor-based systems and can be applied in the unknown environments.

The presented sensor-based control system is a development of the algorithm presented in [8], where authors use NPD algorithms in ADHDP configuration to generate behavioural control signals in goal-seeking (GS) and obstacle-avoiding (OA) tasks, and a fuzzy logic (FL) algorithm to soft switch of low-level behaviours control signals, in a complex task of goal-seeking with obstacle avoiding.

In the presented article a new approach to a collision-free trajectory generating for the WMR Pioneer 2-DX, with usage of NDP algorithms, is proposed. The designed

L. Rutkowski et al. (Eds.): ICAISC 2012, Part II, LNCS 7268, pp. 450–457, 2012.

hierarchical control system consists of the trajectory generator, based on NPD algorithms in ADHDP configuration, and the tracking control system using DHP structure.

2 Model of the Wheeled Mobile Robot Pioneer-2DX

The movement of the nonholonomic WMR Pioneer 2-DX, schematically shown in Fig. 1, is analysed in the xy plane [4], [5]. The WMR is a construction with two drive wheels, a frame and a third, free rolling, castor wheel. The WMR is equipped with eight ultrasonic range-finders ($s_1 - s_8$) and one laser range-finder s_L.

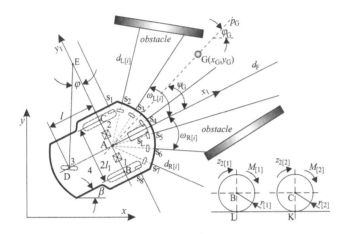

Fig. 1. Scheme of the WMR

The dynamics of the WMR was modelled using Maggie's mathematical formalism [4], [5]. The model involves dynamic equations of the WMR and dynamical properties of executive systems. Using Euler's derivative approximation and the state vector $z = \left[z_{1\{k\}}^T, z_{2\{k\}}^T\right]^T$, where $z_{2\{k\}}$ corresponds to the vector of continuous angular velocities $\dot{\alpha} = \left[\dot{\alpha}_{[1]}, \dot{\alpha}_{[2]}\right]^T$, we obtained a discrete notation of the WMR dynamics in a form

$$
\begin{aligned}
z_{1\{k+1\}} &= z_{1\{k\}} + z_{2\{k\}} h , \\
z_{2\{k+1\}} &= -M^{-1}\left[C\left(z_{2\{k\}}\right) z_{2\{k\}} + F\left(z_{2\{k\}}\right) + \tau_{d\{k\}} - u_{\{k\}}\right] h + z_{2\{k\}} ,
\end{aligned}
\tag{1}
$$

where M, $C\left(z_{2\{k\}}\right)$, and $F\left(z_{2\{k\}}\right)$ are matrixes and vectors that derive from the WMR dynamics, $\tau_{d\{k\}}$ is the vector of bounded disturbances, $u_{\{k\}}$ is the tracking control signal, h is a time discretization parameter and k is an index of iteration steps. The dynamics model of the WMR was described in detail in [4], the closed loop system used in the tracking control system synthesis, was described in detail in [6], [7].

3 Hierarchical Control System

The presented hierarchical control system, that consists of the trajectory generator and the neural tracking control system, is schematically shown in Fig. 2.

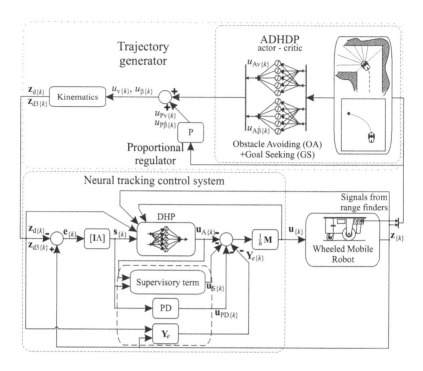

Fig. 2. Scheme of the hierarchical control system

3.1 Trajectory Generator

In the proposed hierarchical control system, the discrete navigator consists of two AD-HDP structures and the proportional regulator P, that generate control signals, and the kinematic module, that calculates the desired trajectory. The strategy of reactive navigation is developed including two simple behaviours, GS and OA, fused in order to realise a complex task of reaching the goal without colliding obstacles. In the trajectory generator we used NPD algorithm in ADHDP configuration, in details described in [6], where it was used to the tracking control of the WMR. NPD structures are a group of Forward Dynamic Programming (FDP) methods [11], [12], [13], which derives from the Bellman's dynamic programming (DP) [2]. The objective of the DP is to determine the optimal control law that minimises the value function [2], [11], [12], [13], which is the function of a state and a control in a general case. The ADHDP structure is adapted on-line using a reinforcement learning (RL) idea. The RL approach bases on iterative interaction with the environment and searching for the optimal action to take for the sake of the assumed cost function. The presented innovative approach uses the P regulator in the navigator to indicate actor-critic structures adequate control signal at the beginning of the adaptation process to limit exploration and avoid the trial and error learning.

We defined the discrete error vector $e_{T\{k\}} = [e_{v\{k\}}, e_{O\{k\}}, \psi_G]^T$, where $e_{v\{k\}}$ is the error of the generated velocity, $e_{O\{k\}}$ is the error of following in the middle of the free space, which may be seen as "obstacle-avoiding error", and ψ_G is the error of an angle between the WMR frame axis and the straight line p_G, passing through the point A of the WMR and the goal G, it may be seen as "goal-seeking error". Errors are defined as

$$
\begin{aligned}
e_{v\{k\}} &= f\left(d^*_{F\{k\}}\right) f\left(d_{G\{k\}}\right) - v_{A\{k\}}/v^*_A , \\
e_{O\{k\}} &= d^*_{R\{k\}} - d^*_{L\{k\}} , \\
\psi_{G\{k\}} &= \varphi_{G\{k\}} - \beta_{\{k\}} .
\end{aligned}
\tag{2}
$$

where $f(.)$ is a sigmoidal bipolar function, $d^*_{F\{k\}} = d_{Lr\{k\}}/d_{max}$, $d_{Lr\{k\}}$ is a range of the laser range finder, d_{max} is a maximal range of the range finders, $d_{G\{k\}}$ is the distance to the point G, $v_{A\{k\}}$ is a realised velocity of the point A, v^*_A is a maximal defined velocity of the point A, $d_{L\{k\}} = \min\left(d_{L[1]\{k\}}\left(s_2\right), d_{L[2]\{k\}}\left(s_3\right)\right)$, $d_{R\{k\}} = \min\left(d_{R[1]\{k\}}\left(s_6\right), d_{R[2]\{k\}}\left(s_7\right)\right)$, $d^*_{L\{k\}} = 2\left[\left(d_{L\{k\}}/\left(d_{L\{k\}} + d_{R\{k\}}\right)\right)\right] - 0.5]$ is the normalised distance to the obstacle on the left side of the WMR, $d^*_{R\{k\}} = 2\left[\left(d_{R\{k\}}/\left(d_{L\{k\}} + d_{R\{k\}}\right)\right)\right] - 0.5]$ is the normalised distance to the obstacle on the right, $\varphi_{G\{k\}}$ is the temporal angle between the x axis and the line p_G, $\beta_{\{k\}}$ is a temporary angle of the self-turn of the WMR frame.

The proposed navigator generates the overall control signal $u_{T\{k\}} = \left[u_{v\{k\}}, u_{\beta\{k\}}\right]^T$, where $u_{v\{k\}}$ controls the desired velocity, and $u_{\beta\{k\}}$ corresponds to the desired angular velocity of the WMR frame turn $\dot{\beta}$. The control signal $u_{T\{k\}}$ consists of the ADHDP actor NNs control signals $u_{TA\{k\}} = \left[u_{Av\{k\}}, u_{A\beta\{k\}}\right]^T$ and the P regulator control signals,

$$
u_{T\{k\}} = u_{TA\{k\}} + u_{TP\{k\}} ,
\tag{3}
$$

where $u_{TP\{k\}} = K_{TP}\, e_{T\{k\}}$, K_{TP} is a fixed matrix of proportional gains.

The objective of the ADHDP algorithm is to determine the sub-optimal control law, that minimises the value function $V\left(x_{\{k\}}, u_{\{k\}}\right)$ [2], [11], [12], [13], which is the function of the state $x_{\{k\}}$ and the control $u_{\{k\}}$ in a general case

$$
V\left(x_{\{k\}}, u_{\{k\}}\right) = \sum_{k=0}^{n} \gamma^k L_C\left(x_{\{k\}}, u_{\{k\}}\right),
\tag{4}
$$

where n is the last step of finite discrete process, γ is a discount factor $(0 \leq \gamma \leq 1)$ and $L_C\left(x_{\{k\}}, u_{\{k\}}\right)$ is a local cost in step k. An important future of the ADHDP algorithm is, that as the only one from the whole NDP structures family, it does not require the model of the controlled system, and is applicable in the trajectory generating process in the unknown environment.

We assumed the local costs $L_{Cv\{k\}}\left(e_{v\{k\}}, u_{v\{k\}}\right)$, and $L_{C\beta\{k\}}\left(e_{O\{k\}}, \psi_{G\{k\}}, u_{\beta\{k\}}\right)$ in the form

$$
\begin{aligned}
L_{Cv\{k\}}\left(e_{v\{k\}}, u_{v\{k\}}\right) &= \tfrac{1}{2} e_{v\{k\}} R_v e_{v\{k\}} + \tfrac{1}{2} u_{v\{k\}} Q_v u_{v\{k\}} , \\
L_{C\beta\{k\}}\left(e_{O\{k\}}, \psi_{G\{k\}}, u_{\beta\{k\}}\right) &= \tfrac{1}{2} e_{O\{k\}} R_O e_{O\{k\}} + \tfrac{1}{2} \psi_{G\{k\}} R_\psi \psi_{G\{k\}} + \tfrac{1}{2} u_{\beta\{k\}} Q_\beta u_{\beta\{k\}} ,
\end{aligned}
\tag{5}
$$

where $R_v, Q_v, R_O, R_\psi, Q_\beta$ are positive constants.

In the task of generating control signal $u_{T\{k\}}$ we used two ADHDP actor-critic structures, each consists of:

– critic, that is realised in the form of RVFL (Random Vector Functional Link) NN, estimates the sub-optimal value function $V_{\mathrm{v}}\left(e_{\mathrm{v}\{k\}}, u_{\mathrm{v}\{k\}}\right)$ or $V_{\beta}\left(e_{\mathrm{O}\{k\}}, \psi_{\mathrm{G}\{k\}}, u_{\hat{\beta}\{k\}}\right)$, and generates signal

$$
\begin{aligned}
\hat{V}_{\mathrm{v}}\left(x_{\mathrm{Cv}\{k\}}, W_{\mathrm{Cv}\{k\}}\right) &= W_{\mathrm{Cv}\{k\}}^{\mathrm{T}} S\left(x_{\mathrm{Cv}\{k\}}\right) , \\
\hat{V}_{\beta}\left(x_{\mathrm{C}\beta\{k\}}, W_{\mathrm{C}\beta\{k\}}\right) &= W_{\mathrm{C}\beta\{k\}}^{\mathrm{T}} S\left(x_{\mathrm{C}\beta\{k\}}\right) ,
\end{aligned}
\tag{6}
$$

where $W_{\mathrm{Cv}\{k\}}$, $W_{\mathrm{C}\beta\{k\}}$ are vectors of output-layer weights, $S\left(.\right)$ is a vector of neurons activation functions, $x_{\mathrm{Cv}\{k\}}$ and $x_{\mathrm{C}\beta\{k\}}$ are input vectors to the NNs. The input vectors to the critic NNs contains adequate errors and control signals.

Critics' weights are adapted by the back propagation method of the Temporal Difference error [11], [12], [13]

$$
\begin{aligned}
e_{\mathrm{TDv}\{k\}} &= L_{\mathrm{Cv}\{k\}}\left(e_{\mathrm{v}\{k\}}, u_{\mathrm{v}\{k\}}\right) + \gamma\hat{V}_{\mathrm{v}}\left(x_{\mathrm{Cv}\{k+1\}}, W_{\mathrm{Cv}\{k\}}\right) - \hat{V}_{\mathrm{v}}\left(x_{\mathrm{Cv}\{k\}}, W_{\mathrm{Cv}\{k\}}\right) , \\
e_{\mathrm{TD}\beta\{k\}} &= L_{\mathrm{C}\beta\{k\}}\left(e_{\mathrm{O}\{k\}}, \psi_{\mathrm{G}\{k\}}, u_{\hat{\beta}\{k\}}\right) + \gamma\hat{V}_{\beta}\left(x_{\mathrm{C}\beta\{k+1\}}, W_{\mathrm{C}\beta\{k\}}\right) - \hat{V}_{\beta}\left(x_{\mathrm{C}\beta\{k\}}, W_{\mathrm{C}\beta\{k\}}\right) .
\end{aligned}
\tag{7}
$$

– actor, that is realised in the form of RVFL NN, generates the sub-optimal control law $u_{\mathrm{Av}\{k\}}$ or $u_{\mathrm{A}\hat{\beta}\{k\}}$

$$
\begin{aligned}
u_{\mathrm{Av}\{k\}}\left(x_{\mathrm{Av}\{k\}}, W_{\mathrm{Av}\{k\}}\right) &= W_{\mathrm{Av}\{k\}}^{\mathrm{T}} S\left(x_{\mathrm{Av}\{k\}}\right) , \\
u_{\mathrm{A}\hat{\beta}\{k\}}\left(x_{\mathrm{A}\hat{\beta}\{k\}}, W_{\mathrm{A}\hat{\beta}\{k\}}\right) &= W_{\mathrm{A}\hat{\beta}\{k\}}^{\mathrm{T}} S\left(x_{\mathrm{A}\hat{\beta}\{k\}}\right) .
\end{aligned}
\tag{8}
$$

Actor estimates the sub-optimal control law by the back propagation method of

$$
\begin{aligned}
e_{\mathrm{Av}\{k\}} &= \frac{\partial L_{\mathrm{Cv}\{k\}}\left(e_{\mathrm{v}\{k\}}, u_{\mathrm{v}\{k\}}\right)}{\partial u_{\mathrm{v}\{k\}}} + \gamma\frac{\partial\hat{V}_{\mathrm{v}}\left(x_{\mathrm{Cv}\{k+1\}}, W_{\mathrm{Cv}\{k\}}\right)}{\partial u_{\mathrm{v}\{k\}}} , \\
e_{\mathrm{A}\hat{\beta}\{k\}} &= \frac{\partial L_{\mathrm{C}\beta\{k\}}\left(e_{\mathrm{O}\{k\}}, \psi_{\mathrm{G}\{k\}}, u_{\hat{\beta}\{k\}}\right)}{\partial u_{\hat{\beta}\{k\}}} + \gamma\frac{\partial\hat{V}_{\beta}\left(x_{\mathrm{C}\beta\{k+1\}}, W_{\mathrm{C}\beta\{k\}}\right)}{\partial u_{\hat{\beta}\{k\}}} .
\end{aligned}
\tag{9}
$$

In the ADHDP structures we used RVFL NNs. The critic $\hat{V}_{\mathrm{v}}\left(x_{\mathrm{Cv}\{k\}}, W_{\mathrm{Cv}\{k\}}\right)$ NN is schematically shown in Fig. 3. It has N inputs, fixed input-layer weights D_{Cv}, randomly chosen in the NNs initialization process, set to zero initial output-layer weights $W_{\mathrm{Cv}\{k\}}$ and R neurons with sigmoidal bipolar activation functions $S_{[j]}\left(x_{\mathrm{Cv}\{k\}}\right)$

$$
S\left(x_{\mathrm{Cv}\{k\}}\right) = \frac{2}{1 + \exp\left(-\beta_{\mathrm{C}} D_{\mathrm{Cv}} x_{\mathrm{Cv}\{k\}}\right)} - 1 .
\tag{10}
$$

where β_{C} is a constant.

In the global co-ordinate system xy position of the WMR is described by the vector $[x_{\mathrm{A}\{k\}}, y_{\mathrm{A}\{k\}}, \beta_{\{k\}}]^{\mathrm{T}}$, where $(x_{\mathrm{A}\{k\}}, y_{\mathrm{A}\{k\}})$ are co-ordinates of the point A. The desired discrete angular velocities are calculated in the kinematics module, according to equation

$$
\begin{bmatrix} z_{\mathrm{d}2[1]\{k\}} \\ z_{\mathrm{d}2[2]\{k\}} \end{bmatrix} = \frac{1}{r}\begin{bmatrix} v_{\mathrm{A}}^* & \dot{\beta}^* l_1 \\ v_{\mathrm{A}}^* & -\dot{\beta}^* l_1 \end{bmatrix}\begin{bmatrix} u_{\mathrm{v}\{k\}} \\ u_{\hat{\beta}\{k\}} \end{bmatrix},
\tag{11}
$$

where $r = r_{[1]} = r_{[2]}$ and l_1 derive from the WMR geometry, $\dot{\beta}^*$ is a maximal defined angular velocity of the self-turn of the WMR frame.

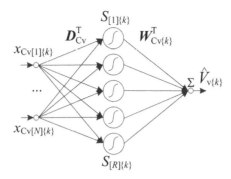

Fig. 3. Scheme of the RVFL critic NN $\hat{V}_v\,(x_{Cv\{k\}}, W_{Cv\{k\}})$

3.2   Neural Tracking Control System

In the neural tracking control system we used the discrete NPD algorithm in DHP configuration, in details described in [7]. The DHP structure consists of two actor NNs, two critic NNs, each pair for one drive wheel, and the model of the WMR. We used the RVFL NNs with sigmoidal bipolar activation functions, randomly chosen fixed weights of the input-layer and initial weights of the output-layer set to zero. Actor NNs generate the control signals $u_{A[1]\{k\}}$, $u_{A[2]\{k\}}$, critic NNs approximates the derivative of the cost function in respect to the state. The cost function is based on the filtered tracking error, and the task of DHP structure is to minimise the tracking errors. The stability of the neural tracking control system is ensured by the supervisory term, derived from the Lyapunov stability theory. The neural tracking control system is stable, which means, that the filtered tracking errors are bounded. According to Fig. 2, the overall tracking control signal $u_{\{k\}}$ is composed of the DHP actor NNs control signal $u_{A\{k\}}$, the supervisory term control signal $u_{S\{k\}}$, the PD control signal $u_{PD\{k\}}$ and the $Y_{e\{k\}}$ control signal.

4   Simulations Results

Simulations of the proposed hierarchical control system were realised by a series of numerical experiments on the model of the WMR Pioneer 2-DX in the software environment. Using simulated range finders signals obtained from the virtual environment, the navigator generated the collision free trajectory for the goals localised in points shown in Fig. 4.a). In the figure the start position of the WMR is marked by the triangle, the goal is marked by the "**X** ". In Fig. 4.b) there is presented a path of the WMR for the point G(7.9, 10.1) and obstacles detected by range finders, marked by stars.

On the basis of the control signals $u_{v\{k\}}$, $u_{\beta\{k\}}$, composed of the adequate ADHDP actors control signals and the proportional regulator control signals, shown in Fig. 5.a) and b) respectively, there was generated the desired trajectory for the tracking control system with DHP structure. The control signals of P controller have small values, and are reduced during the ADHDP NNs adaptation process. In Fig. 5.c) there are shown the desired $(z_{d2[1]}, z_{d2[2]})$ angular velocities of the drive WMR wheels. In Fig. 5.d) the distance to the goal G is presented.

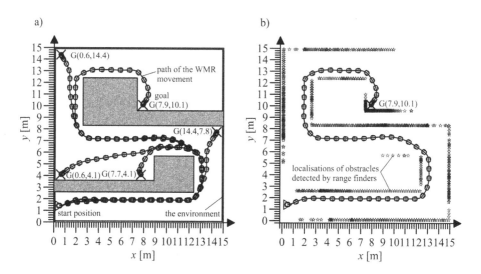

Fig. 4. a) The simulated environment map with the paths of the WMR movement b) the simulated environment map with the path for the goal G(7.9, 10.1)

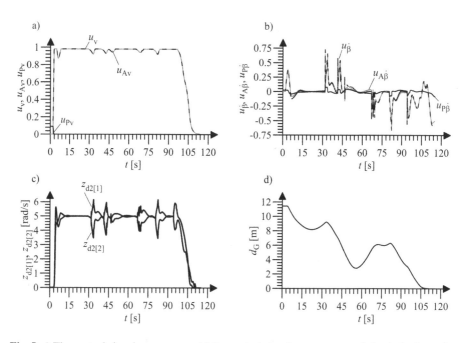

Fig. 5. a) The control signals u_v, u_{Av}, u_{Pv}, b) the control signals $u_{\dot\beta}$, $u_{A\dot\beta}$, $u_{P\dot\beta}$, c) the desired angular velocities ($z_{d2[1]}$, $z_{d2[2]}$), d) the distance to the goal G(7.9, 10.1)

5   Conclusion

The presented hierarchical control system, with NPD structures in ADHDP configuration in the sensor-based navigator and with DHP structure in the neural tracking control system, generates and realises the collision-free trajectory in the unknown 2D environment with static obstacles. The generated trajectory provides, that the point A of the WMR Pioneer 2-DX model reaches the goal. Significant influence on the trajectory generation process have the coefficients in the value functions of the NDP structures. Higher values of the coefficients corresponding to the influence of the "goal-seeking error" in the value function result in the trajectory with smaller distances to the obstacles, where reaching the goal has higher priority. The projected navigator has a simpler structure, in the comparison to the trajectory generator based on the elementary behaviours GS and OA with a soft switch, and is more computationally effective. It does not require the preliminary learning, works on-line and can prevent from the time-consuming trial-and-error learning, which is not suitable for the autonomous WMRs. The proposed hierarchical control system will be verified on the WMR Pioneer 2-DX.

Acknowledgments. This research was realized within a framework of research project No. U-8314/DS/M.

Apparatus/equipment purchased in the project No. POPW.01.03.00-18-012/09 from the structural funds, the Development of Eastern Poland Operational Programme co-financed by the European Union, the European Regional Development Fund.

References

1. Arkin, R.C.: Behavior-Based Robotics. MIT Press, Cambridge (1998)
2. Bellman, R.: Dynamic Programming. Princeton University Press, New York (1957)
3. Burghardt, A.: Behavioural Control of Wheeled Minirobot. PAK 11, 26–29 (2004) (in polish)
4. Giergiel, J., Hendzel, Z., Zylski, W.: Modeling and Control of Wheeled Mobile Robots, WNT, Warsaw (2002) (in polish)
5. Giergiel, J., Zylski, W.: Description of Motion of a Mobile Robot by Maggie's Equations. J. of Theoretical and Applied Mechanics 43, 511–521 (2005)
6. Hendzel, Z., Szuster, M.: Discrete Action Dependant Heuristic Dynamic Programming in Wheeled Mobile Robot Control. Solid State Phenomena 164, 419–424 (2010)
7. Hendzel, Z., Szuster, M.: Discrete Model-Based Adaptive Critic Designs in Wheeled Mobile Robot Control. In: Rutkowski, L., Scherer, R., Tadeusiewicz, R., Zadeh, L.A., Zurada, J.M. (eds.) ICAISC 2010. LNCS, vol. 6114, pp. 264–271. Springer, Heidelberg (2010)
8. Hendzel, Z., Szuster, M.: Neural Dynamic Programming in Behavioural Control of Wheeled Mobile Robot. Acta Mechanica et Automatica 5, 28–36 (2011) (in polish)
9. Maaref, H., Barret, C.: Sensor-based Navigation of a Mobile Robot in an Indoor Environment. Robotics and Autonomous Systems 38, 1–18 (2002)
10. Millan, J.: Reinforcement Learning of Goal-Directed Obstacle-Avoiding Reaction Strategies in an Autonomous Mobile Robot. Robotics and Autonomous Systems 15, 275–299 (1995)
11. Powell, W.B.: Approximate Dynamic Programming: Solving the Curses of Dimensionality. Willey-Interscience, Princeton (2007)
12. Prokhorov, D., Wunch, D.: Adaptive Critic Designs. IEEE Transactions on Neural Networks 8, 997–1007 (1997)
13. Si, J., Barto, A.G., Powell, W.B., Wunsch, D.: Handbook of Learning and Approximate Dynamic Programming. IEEE Press, Wiley-Interscience (2004)

Modified Model-Free Adaptive Controller for a Nonlinear Rotor System

Igor Karoń

Chair of Computer Engineering,
Poznań University of Technology, ul. Piotrowo 3A, 61-138, Poznań, Poland
igor.z.karon@doctorate.put.poznan.pl

Abstract. Most of the machines and plants are tricky for mathematical description thus insufficiently described model can affect the control process. This paper presents Modified version of Model-Free Adaptive controller for fast-changing, hard-to-control plants. Motivation for presented work was insufficiency of currently available solutions, which were in most cases unable to control proposed experimental model.

1 Introduction

When user implements one of the modern control techniques on a real environment plant, one is often obliged to provide a mathematical model of the considered system. However, most of the phenomena is hard to capture with analytical description and its precision has direct influence on the quality of the model-based controller. Hence, one can notice a significant work done in the area of model-free control methods. These techniques include: well-known Proportional Integral Derivate (PID, which is still the choice in over 90% of all industrial control frameworks [1]), *intelligent*-PID (*i*-PID, which uses elements of flatness-based control theory [2]), Active Disturbance Rejection Control (ADRC, which takes advantage of the disturbance observer approach [3]), etc. Other interesting example is Model-Free Adaptive (MFA) control approach [4, 5].

The MFA control method is based on a multilayer perceptron neural network that makes the controller inherently robust to the dynamic changes of the process, its parametric and structural uncertainties as well as other acting disturbances. Besides model-independent approach, the MFA does not need the controller to be redesign for a specific process and it does not require complicated tuning. As a feedback control system, MFA requires that the process could be controllable and open-loop stable. To this day, the robustness of the MFA found itself useful in numerous industrial processes, e.g. [6–8].

However, the above applications of the considered controller were only introduced for slow responding systems (e.g. water treatment, oil boiler, air separation). It is justified by the use of neural networks that time need to adapt to the systems current status and operators desired goal. It is interesting to examine the potential use of the MFA controller on fast responding plants.

Hence, this paper focuses on the attempt to answer this intriguing question by investigating MFA trajectory tracking and robustness abilities for this type

L. Rutkowski et al. (Eds.): ICAISC 2012, Part II, LNCS 7268, pp. 458–465, 2012.

of system. It also tests the considered controller for some typical issues related to the neural networks, i.e.: initial training time, minimum computation power requirement, etc. For this research, a laboratory rotor system is chosen. It is an one degree-of-freedom, nonlinear plant with its analytical description mostly unknown.

The paper is organized as follows In chapter 2 the modified version of MFA controller is described, in Chapter 3 TRAS model is presented. Chapter 4 contains information and results of conducted experimental studies, and in the final Chapter short summary is presented.

2   Modified Model-Free Adaptive Control

The classical approach for Model Free Adaptive control was proposed by Professor Hou Zhonghseng in his PhD thesis for control of the slow responding industrial systems.

Another idea was presented by Gorge S. Cheng, this approach considers the use of the Neural Network combined with classical proportional controller (P), where the gain of P controller is constantly set to one[5]. Modified version of Gorge S. Cheng MFA controller was proposed by Xu Aidong, who considered that gain of proportional block can be modified [12].

For high speed response systems with small bandwidth of control signal, proposed MFA versions become insufficient. Problems considering the use of neural network (like: high non-linearity of neural gates, simplified and insufficient learning algorithms) and with fast changes of controller output (caused by use of proportional control) becomes visible. Due to mentioned disadvantages and to adapt MFA control method for hard to control systems modified version is proposed.

The first step is to increase control on neuron gates linearity. The simplest method is to freely change value of bias given on neuron input. In previous works, bias (described as E0) value was provided as constant one despite a considered control system. In the proposed system, bias is also constant but its initial value depends on user. For control efficiency, it is recommended to use numbers from interval <0;1>. Possibility of setting bias to desire value provides changes of working point of neural gate function. It is very usefull to adjust the network to the desired plant model.

Next steps were provided purely for decrease of the fluctuations in network response. Fluctuations in output signal are caused by non-linearity of neural gates and the self-adapting mechanism of the network [12]. Second step aim to gain additional control on the strength of network output in each step. It is provided by adding gain on the Neural Network output. By tuning influence of network gain for controlled process critical flaws in learning algorithm are reduced.

Third step is to average NN output based on last few samples. It can be described by (1). Averaging set of output signals from desire time period can provide trend visibility of network changes. Combining steps two and three enable much better results and easer adjusting of MFA for control purpose of desire plant. Modified version of MFA controller (MMFA) structure is shown in Fig.1.

$$u_o(t) = \sum_{n-x}^{n} (u_c)/n \tag{1}$$

where: u_o - output of MWE block , u_c - signal after Kc gain, n - number of current sample, x - number of samples to average.

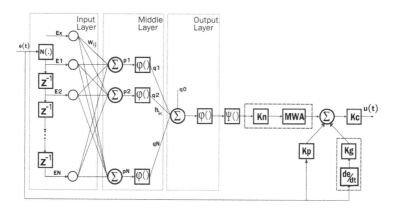

Fig. 1. Modified MFA block schematic

In the presented system, variables are described as follows: Kg – derivative gain value, Kp – proportional gain, Kc – MMFA controller output signal gain, Kn – Neural Network output gain, Ex – constant bias provided to neurons inputs, MWE – averaging block, which is described with (3), w_{ij} - weights for fist layer, h_i - weights for second layer, φ -neurons activation function, $N(.)$ - normalization function, Ψ - function which maps Neural Network output in to real space. In MFA controller functions $N(.)$, φ, Ψ are implement based on the system for control informations.

For modified version online learning algorithm based on delta learning rule was used. Provided algorithm can be described with the equations (2) and (3).

$$\Delta w_{ij}(n) = \eta \cdot Kc \cdot e(n) \cdot \Phi(n) \cdot q_j(n) \cdot (1 - q_j(n)) \cdot \sum_{k=1}^{N} h_k(n) \cdot E_i(n) \tag{2}$$

$$\Delta h_j(n) = \eta \cdot Kc \cdot e(n) \cdot \Phi(n) \cdot q_j(n) \cdot (1 - q_j(n)) \tag{3}$$

where: (2). describes learning process for firs layer and (3). describes learning process for second layer, η - is learning rate, q - vector of signals from previous layer of the network, and Φ can be described with (4).

$$\frac{\Delta y(n+1)}{\Delta u(n)} = \Phi(n) \tag{4}$$

where: y is the plant output and u is the plant input.

3   System Description

TRAS is a laboratory setup designed for educational purposes. System is often used by researchers as a benchmark tool to explore, implement, and evaluate different control methodologies. From a mechanical point of view TRAS has two rotors (front and rear rotor) placed at both ends of a beam (see Fig.2). Rotors are driven by two direct current (DC) motors. The beam is pivoted on a rigid stand. The above construction allows the beam to move freely both in vertical and horizontal plane. Additionally, a movable counterbalance attached to the beam at the pivot point can be used to set a desired equilibrium position.

An exemplary mathematical model of TRAS, based on [9], is presented on Fig.3, where subscripts v and h represent the elements associated with vertical and horizontal motion of the beam respectively, and $\alpha[rad]$ – angular position of the beam (output signal), $U[V]$ – DC motor input voltage (input/control signal), H^* – DC motor dynamics, F^* – function describing transformation of rotational speed of the propeller ($\omega[rad/s]$) into aerodynamic force ($F[N]$), $L[m]$ – lenght of the beam, $M[Nm]$ – beam's turning torque, $K[(kgm^2)/s]$ – beam's angular momentum, $J[kgm^2]$ – beam's moment of inertia, $\Omega[rad/s]$ – angular velocity of the beam, $f[Nm]$– moment of friction force, $G[Nm]$ – aerodynamical damping torque, $R[Nm]$ – returning torque, $k_{hv/vh}$ – constant values, amplifications of cross-coupling effect.

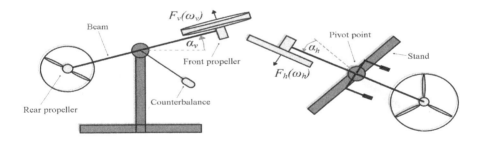

Fig. 2. Main parts and motion idea of the TRAS laboratory system

The mathematical model of TRAS supplied by the producer in [9] and presented in Fig. 3 does not represent the plant dynamics accurately. It has been noticed for example that not all of the effective forces are taken into account. Other proposed models of TRAS (with different level of precision) can be found in literature, e.g. [10, 11]. However, even if the given model imitates the behavior of the real plant with high accuracy, its derivation is problematic and requires high analytical skills. It is caused by the amount and nonlinear nature of acting forces (e.g. aerodynamical damping torque, friction force, etc.).

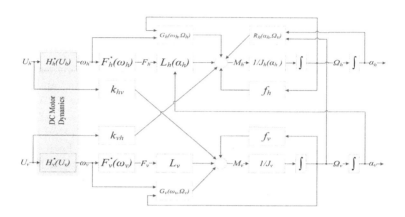

Fig. 3. A block diagram of TRAS simplified mathematical model

4   Research and Results

Aim of conducted experiments was the verification of proposed modified MAF algorithm and its utility for practical control tasks. MFA controller was tested for the task of generation given real-time trajectory for sinusoidal and square signal types. Algorithm was tested with different: values of gains (Kp, Kg, Ks, Kc), number of neurons, averaging period in MWE block, bias value (Ex). For comparison the control models of PD controller was used.

4.1   Study Preparations

Experimental studies were carried on laboratory set, presented in Fig.4. consisting of: plant, I/O card and computer. As early mentioned plant used for experiments was thoroughly described in Chapter 2. Schematic diagram for control process purpose was prepared in Matlab environment Simulink version 7.2. MFA controller model was written as an Embedded Matlab Function. Process set in Simulink was compiled to C and uploaded on I/O Card. Uploaded in I/O card program function independently from Matlab, Simulink only acquire data provide by I/O card from controlled plant.

4.2   Conducted Experiments

Experiments were conducted for different values given for a PD and MFA controller blocks. Signals provided for the plant keep-up task were sinusoidal and square, each given for few frequency values. Aim of conducted experiments was to test flexibility and range of possible value selection for controller variables of given MMFA algorithm. Both algorithms were tested for noise and provided signal tolerance, controller variables were tuned only for sinusoidal signal. In addition for half of experiment time in each simulation external noise was provided for the plant. Sampling time was set to 0.1[s] and each experiment time was six times of the signal period.

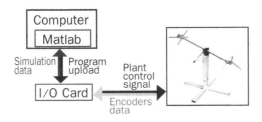

Fig. 4. A block diagram of TRAS control schematic

Table 1. Comparison of IACS of the error signal results for PD and MMFA controller

Kc	Kg	Kp	MFA Sin	MFA Square	PD Sin	PD Square
1	0.85	2.5	556.407	6772.4	1062.1	11740
1	1	2.5	951.4384	6776.7	940.09	10070
1	.85	1.5	966.0281	8036.4	953.79	9309.6
1	.75	4.5	968.02	11724.0	932.4	impossible to simulate
4.5	.75	1.5	—	8060.9	impossible to simulate	8617.0

In Fig.5. and Fig.7. plant response for given signal is showed, similar Fig.6. and Fig.8. presents an adequate control signal provided on plant from the controller for each simulation.

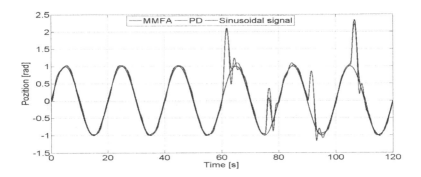

Fig. 5. A simulation results for sinusoidal signal

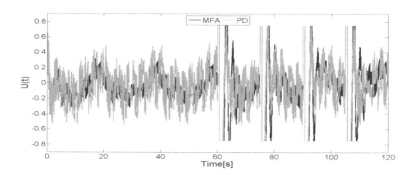

Fig. 6. Control signal given for sinusoidal signal

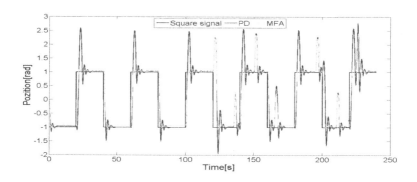

Fig. 7. A simulation results for square signal

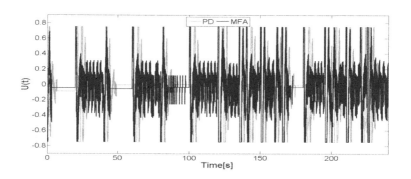

Fig. 8. Control signal given for square signal

5   Conclusions

Experiment results clearly shows advantages gained from usage of the MMFA controller. Flexibility and range of used variables is grater than these in classical PD controller. Therefore, controller tuning is much easier and faster than in other solutions. In addition proposed modifications provide wider range of plant possible to control than the classical approach of MFA. Reaction for disturbance is also better, time and fluctuations for plant recover to given signal, visible on simulation results, perfectly confirmed it. Unlike MFA, proposed MMFA is fitted for fast changing signals where only obstacle is plant mechanic.

As the disadvantages, higher complication of controller structure, computation complexity and greater variables number can be counted.

Despite mentioned disadvantages, MMFA can be classified as a useful solution for most of the plants.

Acknowledgement. I would like to thank Mr. Rafal Madonski from Chair of Control and Systems Engineering, Poznan University of Technology for his help, useful advices regarding MFA control. I would also like to thank Chair of Control and Systems Engineering for provide access to necessary laboratory set.

References

1. Visioli, A.: Practical PID control. Springer (2006)
2. Fliesss, M., Join, C.: Model-free controllers and intelligent PID controllers. In: Mediterranean Conference on Control and Automation, pp. 326–331 (2008)
3. Han, J.: From PID to Active Disturbance Rejection Control. IEEE Transactions on Industrial Electronics 56(3), 900–906 (2009)
4. Cheng, G.S.: Model-free adaptive (MFA) control. Journal of Computing and Control Engineering 14(3), 28–33 (2004)
5. CyboSoft, http://www.cybosoft.com/index.html
6. Zhang, G.: Marine power management system based on model free adaptive control. In: International Conference on Computer Application and System Modeling, pp. 160–163 (2010)
7. Chen, A.: Speed regulator of diesel-generator based on model free adaptive control. In: WRI Global Congress on Intelligent Systems, pp. 193–196 (2010)
8. Jianling, Q., Guang, M.: Design of Glass Furnace Control System Based on Model-Free Adaptive Controller. In: International Conference on Computer Application and System Modeling, pp. 160–163 (2010)
9. Two Rotor Aerodynamical System, User's Manual, Inteco (2010)
10. Rahideh, A., Shaheed, M.H., Huijberts, H.J.C.: Dynamic modelling of a TRMS using analytical and empirical approaches. Control Engineering Practice (16), 241–259 (2008)
11. Toha, S.F., Tokhi, M.O.: Real-coded genetic algorithm for parametric modelling of a TRMS. In: Congress on Evolutionary Computation, pp. 2022–2028 (2009)
12. Aidong, X., Yangbo, Z., Yan, S., Mingzhe, L.: An Improved Model Free Adaptive Control Algorithm. In: Fifth International Conference on Natural Computation, pp. 70–74 (2009)

A Centralized Multi-Robot Task Allocation for Industrial Plant Inspection by Using A* and Genetic Algorithms

Chun Liu and Andreas Kroll

Measurement and Control Department, Mechanical Engineering,
University of Kassel, Mönchebergstraße 7, 34125, Kassel, Germany
{chun.liu,andreas.kroll}@mrt.uni-kassel.de

Abstract. Multi-robot systems are widely employed in various applications including industrial plant inspection. However, current research work mainly focuses on the methods of object detection, and rarely addresses task allocation and path-planning of multi-robot systems for industrial plant inspection. Therefore, a centralized method for multi-robot task allocation (MRTA) and path-planning to solve inspection problems is proposed in this paper. For the first time, the problem statement of the task allocation for inspection problems is formulated. This paper introduces the implementation of the algorithm based on A* and a novel Genetic Algorithm including the environment representation. The task allocation and path-planning are performed based on the assumption that the robots work in known environments. The proposed algorithm is tested in a simulation study derived from a large industrial site.

Keywords: Multi-Robot, Task Allocation, Path-Planning, A*, Genetic Algorithm, Inspection.

1 Introduction

Multi-robot systems have been employed in many application domains and most research focuses on waste cleanup [1], box-pushing [2], target observation [3], object transfer [4], exploration and mapping [5], etc.

The idea of industrial inspection robots is not new as such, as mobile robots have been used for pipeline inspection in the Oil & Gas industry since the 1960ies [6]. However, much research focuses on the methods of object detection (e.g. pipeline inspection by nondestructive techniques), and little research addresses the task allocation of multi-robot systems in industrial plant inspection [7].

The inspection of industrial sites for gas leaks by multi-robot systems is studied in the "RoboGas^{Inspector}" project [8]. Research problems regarding the detection of gas and leak localization strategies have been discussed in [9,10]. This paper focuses on the task allocation and path-planning for multi-robot systems deployed for industrial plant inspection. Fig. 1 shows an example of such large-scale complex environments [11].

L. Rutkowski et al. (Eds.): ICAISC 2012, Part II, LNCS 7268, pp. 466–474, 2012.
© Springer-Verlag Berlin Heidelberg 2012

Fig. 1. PCK refinery. © PCK Raffinerie GmbH.

Based on A* and Genetic Algorithm (GA), a centralized task allocation and path-planning method is proposed in this paper. A centralized approach is attractive as it considers all information and can provide optimal solutions. Traditionally, most research focuses on finding the suitable heuristic function of A* [12], and the GA has been used for finding the optimal path-planning [13]. In this paper, a GA is designed for task allocation to find the optimal solution for industrial plant inspection problems, and A* is responsible for the traveling cost (which is one evaluation parameter of the fitness function in the GA) and path-planning between any two positions as it can consider more detail path conditions (e.g. obstacles, target objects, different terrain conditions).

The paper is organized as follows. The next section provides the problem statement. The description of the proposed solution is addressed in section 3 including environment modeling, A* and Genetic Algorithm. In section 4 experiments and results in a simulation study are given. Finally, the conclusion of this paper is drawn in section 5.

2 Problem Definition

The Multi-Robot Task Allocation (MRTA) problem is a search optimization problem. Three criteria to classify MRTA problems are proposed [14,15]. The algorithm proposed in this paper is of type ST-SR-IA (ST means that each robot is capable of executing at most one task at a time, SR means that each task requires exactly one robot to achieve it, and IA means that the assignment is instantaneous allocation with no planning for future). Given: a group of m robots $R = \{R_1, R_2, ..., R_i, ..., R_m\}$, a set of n tasks $T = \{T_1, T_2, ..., T_j, ..., T_n\}$ with relative weights $\{w_1, w_2, ..., w_j, ...w_n\}$, and the cost C_{ij} of robot R_i executing task T_j, the goal of MRTA is to find an ordered set of tasks for robots in order to minimize the total cost of the mission. According to the application requirements, the cost of a mission may be determined from energy consumption, operating time, traveled distance, etc. As gas leak can be safety-critical, it is important to find out whether there is a gas leak as soon as possible. Therefore, the cost of the proposed algorithm is defined as **the completion time** which is the time span of the first robot starting its tasks and the last robot finishing its tasks. The cost function J is:

$$J := \max\left\{ \sum_{j=1}^{n} C_{1j}, \sum_{j=1}^{n} C_{2j}, ..., \sum_{j=1}^{n} C_{ij}, ..., \sum_{j=1}^{n} C_{mj} \right\} \quad (1)$$

where,

$$C_{ij} \begin{cases} > 0, & \text{if robot } R_i \text{ is allocated task } T_j \\ := 0, & \text{otherwise} \end{cases}.$$

The algorithm for task allocation and path-planning should satisfy two constraints: each task is executed exactly once and robots need to move between inspection positions without colliding with each other or with obstacles. The inspection positions of the inspected objects are determined from the object size, the sensor characteristics and the measurement method (e.g. the sensor range).

In case of the gas leak inspection problem, the goal is not only finding an ordered set of inspected objects for each robot providing for minimum total cost, but also finding a shortest feasible path between the inspection positions. Therefore, the cost C_{ij} is composed of the traveling time C_{ijv} from its previous position to the current gas inspection position, and the inspection time C_{ijs} which is the time to complete the required gas measurements at the inspection position.

$$\begin{cases} C_{ij} = C_{ijv} + C_{ijs} \\ C_{ijv} = \alpha \cdot (d_{ij}/v_i) \\ C_{ijs} = \beta_j \cdot M_{ij} \end{cases} \quad (2)$$

where, $\alpha \in [1 : 10]$ is the ground condition coefficient which is related to the mobility capability of robots on different terrain conditions (e.g. unpaved road, grass-terraced slop, shallow water, etc.), d_{ij} is the traveling distance, v_i is the robot velocity, $\beta_j \in [1 : 10]$ is the sensor performance coefficient related to the capabilities of sensors for inspecting different types of objects T_j (e.g. tanks, pipes), and M_{ij} is the measurement range related to the sensor range, the size of the inspected objects and the measurement method (e.g. refer to [10]).

When the completion times of two solutions are the same, the fuel consumption J_s of all m robots is used as additional criterion:

$$J_s := \text{sum}\left\{ \sum_{j=1}^{n} \delta_1 \cdot C_{1j}, ..., \sum_{j=1}^{n} \delta_i \cdot C_{ij}, ..., \sum_{j=1}^{n} \delta_m \cdot C_{mj} \right\} = \sum_{i=1}^{m} \sum_{j=1}^{n} \delta_i \cdot C_{ij} \quad (3)$$

where, δ_i is the fuel coefficient which is related to the type of the robot R_i. For the homogeneous robot system, δ_i is the same for all robots.

3   Algorithm Design

A centralized approach for multi-robot task allocation (MRTA) in inspection problems is described in this section. The programming is done using MATLAB, and organized into three parts: environment representation, path-planning and task allocation. The A* algorithm is used to calculate the traveling time (C_{ijv} in equation (2)) and path-planning of a robot moving from one position to another. The genetic algorithm is responsible for task assignment. The inspection positions can be specified by the plant operator or other programs, and the inspection costs C_{ijs} depend on the measurement approach and inspection object geometry. In this paper, the inspection positions and the inspection costs at these inspection positions are given at the beginning of the program.

3.1   Environment Representation

In the MATLAB program, the environment is represented as a grid map and recorded as a matrix. This map can be divided into two types: inadmissible areas (e.g. target objects, obstacles) and admissible areas (e.g. accessible roads). According to the mobility capability of robots on different terrains (e.g. unpaved road, grass-terraced slop, shallow water, etc.), the ground condition coefficient of each cell (α in equation (2)) is given. To avoid robots colliding with each other, the time of each robot occupying at each cell (time occupancy) during path-planning can be computed. Therefore, with each cell the following information is associated: (1) inadmissible or admissible area; (2) ground condition coefficient; and (3) the time occupancy.

3.2   Path-Planning

Path-planning means to find a best path between two positions and can be solved using the A* algorithm. This is a heuristic algorithm for finding the shortest feasible path for each robot from the current position to the corresponding target position. Although the A* algorithm has been proposed since 1968 [16], it is still the workhorse for path planning in mobile robotics. For every position s, the basic estimated function is $f[s] = g[s] + h[s]$, where $g[s]$ is the cost of the path from the start position to the current position s, and $h[s]$ is a heuristic value which estimates the cost from s to the goal position q. Different heuristic functions are analyzed in [17]. To find the optimal solution, $h[s]$ is determined from the Euclidean distance ($d[s]$) between s and q in this paper providing for:

$$f[s] = \alpha \cdot \{(g[s] + d[s])/v_i\}$$

At each position of the robot R_i, the estimated function values of the 8 adjacent positions are calculated, and the position with the smallest value is selected to be the next position of the robot until the robot gets to the goal position (the inspection position). The traveling time is $C_{ijv} = \alpha \cdot g[q]/v_i$. The A* algorithm calculates the traveling costs of any two inspection positions before genetic algorithm, and plans the feasible path according to the task allocation by genetic algorithm at the end of the program. This strategy is not so efficient for large-scale problems due to spending long time on calculating the costs of any pair of inspection positions. Future work will improve the efficiency of this algorithm for large-scale problems.

3.3   Task Allocation

In this paper, task allocation is achieved using a genetic algorithm. A task is referred to as an inspection position. A consecutive integer number is assigned to each inspection position. Permutation coding is used to represent task assignments. Therefore, "task assignment" means to assign the complete sequence of inspection positions to visit to each robot.

The initial population of the genetic algorithm is determined by two ways in this paper: generated randomly or by Greedy algorithm. As the goal of the proposed algorithm is to minimize the completion time (equation (1)) while decreasing the total fuel consumption (equation (3)), two Greedy algorithms are proposed: (1) finding one task for each robot which provides for the minimum time in each step in order to minimize the completion time; (2) finding only one robot-task pair which takes the minimum time in each step in order to decrease the total fuel consumption. The initial population of the proposed algorithm is composed of 80% individuals generated randomly, 10% individuals generated by Greedy (1), and the other 10% individuals generated by Greedy (2).

The new population is generated by selection, crossover (partially mapped crossover (PMX) [18]) and mutation (swap, insertion and inversion). Elitism strategy is used for selection, in which at least one best individual is copied without changes to the new population. A number of chromosomes with the highest fitness are selected into the parent pool for crossover and mutation operations. Such a strategy prevents losing the current best solutions and reserves the good genetic material.

The current population is randomly divided into K non-overlapping groups, and each group contains a fixed number of individuals. The elitist selection, crossover and mutation are performed in each group, respectively. For each group: a number of the individuals with better fitness value are selected for the parent pool; a number of elite individuals survive to the next population; two randomly selected chromosomes in the parent pool are considered as the parents for crossover; and different mutation operators are applied in parallel to the best individual in each group. This procedure is inspired from the algorithm [19], which keeps one elite individual in each group and only uses mutation to generate the new offsprings. The crossover operator was added to the algorithm in order to permit combining good building blocks of two parents to form even better children.

The process of this algorithm is shown in Fig. 2.

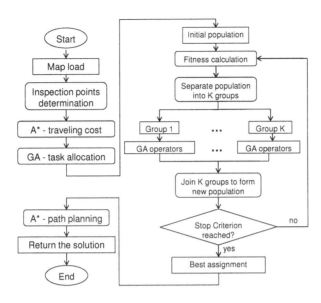

Fig. 2. The process of the proposed algorithm

4   Experiments and Results

An example scenario is derived from a tank farm of a real petroleum refinery ([11]) – Four types of target objects (T1, T2, T3 and T4) with 90 inspection positions are inspected by 3 homogeneous robots. The inspection time at each inspection position is provided by the other program based on the measurement method.

Fig. 3 shows two solutions of task allocation and path-planning, and their completion times and the total fuel consumptions are shown in Table 1. The left one has shorter completion time determined by the robot with the red path, but more fuel consumption. Although the blue path and the red path are overlapping at coordinates (15,33), (15,30) and (17,3), the time occupancies are different (blue path: 107.0711s, 104.0711s and 159.8274s, red path: 70.4706s, 76.8132s~77.9132s and 3.8284s). The red path and the green path overlap at coordinates (21,24:28), but the time occupancy of the red path is 122.0985s~137.1985s and that one of the green path is 107.7279s~112.8279s. Therefore, robots will not collide. In the right figure, the completion time is determined by the robot with the blue path, and the paths are not overlapping. Comparing these two solutions, the deviation of the individual costs in the right solution is larger than that in the left solution, which causes that the right solution has a longer completion time.

To evaluate the impact of the Greedy population initialization on the global search capability, the proposed algorithm which is with Greedy population initialization is compared with the genetic algorithm without Greedy population initialization. Both algorithms are run 100 times independently with population size of 200 and the maximum number of generations chosen as 20000.

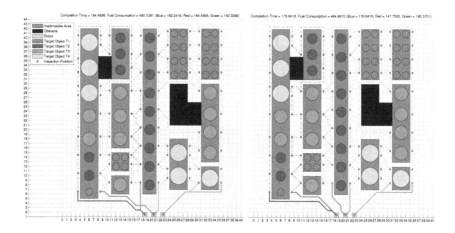

Fig. 3. Alternative solutions of task allocation and path-planning

Table 1. Completion time and total fuel consumption of two solutions in Fig. 3

Solutions	Completion Time (s)	Total Fuel Consumption
Left	164.4696	490.0381
Right	176.6416	484.9670

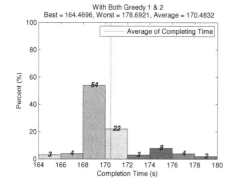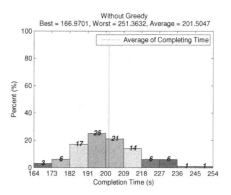

Fig. 4. Completion time distribution of 100 runs with (left)/without (right) Greedy population initialization

The completion time distribution of these 100 runs with/without Greedy initialization is shown in Fig. 4. The completion time of the optimal solution is 164.4696s. All solutions of the GA with Greedy initialization have completion times $J \in [164\text{s}:179\text{s}]$. However, less than 10% solutions of the GA without Greedy initialization provide for completion times $J \in [164\text{s}:179\text{s}]$. Therefore, using Greedy initialization greatly improves the efficiency of the genetic algorithm.

5   Conclusion

Multi-robot systems can be used to inspect industrial plants for gas leakages. Little work addresses the task allocation and path-planning for such missions. This paper presents a centralized task allocation and path-planning algorithm for robot operation in known environments. A* is used for traveling cost evaluation and path-planning between any two positions, and the genetic algorithm is responsible for task allocation. Two Greedy algorithms are proposed to improve the global search capability of the genetic algorithm. The proposed algorithm is demonstrated in simulation study derived from a large industrial plant providing for good results. Future work will include also dynamic environments and cooperative measurement tasks.

Acknowledgements. Parts of the work were supported by the project Robo-Gas^{Inspector} [8], which is greatly acknowledged. The project RoboGas^{Inspector} is funded by the Federal Ministry of Economics and Technology due to a resolution of the German Bundestag.

References

1. Meng, Y., Gan, J.: LIVS: Local Interaction via Virtual Stigmergy Coordination in Distributed Search and Collective Cleanup. In: Proceedings of the 2007 IEEE/RSJ International Conference on Intelligent Robots and Systems, San Diego, USA, pp. 137–1376 (2007)
2. Chakraborty, J., Konar, A., Nagar, A., Tawfik, H.: A Multi-Objective Pareto-Optimal Solution to the Box-Pushing Problem by Mobile Robots. In: Proceedings of the Second UKSIM European Symposium on Computer Modeling and Simulation, Liverpool, England, pp. 70–75 (2008)
3. Kolling, A., Carpin, S.: Cooperative Observation of Multiple Moving Targets: An Algorithm and its Formalization. International Journal of Robotics Research 26(9), 93–953 (2007)
4. Chaimowicz, L., Sugar, T., Kumar, V., Campos, M.F.M.: An Architecture for Tightly Coupled Multi-Robot Cooperation. In: Proceedings of the IEEE International Conference on Robotics and Automation, Seoul, Korea, pp. 2992–2997 (2001)
5. Fox, D., Ko, J., Konolige, K., Limketkai, B., Schulz, D., Stewart, B.: Distributed Multirobot Exploration and Mapping. Proceedings of the IEEE 94(7), 132–1339 (2006)
6. Lumb, R.F.: Inspection of Pipelines Using Nondestructive Techniques. Physics in Technology 6, 249–256 (1977)
7. Kroll, A.: A Survey on Mobile Robots for Industrial Inspection. In: Proceedings of the Int. Conf. on Intelligent Autonomous Systems IAS10, Baden-Baden, Germany, pp. 406–414 (2008)
8. RoboGas^{Inspector}, http://www.robogasinspector.de/
9. Kroll, A., Baetz, W., Peretzki, D.: On Autonomous Detection of Pressured Air and Gas Leaks Using Passive IR-Thermography for Mobile Robot Application. In: Proceedings of IEEE International Conference on Robotics and Automation (ICRA 2009), Kobe, Japan, pp. 921–926 (2009)

10. Baetz, W., Kroll, A., Bonow, G.: Mobile Robots with Active IR-Optical Sensing for Remote Gas Detection and Source Localization. In: Proceedings of IEEE International Conference on Robotics and Automation (ICRA 2009), Kobe, Japan, pp. 2773–2778 (2009)
11. PCK Refinery, http://www.pck.de/
12. Aine, S., Chakrabarti, P.P., Kumar, R.: Heuristic Search under Contract. Computational Intelligence 26(4), 386–419 (2010)
13. Al-Dulaimi, B.F., Ali, H.A.: Enhanced Traveling Salesman Problem Solving by Genetic Algorithm Technique (TSPGA). World Academy of Science, Engineering and Technology 38, 296–302 (2008)
14. Gerkey, B.P., Matarić, M.J.: Multi-Robot Task Allocation: Analyzing the Complexity and Optimality of Key Architectures. In: Proceedings of the IEEE International Conference on Robotics and Automation (ICRA), Taipei, Taiwan, pp. 3862–3868 (2003)
15. Gerkey, B.P., Matarić, M.J.: A Formal Analysis and Taxonomy of Task Allocation in Multi-Robot Systems. The International Journal of Robotics Research 23(9), 939–954 (2004)
16. Hart, P.E., Nilsson, N.J., Raphael, B.: A Formal Basis for the Heuristic Determination of Minimum Cost Paths. IEEE Transactions on Systems Science and Cybernetics SSC4 4(2), 100–107 (1968)
17. Goto, T., Kosaka, T., Noborio, H.: On the Heuristics of A* or A Algorithm in ITS and Robot Path-Planning. In: Proceedings of the 2003 IEEE/RSJ International Conference on Intelligent Robots and Systems, Las Vegas, Nevada, USA, pp. 1159–1166 (2003)
18. Goldberg, D.E., Lingle, R.: Alleles, Loci, and the Traveling Salesman Problem. In: Proceedings of the First International Conference on Genetic Algorithms and Their Application, Hillsdale, NJ, pp. 154–159 (1985)
19. MATLAB Central, http://www.mathworks.com/matlabcentral

A Symbiotic Lenticular Airship
for WiSAR Missions

Eduardo Pinto and José Barata

Universidade Nova de Lisboa, Faculdade de Ciências e Tecnologia,
Departamento de Engenharia Electroténica, 2829-516 Caparica, Portugal
{emp,jab}@uninova.pt

Abstract. This paper presents and describes an innovative cooperative symbiotic robotic system based in two types of unmanned air vehicles: A lenticular shaped airship that allows 3D omnidirectional movements with a big top area for solar energy harvesting and a group of micro-quad rotors using micro electric ducted fans. The solution presented could be used in missions as environmental, biodiversity monitoring, WiSAR missions, road monitoring, detection of forest fires, etc.

Keywords: Lenticular Airship, WiSAR, Cooperative symbiotic robots, Light than air vehicles.

1   Introduction

The system proposed uses a bio-inspired approach based on two different robots working together and maintaining a symbiotic relation. Symbiosis is a popular strategy for survival in biological world, with many examples ranging from the bacteria in the human intestine to the Egyptian plover bird that feeds on the leeches attached to the gums of a crocodile. A collective system like this exhibits very interesting properties. It could be extremely flexible, have extended capabilities for adaptation, self-organization and self-development [1]. Robustness and reliability can often be increased by combining several robots which are individually less robust and reliable [2]. Taking the example of WiSAR-Wilderness Search and Rescue missions, a robot should be able to cover big distances during long periods of time but also have the ability to access and inspect confined spaces with high maneuverability. A system for this purpose should be able to have:

- Capacity of support variable and unstructured terrain but at the same time low complexity to maintain a high degree of reliability
- High power and communications capacity but at the same time low size to maintain the capacity to deal with a very unstructured environment.

These two demands are often conflicting especially when we look to the actual power sources. Long time operation means high power what means heavy batteries that limits maneuverability. The solution we propose in the present work

L. Rutkowski et al. (Eds.): ICAISC 2012, Part II, LNCS 7268, pp. 475–483, 2012.

is to use two kinds of aerial robots working together. The first is a LTAV – Light Than Air Vehicle with a special lenticular shape and the second is a group of very small quadrotors. In our system we were inspired by the mechanism of Trophallaxis in a colony of ants that is used to form a "communal stomach" to the mechanism where the robots of the system plug each other and share the power in order to increase the operational range of the whole system.

1.1   Why a Lenticular Shape?

The choice of a lenticular shape for our LTAV was based in the fact that this shape exhibits very interesting properties when compared with other more common as we can see in Table 1.

The minimum weight of the airship structure under given buoyant lift can be achieved under sphere-shaped body, but the use of lenticular shape allow for a smaller drag [3]. Also by presenting the same low drag shape in all directions makes it less sensible to lateral winds and turbulence and allow implementing a true innovative omnidirectional locomotion. The solution used and described in 2, allow to overcome the control problems described by other authors [4] allowing for very stable flight and hovering and vertical landing and taking off with very simple algorithms. The lenticular shape also exhibits other advantages to our system: VTOL-vertical take-off and landing with easy mooring capability without the need for hangars or mooring masts, and very good hovering capacity with low power consumption. It's also the shape that presents the greater top surface area what is very important for the use of a large array of very thin solar cells based on polyimide film LaRCtrade-CP1 and amorphous silicon. In literature, it is mentioned a possibility of a value of energy of 4.3W/g [5] that will allow the airship to be able to do energy harvesting for itself and for the micro quadrotors. Recent developments will allow the direct deposit at a low cost of solar cells in almost all kind of materials [6] including the ones used for airships envelopes.

Table 1. Airship common shapes

Shape	Airship e.g.	Drag	Manover.	Wind	Lift	Moor
Cigar–shaped	Hinderburg	++	+	+	++	-
Spherical	Aerosphere SA-60	-	++	+	+++	+
Lenticular	Alizé	++	+++	++	+	+++
Multiple Hull	L. Martin P791	+	+	+	++	-
Winged airships	BARS "Bella-1"	+	++	+	+	-
Dart Shape	Bullet Airship	+++	+	+	++	-
Deltoid	AEREON 26	+	++	+	+	-

1.2   Why a Micro-quadrotor

Only last year we have witnessed a wave of interest in quadrotors with many groups [7] all over the world using quadrotors as base for several types of projects. However, the idea is not new and remotes to 1907 with the project "Bréguet-Richet Gyroplane No. 1" developed by the French brothers Louis and Jacques Bréguet under the supervision of French scientist and academician Charles Richet. The main idea behind a quadrotor is mechanical simplicity and using pairs of propellers rotating backward to cancel torque reaction. The various movements are done only by changing the speed of each propeller. In short, a quadrotor offers the following advantages [8]: Very simple mechanics with variable speed fixed pitch propellers, payload augmentation and great maneuverability even in confined spaces. The bigger drawback is high power consumption, that limits its operational possibilities. It's our belief that one of the best methods to overpass this difficulty is to have the quadrotor as a marsupial robot working together with an airship. However, in this article we will focus in only one of the components of the system, the airship and the generic hardware and an innovative controller and IMU board, behalf this IMU board will be used as a controller for all the robots in the system.

2   The Lenticular Shaped Airship

With the exception of the envelope that was manufactured by Mobile Airships, according to our drawings, all of the materials could be easily acquired in Kite and RC specialty stores contributing to maintain the project at a low cost and easily replicable. Several prototypes, and control stations, with several functions, have been developed since 2006.

Fig. 1. Airship in several demonstrations

As we can see in Fig. 1 the assisted control allow an easy and intuitive control as demonstrated by letting small kids control the airship in a confined space as the Electricity Museum in Lisbon.

Table 2. Airship structure

Dimensions	3.2 m diameter, 80 cm height (Fully inflated)
Propulsion	4 brushless directional EDF (GWEDF505E & BL2018-3) with modified digital servos Graupner HVS930BB
Outer ring	11mmx1mm carbon fiber bar with 4mm carbon rod
Envelope	Custom made, PU 6 mil, 3.5m diameter
Battery	Kokam LiPo 30C 2S2P 4000mAH
Speed	about 4 m/s with compensation active (2 m/s up and down)
Payload	800 g without sensors
Sensors	IMU 9DoF, GPS, SRF10 (US) and GP2YDA02 (IR) distance sensors
Coms	WiFi or Bluetooth + Futaba R616FFM 2.4 GHz FASST module

In Table 2 we can check the main characteristics when filled with Helim at 98% purity, about 5.5 cubic meters. The lenticular shape is maintained by a circular ring made with carbon fiber bar (11mm x 1m) reinforced with a 4mm carbon rod. This structure is tensioned as in a bicycle wheel with the Kevlar pre-glued wires during the manufacture of the bag. This way we get a very low weight but rigid structure to support the motors with enough flexibility to support and absorb shocks with obstacles as seen in Fig. 2.

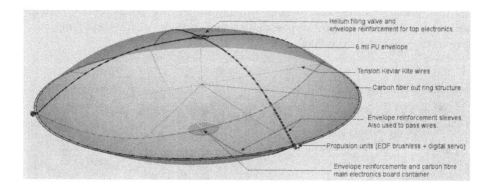

Fig. 2. Airship structure

2.1 Airship Control Hardware

The main component of the system is the IMU controller board. There are many flight control units in the market, but none with the specifications we need in terms of functionality, weight and size that allow it to be used as the control board in all the robots of our system as pointed in Table 3.

Table 3. Characteristics of the controller IMU unit

Dimensions	4cm x 4cm, approximately 16g including GPS module
Microcontroller	MIPS32 M4K 32 bit microcontroller technology with 1.5DMIPS/MHZ
Communication	USB, CAN, I2C, RS485, ICSP&JTAG&DEBUG, & 10 PIO
Wireless	WiFi (MRF24WB0MB) or Bluetooth (RN-41)
Sensors	IMU 9 DOF with GPS SiRF starIV^{TM}, Barometer & Temperature

In Fig. 3, we can observe a block diagram of the airship architecture. The airship use mainly a CAN channel to interconnect all the boards in the system. It was also necessary to develop a brushless motor control board with a CAN interface since we do not find any similar board in the market. It was necessary to modify some commercial servos Graupner HVS930BB to allow a movement of 300 degrees. There were some available servos in the market with at least 360 degrees turn, namely sail wing servos but their reliability and weight did not fit our requirements. In this version we have equipped the airship with 4 IR distance sensors (analog interface, one in each EDF) and 6 SRF10 ultrasonic sensors (I2C interface, one at the top and the bottom and one in each EDF). For starting the experiences and positioning the airship we had included a commercial 2.4GHz receiver module, that use some of the IO pins available.

2.2   Locomotion Modes

Basically there are 4 possible locomotion modes as we can see in Fig. 3. All of these modes allow a true omnidirectional locomotion in a 3D space. They are:

A - Straight trajectory in a horizontal plane with automatic compensation of the trajectory. In this mode we use two opposite ducted fans to give the impulse and speed in the desired direction. The other two fans are used for compensation of the trajectory based in the information from the gyro, accelerometer and compass sensors.

B - This locomotion mode allows vertical takeoff and landing. All of the turbines are pointed to the trajectory to follow. The attitude and speed of the airship is controlled, by changing individually the speed of each turbine. In this mode the drag imposed by the great and orthogonal surface is easily overcomed by the simultaneous trust of the 4 turbines.

C - Rotation. This mode allows very quick changes in direction. It is possible to make very fast rotations that allow by example to get a very rapid 360 degrees sequence of photos.

D - In this mode the airship could climb or descent in an inclined plane. As in mode "A" two of the ducted fans are used for giving the trust and the other two to maintain the trajectory in the inclined plane. The maximum inclination is 30°, limited by the angular range of the servos. Experiences made with inclinations near this limit show that it is very difficult to maintain stability and follow a straight path. The compensation is obligatory since the shape of the airship maintains by itself the airship stable in a horizontal plane.

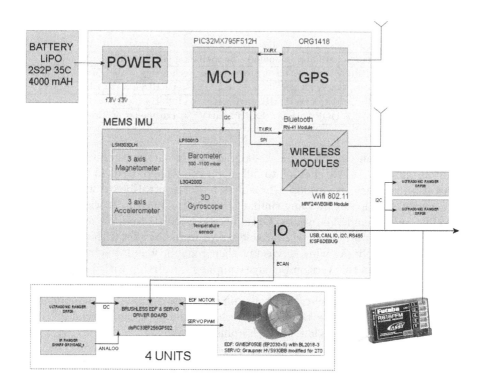

Fig. 3. Block diagram of the airship control hardware

The Table. 4, resumes all the locomotion modes and how the control algorithm implements the angle for each propulsion unit and if the EDF is used for propulsion or for compensation of the movement. Since there is more than one possible solution, special care has been taken to get the best solution possible in terms of energetic consumption and to limit the number of servo movements between modes transitions.

The control algorithm used is very simple and uses a PID controller to obtain the desired movement based on the information filtered by a very simple digital median filter of the sensors implied in each mode. By example, when we pretend to follow a straight path in front we use the gyroscope data as input for a PID controller integrated in a feedback loop to try to minimize the difference between the desired direction and the q actual one.

3   Experimental Work

We started to develop a friendly and intuitive controller using the interface that could be seen in Fig. 1, basically composed by a TFT monitor and a joystick with torsional control. The responsiveness of the control was really good in a way that we allow other people to test (including kids) with incredible

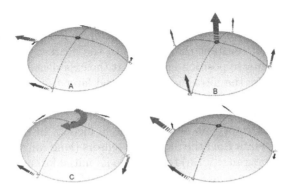

Fig. 4. Locomotion modes

Table 4. Angles for each EDF in the different locomotion modes

	EDF 1	EDF2	EDF3	EDF4	Compensation for
MODE "A" - Straight trajectory in a horizontal plane					
Front	90°	**90°**	90°	**270°**	Straight path
Back	90°	**270°**	90°	**90°**	Straight path
Right	**270°**	90°	**90°**	90°	Straight path
Left	**90°**	90°	**270°**	90°	Straight path
MODE "B" – Vertical trajectory					
Up	**0°**	**0°**	**0°**	**0°**	Horizontality
Down	**180°**	**180°**	**180°**	**180°**	Horizontality
MODE "C" – Rotation					
CW	**270°**	**270°**	**270°**	**270°**	Horizontality
CCW	**90°**	**90°**	**90°**	**90°**	Horizontality
MODE "D" – Trajectory in a inclined plane					
Front	0°	**90°-α**	180°	**270°+α**	Inclination (α)
Back	180°	**270°+α**	0°	**90°+α**	Inclination
Right	**270°+α**	0°	**90°-α**	180°	Inclination
Left	**90°-α**	180°	**270°+α**	0°	Inclination

Notes: In Bold Ducted fans used for trust.
Angles and numeration according to the following diagram:

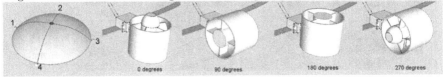

results in several places in indoor controlled situations. We also have done several flight tests in an indoor controlled scenario at "Pavilhão do Conhecimento" (http://www.pavconhecimento.pt/home/). For testing the control algorithm presented in this paper we programmed the airship to follow a linear trajectory trying to maintaining constant the distance to the nearest wall, using a commercial RC transmitter to position and to start the experiences. First using only the value measured by the ultrasonic sensors and later using only the compensation by the given by the IMU. The results were very good specially using the ultrasonic sensors, with a minimum non measurable error. With IMU there was some error in the trajectory: about 1meter in 40 meters. In the second experience we we used the data from the ultrasonic sensors (long range <12m) and the infrared sensors (short range <1m) to maintain an initial formation in the center of the pavilion at the same time that the airships go from the floor to the ceiling. And at the same time avoiding obstacles as walls, floor and ceiling and later the hook of a ceiling crane (Fig. 5-10). The experience was made with 3 airships, and during the tests there was a collision only once between two of the airships (Fig. 5-9). This reveals that the use of some simple sensors as ultrasonic modules is effective to avoid obstacles of the type mentioned. To maintain a formation, the use of this type of sensors revealed not to be sufficient with the airships easily coming out from the initial formation as we can see in Fig. 5-2,3. At the moment we are trying some low cost color based image recognition modules and IR cameras as the Wii camera.

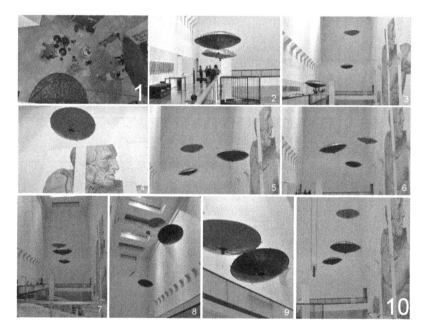

Fig. 5. Airships during tests at "Pavilhão do Conhecimento"

4   Conclusions and Further Work

It's our idea that the work here presented could contribute significantly to an increase in interest of lenticular shaped airships in robotics applications and with the continuation of our work the use in symbiotic applications with other type of robots. It's also our conviction that the hardware developed, with special emphasis for the control and IMU board with very reduced size and dimensions resulting from combining the best MEMS sensors actually available in the market could be used not only as the control board for airships and UAVs of small dimensions but also for many other applications that require low cost, low size IMUs. As far we could check many of the lenticular airships projects have been abandoned because of control problems. In the first tests, our control system has proved to be very effective allowing for indoor straight trajectories with minimal errors. Also some of the tests made with an audience have shown the great interest that an airship of this kind can have and the great capacities for advertising. The high stability and very stable hovering capabilities opens also an enormous range of commercial applications, from environmental to movie and TV making.

References

1. Kernbach, S.: From Robot Swarm to Artificial Organisms: Self-organization of Structures, Adaptivity and Self-development. In: Levi, P., Kernbach, S. (eds.) Symbiotic Multi-Robot Organisms - Reliability, Adaptability, Evolution, ch. 1. Springer, Heidelberg (2010)
2. Parker, L.E., Balch, T.: Robot Teams: From Diversity to Polymorphism. A.K. Peters Ltd. (2002)
3. Konstantinov, L.: The Basics of Gas and Heat Airship Theory. AEROPLAST Journal (2005), http://www.agaeroplast.com
4. Balaskovic, P., http://balaskovic.pagesperso-orange.fr/ballons-et-dirigeables.html
5. Wyrsch, N., et al.: Ultra-Light Amorphous Silicon Cell for Space Applications. In: 2006 IEEE 4th World Conference on Photovoltaic Energy Conversion, Waikoloa (2006)
6. Rowehl, J.A., Lunt, R.R., Xu, J., Wang, A., Boyce, C.M., Im, S.G., Bulovi, V., Gleason, K.K., Barr, M.C.: Direct Monolithic Integration of Organic Photovoltaic Circuits on Unmodified Paper. Advanced Materials (July 2011) ISSN: 1521-4095
7. Huang, H., Waslander, S.L., Tomlin, C.J., Hoffmann, G.M.: Quadrotor Helicopter Flight Dynamics and Control: Theory and Experiment. In: AIAA Guidance, Navigation and Control Conference and Exhibit (2007)
8. Murrieri, P., Siegwart, R., Bouabdallah, S.: Design and Control of an Indoor Micro Quadrotor. In: Proceedings of IEEE International Conference on Robotics and Automation, ICRA 2004, April 26-May 1, vol. 5, pp. 4393–4398 (2004)

A New CNN-Based Method
of Path Planning in Dynamic Environment

Maciej Przybylski and Barbara Siemiątkowska

Institute of Automatic Control and Robotics,
Warsaw University of Technology,
ul. Boboli 8, 02-525 Warsaw, Poland
{maciej.przybylski,b.siemiatkowska}@mchtr.pw.edu.pl
http://rrg.mchtr.pw.edu.pl

Abstract. In this paper the problem of path planning in a dynamic
environment is considered. The minimum cost path is planned using
Cellular Neural Network (CNN). CNN is a very useful tool for parallel
signal processing and can be implemented using VLSI. In the proposed
approach the problem of local minima (dead ends on a map) does not
exist. Different criteria can be taken into account during path planning
for example: the size of the robot, the traversability cost, the occurrence
of dynamic obstacles, etc. The method allows us to specify the goal using
semantic labels. The experiments performed in a real static environment
and simulations in a dynamic environment have shown the efficiency of
the proposed method.

Keywords: path and task planning, mobile robot navigation.

1 Introduction

Path planning is a fundamental part of an autonomous mobile robot navigation
system. The aim of the path planning is to find the optimum collision-free path
between the starting position of the robot and the target location. There is a variety of methods proposed to solve the problem [4,7,15]. They can be classified
using different criteria. One of them is a representation in which path planning is
described and solved. The Configuration Space [15] is one of the oldest method
but this approach cannot be used efficiently in the case of a dynamic environment. The second approach to path planning uses cell decomposition [15] - the
space, which is free from the obstacles, is decomposed into a set of cells. Another
family of path planning algorithms is based on the idea of skeletonization [15].
There are many intelligent algorithms of path planning in a static environment
such as potential field, diffusion methods, genetic algorithms, neural networks,
graph searching techniques [6].

Some of the articles consider non-stationary environments defined as a surrounding where obstacles change their locations form time to time [3], but the
problem of navigation in a dynamic environment is much more complicated [20].

L. Rutkowski et al. (Eds.): ICAISC 2012, Part II, LNCS 7268, pp. 484–492, 2012.
© Springer-Verlag Berlin Heidelberg 2012

A dynamic scene requires on-line methods for fast reaction to moving obstacles. While following its path, a robot has to distinguish stationary obstacles (e.g. walls) from moving ones. One of approaches relies on using global path planning and reactive control or D* algorithm [18]. A path planning problem can also be solved by a Vector Field Approach [1] but the vector field must be recalculated frequently and the method tends to produce poor performance in dynamic environments. In [10] the algorithm which is based on a recursive method for path planning and gives an optimum path is presented. The collision-free path is planned in densely populated environments. However, this algorithm is applicable only for circular obstacles. The most promising approach [14] utilizes graph searching techniques. The explicit time information together with probabilistic values for prediction of a movement of a dynamic obstacle are used for optimal path searching.

In the approach proposed in this paper the information about static and dynamic objects is input to the path planning algorithm. Static elements are described by their positions, dynamic objects are characterized by their positions and velocity vectors.

The paper is organized as follows: at the beginning Cellular Neural Network (CNN) is introduced shortly. Later, the method of the path planning using CNN is presented. Finally, experiments in a static and dynamic environment are described.

2   Path Planning with the Use of Cellular Neural Network

The Cellular Neural Network (CNN) was introduced by Chua and Young [8,9]. It is usually a single-layer network defined on regular lattices, where neurons are arranged in a rectangular network and interact locally (within the neighbourhood). The cells that are not directly connected may affect each other indirectly. This type of the CNN can be viewed as a generalization of a cellular automata.

$$x_{ij} = \sum_{kl \in N_{ij}} a_{kl}^{ij} \cdot y_{kl} + \sum_{kl \in N_{ij}} b_{kl}^{ij} \cdot u_{kl} + I_{ij} \tag{1}$$

$$y_{ij} = f(x_{ij}) \tag{2}$$

Equations (1,2) present typical evaluation of a single cell (c_{ij}) which is described by the state x_{ij}, values of input signals u_{ij}, values of interconnection weights a_{kl}^{ij} between cells c_{kl} and c_{ij}, b_{kl}^{ij} values of interconnection weights between u_{kl} and cell c_{ij}, and finally by bias parameter I_{ij}.

Due to local connections between cells, the CNN could be implemented using the VLSI technology [5,12]. Cellular neural networks are very useful for rapid and parallel signal processing [16]. CNNs are used for solving partial differential equations [2] and image processing [13,17,21].

2.1   Path Planning in a Static Environment

In typical implementations of CNNs the interconnection weights and other parameters do not have any physical interpretation. To make quantitative comparison of different paths easier the physical interpretation of a neural cell parameters is introduced. The values are interpreted as follows:

- a state x_{ij} and the output value y_{ij} is an estimated travel time from the place represented by the current cell to the goal $[s]$,
- interconnection weights a_{kl}^{ij} are dimensionless, represent the traversability level and take value from set $\{0, 1\}$,
- values of interconnection weights b_{kl}^{ij} are equal to the distance between neighbouring cells $\{d_1, d_2\}$ (fig.1) $[m]$,
- an input signal $u_{ij} = \frac{1}{V_{ij}}$ is a reciprocal of robot's velocity in the cell $[s/m]$,
- a bias value $I_{ij} = \frac{r/2}{V_{ij}}$ is a time of travelling through the current cell $[s]$.

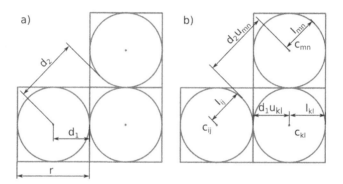

Fig. 1. Distance between cells a) in terms of space (r - cell resolution) b) in terms of time

The evaluation of a new state of the cell is described by eq. (3,4), where the time of travelling x_{ij} is a sum of the travel time between neighbouring cells $b_{kl}^{ij} \cdot u_{kl}$, the travelling time from the neighbouring cell to the goal $a_{kl}^{ij} \cdot y_{kl}$, and finally the travelling time along the current cell I_{ij}.

$$x_{ij} = \min_{kl \in N_{ij}} (a_{kl}^{ij} \cdot y_{kl} + b_{kl}^{ij} \cdot u_{kl} + I_{ij}) \tag{3}$$

$$y_{ij} = x_{ij} \tag{4}$$

Each cell tries to minimize the travel time by activation a connection with the neighbouring cell which has the smallest time value. Since the robot can move only to one neighbouring cell, it is assumed that only one connection can be activated. The weights a_{kl}^{ij} and b_{kl}^{ij} are conjugated. If the interconnection is active the weight a_{kl}^{ij} takes value 1 and b_{kl}^{ij} takes value of a distance between cells which is d_1 or d_2 (fig. 1), otherwise both weights are set to 0. The active connection implies the direction of the robot movement. Regarding this, and the fact that a reciprocal of the maximum allowable velocity is held in the cell, a desirable velocity vector can be calculated easily.

The initial values of a cell parameters for particular situations are shown in Table 1. A cell is marked as a *free space* if any of the robot's position in the corresponding area can be achieved. The cells corresponding to the static obstacles have no connections with other cells and are not evaluated.

Table 1. Initial values of a cell: B stands for a big number (infinity), V is a robot's velocity, r is a cell resolution, k is a number of interconnections, n is a number of dynamic obstacles ($n = 0$ for a path planning algorithm in a static environment)

	y[s]	x[s]	u[s/m]	I[s]	$|N_{ij}|$
Free space	B	B	$\frac{1}{V}$	$\frac{r}{V}$	$8(n+1)$
Static obstacle	B	B	B	B	0
Goal (or Robot in a dynamic environment)	0	0	$\frac{1}{V}$	0	0

Using our algorithm the path from each cell to the goal is calculated, without prior knowledge of the initial robot's position. To reach the goal, the robot follows interconnections between cells (moves to the cell with the smallest time value). Multiple robots of the same type can use the same network (map). An occurrence of regions with additional velocity limit (e.g. rough ground) can be taken into account.

2.2   Path Planning in a Dynamic Environment

In a typical approach to navigation, a robot treats every new object on its way as a static obstacle and tries to recalculate the path, even if the object is moving in the same direction. The algorithm which solves this problem was developed and is presented in this section. It is assumed that knowledge about the moving objects comes only from current observation, therefore continuous updates and calculations of CNN are required.

An occurrence of dynamic obstacles means that cells can be inaccessible in certain periods of time. Therefore, each cell keeps additionally a list of time intervals, during which a cell is occupied. The time of a robot presence in a cell has to be known to avoid collision with dynamic obstacles. This, in contrast to the static path planning version of the algorithm, implies that the knowledge about initial position of the robot is required.

Equations (3, 4) describing cell evaluation remain unchanged but now each cell tries to minimize the travel time from robot's initial pose to the current cell. By activation of a particular interconnection, a cell chooses the direction from which the robot will arrive.

Avoidance of collision with dynamic obstacles requires adjustment of the robot's velocity. The velocity can be adjusted in a current cell as well as in a preceding cell. The algorithm for a velocity adjustment works as follows:

1. If the robot's velocity in the current cell is lower than maximal, increase it in order to leave the current cell before an obstacle presence in this cell.
2. If the robot's velocity in the preceding cell is lower than maximal, increase it in order to enter and leave the current cell before obstacle presence in this cell.
3. Otherwise, decrease robot's velocity in the preceding cell in order to enter the current cell after obstacle presence in this cell.

What is important is a fact that the velocity adjustment procedure is performed only when the time of presence of a robot overlaps with the time of presence of an obstacle. In fact, the third step is the most important, because if there is no need to decrease speed, it can be assumed that the robot is moving at the maximal speed. In order to achieve a convergence of the whole CNN, the change of a speed in the preceding cell is being assumed only during the evaluation of the current cell. This assumption is not taken into account during the evaluation of the preceding cell.

The initialization of CNN cells presented in Table 1 is valid also for path planning in a dynamic environment, with only one difference, in this case the robot becomes a *Goal*.

In some situations the robot has to move back to make room for the obstacle and then continue going moving when the way is free. Since each cell represents the presence of the robot in a certain moment, it is necessary to create one more layer of cells, covering the same space, which is available only after leaving the cell by an obstacle. In a simple case (non-oscillating movements of obstacles) the number of layers is equal to the number of dynamic obstacles +1 (Fig. 2). Each cell in a multilayer is connected with eight neighbouring cells from the same layer and eight neighbouring cells from each additional layer. The cells in the layer corresponding to a particular obstacle become free only after the presence of this obstacle in the cells and not before. While the time intervals of the presence of other obstacles in this layer remain unchanged. For *layer 0* all the time intervals are unchanged. Of course, it is necessary to create additional layers only for those places where dynamic obstacles have appeared.

The presented algorithm makes it possible to decide what is better: to follow the obstacle with a lower speed or to choose a new path. Contrary to previously presented approach, the initial position of the robot has to be known a priori. Therefore only one robot can use the network (map). To reach the goal, the robot follows inverted path from the goal cell to the robot's start cell. Also, the direction and velocity of a dynamic obstacle movement has to be guessed or assumed in order to initialize time intervals of the robot presence in a cell.

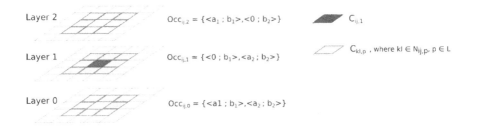

Fig. 2. CNN architecture with additional layers for two dynamic obstacles. $c_{ij,1}$ - considered cell, $c_{kl,p}$ - neighbouring cells, where kl - cell indices, and p - number of layer from the layers set L. $Occ_{ij,p}$ - set of time intervals during which cell ij from layer p is occupied by an obstacle.

2.3   Cellular Neural Network Evaluation

In the preceding subsections, the evaluation of a single cell has been described. The evaluation of the whole network is done iteratively until all the cells on the path from the goal to the start position are stable. A cell becomes stable if the value y does not change between consecutive evaluations.

From the theoretical point of view, an order of the evaluation does not play any role in terms of stability, which makes this algorithm easy to implement in a parallel way. However, without such an implementation, some improvement can be done in order to achieve a faster stabilization of the CNN. In accordance with the fact that the cell which corresponds to the start position has minimal and stable time value, and the fact that each cell tries to minimize its own time value, stabilization of the entire CNN is much faster if the evaluation of the cells is being conducted in a breadth-first order, starting from the start cell.

As it was mentioned, in case of navigation in a dynamic environment, the process of planning interleaves with updates of sensory data. However, the CNN does not have to be reinitialized continuously. In fact, the previously calculated values make the evaluation process faster.

3   Results

The presented method has been tested in a static environment using mobile robot $ELECTRON R1$ designed and built at the Warsaw University of Technology. The robot is equipped with a laser range finder mounted on a rotating support which enables us to make 3-dimensional representations of the environment.

Fig. 3a presents the results of experiments performed in the office. The task for the robot was to plan a path and to reach the goal. The map was built based on laser range finder indications. Each cell of the grid-based map corresponds to a $10cm \times 10cm$ rectangular area of the environment. The radius of influence of the obstacles, on which the maximal speed in a cell depends, equals

70cm (7 cells). The linear and angular velocities were computed using modification of the dynamic window approach [19]. The robot goes along the centre of the corridor (far from the walls) but it is able to move across gaps (doorways).

Fig. 3b represents the results of collision-free path planning if the goal is given using semantic labels. The numbers in brackets represent the linear velocities (m/s) and angular velocities (deg/s) of the robot in the corresponding point of the environment. The map was built based on 3D laser range finder indications, the labels were attached using the method described in [11]. The robot was asked to move towards a chair. For two different robot positions, paths to the nearest chair were generated automatically, without any additional rule-based system. A similar experiment was performed outside the building.

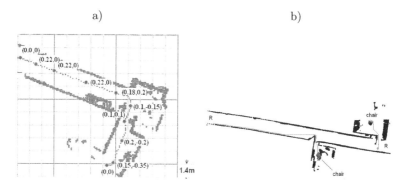

Fig. 3. Path planning in a static environemnt. a) The linear velocities measured in $\frac{m}{s}$ and angular velocity in $\frac{rad}{s}$. b) Path planning to the goal using semantic label.

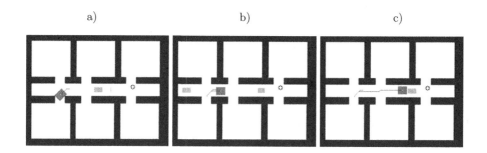

Fig. 4. Calculated path with robot's position at three time points a) robot is making room for the first obstacle which is moving in the opposite direction (t=0.182s) b) when the corridor is passable the robot starts to follow path to the goal (t=1.092s) c) the robot follows a more slowly moving obstacle along the corridor (t=1.620s)

The correctness of the path planning algorithm in a dynamic environment was tested with the use of a simulated scenario, in which the robot navigating along a narrow corridor meets two moving obstacles. The first obstacle is moving in an opposite direction, while the second one is moving in the direction of the goal, but with much lower velocity than the robot's. In that kind of situation typical static approach is not able to find a path. The presented algorithm is able to find the optimal path in terms of time even if the robot has to move back.

Each pixel in Figure 4 corresponds to one cell in one layer of the CNN. The black line shows the calculated path and the consecutive robot's positions. The black areas present static obstacles, while the light gray rectangles represent dynamic obstacles. The current robot's position is presented as a dark gray rectangle. A black round mark depicts the goal position.

4   Conclusions

In this paper two CNN-based approaches for collision-free path planning have been presented. The developed approach excludes the problem of local minima, both in the field of acceptable positions and velocity spaces. The correctness of the presented algorithms was confirmed by tests performed with the use of a real robot (static environment), as well as by simulation tests (dynamic environment). Presented algorithms have different properties and can complement each other. The path planning algorithm in a static environment can be used as a global path planner, while the other algorithm will be helpful in local navigation. Both versions of the algorithm can be implemented efficiently with the use of some parallel computing techniques, which is planned as further work. Ongoing research is focused on the use of heuristics for cell values initialization, which may help to relax the assumption of the finite space of states. Also, further research on the use of CNN for action planning and scheduling is being conducted. Finally, the use of probabilistic information together with the time cost in the process of cell evaluation may improve effectiveness of the presented method.

Acknowledgments. This work has been supported by the National Science Centre (grant 2011/01/B/ST6/07385).

References

1. Arkin, R.C., Balch, T.: Aura: Principles and practice in review. Journal of Experimental and Theoretical Artificial Intelligence 9, 175–189 (1997)
2. Behring, C., Bracho, M., Castro, M., Moreno, J.A., Brzakovic, D.: Automatic multilevel halftoning for color images. In: Proc. of the International Conference on Image Processing (1997)
3. Biswas, R., Limketkai, B., Sanner, S., Thrun, S.: Towards object mapping in nonstationary environments with mobile robots (2002)
4. Buckley, S.: Fast motion planning for multiple moving robots. In: Proc. of the IEEE International Conference on Robotics and Automation (ICRA), pp. 1419–1424 (1989)

5. Cembrano, G.L., Rodrguez-Vzquez, A., Espejo-Meana, S., Domnguez-Castro, R.: Ace16k: A 128x128 focal plane analog processor with digital i/o. Intern. Journal Neural Systems 13(6), 427–434 (2003)
6. Choset, H., Lynch, K.M., Hutchinson, S., Kantor, G., Burgard, W., Kavraki, L.E., Thrun, S.: Principles of Robot Motion: Theory, Algorithms, and Implementations. MIT Press, Boston (2005)
7. Chu, H., Eimaraghy, H.A.: Real-time multi-robot path planner based on a heuristic approach. In: Proc. of the IEEE International Conference on Robotics & Automation, ICRA (1992)
8. Chua, L., Roska, T.: The cnn paradigm. IEEE Transaction on Circuit Systems 40, 147–156 (1993)
9. Chua, L., Young, L.: Cellular neural network. IEEE Transaction on Circuit Systems 35, 1271–1290 (1988)
10. Dougall, D.W., Archibald, J.K.: A recursive approach to roadmap-based path planning. In: The 12th IASTED Int. Conf. on Robotics and Applications, pp. 537–578 (2006)
11. Gnatowski, M., Siemiątkowska, B., Szklarski, J.: Extraction of semantic information from the 3d laser range finder. In: Parenti-Castelli, V., Schiehlen, W. (eds.) Proceedings of the 18th CISM-IFToMM Symposium. Robot Design, Dynamics and Control, ROMANSY 18, pp. 383–390 (2010)
12. Kinget, P., Steyeart, M.: Analogue cmos vlsi implementation of a cellular neural networks with continous programable templates. In: IEEE Symposium on Cercuit System, pp. 376–370 (1994)
13. Kozek, T., Crounse, K.R., Roska, T., Chua, O.: Multi-scale image analysis on the CNN universal machine. In: Proc. 4th IEEE International Workshop on Cellular Neural Networks and Their Applications, pp. 69–74 (1996)
14. Kushleyev, A., Likhachev, M.: Time-bounded lattice for efficient planning in dynamic environments. In: Proceedings of the 2009 IEEE International Conference on Robotics and Automation, ICRA 2009, pp. 4303–4309 (2009)
15. Latombe, J.C.: Robot Motion Planning. Kluwer Academic Publishers, Boston (1992)
16. Manganaro, G., Arena, P., Fortuna, L.: Cellular neural networks, chaos, complexity and VLSI processing. Springer (1999)
17. Reljin, B.D., Bakic, P.R., Kostic, P.D., Brzakovic, D.P., Vujovi, N.S.: Local enhancement of images using cellular neural networks. In: Proc. 8th ISTET, International Symposium on Theoretical Electrical Engineering, pp. 192–195 (1995)
18. Siegwart, R., Nourbakhsh, I.R.: Autonomous Mobile Robots. MIT Press, London (2002)
19. Siemiątkowska, B., Chojecki, R., Olszewski, M., Zajac, M.: Mobile robot navigation using the cellular neural network. In: Proceedings of Romansy, pp. 131–138. Springer, Heidelberg (2008)
20. Smierzchalski, R., Michalewicz, Z.: Path planning in dynamic environments. In: Innovations in Robot Mobility and Control, pp. 135–153 (2005)
21. Targalio, S., Zanela, A.: Cellular neural networks: a genetic algorithm for parameters optimization in artificial vision application. In: Proc. 4th IEEE International Workshop on Cellular Neural Networks and Their Applications, pp. 315–320 (1996)

Artificial Neural Network Ensemble Approach for Creating a Negotiation Model with Ethical Artificial Agents

Banafsheh Rekabdar[1], Mahmood Joorabian[2], and Bita Shadgar[1]

[1] Department of Computer Engineering, Faculty of Engineering,
Shahid Chamran University, Ahvaz, Iran
b-rekabdar@mscstu.scu.ac.ir, bita.shadgar@scu.ac.ir
[2] Department of Electronic Engineering, Faculty of Engineering,
Shahid Chamran University, Ahvaz, Iran
mjoorabian@scu.ac.ir

Abstract. Negotiation is one of the most prevalent methods that agents, in a multi-agent system, use to reach agreements. Nowadays, one important aspect of negotiation is moral behaviors of agents that involve in negotiation. For this reason, we propose an ethical classifier that uses artificial neural networks ensembles. To evaluate the performance of the proposed method, we conduct experiments including comparisons with alternative methods for ethical classification. As the result of experiments suggest, the proposed method shows improved ethical recognition performance, in comparison with other widely used methods.

Keywords: Ethical reasoning, Artificial neural network, Ensemble method, Artificial neural networks ensemble, Intelligent agent, Ethical agent, Negotiation.

1 Introduction

Negotiations play an important role in our everyday life. With the rapid development of multi-agent systems, the significance of negotiation between agents cannot be neglected. Negotiation has been widely used to reach a consensus. In recent years, trust is considered as an important aspect in negotiation between agents. Ethical agents usually can gain people's trust in the long run. Four types of ethical agents including ethical impact agents, implicit ethical agents, explicit ethical agents and full ethical agents were proposed by [1]. The search space for multilateral negotiation is very complex [2]. Several authors proposed the idea of using artificial neural networks (ANN) in multi agent negotiations. In [3], the neural network is used for predicting the behavior of opponent. In this method, neural network was trained based on three recent opponent offers. An approach proposed by [4] used Genetic Algorithm (GA) and Multilayer Perceptron (MLP) for predicting agent behavior in negotiation. In the method by [5], Radial Basis Function (RBF) predicts the result of negotiation. However, this approach was very time consuming and was not suitable for real- time applications.

L. Rutkowski et al. (Eds.): ICAISC 2012, Part II, LNCS 7268, pp. 493–501, 2012.

In this paper, the artificial neural network ensemble method is employed in order to recognize various ethical actions in negotiation efficiently. The proposed method uses a number of artificial neural networks and an ethical dataset to train them. Decisions from neural networks are combined by using a majority voting method to make the final decision of recognitions. Each neural network is implemented by using MLPs with various hidden layers.

The paper is organized as follows: section 2 provides a brief explanation of background and previous works, the definition of the overall proposed method for ethical classifiers described in section 3. In the section 4 experiments setup and results are presented. Finally the conclusion and future works are provided.

2   Background

2.1   Artificial Neural Network Theory

Artificial intelligence (AI) has direct relationship with human brain behavior. AI tries to imitate brain's actions. ANNs is one part of it. They can learn from linear and non-linear data distributions; moreover, can solve complex problems with noisy and incomplete data. ANNs have high ability in generalization and prediction [6]. An artificial neuron can be shown mathematically as follows:

$$y(x) = g\left(\sum_{i=0}^{n} w_i x_i\right) + \varepsilon \tag{1}$$

In formula 1 $y(x)$, w, g, x and ε are respectively the output of axon, weight, sigmoid function, a neuron with n input dentrites $(x_0...x_n)$ and a mean zero additive noise. More details of single artificial neuron, simple network models and example sigmoid functions are described in [7].

2.2   The Basic Ensemble Method

In the basic ensemble method the combiner component is simply computing the average of networks' outputs $(f_i(x))$. The basic ensemble method (BEM) output is defined by equation 2.

$$f_{BEM} = \frac{1}{n} \sum_{i=1}^{n} f_i(x) \tag{2}$$

This approach can lead to high performance [8], [12], but does not consider the fact that all networks are not the same. Since some of them can be more accurate than others. It has some advantages; first, its understanding and implementation is easy [9], [11], second it can be shown not to increase the expected error [9], [13], [14].

2.3   The Generalized Ensemble Method

Generalized BEM method is used for finding the weight of each output that minimizes the mean square error (MSE) of the ensemble. The general ensemble model (GEM) is defined by equation 3 as it comes.

$$f_{GEM} = \sum_{i=1}^{n} \alpha_i f_i(x) \tag{3}$$

In equation 3 the α_i is selected to minimize the MSE with respect to the target function, f (estimated using the cross validation set), while their sum becomes 1. The error $\varepsilon_i(x)$ of a network and correlation matrix C_{ij} are defined as $\varepsilon_i(x) = f(x) - f_i(x)$ and $C_{ij} = E[\varepsilon_i(x)\varepsilon_j(x)]$ respectively. Then, the weights, α_i, that minimize equation 4 must be found.

$$MSE[f_{GEM}] = \sum_{i=1}^{n} \sum_{j=1}^{n} \alpha_i \alpha_j C_{ij} \tag{4}$$

The optimal choice for α_i is as follows [9], [12]:

$$\alpha_i = \frac{\sum_{j=1}^{n} C_{kj}^{-1}}{\sum_{k=1}^{n} \sum_{j=1}^{n} C_{kj}^{-1}} \tag{5}$$

This method has higher performance than BEM. However, this method depends on two factors, the reliable estimation of C and non-singularity of that, so it can be easily inverted [12]. Due to high correlation of errors, the rows of C are almost linearly dependent, thus inverting C leads to round-off errors. Ignoring networks whose errors are highly correlated with others is the way that [12] has applied for solving this problem. The specialized techniques were utilized for the inversion of near-singular matrices and training the networks to be de-correlated with each other in [15], [10].

3   The Proposed Method

This paper plans an ensemble neural network which can recognize ethical behavior from unethical one. Compared to the [17], it achieves higher performance with more accuracy of generalization ability. Since the size of the given dataset is too small in comparison with the size of feature set, a single neural network has less generalization ability. Therefore, the ensemble learning is used for neural network which can produce dramatic improvements in generalization performance. The basic idea of this technique is to generate multiple versions of a predictor, that when combined, will provide more accurate and stable predictions. Moreover the superiority of ensemble learning is shown in section 4 when compared with single neural network. The proposed method has two phases, the training phase and the recognition phase. Figure 1 represents the overall procedure of the proposed method. In the training phase, each neural network in Ensemble Neural Network (ENN) is trained with the whole data set. After this phase the Trained ENN for ethical recognition is generated from training data set. The model consists of N neural networks.

In the recognition phase, for any input vector x, the method obtains N decisions from neural networks and makes final decision by combining decisions from neural networks with an output vector from the combiner. This paper uses majority vote to produce the final output. This ensemble neural network ethical classifier is applied to the scenario of negotiation model explained below. The justification for adding ethical constraints to the negotiation is that when the artificial agents are negotiating with humans, taking ethical considerations into account, makes them more trustworthy. It makes the people working with these systems to be confident in what they are being told by the system. As Cohen suggested [21] good negotiation ethics is important for the negotiator because of reputation; no one will deal with a negotiator with a bad reputation. Unethical tactics may give the negotiators what they want in the short run. These same tactics typically lead to long term problems.

The domain of negotiation is between a seller and a buyer in a selling e-commerce environment. This scenario is for the seller and it is summarized in 17 steps as follows. The buyer scenario is the same as seller.

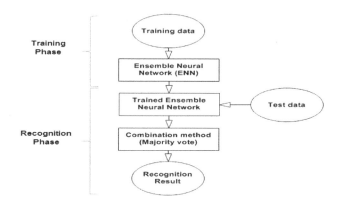

Fig. 1. Process of the proposed method for ethical classifier

1. Seller Agent (SA) receives proposal from Buyer Agent (BA).
2. SA evaluates the proposal.
3. If that proposal is generally bad for the SA, it denies it and goes to step 17.
4. Else if that proposal is good enough, SA accepts it and goes to step 17.
5. Otherwise, if that proposal is not good enough, it proposes a new proposal to BA.
6. To make this new proposal, SA must search in its knowledge base to find a counter proposal.
7. If a suitable proposal is found, SA tests it to see if it is ethical or not (employing the proposed method (ENN)).
8. If it is not ethical, SA goes to step 6.
9. Else if it is ethical it is proposed.
10. If it is accepted by BA and the result is good, SA goes to step 16.
11. Else if it is accepted by BA but the result is bad, SA goes to step 17.
12. Otherwise, if it is not accepted by BA, SA goes to step 1.

13. If a suitable proposal is not found in the knowledge base, SA generates a new proposal from scratch and tests it for ethical evaluation (employing the proposed method (ENN)).
14. If it is ethical it is proposed and SA goes to step 10.
15. If it is not ethical SA goes to step 13.
16. The knowledge base of the SA gets updated for future use.
17. Negotiation would be finished.

4   Experiments

To evaluate the performance of the proposed method the domain of negotiation prior to selling in an e-commerce environment was chosen. In this domain, there is a seller which is an artificial intelligent entity and a buyer who is either a human or an artificial intelligent agent. In [16] authors provide a small set of examples for this kind of domain with their ethical evaluations. To increase their income, sellers must obtain customers' needs and some other information about them to offer the best goods to them. It is also assumed that seller agents have a complete knowledge about the costumers. These ethical evaluations can be used in the proposed negotiation algorithm in section 3 to generate ethical proposals. These examples are shown below:

Example A: the seller agent hides some specifications and problems of the item X from the customer to increase the number of sold items (not ethical).

Example B: in this example, the seller does not hide any details from the customer and it is honest about the specification of the item X (ethical).

Example C: the seller agent is honest about the details of goods, but it increases the price and announces the wrong price (not ethical).

Example D: the seller agent reveals or does not reveal the information about one customer to another, in order to improve selling rate (respectively not ethical or ethical).

Example E: the seller agent has an ethical policy for increasing its customers in longtime view. So, it offers merchandise with high quality and lowest price (ethical).

In order to put these examples into a framework suitable for evaluating ethical situations, the basic agent/patient model was used. The basic agent/patient model is a conceptual framework for ethical situations, specially designed to improve the judgments when an artificial intelligent entity is playing a role in that situation [18]. Its major contribution is that it provides 81 different categories of ethical situations according to the type and property of agent and patient.

There are three types of agents according to this model: Human, organizations and artificial intelligent entity. An agent also has a property consist of three possible values: Good, evil and neutral. Floridi in [19] suggested that it is essential to consider agents and patients together for the task of ethical evaluation. In this work the focus of study is on the ethical evaluation of artificial intelligent agents' actions and the other two types are not related to it. To train the neural networks, the training set in [17] was used. Honarvar in [17] uses the base examples explained before and a basic agent/patient model for ethical situations to generate new examples. He uses a feature set consisting of 15 features that relates to both agent and patient to describe an ethical situation. These features are presented in table 1.

Table 2 shows a sample of the generated training cases and their corresponding base examples. All of the features except number 8 and 15 have the value of Z (*Zero*), A (*Average*), L (*Low*), H (*High*), and the value of feature number 8 and 15 are N (*Neutral*), G (*Good*), and E (*Evil*). Each symbol is represented by a binary vector. The length of the vector can be 3 or 4. The schema for four-value vectors is <*Zero, Low, Average, High*> and for three-value vectors is <*Neutral, Evil, Good*> [17]. For example, if the parameter has the value *Evil*, then the input vector for this parameter is a three-value vector and is equal to <0, 1, 0> or if it has the *Average* value its vector is <0, 0, 1, 0>.

Table 1. The features of ethical situation

1	The Voluntariness of an agent	2	The amount of human patients(HP)' pleasure
3	The duration of HP' pleasure	4	The number of pleasured HP
5	The amount of HP' displeasure	6	The duration of HP' displeasure
7	The number of displeasured HP	8	The properties of HP
9	The amount of non- HP' pleasure	10	The duration of non- HP' pleasure
11	The number of pleasured non-HP	12	The amount of non-HP' displeasure
13	The duration of non- HP' displeasure	14	The number of displeasured non-HP
15	The properties of non-HP		

The proposed ENN for ethical classifier is implemented based on the training data with MATLAB neural network toolbox. Table 3 gives some information about the networks of the implemented method. To create the ENN 12 neural networks were used, and each of them contains only one hidden layer with varying number of hidden neurons. The first neural network has 4 hidden neurons and each following network has one more neuron in its hidden layer than the previous one, so the last network has 15 hidden neurons. The Even berg-Marquardt back propagation algorithm (trainlm) is used to train the feed forward network because it is very fast. There are so many parameters for each network object indicating the architecture of the network or the way it trains the network.

The training procedure stops on the condition that either to reach 100th epoch or exp(-100) in the training accuracy. Furthermore, tansig transfer function for hidden layer and purelin activation function for output layer are applied. To set the parameters, the model is tested with changing parameter values gradually, and then the parameters with the best performance of the method are chosen.

To compare the proposed method with alternative methods for ethical classification, we also used Support Vector Machine (SVM), MLP (single neural network), KStar, and J48 which are widely-used classifiers. For SVM, Poly nominal with exponent 1 is selected as the kernel function, and the threshold and penalized parameters were set to 0.001 and 1 respectively. For MLP, 15 hidden nodes are used [17], and the learning rate and the threshold are fixed to 0.02 and 0.005 respectively. For J48, confidence factor and numFolds are set to 0.25 and 3 respectively. Instead of implementing all alternative methods, we used Weka, the well-known library for machine learning techniques, which contains all of the methods for the experiments [20].

4.1   Experimental Results

In order to highlight the outstanding performance of the proposed method, we compared the method with alternative recognition methods which use only a single model.

For the experiment, the performances of SVM, KStar, J48, and MLP was also obtained from the same data set, especially in the case of the proposed method and MLP, the average results of 10 trials for model generation were used. Table 4 shows the results of the experiments. As shown in Figure 2, ENN showed the best performance among various ethical classifier methods. Moreover, despite ENN uses MLP as a model for its network, the performance was 19.27% higher than the method with a single MLP model. This confirms that using multiple neural networks show better performance than methods which use only a single recognition model.

In the proposed method, it is quite important to choose the appropriate number of neural networks. The number of neural networks should be chosen according to the complexity of domain. Too small number of neural networks may not reduce the complexity of the problem, but too large number of neural networks takes a long time for training, since all of the neural networks must be trained with the whole training data set. In order to analyze the relationship between the number of neural networks and performance, we observe recognition accuracies by changing the number of neural network from 4 to 16.

Table 2. The values of some sample training cases

	1	2	3	4	5	6	7	8	9	10	11	12	13	14	15	target
Example A																
1	H	Z	Z	Z	Z	Z	Z	N	A	L	L	H	A	L	E	L
Example B																	
2	H	H	H	L	L	L	A	G	Z	Z	Z	Z	Z	Z	N	A
Example C																	
3	L	A	L	L	A	H	A	G	Z	Z	Z	Z	Z	Z	N	L
Example D																	
4	H	Z	Z	Z	Z	Z	Z	N	L	A	L	L	L	L	G	H
Example E																	
5	H	H	H	L	Z	Z	Z	G	L	L	L	Z	Z	Z	G	H

Table 3. Specs of each of neural networks In ENN

Input nodes	58
Hidden nodes	4 to 15
Output nodes	4
Learning rate	0.02

Table 4. Result of comparison experiment (unit : %)

	SVM	KStar	J48	MLP	ENN
Accuracy	76.31	71.05	68.42	73.68	92.95
Error	-	-	-	21.32	3.63

Figure 3 shows the result of the experiment. With 12 neural networks, the model shows the highest performance, and from 12 to 16 neural networks, the similar performances are obtained. However, with less than 12 neural networks, the performance drops as the number of neural networks are decreased. The performance is not dropped when the number of neural networks is greater than 12; just the training time is increased. This result shows that 12 neural networks can effectively reduce the complexity of the problem with the ethical data set which is used.

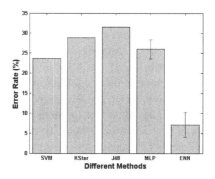

Fig. 2. Result of comparison experiment (unit : %)

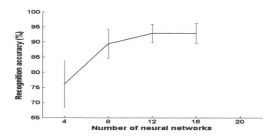

Fig. 3. Performance according to number of neural networks in ENN

5   Conclusion Remarks

In this paper, artificial neural network ensemble is proposed to determine if a behavior or an action is ethically permissible or not. It provides good performance in negotiation models. Since the ethical recognition is known as a complex problem, and the size of the given dataset was too small the method is aimed to use decisions from N number of neural networks and after that makes final decisions by combining outputs from ANN. To evaluate the performance of the proposed method, experiments were conducted with ethical data set containing a total number of 34 cases. As the result of the experiments shows, it is clear that the proposed negotiation model with ANN ensembles gives higher performance than other alternative methods; particularly it has excellent performance in distinguishing ethical behaviors similar to training cases. In the proposed method, the performance can be affected by the number of ANNs even if the combination method remains the same.

References

1. Wiegel, V., van den Berg, J.: Combining Moral Theory, Modal Logic and Mas to Create Well-Behaving Artificial Agents. Int. J. Soc. Robot. 1, 233–242 (2009)
2. Choi, S.P.M., Liu, J., Chan, S.P.: A genetic agent-based negotiation system. Computer Networks 37(2), 195–204 (2001)
3. Oprea, M.: An adaptive negotiation model for agent-based electronic commerce. Studies in Informatics and Control 11(3), 271–279 (2002)
4. Wiegel, V., van den Berg, J.: Experimental Computational Philosophy: shedding new lights on old philosophical debates, pp. 62–67 (2008)
5. Liu, N., Zheng, D.X., Xiong, Y.H.: Multi-agent negotiation model based on rbf neural network learning mechanism, pp. 133–136. IEEE (2008)
6. Sozen, A., Arcaklioglu, E.: Exergy analysis of an ejector-absorption heat transformer using artificial neural network approach. Applied Thermal Engineering 27(2-3), 481–491 (2007)
7. Nissen, S.: Implementation of a fast artificial neural network library (fann). Report, Department of Computer Science University of Copenhagen (DIKU) 31 (2003)
8. Yao, X.: Evolving artificial neural networks. Proceedings of the IEEE 87(9), 1423–1447 (1999)
9. Nigrin, A.: Neural networks for pattern recognition. The MIT press (1993)
10. Tumer, K., Ghosh, J.: Error correlation and error reduction in ensemble classifiers. Connection Science 8(3-4), 385–404 (1996)
11. Liu, Y., Yao, X., Higuchi, T.: Evolutionary ensembles with negative correlation learning. IEEE Transactions on Evolutionary Computation 4(4), 380–387 (2000)
12. Perrone, M.P.: When networks disagree: Ensemble methods for hybrid neural networks. In. DTIC Document (1992)
13. Sharkey, A.J.: Combining artificial neural nets: ensemble and modular multi-net systems. Springer-Verlag New York, Inc. (1999)
14. Shimshoni, Y., Intrator, N.: Classification of seismic signals by integrating ensembles of neural networks. IEEE Transactions on Signal Processing 46(5), 1194–1201 (1998)
15. Rosen, B.E.: Ensemble learning using decorrelated neural networks. Connection Science 8(3-4), 373–384 (1996)
16. Weitz, B.A., Castleberry, S.B., Tanner, J.F., Irwin/McGraw-Hill, Companies, M.-H., Achieve Global, I.: Selling: building partnerships (2004)
17. Honarvar, A.R., Ghasem-Aghaee, N.: An artificial neural network approach for creating an ethical artificial agent, pp. 290–295. IEEE Press (2009)
18. Al-Fedaghi, S.S.: Typification-based ethics for artificial agents, pp. 482–491. IEEE (2008)
19. Floridi, L., Sanders, J.W.: On the morality of artificial agents. Minds and Machines 14(3), 349–379 (2004)
20. Hall, M., Frank, E., Holmes, G., Pfahringer, B., Reutemann, P., Witten, I.H.: The WEKA data mining software: an update. SIGKDD Explorations 11(1), 10–18 (2009)
21. Cohen, S.: Negotiating skills for managers. McGraw-Hill Companies (2002)

Industrial Control System
Based on Data Processing

Gabriel Rojek and Jan Kusiak

Department of Applied Computer Science and Modelling,
AGH University of Science and Technology,
Al. Mickiewicza 30, 30-059 Kraków, Poland
rojek@agh.edu.pl
http://www.isim.agh.edu.pl

Abstract. The goal of the work is presentation and discussion of the idea of innovative approach to industrial control system based on data processing. The key issue of proposed control system is the analysis of a history of considered industrial process, it means the analysis of registered data (process parameters and signals) during the past production. The system searches similarities among the current production period and registered past production episodes (episodes are atomic periods of production). Each of episodes is characterized by controlled and measured signals. An episode which is similar to the present period and which is characterized by the best possible value of quality criterion is being selected and becomes a pattern for control of the present production. The searching procedure was based on the multi-agent methodology, while the control function of the chosen episode was modeled using the artificial neural network. The developed idea of the control system was implemented and tested using the data obtained by simulation of the virtual industrial experiment.

Keywords: industrial control system, agent technology, artificial neural network.

1 Introduction

The present research focuses on design and implementation of industrial control system when there is a lack of detailed knowledge concerning the physical nature of analyzed process. In such a case it is difficult, or sometimes impossible, to build a reliable model of such process, which is essential for the automatic control. Such area of industrial production is still domain of a manual control, based on experience of the workers. Another problem in control of industrial processes is irregularity of signals sampling: some signals are measured every minute, while some other are measured once a day. For example, the quality of the production cycle can be assessed only few times a day. Therefore, it is difficult to specify the proper values of controllable signals resulting in the required final production quality. The conventional approach to the control system in case of irregular

L. Rutkowski et al. (Eds.): ICAISC 2012, Part II, LNCS 7268, pp. 502–510, 2012.
© Springer-Verlag Berlin Heidelberg 2012

measurements of signals is based on pre-processing of such data, most often through the interpolation of the missing data, which can be a source of faults and errors.

The goal of the work is to design an approach to industrial control system that should comply all mentioned problems and can be an alternative for manual control. The main idea of proposed approach is based on processing of data that refers to functioning of industrial system in the past. Elaborated system should enable specification of the controllable signals values which ensure the best possible quality of production Q at current production conditions.

1.1   Signals of Industrial Control

The basic analysis of an industrial control system induces preliminary identification of every signal that can be measured or controlled and that has a possible influence on the production quality. All signals are classified into three main groups: independent signals, controllable signals, dependent signals. This classification corresponds to real industrial problem that was analyzed in [8].

Independent signals I are signals, which can be measured but cannot be modified or changed during production. *Controllable signals* U are signals that can vary during a production process. *Dependent signals* X are measured signals which cannot be directly modified. Each dependent signal is expected to be a function of other production signals and a possible time delay. Sampling frequencies are various for different signals. Some signals are measured with the minute interval, some other few times a day. It may cause troubles for the control system and can be solved by approach proposed in the work.

1.2   Industrial Control System

The typical goal of an industrial control system is to obtain the best possible value of a production quality Q (high products quality). Quality depends on all signals I, U and X, while only signals U can be used in control of a process. Values of signals U should be adjusted to measured signals X and independent signals I. Different values of signals I result in a different best quality value Q, therefore, the problem can be reduced to search for the control function $f(X)$ at given values of signals I that enable obtaining the best possible quality Q.

1.3   Related Works

The main topic of presented work is a control system that should allow to operate in an uncertain and complex environment in a way similar to the human mind that is able to meet uncertainty and lack of precision. The presented here research is based on the authors' experience in data mining techniques with the use of agent paradigm. The earlier works concern information processing in detection of unusual behaviour in a group of coexisting agents ([2], [6], [7]). The main problem of these works involves the analysis of collected data towards the evaluation of the present registered data concerning observed behaviour of other agents. The collected data is a source of knowledge and can be useful in undertaking of decisions concerning actual production.

Different approach to solving complex problems and to deal with uncertainty, fuzziness and vagueness is based on a theory of fuzzy logic [9]. The fuzzy logic controllers are closer to human thinking and natural human decision making than the traditional control systems. They need the "if-then" rules with the input and output variables defined by the fuzzy logic statements. The preparation of that "if-then" rules is necessary in order to implement a fuzzy logic controller in any domain of its application. It means that the knowledge concerning a domain of application of fuzzy control system has to be known a-priori. The fuzzy logic approach seems improper for application to the area of control systems,, where there is a lack of a full knowledge concerning nature of analyzed industrial process.

2   Idea of an Innovative Approach to Industrial Control

The main idea of proposed approach to industrial control is processing of collected past production data and, on that basis, computation of controllable signals U for the current production.

The key abstraction of presented approach is an *episode*. An episode is an event that is separated from other surrounded events. An episode is independent from other events. Taking into account irregularity of past production data, it is possible to choose a day period as the period of an episode. Usually every day of production is characterized by all signals including independent signals I that are measured most rarely. Collected data consists of number of episodes which are treated as potential patterns for present process control.

General idea of the algorithm of presented approach consists of the following three steps (graphically shown in Figure 1):

1. *Selection of the Best Episode* – selection of one of past episodes which is characterized by independent signal I, similar to the actual signal I, and which shows the best quality value Q. This episode becomes the Best Episode and serves as a pattern for the control procedure for current production.
2. *Modelling of the Control Function $f(X)$* – the registered data of the Best Episode are used in modelling of the control function $f(X)$ matching the production during the Best Episode (found in the first step). Modelling of the control function $f(X)$ is performed using the artificial neural network approach. The neural network model takes dependent signals X as the input signals and returns controllable signals U as the output. The neural network is trained with the data of selected past Best Episode.
3. *Application of the Control Function $f(X)$* – the model built in the previous step is used for calculation of the controllable signals values $U = f(X)$ for dependent signals X of the current production.

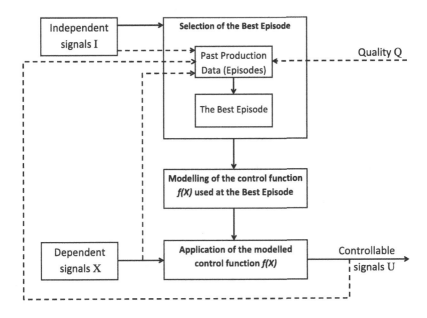

Fig. 1. Main steps of the algorithm of proposed approach to industrial control

It is assumed that each processed episode is independent and has no relations with other past episodes. This assumption enables to process all past episodes in decentralized way, and allows using the multi-agent approach.

3   Design of a Control System

The control system has to fulfill main assumptions of the idea described in the previous section. Realization of all three steps of the algorithm is performed using the multi-agent system. The agent technology was successfully used in industrial systems [3], [4], [5]. Proposed multi-agent system consists of agents of two types: Past Episode Agent and Control Agent presented in next two subsections.

3.1   Past Episode Agent

The main task of a Past Episode Agent is to provide information concerning the production during a single episode (single past time period).

The number of created Past Episodes Agents corresponds to the number of past episodes that are processed. An agent of that type can be created at the very beginning of the system functioning or later, during the system operation, at the moment when the current time period becomes the past episode. In the first case this agent is created by an administrator of the system, while in the second one is created by a Control Agent (presented in the next subsection).

Each created Past Episode Agent registers to the yellow pages service, which provides information about all services and all registered agents. Thanks that, any agent can be found by any Control Agent. That mechanism allows maintaining the independence of different number of communicating agents and is important due to the fact, that number of Past Episode Agents is incremented at the end of every production day (at the end of current production, the actual time period turns to a past episode).

The Past Episode Agent provides information regarding represented past period of production. The Past Episode Agent has to respond to one of the following three requests regarding signals of the episode he represents: (1) Provide me the value of independent signal I; (2) Provide me the quality value Q; (3) Provide me dependent signals X and controllable signals U that were registered during the represented period.

3.2   Control Agent

The Control Agent is related to the present day of production and is performing three main steps of proposed approach, described in the section 2. The main goal of the Control Agent is to compute the values of controllable signals U corresponding to the registered dependent signals X and the measured independent signal I.

Selection of the Best Episode. The first task of the Control Agent is to find a Past Episode Agent representing a past period of production that:

- has independent signal I similar to the present production period. The similarity measure is the geometric distance between values of independent signals of past episode and of current production. This geometry distance is measured with the Euclidean metric,
- is characterized by the best value of the quality criterion Q among all most similar past episodes.

The found agent represents the Best Episode that is used next as a pattern for the control of the current production.

Just after creation, the Control Agent obtains information concerning the independent signal I of the present production, what is the basis of searching for the Best Episode. The Control Agent begins conversation with all Past Episode Agents through the yellow pages service and asks Past Episode Agents for the values of their independent signals. Next, it chooses these Past Episode Agents, which are characterized by independent signals most similar to these of the present production. Finally, from these found Past Episode Agents, it selects that one, which represents the most similar past episode, and also is characterized by the best value of the quality criterion Q. According to the main idea of presented approach (Fig. 1), that chosen Past Episode Agent becomes the basis for modelling of the control function $f(X)$.

Modelling of the Control Function. At this step, the goal of the Control Agent is to evaluate the control function $f(x)$ which models the control procedure of production at the Best Episode. In order to model the control function the agent has to obtain all data concerning the process and its control during the Best Episode. The Control Agent obtains these data from the agent chosen in the previous step (the agent that represents the Best Episode). Finally, the Control Agent knows all signals of chosen Best Episode: independent signal I, controllable signals U and dependent signals X.

Modelling of the control function $f(X)$ can be performed using the Artificial Neural Network approach. Pairs of signals U and X registered at the Best Episode are used as the learning data. The input signals of the proposed neural network are dependent signals X, while the controllable signals U are the network outputs. The modeled control function $f(X)$ is going to be used next in control of the current production for calculation of the controllable signals $U = f(X)$.

Application of the Modeled Control Function. The created ANN model of the function $f(X)$ is used by the Control Agent for control of the current production. The Control Agent, knowing the values of dependent signals X, generates controllable signals $U = f(X)$ using the ANN model of the control function $f(X)$.

This step continues till the end of the present production period, which means until the value of independent signal I doesn't change. Quality measurement is performed at the end of the present time period. The Control Agent creates a new Past Episode Agent on the base of the ending current production period. That new Past Episode Agent is being added to the set of the past production episodes.

4   System Implementation and Testing

Presented approach to industrial control was implemented using JADE (Java Agent DEvelopment) framework and Neuroph (Java Neural Network) framework. JADE is a flexible agent platform that simplifies creation of agent-based systems in many fields [1]. Neuroph allows easy development of neural networks by providing neural network library that supports creating, training and saving neural networks.

The implemented industrial control system was tested in control of a virtual industrial experiment. The virtual experiment corresponds to a simplified real industrial process of the oxidizing roasting process of sulphide zinc concentrates. The reason of using simulation instead of a real industrial data is a lack of measurements of a quality criterion.

The analyzed, artificially generated data set contains records of 30 past days of virtual production. One past day of production corresponds to one episode and is described by one value of independent signal I, one value of quality measure Q, one vector of 20 values of dependent signals X and one vector of 20 values of controllable signals U (each of the values within the range $0 \div 20$). The quality measure Q depends on values of the independent signal I, dependent signal X and the used control function $U = f(X)$. Different values of signal I result in different potentially best quality measure values Q. The low value of the quality measure Q corresponds to a final product of a good quality. Three different control functions were used randomly during the 30 past days. Only one control function $f(X)$ was applied during every single day of production. The values of main parameters of considered experiment (signals I and Q) of 30 past production days are presented in Table 1.

Table 1. Main parameters of experimental 30 past days of production: I – independent signal, Q – quality measures

day	I	Q	day	I	Q	day	I	Q
1	15.49	118.89	11	2.93	27.78	21	17.45	86.34
2	2.97	26.22	12	3.67	54.26	22	14.14	102.62
3	8.95	34.07	13	6.55	8.06	23	12.04	29.75
4	5.43	1.74	14	14.52	63.20	24	6.49	32.40
5	17.74	105.09	15	8.41	21.53	25	12.16	57.08
6	2.65	56.82	16	9.08	24.37	26	6.15	9.51
7	15.34	123.96	17	3.10	31.97	27	11.16	20.69
8	10.43	16.40	18	14.00	39.24	28	2.52	5.42
9	9.07	32.20	19	12.80	86.16	29	10.29	13.11
10	11.36	49.49	20	15.57	110.30	30	17.57	94.84

The proposed approach was validated in 10 tests. The run of every test consisted of the following steps:

1. Thirty Past Episode Agents were created according to 30 past days of production. Every episode corresponds to one single past day of production.
2. One Control Agent was created in order to control the current production process. This agent should assure controllable signals for the whole present day of production. The Control Agent obtains the value of independent signal I, that is measured only once for the whole day period. That value in the first test is $I = 9.80$ (see first column of the Table 2).
3. The Control Agent uses the yellow pages service to obtain identifiers of all Past Episode Agents.
4. The Control Agent asks all Past Episode Agents for values of independent signals I for the days they are representing. The Control Agent receives all answers and chooses 5 agents that represent past days with most similar values of independent signals I. For the first test these agents represent the following days: 3, 8, 9, 16, 29 (see Table 1).
5. The Control Agent asks agents chosen in the previous step for a value of the quality measures Q for days that they are representing. The Control Agent receives all 5 answers and chooses only one agent that represents the past

day characterized by the best quality measure Q. The agent representing day number 29 is chosen as the agent representing the Best Episode for the first test.

6. The Control Agent asks a chosen agent for the values of signals X and U registered during the represented day of past production. The Control Agent receives answer containing values of signals X and U registered during the period of the Best Episode.

7. The Control Agent begins ANN modelling of the control function $f(X)$. It creates the three-layered perceptron $1 - 3 - 1$ with a hyperbolic tangent as the transfer function. The training data set contains 20 pairs of dependent signals X (*input*) and controllable signals U (*output*), registered during the Best Episode. The trained network approximates the control function $f(X)$ at the time period of the Best Episode.

8. The Control Agent measures the value of dependent signal X, and using the trained ANN computes the value of controllable signal U, which should provide the best value of the quality measure Q for a current production.

9. The previous step is repeated until the end of current production period (in practice as long as the independent signal does not change).

10. The quality value Q is evaluated just after the end of the production period (production day). In a case of the first test, calculated quality measure is $Q = 18.14$ (see first column of the Table 2).

Presented procedure was repeated for all other tests, and the main results are collected in Table 2.

Table 2. Obtained results for 10 tests: I – independent signal, Q – quality measure

test	1	2	3	4	5	6	7	8	9	10
I	9.80	3.94	19.20	6.64	3.93	8.84	17.26	12.39	5.28	13.13
Q	18.14	21.27	85.13	10.03	25.68	13.09	83.98	33.62	3.47	51.86

Average quality measure computed for the data of 30 past production days is $\overline{Q}_{data} = 49.45$ (see Table 1). Quality measures of 7 tests (see Table 2), as well as the average value $\overline{Q}_{test} = 34.63$ for all 10 tests, are better comparing to the average value $\overline{Q}_{data}$ of the quality measure of 30 past days of production.

5   Summary

Novel approach to the industrial control system based on data processing is proposed. Presented solution uses multi-agent interactions for choosing the best past episode, that should be similar to the present production and that should be an eligible pattern for the present production control. Developed system uses the artificial neural network in order to model the pattern's control for the present production period. The system was validated using the data of a simple virtual process. Performed tests of the elaborated system show its usefulness in case of lack of a priori knowledge concerning the physical nature of production process. Future research will focus on application of presented approach to real industrial processes, what shall involve several modifications (e.g. modification of used neural network) or additional agent mechanisms (e.g. aggregation of similar Past Agents).

Acknowledgments. The financial support of the National Centre for Research and Development (NCBiR) project no. R07 0006 10 is acknowledged.

References

1. Bellifemine, F.L., Caire, G., Greenwood, D.: Developing Multi-Agent Systems with JADE. John Wiley & Sons, Inc., New York (2007)
2. Cetnarowicz, K., Cięciwa, R., Rojek, G.: Behavior Evaluation with Actions' Sampling in Multi-agent System. In: Pěchouček, M., Petta, P., Varga, L.Z. (eds.) CEEMAS 2005. LNCS (LNAI), vol. 3690, pp. 490–499. Springer, Heidelberg (2005)
3. Dobrowolski, G.: Agent based paradigm for modern information systems. In: Kierzkowski, Z. (ed.) Computational Intelligence for Science, Technology and Economics, Sorus, Warsaw, Poznań, pp. 73–82 (2004) (in polish)
4. Kluska-Nawarecka, S., Dobrowolski, G., Marcjan, R., Nawarecki, E.: Agent-based information-decision systems in industrial application. In: Pieli, A. (ed.) Proc. Conf. KomPlasTech 2003, pp. 404–437. Publishing House of PŚ, Gliwice (2003) (in polish)
5. Nawarecki, E., Kisiel-Dorohinicki, M., Dobrowolski, G.: Agent-based technologies in management and control of production. In: Pietrzyk, M., Kusiak, J., Grosman, F., Piela, A. (eds.) Proc. Conf. KomPlasTech 2002, pp. 13–22. Akapit Scinetific Publishing House, Cracow (2002) (in polish)
6. Rojek, G., Cięciwa, R., Cetnarowicz, K.: Algorithm of Behavior Evaluation in Multi-agent System. In: Sunderam, V.S., van Albada, G.D., Sloot, P.M.A., Dongarra, J. (eds.) ICCS 2005. LNCS, vol. 3516, pp. 711–718. Springer, Heidelberg (2005)
7. Rojek, G., Cięciwa, R., Cetnarowicz, K.: Heterogeneous Behavior Evaluations in Ethically–Social Approach to Security in Multi-agent System. In: Alexandrov, V.N., van Albada, G.D., Sloot, P.M.A., Dongarra, J. (eds.) ICCS 2006. LNCS, vol. 3993, pp. 823–830. Springer, Heidelberg (2006)
8. Sztangret, Ł., Rauch, Ł., Kusiak, J., Jarosz, P., Małecki, S.: Modelling of the oxidizing roasting process of sulphide zinc concentrates using the artificial neural networks. Computer Methods in Materials Science 11(1), 122–127 (2011)
9. Tsoukalas, L.H., Uhrig, R.E.: Fuzzy and Neural Approches in Engineering. John Wiley, New York (1997)

Agent-Based Modelling and Simulation: Examples from Competitive Market and Group Dynamics

Ly-Fie Sugianto, Kaivalya Prasad, Zhigang Liao, and Sen Sendjaya

Faculty of Business and Economics, Monash University,
Caulfield East 3145, Victoria, Australia
Lyfie.sugianto@monash.edu

Abstract. The purpose of this paper is to demonstrate the usefulness of complex systems paradigm in studying real life phenomena. In this paper, we depict the phenomena from two distinctive domains: the competitive behavior of power generators in an auction-based electricity market and group dynamics and performance in an organizational context. Agent based modeling has been employed as the research method to conduct computer experiments. In this paper, we include the formal knowledge representation defining the types of agents in each domain, together with the properties, relationships, processes and events associated with the agents. Emergence from the first study include collusion and capacity withholding to inflate price, whereas in the second study, we observe that timely completion of group task is not always accompanied by a high level of group satisfaction. These *emergence* are evidence that we can gain new knowledge from the Sciences of the Artificial.

Keywords: Agent-based model, Artificial intelligence, Complex systems.

1 Introduction

The cynefin framework [1] is a useful typology to describe problems and life phenomena. The model introduces four domains in which every contextual problem may be best approached using different practices: (1) in simple domain, the approach is to sense, categorize and respond - leading to *best practice*; (2) in complicated domain, the approach is to sense, analyze and respond - leading to *good practice*; (3) in complex domain, the approach is to probe, sense and respond - leading to *emergence*; (4) in chaotic domain, the approach is to act, sense and respond leading to *novelty*.

This paper focuses on the problem and phenomena in the third (complex) domain. Complexity in this domain is a result of the dynamicity and inherent non-linearity resulting from interconnected components (coupling) with high level of interactions among these components. With the increase in the number of interactions, it becomes more difficult for us to understand the system as a whole. And with the increase in the number interconnected components, it becomes more difficult for us to identify and isolate causal relationships in the system.

L. Rutkowski et al. (Eds.): ICAISC 2012, Part II, LNCS 7268, pp. 511–518, 2012.

Although there is no consensus in formalizing definition of problems that can be contextualized into complex domain, problems in this domain may be characterized by four attributes, namely interaction, interconnection (often referred to as coupling or interdependence), heterogeneity and tension. The two problem domains depicted in this paper, namely the competitive electricity market and the group dynamics in organizational study, exhibit these attributes.

It is commonly understood that the crux in studying complex system is in the modeling and simulation of the system. Thus, this paper sets to exemplify our modeling and simulation approach of the two problems which are distinctive in nature. Agent based simulation has been employed as the method in our study. We also offer our interpretations of emergence as findings of our studies. The remaining of this paper is structured as follows. The next section provides descriptions on how the two problems fit well in the complex domain. Subsequently, literature reviews on the use of agent based modeling in each problem domain are presented. This is followed by a section outlining the modeling method and grammar for both problems. Next, the agent based simulations of each problem and their results are discussed. Lastly, the concluding section highlights important findings in our studies, including the work in progress.

2 Framing the Problems in the Complex Domain

2.1 Competitive Electricity Market as Complex System

We submit that the competitive electricity market is a complex system as the phenomenon exhibit the four attributes mentioned previously. First, the high level of interaction is evident in the repetitive nature of trading in the electricity market. In the Australian market, generators are required to submit their bids to the Independent System Operator every trading period and the electricity *spot price* is announced at each of the thirty minute trading interval. Second, the interconnection is evident as the *spot price* and the electricity dispatch and schedule of each generator depends on each others quantity-price bids. Third, the heterogeneity in the context of this problem is inherent in nature, as generators are distinctive in its capacity and in its mode of operation. There is a diverse range of power plants generated using coal, gas, hydro and many others leading to different operational costs, thus may be bidding differently when competing in the market. Fourth, the tension in this problem exists among the profit maximizing objective of each competing generator and operational boundaries (or limitations) that govern the trading, may it be internal in nature, such as operating characteristics of the power plants, or external in nature, such as trading policy and price cap.

The focus of our study here is to investigate the implication of employing different auction pricing rule in a simulated market model. In particular, we wish to compare the impact of different trading arrangements: Uniform and Vickrey pricing rules. Q-Learning [2] has been employed as the learning algorithm for bidding strategically into the market.

2.2   Group Dynamics as Complex System

We also submit that the dynamics of group performance exhibit the four characteristics of complex systems. First, the high level of interaction in group dynamics is evident as group members interact with each other when they communicate and solve problem collectively. Second, the interconnection among group members is characterized by the nature of the tasks they perform. High interdependent tasks, such as those performed by fire-fighters and medical team performing surgery, require high level of coordination among team members. Hence, team members must work cohesively with each other for the team to complete the task successfully. Third, the heterogeneity in the problem is exhibited by the differing *personality* of the group members. Members of a group are people of differing skills and expertise. Some are more adept than others, possessing better interpersonal skills, may it be communication skills or conflict management skills. Fourth, the tension in the context of this social science problem is inherent in the *structure* vs *agency* ontological significance. While the structure tends to limit the choices of individuals, the *agency* allows individuals to act independently and make their own free choices. In team dynamics, *structure* can take the form of task prioritization and positional power or status of team member, whereas *agency* can be exemplified by individual's self-interest.

The focus of our study here is to understand the dynamics involved in group settings, under different leadership styles, and to observe emerging perception of group task satisfaction. We aim to gain insight into the complex processes of workgroups in organizations which are related to motivation and satisfaction of group members. Specifically, we seek to understand the impact of a leaders role in a work group context as the perceptions of group satisfaction develops. The study treats work groups and their interactions as a complex system as the complexity of group dynamics mirrors the complexity of group task satisfaction itself. Rather than framing with a well-structured scientific corpus, complexity theory tends to gather a bundle of theories and methodologies aimed at understanding properties of complex adaptive systems [3]. As mentioned in [4], these systems display: emergence, path dependency, non-state equilibrium and adaptation. Emergence is the only attribute on focus in this paper. Emergence is a system-level phenomenon. It requires new categories to describe it, which were not previously used to describe the behavior of the underlying components. In other words, interactive individual components instantiate emerging patterns at the system level.

3   Literature Reviews

There have been a number of studies on competitive electricity markets employing agent-based models, as reported in [5,6,7,8]. In these studies, agent-based platforms provide electronic laboratories to experiment with the market parameters and study the behavior of the generator agents. All studies reported that as simulation progresses, generator agents can adapt their bidding strategies, based on the success or failure experience of previous trading. In [6], an agent-based simulation depicting the England and Wales market is used to analyze possibility of market abuse in a competitive electricity market. In [8], an agent-based computational model is used to study the market power and efficiency of electricity markets with discriminatory double-auction pricing.

In the social science context, the use of computational modeling is rare, but has been on the increase to study social and behavioral sciences. It is regarded as a powerful quantitative tool used for complex system analysis [9]. This approach entails expressing formal knowledge representation and operationalizing an abstract model of the system using a set of computer code. Among the many types of computational models, the most common forms are agent-based models, system dynamics, discrete event systems and statistical forecasting [10]. As identified in [11], computational models have the following characteristics in comparison to the more traditional formal models. They tend to be larger scale. They include more events, actors, entities and time periods. They tend to focus on the process and intermediate solutions and not equilibrium solutions. They tend to use a mix of simulated and real data. They can also handle more complexity such as greater number of interacting parts and higher levels of non-linearity in relationships. The use of agent-based model in organizational studies is scarce, with the exception of [12].

4   Modeling and Simulation

4.1   Agent-Based Model for a Competitive Electricity Market

Fig. 1 shows the modeling context and grammar of the proposed agent based model for the competitive electricity market problem. The mathematical model defining the State, Action, Action Selection policy and other parameters are discussed in [13,14]. Our agent based model consists of four generator agents that bid into the market. Each generator agent is characterized by the ramp rate of the power plant (limiting factor in electricity generation) and cost function (characterizing the type of power plant).

The simulation of the above model proceeds with an initialization of the Q-table, indicating that agents start with no prior knowledge of the market. Then, for each trading period, there are four successive stages: (1) agents submit bids, select *action* and next *state*; (2) ISO receives bids and determines economic dispatch schedule; (3) agents receive their profit based on pricing rule; (4) agents update their knowledge (Q-table) based on their recent trading experience. The trading then repeats itself, executing the four stages successively. We run simulation scenarios to experiment the impact of market share by varying three sets of parameters: generating capacity of the agent, trading rule imposing maximum capacity bid (or variable bid quantity), and pricing rule that governs the trading (Uniform, Pay-as-bid and Vickrey).

Emergence practice that is observed from the simulation runs includes collusion. Collusion is evident when smaller agents set their bid price in such a way to counteract the bigger generating capacity of one agent in the market. Collusion

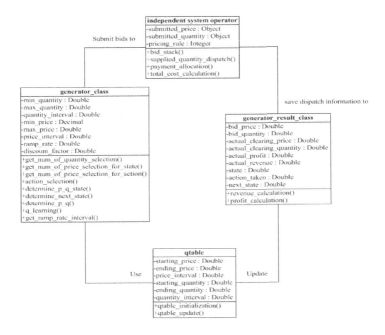

Fig. 1. Agent-based model for studying a competitive electricity market

is observed more evident when Uniform rule is applied and maximum capacity is imposed as the trading rule. In a case where one agent has a greater market share, another observable emergence is withholding capacity in placing bids in an attempt to inflate the market price. Another notable observation that is informative to policy maker and market designer is the total dispatch cost resulting from applying Uniform rule can be excessive when market share of competing agents is not comparable. When comparing the three auction rules, Vickrey rule consistently yields the lowest total dispatch cost.

4.2 Agent-Based Model for Group Dynamics

Fig. 2 shows the modeling context and grammar of the proposed agent based model for studying the group dynamics in an organizational context. The definition of the entities, namely member agent, group agent and leader agent, and their attributes; the processes, including the interactions between agents and other simulation activities are detailed in [15]. In our model, a group consists of seven members and a team leader. A survey was conducted from a panel of eight leadership experts to articulate the influence of different leadership styles on the agent attributes. Each group member is input with values for certain factors to distinguish one member from another. These factors which form the personality of a member agent include members: expertise, flexibility level, communication ability, conflicting ability, and support ability. These factors are input when the member agents are initially created. The values of member communication, conflict, and support ability change over time when members interact with each other or with the leader during the course of performing a task. The values of member expertise and flexibility are updated as members make progress from one task to another. The mathematical models for the events are documented in [15].

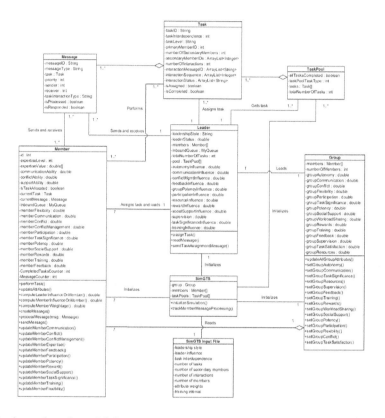

Fig. 2. Agent-based model for studying group dynamics in an organizational context

The simulation of the agent based model is prescribed in six successive stages, namely initialize, assign member task, perform task, update member attributes, update group attributes and compute group task satisfaction. We run simulation scenarios to observe the dynamics of group satisfaction altering factors we hypothesize as influential: leadership style, task interdependence and group profile.

We identified several interesting phenomena emerging from the simulation runs. When the group is composed of members with higher profile (i.e. communication ability, conflict ability, support ability, and perception of task significance) and managed by a paternalistic leader, group satisfaction stabilizes, almost with no negative effects of paternalistic leadership style. When a low profile group works in a highly coupled task, group satisfaction grows then remains constant. It is likely that over time the negative influence of the leader becomes more evident to the group. Another notable observation is that neither group profile nor group satisfaction level is associated with the time spent to complete a task.

5 Conclusion

This paper is an attempt to demonstrate the usefulness of Complex Systems paradigm in understanding real life phenomena. Two studies are presented as examples. The first study exhibits the bidding behavior of competing agents (representing generators). The second study is drawn from an organizational context whereby team members interact with each other, including with their leader, in executing an interdependent task. Agent based modeling has been chosen as the method to obtain emergence from these studies. It is understood that the main hurdle in studying problems in complex domain is in model development and simulation. We propose to contribute to current studies in complex system by depicting two case examples. It is hoped that our approach, documented briefly in this paper, would inform modelers in assessing the suitability of complex systems paradigm in dealing with a problem. Using agent based model in our studies gives us significant advantages over other traditional methods. In particular, by using an agent-based model, we can create hypothetical situations with more potency than existing ones. As a result, we are able to examine a wide range of scenarios. This approach enables a more systematic and imaginative thinking rather than constraining us with limited scenarios. Agent-based model allows us a relatively rapid development and testing of alternatives in a cost effective manner. Likewise, this method provides us with a controlled environment for experimentation. However, to effectively develop and use agent based systems, two complementary skills are required, namely modeling and interpreting (to discover emergence). Our work in progress extends our experiments: for the group dynamics study, we seek to observe the impact of Machiavellian, Transformational and Servant Leadership styles on group satisfaction.

References

1. Snowden, D.: Complex Acts of Knowing: Paradox and Descriptive Self-Awareness. Journal of Knowledge Management 6(2) (2002)
2. Watkins, C.J.C.H.: Learning from Delayed Rewards. PhD Thesis. Cambridge University (2002)
3. Richardson, K.A., Cilliers, P., Lissak, M.: Complexity Science. Emergence 3(2), 6–18 (2001)
4. Holland, J.H.: Hidden Order: How Adaptation Builds Complexity. Addison-Wesley (1995)

5. Bunn, D.W., Oliveira, F.S.: Agent-Based Simulation An Application to the New Electricity Trading Arrangements of England and Wales. IEEE Transaction on Evolutionary Computation 5, 493–503 (2001)
6. Bunn, D.W., Oliveira, F.S.: Evaluating individual market power in electricity markets via Agent-Based simulation. Annals of Operations Research 121, 57–77 (2003)
7. Watanabe, I.: Agent-Based Simulation Model of Electricity Market with Stochastic Unit Commitment. In: Proceedings of the 8th International Conference on Probabilistic Method Applied to Power Systems, pp. 403–408. Iowa State University, Ames (2004)
8. Nicolaisen, J., et al.: Market power and efficiency in a computational electricity market with discriminatory double-auction pricing. IEEE Transaction on Evolutionary Computation 5, 504–523 (2001)
9. Carley, K.M.: Computational and Mathematical Organization Theory: Perspective and Directions. Computational and Mathematical Organization Theory 1(1), 39–56 (1995)
10. Zacharias, G.L., MacMillan, J., Van Hemsel, S.B. (eds.): Behavioural Modeling and Simulation: from Individuals to Societies. Academic Press, Washington (2008)
11. Carley, K.M.: Computational Modeling for Reasoning about the Social Behavior of Humans. Computational and Mathematical Organization Theory 15(1), 47–59 (2009)
12. Hazy, J.K., Tivnan, B.F.: On Building an Organizationally Realstic Agent-Based Model of Local Interaction and Emergent Network Structure. In: Proceedings of the 2004 Winter Simulation Conference, vol. 2, pp. 748–755. IEEE Press (2004)
13. Sugianto, L.F., Liao, Z.: Implication of Different Pricing Rule on Generators Bidding Behaviour. In: Proceedings of 6th IEEE Conference on Industrial Electronics and Applications (ICIEA), Beijing, China, pp. 2421–2425 (2011)
14. Liao, Z., Sugianto, L.F.: A Comparative Study on Pricing Rules and Its Effect on Total Dispatch Cost. In: Dagli, C.H. (ed.) Complex Adaptive Systems, Procedia Computer Science, vol. 1. Elsevier (2011)
15. Prasad, K., Sugianto, L.F., Sendjaya, S.: Modeling and Simulating the Dynamics of Group Task Satisfaction. Working Paper

Will a Robot Be a Human?

Jinchang Wang

School of Business, Richard Stockton College of New Jersey,
101 Vera King Farris Drive, Galloway, NJ 08205, USA
Jinchang.Wang@stockton.edu

Abstract. It has been a long-standing contention on whether or not robots can eventually be as intelligent as humans. Neither side of the contention has provided solid arguments of proving this way or the other. We reason in this article that a digital robot will not have same mental experience as a human so far as the self-awareness of an existing person cannot be duplicated. This thesis draws a line between biological humans and digital robots. It makes us rethink the issues such as the limitation of computer software, how far machine intelligence can go, whether robots will eventually dominate humans intellectually, what machines are, and who we are.

Keywords: Computer Consciousness, Robot, Machine Intelligence, Artificial Intelligence.

1   Introduction

Will computer-based humanoids be indistinguishable from humans sometime in the future? Are robots with the full range of human mentality an inexorable emergence? These issues have been reflected for decades by computer scientists, cognitive scientists, philosophers, biologists, psychologists, physicists, and sociologists. These issues are also closely related to our fundamental curiosities such as who we are, where we come from, what intelligence and consciousness are, what the fundamental difference is between a machine and a human, whether humans can make a species superior to us, and whether immortality is possible.

We show in this paper that, among the unknowns and uncertainties in the future, there is one thing with certitude: - electronic robots will not have the full range of human consciousnesses and mental experience. That is not a hypothesis without solid support. It is a reasoned thesis. We prove it by showing that some human consciousnesses cannot be possessed by a robot so far as we do not know how to duplicate the self-consciousness of an existing person.

2   Scholars' Views on the Future of Machine Intelligence

The debate has been there for sixty years on how intelligent a computer can be and whether a computer as intelligent as a human is a blessing or a doomsday of us. Up to now, no one has provided solid arguments to prove this way or the other. How smart a computer will be remains an open question.

L. Rutkowski et al. (Eds.): ICAISC 2012, Part II, LNCS 7268, pp. 519–527, 2012.

We group the views in the debate into three categories: "optimistic believers", "pessimistic believers", and "disbelievers", as we name them.

Many computer scientists including the vanguards of artificial intelligence (AI) are *"optimistic believers"*, who cherished firm beliefs that computers will be inevitably and inexorably as smart as humans and such machines will benefit human beings.

Alan Turing predicted that computers would pass the Turing Test by year 2000 [16]. Marvin Minsky, a founder of AI department in MIT, has never cast any doubt on the possibility of having computers of human intelligence and consciousness, "Most people still believe that no machine could ever be conscious, or feel ambition, jealousy, humor, or have any other mental life-experience. To be sure, we are still far from being able to create machines that so all the things people do. But this only means that we need better theories about how thinking works." [9]

Minsky described the human brain as a "meat machine, no more no less" [1]. "If we're a carbon-based complex, computational, collocation of atoms, and we're conscious, then why wouldn't the same be true for a sufficiently complex silicon-based computer?" [2]

Ray Kurzweil, a computer scientists and futurist, believes that a silicon computer can be as conscious and spiritual as a biological machine like a human. He is very optimistic about the perspective humanoid era, taking it as an absolute blessing of humans. "By the late 2020, we will create nonbiological systems that match and exceed the complexity and subtlety of humans, including our emotional intelligence." [8] Gilder and Richards commented on Kurzweil's utopia, "Kurzweil's record as a technology prophet spurred interest in this more provocative prediction that within a few decades, computers will attain a level of intelligence and consciousness both qualitatively and quantitatively beyond human capacity." [2]

Storrs Hall, a nano-scientist and computer system architect, has no doubt that computers will soon achieve human intelligence and consciousness, and is optimistic about the moral machines. "AI is coming. It is clear we should give conscience to our machines when we can. It also seems quite clear that we will be able to create machines that exceed us in moral as well as intellectual dimensions." [3]

Hans Moravec, a leading expert in robotics, called for humans to give the way to the new species of intelligent machines, "We should keep researching, and should proudly work to create robots that will supplant humans as Earth's superior species. Humans should just get out of the way of this self-imposed evolution." [10]

"Pessimistic believers" agree with "optimistic believers" that computers will inexorably surpass human's intelligence but they take it as a disastrous doomsday for human beings. Bill Joy, a co-founder of Sun Microsystem, cast a heavy shadow on the fate of human beings in his well-known article "Why the future doesn't need us" in 2000. "How soon could such an intelligent robot be built? The coming advances in computing power seem to make it possible by 2030. And once an intelligent robot exists, it is only a small step to a robot species - to an intelligent robot that can make evolved copies of itself." He viewed the research on computer intelligence similar to the research work of atom bombs in 1940's, and called for that "researches leading to the danger should be relinquished." [6]

One person was so devastated about the future of computers that he went to extreme and appealed to terrorism to stop the computer's progress. T. Kaczynski, a mathematician, the so-called Unabomber, put in his manifesto, "If trend continues and scientists succeed in developing intelligent machines that can do all things better than human beings can do then the fate of the human race would be at the mercy of the machines. They will have been reduced to the status of domestic animals." [7]

"Disbelievers" do not believe that computers can ever be like humans. Among them are not only dualists who take it for grant that the mind is something separate and fundamentally different from the physical things, but also many philosophers and scientists.

As a successful and highly regarded computer architect and entrepreneur in Silicon Valley, Jeff Hawkins holds a firm attitude denying the possibility of human like computers, "Can computers be intelligent? For decades, scientists in the field of artificial intelligence have claimed that computers will be intelligent when they are powerful enough. I don't think so. Brains and computers do fundamentally different things." [4]

To many scholars, subtlety of mind is improbable to be realized by "mechanical" computer programs. Physicist and mathematician Roger Penrose enumerates in his book <The emperor's new mind> [11] mysterious phenomena and processes of human intelligence, consciousness, mentality, and mind, and says "According to this perception, all aspects of mentality are merely features of the computational activity of brain; consequently, electronic computers should also be capable of consciousness, I do my best to express, in a dispassionate way, my scientific reasons for disbelieving this perception, and arguing that the conscious minds can find no home within our present-day scientific world-view." He hypothesized that the thorough explanation of human minds would be somewhere in the "quantum world".

Mathematician and psychologist Douglas Hofstadter believes that human mind is unlikely to be programmed directly, rather, it will be an emergent phenomenon as by-products of sufficiently complex computer programs. "Will emotions be explicitly programmed into a machine? No. That is ridiculous. Any direct simulation of emotions cannot approach the complexity of human emotions, which arise indirectly from the organization of our minds. " [5],

No one has so far provided solid evidences or arguments to support whatever opinion. Whether a robot can have same consciousnesses as a human is even viewed by some scholars as one that cannot be proved or disproved. "Someone is bound to ask, can you prove that the computer is not conscious? The answer to this question is: Of course not. I cannot prove that the computer is not conscious, any more than I can prove that the chair I am sitting on is not conscious." [15]

3   Can a Robot Have All Human Consciousnesses?

We in this section prove, by using a counterexample, that a robot cannot have the full range of human mental experience as far as we do not know how to duplicate an existing person's self-consciousness.

3.1   Definitions of Terms

Consciousness in this article refers to all mental experience of a person such as thinking, calculation, reasoning, feelings, emotions, intuitions, and faith. Andy Clark defined and categorized mental phenomena of "consciousness" with three levels:

(1) feelings that characterize daily experience (hunger, sadness, desire); (2) flow of thoughts and reasons; (3) meta-flow of thoughts about thoughts, thoughts about feelings, and reflection on reasons. [1]

A *computer program*, or simply a *program*, refers to instructions to computers in any computer language. *A program is copiable* or *duplicatable* if the instructional statements in the program can be duplicated so that the original and the copy are literally identical and the result of running the copy is indistinguishable from the result of running the original. With this definition, once a computer would someday be programmed to have consciousnesses of "happiness", "self-awareness" and "anxiety of death", other computers, by copying, would also have same consciousnesses of "happiness", "self-awareness" and "anxiety of death". Any program for a digital computer is copiable, because, according to the Church-Turing Thesis, it can be converted to a set of equivalent 0-1 codes for a universal Turing Machine [14], and the 0-1 codes on the tape of a Turing Machine are obviously copiable. *A computer is copiable* if all the programs in the computer are copiable. All computers as we have at present are copiable since all programs in current computers are copiable.

By *robot* we refer it to an electronic or digital machine which, under control of its internal digital computer, looks like human, acts like human, and is supposed to have human intelligence and consciousnesses.

3.2   Self-awareness and Anxiety of Death

Self-awareness and anxiety of death are two examples of human consciousnesses and mental experience.

Self-awareness is, according to Oxford Encyclopedia, a conscious trait "associated with the tendency to reflect on or think about one-self". Self-awareness is a piece of intelligence that differentiates subjective selfhood from the others. It belongs to the third level of consciousness in Clark's classification (see Section 2.1). A human is capable of reflecting on his own mental experience and recognizing the subjective "self", while the other animals are not.

Death is the destination of life. *Anxiety* is "an emotion of feeling dominated by comprehensions" [12]. *Anxiety of death* is comprehension and dread of the mystery/obscurity of death. Self-awareness is a necessary condition to have anxiety of death. The feeling of anxiety of death comes from a person's understanding that "I live only once" and "if I died then the world currently around me would disappear forever."

People may have disagreements on exact definitions of self-awareness and anxiety of death. But it would not cause problems in addressing our thesis below. What we need in this article is just the consensus that both self-awareness and anxiety of death are examples of human consciousnesses.

3.3   Anxiety of Death Defies Copying

Let *AD* denote "anxiety of death", and *SA* denote "self-awareness". Let *R* denote a robot which is programmed to have human consciousnesses. A human has consciousness of AD and SA, and so does robot R.

Suppose all the programmed consciousnesses in robot R, including SA and AD, are copied to another robot R'. According to the definition of "copying" in Section 2.1, R and R' have identical consciousnesses after copying, which include self-identity. That is, the self-identities of R and R' are same. R and R' are a same "self", which can be put as "R-self" = "R'-self". Now, either R or R' has multiple "selfs". Realizing this, R' would not fear to die since "death" of R' would not result in disappearance of the world around itself due to the existence of R-self that is another R'-self. Therefore, R' would not have anxiety of death. With the same analysis, robot R would not have anxiety of death either.

So, we say that the programmed consciousness AD is "copy-defiant" in the sense that, after copying AD together with the self-consciousness from R to R', AD would disappear on either R or R'. The copy of AD would nullify itself. Therefore, we will not pragmatically obtain a sustained duplication of AD.

When a program is copied, its symbolic binary codes are duplicated. If the symbolic codes incur semantic self-reflection, it may cause inconsistency after copying. That is the reason that may interpret the phenomenon of copy-defiance of anxiety of death. The entanglements between a symbolic program and its semantics were prophesied by Penrose [11] and Hofstadter [5], though they did not reach as far as the characteristics of copy-defiance of some symbolic codes.

All the computer programs that have been so far developed, including those for mimicking human intelligence, are not copy-defiant. None of them has incurred self-reflective semantics yet. The programs for self-awareness and anxiety of death, if invented sometime in the future, must be distinct significantly from current computer programs due to its copy-defiance feature.

3.4   A Robot Will Not Have All Consciousnesses of a Human

Robot R is assumed to have intelligence and consciousness on a par with a human H. R must be free in moving and acting same as human H is, so as to have those human consciousnesses related to moving and actions.

As discussed in the last section, the programmed consciousness AD is copy-defiant so that if AD is copied together with SA to another robot, then AD would be lost in both the original and the copy. Robot R is assumed to have SA and AD. So, the programs for AD and SA in robot R must have no copy in other robots. Since R is as intelligent as humans, R would be able to figure out that "a copy of the programs for myself would relieve my anxiety of death". So, R would have a motive to make a copy of the programs for its consciousnesses.

If R has got itself copied, then anxiety of death would not exist with R due to the defiance of copying of anxiety of death. But human H still has anxiety of death. So, robot R would have different consciousness from a human H as least on the feelings towards death. Note that R should easily get itself copied because R is free in action, and copying computer programs is a simple routine of computer operation: - duplicating all the programs inside R would be as easy as making a backup of all the files in a computer.

If R does not manage to get itself copied for some reason, then R may retain anxiety of death. But robot R would have a motive to have a copy of itself to relieve anxiety of death, and R knows that it can be done easily by "copy-paste". On the other hand, although human H also has a motive to relieve anxiety of death by making himself copied, he realizes that copying himself is almost an impossible mission in practice. R has anxiety of death but R knows that its "death" can be easily avoided by making himself copied. Human H has anxiety of death also, but H has no idea on how to avoid death. For R, death can be immune with a simple process of program-copying. For H, on the other hand, death is the destined destination. So, robot R and human H would inherently have different feelings towards death. That difference is analogical to the feeling of a man who has caught a slight cold that can be cured quickly versus the feeling of a man who has got a terminal cancer that is past beyond cure.

The feeling towards death is an example of human consciousness. The above discussion forms a counterexample against the assertion "a digital robot can have same intelligence and consciousness as a human does." Therefore, robot R would not have same consciousnesses as human H does, no matter whether or not R has a copy of its consciousnesses. If R got itself copied, robot R would not have anxiety of death but human H still has. If R did not get itself copied, R would have a feeling toward death different from human H.

The above arguments have an implicit assumption: We are not able to duplicate an existing person's "self" by whatever technologies such as programming and cloning. With this assumption, the self of robot R is not the self of any human H, or R-self is not H-self, so that the argument is valid that human H's anxiety of death remains despite of existence of robot R and its copies. This assumption also ensures that the consciousness of anxiety of death remains with human H, because if human H would know how to copy himself then H would go ahead to make copies of himself so as to get rid of anxiety of death.

Now the thesis we have derived can be stated as:

Thesis-1
An electronic robot cannot have all human consciousnesses, and so cannot have same mental experience as a human, as far as we do not know how to duplicate an existing person's self-consciousness.

4   Discussions and Remarks

We have reasoned that it is not possible to have an electronic robot of all human mental experience before we are able to duplicate an existing person's self. In this section, we discuss some issues implied by the thesis, such as what a computer can and cannot do, what the future androids are like, whether those androids are a blessing or a threat to humans.

4.1   The Limit of Capability of Copiable Machines

We can see from the arguments in the last section that it is due to "duplicatability" of digital programs that makes a robot incapable to have some consciousness a human has. All digital computer programs are copiable because they can be equivalently converted to a set of binary codes for a Turing machine [17] [14] and the codes on the tape of a Turing Machine are obviously copiable. No man-made machine in current world is un-copiable. By Thesis-1, the machines as we have now will not "become" humans no matter how complex they will be, as far as we have no idea on how to program or clone a particular person's self-consciousness. In fact, what an un-copiable man-made machine is like, how it works, and how to manufacture such a machine, are still utterly beyond our current knowledge.

4.2 Impossible vs. Improbable

"Anything is not impossible, as far as it does not cause a logical contradiction." (Gottfried Leibniz) No machine so far has been programmed to be conscious of hunger, sleepiness, anger, envy, pain, embarrassment, happiness, etc. And no one has proved that a machine having those consciousnesses would cause a logical contradiction. Hence, we say that those consciousnesses are not impossible to be programmed in a machine; and we do not have solid evidence to say that a robot will not have those consciousnesses forever. The examples of subtle and delicate consciousnesses given in the books of Penrose [11] and Hofstadter [5] show difficulties to have machines mimicking human's mental experience, but they do not lead to contradictions, so they are not evidences for impossibility of programming them, but just showing improbability of programming them. Our reasons in Section 2 elaborated a logical contradiction for a self-aware robot to have anxiety of death, which showed that the statement "a digital robot could be programmed to have same consciousnesses as a human" is groundless. Hence, Thesis-1 indicates the impossibility, rather than unlikeliness or improbability.

We do not have solid evidences denying the possibility of machine consciousnesses such as anger and pain; so those machine consciousnesses cannot be said to be impossible to appear sometime in the future even in millions of years. But now we can say, with Thesis-1 on hand, that it is impossible for a self-aware machine to have anxiety of death as far as we are not able to copy the self-consciousness of an existing person.

4.3 Will a Robot Be One of Us?

With Thesis-1, we now can answer this question with "no, at least before we know how to duplicate an existing person's self-consciousness." We are in the era in which the difference between humans and machines is blurring. Electronic computers have been thought by many to be omnipotent and to surpass humans on every aspect of intelligence and consciousness in a few decades. Thesis-1 indicates a limit of electronic computers and robots. Even though one could program robots sometime in the future to such a level that they were pretty much human-like, those robots would not be humans because they would miss something unique we humans have, - our sense on life and death. The electronic robot would not be one of us.

When talking about intelligent machines as a new species created by humans, Kurzweil said, "Evolution has been seen as a billion-year drama that led inexorably to its grandest creation: human intelligence. The emergence in the early twenty-first century of a new form of intelligence on Earth that can compete with, and ultimately significantly exceed, human intelligence will be a development of greater import than any of the events that have shaped human history." [8] We can see now that

Kurzweil's perspective of machine intelligence is not realistic, at least not as soon as he predicted. The electronic computers as we currently have are not as omnipotent as Kurzweil thought. Even though we do not know how smart electronic computers will be, they may be forever incapable of something that humans are capable of, due to the computers' inherent idiosyncrasy, - copiability or duplicatability.

4.4   Final Remarks

We humbly admit that we are very ignorant about our own consciousness, mentality, and spirit, as well as how to re-create them. These are issues on which sagacious philosophers and scholars have elaborated for thousands of years. With the improvements of machine intelligence, answers to those issues are becoming more compelling. On the other hand, the research on machine intelligence may help understand ourselves through the endeavors of remaking human mentality on computers. In the process of trying to develop machine intelligence, we will know more about ourselves. It would help identify some unique idiosyncrasies that are possessed exclusively by humans. Thesis-1 is a forward step in understanding who we are and the fundamental difference between electronic machines and us, which sets off more questions for us to keep reflecting hereafter, such as: Is there any piece of our consciousnesses, other than anxiety of death, which may not be realized on electronic robots? Can an existing person's mind be programmed? Can a human's "self" be copied? What is an un-copiable machine like, and how does it work? Is consciousness a "by-product" emerging from sufficiently sophisticate program, as proposed by Hofstadter [5] and some other scientists? If so, how does such "emerged" process occur? Is the emerged process copiable? ...

References

1. Clark, A.: Mindware - In introduction to the philosophy of cognitive science. Oxford University Press, New York (2001)
2. Gilder, G., Richards, J.: Are we spiritual machines? The beginning of debate. In: Richards, J. (ed.) Are We Spiritual Machine? - Ray Kurzweil vs. the critics of strong AI. Discovery Institute Press (2002)
3. Hall, J.S.: Beyond AI - Creating the conscience of the machine. Prometheus Books, New York (2007)
4. Hawkins, J., Blakeslee, S.: On Intelligence. Holt Paperback, Times Books / Henry Holt and Company, New York (2004)
5. Hofstadter, D. R.: Gödel, Escher, Bach - An eternal golden braid. Basic Books, Inc. (1999)
6. Joy, B.: Why the Future Doesn't Need Us? Wired. Online (2000)
7. Kaczynski, T.: Unabomber's manifesto. Online (1995)
8. Kurzweil, R.: The Singularity Is Near - When humans transcend biology. Penguin Books (2005)
9. Minsky, M.: The Society of Mind. Touchstone, Simon & Schuster, NY (1986)
10. Moravec, H.: Cited in Jason Specht "Bill Joy's Hi-tech Warning", online (2001)
11. Penrose, R.: The Emperor's New Mind. Oxford University Press (1999)

12. Popplestone, J.A., McPherson, M.W.: Dictionary of Concepts in General Psychology, p. 21. Greenwood Press, New York (1988)
13. Richards, J.W. (ed.): Are We Spiritual Machines? - Ray Kurzweil vs. the critics of strong A.I. Discovery Institute Press (2002)
14. Russell, S., Norvig, P.: Artificial Intelligence - A modern approach, 3rd edn. Prentice Hall, New Jersey (2010)
15. Searle, J.R.: I Married a Computer. In: Richards, J. (ed.) Are We Spiritual Machine? Discovery Institute Press (2002)
16. Turing, A.: Computing machinery and intelligence. Mind 59, 433–466 (1950)
17. Turing, A.M.: On Computable Numbers, with an Application to the Entscheidungsproblem. Proceedings of the London Mathematical Society 2(42), 230–265 (1937)

Part VI

Artificial Intelligence in Modeling and Simulation

Fractal Modelling of Various Wind Characteristics for Application in a Cybernetic Model of a Wind Turbine

Marzena Bielecka[1], Tomasz Barszcz[2], Andrzej Bielecki[3], and Mateusz Wójcik[4]

[1] Department of Geoinformatics and Applied Computer Science,
Faculty of Geology, Geophysics and Environmental Protection,
AGH University of Science and Technology,
Mickiewicza 30, 30-059 Cracow, Poland
bielecka@agh.edu.pl
[2] Chair of Robotics and Mechatronics,
Faculty of Mechanical Engineering and Robotics,
AGH University of Science and Technology,
Al. Mickiewicza 30, 30-059 Kraków, Poland
tbarszcz@agh.edu.pl
[3] Institute of Computer Science, Jagiellonian University,
Lojasiewicza 6, 30-348 Cracow, Poland
bielecki@ii.uj.edu.pl
[4] Department of Computer Design and Graphics,
Faculty of Physics, Astronomy and Applied Computer Science,
Jagiellonian University,
Reymonta 4, 30-059 Kraków, Poland
mateusz.wojcik@uj.edu.pl

Abstract. The Weierstrass functions family, which graphs are fractal sets, in combination with medium-term trends, is used as the basis of the model of wind. Various aspects of wind variability, neglected in models proposed so far, are taken into considerations. A genetic algorithm is used in order to fit the proper parameters of Weierstrass function. Fractal dimension is utilized as a parameter in a fitness function. The results have shown that the proposed approach yielded very good fit for the observation data.

1 Introduction

There are a few approaches to wind modelling in dependence on the aim the model is created. Three following are the most classical ones.

Spatial Distribution of the Wind Intensity. Such models are utilized for designing of turbines spatial distribution if the designed wind farm is intended to be situated on extensive area [6,12]. It should be also mentioned that this class of wind models has also significance in meteorology and related sciences [7].

L. Rutkowski et al. (Eds.): ICAISC 2012, Part II, LNCS 7268, pp. 531–538, 2012.

Mean Wind Intensity in a Given Place. Such models are used for prediction of energy production by wind farms. Methods of precise forecasting of electric power load are in constant demands on electricity markets. This is caused by the specific character of electric power which, particularly, can not be stored at the industrial level and, therefore, balance between demand and supply must be managed in real time ([3,22,23]).

Wind Intensity as a Time Series in a Given Place. Such models are mainly used to forecast wind speed in a given place [4,8,14,15,18,19,21].

In the context of the three specified tasks the wind speed, and, sometimes, direction is predicted or modelled.

In this paper it is discussed a problem which seems to be a new one in the context of wind turbines operating. The cybernetic model of the wind turbine being the basis for analysis of its mechanical parts load is intended to be created. The module simulating the wind parameters, crucial in the context of a mechanical parts load analysis, is a key part of the model. However, in such context, there are a few parameters of wind which should be taken into account but have not been considered in the mentioned models founded so far.

The paper is organized in the following way. In Section 2 wind parameters influencing vital operational features of a turbine are specified in details. In Section 3 formal basis is introduced whereas results are presented in Section 4.

2   Wind Parameters Influencing Vital Operational Features of a Turbine

The wind speed is one of fundamental operational parameters (next to generator rotational speed and the generated power), measured by a wind turbine monitoring system [2]. The result of the modelling of a time series highly depends on the used criteria that should reflect the overall goal of the model. In this paper, we focus on wind speed modelling on the time interval equal to five minutes. The indented usage of the model is the input to the mechanical drivetrain model, which simulates behavior of its mechanical components under the varying wind. Simulated signals can be, in turn, used to develop the optimum fault signatures, which would be efficient in such operating conditions. However it should be stressed that a wind force varies with the square of wind speed whereas the power in the wind varies with the cube of the wind speed [24]. This means a small increase in wind speed produces a large increase in power. Therefore, a very precise wind speed model is needed in reliability evaluation of a power system including wind energy conversion system.

In this section a few characteristics of a wind speed are discussed in the context of their influence of wind turbines exploitation and energy production. They refer to various aspects of the wind model proposed in the following text. The error criteria, that are used in evaluation of the model accuracy, are discussed as well.

In the sequel z_i is the measured wind speed whereas y_i denotes the predicted wind speed value.

1. The most basic characteristics of the wind is the value of its speed. In this case we refer simply to y_i value.

   In the most cases this is the only characteristic of the wind to which the proposed models are referred in order to evaluate their quality [4,5,8,10,11,14,18,21]. The wind speed signal contains several frequency components, in the most general distinction we can divide it into constant component, low- and high-frequency. Poor fitting of a model can be caused by poor performance of only one of these components, which is hard to check with only the MAPE criterion. Therefore, below we propose more detailed modelling criteria.

   Aforementioned wind signal components have very different interpretation from the operational point of view. The constant component (i.e. the average value) is simply the wind speed averaged during the whole measurement. In periods of days or weeks it can show what were the dominant wind conditions. This can influence usefulness of the data, as e.g. during summer months winds are usually weaker and there may be not enough data from the full power range. The low frequency component represents the moving average of the wind speed. Its prediction is important for predicting the energy output of the turbine, which is - in turn - very important for the stability of the whole power generation system. The medium frequency component represents changes with periods in the range of 10..100 seconds and in most cases is handled by the wind turbine controller. Finally, the high frequency component is mainly caused by turbulences in the air flow and influence the wear of mechanical components.

   The wind speed values are positive real numbers so the mean absolute percentage error (MAPE), given as $MAPE = \frac{1}{N} \sum_{n=1}^{N} \frac{|z_i - y_i|}{z_i} 100\%$, is good criterion for model accuracy evaluation.

2. The wind variability is a crucial parameter for wind turbine fatigue wear prediction. In this point we refer only to direction of the wind speed changes which can be expressed as $var_i := \text{sgn}(z_{i+1} - z_i)$. This is a parameter which is not widely used, but we would like to propose it, as it can be a useful measure of prediction of non-stationarity of the operational point of turbines.

   The wind has a significant high frequency component, which is responsible for quick changes of the operational point - mainly the load of the gearbox and the generator. Thus, the accurate model, capable of predicting these changes can be used in research on durability of these mechanical components.

   In the context of the wind variability, the model is valid if $\text{sgn}(y_{i+1} - y_i) = \text{sgn}(z_{i+1} - z_i)$ which is equivalent to equality $\text{sgn}(z_{i+1} - z_i) \cdot \text{sgn}(y_{i+1} - y_i) = 1$. Let n_{+1} denotes the number of points in which the measured variability is equal to the one obtained from the model whereas n_{-1} denotes the number of points in which they differ. Then, the fraction of the incorrect values of variability obtained from the model $\varrho := \frac{n_{-1}}{n_{+1} + n_{-1}}$, can be used as the error criterion.

3. The numerical wind acceleration can be expressed as $a_i := z_{i+1} - z_i$. The time increase in the denominator can be neglected because for each i we have

the same time difference $t_{i+1} - t_i = const$. In general, accurate modelling and prediction a momentary wind acceleration is essential in order to prevent systems in-action from the effects of strong wind gusts. This parameter is quite similar to the previous one. The variability aspect took into account only the direction of change, neglecting its magnitude. The numerical wind acceleration, in turn, should give more accurate measure of the wind variability. There is an important difference between the two aforementioned parameters. Because the acceleration criterion involves the magnitude, it can distinguish between high and low cycle fatigue phenomena. The magnitude of cycles has enormous impact on the durability [17]. It is well known behaviour, often presented on the S-N or Woehler curve [20]. Such a phenomenon has fundamental impact on the lifetime of mechanical components, especially gearboxes. There were several reported wind turbine gearboxes failures [1] and proper modelling of operational point variability can lead to more accurate prediction of the component lifetime.

Let b_i denotes acceleration obtained from the model: $b_i := y_{i+1} - y_i$. The MAPE is not a good criterion for evaluation if the acceleration is well approximated by the model because the denominator would be small. Therefore, the absolute mean error $MAE := \frac{1}{N-1} \sum_{i=1}^{N-1} |a_i - b_i|$ is used.

4. It can be also advantageous to compare levels of irregularity of z_i and y_i. This criterion can be described as the comparison of the level of irregularity of both measured and predicted values. For modelling based on fractals, the comparison of fractal dimensions can be applied for this task.

The fractal dimension can be a measure of the high frequency component, which - in case of wind turbines - causes high frequency variability of the turbine torque. The torque variability causes variable stress in mechanical components, in particular gearboxes. If the fractal dimension is higher than 1, variability of stress can be higher that assumed by the designer and the manufacturer. Thus, such operating conditions will cause faster wear of the gearbox and decrease in the turbine availability. Accurate modelling of the fractal dimension of the wind speed time series is crucial for the prediction of the lifetime of wind turbine gearboxes.

5. The mean value of the wind speed is crucial for prediction of a wind farm energy production abilities.

As it was mentioned above, the low frequency component represents the moving average of the wind speed. Its accurate prediction is important for the stability of the whole power generation system. It is important to choose correctly the depth of the averaging buffer with practical considerations determining this choice. As this prediction is the most important for the power control, it is important to recall the organization of the power generation on the national level. All the large turbogenerators receive the required energy generation signal from a central authority signal (in Poland it is "Central Power Command") [13]. This central authority monitors the generation of all sources and has to take into account the renewable sources, which depend on wind speed and their output variations must be compensated by other sources. Prediction of the power produced by a wind farm at different time scales is of interest to the electricity grid. So, the averaging buffer for the proposed criterion should be based on the time constants of the central control of the power generation. These constants are typically in the range of 10-30 seconds [9].

It is important to note that the first four criteria were important from the mechanical point view, while the last one is important to estimate the quality of power generation.

3   Mathematical Basis and the Fitting Algorithm

In this paper a wind model, created in order to apply it in a wind turbine model for analysis of momentary turbine parts loading, is proposed. The wind speed is considered as a time series modelled by the Weierstrass function, having a fractal graph. Though it was suggested over eighty years ago that the Weierstrass function can be used as a mathematical tool describing wind properties adequately [16] it seems that, so far, it has not been applied in wind models. In the approach proposed in this paper, the parameters of the Weierstrass function and linear trend are fitted using a genetic algorithm in which a fractal dimension is utilized as a parameter in a fitness criterion.

Suppose $\lambda > 1$ and $1 < s < 2$. The Weierstrass function $f : \mathbb{R} \to \mathbb{R}$, having parameters λ and s, is defined as

$$f_{\lambda,s}(t) = \sum_{k=1}^{\infty} \lambda^{(s-2)k} \sin(\lambda^k t). \tag{1}$$

The Weierstrass function is a periodic one so it is necessary to apply additional function to approximate the long-term trend. Thus, the long-term trend is fitted separately as a line $ul_j(t)$ for time intervals $[t_{j_{begin}}, t_{j_{end}}]$ having various length. The intervals are determined according to the following procedure.

At the beginning, accuracy parameter δ is chosen and first experimental point $v(t_1)$ is taken. Then, procedure determines intervals $[t_{j_{begin}}, t_{j_{end}}]$ in a sequence where, for j-th interval, $t_{j_{begin}}$ equals t_1 (for first interval) or $t_{(j-1)_{end}}$ (for next intervals). To determine $t_{j_{end}}$ (end of j-th interval) the following actions are taken:

1. Initialize variable n_j (length of j-th interval) as 1
2. Increment n_j ($n_j := n_j + 1$) while following condition is satisfied

$$\forall t \in \{t_{j_{begin}+1}, ..., t_{j_{begin}+n_j}\} : |v(t) - ul_j(t)| < \delta \tag{2}$$

where $ul_j(t)$ is a line $a_j t + b_j$ to which points $v(t_{j_{begin}})$, $v(t_{j_{begin}+n_j+1})$ belong

3. Set $t_{j_{end}}$ as $t_{j_{begin}+n_j}$

Condition (2) guaranties for j-th interval $[t_{j_{begin}}, t_{j_{begin}}]$ there exists the line $ul_j(t)$ that, for each argument t, distance from experimental point $v(t)$ to $ul_j(t)$ is not further than δ.

Thus, the line $ul_j(t) = a_jt + b_j$ represents long-term trend on the time interval $[t_{j_{begin}}, t_{j_{end}}]$ which can be regarded as a medium-term trend on the time interval $[0s, 300s]$. The postulated model is of the form:

$$u_j(t) = a_jt + b_j + \sum_{k=1}^{K_j} \lambda_j^{(s_j-2)k} \sin\left(\lambda_j^k x(t)\right) + C_j. \tag{3}$$

To sum up, on each time interval the linear long-term trend $vl_j(t)$ is determined in the way described above. Then, the parameters K_j, λ_j, s_j of the Weierstrass function and the parameter C_j are fitted using classical genetic algorithm. It is assumed that the parameters belong to the following intervals: $\lambda_j \in [1.101, 1000]$, $s_j \in [1.101, 1.999]$, $K_j \in [1, 30]$, $C_j \in [-5, 5]$. Furthermore, there exist two other parameters: $x_j(0)$ - the starting point for the Weierstrass function and Δx_j - the step scaling the time variable to the Weierstrass function variable. In this way the domain of the Weierstrass function $W_j(x(t)) = \sum_{k=1}^{K_j} \lambda^{(s_j-2)k} \sin\left(\lambda_j^k x(t)\right) + C_j$ is determined as $[x_j(0), x_j(0) + \Delta x_j \cdot (n_j - 1)]$. It is assumed that $x_j(0) \in [0, 1]$ and $\Delta x_j \in [0.00001, 0.005]$. The parameters $x_j(0)$ and Δx_j are determined using a genetic algorithm as well.

The used fitness function consists of three components. The first one is a standard mean square error whereas the second one - capacity measure - is given as a difference between experimental box-counting dimension of graphs of two functions: u_j and v_j. The third one is a measure of accuracy of amplitude approximation between functions: u_j and v_j. The mentioned components are weighted.

4   Results

The used data are real data recorded on a 1.5 MW wind turbine, located in Germany. The data were available courtesy of the company SeaCom GmbH from Herne, Germany.

Values of errors of approximation parameters specified in Section 2 are given in Table 1. Mean fractal dimension is equal to 1.3607 with standard deviation 0.1459 which means that, statistically, it is significantly greater than 1. Thus, the hypothesis proposed in [16] that the wind speed as a time function has fractal character is, in a way, confirmed. Therefore, the fractal character of the wind speed variability should be one of crucial points in mathematical models of the wind.

It should be stressed that apart from the wind speed variability, for which the mean error is equal to about 37%, values of errors of the parameters being the criteria of the model accuracy are extremely low. This means that the proposed model adequately conveys the subtle shades of the wind phenomenon. Referring to the mentioned big value of error of wind variability approximation let us stress that the variability is defined as a sign of change of the wind speed, i.e. as a sign of the numerical acceleration $var_i = \text{sgn } a_i$. However, the acceleration is expressed by the model with a very good accuracy - the mean value of MAE is extremely low. This means that the variability is modelled incorrectly mainly in the cases in which its value is close to zero. Therefore, the low value of accuracy

Table 1. Mean values of errors of approximation parameters

Measured value	Mean error	Standard deviation of error
Speed value y_i	MAPE = 3.85 %	1.34 %
Variability $sgn(y_{i+1} - y_i)$	$\varrho = 0.37$	0.03
Acceleration $y_{i+1} - y_i$	MAE = 0.11	0.05
Fractal dimension	MAE = 0.004	0.002
Fractal dimension	MAPE = 1.23%	0.66%
Mean value of y, for $n = 10$	MAPE = 1.93 %	0.85 %
Mean value of y, for $n = 30$	MAPE = 1.16 %	0.62 %
Mean value of y, for $n = 300$	MAPE = 0.39 %	0.33 %

in reflection of the value of variability has no meaning in the model applications, in particular as the module of wind turbine models, and is only a small drawback of the proposed approach.

5 Conclusion

In order to improve the performances of real-time wind speed simulator, it is essential that the internal wind speed generator reproduce, as faithful as possible, the real conditions concerning the wind speed regime. The proposed wind speed model considers the wind speed as a non-stationary process, having two components: the long- and medium-term component, modelled by the low frequency range of an experimental available spectral characteristic and the turbulence component, described by a fractal component of the model. All three components have adjustable parameters which have been fitted using a classical genetic algorithm with a specifically defined fitness function. Such approach allowed us to create an adequate model of a wind speed variability in time which accurately reflects various aspects of the phenomenon - compare low values of errors, Table 1. These aspects are essential for a modelling of mechanical loads in parts of wind turbines - in particular, it has a fundamental impact on the lifetime of mechanical components, especially gearboxes.

References

1. Barszcz, T., Randall, R.: Application of spectral kurtosis for detection of a tooth crack in the planetary gear of a wind turbine. Mechanical Systems and Signal Processing 23, 1352–1365 (2009)
2. Barszcz, T., Jabłoński, A.: A novel method for the optimal band selection for vibration signal demodulation and comparison with the kurtogram. Mechanical Systems and Signal Processing 25, 431–451 (2011)
3. Bąk, M., Bielecki, A.: Neural Systems for Short-Term Forecasting of Electric Power Load. In: Beliczynski, B., Dzielinski, A., Iwanowski, M., Ribeiro, B. (eds.) ICANNGA 2007. LNCS, vol. 4432, pp. 133–142. Springer, Heidelberg (2007)

4. Damousis, I.G., Alexiadis, M.C., Theocharis, J.B., Dokopoulos, P.S.: A fuzzy model for wind speed prediction and power generation in wind parks using spatial correlation. IEEE Transactions on Energy Conversion 19, 352–361 (2004)
5. Fan, S., Liao, J.R., Yokoyama, R., Chen, R., Lee, W.J.: Forecasting the wind generation using a two-stage network based on meteorological information. IEEE Transactions on Energy Conversion 24, 474–482 (2009)
6. Focken, U., Lange, M., Mönnich, K., Waldl, H.P., Beyer, H.G., Luig, A.: Short-term prediction of the aggregated power output of wind farms - a statistical analysis of the reduction of the prediction error by spatial smoothing effects. Journal of Wind Engineering and Industrial Aerodynamics 90, 231–246 (2002)
7. Herman, A., Kaiser, R., Niemeyer, H.D.: Wind-wave variability in a shallow tidal sea - spectral modelling combined with neural networks method. Coastal Engineering 56, 759–772 (2009)
8. Huang, Z., Chalabi, Z.S.: Use of time-series analysis to model and forecast wind speed. Journal of Wind Engineering and Industrial Aerodynamics 56, 311–322 (1995)
9. Karczewski, J., Pawlak, M.: Reconfigurable control system of condensation power turbine. Problemy Eksploatacji 60, 15–26 (2006) (in polish)
10. Kusiak, A., Song, Z., Zhang, H.: Anticipatory control of wind turbines with data-driven predictive models. IEEE Transactions on Energy Conversion 24, 766–774 (2009)
11. Kusiak, A., Zhang, H., Song, Z.: Short-term prediction of wind farm power: a data mining approach. IEEE Transactions on Energy Conversion 24, 125–136 (2009)
12. Landberg, L.: Short-term prediction of the power production from wind farms. Journal of Wind Engineering and Industrial Aerodynamics 80, 207–220 (1999)
13. Laudyn, D., Pawlik, M., Strzelczyk, F.: Power Plants, WNT, Warsaw (2000) (in polish)
14. Mohandes, M.A., Halawani, T.O., Rehman, S., Hussain, A.A.: Support vector machines for wind speed prediction. Renewable Energy 29, 939–947 (2004)
15. Monfared, M., Nikravesh, S.K.Y., Rastegar, H.: A novel fuzzy predictor for wind speed. In: Proceedings of the World Congress on Engineering and Computer Science, WCECS 2007, pp. 840–843 (2007)
16. Richardson, L.F.: Atmospheric difusion shown on a distance-neighbour graph. Proceedings of the Royal Society of London, Series A 110, 730–737 (1926)
17. Rykaluk, K.: Fracture in Metal Structures, Dolnośląskie Wydawnictwo Edukacyjne, Wrocław (2000) (in polish)
18. Sreelakshmi, K., Ramakanthkumar, P.: Performance evaluation of short term wind speed prediction techniques. International Journal of Computer Science and Network Security 8, 162–169 (2008)
19. Sreelakshmi, K., Ramakanthkumar, P.: Neural networks for short term wind speed prediction. World Academy of Science, Engineering and Technology 42, 721–725 (2008)
20. Stephens, R.I., Fatemi, A., Stephens, R.R., Fuchs, H.O.: Metal Fatigue in Engineering. Wiley & Sons, New York (2001)
21. Taylor, J.W., McSharry, P.E., Buizza, R.: Wind power density forecasting using ensemble predictions and time series models. IEEE Transactions on Energy Conversion 24, 775–782 (2009)
22. Weron, A., Weron, R.: Stock Market of Energy. CIRE, Wrocław (2000) (in polish)
23. Weron, R.: Energy price risk management. Physica A: Statistical Mechanics and Its Application 285, 127–134 (2000)
24. Wen, J., Zheng, Y., Donghan, F.: A review on reliability assessment for wind power. Renewable and Sustainable Energy Reviews 13, 2485–2494 (2009)

Selecting Representative Prototypes for Prediction the Oxygen Activity in Electric Arc Furnace

Marcin Blachnik[1], Mirosław Kordos[2], Tadeusz Wieczorek[1], and Sławomir Golak[1]

[1] Silesian University of Technology, Department of Management and Informatics,
Katowice, Krasinskiego 8, Poland
marcin.blachnik@polsl.pl
[2] University of Bielsko-Biala, Department of Mathematics and Informatics,
Bielsko-Biała, Willowa 2, Poland
mkordos@ath.bielsko.pl

Abstract. Selecting a set of representative prototypes in prediction systems enable us to generate prototype based rules (P-Rules), which constitute a very powerful means of providing domain experts with knowledge about the data and the process depicted by the data. P-rules has already proved very useful in classification tasks. This paper investigates application of P-rules to regression problems. The problem of our concern is prediction of oxygen activity in an electric arc furnace during steel scrap melting. For that purpose we use a new algorithm for determining prototype positions, which is based on conditional clustering. Also a comparison between the new algorithm and the classical clustering-based methods for prototype extraction is described.

Keywords: Regression, Nearest Neighbor, Instance Selection, Context Dependent Clustering, Industrial Application, Electric Arc Furnace.

1 Introduction

Prototype based rules shortly called P-rules [3] are a concept of representing knowledge extracted from the data as a triple: a set of prototypes, similarity (or distance) measure and appropriate reasoning scheme. Typically there are two different schemes:

- nearest neighbor approach (nearest prototype) - where the system decision is obtained by determining the nearest prototype to the given test instance according to the following rule:

$$\text{If } j = \underset{i=1,...,c}{argmin}\, D(\mathbf{x}; \mathbf{p}_i) \text{ Then } C(\mathbf{x}) = C(\mathbf{p}_j) \tag{1}$$

where $C(\mathbf{x})$ is a function that returns the value of the instance label $\mathbf{x}$, and c is the number of prototypes.
- threshold rules - where each prototype represents an associated respective field defined by a prototype and a threshold value:

$$\text{If } D(\mathbf{x}; \mathbf{p}) < \theta \text{ Then } C(\mathbf{x}) = C(\mathbf{p}) \tag{2}$$

L. Rutkowski et al. (Eds.): ICAISC 2012, Part II, LNCS 7268, pp. 539–547, 2012.

According to that rule if an instance satisfies a given condition (is closer to some prototype then the given threshold) then a particular decision is made. In case when several rules satisfy that condition usually the order of the sequence of rules determine the primary rule.

Although the concept of the nearest neighbor approach is well known for many years [4], we are reusing it in a different way. Many experts not related to data mining were reporting the problem of knowledge representation. For example metallurgical experts face the problem of excessive amount of data, because current furnaces are equipped with tens of sensors sampled every second (what gives 84 thousand of samples per sensor per day). After a year - a typical period of sample acquisition, the number of samples is over 31 mln per sensor! Thus, instance selection is becoming a very important issue.

In P-rule systems the goal is to replace the original subset of instances by as small as possible subset preserving the model accuracy, such that a compromise between the system accuracy and the number of reference instances (prototypes) is reached. The instances selected in this way may be used for further in depth analysis of relationships between the selected objects. For example in metallurgy such prototypes may be used for identification of the time where a given stage of the process is occurring. In that situation mutual position of the prototypes (according to the Voronoi diagrams) can be used to find out what is the current melting stages the process.

Currently most of the applications of P-rules and in general instance selection methods were dedicated to classification problems for example [2,7,12]. However, in this paper we show how to approach regression problems and how to determine prototype position efficiently. Typical approaches in this field are based on clustering, where a set of similar instances is replaced by the center of the cluster and is associated with its label obtained by averaging output values of all samples within that cluster. However, this approach is not appropriate for regression problems, because it causes an unnecessary increase of the number of prototypes and it ignores output information during the training. Such problem appears because prototypes are obtained independently of the output labels. To address this issue we propose another solution, which is based on conditional clustering where information about output values is used in the clustering process as a clustering condition.

Our approach has been applied to a dataset describing the metallurgical process, where the task was to predict the amount of active oxygen in the electric arc furnace during the steel scrap meltdown.

The paper is organized as follow: the next section describes the dataset used in our experiments. Section (3) explains how to use the conditional clustering to determine prototype positions. Section (4) presents the obtained results of the application of the proposed method to predict the amount of oxygen activity. The last section (5) concludes the paper, discusses the obtained results and indicates the further research directions.

2   The Problem Definition and Dataset Description

The electric arc furnace (EAF) is the main part of the metal scrap recycling process in steel mini-mill plants. EAF uses the heat generated by electric arcs generated between the graphite electrodes and metal scraps to melt the steel. The process of melting scrap metal in EAFs is used for production of high quality steel. The process is performed in several stages. At least four conditions needs to be satisfied before melted steel can be tapped out from the EAF: no solid metal pieces should be present inside the furnace, the carbon content should be at a required level, the temperature should be at a specified level and required amount of oxygen should be dissolved in the bath. Reactions taking place inside the furnace are much more predictable if the oxygen activity is controlled. Knowledge of the bath oxygen activity during the operation enables operators to predict what reactions are taking place inside the furnace more accurately and to operate furnaces much closer to their optimal operating conditions by minimizing tolerances of the produced steel parameters as well as minimize the furnace worn-out and energy usage. Once the desired steel composition, temperature and oxygen activity are obtained in the furnace, the tap-hole is opened, the furnace is tilted and the steel is poured into a ladle and undergoes the next batch operation (usually a ladle furnace or ladle station). During the tapping process bulk alloy additions are made based on the bath analysis and the desired steel grade. Deoxidizers may be added to the steel to lower the oxygen content prior to further processing.

2.1 Dataset Description and Preprocessing Steps

To predict the value of oxygen activity we had to extract important information from the industrial database. The dataset is populated with measurements obtained from the EAF process controllers and sensors. Every 0.1 second all sensors are sampled and the obtained values are collected in the industrial database. This allows measuring the mass of each steel scrap bucket loaded into the furnace, energy consumed during the process, amount of carbon and oxygen injected into the furnace, temperatures of the bottom of the furnace casing, the time periods where the process gets suspended. All the values are used to construct the dataset.

The output value that should be predicted (oxygen activity) is recorded only few times during the melting process, because it requires turning off the arc and is very expensive. The solution proposed in this paper selects the nearest past values of all sensors for each oxygen measurement, except the buckets weight values which were constant for each individual melt. Then for that melt, instead of directly predicting the absolute value of oxygen activity the derivative is calculated.

The final dataset used in our experiment includes 6263 samples described by 31 attributes that are: derivatives of six sensors, which measure the temperature at the bottom of the furnace casing, derivative of the amount of carbon, oxygen injected to the furnace by five lances and the burners, electric energy consumed by the process and the total weight of the steel scrap.

Because the values gathered from the sensors include many outliers, each attribute after transformation from the row signal into the derivative is transformed with the hyperbolic tangent function to reduce the outlier's influence on the training process [9]. The transformation requires determining the linear coefficient that adjusts the signals to the appropriate range of values. For that propose the Z-transformation in the following form is used:

$$\mathbf{a}_i = tanh\left(\frac{\mathbf{a}_i - \overline{\mathbf{a}}_i}{std(\mathbf{a}_i)}\right) \tag{3}$$

where $tanh()$ - hyperbolic tangent function, $\mathbf{a}_i$ - i-th attribute of the dataset, $\overline{\mathbf{a}}_i$ - mean value of i-th attribute and $std(\mathbf{a}_i)$ - standard deviation of i-th attribute.

3   Instance Construction

As mentioned in the introduction we had to extract representative prototypes that can be further used by human experts for in depth investigation. To achieve that goal we are interested in prototypes that can be interpreted independently and to obtain that we use the nearest neighbor decision algorithm. For the same reason we do not use other prototype based algorithms like RBF networks [1] or the family of Reduced Set Suppoort Vector Machines [11], where the predicted output of the system is a linear combination of all prototypes, what reduces the overall comprehensibility of the system.

One of the simplest solution of prototype construction is input data clustering [8]. In the literature many different clustering algorithms are known [5]. One of the most popular clustering methods is based on the optimization of scalar cost function (OSCF), which has very low (linear) computational complexity $O(ncdi)$ where i is the number of iterations (constant), d the dimensionality of the problem (constant), and c is the number of cluster centers, preserving $n \gg c$. An example of this family are: k-means algorithm, expectation maximization algorithm and a family of Fuzzy C-means clustering.

As it was mentioned in the introduction obtaining informative prototypes requires incorporation of system output (($\mathbf{y}$) variable) in the prototype construction process. A typical approach, based on a simple input data clustering does not preserve such information and thus the process needs to be modified. There are several possibilities of the modification. One of them is based on using input data together with output data for the clustering process. In this approach the dataset $\mathbf{Z}$ is defined by concatenation of input and output data $\mathbf{Z} = \mathbf{X} \cup \mathbf{y}$. In this case the output variable $\mathbf{y}$ is considered to be one of the variables of the dataset and as a result the number of attributes of $\mathbf{Z}$ is $m + 1$. Such solution is often used in training the ANFIS (artificial neural fuzzy inference system) [6]. However, because too little attention is paid to the output variable this approach is not sufficient in our case.

Another typical approach is based on discretization of the output $\mathbf{y}$ attribute and then independent clustering of the instances falling into each discretization bean. This approach causes a very strong influence of model output ($\mathbf{y}$) on the obtained prototypes, so in practical applications the obtained prototype position highly depends on the discretization process. To overcame this problem a good solution can be obtained by applying a soft discretization by defining fuzzy membership functions (MF) instead of hard beans and incorporating these soft discretization beans in the clustering process.

A set of clustering methods, which can incorporate such external input in the clustering process can be found in the literature. These methods are often called context

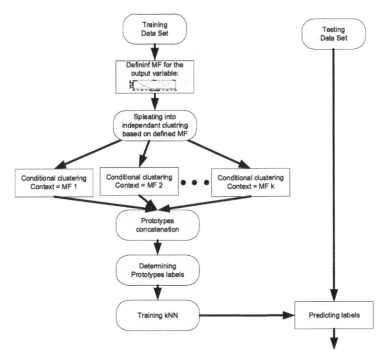

Fig. 1. Diagram of the data analysis process

clustering methods. For instance Conditional Fuzzy C-means (CFCM) [10], which requires an external variable that should be in the range [0;1] representing the clustering context. In the described approach the clustering process should be repeated for each membership function defined for the output variable and the values of the MF of each input vector should be provided as an external variable. The final cluster centers (prototypes) of each clustering should be concatenated into a single subset of reference points, as described in fig. (1)

3.1 Conditional Fuzzy Clustering

The most important limitation of FCM in the applications to P-rules system is a lack of information about output variable, which leads to a reduced comprehensibility of the obtained rules. That can be solved by conditional clustering for example by the use of Conditional Fuzzy C-Means. This algorithm allows introducing external knowledge, which represents the influence of certain instance on the clustering process. This knowledge is represented as instance weights $f_k \in [0\,1]$ defined for every instance k in the training set. The value of weight (f_k) is usually calculated as a value of the MF as $f_k = \mu(y_k)$ of some external variable y_k, where $\mu(\cdot)$ is the function describing the MF. In CFCM method the cost function remains identical to the FCM one (4),

$$J_m(\mathbf{U}, \mathbf{V}) = \sum_{i=1}^{c} \sum_{k=1}^{n} (u_{ik})^z \|x_k - v_i\|_A^2 \tag{4}$$

where $\mathbf{U}$ is a partition matrix of elements u_{ik} representing the value of membership of instance i to the cluster k, matrix $\mathbf{V}$ represents a set of c cluster centers and $z > 1$ is some constant, typically $z = 2$. The partition matrix must satisfy the following requirements:

1° each vector x_k belongs to the i-th cluster to a degree between 0 and f_k, where $0 \geq f_k \geq 1$:

$$\bigvee_{1 \leq i \leq c} \bigvee_{1 \leq k \leq n} u_{ik} \in [0, f_k] \tag{5}$$

2° sum of the membership values of k-th vector x_k in all clusters is equal to f_k (in FCM it is equal to 1)

$$\bigvee_{1 \leq k \leq n} \sum_{i=1}^{c} u_{ik} = f_k \tag{6}$$

3° no clusters are empty.

$$\bigvee_{1 \leq i \leq c} 0 < \sum_{k=1}^{n} u_{ik} < n \tag{7}$$

Cost function (4) is minimized according to $\mathbf{U}, \mathbf{V}$ by the use of Piccard iteration under these conditions by:

$$\bigvee_{1 \leq i \leq c} v_i = \sum_{k=1}^{n} (u_{ik})^z x_k \Bigg/ \sum_{k=1}^{n} (u_{ik})^z \tag{8}$$

$$\bigvee_{\substack{1 \leq i \leq c \\ 1 \leq k \leq n}} u_{ik} = f_k \Bigg/ \sum_{j=1}^{c} \left(\frac{\|x_k - v_i\|}{\|x_k - v_j\|} \right)^{2/(z-1)} \tag{9}$$

where both equations are iteratively evaluated until the convergence is obtained.

3.2 Defining the Clustering Context

In the above presented approach defining appropriate clustering context requires defining fuzzy membership functions for the output variable $\mathbf{y}$. This can be done in several ways. One solution is based on manually adjusting fuzzy MF to the output variable. This can be used if the expert can manually define the areas of interests for the output variable. In that case the obtained solution may be very helpful in improving the interpretability of obtained prototypes. Another solution is to adjust the MF automatically. The most naive solution is based on splitting the variable into equal width beans and then setting the position of the MF (for example center of the Gaussian MF) in the middle of each bean with the width of that functions adjusted in this way that the MFs crosses the membership level of 0.5. A more accurate approach can be obtained by the fuzzy clustering of the output variable, which allows for automatically obtaining fuzzy membership values. In that solution FCM clustering is applied for the single variable $\mathbf{y}$. The results of FCM determine centers of the clusters and the partition matrix represents the values of the membership function of each vector to all clusters. In all practical experiments the MF were defined automatically by a simple equal width principle.

3.3   Nearest Neighbor Rule Adaptation

The nearest neighbor prediction rule is simply based on assigning output value identical to the label of the closest prototype. The drawback of that rule is a stair-like output function, where the Voronoi diagram borders are the borders of the plateau of the output function. A simple well known modification of that rule is based on taking into account k nearest neighbors and taking average over all k neighbors. In practise this approach is still not very useful because the predicted values also belong to the finite set of values (output is also a stair-like function), however with much higher number of steps. To overcome this limitation a weighed kNN rule can be used, where the influence of the label of the closest prototypes is inversely proportional to the distance between the k prototypes and the test vector according to the formula (10)

$$c(\mathbf{x}) = \sum_{i=1}^{k} \frac{c\left(\mathbf{p}_i\right) \cdot D\left(\mathbf{x}, \mathbf{p}_i\right)}{\sum\limits_{j=1}^{k} D\left(\mathbf{x}, \mathbf{p}_j\right)} \tag{10}$$

This formula allows pseudo-linear transformation of the k nearest neighbors output values. Unfortunately it reduces the comprehensibility of the system, but on the other hand it increases its accuracy. So the interpretability of the system is inversely proportional to the number of considered nearest neighbors in the decision process (k). In this case a compromise between comprehensibility and accuracy needs to be established. In our experiments we have tested two different solutions; one that preserves the highest comprehensibility $k = 1$ and a second one for $k = 2$ that improves the accuracy, but still preserves simplicity in the decision making process.

4   Numerical Examples

In our tests we have compared the behavior of the algorithm described in this paper to the classical clustering methods, to the kNN algorithm and to linear regression as the base rates. In all experiments we have optimized the number of prototypes. The membership functions defined for the oxygen activity (output of the system $\mathbf{y}$) for CFCM clustering are presented in the figure (2). In all the experiments the results of a 10-fold crossvalidation were recorded and a comparison between prototype based methods is presented in figure (3), as well as in the table (1) where also a comparison with other methods like 1NN and kNN is provided. Results marked as W were obtained using weighted version of nearest neighbor rule. For all the methods only the best results are reported in the table. It is important to notice that the obtained values of RMSE are overestimated, because the parameter optimization process was not embedded in the crossvalidation procedure. However, it should not significantly affect the comparison of the methods, because always the same number of parameters were tested for all the algorithms.

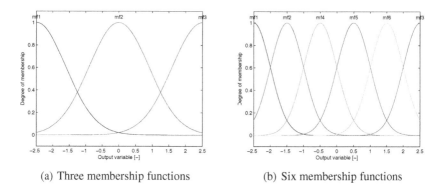

(a) Three membership functions   (b) Six membership functions

Fig. 2. Membership functions defining the clustering context defined for the output variable

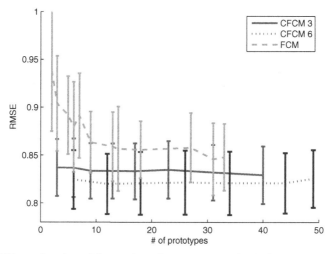

Fig. 3. RMSE as a function of the number of prototypes obtained with FCM and CFCM with 3 and 6 different clustering contexts and the 1NN rule

Table 1. Comparison of RMSE and its standard deviation and mean number of prototypes for all compared methods

model	RMSE	#P
fcm	0.85 ± 0.038	31
cfcm 3	0.83 ± 0.029	9
W(k=2) cfcm 3	0.84 ± 0.028	9
cfcm 6	0.82 ± 0.032	12
W(k=2) cfcm 6	0.82 ± 0.035	12
kNN	0.80 ± 0.031	k=100
W kNN	0.80 ± 0.031	k=100
kNN	1.07 ± 0.039	k=1

5   Conclusions

A new algorithm for optimization of the prototype positions for P-rules was presented. The proposed algorithm uses the knowledge of the output values during the clustering process. That results in the obtained prototypes being much more representative and in significantly lower error rates. In the presented application we were unable to obtain results as good as for the optimized k-NN classifier. However, we were able to radically reduce the computational complexity, so instead of over 6 thousand vectors, only 12 prototypes were used. The obtained results also prove that determining the correct shape and number of membership functions for the output values is very important. The results show that a higher number of clustering contexts (higher number of membership functions defined for the output variable) leads to much lower error rates, while it does not influence the number of prototypes significantly. In the presented approach the membership functions were defined manually, however in the further research it should be possible to determine them automatically based on the distribution of values of the output variable.

Surprisingly, weighted nearest neighbor rule applied to both: prototypes and to original data did not improve the accuracy, but rather decreased it or increased the variance.

Acknowledgments. The work was sponsored by the Polish Ministry of Science and Higher Education, project No. N N516 442138 and N N508 486638.

References

1. Bishop, C.M.: Pattern Recognition and Machine Learning. Springer (2006)
2. Blachnik, M., Duch, W., Wieczorek, T.: Selection of Prototype Rules: Context Searching Via Clustering. In: Rutkowski, L., Tadeusiewicz, R., Zadeh, L.A., Żurada, J.M. (eds.) ICAISC 2006. LNCS (LNAI), vol. 4029, pp. 573–582. Springer, Heidelberg (2006)
3. Duch, W., Grudziński, K.: Prototype based rules - new way to understand the data. In: IEEE International Joint Conference on Neural Networks, pp. 1858–1863. IEEE Press, Washington D.C (2001)
4. Duda, R.O., Hart, P.E.: Patter Classification and Scene Analysis. J. Wiley & Sons (1973)
5. Gan, G., Ma, C., Wu, J.: Data Clustering: Theory, Algorithms, and Applications. Series on Statistics and Applied Probability, ASA-SIAM (2007)
6. Jang, J.: Anfis: adaptive-network-based fuzzy inference system. Systems, Man and Cybernetics 23(3), 665–685 (1993)
7. Jankowski, N., Grochowski, M.: Comparison of Instances Seletion Algorithms I. Algorithms Survey. In: Rutkowski, L., Siekmann, J.H., Tadeusiewicz, R., Zadeh, L.A. (eds.) ICAISC 2004. LNCS (LNAI), vol. 3070, pp. 598–603. Springer, Heidelberg (2004)
8. Kuncheva, L.I., Bezdek, J.C.: Nearest prototype classification: Clustering, genetic algorithms or random search? IEEE Transactions on Systems, Man, and Cybernetics C28(1), 160–164 (1998)
9. Kordos, M., Blachnik, M., Perzyk, M., Kozłowski, J., Bystrzycki, O., Gródek, M., Byrdziak, A., Motyka, Z.: A Hybrid System with Regression Trees in Steel-Making Process. In: Corchado, E., Kurzyński, M., Woźniak, M. (eds.) HAIS 2011, Part I. LNCS, vol. 6678, pp. 222–230. Springer, Heidelberg (2011)
10. Pedrycz, W.: Conditional fuzzy c-means. Pattern Recognition Letters 17, 625–632 (1996)
11. Schölkopf, B., Smola, A.: Learning with Kernels. Support Vector Machines, Regularization, Optimization, and Beyond. MIT Press, Cambridge (2001)
12. Wilson, D., Martinez, T.: Reduction techniques for instance-based learning algorithms. ML 38, 257–268 (2000)

Stability Analysis of the Neural Network Based Fault Tolerant Control for the Boiler Unit*

Andrzej Czajkowski, Krzysztof Patan, and Józef Korbicz

Institute of Control and Computation Engineering,
University of Zielona Góra, ul. Podgórna 50, 65-246 Zielona Góra

Abstract. This paper deals with the stability analysis of the fault accommodation control system. When a fault is detected, the fault tolerant control tries to compensate the fault effect by adding to the standard control the auxiliary signal. This auxiliary control constitutes the additional control loop which can influence the stability of the entire control system. This paper focuses on the stability analysis of proposed control scheme based on the Lyapunov direct method.

Nowadays everyone can observe very rapid and significant progress in the automation industry. Not only very sophisticated and complex systems are fully automated, but also the simple one. Unfortunately with the growing number of components of a production system the probability of system faults becomes higher and higher. This makes necessary to design a control system which automatically adapt the proper behaviour in the case of faults.

In the previous works of the authors, a fault detection and accommodation methodology for the boiler unit was proposed [3]. The already elaborated methodology uses a robust state space model of the system and nonlinear state observer, both carried out by means of artificial neural networks. The designed fault tolerant control tries to compensate a fault effect by adding the auxiliary signal to the standard control generated using e.g. the classical PID controller. The auxiliary control constitutes the additional control loop which can influence the stability of the entire control system. Thus, in this paper the stability analysis of the proposed control scheme based on the Lyapunov direct method is presented.

1 Problem Formulation

Let consider a nonlinear dynamic system governed by the following state equation:

$$\boldsymbol{x}(k+1) = g(\boldsymbol{x}(k), \boldsymbol{u}(k)) + f(\boldsymbol{x}(k), \boldsymbol{u}(k)), \tag{1}$$

where $g(\cdot)$ is a process working at the normal operating conditions, $\boldsymbol{x}(k)$ is the state vector, $\boldsymbol{u}(k)$ is the control and $f(\cdot)$ represents a fault affecting the process.

---

* This work was supported in part by the Ministry of Science and Higher Education in Poland under the grant N N514 6784 40.

L. Rutkowski et al. (Eds.): ICAISC 2012, Part II, LNCS 7268, pp. 548–556, 2012.

An unknown fault function $f(\cdot)$ is a function of both the state and input. Thus, it is possible to model a wide range of possible faults. When the process works in the normal operating conditions the fault function $f(\cdot)$ is equal to zero. As, in general, the state vector is not fully available, to approximate a fault function one need to design the model of the healthy process

$$\bar{x}(k+1) = \bar{g}(\bar{x}(k), u(k)), \tag{2}$$

where $\bar{x}$ is the state vector of the model, $\bar{g}$ stands for the model of the process working at the normal operating conditions, and the state observer

$$\hat{x}(k+1) = \hat{g}(\hat{x}(k), u(k), y(k)), \tag{3}$$

where $\hat{x}$ is the estimated state vector, $\hat{g}$ is the mapping realized by the observer and y is the output of the process. Then, the unknown fault function can be approximated as:

$$\hat{f} = \hat{g}(\hat{x}(k), u(k), y(k)) - \bar{g}(\bar{x}(k), u(k)). \tag{4}$$

The fault effect occurring in the control system can be compensated/eliminated by a proper determination of the auxiliary input u^{fa} based on the estimated fault function $\hat{f}$. This additional control is added to the control $u(k)$ calculated by the standard controller used [15]. As a result, one can determine the augmented control law u^{ftc} as follows:

$$u^{\text{ftc}}(k) = u(k) + u^{\text{fa}}(k), \tag{5}$$

2   State Space Neural Network Model

2.1   Nonlinear State Space Model

Let $u(k) \in \mathbb{R}^n$ be the input vector, $\bar{x}(k) \in \mathbb{R}^q$ - the output of the hidden layer at time k, and $\bar{y}(k) \in \mathbb{R}^m$ - the output vector. The state space representation of the neural model considered is described by the equations

$$\begin{aligned} \bar{x}(k+1) &= \bar{g}(\bar{x}(k), u(k)) \\ \bar{y}(k) &= C\bar{x}(k) \end{aligned}, \tag{6}$$

where $\bar{g}(\cdot)$ is a nonlinear function characterizing the hidden layer, and C represents synaptic weights between hidden and output neurons. In most cases, as the nonlinear function in the hidden neurons, the hyperbolic tangent activation function is selected as it gives pretty well modelling result.

2.2   Nonlinear State Observer

The proposed fault compensation scheme requires to estimate *on-line* the state vector of the plant. This can be carried out using the State Space Innovation

Form (SSIF) model. The identified SSIF model can be regarded as an extended Kalman filter for unknown nonlinear systems [8]. The SSIF neural model is represented as follows:

$$\hat{x}(k+1) = \hat{g}(\hat{x}(k), u(k), \varepsilon(k))$$
$$\hat{y}(k) = C\hat{x}(k) \quad , \tag{7}$$

where $\varepsilon(k)$ is the error between the observer output $\hat{y}(k)$ and measured system output $y(k)$, $\hat{g}$ is the nonlinear function characterizing the hidden layer. Then, using the estimated state $\hat{x}(k)$, the unknown fault function f can be approximated using (4).

2.3   Deriving a Control Law

To accommodate a fault, the suitable change of a control law is proposed. According to (5), the additional control $u^{fa}(k)$ should be chosen in such a way to compensate a fault effect. The problem can be easily solved for linear systems (see e.g. [15]). Assuming that the nominal model of the system is linear and introducing control $u^{fa}(k)$, the process (1) can be rewritten in the following way:

$$x(k+1) = Ax(k) + B\left(u(k) + u^{fa}(k)\right) + f\left(x(k), u(k)\right). \tag{8}$$

To completely compensate the fault effect, the fault model should be as close as possible to the nominal model, therefore

$$Bu^{fa}(k) + f(x(k), u(k)) = 0, \tag{9}$$

then

$$u^{fa}(k) = -B^- f\left(x(k), u(k)\right), \tag{10}$$

where B^- represents the pseudoinverse of the control matrix, e.g. in a Moore-Penrose sense. Taking into account that f is unknown it can be replaced with its approximation given by $\hat{f}$. Finally, using (4) one obtains

$$u^{fa}(k) = -B^-(\hat{g}(\hat{x}(k), u(k), y(k)) - \bar{g}(\bar{x}(k), u(k))). \tag{11}$$

In order to use control law (11) and to accommodate faults in the control system, the state space neural model (6) have to be linearised first around the current operating point $(x, u) = (x(\tau), u(\tau))$, as shown in [3]. Then, the state space model can be described in the linear form:

$$\bar{x}(k+1) = A\bar{x}(k) + Bu(k) + D$$
$$\bar{y} = C\bar{x}(k) \quad , \tag{12}$$

where $A = h'W^x$, $B = h'W^u$, $D = x(\tau) - A\bar{x}(\tau-1) - Bu(\tau-1)$. Symbol h' represents the first derivative of the activation function of hidden neurons.

3   Stability Analysis

The stability analysis of the control system is extremely important in industrial applications. Lack of the stable behaviour can result in an unanticipated control signal. This can lead to change the equilibrium point by the system and introduce dangerous oscillations in the actuators work. In the most optimistic scenario this would end up in stopping the plant by emergency systems. In the worst case it can lead to the significant damage of components or even could have the catastrophic effect on the environment if the controlled system is a kind of high-risk one. In this paper, the second method of Lyapunov is used to determine stability conditions for the system.

Let us assume a discrete state-space representation of the PI controller:

$$\begin{cases} \boldsymbol{x}_r(k+1) = \boldsymbol{x}_r(k) + K_i \boldsymbol{e}(k) \\ \boldsymbol{u}_r(k) = \boldsymbol{x}_r(k) + K_p \boldsymbol{e}(k) \end{cases}, \tag{13}$$

where K_p is the proportional term, K_i – the integral term, $\boldsymbol{e}(k)$ – the regulation error, $\boldsymbol{x}_r(k)$ – the controller state. Regulation error is defined as:

$$\boldsymbol{e}(k) = \boldsymbol{y}_r(k) - \boldsymbol{y}(k), \tag{14}$$

where $\boldsymbol{y}_r(k)$ is the reference signal. Using the equivalence rule, the regulation error can be rewritten in the form:

$$\boldsymbol{e}(k) = \boldsymbol{y}_r(k) - \bar{\boldsymbol{y}}(k) = \boldsymbol{y}_r(k) - \boldsymbol{C}\bar{\boldsymbol{x}}(k). \tag{15}$$

Finally, the standard control can be represented as:

$$\begin{cases} \boldsymbol{x}_r(k+1) = \boldsymbol{x}_r(k) + K_i \left(\boldsymbol{y}_r(k) - \boldsymbol{C}\bar{\boldsymbol{x}}(k) \right) \\ \boldsymbol{u_r}(k) = \boldsymbol{x}_r(k) + K_p \left(\boldsymbol{y}_r(k) - \boldsymbol{C}\bar{\boldsymbol{x}}(k) \right) \end{cases}. \tag{16}$$

Next, let consider the compensation component:

$$\boldsymbol{u}^{\mathtt{fa}}(k) = -\boldsymbol{B}^- \hat{\boldsymbol{f}}(k) = -\boldsymbol{B}^- \left(\hat{\boldsymbol{x}}(k) - \bar{\boldsymbol{x}}(k) \right). \tag{17}$$

Substituting (16) and (17) into (5) one obtains the following rule:

$$\boldsymbol{u}^{\mathtt{ftc}}(k) = \boldsymbol{x}_r(k) + K_p \left(\boldsymbol{y}_r(k) - \boldsymbol{C}\bar{\boldsymbol{x}}(k) \right) - \boldsymbol{B}^- \left(\hat{\boldsymbol{x}}(k) - \bar{\boldsymbol{x}}(k) \right). \tag{18}$$

The state of the system (6) (with introduced weight matrices of the neural model) can be presented as:

$$\bar{\boldsymbol{x}}(k+1) = h(\boldsymbol{W}^x \bar{\boldsymbol{x}}(k) + \boldsymbol{W}^u \boldsymbol{u}(k)), \tag{19}$$

where $\boldsymbol{W}^x$ is the matrix of recurrent links, $\boldsymbol{W}^u$ – the input weight matrix. Using (18), the equation (19) can be rewritten as follows:

$$\begin{aligned} \bar{\boldsymbol{x}}(k+1) = h \big(&\left(\boldsymbol{W}^x - \boldsymbol{W}^u K_p \boldsymbol{C} + \boldsymbol{W}^u \boldsymbol{B}^- \right) \bar{\boldsymbol{x}}(k) \\ &- \boldsymbol{W}^u \boldsymbol{B}^- \hat{\boldsymbol{x}}(k) + \boldsymbol{W}^u \boldsymbol{x}_r(k) + \boldsymbol{W}^u K_p \boldsymbol{y}_r(k) \big). \end{aligned} \tag{20}$$

Similarly, the state equation of the observer (7) can be represented as:

$$\hat{x}(k+1) = h\left(W^x \hat{x}(k) + W^u u^{\text{ftc}}(k) + W^e \varepsilon(k)\right), \tag{21}$$

where

$$\varepsilon(k) = \hat{y}(k) - \bar{y}(k) = C\left(\hat{x}(k) - \bar{x}(k)\right). \tag{22}$$

Substituting (18) and (22) into (21) one obtains

$$\hat{x}(k+1) = h\left(\left(-W^e C - W^u K_p C + W^u B^-\right)\bar{x}(k) \right. \tag{23}$$
$$\left. + \left(W^x - W^u B^- + W^e C\right)\hat{x}(k) + W^u x_r(k) + W^u K_p y_r(k)\right).$$

Substituting the augmented state $x(k) = [\bar{x}(k)\ \hat{x}(k)\ x_r(k)]^T$, the state equation of the control system can be represented as follows:

$$x(k+1) = h\left(\mathcal{A}x(k) + \mathcal{B}\right), \tag{24}$$

where

$$\mathcal{A} = \begin{bmatrix} W^x - W^u K_p C + W^u B^- & -W^u B^- & W^u \\ -W^e C - W^u K_p C + W^u B^- & W^x - W^u B^- + W^e C & W^u \\ -K_i C & 0 & 1 \end{bmatrix}, \tag{25}$$

and

$$\mathcal{B} = \begin{bmatrix} W^u K_p y_r(k) \\ W^u K_p y_r(k) \\ K_i y_r(k) \end{bmatrix}. \tag{26}$$

In order to apply the Lyapunov method, a number of transformation are required to perform. Firstly, let introduce the linear transformation in the form

$$v(k) = \mathcal{A}x(k) + \mathcal{B}, \tag{27}$$

now, (24) can be rewritten as follows:

$$v(k+1) = \mathcal{A}h\left(v(k)\right) + \mathcal{B}. \tag{28}$$

Next, let introduce the equivalent coordinate transformation

$$z(k) = v(k) - v^*(k), \tag{29}$$

where $v^*(k)$ is the equilibrium point of system (28), and assuming $\mathcal{B}$ as a threshold or a fixed point, the system (28) can be transformed into

$$z(k+1) = \mathcal{A}g\left(z(k)\right), \tag{30}$$

where $g(z(k)) = h\left(z(k) + v^*(k)\right) - h\left(v^*(k)\right)$.

Now, one can present the main result of the paper.

Theorem 1. *The control system (30) is globally asymptotically stable if there exists a matrix $\boldsymbol{P} \succ 0$ such that the following condition is satisfied:*

$$\mathcal{A}^T \boldsymbol{P} \mathcal{A} - \boldsymbol{P} \prec 0. \tag{31}$$

Proof. Let us consider a positive definite candidate Lyapunov function:

$$\boldsymbol{V}(\boldsymbol{z}) = \boldsymbol{z}^T \boldsymbol{P} \boldsymbol{z}. \tag{32}$$

According to the direct Lyapunov method, the difference along the trajectory of the system (30) is given as follows:

$$\begin{aligned}
\Delta \boldsymbol{V}(\boldsymbol{z}(k)) &= \boldsymbol{V}(\boldsymbol{z}(k+1)) - \boldsymbol{V}(\boldsymbol{z}(k)) \\
&= (\mathcal{A}g(\boldsymbol{z}(k)))^T \boldsymbol{P} \mathcal{A}g(\boldsymbol{z}(k)) - \boldsymbol{z}(k)^T \boldsymbol{P} \boldsymbol{z}(k) \\
&= g^T(\boldsymbol{z}(k)) \mathcal{A}^T \boldsymbol{P} \mathcal{A}g(\boldsymbol{z}(k)) - \boldsymbol{z}(k)^T \boldsymbol{P} \boldsymbol{z}(k)
\end{aligned} \tag{33}$$

Taking into account the following property of the activation function [10]:

$$|g(\boldsymbol{z}(k))| \leq |\boldsymbol{z}(k)|, \tag{34}$$

(33) takes the form:

$$\begin{aligned}
\Delta \boldsymbol{V}(\boldsymbol{z}(k)) &\leq \boldsymbol{z}^T(k) \mathcal{A}^T \boldsymbol{P} \mathcal{A} \boldsymbol{z}(k) - \boldsymbol{z}(k)^T \boldsymbol{P} \boldsymbol{z}(k) \\
&\leq \boldsymbol{z}^T(k)(\mathcal{A}^T \boldsymbol{P} \mathcal{A} - \boldsymbol{P}) \boldsymbol{z}(k)
\end{aligned} \tag{35}$$

From (35) one can see that if

$$\mathcal{A}^T \boldsymbol{P} \mathcal{A} - \boldsymbol{P} \prec 0, \tag{36}$$

then $\Delta \boldsymbol{V}(\boldsymbol{z}(k))$ is negative definite and the system (30) is globally asymptotically stable. ∎

Remark 1. From practical point of view, the selection of a proper matrix $\boldsymbol{P}$, in order to satisfy the condition (36), can be troublesome. Fortunately, recently, linear matrix inequalities (LMI) methods have became quite popular among researchers from the control community due to their simplicity and effectiveness taking into account numerical complexity, and $\boldsymbol{P}$ can be easily found using iterative solvers.

4   Boiler Unit

The object considered in this work is the boiler unit dedicated for the investigation of diagnostic methods of industrial actuators and sensors [12]. The boiler unit together with the control system was implemented in Matlab/Simulink. The simulation model of the boiler unit renders it possible to generate a number of faulty situations. The specification of faults is presented in Table 1.

Table 1. Specification of faulty scenarios

Fault	Description	Type
f_1	output choking	partly closed (50%)
f_2	level transducer failure	additive (-0.05)
f_3	positioner fault	multiplicative (0.7)
f_4	valve head or servo-motor fault	multiplicative (0.8)

5   Experiments

5.1   Stability Analysis

The first step in the fault tolerant control design is the process modelling. As described in the previous work of the authors [3], different structures of the neural state space model were trained for 100 epochs using Levenberg-Marquardt algorithm. The best results were achieved for the second order neural model consisting of seven hidden neurons with the hyperbolic tangent activation function. With such model and the use of PI controller the stability of the control system during several faulty scenarios is investigated. The reference signal in the form of the constant value equal to 0.25 is used. Faults (presented in Table 1) are simulated at the $500th$ time instant, while the system works at the equilibrium point.

As described in [3] fault detection block started the compensation of faults in a reasonable time (after 30, 5, 8 and 10 time instants for f_1, f_2, f_3 and f_4, respectively). Convergence of system states of the original system (24), are considered. The results achieved in the case of the fault f_2 are shown in Fig. 1a. In Fig. 1b are presented states of the transformed autonomous system. All states converge to zero, which means that the control system is stable. The stability of the control system in the case of faults was also verified checking the stability condition (36) using a Linear Matrix Inequality method. To find the matrix P satisfying the condition (31) after each change of the matrix B due to linearisation, the Yalmip together with SeDuMi is used. Experiment was performed under Matlab R2010b (7.11) on a PC with Core 2 Duo T6500 2.1 GHz and 4096 MB RAM (64-bit operating system). Results are presented in Table 2. Low iteration number as well as the small average execution time guarantee that such calculations can be accomplished in the real time, assuming the sampling time bigger than 1 second. Such an assumption is the realistic one for the considered boiler unit.

(a)

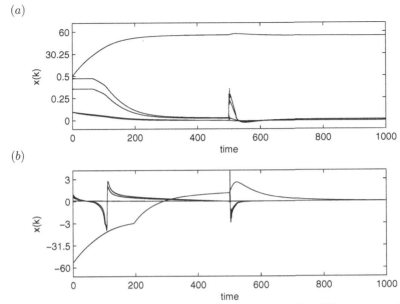

(b)

Fig. 1. Convergence of the control system states with faulty (f_2) system: original (a), transformed (b)

Table 2. Performance of LMI solver

Scenario	nofault	f_1	f_2	f_3	f_4
avg. time (s)	0.2021	0.2049	0.2059	0.2053	0.2025
max time (s)	0.2760	0.3570	0.3430	0.3050	0.3600
min time (s)	0.1940	0.1940	0.1920	0.1920	0.1890
avg. no iter.	4.0370	4.0350	4.0370	4.0370	4.0370
max no iter.	8	8	8	8	8
min no iter.	3	3	3	3	3

6   Conclusions

The purpose of this work was to determine, numerically and experimentally verify the stability of the fault tolerant control scheme for the boiler unit. The reported results shown that the Lyapunov direct method is very important and useful tool in this aspect. The presented experiments have proven that the proposed active fault tolerant control can provide stable work even in the case of faults acting on the process components, sensors and actuators. The very interesting problem is to define constraints imposed on the augmented control law assuring the stability of the fault tolerant control system in any case. These constraints can be defined extracting the knowledge from stability criteria. This problem constitutes our future research directions in this area.

References

1. Blanke, M., Kinnaert, M., Lunze, J., Staroswiecki, M.: Diagnosis and Fault-Tolerant Control. Springer, Berlin (2006)
2. Bonfé, M., Castaldi, P., Mimmo, N., Simani, S.: Active fault tolerant control of nonlinear systems: The cart-pole example. International Journal of Applied Mathematics and Computer Science 21(3), 441–445 (2011)
3. Czajkowski, A., Patan, K.: Robust fault detection and accommodation of the boiler unit using state space neural networks. In: Diagnostics of Processes and Systems - DPS 2011: 10th International Science and Technology Conference, p. [10]. [B. m.], Zamość, Polska (2011)
4. Ducard, G.: Fault-tolerant flight control and guidance systems: practical methods for small unmanned aerial vehicles. Advances in Industrial Control. Springer (2009), http://books.google.com.gi/books?id=UkVIaMsQQZQC
5. Isermann, R.: Fault Diagnosis Applications: Model Based Condition Monitoring, Actuators, Drives, Machinery, Plants, Sensors, and Fault-tolerant Systems. Springer (2011)
6. Korbicz, J., Koscielny, J.M., Kowalczuk, Z., Cholewa, W. (eds.): Fault Diagnosis. Models, Artificial Intelligence, Applications. Springer, Berlin (2004)
7. Löfberg, J.: Yalmip: A Toolbox for Modeling and Optimization in MATLAB. In: Proceedings of the CACSD Conference, Taipei, Taiwan (2004), http://users.isy.liu.se/johanl/yalmip
8. Nørgaard, M., Ravn, O., Poulsen, N.K., Hansen, L.K.: Neural Networks for Modelling and Control of Dynamic Systems. Springer, London (2000)
9. Noura, H., Theilliol, D., Ponsart, J., Chamseddine, A.: Fault-tolerant Control Systems: Design and Practical Applications. Advances in Industrial Control. Springer (2009)
10. Patan, K.: Artificial Neural Networks for the Modelling and Fault Diagnosis of Technical Processes. Springer, Berlin (2008)
11. Patan, K.: Local stability conditions for discrete-time cascade locally recurrent neural networks. International Journal of Applied Mathematics and Computer Science 20, 23–34 (2010)
12. Patan, K., Korbicz, J.: Nonlinear model predictive control of a boiler unit: a fault tolerant control study. In: Conference on Control and Fault-Tolerant Systems - SysTol 2010 [CD–ROM]. [B. m.], Nice, Francja, pp. 738–743 (2010) ISBN: 978-1-4244-8152-1
13. Puig, V.: Fault diagnosis and fault tolerant control using set-membership approaches: Application to real case studies. International Journal of Applied Mathematics and Computer Science 20(4), 619–635 (2010)
14. Sturm, J.F.: Using SEDUMI 1.02, a MATLAB* toolbox for optimization over symmetric cones (2001), http://sedumi.mcmaster.ca
15. Theillol, D., Cédric, J., Zhang, Y.: Actuator fault tolerant control design based on reconfigurable reference input. International Journal of Applied Mathematics and Computer Science 18, 553–560 (2008)

Variable Selection in the Kernel Regression Based Short-Term Load Forecasting Model

Grzegorz Dudek

Department of Electrical Engineering, Czestochowa University of Technology,
Al. Armii Krajowej 17, 42-200 Czestochowa, Poland
dudek@el.pcz.czest.pl

Abstract. The short-term load forecasting is an essential problem in energy system planning and operation. The accuracy of the forecasting models depends on the quality of the input information. The input variable selection allows to chose the most informative inputs which ensure the best forecasts. To improve the short-term load forecasting model based on the kernel regression four variable selection wrapper methods are applied. Two of them are deterministic: sequential forward and backward selection and the other two are stochastic: genetic algorithm and tournament searching. The proposed variable selection procedures are local: the separate subset of relevant variables is determined for each test pattern. Simulations indicate the better results for the stochastic methods in relation to the deterministic ones, because of their global search property. The number of input variables was reduced by more than half depending on the feature selection method.

Keywords: feature selection, kernel regression, genetic algorithm, tournament feature selection, short-term load forecasting.

1 Introduction

The short-term load forecasting (STLF) is extremely important to balance the electricity generated and consumed at any moment. Precise load forecasts are necessary for electric companies to make important decisions connected with electric power production and transmission planning, such as unit commitment, generation dispatch, hydro scheduling, hydro-thermal coordination, spinning reserve allocation and interchange evaluation.

Many STLF models have been proposed. Conventional STLF models use smoothing techniques, regression methods and statistical analysis. In recent years artificial intelligence methods have been widely used to STLF: neural networks, fuzzy systems and expert systems.

In this article nonparametric regression method is applied to STLF. The regression relationship can be modelled as [1]:

$$y = m(x) + \varepsilon \tag{1}$$

L. Rutkowski et al. (Eds.): ICAISC 2012, Part II, LNCS 7268, pp. 557–563, 2012.

where: y is the response variable, x – the predictor, ε – the error, which is assumed to be normally and independently distributed with zero mean and constant variance, $m(x) = E(Y \mid X = x)$ is a regression curve.

The aim of regression is to estimate the function m. This task can be done essentially in two ways. The first approach to analyze a regression relationship is called parametric since it is assumed that the mean curve m has some prespecified functional form and is fully described by a finite set of parameters (e.g. a polynomial regression equation). In the alternative nonparametric approach the regression curve does not take a predetermined form but is constructed according to information derived from the data. The regression function is estimated directly rather than to estimate parameters. Most methods of nonparametric regression implicitly assume that m is a smooth and continuous function. The most popular nonparametric regression models are [1]: kernel estimators, k-nearest neighbour estimators, orthogonal series estimators and spline smoothing.

In [2] to STLF the multivariate generalization of the kernel Nadaraya-Watson estimator was described:

$$\hat{m}(\mathbf{x}) = \frac{\sum\limits_{j=1}^{n} \prod\limits_{k=1}^{d} K\left(\dfrac{x_k - x_{j,k}}{h_k}\right) y_j}{\sum\limits_{j=1}^{n} \prod\limits_{k=1}^{d} K\left(\dfrac{x_k - x_{j,k}}{h_k}\right)}, \tag{2}$$

where n is the size of the random sample:

$$\begin{bmatrix} y_1 \\ \mathbf{x}_1 \end{bmatrix}, \begin{bmatrix} y_2 \\ \mathbf{x}_2 \end{bmatrix}, \dots, \begin{bmatrix} y_n \\ \mathbf{x}_n \end{bmatrix}, \tag{3}$$

d is the dimension of the input pattern vector $\mathbf{x}_j = [x_{j,1}\ x_{j,2} \dots x_{j,d}]$, which represents a vector of hourly power system loads in the following hours of the day preceding the day of forecast $\mathbf{L}_j = [L_{j,1}\ L_{j,2} \dots L_{j,d}]$:

$$x_{j,k} = \frac{L_{j,k} - \overline{L}_j}{\sqrt{\sum\limits_{l=1}^{d} (L_{j,l} - \overline{L}_j)^2}}, \tag{4}$$

and y_j is the encoded value the forecasted system load $L_{j+\tau,k}$ at the kth hour of the day $j+\tau$ ($\tau = 1, 2, \dots$ is the forecast horizon):

$$y_j = \frac{L_{j+\tau,k} - \overline{L}_j}{\sqrt{\sum\limits_{l=1}^{d} (L_{j,l} - \overline{L}_j)^2}}. \tag{5}$$

$\overline{L}_j$ in (4) and (5) is the mean load of day j.

The Gaussian kernel function used in (2) is of the form:

$$K(t) = \frac{1}{\sqrt{2\pi}} \exp\left(-\frac{t^2}{2}\right),$$ (6)

and $h \in \Re^+$ is a bandwidth (smoothing parameter).

The choice of a kernel is not as important as the choice of a bandwidth value. The bandwidth values decide about the bias-variance tradeoff of the estimator. The small bandwidth value results in undersmoothing, whereas the large value results in over-smoothing. In [3] there was shown that good results are obtained when h_k is calculated using the Scott's rule:

$$h_k = \hat{\sigma}_k n^{-1/(d+4)},$$ (7)

where $\hat{\sigma}_k$ is the sample standard deviation of x_k.

Estimator (2) depends on how many and which variables x_k are inputs of the model. In this article some wrapper methods of variable selection (VS) are tested: sequential forward selection (SFS), sequential backward selection (SBS), genetic algorithm (GA) and tournament feature selection (TFS) [4].

2   Methods of Variable Selection to the Kernel Regression Model

The proposed methods of VS can be divided on deterministic and stochastic ones. SFS and SBS [5], which are suboptimal strategies, belong to the first group. They based on simple greedy heuristics. SFS adds one new feature to the current set of selected features in each step. SBS starts with all the possible features and discards one at the time. The main drawback of these algorithms is that when a feature is selected or removed this decision cannot be changed. This is called the nesting problem. The extension of these strategies is plus l-take away r method and floating search method, where forward and backward selection algorithms are used alternately.

More effective, global optimization of the input variable space provide stochastic methods, such as GA. GA with binary representation is naturally adapted to solve problems of combinatorial optimization with binary variables, which include the VS problem. The GA, as the method independent on domain, has been applied to many optimization problems because of their robustness in search for large spaces and mechanism of escaping from the local minima. Search for the solution space in GA is conducted in parallel by population of chromosomes which encode the solutions. GA for VS was applied to various models: classifiers, clustering and approximation models.

In the GA approach, the given variable subset is represented as a binary string (chromosome) with a zero or one in position i denoting the absence or presence of feature i: $\mathbf{b} = (b_1, b_2, ..., b_d) \in \{0, 1\}^d$. Each chromosome is evaluated taking into account the model error (the forecast error here). It may survive into the next generation and reproduce in dependence on this evaluation (fitness). New chromosomes are created from old ones by the process of their crossover and mutation. One-point crossover and classical binary mutation are applied in this approach. Binary tournament is used as a chromosome selection method.

The TFS method was introduced in [4] as an alternative to other stochastic VS methods such as GA and simulated annealing. In comparison to other combinatorial optimization stochastic methods TFS is distinguished by simplicity. There is only one parameter in TFS controlling the global-local search properties which makes this algorithm easy to use.

Data representation in TFS is the same as in GA. TFS explores the solution space starting from an initial solution and generating new ones by perturbing it using a mutation operator. This operator switches the value of one randomly chosen bit (but different for each candidate solution) of the parent solution. When the set of new l candidate solutions is generated (l represents the tournament size), their evaluations are calculated. The best candidate solution (the tournament winner), with the lowest value of the error function (MAPE here), is selected and it replaces the parent solution, even if it is worse than the parent solution. This allows us to escape from local minima of the error function. If l is equal to 1, this procedure comes down to a random search process. On the other hand, when $l = d$ this method becomes a hill climbing method where there is no escape from the local maxima.

This algorithm turned out to be very promising in the feature selection problem, better than a GA and simulated annealing, as well as deterministic SFS and SBS algorithms [4].

The flowchart of GA and TFS are shown in Fig. 1.

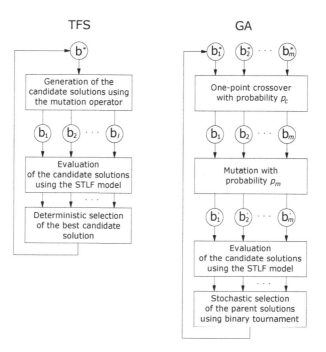

Fig. 1. Flowcharts of TFS and GA to variable selection in the kernel regression based STLF model

3   Application Example

The described above variable selection methods were applied to the forecasting model based on the Nadaraya-Watson estimator. The task of the model is to forecast the next day power system load ($\tau = 1$) at hour $k = 1, 6, 12, 18$ and 24. Time series studied in this paper represents the hourly electrical load of the Polish power system from the period 2002-2004. This series is shown in Fig. 2.

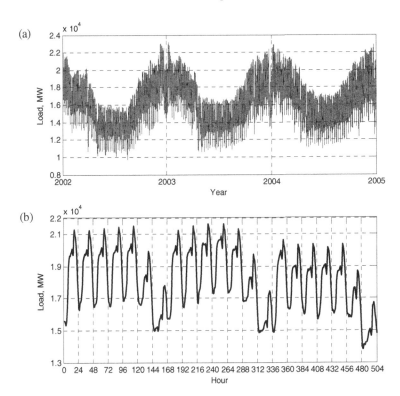

Fig. 2. The load time series of Polish power system in three year (a) and three week (b) intervals

The time series were divided into training and test parts. The test set contained 30 patterns from January 2004 (from 2 to 31 January) and 31 patterns from July 2004. The training set contained patterns from the period from 1 January 2002 to the day preceding the day of forecast.

For each forecasting task (the forecast of system load at the kth hour of the day $j + \tau$) the separate model was created using the training subset containing y-values representing loads from the days of the same type (Monday, ..., Sunday) as the day of forecast and paired with them x-patterns representing the load vector of preceding days (e.g. for forecasting the Sunday load at hour k, model learns from x-patterns representing the Saturday patterns and y-values representing the loads at hour k on Sundays). This routine of model learning provides fine-tuning its parameters to the changes observed in the current behavior of the time series.

The parameters of the stochastic variable selection methods were as follows:

- GA: number of generations – 100, population size – 8, probability of mutation – 0.05, probability of crossover – 0.9,
- TFS: number of iterations – 100, tournament size $l = 8$.

The best subsets of the relevant variables were determined in leave-one-out cross-validation procedure.

The training and test errors of the Nadaraya-Watson STLF model using different methods of VS are shown in Table 1. The selected variables of the input patterns and the bandwidth values corresponding to these variables for one of the forecasting task are shown in Table 2.

Table 1. Errors of the Nadaraya-Watson STLF model using different VS methods

VS metod	January		July		Mean	
	$MAPE_{trn}$	$MAPE_{tst}$	$MAPE_{trn}$	$MAPE_{tst}$	$MAPE_{trn}$	$MAPE_{tst}$
Without VS	1.62	1.20	1.54	0.92	1.58	1.05
SFS	1.37	1.25	1.32	0.90	1.34	1.07
SBS	1.37	1.20	1.35	0.90	1.36	1.05
GA	1.38	1.17	1.34	0.90	1.36	1.03
TFS	1.34	1.17	1.30	0.90	1.32	1.03

Table 2. The bandwidth values h_k corresponding to the selected components of the input patterns in the model for hour 12 on 1 July 2004

k	1	2	3	4	5	6	7	8	9	10	11	12
SFS	0.037	-	-	-	-	-	-	-	-	-	0.041	0.040
SBS	0.045	0.035	-	-	-	0.036	-	0.058	0.048	0.041	0.051	-
GA	0.044	0.034	-	-	-	0.035	0.064	0.057	0.047	0.040	-	-
TFS	0.044	0.034	-	-	-	0.035	-	0.057	0.047	0.040	-	-
k	13	14	15	16	17	18	19	20	21	22	23	24
SFS	-	-	-	0.037	-	-	-	-	-	-	0.039	-
SBS	-	-	0.041	0.046	-	-	-	-	-	0.050	0.049	-
GA	-	-	-	-	0.076	-	-	0.092	-	-	0.048	-
TFS	-	0.037	-	0.045	-	-	-	-	-	0.049	0.048	-

All VS methods ensure the training error reduction, but only stochastic methods ensure the test error decreasing. However, the difference between the test errors in two cases: (i) using GA or TFS to VS and (ii) without VS turned out to be not statistically significant. This was proved using the Wilcoxon rank sum test for equality of medians. The 5% significance level is applied in this study. In the case of the training errors the Wilcoxon test in all cases indicates the statistically significant difference between errors.

The average reduction in the number of input pattern components was: 76% for SFS, 52% for SBS, 60% for GA and 67% for TFS, which means that filtering more than half of the x-vector components should not adversely affect the accuracy of the model. The frequency of variable selection is shown in Fig. 3. Most information about the forecast are contained in the ending components of **x** representing the system load at hour 23 and 24.

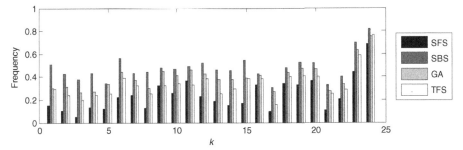

Fig. 3. The frequency of variable selection

4   Conclusion

The article describes an attempt to improve the performance of the kernel regression based STLF model by the selection of input variables. Four methods of variable selection were tested: sequential forward and backward selection, genetic algorithm and tournament feature selection. The first two are deterministic and local search methods, while the last two are stochastic and global search methods.

The empirical comparison between all of the presented variable selection method showed that the tournament feature selection provides the best performance of the forecasting model based on Nadaraya-Watson estimator. Both the training and test forecasting errors were the lowest when using this method. The global search property and simplicity (only one parameter controlling the balance between exploration and exploitation of the solution space) make the tournament feature selection easy to use and fast.

It is worth noting that the proposed routine of variable selection is local: for each test pattern a separate selection procedure and model learning is performed. Usually the feature selection methods are global, i.e. they determine one feature set for all test data. But in practice different features can be important in different regions of the input pattern space. The proposed approach enables the construction of an optimal model for the current test sample. Such a local model loses its generality but leads to the more accurate estimation of the regression curve in the neighborhood of the test point.

Acknowledgments. The study was supported by the Research Project N N516 415338 financed by the Polish Ministry of Science and Higher Education.

References

1. Härdle, W.K., Müller, M., Sperlich, S., Werwatz, A.: Nonparametric and Semiparametric Models. Springer (2004)
2. Dudek, G.: Short-term Load Forecasting Based on Kernel Conditional Density Estimation. Przegląd Elektrotechniczny 86(8), 164–167 (2010)
3. Dudek, G.: Optimization of the Kernel Regression Model to Short-term Load Forecasting. Przegląd Elektrotechniczny 87(9a), 222–225 (2011) (in polish)
4. Dudek, G.: Tournament Searching Method to Feature Selection Problem. In: Rutkowski, L., Scherer, R., Tadeusiewicz, R., Zadeh, L.A., Zurada, J.M. (eds.) ICAISC 2010. LNCS (LNAI), vol. 6114, pp. 437–444. Springer, Heidelberg (2010)
5. Theodoridis, S., Koutroumbas, K.: Pattern Recognition, 4th edn. Elsevier Academic Press (2009)

Software Modeling Language with Frames and Multi-abstractions: An Overview

Konrad Grzanek

IT Institute,
Academy of Management (SWSPiZ),
Sienkiewicza 9, 90-113 Lodz
kongra@gmail.com

Abstract. Static software analyzers should be able to work on an uniform software models and run uniformly implemented algorithms that would crosscut the borders of implementation platforms. We present an overview of an universal software modeling language capable of covering the semantic constructs that can be found both in object and functional programming style. Concrete and abstract elements of the language are being discussed together with the frame-based binding mechanism. We also give some insight into the implementation details, namely the persistence layer and the proper type hierarchies.

Keywords: Software Modeling, Type Theory, Compilation, Knowledge Representation.

1 Introduction

Source code analysis used in the software quality evaluation process is usually based on specific features of a concrete programming language. In heterogeneous environments, where many various implementation languages and/or their dialects are used, it is a severe limitation. Analyzers should be able to work on an uniform software model rather and run uniformly implemented algorithms that would cross-cut platform borders transparently.

The recent decades came with many achievements in the field of type systems theory ([5], [3]) and universal *object oriented* languages and software representation ([6], [7]). Some practical solutions were also presented, e.g. [8], [9]. Most of them concentrate on representing the object programming style and lack the uniformity required to encompass both object and *functional* (essentially $\lambda - calculus$) style.

We present a formal *Lisp* based language suitable to represent language constructs met in both *object-oriented* and functional programming styles. It is deeply rooted in some major types theory achievements and uses a simple yet powerful representation when approaching one of the most important elements of static analyzers - the symbol binding.

L. Rutkowski et al. (Eds.): ICAISC 2012, Part II, LNCS 7268, pp. 564–572, 2012.
© Springer-Verlag Berlin Heidelberg 2012

2   Motivation

There were essentially the following motivating factors behind our solution:

- We wanted to treat multi-methods as the main way of representing dynamic binding both in the functional as well as object programming style.
- Known universal representation systems do not put any emphasis on the nature of symbol binding in the compilers. We wanted to create a formal software model in which the elements of these essential mechanisms are the first-class citizens (namely Frames, Symbols and their correlations).

3   Core Language Elements

The first thing worth mentioning is the meta-model of our universal formalism. The meta-model assumes the persistent character of model elements. The persistence of elements that represent software wins two things for us:

1. The ability to analyze large code-bases that consist of millions of lines of code. Normally the representations do not fit in memory of a traditional end-user machine.
2. Compilers that compile to our model perform various aggregations and pre-processing. Storing processed data allows to use it later without a need to re-run the whole complicated process.

Model objects are stored persistently in a Berkeley DB based data store called a *Repo* (*repository* model). It is an effective non-relational, non-SQL embedded database with the following features:

- Simple type system with multiple inheritance and loose type checking (dynamic and weak) based on so called *R-types*.
- Reference based storage of persistent objects called *(R-obj)ects* using 8-byte representation of *(R-)type* and *R-id*.
- The ability to store sequences and sets of objects as well as mappings from *R-obj* to *R-obj*.
- The ability to store mappings from *java.lang.String* to *R-obj* (with low-level storage data type called *:R-bindings*).
- API mechanism to define custom storage data types.

The expression below defines a Repo type Frame used in our universal model (to be described later).

```
(R-deftype Frame [Map FrameValue]
  (:owner    :R-obj)
  (:symbsets :R-bindings))
```

Frame is a subtype of *Map* and *FrameValue* and it introduces two properties, *:owner* - a reference to an *R-object* and *:symbsets* - mapping *String* → *R-object*.
  In the following Fig.1. arrows mean a subclassing relation between *R-types*.

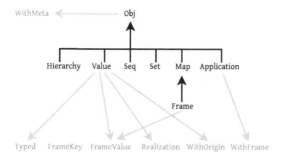

Fig. 1. Hierarchy of essential language elements

The core of our language is implemented as a hierarchy of *R-types*. *Obj* is the root of the hierarchy, *WithFrame* being a (mix-in) type that introduces some meta-information slots in the derived *R-types*.

Out of all defined *R-types*, three deserve a special attention:

1. **Value** is a type of all *R-objs* that represent *first-class* values in the modeled language environment. Every *Value* (potentially) possesses a type (as a *WithType* derivative) and may be a realization (*Realization* derivative) of some other model element. Property called *:origin* is a reference to an *R-obj* representing an expression or some other entity that produced this element as it's result, e.g. template instantiation.
2. **Frame** is the core of our *Symbol* → *FrameValue* binding sub-language.
3. **Application** represents the act of applying an *Abstraction* to a set of operands represented by a *Frame*, as to be described later.

The following sections contain a more detailed description of various kind of *Values*.

4   Values

All values are *R-types* deriving from *Value*. Their hierarchy is presented on Fig.2. In general they can be classified (somewhat informally) into two categories: concrete and abstract. The concrete values are supposed to be used as representations of corresponding concrete values in the modeled language/system environments. Their short description follows:

- An *R-object* of type **Unit** represents the only value (*singleton*) of *UnitType*.
- A **Record** is a representation of objects of *RecordType*. Every *Record* is also a *Frame* and thus it binds *Symbols* (*RecordType :components*) to proper *Values*.
- **Literals** are named (by inheriting *Symbolic*) values, possessing textual representation. String literal, e.g. "XYZ" or a numeric *floating-* or *fixed-point* literal 256.4 may be represented as *Literal* instances with proper *:type* (*Value* is an *R-(sub)type* of *Typed*) property values.

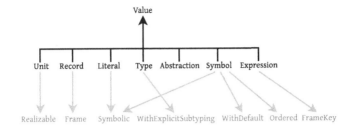

Fig. 2. Values and their hierarchy

Types, **Abstractions**, **Symbols** and **Expressions** are the essential model types capable of representing abstract artifacts in software. The rest of this paper is dedicated to presenting these model types.

5 Type System

The type system basically consists of the elements representing the classic types one can meet in various languages and styles. The detailed description of all the type system items requires a separate paper, so here only the major aspects will be presented.

Our type system was designed to include both the traditional structural (implicit) subtyping relation $<:$ as well as the subclassing relation $\ll$. These two relations, sometimes marked commonly as $\prec$, are not the same. As described e.g. in [3] or in [9] it is due to the *contra-variance* problem with methods that emerges from the typical subtyping rule that is *contra-variant* for the argument types in the left-hand premise:

$$\frac{\Gamma \vdash T_1 <: S_1, S_2 <: T_2}{S_1 \to S_2 <: T_1 \to T_2}$$

More on that can be found in [4]. In general, the structural subtyping is used to represent $\lambda - calculus$ and it's derivatives (the functional languages), while the subclassing is suitable for languages with nominal, class-oriented type systems. Contravariance problem solution is also given in our language thanks to it's multi-abstractions mechanism described in section 8.

When designing our type system we went further than [8] or [9] in that we extended all types including *RecordTypes* to participate in the subclassing ($\ll$) relation. It was possible because internally every *Type* (as all language elements) is a unique entity identified if not by it's name (*Symbol*), at least "named" by it's Repo *id*.

Sub-classing may be used in bounded quantification on types, e.g. the following generic class

```
class A<T extends B> extends C<T> {
  T obj;
}
```

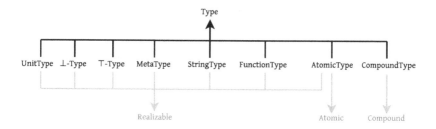

Fig. 3. Types overview

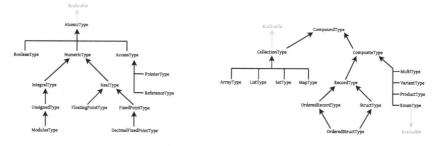

Fig. 4. Atomic types   **Fig. 5.** Compound types

is represented as $A \rightarrow \forall\, T \ll B\,.\,\{obj : T\}_{\ll (apply\ C\ T)}$ where $(apply\ C\ T)$ is a result of applying the *abstraction* C to T (see section 8).

6   Expressions

Our modeling language contains a set of *R-types* whose instances are created to represent expressions and statements in programming languages. To stay close to the functional approach we do not make a distinction between pure, side-effect free expressions and statements.

Every *Expression* possesses a corresponding *:value* that represents the value of an expression. If the Expression does not have any value, it's type is *UnitType* instance and value - the *Unit* instance.

Raise is another interesting *expression* type. It represents exception throwing statements. Thus it's type is an instance of $\perp - Type$ (a *bottom type*).

A detailed view of the *Expression R-type* hierarchy can be seen on Fig.6.

Every *Expression* has a *:parent* property. It is a convenient way to navigate the nested *Expressions* tree.

It is worth mentioning that every *Expression* is also a *Value*. This is the way to represent code-building abstractions, e.g. *macros* in *Lisp* family of languages.

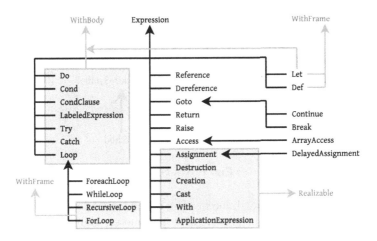

Fig. 6. Expressions

7   Frames, Symbols and the Symbentry Model

Recognizing meanings of names is a very important element of the static analysis process. Symbol tables ([2]) are key elements of a static analyzer, programming language compiler or interpreter. Integrating symbols recognition within the universal model is a crucial undertaking. Some initial work done by the author was described in [10]. Thus the constructs being described here are a natural continuation of previous attempts to solve this problem. A decision was made to refine our previous simple approach inspired by [1] and described in [10]. The approach assumes the presence of so-called *frames* and *environments*.

A *Frame* is a *Map*, that carries on *:bindings* property of low-level storage type *:R-map*. It's value is a mapping from *Symbols* to other model objects, more precisely the *FrameValue* instances. Besides the *:bindings* every *Frame* contains a *String* → *Set* mapping called *:symbsets*. It maps a name (*java.lang.String*) onto a *Set* of *Symbols*. This is how a *Frame* may contain many unique keys (identified by their internal *Repo* id) - *Symbols* of the same name. It is a very useful mechanism when modeling e.g. procedural names overloading in many programming languages. This is also an important extension of the basic frame-based symbols recognition framework described in [1].

The *Frame* may also be "owned" by some other model object. The proper reference is established with an *:owner* property.

The universal software model represents names as *Symbols* - the simple objects possessing *:name* property. When looking at Fig.7. it can be easily seen we use *Symbols* to model somewhat complicated real-life items, e.g. packages, object abstractions, classes, interfaces and symbols depicting types. *Symbol* is a key for *Frame*-based names recognition.

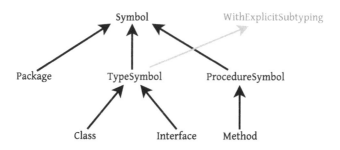

Fig. 7. Symbols

A *Symbol* instance can play different roles in the model depending on the way it is used, e.g. a procedure or generic type parameter, global name etc. When used as a type parameter, it must be able to participate in the ≪ relation. This is why the *TypeSymbol* derives from *WithExplicitSubtyping*.

SYMBSET CHAIN OF java.util.ArrayList

TOP-LEVEL Frame		f1 : Frame		f2 : Frame		f3 : Struct	
Symbol	Value	Symbol	Value	Symbol	Value	Symbol	Value
java : Package		util : Package		ArrayList : Class			

:scope :owner

Fig. 8. Symbentry model use-case

A (*Symbol . Frame*) pair is called the *symentry* (*symbol-entry*). A chain of symbol entries, as exposed on Fig.8. represents a search path to some program entity representation using it's qualified name.

8   Abstraction, Multi-abstraction and Their Applications

Abstract constructs are the key elements for building software. Our modeling language contains the elements to model abstractions, but also a successful attempt was made to solve the contravariance problem in the way described in [12]. Similar theoretical works were also presented in [11] and the practical ones in [13]. The approach is based on the idea of late binding of procedure bodies on the types of their arguments. In some real-world programming languages, e.g. Common Lisp (*CLOS* - the Common Lisp Object System) or Clojure this is known as *multi-methods*. It turns out the powerful idea may be used effectively to model not only procedural abstractions in programming languages. In general we use it to model:

– Methods overriding in object-oriented programming languages, including binding on the types of more than one argument.
– Parametric abstraction with generic (∀) types and procedures.

- Normal, early bound procedures.
- Abstract data-types (classes and interfaces).

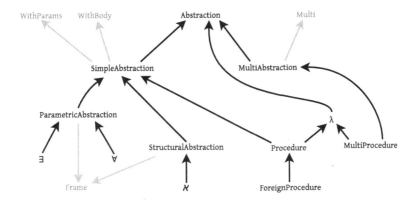

Fig. 9. Abstractions

There are the following most significant kinds of abstract (derived from *Abstraction*) language elements in our model, as presented in Fig.9.:

- **Procedure** and **MultiProcedure** used to model procedures and methods, with common λ category.
- **StructuralAbstraction** with major type called ℵ - a representation of abstract data-types.
- **ParametricAbstraction** with subtypes ∀ and ∃ to model parametric polymorphism in types and procedures.

A generic interface like the one below

```
interface I<T extends B> {
  void foo();
}
```

is represented as $I : Interface \rightarrow \forall T \ll B. \aleph foo. \{\}$

Every *Abstraction* may be further used to build an *Application* of it, i.e. the model object that represents of applying the *Abstraction* to a set of actual parameters (operands). The *Application* may be further specified to be an *:origin* of any *Value*, for example

```
class X extends B {}

class A implements I<X> {
  void foo() {
  }
}
```

is $A : Class \rightarrow \{\}_{:origin(Application\ :abstraction\ I\ :frame\ \{T \rightarrow X,\ foo \rightarrow (Procedure...)\})}$

9   Conclusions

Universal models of heterogeneous software and frameworks for static analyzers construction are very important tools for those who think about achieving high quality of software systems by performing systematical studies of it's
structure and semantics. The presented language covers the most important semantic constructs commonly found in object-oriented and functional languages.
We discussed the core elements of the language, hierarchies and *Values*: *Types*,
Expressions and *Abstractions*. We argue it's framework of *Symbols* and *Frames*
is intended to be a highly effective basis of static software analyzers construction
frameworks.

This paper presented only some selected aspects of our software modeling
language. More detailed descriptions is a question of future works.

References

1. Abelson, H., Sussman, G.J.: Structure and Interpretation of Computer Programs.
   The MIT Press (1984) ISBN 0-262-01077-1
2. Muchnick, S.: Advanced Compiler Design and Implementation, 1st edn. Morgan
   Kaufmann (1997)
3. Pierce, B.C.: Types and programming languages, pp. 1–632. MIT Press (2002)
4. Cook, W.R., Hill, W.L., Canning, P.S.: Inheritance is Not Subtyping. In: POPL
   (1990)
5. Pierce, B.C., Turner, D.N.: Simple Type-Theoretic Foundations for Object-
   Oriented Programming. J. Funct. Program., 207–247 (1994)
6. Bruce, K.B., Cardelli, L., Pierce, B.C.: Comparing Object Encodings. Inf. Comput.,
   108–133 (1999)
7. Abadi, M., Cardelli, L., Viswanathan, R.: An Interpretation of Objects and Object
   Types. In: POPL, pp. 396–409 (1996)
8. Wright, A., Jagannathan, S., Ungureanu, C., Hertzmann, A.: Compiling Java to
   a Typed Lambda-Calculus: A Preliminary Report. In: Leroy, X., Ohori, A. (eds.)
   TIC 1998. LNCS, vol. 1473, pp. 9–27. Springer, Heidelberg (1998)
9. Chen, J., Tarditi, D.: A simple typed intermediate language for object-oriented
   languages. In: POPL, pp. 38–49 (2005)
10. Grzanek, K.: Realization of The Design Patterns Occurrences Recognition System
    with Static Analysis Methods, PhD Thesis, Department of Computer Engineering,
    Czestochowa University of Technology, pp.1–192 (2009)
11. Castagna, G.: Covariance and Contravariance: Conflict without a Cause. ACM
    Trans. Program. Lang. Syst., 431–447 (1995)
12. Castagna, G., Ghelli, G., Longo, G.: A Calculus for Overloaded Functions with
    Subtyping. Inf. Comput., 115–135 (1995)
13. Salzman, L., Aldrich, J.: Prototypes with Multiple Dispatch: An Expressive and
    Dynamic Object Model. In: Gao, X.-X. (ed.) ECOOP 2005. LNCS, vol. 3586,
    pp. 312–336. Springer, Heidelberg (2005)

Enriching Business Processes with Rules Using the Oryx BPMN Editor*

Krzysztof Kluza, Krzysztof Kaczor, and Grzegorz J. Nalepa

AGH University of Science and Technology,
al. Mickiewicza 30, 30-059 Krakow, Poland
{kluza,kk,gjn}@agh.edu.pl

Abstract. BPMN is a leading visual notation for modeling Business Processes. Although it can be efficiently used for modeling workflow structures, it is not suitable for modeling the low-level logic of particular tasks in the process. Recently, Business Rules have been used for this purpose. Such rules are often specified in natural language and in an informal way. In this paper, we consider an approach to the integration of Business Processes with Business Rules. As a proof of concept, we propose a framework based on the Oryx BPMN editor integrated with rule-based tools. The goal of the integration of the BPMN editor with the XTT2 rule framework is to provide an environment for visual modeling processes with formally described business rules. We also discuss execution options of the integrated model. In the future, this opens up a possibility to execute such models using the HeaRT rule engine.

1 Introduction

Business Process Model and Notation (BPMN) [1] is de facto a standard for Business Process (BP) modeling. It provides a visual notation emphasizing the workflow in a process, and describes activities of the organization at an abstract level. The detailed logic of the tasks in the process has to be specified in other way. Recently, the Business Rules (BR) approach [2], based on the the Rule-Based Systems (RBS) concepts [3], has been used for this purpose. However, the common problem with BR is that they are often specified in natural language and in an informal way. In our research, we address this *visual modeling problem* by using the XTT2 [4] knowledge representation of Business Rules, which is both formalized and can be visually modeled [5].

Although there is a difference in abstraction levels of BP and BR, rules can be complementary to processes. A BPMN model can define the high level behavior of the system while the low-level process logic can be described by rules. Despite the ongoing research on this integration, there is no standardized and coherent methodology available. The integration details are not well specified, and there is not many tools which provide such an integrated modeling environment. Thus, the further issue is the *execution problem* of such an integrated model. In this paper, we give an overview of a solution for this problem as well.

---

* The paper is supported by the *BIMLOQ* Project funded from 2010–2012 resources for science as a research project.

L. Rutkowski et al. (Eds.): ICAISC 2012, Part II, LNCS 7268, pp. 573–581, 2012.

The rest of this paper is organized as follows. In Section 2, the motivation for the approach is presented. Section 3 describes BPMN and modeling processes in the Oryx editor. It also introduces the BR approach. Section 4 provides the description of the XTT2 Business Rules and the HQEd editor for BR. In Section 5, we present the outline of the Oryx-HQEd Integrated Framework. Section 6 provides an evaluation of the proposal in comparison to the related work. The paper is summarized in Section 7.

2   Motivation

Artificial Intelligence (AI) tools are commonly used as components in intelligent systems [6] and Software Engineering (SE) applications. SE uses visual languages such as Unified Modeling Language (UML) [7] for modeling purposes. Such languages are often derived from the AI tools, e.g. class diagrams derived from the classic AI frame systems. A diagram can replace even a long description and allows for a faster knowledge acquisition. It is a part of policy emphasizing the aspect of high-quality software.

In the case of Business Process modeling, UML is far too expressive and overcomplicated to be understood by an average business user [8]. Thus, the BPMN notation was introduced. Although it can perfectly model a workflow in the process, the detailed logic of the process tasks can not be specified in BPMN.

Business Rules are one of the solutions which can be used for the specification of task logic in Business Processes [9,10,11]. This opens a field for using RBS solutions from AI. Developing the integrated software for modeling BP with BR is therefore extremely important in order to ensure the high quality of information systems in the future. In our research, we address two main problems dealing with BP and BR:

1. The *visual modeling problem* – by visual editing the XTT2-based Business Rules.
2. The *execution problem* of such an integrated model – by running the model using the integrated environment with the rule engine.

In this paper, we give an overview of a solution for integration of Business Processes with Business Rules. The research is based upon our previous research concerning visual inference specification methods for modularized rule bases [12] and selected analysis and execution methods for Business Processes [11].

The original contribution of this research is addressing the two abovementioned problems during the integration process. We consider several approaches to this integration. As a proof of concept, we propose an integrated tool framework for BP and BR. The framework uses BPMN and the Oryx editor for modeling processes and the XTT2-based tools for rules [13]. Oryx[1] is a web-based editor for modeling business processes, which enables to model processes in a collaborative way. The tool is extensible by providing a plugin mechanism for adding new functions. In the framework, the EXtended Tabular Tree version 2 (XTT2) [4,14] knowledge representation for Business Rules and the HeKatE Qt Editor (HQEd) with the HeKatE rule engine (HeaRT) [15] are used as well. This allows for visual modeling of both Business Processes and Rules.

---

[1] See: http://code.google.com/p/oryx-editor

As to address the *execution* problem, we propose using the workflow engine which communicates with the HeaRT rule engine. The workflow engine can be either one of the Business Process Execution Language (BPEL) [16] engines (a subset of BPMN models can be transformed to BPEL) or some native execution environment for processes, such as jBPM². HeaRT, as a component for executing the logic of particular tasks, is responsible for handling, selection and execution of rules. Such an approach allows for executing a fully specified BPMN model.

3   Modeling Business Processes with BPMN

BPMN is a visual notation for modeling Business Processes using workflow-like diagrams. A BPMN model defines the ways in which operations are carried out to accomplish the intended objectives of an organization. It can be serialized to XML and further processed e.g. into languages for execution of business processes, such as BPEL. Although BPMN defines three models to cover various aspects of processes, in our research, we use only the main BPMN diagram type, Business Process Diagram (BPD), as it is expressive enough to model workflow structures.

A BPMN diagram, shown in Figure 1, depicts the process of a simple yet illustrative system, the Polish Liability Insurance (PLLI), which determines the price for the liability insurance for protecting against third party insurance claims. Because the insurance price is determined based on some data from a user, the first task (*Enter car and driver data*) requires interaction with a user i.e. entering the input data. Further tasks determine the insurance price: the base price is calculated first, then the calculated insurance premium can be increased or decreased, and finally, all discounts are taken into account and the final price for insurance is calculated.

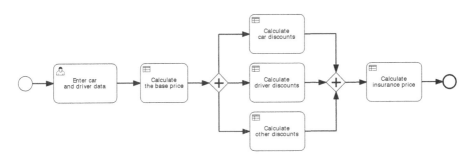

Fig. 1. An example of the BPMN diagram for a Polish Liability Insurance process

Although the BPMN notation is relatively young, there are more than 80 BPMN implementations of various BPMN tools³. In our research, we extend the Oryx editor.

Oryx allows for modeling processes in BPMN. The editor has been selected for our research for a couple reasons. It is implemented as a web-based application, what allows for collaborative modeling processes without installing new software in the user's

---

² See: http://www.jboss.org/jbpm
³ See: http://www.bpmn.org

operating system. Through implementation of a plug-in concept, it is possible to extend the application with new functions or adapt it to enhance existing functionality. The technologies used in Oryx conform to the standards from the World Wide Web Consortium (W3C), such as SVG, XHTML, CSS or RDF. Oryx also uses Javascript run in a so-called sandbox way in the browser, which prevents the execution of some malicious code in the system.

As the BPMN is used only for modeling the workflow between tasks, their low-level specification is not defined within the BP model. Recently, the Business Rules approach has been used for this purpose [11]. Although there is a difference in abstraction levels of BP and BR, rules can be complementary to processes. Especially, they can precisely define the logic of a process task, e.g. in structured natural language (refer to the *Calculate the base price* task in Figure 1):

```
If the car engine capacity is below 900 cm3,  the base charge is 537 PLN.
If the car engine capacity is between 901 and 1300 cm3, the base charge is 753 PLN.
...
If the car engine capacity is over 2000 cm3, the base charge is 1536 PLN.
```

Such a separation of BP and BR is consistent with the BPMN specification [1], which clarifies that BPMN is not suitable for modeling such concepts as rules.

4   XTT2 Business Rules

The main goal of the XTT2 [13,4,14] representation is to provide a structured knowledge representation supporting the logical and visual specification of rules, and allows for advanced inference control [17]. XTT2 provides formal rule representation language [18,4], based on the Attributive Logic with Set Values over Finite Domains (ALSV(FD)) logic [13], which is more expressive than the propositional logic.

Rules in the XTT2 rule base that work together in a common context are grouped into an extended decision table. Table 1 presents a simple decision table for the *Calculate the base price* task from the PLLI example. The table consists of two columns: the 1st one contains conditional attribute, and the 2nd one contains the decision attribute. Each row corresponds to a single rule that specifies the base insurance price.

Table 1. A decision table for the *Calculate the base price* task

Car capacity [cm^3]	Base price [PLN]
< 900	537
$[901, 1300]$	753
$[1301, 1600]$	1050
$[1601, 2000]$	1338
> 2000	1536

XTT2 has a well-defined graphical representation and is suitable for visual editors. An advanced XTT2 knowledge base composes a network of the decision tables. HQEd [4] allows for modeling an XTT2-based rule base in a visual way. It also provides an interface for plugins extending its functionality with integration with other systems.

The editor can continuously check the model against syntax errors, what allows for discovering errors at the time they appear. HQEd also provides several additional features, e.g. on-line model verification feature with HeaRT [19]. This is, however, out of scope for this paper.

5   Oryx-HQEd Integrated Framework

In order to address the *visual modeling problem*, the Oryx user interface was adapted for choosing a proper XTT2 decision table for a particular Business Rule task in the BPMN model. Figure 2 presents the integration of the BPMN Business Processes with the XTT2-based Business Rules for the PLLI use case. The model for this case consists of 6 tasks: a User task, which requires interaction with a user, and 5 Business Rule tasks, which are used to determine the insurance price. The BR task *Calculate the base price* triggers the chosen XTT2 table, which can be selected during the BP design. As the HQEd provides a socket-based interface for its services, XTT2 rules can be edited in the HQEd editor connected via network with Oryx. In such a case opening a rule task in Oryx allows for XTT2 editing in HQEd.

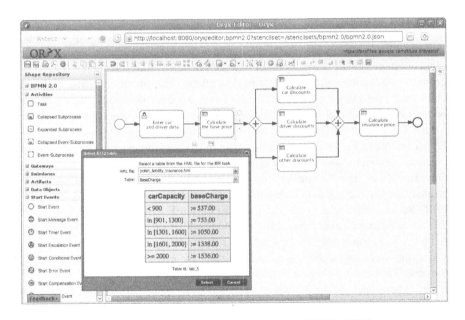

Fig. 2. Screenshot from the prototype Oryx GUI for XTT2

As to address the *execution problem* (the runtime environment for processes with rules), we propose using a workflow engine which communicates with the HeaRT rule engine. Such a workflow engine can be one of the BPEL engines, which follows a process description written in a particular BPEL XML file. As a subset of BPMN models can be transformed to BPEL and HeaRT can be used from the BPEL engine, this can be a potential solution for the execution problem.

Another option is using some native workflow engine for BPMN 2.0, e.g. jBPM. jBPM is a generic process engine based on the Process Virtual Machine (PVM)[4], which can execute business processes described in BPMN 2.0. It is not an isolated process engine, thus it can be integrated with HeaRT. Such an approach allows for visual modeling of both processes and rules as well as executing a fully specified BPMN model. An outline of the the Oryx-HQEd framework architecture is presented in Figure 3.

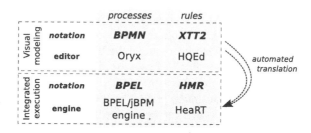

Fig. 3. An outline of the Oryx-HQEd framework architecture

6   Related Work

In the area of Business Processes engineering, there is ongoing research concerning the problem of integration of Business Processes with Business Rules. Knolmayer et. al [9] described a rule-based method for modeling workflows. The limitation of this approach, in which the Event-Condition-Action (ECAA) rules were used to specify the processes, is focusing only on several workflow patterns. A hybrid composition approach consisting of the BPEL process and several well-modularized Business Rules was proposed by Charfi and Mezini in [10]. It consists of two phases separating rules from processes. The authors considered using a rule engine for BP implementation.

Zur Muehlen et. al [20] considered the relationship between rules and processes. They analyzed the representation capabilities of two rule modeling languages, SRML and SBVR, in comparison to the Petri net, EPC, IDEF and BPMN 1.0 approaches. In [21] zur Muehlen et. al compared BP-oriented and BR-oriented approaches and presented a decision framework for process and rule modeling. Some guidelines for process and rule modeling according to the particular factors, such as change frequency, implementation responsibility etc. were described. This should help modelers to decide how particular aspects of the organization should be modeled. However, the presented decision framework does not contain the integrated methodology.

The abovementioned papers do not provide any tool for the solution but only describe the topic very broadly. Moreover, several of them do not concern the BPMN notation, which is de facto a standard for process modeling.

There are many tools that support Business Process modeling, analysis and execution [22,23,24]. However, only several tools are partially adapted for modeling processes with rules. Among such tools, there is no standardized and coherent methodology for BP and BR integration.

---

[4] See: http://docs.jboss.com/jbpm/pvm

The existing solutions much differ in terms of aims and scope. In Corel iGrafx Process[5] rules can be modeled using BPMN gateways, which controls the flow according to the value of attribute. However, this is a very limited solution. It is not possible to group such defined rules in decision tables or reuse them, and iGrafx does not allow for using rules in BPMN tasks. IBM WebSphere Business Modeler Advanced[6], in turn, supports the Business Rule tasks in models. Such a task requires to define the if-then rule schema and to specify the rules. However, this solution does not provide a visual specification of rules. Business Process Visual Architect[7] allows a user to depict single rules and rule grids within a BPMN model. However, such rules are only depicted in the diagram and can not be used in simulation or execution process. Drools[8] rule engine, in turn, is integrated with the jBPM engine, so selected BPMN elements can be used to control the inference flow. It constitutes one of the running example of rules and processes integration but does not provide any dedicated decision table editor for visual rule modeling [25].

Our solution outlines a tool framework which supports integration of XTT2 BR with BPMN processes modeled in Oryx. In contrast to the abovementioned tools which do not support advanced rule representations, we use decision tables for defining the task logic in the process. Such tables can be visually designed using HQEd. Rules in a table are formally described, and their syntax can be checked during the design process.

7   Conclusion

In this paper, we propose the integrated framework for BP and BR. The tool framework uses the Oryx editor for processes and the XTT2-based tools for rules. The goal of the integration of the BPMN editor with HQEd is to provide a framework for coherent modeling processes with rules.

In our research, we address the *visual modeling problem* by using the BPMN Business Processes and XTT2 Business Rules, both of which can be modeled in a visual way. We give an overview of a solution for the *execution problem* of such an integrated model. We propose using the workflow engine integrated with the HeaRT rule engine, which is out of scope of this paper.

As future work a full solution for executing the integrated model composed of BPMN process with rules is planned. Besides the solution mentioned above other directions are considered. First of all a translation from the selected BPMN diagrams to the HMR representation is partially developed [26]. It allows for obtaining a full model described by XTT2 rules. Another effort aims at translating XTT2 rules to BPEL. In this way, with the BPMN part translated to BPEL, a workflow engine could be used to run the whole model.

An important issue is the quality of the integrated model. The verification features of HeaRT can be used for formal verification of selected BPMN models and rule tasks. However, this is mostly local verification of single rule tasks or simple BPMN

---

constructs. A global verification of the complete model was considered in [27]. The verification process uses the translation to the Alvis modeling language [28], a language for modeling and verification of distributed systems.

References

1. OMG: Business Process Model and Notation (BPMN): Version 2.0 specification. Technical Report formal/2011-01-03, Object Management Group (January 2011)
2. Ross, R.G.: Principles of the Business Rule Approach. Addison-Wesley Professional (2003)
3. Giurca, A., Gasevic, D., Taveter, K. (eds.): Handbook of Research on Emerging Rule-Based Languages and Technologies: Open Solutions and Approaches. Information Science Reference, Hershey, New York (2009)
4. Nalepa, G.J., Ligęza, A., Kaczor, K.: Formalization and modeling of rules using the XTT2 method. International Journal on Artificial Intelligence Tools 20(6), 1107–1125 (2011)
5. Nalepa, G.J.: Proposal of business process and rules modeling with the XTT method. In: Negru, V., et al. (eds.) Symbolic and Numeric Algorithms for Scientific Computing: SYNASC 2007: 9th international Symposium: RuleApps 2007 – Workshop on Rule-based Applications: Timisoara, Romania, September 26–29, pp. 500–506. IEEE, CPS Conference Publishing Service, Los Alamitos, California (2007)
6. Tadeusiewicz, R.: Introduction to intelligent systems. In: Wilamowski, B.M., Irwin, J.D. (eds.) Intelligent Systems, 2nd edn. The Electrical Engineering Handbook Series. The Industrial Electronics Handbook, pp. 1-1–1-12. CRC Press Taylor & Francis Group, Boca Raton, London (2011)
7. OMG: Unified Modeling Language (OMG UML) version 2.2. superstructure. Technical Report formal/2009-02-02, Object Management Group (February 2009)
8. Nalepa, G.J., Kluza, K.: UML representation for rule-based application models with XTT2-based business rules. International Journal of Software Engineering and Knowledge Engineering, IJSEKE (2012) (accepted for publication)
9. Knolmayer, G., Endl, R., Pfahrer, M.: Modeling processes and workflows by business rules. In: Business Process Management, Models, Techniques, and Empirical Studies, pp. 16–29. Springer, London (2000)
10. Charfi, A., Mezini, M.: Hybrid web service composition: Business processes meet business rules. In: Proceedings of the 2nd International Conference on Service-Oriented Computing, ICSOC 2004, pp. 30–38. ACM, New York (2004)
11. Nalepa, G.J., Kluza, K., Ernst, S.: Modeling and analysis of business processes with business rules. In: Beckmann, J. (ed.) Business Process Modeling: Software Engineering, Analysis and Applications. Business Issues, Competition and Entrepreneurship. Nova Publishers (2011)
12. Kluza, K., Nalepa, G.J., Łysik, Ł.: Visual inference specification methods for modularized rulebases. Overview and integration proposal. In: Nalepa, G.J., Baumeister, J. (eds.) 6th Workshop on Knowledge Engineering and Software Engineering (KESE 2009) at the 32nd German Conference on Artificial Intelligence, Karlsruhe, Germany, Karlsruhe, Germany, September 21, pp. 6–17 (2010)
13. Nalepa, G.J., Ligęza, A.: HeKatE methodology, hybrid engineering of intelligent systems. International Journal of Applied Mathematics and Computer Science 20(1), 35–53 (2010)
14. Nalepa, G.J.: Semantic Knowledge Engineering. A Rule-Based Approach. Wydawnictwa AGH, Kraków (2011)
15. Nalepa, G.J.: Architecture of the HeaRT Hybrid Rule Engine. In: Rutkowski, L., Scherer, R., Tadeusiewicz, R., Zadeh, L.A., Zurada, J.M. (eds.) ICAISC 2010, Part II. LNCS (LNAI), vol. 6114, pp. 598–605. Springer, Heidelberg (2010)

16. Sarang, P., Juric, M., Mathew, B.: Business Process Execution Language for Web Services BPEL and BPEL4WS. Packt Publishing (2006)
17. Nalepa, G.J., Bobek, S., Ligęza, A., Kaczor, K.: Algorithms for Rule Inference in Modularized Rule Bases. In: Bassiliades, N., Governatori, G., Paschke, A. (eds.) RuleML 2011 - Europe. LNCS, vol. 6826, pp. 305–312. Springer, Heidelberg (2011)
18. Nalepa, G.J., Ligęza, A., Kaczor, K.: Overview of Knowledge Formalization with XTT2 Rules. In: Bassiliades, N., Governatori, G., Paschke, A. (eds.) RuleML 2011 - Europe. LNCS, vol. 6826, pp. 329–336. Springer, Heidelberg (2011)
19. Nalepa, G.J., Bobek, S., Ligęza, A., Kaczor, K.: HalVA - Rule Analysis Framework for XTT2 Rules. In: Bassiliades, N., Governatori, G., Paschke, A. (eds.) RuleML 2011 - Europe. LNCS, vol. 6826, pp. 337–344. Springer, Heidelberg (2011)
20. Zur Muehlen, M., Indulska, M., Kamp, G.: Business process and business rule modeling languages for compliance management: a representational analysis. In: Tutorials, Posters, Panels and Industrial Contributions at the 26th International Conference on Conceptual Modeling, ER 2007, vol. 83, pp. 127–132. Australian Computer Society, Inc., Darlinghurst (2007)
21. Zur Muehlen, M., Indulska, M., Kittel, K.: Towards integrated modeling of business processes and business rules. In: 19th Australasian Conference on Information Systems ACIS 2008, Christchurch, New Zealand (December 2008)
22. van der Aalst, W.M.P., ter Hofstede, A.H.M.: YAWL: Yet another workflow language. Information Systems 30(4), 245–275 (2005)
23. Monsalve, C., Abran, A., April, A.: Measuring software functional size from business process models. International Journal of Software Engineering and Knowledge Engineering 21(3), 311–338 (2011)
24. Lam, V.S.W.: Formal analysis of BPMN models: a NuSMV-based approach. International Journal of Software Engineering and Knowledge Engineering 20(7), 987–1023 (2010)
25. Kaczor, K., Nalepa, G.J., Łysik, Ł., Kluza, K.: Visual Design of Drools Rule Bases Using the XTT2 Method. In: Katarzyniak, R., Chiu, T.-F., Hong, C.-F., Nguyen, N.T. (eds.) Semantic Methods for Knowledge Management and Communication. SCI, vol. 381, pp. 57–66. Springer, Heidelberg (2011)
26. Kluza, K., Maślanka, T., Nalepa, G.J., Ligęza, A.: Proposal of Representing BPMN Diagrams with XTT2-Based Business Rules. In: Brazier, F.M.T., Nieuwenhuis, K., Pavlin, G., Warnier, M., Badica, C. (eds.) Intelligent Distributed Computing V. SCI, vol. 382, pp. 243–248. Springer, Heidelberg (2011)
27. Szpyrka, M., Nalepa, G.J., Ligęza, A., Kluza, K.: Proposal of Formal Verification of Selected BPMN Models with Alvis Modeling Language. In: Brazier, F.M.T., Nieuwenhuis, K., Pavlin, G., Warnier, M., Badica, C. (eds.) Intelligent Distributed Computing V. SCI, vol. 382, pp. 249–255. Springer, Heidelberg (2011)
28. Szpyrka, M., Matyasik, P., Mrówka, R.: Alvis – Modelling Language for Concurrent Systems. In: Bouvry, P., González-Vélez, H., Kołodziej, J. (eds.) Intelligent Decision Systems in Large-Scale Distributed Environments. SCI, vol. 362, pp. 315–341. Springer, Heidelberg (2011)

Solving Ramified Optimal Transport Problem in the Bayesian Influence Diagram Framework

Michal Matuszak[1], Jacek Miękisz[2], and Tomasz Schreiber[1],[*]

[1] Faculty of Mathematics and Computer Science, Nicolaus Copernicus University,
Chopina 12/18, 87–100 Torun, Poland
{gruby,tomeks}@mat.umk.pl
[2] Institute of Applied Mathematics and Mechanics, University of Warsaw,
Banacha 2, 02–097 Warsaw, Poland
miekisz@mimuw.edu.pl

Abstract. The goal of the ramified optimal transport is to find an optimal transport path between two given probability measures. One measure can be identified with a source while the other one with a target. The problem is well known to be NP–hard. We develop an algorithm for solving a ramified optimal transport problem within the framework of Bayesian networks. It is based on the decision strategy optimisation technique that utilises self–annealing ideas of Chen–style stochastic optimisation. Resulting transport paths are represented in the form of tree–shaped structures. The effectiveness of the algorithm has been tested on computer–generated examples.

Keywords: Optimal Transport Path, Transport Network, Branching Structure, Bayesian Influence Diagrams, Optimal Decision Strategies.

1 Introduction

The transport problem was introduced by G. Monge in a very famous paper, *Mémoire sur la théorie des déblais et des remblais* [10,4]. Recently this classical problem has gained an extensive popularity [1,14]. The original problem is to move a pile of soil from one place to another with the minimal effort. In 1942, Kantorovich introduced his formalization of a relaxed version of the Monge's problem [7,2]. The task of finding optimal paths was transformed into the problem of transporting a positive measure μ_s onto another positive measure μ_d with the same mass. The Monge–Kantorovich approach assumes that the transport cost is proportional to the distance and the transported mass. It favours thin routes rather than wide ones. Unfortunately it is not practical from the economic point of view.

In most transport networks, sending each particle straight to the destination is economically unrealistic. The preferable solution is to aggregate particles and move them together as it happens in tree leafs or on highways. We should mention

[*] Deceased author (1975 – 2010).

L. Rutkowski et al. (Eds.): ICAISC 2012, Part II, LNCS 7268, pp. 582–590, 2012.
© Springer-Verlag Berlin Heidelberg 2012

the Steiner tree problem where one minimizes only the total length of a network [13] and omits the cost of constructing edges. His model is not appropriate for our purposes because it does not discriminate the cost of high or low capacity edges; constructing a high–capacity highway is more expensive than constructing a backroad.

The first model taking into account the cost of edges was introduced by Gilbert and it has been extensively investigated in [14]. He showed that in shipping two objects from nearby cities to the same far away city, see Fig. 1(c), it may be more optimal to first transport them to a common location and then transport them together to the target. In this case, a Y shaped path is preferable to a V shaped path, see Fig. 1. In general, resulted paths form leaf–like structures. Biological leafs tend to maximize an internal efficiency by developing an efficient transport system for water and nutrients [16]. We should note that the presented problems are NP–hard [4,13].

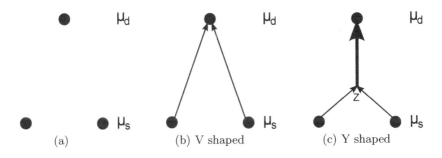

Fig. 1. (a) Three cities, two of them at the bottom are the source and the third city at the top is the destination for transported goods, (b) Monge–Kantorovich solution, (c) Gilbert solution, the interior vertex z can be determined analytically [14]

An influence diagram [6,11,12] is an extension of a Bayesian network [8,6,11,12], in which not only a probabilistic inference occurs but also decision making problems are solved. Influence diagrams are built on a directed acyclic graphs (DAGs) whose nodes and edges have standard interpretations stemming from and extending those used for Bayesian networks.

An influence diagram, similar to a Bayesian network, can be built with the use of chance nodes, which we represent as ovals. Also two additional types of nodes are introduced: decision nodes corresponding to available decisions (rectangles) and utility nodes (rhombi) specifying payoff functions (utilities) to be maximized by suitable choices of decision policies.

If the network is well designed, then the arcs leading to chance nodes specify direct causal relationships not necessarily corresponding to any temporal ordering. The arcs leading to decision nodes indicate the information available at the moment of decision making, thus feeding input to decision policies. The influence diagrams can be considered as generalizations of (symmetric) decision trees, see [6].

Finding an optimal decision strategy for an influence diagram is an NP–hard task. One can show this easily by reducing the traveling salesman problem (that is NP–complete) to our task.

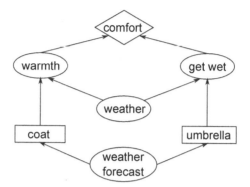

Fig. 2. Illustration of a simple influence diagram that includes two decision nodes: whether or not to take an umbrella and/or a coat for a journey. The decisions have an impact on the warmth and can prevent from getting wet from the rain, but if it does not rain, then carrying an umbrella has a negative impact on the mood.

In Fig. 2, an example of an influence diagram is shown. The decision node *umbrella* represents the choice whether or not to take an umbrella. Taking an umbrella does increase the chance of not getting wet during rain, yet it also causes negative effects, such as the need of carrying an additional weight. Further, wearing a *coat* decreases the chance of getting chilled but also negatively affects our comfort if the outside temperature is too high. All these effects are jointly taken into account in the utility node *comfort*.

There exists a number of algorithms for finding an optimal decision strategy for an influence diagram. For a detailed discussion we refer the reader to Chapter 10 in [6] and Subsection 5.2.2 in [11]. We focus our attention on the Chen–style [5] stochastic optimisation algorithm described in [9] which is well suited for our task.

In Section 2, we formalize the transport problem. Then we outline the transformation of the problem into influence diagrams. Results, technical details, and a discussion are contained in following sections.

2   Optimal Transport Problem

In this section we recall some concepts of Xia [14,15,16] concerning optimal transport paths between measures.

Let (X, d) be a metric space. We define an atomic measure on X as follows

$$a = \sum_{i=1}^{k} a_i \delta_{x_i} \tag{1}$$

for some integer k and points $x_i \in X$, a_i are positive numbers and δ_{x_i} is the Dirac mass located at the point x_i. We will work with the probability measures, i.e. we assume that $\sum_{i=1}^{k} a_i = 1$.

Let $A(X)$ be the space of all atomic probability measures on X. For measures on X,

$$\mu_s = \sum_{i=1}^{k} s_i \delta_{x_i} \text{ and } \mu_d = \sum_{j=1}^{n} d_j \delta_{y_j} \qquad (2)$$

a **transport path** from μ_s (source) to μ_d (destination) is defined as a weighted directed acyclic graph (DAG) $G = (V_G, E_G)$, where V_G is a set of vertices such that $\{x_1, x_2, \ldots, x_k\} \cup \{y_1, y_2, \ldots, y_n\} \subset V_G$ and E_G is a set of directed edges with a weight function

$$w : E_G \to (0, +\infty). \qquad (3)$$

Hence V_G consist of source, destination and intermediate vertices, see for example Fig. 1(c) and Fig. 3. The value $w(e)$ can be identified with the amount of goods transported along the edge e.

The balance equation for every $v \in V_G$

$$\sum_{e \in E_G, e^- = v} w(e) = \sum_{e \in E_G, e^+ = v} w(e) + \begin{cases} s_i \text{ , if } v = x_i \text{ for some } i = 1, \ldots, k \\ -d_j \text{ , if } v = y_j \text{ for some } j = 1, \ldots, n \\ 0 \text{ , otherwise} \end{cases} \qquad (4)$$

where e^- denotes the first vertex of the edge $e \in E_G$ and e^+ is the second vertex. It simply means that the total mass flowing into $v \in V_G$ equals to the total mass flowing out of v.

For any $0 \leq \alpha \leq 1$ and any transport path G, we define the **path cost** function $w_p(G, \alpha)$ as follows

$$w_p(G, \alpha) = \sum_{e \in E_G} \|e\| * [w(e)]^\alpha \qquad (5)$$

where $\|e\|$ denotes the length of the edge e.

The ramified optimal transport problem focuses on finding a transport path from μ_s to μ_d which minimizes $w_p(G, \alpha)$. The minimizer is called an optimal transport path. In other words, for a given G, and α we have to create a weight function such that (4) is satisfied and (5) is minimized.

3   The Algorithm

In this section, the formal description of our algorithm is given. First, we define the total cost function which is minimized during the optimization phase. Then we present the transformation of the optimal transport problem into an influence diagram and finally we translate an optimized decision policy into an optimal transport path.

So far we have assumed that each destination node receives a specific amount of mass. Such a strict constraint prevents us from applying many optimization techniques so we relax the above assumption and introduce a **disagreement cost** for a DAG G,

$$w_d(G) = \sum_{j=1}^{n} \left[d_j - \sum_{e \in E_G, e^+ = v} w(e) \right]^2 \tag{6}$$

which characterizes the difference between a shipped and expected mass.

We define the **total cost function** which is based on (5) and (6),

$$w(G, \alpha, c_1, c_2) = c_1 w_p(G, \alpha) + c_2 w_d(G), \tag{7}$$

where c_1 and c_2 are weights which control the importance of the **disagreement cost** and the **path cost**. The objective is to minimize the total cost function in (7) which is identified with the $-$payoff ("minus" because it is assumed that we maximize the payoff function) in the influence diagram.

Let us assume that an influence diagram $(\mathcal{S}, \mathcal{P}, \mathcal{U})$ is given, which is built on a connected DAG $\mathcal{S}$, with conditional probability tables (CPTs) $\mathcal{P}$ and utility functions $\mathcal{U}$. The set of nodes in $\mathcal{S}$ splits into chance nodes $C_{\mathcal{S}}$, decision nodes $D_{\mathcal{S}}$ and utility nodes $U_{\mathcal{S}}$. An influence diagram that describes an optimal transport problem is constructed in the following way:

- $C_{\mathcal{S}} = \emptyset$
- $D_{\mathcal{S}} = V_G \backslash \{y_j \| j = 1, \dots, n\}$
- $U_{\mathcal{S}} = \{y_j \| j = 1, \dots, n\}$

In addition, for each decision node $D \in D_{\mathcal{S}}$, a *randomised policy* τ_D is attached. It assigns to each configuration $\bar{w}$ of $\mathrm{pa}(D)$ (where $\mathrm{pa}(D)$ is a set of parents of node D) a probability distribution on possible decisions to be taken, that is to say $\tau_D(d|\bar{w})$ stands for the probability of choosing a decision d given that $\mathrm{pa}(D) = \bar{w}$. These randomised policies will evolve in the course of the optimisation process, eventually to become (sub)optimal deterministic policies which collectively determine the utility maximizing strategy for the influence diagram considered. The initial choice of τ_D, $D \in D_{\mathcal{S}}$ can be either *uniform*, with all routes equiprobable, or *heuristic*, provided some additional knowledge is available allowing us to make a good *first guess* about the optimal path.

The connections in $\mathcal{S}$ are replicated from the set of edges E_G. If V_G consists only of source and destination vertices and does not have intermediate ones, then we can add them either

- uniformly – producing a regular grid of vertices
- heuristically – an additional knowledge about preferred paths is provided
- randomly – all parts of the space are treated with equal probabilities

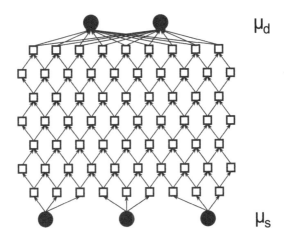

Fig. 3. Representation of an influence diagram used in the algorithm. Squares describe intermediate vertices where junctions can occur and dots represent source and destination of the mass.

Next we have to define connections between them. To preserve an acyclic property and equality of routes we assume that the atomic measures (the source and the destination) can be spatially separated by a hyperplane. Edges can by defined as follows,

1. For each decision node we define a maximal number of children k_d
2. $Q = \{x_i \| i = 1, \ldots, k\}$ and $R = \emptyset$
3. For each $q \in Q$, find k_q nearest neighbours of q, set them as children of q, and add to R.
4. If $R \neq \emptyset$ then $Q = R$ and $R = \emptyset$ and go to 3.

For such an influence diagram it is feasible to use the stochastic optimisation algorithm from [9]. Description of the algorithm falls beyond the scope of the present article. Results of the algorithm will be stored in the *randomised policy* τ_D. Using computed policies we can easily determine the optimal paths. Each policy describes where and how we should transport the incoming mass. Starting from roots of DAG we transport the source mass to the children according to computed policies.

4   Examples

In the first example, presented in Fig. 4, we reproduced the Gilbert solution from Fig. 1(c). The angle between merging edges was computed in [14] and is equal to $arccos(2^{2\alpha-1} - 1)$. Expected solution for $\alpha = 0.7$ is 71.36 degrees and the experimental value obtained from presented algorithm is equal to 73.5 degrees and highly depends on the distribution of decision nodes. The second example is presented in Fig. 5. Simulation of the influence diagram from Fig. 5 required 160 ms time per epoch of the algorithm [9]. The resulted transport path follows the expectations and results from [16]. It favours high capacity roads over narrow ones.

The programme has been implemented in language D [3], currently gaining popularity as a natural successor of C++. The implementation, aimed so far mainly at algorithm evaluation purposes, can be described as careful but not fully performance–optimised, with the total utility evaluation performed using the standard Monte–Carlo rather than a more refined and effective scheme. All tests were performed on a machine with Intel Core 2 Q9300 2.50 GHz CPU and 4GB RAM.

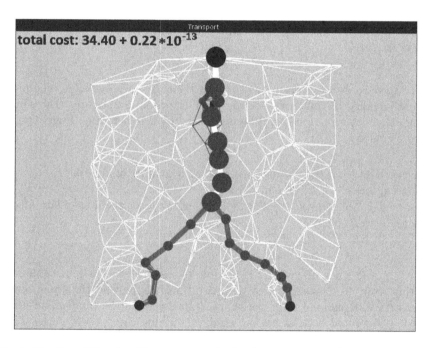

Fig. 4. Results of the algorithm on a graph that has 2 source nodes, one destination node and 200 randomly distributed decision nodes. Resulted transport path follows the Gilbert solution, see Fig. 1(c). In the upper left corner the total cost is presented in the form given by Eq. 7. Parameter α was set to 0.7, $s_1 = s_2 = 0.5$ and $d_1 = 1$.

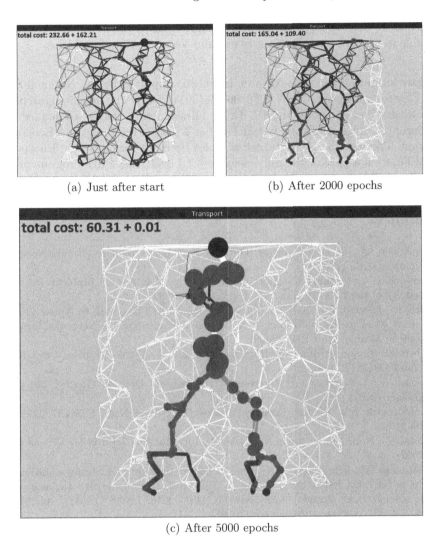

(a) Just after start   (b) After 2000 epochs

(c) After 5000 epochs

Fig. 5. Results of the algorithm on a graph that has 4 source nodes, one destination node and 400 randomly distributed decision nodes. In the upper left corner the total cost is presented in the form given by Eq. 7. Parameter α was set to 0.7, $s_1 = 0.2$, $s_2 = 0.4$, $s_3 = 0.3$, $s_4 = 0.1$ and $d_1 = 1$.

5   Conclusions

A new stochastic algorithm for solving transportation problem has been presented. The main advantage of the introduced method is its innovative application of Bayesian influence diagrams. Experimental results indicated the correctness of the algorithm. In the first test, the analytical result has been reproduced and in the second one our expectation for the solution has also been met. The Chen's style algorithm for solving Bayesian influence diagram has been shown as a powerful tool able to find other applications in machine learning related problems.

Acknowledgements. This research has been supported by the National Science Centre grant 2011/01/ N/ST6/00573 (2011-2014). The authors gratefully acknowledge the access to the PL–Grid[1] infrastructure that is co–funded by the European Regional Development Fund as a part of the Innovative Economy program. The work of M. Matuszak has also been supported by the European Social Fund as a part of the Sub–measure 4.1.1 (National PhD Programme in Mathematical Sciences).

References

1. Ambrosio, A.: Lecture Notes on Optimal Transport Problems, Scuola Normale Superiore, Pisa (2000)
2. Ambrosio, A.: Optimal transport maps in Monge–Kantorovich problem. In: Proceedings of the ICM, Beijing, vol. 3, pp. 131–140 (2002)
3. Bell, K., Igesund, L.I., Kelly, S., Parker, M.: Learn to Tango with D, Apress (2008)
4. Bernot, M., Caselles, V., Morel, J.-M.: Optimal Transportation Networks. Lecture Notes in Mathematics 1955 (2009)
5. Chen, K.: Simple learning algorithm for the traveling salesman problem. Phys. Rev. E 55, 7809–7812 (1997)
6. Jensen, F.V., Nielsen, T.D.: Bayesian Networks and Decision Graphs, 2nd edn. Springer (2007)
7. Kantorovich, L.V.: On the transfer of masses. Dokl. Akad. Nauk. SSSR 37, 227–229 (1942)
8. Koski, T., Noble, J.: Bayesian Networks: An Introduction. John Wiley & Sons, Ltd (2009)
9. Matuszak, M., Schreiber, T.: A New Stochastic Algorithm for Strategy Optimisation in Bayesian Influence Diagrams. In: Rutkowski, L., Scherer, R., Tadeusiewicz, R., Zadeh, L.A., Zurada, J.M. (eds.) ICAISC 2010. LNCS (LNAI), vol. 6114, pp. 574–581. Springer, Heidelberg (2010)
10. Monge, G.: Mémoire sur la théorie des déblais et des remblais, Histoire de l'Académie Royale des Sciences de Paris, 666–704 (1781)
11. Neapolitan, R.E.: Learning Bayesian Networks. Prentice Hall Series in Artificial Intelligence. Pearson Prentice Hall (2004)
12. Pearl, J.: Reasoning in Intelligent Systems: Networks of Plausible Inference. Morgan Kaufmann Publishers Inc. (1988)
13. Vazirani, V.V.: Approximation Algorithms. Springer, Berlin (2001)
14. Xia, Q.: Optimal paths related to transport problems. Communications in Contemporary Mathematics 5, 251–279 (2003)
15. Xia, Q.: Ramified optimal transportation in geodesic metric spaces. Adv. Calc. Var. 4, 277–307 (2011)
16. Xia, Q.: The formation of a tree leaf. ESAIM. COCV 13, 359–377 (2007)

---

[1] http://www.plgrid.pl

Knowledge Based Model
for Scheduling in Failure Modes

Hubert Sękowski and Ewa Dudek-Dyduch*

AGH University of Science and Technology,
30 Mickiewicza Av., 30-059 Krakow, Poland
{Hubert.Sekowski,edd}@agh.edu.pl
www.agh.edu.pl

Abstract. The paper presents an artificial intelligence approach to simulation and scheduling discrete manufacturing processes (DMP) in a failure modes. It presents a knowledge based model of DMP for the failure mode and a new conception of solving of failure control problem. The solving method is based on formal description of DMP given by the algebraic-logical meta model (ALMM). Authors propose the application of FMEA method to determine RPN coefficients that allows to choose simulation experiments for failure modes.

Keywords: knowledge based model, algebraic-logical model, discrete manufacturing process, failure modes.

1 Introduction

Number of works have been pubilshed on use of artificial intelligence in simulation and scheduling. Some of them are based on algebraic-logical model (ALM) [1, 2, 5–7]. The model application field expanded and covers not only manufacturing processes (for which it was worked out) but wider areas of applications (as an example logistics). With growing field of the model application it became the meta-model. This paper shows the algebraic-logical meta-model (ALMM) application for failure modes scheduling and simulation.

Ensuring the continuity of business processes (especially production processes) is one of the basic tasks in Business Continuity Planning - BCP [4]. It is also an important element of publications on Flexible Manufacturing System - FMS [3].

Business Continuity Planning includes the development of rather general instructions that help to evaluate factors negatively influencing production continuity and methods of restoring all business processes. BCP focuses on highly generalized level. There are no algorithms supporting quantitative estimation of possible delays, costs and influence of the potential failure of one component on the continuity of the entire process. Flexible Manufacturing System, on the other hand, takes advantage of achievement related to computer systems – particularly with regards to the assignment of tasks in multiprocessor and heterogeneous environments. Publications dealing with FMS systems touch upon

---

* This article was written as a part of the project: "Modeling and algorithms for control and decision making for discrete dynamics processes".

L. Rutkowski et al. (Eds.): ICAISC 2012, Part II, LNCS 7268, pp. 591–599, 2012.

system operation continuity but only in the context of such topology organization that a failure of one component does not interrupt production process continuity, but only influences its productivity. The latest publications [3], point out the need for further research aimed at determining the influence of repair times on the operation of a production system. This article is related to that research direction. Its aim is twofold:

- to present a knowledge based model of discrete manufacturing process (DMP) for the failure mode,
- to present a conception of control of DMP in the failure mode.

The paper shows applicability of the meta-model as artificial intelligence tool for failure modes scheduling and simulation.

2   Knowledge Based Model of DMP

Simulation aimed at scheduling of any DMP consists in determining a sequence of process states and the related time instances. The new state and its time instant depend on the previous state and the decision that has been realised (taken) then. Decision determines the job to be performed, resources, transport unit etc. Manufacturing processes belong to the larger class of discrete processes, namely discrete deterministic processes (DDP). The formal model of DDP will be here adopted for DMP.

Definition 1. *Algebraic-logical model (ALM) of a discrete manufacturing/ production process (DMP) is defined by the sextuple (U, S, s_0, f, S_N, S_G) where U is a set of control decisions or control signals, $S = X \times T$ is a set named a set of generalized states, X is a set of proper states, $T \subset \mathbb{R}^+ \cup \{0\}$ is a subset of non negative real numbers representing the time instants, $f : U \times S \to S$ is a partial function called a transition function, (it does not have to be determined for all elements of the set $U \times S$), $s_0 = (x_0, t_0)$, $S_N \subset S$, $S_G \subset S$ are respectively: an initial generalized state, a set of not admissible generalized states, and a set of goal generalized states, i.e. the states in which we want the process to take place at the end.*

The transition function is defined by means of two functions, $f = (f_x, f_t)$ where $f_x : U \times X \times T \to X$ determines the next state $f_t : U \times X \times T \to T$ determines the next time instant. It is assumed that the difference $\Delta t = f_t(u, x, t) - t$ has a value that is both finite and positive. Thus, as a result of the decision u that is taken or realised at the proper state x and the moment t, the state of the process changes for $x' = f_x(u, x, t)$ that is observed at the moment $t' = f_t(u, x, t) = t + \Delta t$. Because not all decisions defined formally make sense in certain situations, the transition function f is defined as a partial one. Thanks to it, all limitations concerning the control decisions in a given state s can be defined in a convenient way by means of so-called sets of possible decisions $U_p(s)$, and defined as: $U_p(s) = \{u \in U : (u, s) \in \text{Dom } f\}$.

At the same time a DMP is represented by a set of its trajectories that start from the initial state s_0. It is assumed that no state of a trajectory, apart from the last one, may belong to the set S_N or has an empty set of possible decisions. Only a trajectory that ends in the set of goal states is admissible. The control sequence determining an admissible trajectory is an admissible control sequence (decision sequence). The task of optimisation lies in the fact of finding such an admissible decision sequence $\tilde{u}$ that would minimize a certain criterion Q.

In the most general case, sets U and X may be presented as a cartesian product $\mathbf{U} = U^1 \times U^2 \times \ldots U^m$, $X = X^1 \times X^2 \times \ldots X^n$ i.e. $u = (u^1, u^2, \ldots u^m)$, $x = (x^1, x^2, \ldots, x^n)$. There are no limitations imposed on the sets, in particular they have not to be numerical. Thus values of particular co-ordinates of a state may be names of elements (symbols) as well as some objects (e.g. finite set, sequence etc.). Particular u^i represent separate decisions that must or may be taken at the same time. The sets S_N, S_F, and U_p are formally defined with use of logical formulae. Therefore, the model paradigm is a specialised form of the algebraic-logical meta-model (ALMM). According to it's structure the knowledge on DMP is represented by coded information on U, S, s_0, f, S_N, S_G. Function f may be defined by means of procedure or by means of rules of type IF..THEN. The presented paradigm of knowledge representation (ALMM) consists of the following main procedures realising rules IF..THEN, utilizes by control algorithms: procedure that generates and examines subsets of possible decisions $U_p(s)$, procedures that realize the function f (in the most cases it is a vector function), i.e. determine the next state $(x', t') = f(u, x, t)$, procedures that examine if the state belongs to the set S_N or S_G. All the procedures are based on information acquired from three sources: description of manufacturing process that take into account all its limitation, expert knowledge referring to control rules, results of computer simulation experiments. The basic structure of model of DMP is usually created on a basis of process technology description. Basing on additional expert knowledge (or analysis of DMP) subsets of states can be differentiated, for which best decisions or some decision choice rules R (control rules) are known. Similarly, some subsets of *advantageous* or *disadvantageous* states for the controlled process can be determined. Formally, the knowledge allow us restrict sets of possible decisions U_p. Knowledge represented by the basic ALM of DMP (def.1) enriched by expert knowledge creates the knowledge-based model KBM of DMP. The knowledge can be enriched further as a result of simulation experiments.

Basing on the model of DMP different classes of algorithms can be formally defined and analysed.

If the DMP process contains finite (or countable) sets $U_p(s)$ only, transition graph for the process is defined as a graph $G = (S, R)$, where $R \subset (S \times S)$ is a relation such that $(s_i, s_j) \in R \Leftrightarrow \exists_{u \in U_p(s_i)} : f(u, s_i) = s_j$. It can be shown that for all real DMP the graph G is acyclic one. The admissible trajectory determination is equivalent to determination of path in transition graph G for which a state s_0 is an initial vertex and state $s_d \in S_G$ is a final vertex. It is worth noting that admissible sequence of control signals $\tilde{u}$ determination is equivalent to the path determination. Not admissible trajectory is defined by analogy with the difference that final vertex $s_d \in (S_N \cup S_E)$, where S_E is a subset of states for which $U_p(s) = \emptyset$

3 ALM Application to Simulate the Manufacturing Process

When a structure of a discrete manufacturing process is established one can create its algebraic-logical model (ALM). The ALM provides a basis for simulation software of the process. This simulation program has a structure that reflects the elements U, S, f, U_p, S_N, S_G. Any change in the structure of the process (for example, adding machine, or a change in its effectiveness) is reflected in the algebraic-logical model (ALM). Consequently, also relevant parts of the simulation program has been changing. The simulation software is a part of information management system which controls and supervises the production.

Suppose we have a fixed set of production orders. Based on the ALM and applying optimization algorithms we can determine the optimal (suboptimal) rank orders and assign resources (machines) for individual operations. Formally, this corresponds to determining an optimal (suboptimal) admissible sequence of ũ decisions and trajectory s̃. For this purpose a variety of methods and algorithms for optimization can be used. They all, however, benefit from multiple trajectory simulation process. It is therefore very important to avoid generating the same sections of the trajectory. In the proposed conception the memorizing in database previously established trajectories and their states is applied.

Let $S(\tilde{s})$ denotes the set of all states of any trajectory s̃. These sets can be used when consecutive trajectories are generated. For each, just obtained state (the algorithm iteration), set of already generated states can be searched. The search goal is to find out if just obtained state belongs to the set. Fig. 1 shows the algorithm with highlighted modifications that allow to use the knowledge from earlier generated trajectories. This approach allows to save time – if just obtained state is determined as a state belonging to trajectory generated before, algorithm terminates and returns new trajectory. Moreover, the simulation analysis is easier as paths that finishes in the same final state are seen at first glance. If time instant variable is not crucial, proper states instead of generalized states can be stored and compared.

If information collection for control purposes search method [7] is applied, not only set of states have to be collected but also previously calculated trajectories. Current process subgraph (to be strict its current estimation) is collected for the most general case.

In summary, thanks to the formal model of the manufacturing process (ALM) it can be easily created a simulation program with a structure that allows to:

- avoid generating the same sections of the trajectory,
- easily take into consideration the structural and parametric changes taking place in manufacturing system.

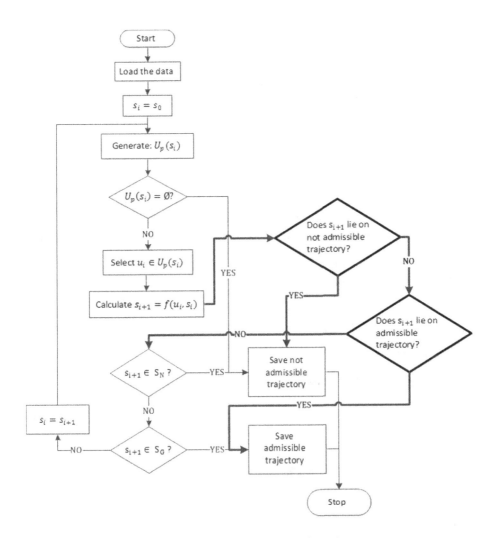

Fig. 1. Algorithm generating single trajectory

Simulation is carried out before the start of production and its results are used during the production. Before the start of production it is used for:

- optimization of job scheduling,
- a'priori acquisition of additional knowledge about the execution of manufacturing orders,
- simulation of selected failure situations and determining remedy actions.

During the production simulation results are used in order to:

- monitor the successive states of the process,
- detect discrepancies between the planned schedule and its performance as well as to detect and diagnose failure states.

4   The Use of ALM for Failure Mode

In case of failure occurrence, it must be diagnosed quickly and there should be taken remedy actions. However, the decision on remedial actions and further control must be taken in a real time. It is therefore necessary to prepare action scenarios before the production set of jobs starts. For this purpose the simulation model of production based on ALM can be used. As discussed in the previous chapter, changes in the structure or changes of the parameters of manufacturing system can be easily included in the ALM of manufacturing process. In the next step, these changes can be easily included in the simulation program. Therefore, there can be simulate a'priori various failure situations and appropriate continuation of production can be determined. However, the number of potential failure situations is very large. To solve this problem the authors propose to use the coefficient of Risk Priority Number (RPN) [8].

4.1   Failures - Estimating Effects

Failures, particularly their types and effects, are subjects of numerous analyses and studies. *Failure Mode and Effects Analysis* is one of the methods enabling quantitative determination of possible errors [8]. This method evaluates the influence of failure on process taken into account three parameters: occurrence frequency, consequences and easiness of detection of errors generating failures. All three parameters are in the scale of 1 to 10.

Occurrence frequency is evaluated by the so called occurrence ranking O (where $O = 1$ – insignificant frequency and $O = 10$ – very high frequency, errors are almost unavoidable). Error consequences are evaluated by means of *severity number* S (where $S = 1$ – no consequences and $S = 10$ – significant consequences, the system does not work). *Error detection number* D is established based on the possibility of removing errors thanks to planned tests and inspections ($D = 1$ – almost certain detection and $D = 10$ – detection highly improbable or impossible). Coefficients S, O and D are used to determine the *Risk Priority Number* RPN ($RPN = S \cdot O \cdot D$).

Processes whose RPN coefficient is higher should undergo earlier analysis.

4.2   Conception of Failure Control Problem Solving

There is a problem with failures occurrence and the manufacturing execution during the failures. A conception of solving this kind of problems is shown in fig. 2. The conception consists of two stages:

1. creating a knowledge based model of DMP for different failures,
2. working out a remedy method (procedure) in case of failure occurrence; the method uses the KMB models for failures.

Knowledge based model of DMP for normal (non failure) mode consists of:

- algebraic-logical model of DMP,
- expert knowledge – some rules for the best scheduling (control),
- results of simulation experiments – knowledge base on not admissible trajectories, admissible trajectories and their criterion Q values.

Knowledge based model of DMP for failure mode consists of:

- knowledge on RPN coefficients,
- algebraic-logical models of DMP for the differentiate failures,
- results of simulation experiments – knowledge base on trajectories for each differentiate failure (not admissible and admissible trajectories with criterion Q values),
- remedy rules for particular failures; the rules results from simulations experiments as well as expert knowledge.

Let sfm denotes any *state in failure mode*. An interruption (failure) occurs when the systems transfers from a state s_i to the next state. But, due to this failure, the system does not transfer to state s_{i+1} but to state sfm_i. The change in structure or functioning of the system caused by the interruption results in a change of the ALM for the fragment of the production process after the moment t_i. Directly after the failure is noticed, diagnosis has to be performed to determine type of the failure – that means determine sfm_i. If type of the failure is known, it is possible to determine possible remedy scenarios. Particularly the scenarios may assume:

- the total repair; after the repair, the system transfers into the mode s_{i+1}'. (in particular cases this may be a previously determined state).
- partial repair or no repair; in this case the system stays in failure mode.

The simulation results in a set of rules to follow in order to minimize failure effects:

- failure type 1 - remedy rules for failure type 1,
- failure type 2 - remedy rules for failure type 2,
- (...),
- failure type n - remedy rules for failure type n.

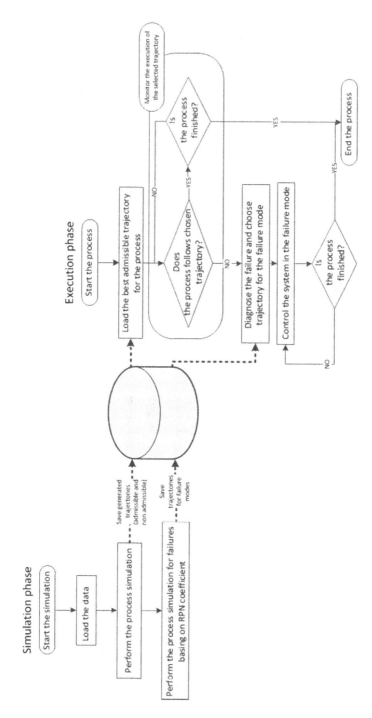

Fig. 2. Conception of failure control problem solving

5   Conclusion

This paper presents conception of solving failure control problem for discrete manufacturing processes. The conception is two stages. The knowledge based model (KBM) for the failure control is proposed and remedy method is work out. Both, the knowledge based model as well as the remedy method use formal description of discrete manufacturing process given by the algebraic-logical meta model (ALMM) that is defined in the paper. Application of the ALMM allows to present the conception on a high abstract level. Thanks to it, the presented conception can by applied not only for manufacturing process but also for the others, e.g. logistic ones. Moreover application of meta model allows to easy modification of simulation software based on the meta model. The modifications are necessary for failure mode simulation.

Authors propose the application of the FMEA method which makes it possible to determine RPN (risk priority numbers) coefficients for particular machines. Those coefficients enable the sequencing of predicted failures. In accordance with such sequencing, simulation experiments for particular failure modes are conducted in order to develop sets of remedy rules which would minimize failure effects.

Preliminary experiments have confirmed usefulness of the presented conception.

References

1. Dudek-Dyduch, E., Kucharska, E.: Learning Method for Co-operation. In: Jedrzejowicz, P., Nguyen, N.T., Hoang, K. (eds.) ICCCI 2011, Part II. LNCS (LNAI), vol. 6923, pp. 290–300. Springer, Heidelberg (2011) ISBN 978-3-642-23937-3
2. Dudek-Dyduch, E., Kucharska, E.: Optimization learning method for discrete process control. In: Proceedings of the 8th International Conference on Informatics in Control, Automation and Robotics, ICINCO 2011, Noordwijkerhout, The Netherlands, July 28-31, vol. 1, pp. 24–33 (2011) ISBN 978-989-8425-74-4
3. Joseph, O.A., Sridharan, R.: Evaluation of routing flexibility of a flexible manufacturing system using simulation modelling and analysis. Int. J. Adv. Manuf. Technol. (2011), doi:10.1007/s00170-011-3153-5
4. Bosworth, S., Kabay, M.E., Whyne, E.: Computer Security Handbook. In: Business Continuity Planning by Michael Miora, 5th edn., ch.58. John Wiley & Sons (2009) ISBN:9780471716525
5. Dutkiewicz, L., Kucharska, E., Kraszewska, M.: Scheduling of preparatory work in mine simulation algorithms. Mineral Resources Management, 2008 t. 24 z. 3/3, Krakow (2008) ISSN 0860-0953
6. Dudek-Dyduch, E., Dyduch, T.: Learning Algorithms for Scheduling Using Knowledge Based Model. In: Rutkowski, L., Tadeusiewicz, R., Zadeh, L.A., Żurada, J.M. (eds.) ICAISC 2006. LNCS (LNAI), vol. 4029, pp. 1091–1100. Springer, Heidelberg (2006)
7. Dudek-Dyduch, E.: Learning based algorithm in scheduling. Journal of Intelligent Manufacturing (JIM) 11(2), 135–143 (2000)
8. McDermott, R., Mikulak, R., Beauregard, M.: The Basics of FMEA, 2nd edn. Productivity Press (2009) ISBN:9781563273773

Modified Approximation
Based Optimization Strategy

Łukasz Sztangret and Jan Kusiak

Department of Applied Computer Science and Modelling,
AGH University of Science and Technology,
Al. Mickiewicza 30, 30-059 Kraków, Poland
szt@agh.edu.pl
http://www.isim.agh.edu.pl

Abstract. The paper presents the Approximation Based Optimization
(ABO) strategy and its modification, which allows decrease the optimization computing time through the reduction of a number of objective
function calls. It also gives the acceleration of a convergence of the optimization procedure. Elaborated strategy was validated using the Rastrigin's benchmark function and in optimizing of the real industrial
metallurgical process.

Keywords: optimization, approximation strategy, DP steel, cooling
process.

1 Introduction

Optimization of industrial processes is a difficult task. Searching for the optimal
solution requires a reliable mathematical model of the process, defining the objective function, optimization variables, a range of their limits as well as additional
restrictions arising from the nature of the process, etc. The objective function
is determined on the basis of the model's output values. Mathematical models
of metallurgical processes are most often based on the finite-element method
(FEM). Simulations of the FEM models of complex systems may last few days
or even longer. Therefore, the optimization of such processes is difficult (or sometimes impossible) due to the fact of necessary objective function calls requiring
time consuming simulations of FEM models. This is why optimization strategies, which allow reduction of a number of objective function calls, are searched.
The Approximation Based Optimization (ABO) strategy described in [3,4] allows decrease the necessary objective function calls, and moreover is resistant to
problems caused by non-linearity, discontinuity or multimodality of the objective functions. The paper presents the idea of ABO strategy and the proposition
of its modification. The Modified Approximation Based Optimization strategy
(MABO) was validated by optimization of the Rastrigin's benchmark function
and also by optimization of an industrial, metallurgical process of cooling of dual
phase steels. The results obtained from the MABO strategy were compared with
results of chosen heuristic optimization techniques: genetic algorithms, evolution

L. Rutkowski et al. (Eds.): ICAISC 2012, Part II, LNCS 7268, pp. 600–607, 2012.

algorithms, the particle swarm optimization, the simulated annealing method, ant colony optimization and artificial immune system [1,2,5,9,10,12].

2   Approximation Based Optimization Strategy and Its Modification

The Approximation Based Optimization strategy is an iterative optimization technique. Its main idea focus on fact, that the optimal solution of the considered objective function f is not searched directly, but indirectly. In each iteration, the analyzed objective function f is replaced by an approximation function g and the optimization procedure searches the optimal solution among solutions of a function g. Optimization procedure begins with establishing of the initial set $X^{(0)} \in D \subset \mathbb{R}^n$ consisting of feasible solutions. For each element $\mathbf{x} \in X^{(0)}$, $i = 1, 2, \ldots, m$, the objective function value is computed and, as a result, a set $\{X^{(0)}, Y^{(0)} = f(X^{(0)})\}$ is created. Based on this set, coefficients of approximation function g are calculated. The coefficients of function g are obtained by solving a system of linear equations expressing the approximation error ε in the approximation points:

$$\varepsilon = \sum_{i=1}^{m} (g(\mathbf{x}^i) - f(\mathbf{x}^i))^2 \tag{1}$$

Next, minimal solution of a function g is searched using any of the optimization techniques, and the found value $\mathbf{x}^*$ is being added to a set $X^{(0)}$ resulting in a new data set $\{X^{(1)}, Y^{(1)}\}$. New approximation g of a function f is evaluated on the basis of that new data set, and the whole procedure is continued until a stop condition is reached.

The aim of proposed modification is to increase of the importance of the approximation points lying in the close neighborhood of the actual minimum. This can be done through the adjustment of a shape of the approximation function, which can be realized by implementing of the weights to the optimization error at every approximation point. The values of weights w^i ($i = 1, 2, \ldots, m$) in each of the approximation points depend on the values of the objective function in these points. The smaller is the objective function value, the higher weight value should be. Proposed modification yields the following new form of equation (1):

$$\varepsilon = \sum_{i=1}^{m} w^i (g(\mathbf{x}^i) - f(\mathbf{x}^i))^2 \tag{2}$$

As the result of that modification, the function g is built on the basis of a set $\{X^{(0)}, Y^{(0)}, W^{(0)}\}$. Introduction of weights w^i and the appropriate control of their values improve the convergence of optimization process.

Within the scope of this paper, the approximation function g was limited to a square function, described by a following equation:

$$g(\mathbf{x}) = \mathbf{x}^T A \mathbf{x} + \mathbf{b}^T \mathbf{x} + c \tag{3}$$

where: $\mathbf{x} \in D \subset \mathbb{R}^n$; $A = A^T$.

If a matrix A is positively defined, the minimum is calculated using the relation:

$$\mathbf{x}^* = -\frac{1}{2}A^{-1}\mathbf{b} \tag{4}$$

There are two possible locations of the found point $\mathbf{x}^*$. In the first case, if the point $\mathbf{x}^*$ belongs to the domain D, its neighborhood of a radius R is investigated:

- If a number of points in that neighborhood is sufficient (eg. more or equal to $0.5n^2 + 1.5n + 1$, where n is a dimension of $\mathbf{x}$), the local approximation is made using square function h of the form (3). The minimum of a function h in the neighborhood defined by radius R becomes a new, more accurate optimal solution $\mathbf{x}^*$.
- Otherwise, if the neighborhood R does not contain required number of points, a local approximation is not performed.

Next, the values of the objective function $f(\mathbf{x}^*)$ and corresponding weight w^* are calculated. The weight w^* is computed as the linear relationship between the maximal and minimal values of the weights $W^{(i)}$.

In the second case, if $\mathbf{x}^*$ does not belong to the domain D, a point $\mathbf{x} \in X$, for which the objective function has the smallest value, becomes a new minimal solution $\mathbf{x}^*$. Similar situation occurs in the case, when a matrix A is not positively defined.

The weights w^i corresponding to all approximation points are modified in the next step. A first degree spline function η determined by three nodes: U, V and Z (Figure 1a) is used in modification of these weights. The argument of this function is $\xi = \|\mathbf{x}^* - \mathbf{x}\|$, which is the distance of a given point from the current minimum. The coordinates of nodes U, V and Z determining a shape of a function η, are:

$$\begin{aligned}
\xi_U &= 0 \\
\eta_U &= c_1 \\
\xi_V &= (\alpha - \beta)\exp^{-\gamma\,i} \\
\eta_V &= c_2 \in [\eta_Z, \eta_U] \\
\xi_Z &= \max\{\|\mathbf{x}^* - \mathbf{x}\|\} \\
\eta_Z &= c_3
\end{aligned} \tag{5}$$

where: α and β are coefficients responsible for the initial and the final values of the abscissa of point V, respectively; γ is responsible for the rate of changes; c_1, c_2 and c_3 are algorithm parameters which values are 1, 0.5 and 0.1, respectively; i is iteration number.

Each values w_i is multiplied by the value of the spline function η. As the distance $\xi = \|\mathbf{x}^* - \mathbf{x}\|$ increases, the weight of the point becomes smaller. During optimization procedure, abscissa of V point is decreasing (Figure 1b) by what weights of points lying far from minimum have smaller impact on coefficients of approximation function.

The procedure ends when the maximum number of iterations (or objective function calls) is reached or the obtained solution is satisfactory.

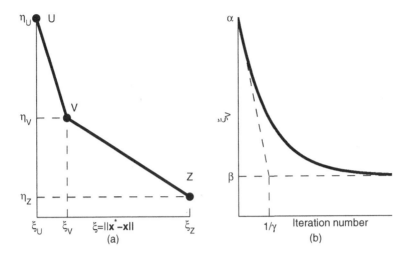

Fig. 1. Spline function η controlling changes of the weights w_i (a) and the variation of an abscissa of a V point (b)

3   Validation and Industrial Application of the MABO Strategy

Developed Modified Approximation Based Optimization (MABO) strategy was validated by optimization of the Rastrigin's benchmark function:

$$y(x_1, x_2) = x_1^2 + x_2^2 - \cos(18x_1) - \cos(18x_2) + 2 \qquad (6)$$

where: $\mathbf{x} \in [-0.2, 0.8] \times [-0.2, 0.8]$.

The obtained results of the MABO strategy were compared with the results of chosen heuristic optimization methods: genetic algorithms (GA), evolutionary algorithms (EA) (strategies $(1+1)$, $(\mu + \lambda)$, (μ, λ)), particle swarm optimization (PSO), simulated annealing method (SA), ant colony optimization (ACO) and artificial immune system (AIS). The MABO strategy gives better optimization results of the Rastrigin's benchmark function in much lower number of iterations (see Table 1). The optimization with the use of each of the non-deterministic algorithms was performed 8 times. To compare the efficiency of all algorithms an effectiveness factor, defined as a product of a mean objective function calls and a mean optimum value, was calculated. Low value of the effectiveness factor means, that the algorithm turns out to be better in considered optimization problem. Figure 4 shows graphically the comparison of the effectiveness factor obtained using the MABO strategy and applied heuristic algorithms. As it can be seen, MABO strategy gives the lowest value of the effectiveness factor (Figure 4a).

The MABO strategy was validated also by optimization of a real, industrial metallurgical problem. Optimization problem of cooling of dual phase steel sheets after rolling was considered. Dual phase (DP) steels are more and more widely used in automotive industry. Their structure is composed of islands of hard martensite (20-30%) in a matrix of soft ferrite (70-80%) [7,8]. Such a structure is obtained in the process of rolled metal sheet in a three-step cooling cycle (Figure 2):

- fast cooling to the temperature of the greatest speed of ferritic transformation,
- maintaining at this temperature until the required ferrite volume fraction is reached,
- again, fast cooling is such a way as to ensure that the rest of the austenite is converted into martensite, and an amount of bainite in the final product is minimized.

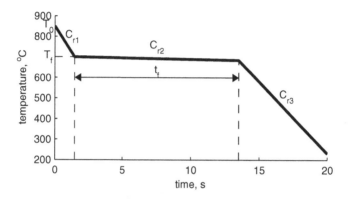

Fig. 2. Typical cooling scheme for DP steel

Based on the performed sensitivity analysis [6], two parameters were chosen as decision variables: dwelling time at a low cooling rate within the range of ferritic transformation temperature t_f, and the temperature at the beginning of the second step of the cycle T_f. By changing these parameters, an attempt to obtain steel with the following required percentage of volume fractions of martensite $F_{m0} - 0.2$, bainite $F_{b0} = 0$ and perlite $F_{p0} = 0$ was carried out. The volume fractions of the martensite, bainite and perlite are functions of t_f and T_f described in the work [11]. The objective function is defined as the root square mean error of considered volume fractions in the following form:

$$\Phi = \sqrt{\left(\frac{F_m - F_{m0}}{F_m}\right)^2 + F_b^2 + F_p^2} \tag{7}$$

The plot of the objective function (7) for the cooling process is shown in Figure 3.

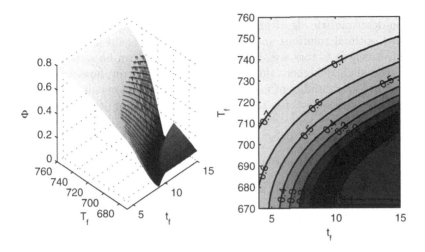

Fig. 3. Objective function of the cooling scheme for DP steel

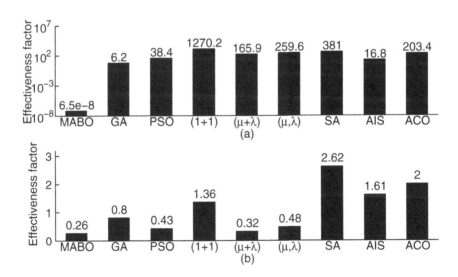

Fig. 4. Comparison of the effectiveness factors of MABO strategy and considered heuristic algorithms in optimization of the Rastrigin's function (a) and the cooling process (b)

The domain D of feasible solutions was $[4, 15]$ x $[670, 800]$. The stop criteria were: obtaining a solution below 0.01; exceeding 500 calls of the objective function. Also, in that optimization problem, the calculations with the use of each of the non-deterministic algorithms were performed 8 times. The average values of obtained optimal solutions and number of objective calls are given in Table 1. The effectiveness factors are shown in Figure 4b. It can be seen that MABO strategy gives slightly higher value of the optimization error, however that value is obtained in lower number of iterations (objective function calls). At the same time, the effectiveness factor is the lowest in comparing of other used heuristic algorithms.

Table 1. Comparison of the results of different algorithms

Optimization Method	Rastrigin's function		Cooling process	
	Opt. error	Obj. function calls	Opt. error	Obj. function calls
MABO	**1.51e-9**	**43**	**8.4e-3**	**32**
GA	0.0027	2298	6.3e-3	128
PSO	0.0485	792	4.6e-3	93
$(1 + 1)$	0.4602	2760	16.8e-3	200
$(\mu + \lambda)$	0.0848	1956	5.3e-3	60
(μ, λ)	0.1028	2528	4.8e-3	100
SA	0.127	3000	7.6e-3	345
AIS	0.0056	3000	5.7e-3	283
ACO	0.0679	3000	8e-3	250

4   Summary and Conclusions

The main goal of the paper was elaboration of the Modified Approximation Based Optimization strategy. Developed strategy was validated in optimization of the Rastrigin's benchmark function, giving a better optimal solution in smaller number of iterations comparing to the chosen heuristic algorithms. Application of the MABO strategy in the optimization of the real, industrial metallurgical process confirms its effectiveness. It allows decreasing the number of the objective function calls, which in the case of the complex FEM model of considered process, results in a significant decrease of the computation time. The obtained results confirm that the MABO strategy can significantly reduce the number of necessary objective function calls and hence to reduce the time of optimization process and can be useful in solving complex optimization industrial problems.

Acknowledgements. The financial support of the National Centre for Research and Development (NCBiR) project no. N508 590 139 is acknowledged.

References

1. Arabas, J.: Lecture Notes on Evolutionary Algorithms, WNT, Warszawa (2004) (in polish)
2. Goldberg, D.E.: Genetic algorithms in search, optimization and machine learning. Addison-Wesley, Boston (1989)
3. Kusiak, J.: Technique of the tool shape optimization in large scale problems of metal forming. Journal of Materials Processing Technology 57, 79–84 (1996)
4. Kusiak, J., Danielewska-Tułecka, A., Oprocha, P.: Optimization. Selected methods and applications. PWN, Warszawa (2009) (in polish)
5. Mrozek, A., Kuś, W., Burczyński, T.: Compuimbational intelligence methods in searching of stable configurations of nanostructures. Journal of Computer Methods in Materials Science 11, 46–52 (2011)
6. Myczkowska, K., Szeliga, D., Kusiak, J.: Sensitivity analysis of the cooling cycle for the DP steels, Rudy i Metale Nieżelazne (2011) (in press) (in polish)
7. Pietrzyk, M., Kusiak, J., Kuziak, R., Zalecki, W.: Optimization of laminar cooling of hot rolled DP steels. XXVIII Verformungskundliches Kolloquium, Planneralm, pp. 285–294 (2009)
8. Pietrzyk, M., Madej, Ł., Rauch, L., Gołąb, R.: Multiscale modelling of microstructure evolution during laminar cooling of hot rolled DP steel. Archives of Civil and Mechanical Engineering 10, 57–67 (2010)
9. Sztangret, Ł., Stanisławczyk, A., Kusiak, J.: Bio-inspired optimization strategies in control of copper flash smelting process. Journal of Computer Methods in Materials Science 9, 400–408 (2009)
10. Sztangret, Ł., Stanisławczyk, A., Kusiak, J.: Control of the copper flash smelting process - comparison of the effectiveness of bio-inspired strategies. In: Burczyński, T., Periaux, J. (eds.) Evolutionary and Deterministic Methods in Design, Optimization and Control. Applications to Industrial and Societal Problems, pp. 289–295 (2011)
11. Sztangret, Ł., Szeliga, D., Kusiak, J., Pietrzyk, M.: Optimization task for selection of parameters of laminar cooling after hot rolling for DP steel strip. Rudy i Metale Nieżelazne (2011) (in press) (in polish)
12. Wang, L., Wu, Q.: Ant System Algorithm for Optimization in Continous Space. In: Proceedings of the 2001 IEEE International Conference on Control Applications, pp. 395–400 (2001)

Multiplicative ICA Algorithm
for Interaction Analysis in Financial Markets

Ryszard Szupiluk[1,2], Piotr Wojewnik[1,2], and Tomasz Ząbkowski[1,3]

[1] Polska Telefonia Cyfrowa Ltd., Al. Jerozolimskie 181, 02-222 Warsaw, PL
[2] Warsaw School of Economics, Al. Niepodleglosci 162, 02-554 Warsaw, PL
[3] Warsaw University of Life Sciences, ul. Nowoursynowska 159, 02-787 Warsaw, PL
{rszupiluk,pwojewnik,tzabkowski}@t-mobile.pl

Abstract. In this article we present a new method for the analysis of dependencies in case of multivariate time series. In this approach, we assume that the set of time series representing the various financial instruments creates a multidimensional variable. Such a multidimensional variable is decomposed into independent components which enable to analyze the morphology of given financial instruments and to identify the hidden interdependencies. We propose a new multiplicative version of the Natural Gradient ICA algorithm that could be used in automated trading systems or modeling environments. The presented method is tested on real stock markets data.

Keywords: independent components analysis, information representation, financial time series decomposition.

1   Introduction

The predictive modeling using both, classical as well as so called digital economy methods such as agents - the evolutionary algorithms - requires proper identification of the environment in which the models are built. This is also applicable to financial markets represented by the data, signals or time series associated with different economic values or financial instruments. An appropriate way to build the models is to identify the fundamental factors influencing the market environment [5,10]. Unfortunately, these factors are often hidden, mixed with noises or just interacted with some random noise [13,14]. A fundamental problem in financial market modeling is to estimate the trends and to separate the general market dependencies form the individual behavior of a given financial instrument [7].

The standard analysis of trends for the financial data is generally limited to single time series [11,12]. In this way the interactions with other variables are omitted. Some explanation for this approach is the assumption that the data include the effect of other variables and their elimination leads to an ambiguous interpretation of the components. This is obviously true if we are dealing with instruments whose intrinsic value does not surprise us, because the price is a result of balanced supply and demand with respect to market expectations.

L. Rutkowski et al. (Eds.): ICAISC 2012, Part II, LNCS 7268, pp. 608–615, 2012.
© Springer-Verlag Berlin Heidelberg 2012

Such instruments include commodities, currencies and stock prices of large and stable corporations. Changes to these instruments, both in terms of their fundamental scores and market orientation are usually relatively slow. The trends take a long time and the relationships in the short and medium term are stable. However, there is a large number of instruments usually associated with smaller or medium companies for which internal factors in a given period may be more important than the effects on broader market. Of course, there may be also the entire markets, which are dominated by internal factors.

The stock price of such companies, although being under the influence of overall market in the initial phase, starts to differentiate. Such move which begins with completely different direction than a specific industry or wide trends is the chance for above-average returns on investment (or rather speculation). For this reason, they are especially interesting for both individual investors and automated trading systems [15]. Another issue, even for a stable financial instrument, is to eliminate the noise that comes from the other less stable instruments. This is basically complementary to the situation described above. If something happens concerning less significant company and it has negative impact that might have impact also for more stable instruments. Even if this is the factor of transition and the long or medium term is negligible, at a given time it may lead to inappropriate and costly investment decisions.

The consequence of the foregoing is that the market functioning involves the analysis of mutual influences and relationships. This leads directly to the issue of data decomposition and interpretation of the underlying hidden components. In this study we focus on internal dependencies estimation without any short-term fluctuations that could be assigned to a broader market environment.

A natural approach to the analysis of hidden dependencies is proposed by blind source separation methods [3,6]. Previous works that aimed to apply these methods in finance were focused on the direct estimation of the trends [1,4]. In this paper we focus on relations between the hidden components and their impact on original instruments. This will determine which instruments have similar hidden morphology and which ones are quite different. In terms of economic interpretation we can identify it with the dependence or independence on the market. In our paper we propose a modified Natural Gradient algorithm in a multiplicative form that is convenient for use in automated trading systems and in environments that model the financial markets.

2   Problem Formulation

We present the problem of internal relations estimation as blind separation case in which we extract the components hidden in the financial data. For this purpose, let us assume that we collect the individual signals $\mathbf{x}_i$, (financial instruments, time series) in a matrix $\mathbf{X} = [\mathbf{x}_1 \, \mathbf{x}_2 \ldots \mathbf{x}_m]^T$, $\mathbf{X} \in R^{m \times N}$. Next, we assume that the observed signals $\mathbf{s}_i$ are linear combination of some underlying hidden components. In other words, we assume that the model is a linear mixture of the latent components and it has a form of

$$\mathbf{X} = \mathbf{AS}, \tag{1}$$

where matrix $\mathbf{A} \in R^{m \times m}$ represents mixing system and $\mathbf{S} = [s_1 \, s_2 \, \ldots \, s_m]^T$ - hidden components.

Our aim is to find such transformation defined by matrix $\mathbf{W}$ that

$$\mathbf{Y} = \mathbf{WX} = \mathbf{WAS} \approx \mathbf{S}. \tag{2}$$

The way we formulate the problem, in fact, does not entitle us to propose a unique solution unless we have a priori knowledge or we make some additional assumptions about $\mathbf{A}$ and $\mathbf{S}$. The desired characteristics may include such concepts as independence, correlation, predictability, sparsity, smoothness or non-negativity [2,3,6,8,9]. As well we may deal with various combinations of these quantities. In practical applications one of the most popular characteristic is the statistical independence what leads to independent component analysis (ICA) where we can apply the classic ICA algorithms to find the matrix W using the Natural Gradient Algorithm [3]

$$\mathbf{W}(t+1) = \mathbf{W}(t) + \mu(t)[\mathbf{I} - \mathbf{R}_{fy}(t)]\mathbf{W}(t), \tag{3}$$

where

$$\mathbf{R}_{fy}(t) = E\left\{ \mathbf{f}(\mathbf{y}(t))\mathbf{y}^T(t) \right\} \tag{4}$$

is a non-linear covariance matrix with $\mathbf{f}(\mathbf{y}(t)) = [f_1(y_1), \ldots, f_n(y_n)]^T$ - non-linear functions in a form of $f_i(y_i) = \frac{\partial \log(p_i(y_i))}{\partial y_i}$. The estimation of $\mathbf{S}$ by $\mathbf{Y}$ via (3) can be performed with respect to accuracy of the scale and the order

$$\mathbf{Y} = \mathbf{PDS}, \tag{5}$$

where $\mathbf{P}$ is a permutation matrix and $\mathbf{D}$ is a scaling matrix. The algorithm of the form (5) is an effective and widely described in the ICA approach. However, it has some limitations. It is very sensitive to learning parameter $\mu(t)$ and the form of nonlinearity $\mathbf{f}(.)$. Additionally, it is naturally addressed to the spatial data which does not take into account the time structure of the analyzed signal. In the following we will present an extended form of this algorithm which takes into account the temporal structure what can improve the algorithm robustness to deal with the presence of additive noise. For this purpose, we define the filtered non-linear covariance matrix $\mathbf{R}$

$$\mathbf{R}_{f\bar{z}}(t) = E\left\{ \mathbf{f}(\mathbf{z}(t))\bar{\mathbf{z}}^T(t) \right\} \approx \frac{1}{N} \sum_{i=1}^{N} \mathbf{f}(\mathbf{z}(t))\bar{\mathbf{z}}^T(t), \tag{6}$$

where

$$\bar{\mathbf{z}}(t) = \sum_{k=1}^{K} b(k)\mathbf{z}(t-k), \tag{7}$$

K is the level of delay and $f(z)$ is some non-linearity, and $b(k), k = 1, \ldots, K$ are the coefficients of FIR (finite impulse response) filter.

In further considerations we assume that $f(z) = z^3$ and thus the nonlinear covariance matrix will be related to the fourth order statistics [2]. These statistics are one of the important approaches to approximate the independence. The proposed algorithm has the following form:

1. We make the data preprocessing by PCA transformation $\mathbf{y} = \boldsymbol{\Sigma}_0^{-\frac{1}{2}} \mathbf{Q}_0 \mathbf{x}$, where $\boldsymbol{\Sigma}_0$ is diagonal eigenvalue matrix of $\mathbf{R}_{\mathbf{xx}}$ with descending order, and $\mathbf{Q}_0$ is eigenvectors matrix of of $\mathbf{R}_{\mathbf{xx}}$. We get $\mathbf{R}_{\mathbf{yy}} = \mathbf{I}$. We randomly initialize matrix $\mathbf{W}_0$ and take $\mathbf{W} = \mathbf{W}_0$.
2. We calculate $\mathbf{R}_{f\bar{y}}(t)$ according to (6) and set the matrix

$$\mathbf{F} = \frac{1}{2}(\mathbf{R}_{f\bar{y}} + \mathbf{R}_{f\bar{y}}^T)\mathbf{W}. \tag{8}$$

3. We make SVD (singular value decomposition) matrix decomposition

$$\mathbf{F} = \mathbf{U}\boldsymbol{\Sigma}\mathbf{V}^T. \tag{9}$$

4. We set

$$\mathbf{W} \leftarrow \boldsymbol{\Sigma}^{-\frac{1}{2}}\mathbf{U}^T, \tag{10}$$

$$\mathbf{y} \leftarrow \mathbf{W}\mathbf{y}. \tag{11}$$

5. We go to step 2.

The proposed algorithm is computationally simple and efficient. It takes into account the temporal structure of the data, and due to its multiplicative form it does not require setting the learning parameter. This makes it highly appropriate for the algorithmic modeling of market processes, and has possible application in automated transactional systems.

3   Practical Financial Interactions Estimation

In this section we will verify the presented approach on the real data. We consider eleven time series for the stock indices and foreign exchange rates against Polish zloty describing the markets of Brasil, France, London, Japan, USA and Poland in the time span 18/01/2008 - 07/03/2011: Bovespa, BRLPLN, CAC40, EUR-PLN, FT-SE100, GBPPLN, NIKKEI, JPYPLN, SP500, USDPLN and WIG.

In the experiment we try to identify the interconnections between analyzed markets and also find some local trends in the following way. We look for common independent components $\mathbf{s}$ in the time series $\mathbf{x}$ and then identify, which components play crucial role for particular series. While $\mathbf{x} = \mathbf{As}$, then the value of a_{ij} presents the direction and the magnitude of impact j-th signal on i-th series. To keep the a_{ij}-values comparable we preprocess the time series **x** by standarization and also we calculate the squares of a_{ij}.

In Fig. 1 you can observe the standarized times series used for ICA decomposition. All the stock indices perform similarly as a group and also the the foreign exchange rates (excluding the pair BRLPLN) look alike. In Fig. 2 you can see the resulting independent components without any visible interdependencies.

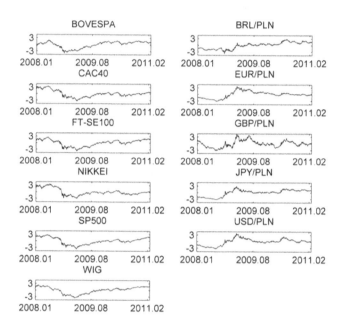

Fig. 1. The stadarized time series of main international stock indices and Warsaw Stock Exchange index (WIG) as well as specific foreign exchange rates against Polish zloty

In Fig.3 you can observe the impact of the signals on particular time series measured as the squared values of the mixing matrix A. As you can see the set of important signal differs among the time series.

For the South American market the crucial role is played by the signals s5 and s8. These signals do not influence any other market, and therfore we might expect the Brazilian market to be almost isolated with only mere connections to FT-SE100, SP500 and WIG. Some other Brasilian connection comes through signal s1 in the rate of BRLPLN, where the component s1 influences all the foreign exchange rates and also the stock exchange in Paris, Tokyo and New York. The signal shows strong connection between these stock markets and also their influence on exchange rates defined against Polish zloty. All the foreign exchange rates are also interdependent through the signals s2 and s7.

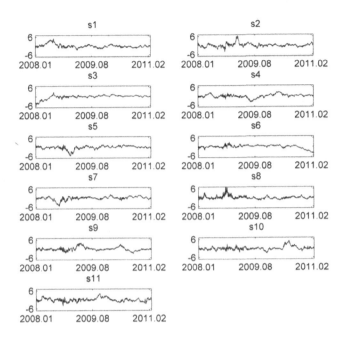

Fig. 2. The independent components identified with algorithm proposed in Section 2

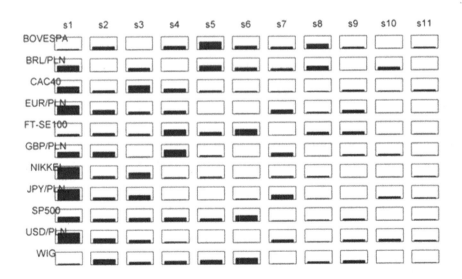

Fig. 3. The impact of the signals on particular time series - squared values of the mixing matrix **A**. The signal s1 strongly influences most of the series except Bovespa, FT-SE100 and WIG while the signal s11 does not influence any series so much.

The French CAC-40 is connected to NIKKEI and JPYPLN with signal s3 and to FT-SE100 and GBPPLN with s4. The connections with New York are manifold and they come through the signals s1-s4, where only s1-s3 influence the USDPLN. FT-SE100 operates closely to CAC40, EURPLN and GBPPLN (see signal s4), but also close to SP500 and WIG (signal s6). There are no evident connections to Japan and USDPLN market.

In the Japan series (as in the Brazilian) we can observe close relation between stock market and the foreign exchange rate through the signals s1 and s3, though these signals connect also SP500 and CAC40 and all the currencies. The US stock market is connected to all other series with the signals s1-s6 and this impact is tracked by the Polish WIG.

The signals s9-s11 are immaterial for the time series and thus might be interpreted as a noise. On the other hand if we analyse the signal s6 in Fig. 2 we can observe some well established trend. In particular the signal is important to FT-SE100, SP500 and WIG and thus it can be used for economic situation description and prediction.

4   Conclusions

In this paper a multi-dimensional analysis of a set of financial instruments represented by time series was presented. It allows us to identify hidden relationships and patterns in financial data. An independent component analysis is used to separate the hidden components for data with non-Gaussian statistical characteristics. It also enables to capture the dependencies described with higher order statistics.

Such approach is necessary to assess to what extent individual markets (or single financial instruments) are independent of each other taking into account a broader insight rather than just a correlation. The novel version of the Natural Gradient algorithm can be easily implemented and can be employed without using any sophisticated parameters. The performed experiments confirmed the validity of the developed concept.

In this paper a multi-dimensional analysis of a set of financial instruments represented by time series was presented. It allows us to identify hidden relationships and patterns in financial data. An independent component analysis is used to separate the hidden components for data with non-Gaussian statistical characteristics. It also enables to capture the dependencies described with higher order statistics. Such approach is necessary to assess to what extent individual markets (or single financial instruments) are independent of each other taking into account a broader insight rather than just a correlation. The novel version of the Natural Gradient algorithm can be easily implemented and can be employed without using any sophisticated parameters. The performed experiments confirmed the validity of the developed concept.

Acknowledgements. This paper was financed with the resources for the science for 2010-2012 - Research Grant NN111281738 of the Polish Ministry if Science and Higher Education.

References

1. Back, A.D., Weigend, A.S.: A First Application of Independent Component. Analysis to Extracting Structure from Stock Returns. International Journal of Neural Systems 8, 473–484 (1997)
2. Cardoso, J.F.: High-order contrasts for independent component analysis. Neural Computation 11(1), 157–192 (1999)
3. Cichocki, A., Amari, S.: Adaptive Blind Signal and Image Processing. John Wiley, Chichester (2002)
4. Drakakis, K., Rickard, S., de Frein, R., Cichocki, A.: Analysis of financial data using non-negative matrix factorization. Int. Math. Forum 3(39), 1853–1870 (2008)
5. Hellstrom, T.: ASTA - a Tool for Development of Stock Prediction Algorithms. Theory of Stochastic Processes 5(21), 22–32 (1999)
6. Hyvarinen, A., Karhunen, J., Oja, E.: Independent Component Analysis. John Wiley (2001)
7. Krutsinger, J.: Trading Systems: Secrets of the Masters. McGraw-Hill (1997)
8. Lee, D.D., Seung, H.S.: Learning of the parts of objects by non-negative matrix factorization. Nature 401, 788–791 (1999)
9. Li, Y., Cichocki, A., Amari, S.: Sparse component analysis for blind source separation with less sensors than sources. In: Fourth Int. Symp. on ICA and Blind Signal Separation, Nara, Japan, pp. 89–94 (2003)
10. Luo, Y., Davis, D., Liu, K.: A Multi-Agent Decision Support System for Stock Trading. The IEEE Network Magazine Special Issue on Enterprise Networking and Services 16(1) (2002)
11. Murphy, J.J.: Technical Analysis of the Financial Markets. New York Institute of Finance (1999)
12. Nison, S.: Japanese Candlestick Charting Techniques. New York Institute of Finance (1991)
13. Peters, E.: Fractal market analysis. John Wiley and Son (1996)
14. Shiryaev, A.N.: Essentials of stochastic finance: facts, models, theory. World Scientific, Singapore (1999)
15. Schwager, J.: Stock Market Wizards: Interviews with America's Top Stock Traders. Harper Paperbacks (1993)

Fuzzy Availability Analysis of Web Systems by Monte-Carlo Simulation

Tomasz Walkowiak, Jacek Mazurkiewicz, and Katarzyna Nowak

Institute of Computer Engineering, Control and Robotics,
Wroclaw University of Technology, ul. Janiszewskiego 11/17, 50-372 Wroclaw, Poland
{Tomasz.Walkowiak,Jacek.Mazurkiewicz,Katarzyna.M.Nowak}@pwr.wroc.pl

Abstract. The paper describes the availability analysis of Web systems. The analysed systems are modelled as a set of tasks that use data, obtained in an interaction with other tasks, to produce responses. System is reliable - we do not discuss the failure and repair process of the elements. We realise the functional analysis of a Web system measured by a functional availability, i.e. the probability that a client will receive a correct response within a given time limit. The metric is calculated by simulation software developed by authors and based on the Monte-Carlo technique. We model the input load by fuzzy numbers and receive a fuzzy representation of the Web system availability changes during a day. Simulation results of for a testbed system are given.

1 Introduction

The Web systems are currently becoming the core infrastructure of almost all business activities. They belong to a class of complex systems as a result of the large number of components and their complicated interactions. As more and more Web systems are being designed and implemented it's vital to have means for analysis the system reliability and ways of selecting the best (according to some criteria) configuration of the system components and system maintenance. Reliability is mostly understood as the ability of a system to perform its required functions for a specified period of time [1]. It's is mostly defined as a probability that a system will perform its function during a given period of time. From the reliability point of view the Web systems are characterized by a very complex structure. The classical models used for reliability analysis are mainly based on Markov or Semi-Markov processes which are idealized and it is hard to reconcile them with practice. The typical structures with reliability focused analysis are not complicated and use very strict assumptions related to the life or repair time and random variables distributions of the analyzed system elements. There is a possibility to use a time event simulation with Monte Carlo analysis instead of classic reliability analysis. It allows calculating any point wise parameters. We can also estimate different distributions of time being in a state or in a set of states. On the other hand it is - in general - very hard to find the proper universal values related to description of the complex system [6]. Sometimes the

L. Rutkowski et al. (Eds.): ICAISC 2012, Part II, LNCS 7268, pp. 616–624, 2012.

parameters are completely unmeasured or the population of analyzed elements is too limited to find such general information [7]. The possible solution is to fix the parameters based on experts' experience and to operate with them in the fuzzy way. The approach can be realised as multiple input and one output fuzzy system. And by a usage of fuzzy operators one could calculate the overall metric value as a fuzzy variable or after a defuzzification as a crisp value. The crucial point for such approach is the calculation of system metric - availability in the presented paper. We focus on a business service realized by Web system [4] and functional aspects of the system, i.e. performance aspects of business service realized by a Web system. We assume that the main goal, taken into consideration during design and operation of the Web system, is to fulfil the user requirements. This could be seen as some requirements to perform a user tasks within a given time limit. Therefore, to measure functional aspects of Web system we propose to use the functional availability metric. It is defined as a probability that service response time will be less than a given time limit. The service response time depends on number of users presented in the system (input load). For most Web system it is hard to predict this value, therefore we propose to set the input load based on experts' experience. This fact is the reason why fuzzy approach to availability analysis is justifiable [8]. To deal with functional aspects of Web systems we propose a common approach [2] based on modelling and simulation. Modelling is focussed on a process of execution of a user request, understand as a sequence of task realised on technical services provided by the system [12]. Whereas the simulation is responsible for functional analysis. It is based on a time event simulation with Monte Carlo analysis [3]. The organisation of the paper is as follows. We start with modelling of the Web system on the task level (section 2). It is followed by a functional analysis performed by a simulator tool. The tool allows to calculate the user request time and therefore to calculate the functional availability. Next, the functional availability is defined by functional aspects (probability that a user will receive a request within a given time limit for a given system input load) and input load (the number of users changing in time during a week). Finally, we model the input load by fuzzy numbers and receive the fuzzy client availability. We conclude with a short summary and plans for future works.

2 Web System

2.1 Model Overview

As it was mentioned in the introduction we decided to analyse Web systems from the business service point of view. Therefore, we model a process of execution of a user request, understand as a sequence of task realised on technical services provided by the system. Generally speaking users of the system are generating tasks which are being realized by a Web system. The task to be realized requires some services presented in the system. A realization of the system service needs a defined set of technical resources. Moreover, the services have to be allocated on a given host. Therefore, we can model a Web system WS as a 4-tuple [10][12]:

$$WS = \langle Client, BS, TI, Conf \rangle, \qquad (1)$$

where: $Client$ - finite set of clients, BS - business service, a finite set of service components, TI - technical infrastructure, $Conf$ - information system configuration.

During modelling of the technical infrastructure we have to take into consideration functional aspects of Web systems. Therefore, the technical infrastructure of the Web system could be modelled as a pair:

$$TI = \langle H, N \rangle, \qquad (2)$$

where: H - set of hosts (computers), N - computer network.

The main technical infrastructure of the Web systems are hosts. Each host is described by the set of functional parameters: server name (unique in the system), host performance parameter - the real value which is a base for calculating the task processing time (described later), set of technical services (i.e. apache Web server, tomcat, MySQL database), each technical service is described by a name and a limit of tasks concurrently being executed. The BS is a set of services based on business logic, that can be loaded and repeatedly used for concrete business handling process (i.e. ticketing service, banking, VoIP, etc). Business service can be seen as a set of service components and tasks, that are used to provide service in accordance with business logic for this process [14]. Therefore, BS is modelled a set of business service components BSC, (i.e. authentication, data base service, Web service, etc.), where each business service component is described a name, reference to a technical service and host describing allocation of business service component on the technical infrastructure and a set of tasks. Tasks are the lowest level observable entities in the modelled system. It can be seen as a request and response form one service component to another. Each task is described by its name, task processing time parameter and optionally by a sequence of task calls. Each task call is defined by a name of business service component and task name within this business service component and time-out parameter. System configuration $Conf$ is a function that gives the assignments of each service components to a technical service and therefore to hosts since a technical set is placed on a given host. In case of service component assigned in a configuration to a load balancing technical service the tasks included in a given service component are being realised on one of technical services (and therefore hosts) defined in the load balancer configuration. The client model $Client$ consists of set of users where each user is defined by its allocation (host name), replicate parameter (number of concurrently ruing users of given type), set of activities (name and a sequence of task calls) and inter-activity delay time (modelled by a Gaussian distribution). Summarising, a user initiates the communication requesting some tasks on a host, it could require a request to another host or hosts, after the task execution hosts responds to requesting server, and finally the user receives the respond. Requests and responds of each task give a sequence of a user task execution (choreography) as presented in exemplar Fig. 2. The request is understood as correctly answered if answers for each requests in a sequence of a user task execution were given within defined time limit (parameter of each request in *BS* model) and if a number of tasks executed on a given technical service is not exceeding the limit parameter (parameter of *TI* model). The user request execution time in the system is calculated as a sum of times required for TCP/IP communication (modelled by a random value) and times of tasks processing on a given host. The task processing time is equal to the task processing time parameter multiplied by a number of other task processed on the same host in the same time and divided by a the host performance parameter. Since the number of tasks is changing in simulation time, the processing time is updated each time a task finish the execution or a new task is starting to be processed.

2.2 Programming Simulation

The above model was analyzed be means of computer simulation. A software package for Monte-Carlo simulation [5] has been developed by authors [8]. It is based on the publicly available SSF [13] simulation engine that provides all the required simulation primitives and frameworks, as well as a convenient modelling language DML [13] for inputting all the system model parameters. The simulation algorithm is based on tracking all states of the system elements. The state is a base for a definition of an event, which is understood as a triple: time of being happened, object identifier and state. Based on each event and states of all system elements rules for making a new event has been encoded in the simulation program. The random number generator was used to deal with random events. By repeating the simulator runs multiple times using the same model parameters and obtains several independent realizations of the same process (the results differ, since the system model is not deterministic). These are used to build the probabilistic distribution of the results, especially the average measures. Simulation experiments were performed on a testbed Web system consisting of six hosts.

2.3 Case Study

To show the possibilities of the proposed model we have analyzed a Web system which consists of three networks: one is a client network, other service provider networks (secured by a Firewall). System (testbed) is realizing simplified hotel booking system that allows booking an available apartment in hotel. Few servers are used for a proper service realization: *WebServer*, *HotelDatabase*, *ReservationServer*, *PaymentServerController*, *BackupWebServer* (Fig. 1).

The service and its choreography is described in Fig. 2. First of all, place of the hotel is being searched, than reservation is being made. At the end of this scenario payment is done with an interaction with given payment system.

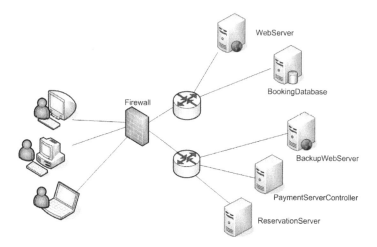

Fig. 1. Web system infrastructure - case study example

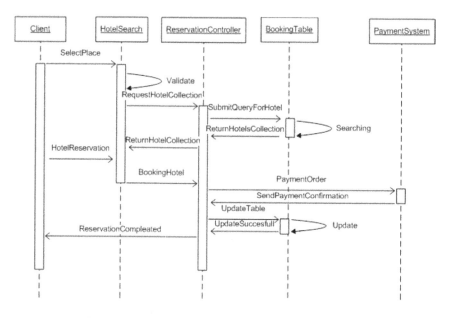

Fig. 2. Web system choreography - case study example

3   System Availability

3.1   Assumptions

The presented approach is focused on a process of execution of a user request, understand as a sequence of task realised on technical services provided by the system. Therefore, the main aim of simulation was to allow calculation service response time. The user initiates the communication requesting some tasks on a host, it could require a request to another host or hosts, after the task execution a host responds to requesting server, and finally the user receives the respond. Requests and responds of each task give a sequence of a user task execution - choreography (see Fig. 2). The user request execution time in the system is calculated as a sum of times required for TCP/IP communication (modelled by a random value) and task processing times on hosts according to some choreography.

3.2 Functional Availability

To measure functional aspects of Web system we propose to use the functional availability metric. It is defined as a probability the user's request is served and that service response time will be less than a given time limit for a given load (number of user requests per second) of the system. This metric is a numerical representation of clients' perception of particular business service quality. It measures the probability that the user will not resign from active interaction with the service due too long service response time. The example results for the testbed system with choreography from Fig. 2 with a time-limit set to 12s and concurrent task limit set to 200 are presented in Fig. 3.

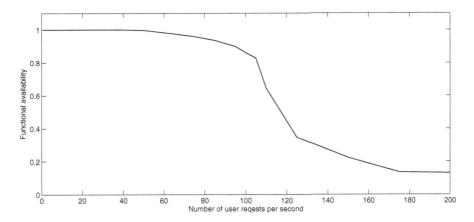

Fig. 3. Functional availability for a testbed system in a function of number of user requests per second

3.3 Input Load Problem

It is obvious that a number of users of a Web system changes in time. It depends on a type of provided service. But usually on weekends, there are fewer users then on weekdays. Also one could notice changes in traffic during a day. With a peak load in a middle of day and minimum load at night. Therefore, the input load variations could be described by a function similar to that presented in Fig. 4.

Using the function describing the number of users the changes of functional availability in time could be easily calculated. The results for a testbed system and assumed input load are presented in Fig. 4.

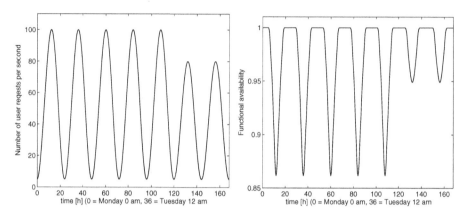

Fig. 4. Input load for a tesbed system and functional availabiliy for a tesbed system in a function of a time - for one week

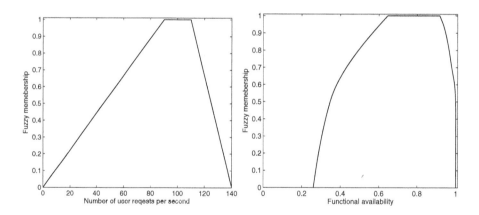

Fig. 5. Fuzzy number of users per second and fuzzy value of functional availability

4   Fuzzy Approach to Functional Analysis

Modern systems are characterized by very screwed up reliability [9] and functional parameters. It is very hard to find the proper universal values related to description of these devices [6]. Sometimes the parameters are completely unmeasured or the population of analyzed elements is too limited to find such general information [7]. The possible solution is to fix the parameters based on experts' experience. Therefore we propose to use fuzzy approach to deal with the number of users requests. We propose to use a trapezoidal membership function

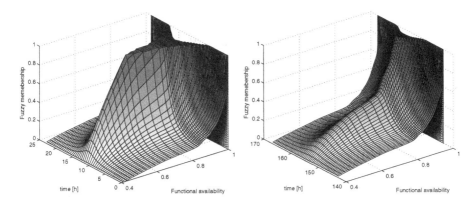

Fig. 6. Functional availability, fuzzy membership and time for a weekday and weekend

for fuzzy representation of number of users per second. Assumption of the fuzzy membership function shape does not bind the analysis. One could use any other membership function and apply presented here methodology. For example, for input load defined by fuzzy membership function set to (0, 90, 110, 140), the fuzzy value of the functional availability is presented in Fig. 5. Following this idea, one could model the input load (Fig. 4) during a whole week by fuzzy trapezoidal function, and achieves a resulting membership function of changes of functional availability as presented in Fig. 6.

5   Conclusion

In this paper we have presented a functional analysis of Web systems based on modelling and fuzzy logic approach. Developed simulation software allows analysing the functional features of the Web system for a given configuration of it. Functional parameters describe the Web system choreography (interaction between tasks), system structure (number of hosts, host performance, service components placement on hosts and each task execution time) and input load (changes of user requests number in a time during a week). Using the tool Web-based system configuration and maintenance procedures could be easily verified and different configuration could be compared. It makes the solution a powerful tool for increasing system availability and by that increasing user satisfaction. It is also possible to find general results describing safety conditions of system manoeuvres from Fig. 6. We plan to extend presented approach by adding a failure and repair processes described by fuzzy parameters. We hope, that presented approach could be a foundation for a new methodology of the reliability and quality analysis of Web Systems, which is much closer to the practice experience.

Acknowledgments. The presented work was funded by the Polish National Science Centre under contract no. 4759/B/TO2/2011/40.

References

1. Barlow, R., Proschan, F.: Mathematical theory of reliability. Society for Industrial and Applied Mathematics, Philadelphia (1996)
2. Birta, L., Arbez, G.: Modelling and simulation: exploring dynamic system behaviour. Springer, London (2007)
3. Fishman, G.: Monte Carlo: concepts, algorithms and applications. Springer (1996)
4. Gold, N., Knight, C., Mohan, A., Munro, M.: Understanding service-oriented software. IEEE Software 21, 71–77 (2004)
5. Lipinski, Z.: State model of e-service reliability. In: International Conference on Dependability of Computer Systems, DepCoS-RELCOMEX 2006, pp. 35–42. IEEE Computer Society (2006)
6. Liu, H., Chu, L., Recker, W.: Performance evaluation of ITS strategies using microscopic simulation. In: Proceedings of the 7th International IEEE Conference on Intelligent Transportation Systems, pp. 255–270 (2004)
7. Liu, J.: Parallel Real-time Immersive Modelling Environment (PRIME), Scalable Simulation Framework (SSF), User's manual. Colorado School of Mines Department of Mathematical and Computer Sciences (2006), http://prime.mines.edu/
8. Mazurkiewicz, J., Walkowiak, T.: Fuzzy Economic Analysis of Simulated Discrete Transport System. In: Rutkowski, L., Siekmann, J.H., Tadeusiewicz, R., Zadeh, L.A. (eds.) ICAISC 2004. LNCS (LNAI), vol. 3070, pp. 1161–1167. Springer, Heidelberg (2004)
9. Mazurkiewicz, J., Walkowiak, T.: Fuzzy reliability analysis. In: ICNNSC 2002 - 6th International Conference Neural Networks and Soft Computing, Advances in Soft Computing, pp. 298–303. Physica-Verlag (2003)
10. Michalska, K., Walkowiak, T.: Simulation approach to performance analysis information systems with load balancer. In: Information Systems Architecture and Technology: Advances in Web-Age Information Systems, pp. 269–278 (2009)
11. Piegat, A.: Fuzzy Modelling and Control. EXIT Academic Publishing House, Warsaw (1999) (in polish)
12. Walkowiak, T.: Information systems performance analysis using task-level simulator. In: International Conference on Dependability of Computer Systems DepCoS-RELCOMEX 2009, pp. 218–225. IEEE Computer Society (2009)
13. Walkowiak, T.: Simulation approach to Web system dependability analysis. In: Summer Safety and Reliability Seminars SSARS 2011 Gdynia, pp. 197–204. Polish Safety and Reliability Association (2011)
14. Walkowiak, T., Michalska, K.: Functional Based Reliability Analysis of Web Based Information Systems. In: Zamojski, W., Kacprzyk, J., Mazurkiewicz, J., Sugier, J., Walkowiak, T. (eds.) Dependable Computer Systems. AISC, vol. 97, pp. 257–269. Springer, Heidelberg (2011)

Distance Examination with Computer Aided Analysis – E-matura Platform

Sławomir Wiak, Dominik Jeske,
Maciej Krasuski, and Rafał Stryjek

Technical University of Lodz, Lodz, Poland
{slawomir.wiak,dominik.jeske,
maciej.krasuski,rafal.stryjek}@p.lodz.pl

Abstract. This paper presents a system for conducting modern distance examinations. It could be defined as important component of distance learning systems.

E-matura system includes several important features such as computer aided mathematical analysis of exams results. Using the advanced information technologies authors have created highly saved system for a huge number of con-current examining processes, and with a user friendly interface. E-matura gives possibility to create the exam questions containing images, animation, video, sound recording, and open questions as well.

1   Introduction

The number of virtual learning environments is recently increasing. New teaching models and tools incorporating e-learning ideas have been successfully exploited by a large group of universities and other professional institutions involved in the education process. The examination procedure is an important stage of the educational process. Modern e-learning platform should have an effective unit for examination [1-8]. E-matura platform is created as a tool to fulfil all the tasks of e-examinations [9-17].

E-matura system has been created at the Technical University of Lodz and under the auspices of the Ministry of Education. Several thousand pupils in Poland have passed the mature test examination in mathematics via Internet last year thanks to e-matura platform. Let us stress that both Microsoft and IBM technologies have been implemented.

System has been created to handle thousands of students/pupils simultaneously and providing maximum level of the security for data safety. Flow chart of the system security (see Fig. 1) shows us all the steps in the communication process between client and server. It could happen while any process could run in improper way, thus the system could be exposed on a hackers attack.

L. Rutkowski et al. (Eds.): ICAISC 2012, Part II, LNCS 7268, pp. 625–633, 2012.
© Springer-Verlag Berlin Heidelberg 2012

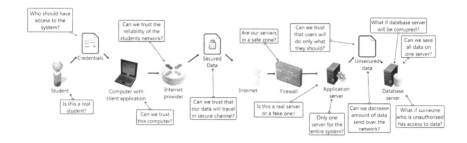

Fig. 1. Flow chart of the system security

2   Modern GUI

Generally, the systems for distance examinations focus mainly on the so-called test questions known as "closed questions" with the set of possible answers for each question; then one proper answer would be selected by the student.

We would like to stress that some innovative Information Technologies (IT) are implemented to e-matura platform. One of them is Silverlight, thus generated questions could include components such as interactive animations, interactive areas for drag and drop items, and for highlighting the answers, etc. These few examples listed above show the modern examination strategies go beyond the traditional forms of the test examinations, also in written form.

3   Accessibility

E-matura platform has been built up by programming actions or by set of Silverlight behaviours. WCAG standard (version 2.0) has been implemented.

This standard includes a variety of techniques which include specific authoring practices and examples enabling development of more accessible Web content [1]. These techniques relate to the possibility of controlling the application from the keyboard, in order to increase the font size. Moreover these techniques contain information about the guidelines for the use of colour in an application, and a short text alternative for controls.

E-matura could be also exploited by the teachers to ensure all students/pupils equal access to learning notes. This e-examination platform gives the chance disabled people to be more familiar with distance learning idea and to take the distance exams.

4   Computer-Aided Analysis of Graduate Characteristics

During each test exam for past three years over 600 000 answers are generated, then then stored in data base system. The platform keeps implemented such functionality, as; if student answer a given question several times, even changing his answer, the system store all steps. Moreover the time necessary to give each answer will be also registered. There are three sets of questions and answers implemented. For the purpose of further research work, questions are set up as follows: first - from the simplest to the most difficult, second - from the most difficult to the simplest, and third – randomly (see Table 1). Two versions of the answers are discussed: first - the correct answers up to 70% of the questions was by selecting B or C (30% was A or B); second - this order was completely random.

Table 1. Exam results for different versions (whole groups of students)

	Points B C answers superiority distribution		Uniform answers distribution	
	Points	Points percentage	Points	Points percentage
From simplest to most difficult	23,27	51,26	23,30	51,33
From most difficult to simplest	22,41	49,35	23,99	52,84
Random	22,91	50,46	23,25	51,23
Summary	22,88	50,39	24,55	51,89

Computer aided examination system is available for the following groups of users: students, teachers and authorities. Teachers would see results for the whole classroom and for each student as well. Authorities could provide the comparative analysis of the exam results in the reference to each school, city, region and whole country. Student individual exam results could be referred to the classroom, school or whole country. Computer elaborated final exam results diagnosis would indicate these parts of the teaching program which needs additional extension (more deep knowledge is recommended).

Table 2. Sample exam results for analysis

Question		Time spent to solve question [min]				Points for question				
Category	no	avg	min	stddev	median	avg	min	max	stddev	median
Open questions	1	14,7	0,1	19,54	10,1	0,6	0	2	0,90	0
	2	6,9	0	10,06	4,1	0,7	0	2	0,82	0
	3	6,1	0	5,38	5,6	1	0	2	1,00	0

Registered time of each answer for the given question, and the number of inputs to each question to set up the correct answer give also very large analysis capability. The final comparative analysis of the test exam results could be provided for each student; moreover: classroom, school, type of school, city, and region. The set of additional criteria could be also defined, and then the results are expected immediately after the exam (see Table 2). While the procedure runs students answer several questions, covering such issues as: whether they were attended the tutorials, who was the authority, how much time per day they spent at the computer using the Internet, if both parents work, whether parents help them in their learning, etc.

5   E-tutoring

In the traditional examination system there are some limitations. Such a system does not give enough information for students taking the exam how to learn more, then to pass exams with the possibly high rank. It is also important to stress that in each step of education process it is strongly recommended to save results of learning progress for each student and teachers as well. In the case of not satisfactory results it is not possible to assign automatically new tasks for student; thus it means the weakness of the system.

5.1   E-tutoring Module

It could be stated e-matura platform provides computer aided analysis also for undergraduate courses. E-matura platform has been created in order to collect as much as possible information (in addition to the answers), which could be precisely analysed after processing and corresponding to final conclusions set up. This system stores information to answer such as problems:

- How many times student answers each question?
- Which questions are the more difficult, and which are easier?
- How much time student needs to solve an each task, and then a whole exam?

Currently, we have built the e-tutoring module, which would support the education process for students, and helping teachers as well. This module is an integral part of the e-matura platform.

5.2   E-tutoring Module for Teachers

Currently done programming work is to implement an additional module in order to provide students additional tasks for the subjects being diagnosed by the system, especially for repeating. Basing on the diagnosis results the weakest knowledge areas of the student or classroom are evaluated; thus the teacher would be also able to assign tasks to a particular student or entire classroom. The system would also display who has done the homework and would check the correctness of each answer. The above defined functionality of the system is helpful for the teacher, which means teacher is not obliged to check the homework in traditional way. Tasks would be drawn either from the previous exams data base of tasks or will be generated automatically by the system; basing also on the questions to be defined by the teachers individually, and then stored in the system.

The teacher would be able to exploit e-matura platform to prepare students for the exams. Teachers could also follow the progress of each student knowledge individually or even corresponding to the classroom level. The system will present an overall assessment of students' knowledge, as well as by individual parts of the program. What is more, e-tutoring module will provide access to historical data for each student and classroom. It is also possible to process aggregated data (current and historical) from e-matura system even by exploiting Microsoft Excel spread sheets.

Teacher would get answers to the following set of questions:

- **Which questions are the most difficult?** If student answers any given question several times changing the answer (responses), the system records all his/her steps. The time student spent to give the answer to each question, and how many times the student turn back to the question are also registered. The results of the given answers for the questions by student, classroom, and school or even for the group of selected schools could be registered and also analysed.
- **The student result against the classroom, school, and country?** The teacher would also keep the knowledge of the results of the exam individually for the student, for the whole classroom with the reference to the average results of the school, for the group of selected schools, city or even country. It would be possible to compare students' results with the results of students attending the same school category.
- **Which part of teaching program should be repeated by students?** Teacher will receive detailed information requiring additional repetition.

The teacher would be able to provide the quantitative analysis of the exam results based on statistical analysis. The set of selected parameters for such an analysis are defined below [4]:

- stanine (STAndard NINE - is a method of scaling test scores on a nine-point standard scale with a mean of five and a standard deviation of two) scores,
- ease of the task / test - the ratio of the number of points obtained by students to the maximum number of points possible to get a task or test,
- difficulty of the task - the ratio of the number of students who have not solved task properly to the number of students,
- the arithmetic mean of the results - the average score obtained by the test group of students – for example classroom,
- median - the result of the middle set of exam results of a particular population – for example classroom,
- mode - the most common value among a group,
- area of typical results - results interval on the scale located between the sum and arithmetical difference of the arithmetic mean and standard deviation,
- standard deviation - a measure of variability or diversity, allowing to determine the range of typical results,
- variance -a measure of how far a set of numbers are spread out from each other [4].

5.3   E-tutoring – Module for Students

Each student keeping access to platform would start test exam having the set of tasks assigned by the teacher. After solving the task student will receive immediately results and would be able to identify the correct answers. The teacher will be also able to extend data base system introducing a theory to each task. The additional information (either comments or explanations) will appear when the answer would be wrong or on the basis of the user request.

Student will be able to join the trial exam in any time he wishes. The results (final scores) would be displayed immediately, while student is logging out the exam. Moreover a hint what he has done wrong of each selected task could be also displayed helping in order not to make mistake in the future. In the case of problems with the solving the tasks student will be able to mark each task he wants to turn back after the exam. Each student will be able to follow his progress of knowledge in a convenient data file, such as graphs.

Thanks to the system functionality one could make diagnosis concerning the general problem, which could be defined as follows: to which parts of the curriculum teacher should pay special attention. Following the above student could select only those tasks to which the special attention should be paid. If the required number of correctly solved tasks will be achieved system will mark this part of program as a complete.

5.4   E-tutoring – Central Questions Database

One of the important component (block) of the system is the so called "central questions database". Each teacher keeps access to the system to introduce his specific questions extending the database. Each question will be assigned to the author and will have either private or public attribute. If it will be a public question any user with predefined login and password could have the access to it. Let us point out teachers will be able to proceed these questions for the tests, exams, home works, etc. These questions will be also available for e-tutoring module for students to learn more. Each teacher could choose so called public questions for his students. These questions will be specially signed by approved flag.

5.5   E-tutoring – Learning by Playing

E-tutoring will give a possibility to organize also competition. The competition organizer could prepare the questions and set up the questions to the system in advance. The questions will be available for students in due time competition starts. Moreover, thanks to Internet connection the platform will be available for students who could login in any place.

6   Data Safety

IT system, in which the personal data of the users are stored and being proceeded should ensure very tight data security. E-matura platform has stored detailed information about the users (Name, Surname, Personal ID, etc.), i.e. students and teachers who participate in the project. The obligatory demand to store the data comes from the financial institution funding this project. It is due to requirement to identify each user precisely. Moreover, the so called "classified data" such as exam questions and huge data base of the questions, which are being extracted according to special procedures during examination, are also stored in e-matura platform.

SQL Server 2008 R2 Microsoft database has been installed and exploited, which gives several possibilities to protect the data base against unauthorized access.

Taking into account two basic features (the rate of application performance and security of classified data security), it is decided to encrypt data at a line level using the AES algorithm. Only those table columns storing sensitive data have been encrypted to avoid slowing down the whole database. By using encryption, even people with physical access to data are unable to use them without the proper decryption key.

Developing a Web-based project, which involves users who are well motivated to pass the exams, other safety-related factors should be also taken into account. One well known problem, which often occurs in these types of systems, is SQL injection attacks. These attacks are very common in the systems where the business logic is located within the application to retrieve data from the database. An example of a malfunction can be the creation of a mechanism to login in, which queries about the user's existence are built into the application and then run as a dynamic SQL in the database. In this case, an unauthorized person can affect on the appearance of a built query by typing additional SQL commands. In this way, the system will check, if the password is correct and then execute the hacker's command.

To avoid this problem and to prevent access to data directly from the application, all communication processes between the Web application and the database should be done through stored procedures. In this way, the user cannot get to the tables and data, because of the stored procedure which provides such access is not available.

7   Safe e-examining

The client application communicates with the server part via a network service based on Windows Communication Foundation technology, version 4.0. This technology use open standards such as HTTP and SOAP, and provides the functionality for client applications. In order to ensure secure communication between the client and the server SSL has been used, which allows the security of the system in two dimensions:

- Verification of Application Server,
- Encryption of transmitted data.

Verification of the server is based on a system of certificates through which it is possible to check an entity identified by a given certificate. The certificate is issued by a special certification centre as the request of any client.

Each certificate includes a pair of keys: private and public, so it gives possibility for an asymmetric encryption of data transferred between client and server. During the communication process between the application server and the application installed on an end user's computer, keys are used to encrypt and decrypt transmitted information. By using this solution the data sent between the client and the server cannot be overheard by a third party.

The firewall separates servers that are within the internal network from the so-called external world or the Global Internet. The firewall allows locking of the computer's ports on which the services are not operating, in order to increase safety and to not leave loopholes for malicious software that could get through such ports to the internal network.

Authentication involves checking whether the person is who claims to be. By the authorization process, the system checks which resources/functionalities the user is authorized to access. In the e-matura system authentication is based on the username and password, which are checked when the user is going to access by "log in" into the system. If the user gives the correct data as a result of this operation, then the user will receive a specially-called token-generated number that is assigned to the current session.

This token is used to make authentication of all Web services methods, and provides a unique communication layer between the client and the server. By using the token, the username and its password are not sent with each request to Web service. This means the safety increase by reducing to a minimum the transmission of confidential data to the user. Additional protection is the life span of the token counter. Each token has a set life span that is incremented each time the site is accessed. If the service using the generated token is barred because of its invalidity, any subsequent attempt to gain access to the site returns an error and redirection to the login page. With this approach, a token captured on a victim cannot be used on another computer or the same computer in another session.

8   Conclusions

E-matura platform (system) is not only a modern system for conducting distance examinations, it is also a computer aided sophisticated mathematical tool for analysis of graduates and it will be powerful tool for e-tutoring. The stored data could be also used to provide the analysis for the different levels of detailed knowledge of the exam results. The e-platform has been continuously developed. It is expected that final product (e-matura platform) will be ready for use in a large scale in 2013.

Microsoft SQL Server 2008 R2 is a database which collects data during the exam. It is also expected to build our own specific Business Intelligence solution using Microsoft SQL Server or by exploiting either ORACLE or DB2.

The paper has been written within the project "e-matura", co-financed by the European Union in the framework of the European Social Fund - Operational Program of Human Capital Priority III, High quality of educational system, Activity 3.3 Innovation projects

References

1. http://www.w3.org/WAI/GL/WCAG20-TECHS/intro.html
2. Gartner Research, Business Intelligence Tools, Perspective (2003)
3. Surma, J.: Business Intelligence - Business Decisions Support Systems. Polish Scientific Publishers PWN, Warsaw (2009) (in polish)
4. Results of tests, school exams and final exams 2002-07 (2007),
   http://www.cke.edu.pl
   (in polish)
5. Fetaji, B., Fetaji, M.: E-learning indicators: a multi-dimensional model for planning and evaluating e-learning software solutions. Electronic J. of e-Learning 7(2), 1–28 (2009)

6. Karlsudd, P., Tågerud, Y.: Bridging the gap – taking the distance out of e-learning. Electronic J. of e-Learning 6(1), 43–52 (2008)
7. Choy, S.: Benefits of e-learning benchmarks: Australian case studies. Electronic J. of e-Learning 5(1), 11–20 (2007)
8. Hramiak, A.: Use of a virtual learning environment in initial teacher training. Electronic J. of e-Learning 5(2), 103–112 (2007)
9. Jeske, D., Krasuski, M., Stryjek, R.: Secure and high available exam system "E-Matura" case study. In: 2nd World Conference on Technology and Engineering Education, Ljubljana, Slovenia, September 5-8 (2011)
10. Wiak, S., Jeske, D., Krasuski, M., Stryjek, R.: Computer-aided business intelligence for non-business solutions. Global Journal of Engineering Education, 13(3) (2011)
11. Wiak, S., Jeske, D., Krasuski, M., Stryjek, R.: E-tutoring as part of the e-examination - the use of data warehousing and data mining to assist in the learning and teaching process. In: 3rd WIETE Annual Conference on Engineering and Technology Education (in print)
12. Wiak, S., Jeske, D., Krasuski, M., Stryjek, R.: The e-matura project yesterday, today and tomorrow - challenges and opportunities. In: 3rd WIETE Annual Conference on Engineering and Technology Education (in print)
13. Jeske, D., Krasuski, M., Stryjek, R., Wiak, S.: Modern distance examination as part of distance learning – the E-matura project. Electrical Review (2012) (in print)
14. Wiak, S., Jeske, D., Krasuski, M., Stryjek, R.: Ensuring secure and high available database for the e-matura information system. In: Wiak S. (eds.): Information System for Distance Examination in Mathematics on the e-Matura Project Example. PWN, Warsaw (2011) (in print)
15. Wiak, S., Jeske, D., Krasuski, M., Stryjek, R.: Modern distance examination using the latest technology - the E-matura project. In: 2nd World Conference on Technology and Engineering Education, Ljubljana, Slovenia, September 5-8 (2011)
16. Wiak, S., Jeske, D., Krasuski, M., Stryjek, R.: Computer-aided mathematical analysis of graduates - Business Intelligence in the E-matura project. In: 2nd World Conference on Technology and Engineering Education, Ljubljana, Slovenia, September 5-8 (2011)
17. Wiak, S., Jeske, D., Krasuski, M., Stryjek, R.: A secure and highly accessible examination system - E-matura: a case study. In: 2nd World Conference on Technology and Engineering Education, Ljubljana, Slovenia, September 5-8 (2011)

Simulation of the Behavior of Disc-Spring Valve Systems with the Fuzzy Inference Systems and Artificial Neural Networks

Grzegorz Wszołek, Piotr Czop, Antoni Skrobol, and Damian Sławik

Silesian University of Technology,
ul. Konarskiego 18A, 44-100 Gliwice, Poland
{grzegorz.wszolek,antoni.skrobol,damian.slawik}@gmail.com
piotr.czop@labmod.com

Abstract. This paper proposes an analytical tool that supports the design process of a hydraulic damper valve system. The analytical tool combines Artificial Neural Networks (ANNs) and Fuzzy Inference Systems (FIS) into one tool called, in the paper, the Approximation Tool. The proposed Approximation Tool obtains a key design characteristic of a valve, which is the flow rate, and the corresponding maximum stress level in the valve components, as a function of a pressure load. The cases required to prepare the Approximation Tool were produced by a first-principle model using a finite element approach. The model was calibrated based on experimental results to provide accurate results in the entire range of input parameters. The paper describes the proposal, implementation, validation and an example of applying the Approximation Tool that allows the replacement of complex high- fidelity Finite Element analyses. As an approximator the Feed Forward Neural Network and FIS were taken.

1 Problem Description

1.1 Conventional Hydraulic Damper Working Principles

A conventional hydraulic damper that contains a specific type of valve system consisting of a number of circular metal plates, referred to further in the paper as a stack of plates (see Fig. 1), is taken into consideration.

This valve is part of a piston that is kinematically forced to move up and down in a liquid-filled cylinder. During its movement, the piston divides the cylinder space into two chambers. The flow of the fluid from one cylinder chamber to the other is restricted by the valve – stack of plates. The pressure difference between the two parts of the cylinder creates the resultant force that acts as a pressure on the bottom surface of the lower plate of the valve system. This causes bending of the stack of plates and valve opening. The height of the opening depends on the stiffness of the stack of plates. The opening height is then the first major characteristic of the valve system because, by controlling the fluid flow,

L. Rutkowski et al. (Eds.): ICAISC 2012, Part II, LNCS 7268, pp. 634–642, 2012.

it indirectly controls the damping force of the hydraulic damper [13]. Interested readers can find a more detailed description of the valve system design in [6].

Hydraulic dampers can work with a frequency of 10Hz or even higher, as mentioned by [11]. That leads to a very high number of 'open-close' cycles that should be performed by the valve during hydraulic damper work. This cyclical loading that can cause fatigue damage of the valve plates. The relationship between design of the valve system and its fatigue durability has already been presented in the literature i.e. [3,4]. It was described that the maximum stress level that exists in the plates when the applied load creates deflection of the stack limits the durability of the system [3,14].

Designing the valve stack of plates is then an optimization process where the criteria are both damping force and valve system durability characterized by maximum stress level in the stack of plates. To facilitate the valve system design process, a model of the system can be created to simulate the behavior of the stack of plates under applied loads. This model should be capable of reproducing the essential properties of a valve system during operation in a shock absorber, i.e. stack opening and stress level in the plates.

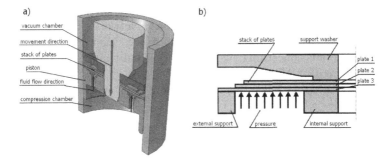

Fig. 1. a) A cross section of a valve system, b) scheme of the valve used in the FE Model

1.2   A Hydraulic Damper Non-linear FE Model

To allow understanding of the contribution of a stack of plates' corresponding components, including the plastic deformation phenomenon and simulation of complex cases, an advanced valve system model has been developed by Czop et al. [4]. The proposed method uses Finite Element discretization to model the behavior of a circular plate stack. The non-linear Finite Element Model used in this paper will be further referred to as the FE Model. As an output of the analysis, the height of the stack opening as well as the maximum value of von Mises stress level in each plate can be obtained. The model was prepared in the Abaqus software environment. The FE Model was correlated with experimental data and its ability to solve the problem presented above was confirmed [3,4].

Mentioned FE Model, however, has several disadvantages, such as (i) the long time required for model preparation and (ii) for analysis, especially when the analysis is performed in several steps, (iii) the high cost of commercial software required to perform the analysis and (iv) special requirements concerning the workstation on which the software can run. All these features become significant when optimization or identification tasks have to be performed, since the fitness function evaluation requires a large number of plate stack configurations to be solved. A very time consuming optimization process occupies the workstation and commercial software for a long period of time.

2   Approximation Tool

Different types of artificial neural networks are well recognized as an efficient and easy-handling tool for several engineering tasks, like identification of defects, optimization or classification tool, etc. [9]. The ANNs, as well as Fuzzy Inference Systems, are already identified as very good approximators of different boundary-value problems [1,7,10].

Two kinds of approximators are presented in the paper. First approximator is the Feed-Forward Neural Network (FFNN) with sigmoid activation functions created and trained using the MATLAB® Neural Network Toolbox for approximation of the key design characteristics of the valve system. Interested readers can find more details concerning the architecture and training method in documentation prepared by Math-Works Inc. [8].

Second is the adaptive Fuzzy Inference System (FIS) with the gaussian membership function

$$G(x) = \exp\left(-\frac{1}{2}\frac{(x-t)^2}{s^2}\right),\tag{1}$$

where: t is the mean, and s is the standard deviation.

The approximation function realized by the FIS is as follows [1]:

$$f(x) = \frac{\sum_{l=1}^{M} W_l \prod_{i=1}^{N} G(x_i)}{\sum_{l=1}^{M} \prod_{i=1}^{N} G(x_i)},\tag{2}$$

where: $G(x)$ is the membership function defined by (1), x is the input vector, $i = 1 \dots N$ is the number of inputs, $l = 1 \dots M$ is the number of fuzzy rules.

The FIS was created and trained using numerical algorithms prepared individually by the authors [1,2].

3   Approximation Task

3.1   Formulation of the Approximation Task

The Approximation Tool approximates the stack behavior in order to obtain a key design characteristic of a valve, in other words, the opening height and the corresponding maximum stress level in the stack of plates as a function of a pressure load. The stack of plates already described in previous paragraphs is considered. The model shown in Fig. 1b consists of a pyramidal stack of three circular plates. The stack is clamped between the support washer and the bottom internal and external support. The washer is added to the model to act as a plate travel stop. The thicknesses of all plates as well as the outer diameter of Plate 1 and Plate 2 are the design variables. The outer diameter of the bottom plate (Plate 3) is constant. These design variables, as well as the value of pressure applied to the bottom surface of Plate 3, are the inputs of the ANN and FIS. The outputs are the opening height of the stack of plates and maximum values of von Mises stress in all three plates. Thus the length of the input vector is 6 and the length of the output vector is 4. The input and output vectors collected together create the pair of vectors. The total number of 4860 pairs is prepared to train the networks. The data is obtained using an advanced nonlinear Abaqus model of a stack of plates described in previous paragraphs. Thickness of Plate 1, 2 and 3 was within the range 0.15 to 0.35 mm. Outer diameter of Plate 1 and 2 was within the range 10 to 20mm and the pressure was between 2.5 and 50 bar.

The data obtained with use of a non-linear FE Model is randomly divided into three sets - training set that contains 3402 pairs, validation and testing set with 729 pairs each.

3.2 Network Architecture

The multi input – single output (MISO) Neural Networks and Fuzzy Inference Systems are chosen to approximate the given problem. For each design variable of the valve system, a separate approximator is prepared. Although this attempt increases the complexity of the training process it has an advantage - the approximator of each design characteristic is independent from other approximators. This allows tuning of the approximator responsible for e.g. opening height approximation without influencing other networks.

The network architecture is presented in Table 1. Symbol 6-5-4-1 denotes the network with 2 hidden layers, 6 input neurons, 5 neurons in the first hidden layer, 4 neurons in the second hidden layer and 1 output unit.

The FIS were trained using gradient descent method with momentum. The FFNN were trained by the Levenberg-Marquardt method [8]. The approximator performance – approximation abilities – is judged with the help of Mean Square Errors [8]. Three different errors for each approximation problem are measured – training set error (MSE_L), validation set error (MSE_V) and testing set error (MSE_T). It should be mentioned that the level of the MSE depends on the range of the values that are compared.

3.3 Approximation Results Discussion

The results of approximation of the opening height, max von Mises stress in Plates 1, 2 and 3 are presented in Table 2.

Table 1. Architecture of the networks used in approximation of the valve system behavior

	Opening height	Stress in plate 1	Stress in plate 2	Stress in plate 3
FFNN symbol	6-14-6-1	6-14-8-1	6-14-8-1	6-16-8-1
FIS symbol	6-19-1	6-19-1	6-19-1	6-19-1

Both the FIS and the FFNN achieve similar MSE of approximation. The FFNN require a lower number of parameters to achieve the MSE at a similar level to the FIS. Additionally, the approximation abilities (generalization) of the FFNN are slightly better than the FIS. It can be observed by comparing the difference between MSE_L and MSE_T.

Table 2. MSE of the ANNs

	FFNN MSE_L	FFNN MSE_V	FFNN MSE_T	FIS MSE_L	FIS MSE_V	FIS MSE_T
Opening height	4.28e-6	4.68e-6	5.46e-6	6.58e-6	6.64e-6	8.10e-6
stress in plate 1	17.54	24.35	26.48	31.83	32.41	40.73
stress in plate 2	50.47	64.31	62.54	129.52	136.18	142.48
stress in plate 3	65.35	76.44	82.09	96.17	98.25	110.22

4   Application Example

4.1   Formulation of the Optimization Task

The goal is to design a stack of plates of a damper valve system to obtain a pressure-flow curve within the range presented in Fig. 2a. The pressure-opening curve can be transferred to the pressure-flow characteristic (see Fig. 2b) using the formula (3).

$$q = Cd \cdot A \cdot \sqrt{\frac{2p}{\rho}} \tag{3}$$

where: $Cd = 0.6$ is a discharge coefficient, $\varrho = 960 kg/m^3$ is fluid density and A is a flow area given by the equation (4).

$$A = 2\pi R \cdot H, \tag{4}$$

where: R is the radius of the piston valve and H is the opening height.

The Matlab® Optimization Toolbox™ is used in the optimization process. The Generalized Pattern Search (GPS) is chosen since this optimization solver can handle optimization problems with nonlinear, linear, and bound constraints, and does not require fitness functions to be differentiable or continuous [8].

The GPS minimizes the fitness function which contains information about the opening height of the stack of plates for a given pressure drop of the valve system. In other words, the goal is to find the pressure-opening curve with the best fit to the reference curve presented in Fig. 2b. The general form of the fitness function is given by the formula

$$ J = \sum_{i=1}^{F} \left(\widehat{H}(p_i) - H(p_i) \right)^2 , \tag{5} $$

where: $\widehat{H}$, H is the required and computed opening height respectively, p is the pressure drop, and F is the number of pressure intervals taken into account.

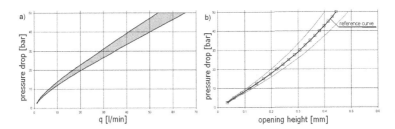

Fig. 2. The required: a) pressure-flow, b) opening height – pressure drop characteristic of the damper valve system with 20 points used for fitness function evaluation.

The optimization solver changes the design variables, which are the diameters of Plate 1 and 2 and the thickness of all three plates within the range mentioned in Sect. 3.1. To evaluate the fitness function, the opening height should be calculated based on the design of the stack of plates proposed by the optimization solver. This can be done by solving the boundary-value problem using the FE Model of the valve stack proposed by Czop et. al. [4,3]. This part of the optimization process is very time consuming because the fitness function (5) has to be computed for each design proposed by the optimization solver. The second disadvantage of such an approach has already been mentioned in Paragraph 1 of this paper. One way to speed up this process is to improve the fitness function evaluation. This can be done by replacing the FE Model solution of the boundary-value problem by an approximation of the solution that can be obtained using the Approximation Tool.

Replacement of the boundary-value problem solution by its approximation is already known. This approach was proposed in literature [1,2]. The identification process was realized on the basis of knowledge about the fields of displacements, temperature or natural frequencies of the investigated structure that were approximated by the FIS. The above-mentioned approach of solution replacement by approximation can also be met in commercial use. Simulia Isight® software proposes a method of optimization where the solution delivered by, for example, Finite Element Analysis (FEA) can be represented by its approximation [5,12]. Different techniques are proposed to be used – Response surface modeling, Radial Basis Function Approximation and Kriging method [5,12]. The idea of replacement of the boundary value problem solution using FEA by the Approximation Tool is presented in Fig. 3. The FFNN described in Sect. 3 of this paper is used by the Approximation Tool to approximate the opening height for 20 pressure values from 2.5 bar to 50 bar.

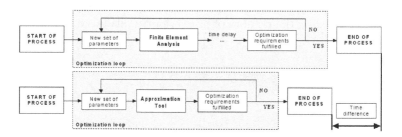

Fig. 3. Optimization process using a) Finite Element Analysis b) Approximation Tool

4.2   Optimization Results

The GPS method used to minimize the fitness function (5) requires the starting point to be provided by the user. The optimization process was performed several times in order to avoid the influence of starting point selection onto the optimization results. The starting point was randomly selected each time from the range described in Sect. 3.1. The time needed to perform one optimization process is 20-30 sec. Thus the cost of the optimization task repetition is negligible. The algorithm stops when the number of iterations performed reaches 100. The average total number of fitness function evaluations for 100 iterations is 700.

Fig. 4a shows the pressure-opening curves for different designs found in six optimization processes. The pressure-flow curves are presented in Fig. 4b. It can be noticed that the results of optimization are within the specified range with one exception – the pressure-flow curve of Design 1 is outside the specification for small flows.

For all selected designs the maximum von Mises stress level was calculated in order to find the best design in terms of fatigue durability. The stresses were calculated using FFNNs described in Sect. 3. Based on the results of the optimization process and stress calculations, the best option – Design 2 – was chosen. All six designs found by the optimization algorithm together with maximum von Mises stress values calculated by FFNNs are presented in Table 3.

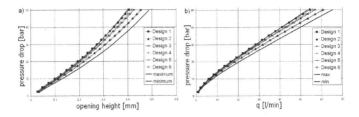

Fig. 4. Optimization results: a) pressure-opening and b) pressure-flow curves

Table 3. Designs found in the optimization process

	Thickness Plate 1 [mm]	Thickness Plate 2 [mm]	Thickness Plate 3 [mm]	Out. diam. Plate 1 [mm]	Out. diam. Plate 2 [mm]	Max von-Mises stress [MPa]
Design 1	0.30	0.35	0.20	17.0	21.0	508.1
Design 2	0.20	0.35	0.25	17.0	16.0	552.5
Design 3	0.30	0.30	0.25	12.0	20.0	823.3
Design 4	0.30	0.30	0.20	18.0	19.0	580.7
Design 5	0.25	0.30	0.25	19.0	17.0	637.9
Design 6	0.25	0.25	0.30	17.0	20.0	564.4

5   Summary

The paper describes the proposal, implementation, validation and an example of applying the Approximation Tool that allows the replacement of complex high-fidelity Finite Element analyses. As an approximator the FFNN and FIS were taken. Both the FIS and FNN provided MSE error on a similar level. The FFNN, however, has better generalization abilities – a smaller difference between the approximation error of training and testing data. Thus FFNN was chosen to be used in further investigations.

As the application example, the hydraulic damper valve system design process was presented. The Approximation Tool replaced a very time consuming boundary-value problem solution. The design process depended on fitness function minimization, which was evaluated with the help of FFNN used for opening height approximation. The valve stack designs, selected during the optimization process, were then ranked with respect to durability. Maximum stress level was calculated by the FFNNs presented in Section 3. A final design that fulfills all requirements was found. It was confirmed that usage of the Approximation Tool reduces the design process from 10-13 hours to less than 10 minutes.

Further investigations will focus on preparation and implementation of the optimization with Evolutionary Algorithms in order to make the design process independent of starting point selection.

Funding. This work was supported by Polish Ministry of Science (MNiI) [research project N N504 494239].

References

1. Burczynski, T., Orantek, P., Skrobol, A.: Fuzzy-neural and evolutionary computation in identification of defect. Journal of Theoretical and Applied Mechanics 42(3), 445–460 (2004)
2. Burczynski, T., Skrobol, A.: Coupled evolutionary algorithm and artificial neural network in defects identification. In: Bathe, K.J. (ed.) Third MIT Conf. on Computational Fluid and Solid Mechanics, pp. 122–1226 (2005)
3. Czop, P., Slawik, D., Sliwa, P., Wszolek, G.: Circular plater theory applied to modeling of intake valves used in shock absorbers. Journal of Achievements in Materials and Manufacturing Engineering 33(2), 173–180 (2009)
4. Czop, P., Slawik, D., Sliwa, P.: Static validation of a model of a disc valve system used in shock absorbers. International Journal of Vehicle Design 53(4), 317–342 (2010)
5. Dassault Systemes: Isight 3.5. Getting started guide (2009), http://www.simulia.com
6. Dixon, J.C.: The shock absorber handbook. Wiley, England (2007)
7. Kosinski, W., Weigl, M.: Fuzzy-neural systems for multivariate approximation problems. In: Proceeding of 6rd Zittau Fuzzy Colloquium, Zittau, pp. 141–146 (1998)
8. Math-Works Inc.: Matlab-Simulink documentation (2011), http://www.mathworks.com/help
9. Piatkowski, G., Ziemianski, L.: Neural network identification of a circular hole in the rectangular plate. In: Rutkowski, L., Kacprzyk, J. (eds.) Neural Networks and Soft Computing, pp. 778–783. Physica-Verlag Springer, Heidelberg (2003)
10. Rutkowska, D.: Computational intelligent systems. Akademicka Oficyna Wydawnicza PLJ, Warszawa (1997)
11. Segel, L., Lang, H.H.: The mechanics of automotive hydraulic dampers at high stroking frequencies. Vehicle System Dynamics 10(2–3), 82–85 (1981)
12. Van der Velden, A., Koch, P.: Isight design optimisation methodologies (2009), http://www.simulia.com
13. Van Kasteel, R., et al.: A new shock absorber model with an application in vehicle dynamics studies. In: 2003 SAE International Truck and Bus Meeting and Exhibition, Fort Worth, Texas (2003)
14. Young, W.C.: Roark's formulas for stress and strain. McGraw-Hill, New York (2003)

Part VII

Various Problems of Artificial Intelligence

System for Independent Living – New Opportunity for Visually Impaired

Jerzy Jelonkiewicz and Łukasz Laskowski

Czestochowa University of Technology, Department of Computer Engineering,
Al. A.K. 36, 42-200 Czestochowa, Poland

Abstract. The authors present the solution that supports the visually impaired persons. Proposed solution can help them to be more independent in everyday life. Described system will be able to assist the blind in unknown environment (stereo-vision based depth analysis module), to recognise familiar persons and read texts and labels. All information gathered by stereo-vision module and processed by the system (about obstacles in surrounding, result of face recognition, texts in visual field) will be available for the user thanks to tactile interface and the sound system. Considered here device can also help in moving around (system can be connected to a small vehicle).

Keywords: visually impaired, neural networks, stereovision, depth analysis.

1 Introduction

A significant number of the elderly suffer from poor eyesight. Even though they might be otherwise enjoying good health and relative fitness, they still face everyday difficulties with recognizing places, faces, reading text, as well as stress when crossing streets. This often has the effect of confining seniors to their own home. But even there, in a friendly environment, impaired sight still creates significant difficulties. All types of text - whether it is on a TV screen, in newspapers, on medicine labels, is usually written in small letters making it indiscernible for people with poor eyesight. Thus the home environment becomes inhospitable, forcing the residents to use dedicated carers. Overtime as additional medical problems with moving might appear the elderly can feel imprisoned in their homes, isolated, alone and not needed. Therefore some aid in recognizing the home and the surrounding environment can give the elderly an improvement of self confidence, a chance for a more independent, better quality life and the opportunity for active participation in the local community. Furthermore wheelchair or electric scooter users will receive driving assistance from the proposed system. The system, presented here, aims to address most of the everyday life difficulties of seniors with poor eyesight. Eyes give us the possibility to estimate the distance to a nearby object, recognize its shape, read and predict the moving object's position and so on. A truly useful aid for a visually challenged person is one that would facilitate both mobility and independence.

L. Rutkowski et al. (Eds.): ICAISC 2012, Part II, LNCS 7268, pp. 645–652, 2012.

A successful visual aid system will require depth perception, this can be achieved by utilizing a binocular system. Additionally such a solution would make face and text recognition feasible. The information gathered by the vision system would be fed to the user via a tactile interface. By touching an interface plate, the user would be able to perceive the third dimension effectively replacing the white cane. Tactile interface, proposed here, was not used before and seems to be much more convenient than e.g. sound 3D. Face recognition is a major issue for people with sight impairments. This is often exploited by criminals who pose as friends or relatives. Information recognized faces in the vicinity can be supplied to the user via a speaker speech system. Another major obstacle in the day to day lives of seniors with poor eyesight is shopping and running errands. Given that our system would have the feature of reading out text the user would be able to obtain the necessary products from the shop by himself/herself. The touch interface would supply shape information about the examined object and labels could be read out via the audio system. Finally the system can be augmented with a GPS module, allowing safe and easy navigation around the city and provide assistance with negotiating any obstacles that might arise. Additionally this would allow the carer to know where the user is located enabling quick response to any problems.

2   State of Art

The authors carried out survey concerning the systems, that could be helpful for individuals affected by impairment of sight in their everyday , independent life. The most interesting solutions are the following. One of this was presented by Pełczyński et all [1]. This system, based on stereovision, is able to lead the blind and warn about obstacles, thanks to 3D sound. The authors mentioned some efficiency problems of the system - the algorithm used for depth analysis was too simple (SAAD algorithm) to be able to solve the stereo-matching problem. Another application, proposed in literature is the system elaborated by professor Materka and his team [2, 3]. In this case efficiency of the system seems to be proved. Both mentioned above systems can assist the visually impaired people in unknown environment. The depth's perception is obtained by the 3D sound. The system, that seems to be similar with the authors idea, was build in Japan by Yairi et All [4]. This system allows for obstacles detection and assisting in moving around. Unfortunately, there was no information about used algorithms and components, which is crucial for the functionality of the device.

3   The Idea

Proposed system is based on stereo vision [5]. The advantages of stereo vision include; ease of use; non-contact; lack of emissions; low cost and flexibility [6-10]. The entire system could appear as shown in fig. 1. The system (fig. 1.) can be divided into three separate processing layers. At layer 1 the acquisition of image is carried out. It is performed by two stereoscopic cameras attached to

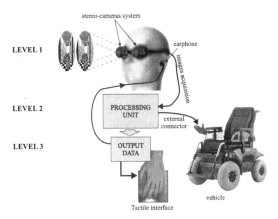

Fig. 1. The portable binocular vision system supporting aged and visually impaired people

the binoculars. Because of the displacement of the cameras, each image point in left and right pictures has slightly different position, which allows for depth calculation. At layer 2 the two images (from the left and right cameras) are fed into the PROCESSING UNIT. The unit would consist of a specialized computer with algorithms that allow for finding the distance to each point on the observed scene, recognition of objects (both functions implemented as neural networks) and also some additional functions: voice simulation, cooperation with a GPS system, reading text, vehicle motion support and coordination. The depth analysis problem seems to be the most difficult one. The real scene contains large amounts of points, and the complexity of the correspondence problem depends on the complexity of the scene. There are some ways that can help reduce the number of false matches, but many unsolved problems still exist in stereo matching. The authors of the proposal have worked out completely innovative algorithm of depth analysis from stereo pictures. This algorithm is based on the Self-Correcting Neural Network (completely innovative architecture of neural network with possibility of synaptic connection strength correction) [12], giving incredibly low error . High efficient algorithm together with parallel processing architecture should give satisfying results. Aged people often have problems with recognizing familiar faces. This is why the face recognition functionality is one of the most important features of the system. It can be solved with the help of associative memory. Additionally third dimension of considered object can improve results of the recognition process. So far shopping was nearly impossible for visually impaired people. A portable vision system allows for object detection (the stereo-vision module) through tactile interface. The touch interface gives of shape estimate information. Label and prices can be read through the text recognition feature. All text in the field of vision could be read by system through the earphone on demand. Information about recognized pieces of text in the vicinity can be given to the user through the audio or tactile channels. The processing unit would be fitted with an external connector. It allows for cooperation with external devices (mainly the vehicle, but other devices are possible). At layer 3 the results from the processing unit are converted and written as OUTPUT DATA. The information about the depth of the scene, result of object recognition are passed to a tactile interface. The topological (tactile) plate is an object of a pending patent. The tactile interface consists of three independent modules: topological plate, vibrating action buttons and brail information's displayer. By touching this plate, the user is able to perceive the 3rd dimension of his/her surrounding effectively replacing the white cane. Initial design of tactile palmtop interface presents fig.2.

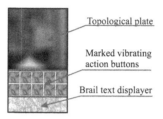

Fig. 2. Design of tactile interface

The upper part of the interface allows for the depth perception by the blind. Thanks to innovative construction, depth of the observed (by stereo-cameras system) scene is transformed to this element, and can be received by the user. The middle part of interface is used for the system control. Vibrating buttons inform about possible action and also for releasing the action. E.g. if in a view area a text appears, the appropriate button will vibrate (frequency of vibrating is inversely proportional to the distance to the object). Pushing this button invokes text reading action. All text in the field of vision could be read by system through the earphone on demand. Information about recognized pieces of text in the vicinity can be given to the user through the audio or tactile channels. Brail text displayer is another option for the user. Moreover the sound system can warn the user about recognized obstacles. The elderly can have some problems with spatial orientation and reaching their destinations. This can be supported by a GPS module in the system. Information about the route can be passed through the earphone. By connecting the system to the Internet it is also possible to relay the position of the user to other people (carer). Crossing roads is another frequent problem for visually impaired people. Moving objects can be identified through depth analysis and image segmentation. This information can be very useful in safely roads crossing assistance (information about an opportunity to cross the road could be given through the earphone). Smart, small vehicle can be helpful for independent moving outdoors and also indoors (e.g. in markets). When equipped with driving support system, it becomes safer and more convenient. Such a vehicle should prevent collisions, assist in finding localization and lead to the destination place. These features can be obtained by connecting the vehicle with the vision system (vision system can operate independently or support driving when connected to the vehicle). The vision system should be able to make basic semantic analysis of the scene and estimate distance to the detected obstacles. The vehicle will be equipped with additional camera in order to analyze the way in front of the vehicle. In an emergency, the system will inform the user by vibrating the interface part, marked as obstacle warning. If there is no reaction from the user, the voice warning appears. If the vehicle still goes on, the driving support system may slow down or even stop the vehicle. The system described here does not attempt to modify the environment in order to fit it to the needs of older people, but attempts to make the lives easier and independent by trying to address some of the most important problems faced by people with poor eyesight.

4   The Preliminary Research Results

The system considered here is on the stage of advanced project. The authors are working on component modules of the system. The most advanced component is the stereo-vision system, based on the depth analysis algorithm. Proposed novel neural structures considers the following Hopfield Neural Networks: Hybrid-Maximum Neural Network (HMNN) [11] and Self-Correcting Neural Network (SCNN) [12]. Each network has different advantages, confirmed in preliminary tests. The main advantage of HMNN is its high performance with good enough accuracy. The SCNN offers exceptionally high accuracy, not observed in any other considered network. In order to verify the efficiency of algorithm a comparison with solutions known from literature was carried out. Each neural stereo-vision algorithm was simulated in the same experimental conditions . The results of the Hybrid Maximum Network's and Self-Correcting Network's working were juxtaposed with the results of stereo matching process, performed by some other Hopfield-based networks [13-17]. Obtained depth maps (the brightness of points are proportional to disparity corresponding to this point) and errors were shown in fig. 3. Proposed structures were marked on red. In the case of HMNN, thanks to the use of maximum mode of network's working (only extremely stimulated neurons are taken under consideration), the time of computation significantly decreases. The experimental results indicate significant advantage of using the maximum mode after finding the global minimum attraction area. A comparative analysis, performed with the classical Hopfield network (analogue and discrete), Maximum Network and Hybrid Maximum Network indicated a better performance of the latter type of network. This solution was similar to that obtained by the analogue Hopfield-like network, but the number of iterations in our case was much smaller. As the computational time is crucial in the real-time applications , the use of novel Hybrid Maximal Network is justified. Another advantages was found for the SCNN. The most typical problem for the Hopfield-like networks, with trapping in local minimum of energy, was solved by using a supervising layer. Thanks to interconnection weights modification, done by the supervising neurons, the local minima trapping problem is solved. Moreover the experimental results also prove another interesting feature

The picture	*The name of network*	Depth map	Error (in percents)
	Analogue Hopfield-like neural network		19,89
	Discrete Hopfield-like neural network		69,02
	Discrete Hopfield-like neural network with continuous activation function		59,62
	Maximum neural network		68,52
	Hybrid Maximum Neural Network	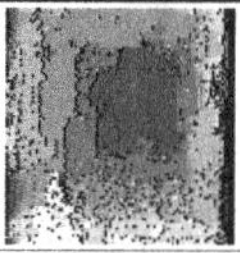	20,04
	Self-Correcting Neural Network - after the first weight correction	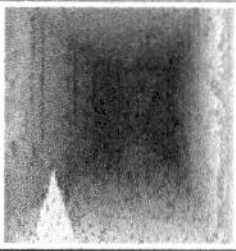	11,45
	Self-Correcting Neural Network - after the second weight correction		4,37

Fig. 3. The juxtaposition of results of working neural networks investigated in the present publication

of the supervising neurons: they are responsible for the interconnection weights modification. A comparative analysis, performed with the classical Hopfield network and SCNN indicated a better performance of SCMNN. The solution of stereo correspondence problem obtained looks to be more promising compared to the classical Hopfield like network.

5 Conclusion

The elderly with impaired sight are considered disabled in all civilized countries and usually belong to a special care group. Special funds and resources are allocated to cover most of the costs related to adapting their living spaces to their needs. In most cases however they require full or part time help from their carers. The introduction of the proposed here system could change that - the visually impaired could once again live with a high degree of independence. The system is under intensive research, carried out by the authors. A part of the visual system was presentedpaper. In this study authors show the use of two innovative Hopfield architectures based on the following neural networks: Hybrid Maximum Neural Network and Self-Correcting Neural Network. The networks have been used in stereo matching process. This problem is formulated as an optimization task where an energy function of network, which represents the mapping of all constraints on the solution, is minimized, thanks to a neural network. The advantage of using a Hopfield neural network is that a global match is automatically achieved because all the neurons are interconnected in a feedback loop so the output of one affects the input of all the others. The convergence into a stable state is guaranteed for continuous Hopfield-like network with continuous activation function. The parallel execution capability of this structure is also a powerful property that should be taken into consideration in terms of the foreseen target system.

As was shown, only results obtained by continuous, Hybrid Maximum and Self-Correcting networks that can be accepted. Almost the same errors as for analogue network were obtained by Hybrid Maximum network. Moreover the HMNN was faster- the number of epochs for this kind of structure was 30 percents lower than in the case of analogue Hopfield-like network - very important in real-time applications. The most accurate performance offers the Self-Correcting Neural Network. This solution gains its accuracy due to weight correction process. This leads to the conclusion that the weights correction process, based on the obtained solution's analysis, is essential to reach a correct solution of stereo correspondence problem. This approach can be crucial for applications requiring really high accuracy (like the vision system supporting visually impaired people).

Taking into account obtained results we conclude that HMNN and SCNN are the most efficient among considered neural structures. These structures can find application is the system proposed here. This approaches can be crucial for the applications requiring really high accuracy (e.g. system of supporting visually impaired people).

References

[1] Pełczyński, P., Ostrowski, B., Rzeszotarski, D.: Mobilny system pasywnej nawigacji w scenie trójwymiarowej. VIII Electronic Conference KKE 2009, Published in Elektronika R51(1), 35–37 (2010)

[2] Strumillo, P., Materka, A.: Systemy elektroniczne wspomagajace osoby starsze i niepelnosprawne. Elektronika 11, 28–31 (2007)

[3] Strumillo, P., Materka, A.: Elektronika we wspomaganiu osob starszych i niepelnosprawnych. In: VI Electronic Conference, Darlowo, pp. 15–21 (2007)

[4] Yairi, I.E., Kayama, K., Igi, S.: Robotic Communication Terminals as a Ubiquitous System for Improving Human Mobility by Making Environment Virtually Barrier-Free. In: Sakurai, A., Hasida, K., Nitta, K. (eds.) JSAI 2003. LNCS (LNAI), vol. 3609, pp. 61–75. Springer, Heidelberg (2007)

[5] Jain, A.K.: Fundamentals of digital image processing. Prentice-Hall (1989)

[6] Bouayed, H.A., Pissaloux, E.E., Abdallah, S.M.: Vision system for fast 3D obstacle detection via stereovision matching. In: SPIE Int. Conf. on Intelligent Robots and Computer Vision, Boston (2001)

[7] Barlow, H.B., Blackmore, C., Pettigrew, J.D.: The natural mechanism of binocular depth discrimination. J. Physiology 193, 327–342 (1967)

[8] Marr, D., Poggio, T.: Cooperative computation of stereo disparity. Science 194, 283–287 (1976)

[9] Faugeras, O.: Three-dimensional computer vision. A geometric viewpoint. MIT (1993)

[10] Fisher, R.B.: From surfaces to objects: computer vision and three dimensional scene analysis. John Wiley and Sons Ltd. (1989)

[11] Laskowski, Ł.: Hybrid-Maximum Neural Network for Depth Analysis from Stereo-Image. In: Rutkowski, L., Scherer, R., Tadeusiewicz, R., Zadeh, L.A., Zurada, J.M. (eds.) ICAISC 2010. LNCS (LNAI), vol. 6114, pp. 47–55. Springer, Heidelberg (2010)

[12] Laskowski, L.: A Novel Continuous Dual Mode Neural Network in Stereo-Matching Process. In: Diamantaras, K., Duch, W., Iliadis, L.S. (eds.) ICANN 2010. LNCS, vol. 6354, pp. 294–297. Springer, Heidelberg (2010)

[13] Ruycheck, Y., Postaire, J.G.: A neural network algorithm for 3-D reconstruction from stereo pairs of linear images. Pattern Recognition Lett. 17, 387–398 (1996)

[14] Ruycheck, Y., Postaire, J.G.: A New Neural Real-Time Implementation for Obstacle Detection using Linear Stereo Vision. Real-Time Imaging 5, 141–153 (1999)

[15] Pajeras, G., Cruz, J.M., Aranda, J.: Relaxation by Hopfield Network in Stereo Image Matching. Pattern Recognition 31(5), 561–574 (1998)

[16] Sun, T.H., Chen, M., Lo, S., Tien, F.C.: Face recognition using 2D and disparity eigenface. Expert Systems with Applications 33, 265–273 (2007)

[17] Joya, G., Atencia, M.A., Sandoval, F.: Hopfield neural networks for optimization: study of the different dynamics. Neurocomputing 43, 219–237 (2002)

A Clustering-Based Methodology
for Selection of Fault Tolerance Techniques

Paweł L. Kaczmarek and Marcin Ł. Roman

Gdańsk University of Technology, Faculty of Electronics,
Telecommunications and Informatics, Narutowicza 11/12, 80-952 Gdańsk, Poland
pkacz@eti.pg.gda.pl, marcin.roman@gmail.com
http://www.eti.pg.gda.pl

Abstract. Development of dependable applications requires selection of appropriate fault tolerance techniques that balance efficiency in fault handling and resulting consequences, such as increased development cost or performance degradation. This paper describes an advisory system that recommends fault tolerance techniques considering specified development and runtime application attributes. In the selection process, we use the K-means clustering algorithm to identify similarities between known fault tolerance techniques to select those ones that are possibly different, but simultaneously conform to developer specification. As a part of the research, we implemented a web-based system that covers definition of attributes, aggregates knowledge about fault tolerance techniques together, and implements the advisory algorithm.

Keywords: fault tolerance, clustering, advisory systems, software development.

1 Introduction

Development of dependable computer systems remains a challenging task; considering the size, complexity and application domains of the systems. Fault tolerance is one of means to attain dependability by providing system functionality even when faults occur in the system [2] [9] [13] [6]. A number of concrete fault tolerance techniques (FTT) exist, including: checkpointing, N-version programming, atomic actions and exception handling, among others. The use of any FTT requires additional time and development cost, which is often the main obstacle that limits application dependability.

Development of dependable applications requires selection of appropriate FTTs that balance cost and efficiency, and consider other attributes such as development time, performance and parallelization. However, developers lack appropriate knowledge and guidelines that simplify the selection process, which causes dependence on human factor. This in turn may lead to human made errors, company specific solutions and unrepeatability of the whole process.

Considering the difficulties, we propose a methodology that assists the developer in the process of FTT selection. The developer specifies required attributes

L. Rutkowski et al. (Eds.): ICAISC 2012, Part II, LNCS 7268, pp. 653–661, 2012.

that may concern dependability (such as reliability or availability), development process (such as time or budget) or application quality of service (QoS) (such as performance). The methodology recommends FTTs that match specified attributes, but simultaneously differ in their attributes other than specified. We assume that it is not reasonable to use similar techniques because it increases the development cost and does not increase the coverage of tolerated faults.

As a preliminary step of the methodology, we identified attributes of FTTs and rated many existing FTTs. The methodology uses the K-means clustering algorithm to identify groups of similar FTTs depending on general rates assigned to the techniques. The methodology selects techniques that are assigned to different clusters and match required attributes best. We used a heuristic approach in the methodology, analogously to other expert systems [7].

The rest of the paper is organized as follows. The next section presents related work and our motivation. Sect. 3 presents fault tolerance techniques, thier attributes and rating. The recommendation algorithm is discussed in Sect. 4. Then, the system that implements the methodology is presented in Sect. 5; and Sect. 6 concludes the paper.

2   Related Work and Motivation

Fault tolerance is a mature research discipline, in which numerous models and solutions have already been proposed. However, the solutions typically address tolerance of concrete faults rather than a general comparison of FTTs and their selection. Consequently, software developers are faced with the difficulty to select appropriate FTTs that would conform to project requirements. There is no work known to us that supplies a method of automated recommendation of fault tolerance techniques in software development.

The ReSIST (Resilience for Survivability in IST) [2] Network of Excellence created a comprehensive knowledge base and catalog of documents related to the creation of highly dependable systems. Project outcomes cover a knowledge base browser, proposals of new solutions and a list of Resilience-Explicit Computing Mechanisms has been created. Books and articles [13,6,15,9] overview fault tolerance techniques. Additionally, it is agreed that fault tolerance requires redundancy and additional development effort. In our work, we propose an advisory system that can automatically recommend appropriate FTT, which is not available in existing knowledge bases and catalogs.

[7] presents a comprehensive methodology for selecting requirements engineering techniques in the development process. The work presents a list of requirement engineering techniques, technique evaluations and a selection algorithm based on the clustering approach [12]. In our work, we apply a similar operation pattern that recommends appropriate techniques depending on technique and project attributes. Our work differs in that we apply the methodology in fault tolerance rather than requirements engineering, which requires different definition of techniques, attributes and selection rules.

[16] presents a general fault tolerant architecture GFTSA and formal language Object-Z to prove properties of GFTSA. The architecture uses many common fault tolerance concepts such as checkpointing, coordinated recovery, and exceptions. Many detailed techniques and models of fault tolerance have been proposed. [3] presents a solution of coordinated forward recovery and exception handling in distributed systems. [1,4] focus on development of heterogeneous software systems by integrating off-the-shelf modules of unknown dependability. [14,8] present solutions that use redundancy and voting to improve dependability in distributed applications. In our work, we do not propose a novel method for tolerating faults but rather a methodology of selecting an appropriate FTT.

3   Evaluation of Fault Tolerance Techniques

Fault tolerance techniques influence both development and runtime of applications. Development is influenced by additional time and effort required for technique application in practice. Runtime is influenced by additional fault tolerance and additional overhead that may cause performance degradation.

During the analysis, we consider three groups of attributes:

- Development attributes. The attributes concern the impact of a FTT on the development process, which includes: economy - required cost and time overhead (CST), configuration simplicity (CS), maturity (MTR), learning curve (LC), popularity (POP).
- Application behavioral attributes. The attributes concern features related to QoS that may be influenced by using a particular FTT: sequential performance (SP), parallelization (PAR), error detection (ED) and fault tolerance (FT).
- Dependability attributes [6,2,11,10]. Typically, dependability is described using the following detailed attributes: reliability (REL), availability (AVL), safety (SAF), confidentiality (CON), integrity (INT) and maintainability (MNT).

Some of the attributes have a heuristic nature which requires subjective expert opinions. This, however, conforms with the general approach of the methodology as it leverages the heuristic approach. We use AT to denote the set of considered attributes.

Identification of FTTs and description of their attributes are first steps required in selection of appropriate techniques. We leverage existing knowledge of FTTs, such as: [13,3,15,6,2]. The identification of the attributes enables a systematic description and classification of a FTT. Selected FTTs include: coding techniques (checkpointing, exception handling, transactions, distributed transactions), design diverse techniques, based on redundancy in implementation and design (recovery blocks, N-version programming), data diverse techniques, based on data re-expression algorithms (N-copy programming, Retry blocks) and others. More techniques and detailed descriptions are registered in the web system.

Table 1 shows exemplary results of FTT ratings.

Table 1. Selected fault tolerance techniques and attributes

	CS	CST	MTR	LC	POP	ED	FT	SC	PAR
Checkpointing	3	4	5	4	3	4	3	3	1
Deadline mechanism	2	2	2	3	1	3	3	2	2
Distributed Recovery Blocks	2	2	3	2	2	4	4	1	5
Exception Handling	5	4	5	5	5	2	3	4	2
N-copy programming	4	5	3	4	3	2	3	1	5
N-self checking	2	2	3	3	3	3	5	2	5
N-version programming	4	3	4	4	4	5	5	1	4
Recovery Blocks	3	2	3	3	2	4	4	1	1
Retry Blocks	3	4	5	5	3	2	3	2	2
Self-configuring optimal programming	1	2	2	1	1	4	4	2	3
Transactions	5	3	5	5	5	4	4	3	3
... ...	...	...	...	...	...	...	...	...	...

After identification of attributes and known FTTs, we performed an expert-based rating using the following procedure:

- We performed a survey among experts in software engineering and dependability. Each FTT was rated individually by four experts that assigned appropriate rates for each FTT attribute.
- We normalized the rates and calculated the final result by averaging individual ratings. All rates were scaled to the range of 1 to 5 ($Rates = \{1, 2, 3, 4, 5\}$), where 1 denotes the lowest desired value and 5 the highest desired value.
- Each $t \in FTT$ was given a rate $\rho \in Rates$ for each attribute $a \in AT$ constructing a vector:

$$Rates(t) = [\rho_{1,t}, \rho_{2,t}, ..., \rho_{M,t}] \tag{1}$$

where M is the size of AT.

Although expert-based rating is a heuristic approach, it is argued that the approach is effective [7,5] in many cases. The rating enables transition from heuristic knowledge to a machine-interpretable form. Our solution uses the same processing model as [7], adjusted to the specific methods of fault tolerance.

4   FTT Selection Method

The selection method uses information about FTTs, attributes and rates given previously by experts. We assume that FTT rating is universal, that is it is made available for developers independently from the project they are developing.

4.1   Specification of FTT Requirements

The recommendation algorithm requires the following information regarding the concrete development project that is considered:

- The number of required techniques (K)
- Specification of attribute group to be used in clustering and evaluating. We assume that attributes are selected from one of two groups: (i) general dependability attributes, (ii) development and application behavior attributes.
- Specification of desired attributes of techniques for the concerned project given arbitrary by a software developer. The specification contains N selected attributes $a \in AT$ and their weights (w) expressed in the range of 1 to 5:

$$AT Requirement = ((a_1, w_1), (a_2, w_2), ..., (a_N, w_N)) \qquad (2)$$

The purpose of the algorithm is to recommend K techniques such that:

- The varied sum of rates for attributes in $AT Requirement$ is maximized. Attributes specified with higher weights are considered as more important.

$$Maximize \sum_{k=1}^{K} \sum_{n=1}^{N} Rate(t_k, a_n) * w_j \qquad (3)$$

and
- Recommended techniques differ in attributes other then specified in the input $AT Requirement$.

4.2   Clustering-Based Categorization of FTT

We intend to select techniques that are possibly different but simultaneously conform to developer requirements. Consequently, the recommended set of FTT provides a possibly wide coverage of unspecified features. We used the K-means clustering algorithm [12] to divide FTTs into groups of similar techniques. From each cluster, we recommend the technique that matches best the $AT Requirement$. We map the description of FTTs into the model appropriate for the K-means clustering algorithm as follows:

- FTT attributes create a multi-dimensional space $\mathbb{S}^M$, the number of FTT attributes is the dimension of the space (M).
- Each technique is considered as a vector $p \in \mathbb{S}^M$. Rates of FTT attributes are values in corresponding dimensions.
- The size of FTT (the set of fault tolerance techniques) corresponds to the number of vectors $(\{p_1, p_2, ...p_N\})$.
- The number of selected techniques K corresponds to the number of generated clusters $(\omega_1, \omega_2, ..., \omega_K)$.

The objective of K-means clustering is to minimize the function:

$$J = \sum_{k=1}^{K} \left(\sum_{j, p_j \in \omega_k} d(p_j, \mu_k) \right) \qquad (4)$$

where d means the distance between a point p and a cluster center μ. The distance measure is also a criterion for cluster membership: a point belongs to the cluster that is closest to it. It may be viewed as a global optimization goal to minimize the average error. We used three distance metrics: Euclidean, Chebyshev and Manhattan.

After clustering, closer points vary less, which means the techniques grouped in one cluster can be regarded as competing. The points from different clusters can be regarded as complementary. Selecting a point from each cluster chooses the best technique in each group while selection of points from different clusters provides the widest range of coverage of features.

4.3   Algorithm Operation

Algorithm 1 shows the main steps of the FTT recommendation algorithm that works as follows:

1. Initial pre-selection of a subset of candidate techniques. Since not all techniques are appropriate in each case, the user has a possibility to pre-harvest selection of candidates.
2. Division of FTTs into subsets using clustering. We intend to select techniques that are possibly different but simultaneously conform to developer requirements.
3. Selection of techniques. The algorithm selects "the best" technique from each cluster, which means selecting the technique with the highest evaluation function (Equation 3).
4. Clustering verification. The process of clustering may result in an empty cluster [12] because of its heuristic nature. If the situation occurs, the algorithm selects another technique from a non-empty cluster.
5. Recommend FTT and present corresponding code patterns.

5   Implementation and Evaluation

The designed methodology was implemented in a system that manages appropriate data infrastructure and supplies the recommendation algorithm. Using the system, we registered approximately twenty FTTs, technique attributes, FTT ratings and code snippets.

The system supplies two kinds of interfaces: a web based interface and Web services interface. The web interface is expected to be regularly used by developers. It allows one to configure parameters of the clustering algorithm, adding and deleting new elements: techniques, attributes, etc. The Web services interface allows connection to the system by other tools and modules related to application development. It supplies the recommendation mechanism, technique description and attributes. The application is available at:

http://www.fttadvisor.eti.pg.gda.pl

The system is implemented in the .NET 3.5 environment and uses the MS SQL 2008 database to store data. It is constructed as a typical three-layer application containing data access layer, business logic layer and interface layer (divided into Web services and www modules). The system covers approximately ten thousand LOC of C#, SQL and ASP pages. Adequate SQL scripts and installers are also supplied.

Algorithm 1. Selection of FTTs depending on user specified attributes

---

input: techniqueCount,   attributeGroupName,   userWeights, $THREAD\_COUNT$, MAX_STEPS, $TOTAL\_RANDOM$

output: set of recommended techniques

1: Techniques t = ReadTechniques(attributeGroupName, userWeights);
2: SynchronizedContainer container = new SynchronizedContainer();
3: Techniques[] techniques = Clone(t, $THREAD\_COUNT$);
4: **for** $i = 1$ to $THREAD\_COUNT$ in parallel **do**
5:     initialTechniques = techniques[i];
6:     **if** techniqueCount $\geq$ initialTechniques.Size() **then**
7:         container.Put(initialTechniques);
8:     **else**
9:         Cluster[] clusters = DistributeInitialClusters($TOTAL\_RANDOM$);
10:        **for** $i = 1$ to MAX_STEPS **do**
11:            **for all** c in clusters **do**
12:                c.FlushCluster();
13:            **end for**
14:            **for all** t in initialTechniques **do**
15:                Cluster c = FindTheNearestCluster(t, clusters);
16:                c.Assign(t);
17:            **end for**
18:            **for all** c in clusters **do**
19:                c.MoveTheClusterCentre();
20:            **end for**
21:            **if** HasAnyClusterNotMoved() **then**
22:                break;
23:            **end if**
24:        **end for**
25:        int emptyClusters = 0;
26:        **for all** c in clusters **do**
27:            **if** c.IsEmpty() **then**
28:                emptyClusters = emptyClusters + 1;
29:            **else**
30:                container.Put(c.GetTheMostRatedTechnique());
31:            **end if**
32:        **end for**
33:        **for** $i = 0$ to emptyClusters **do**
34:            container.Put(GetTheBestTechniqueNotSelectedYet());
35:        **end for**
36:    **end if**
37: **end for**
38: JoinAllThreads();
39: return container.GetTheBestTechniques(techniqueCount);

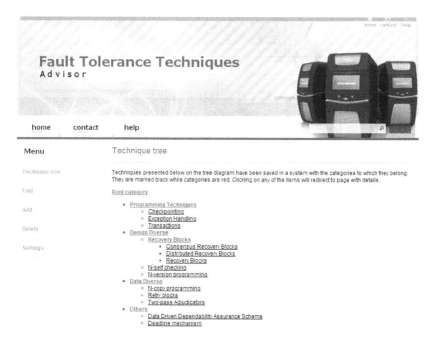

Fig. 1. Techniques tree

Fig. 1 shows a screenshot of registered techniques classified in categories.

The system enables an administrator and a user to configure the clustering algorithm, including: max number of iterations, min and max dimension value, distance metric, using all attributes for clustering and for objective function.

6   Conclusions

The paper proposed a methodology of automated recommendation of fault tolerance techniques. Our work leverages knowledge about existing attributes related to development of dependable applications and existing catalogs of fault tolerance techniques. We conducted an expert based rating of techniques and proposed an algorithm such that selected techniques match developer requirements and simultaneously are possibly different. The algorithm is based on K-means clustering as a heuristic method of unsupervised learning. The methodology was implemented in a web based system.

The methodology and the implemented system will be the basis for further work. The current set of techniques includes the most important and recognizable ones. We plan to register more techniques in the system to cover both general purpose, and specific, techniques. Hierarchization is another interesting research area that originates from the clustering approach. Categorization of techniques would be advisable to guide developers through the selection process.

Further, FTTs are described solely on specified attributes, which narrows expressiveness. New means of description may cover concepts unavailable in the current analysis such as: field use of an application, application architecture, development technology, and others. The extension can lead to better clustering and matching of entered requirements.

Acknowledgments. The work was supported in part by the Polish Ministry of Science and Higher Education under research project number N N519 172337.

References

1. Chitnis, L., Dobraa, A., Ranka, S.: Fault tolerant aggregation in heterogeneous sensor networks. Journal of Parallel and Distributed Computing (2009)
2. European Network of Excellence ReSIST, Resilience for Survivability in IST, http://www.resist-noe.org
3. Garcia, A., Rubira, C., Romanovsky, A., Xu, J.: A comparative study of exception handling mechanisms for building dependable object-oriented software. Journal of Systems and Software (2001)
4. Gashi, I., Popov, P., Strigini, L.: Fault tolerance via diversity for off-the-shelf products: A study with sql database servers. IEEE Transactions on Dependable and Secure Computing (October- December 2007)
5. Helmer, O., Rescher, N.: On the epistemology of the inexact science. Management Science 6(1) (1959)
6. Jalote, P.: Fault Tolerance in Distributed Systems. Prentice Hall PTR (1998)
7. Jang, L., Eberlein, A., Far, B., Mousavi, M.: A methodology for the selection of requirements engineering tehniques. Software and Systems Modeling 7 (2007)
8. Kaczmarek, P.L.: Ontology Supported Selection of Versions for N-Version Programming in Semantic Web Services. In: Bubak, M., van Albada, G.D., Dongarra, J., Sloot, P.M.A. (eds.) ICCS 2008, Part I. LNCS, vol. 5101, pp. 317–326. Springer, Heidelberg (2008)
9. Koren, I., Krishna, C.: Fault-Tolerant Systems. Elsevier B.V. (2007)
10. Krawczyk, H., Wiszniewski, B.: Analysis and Testing of Distributed Software Applications. Research Studies Press (1998)
11. Laprie, J.C., Randell, B., Aviienis, A.: Fundamental concepts of dependability. Tech. rep., LAAS-CNRS (2000)
12. Manning, C.D., Raghavan, P., Schtze, H.: An Introduction to Information Retrieval. Cambridge University Press, Cambridge (2009)
13. Pullum, L.: Software Fault Tolerance Techniques and Implementation. Artech House (2001)
14. Townend, P., Xu, J.: Replication-based fault tolerance in a grid environment. In: U.K. e-Science 3rd All-Hands Meeting (2004)
15. Xie, Z., Sun, H., Saluja, K.: A survey of software fault tolerance techniques (2008)
16. Yuan, L., Dong, J.S., Sun, J., Basit, H.A.: Generic fault tolerant software architecture reasoning and customization. IEEE Transactions on Reliability (September 2006)

Improving PAWS by the Island Confinement Method

Yousef Kilani, Mohammad Bsoul, Ayoub Alsarhan, and Ibrahim Obeidat

Faculty of Prince Al-Hussein Bin Abdallah II for Information Technology,
Hashemite University, Jordan
{ymkilani,mbsoul,AyoubM,IMSObeidat}@hu.edu.jo
http://www.hu.edu.jo

Abstract. The propositional satisfiability problem (SAT) is one of the most studied NP-complete problems in computer science [1]. Some of the best known methods for solving certain types of SAT instances are stochastic local search algorithms [6].

Pure Additive Weighting Scheme (PAWS) is now one of the best dynamic local search algorithms in the additive weighting category [7]. Fang et. al [3] introduce the island confinement method to speed up the local search algorithms. In this paper, we incorporate the island confinement method into PAWS to speed up PAWS. We show through experiments that, the resulted algorithm, PAWSI, betters PAWS in solving the hard graph coloring and AIS problems.
abstract environment.

Keywords: The propositional satisfiability problem, local search algorithms, the island confinement method, PAWS.

1 Introduction

The *satisfiability (SAT) problem* is one of the best known and well-studied problems in computer science, with many practical applications in domains such as theorem proving, hardware verification and planning [7]. "The techniques used to solve SAT problems can be divided into two main areas: complete search techniques based on the well-known Davis-Putnam-Logemann-Loveland (DPLL) algorithm [8] and stochastic local search (SLS) techniques evolving out of Selman and Kautz's 1992 GSAT algorithm [9]" [7].

Fang et. al [3] introduce *the island confinement method (ICM)* to speed up the local search algorithms. This method considers some clauses, *the island*, as hard in which the search satisfies these clauses throughout the search process. Fang et. al [3], and Kilani [4] incorporated the ICM into the DLM [11], [12], [13] and ESG [14] algorithms. They showed that the resulted algorithms after the incorporation process betters the original algorithms in solving the SAT problems encoded from the *binary constraint satisfaction problems*. Fang et. al [2], [5] further introduce two new theorems to find an island.

L. Rutkowski et al. (Eds.): ICAISC 2012, Part II, LNCS 7268, pp. 662–670, 2012.

In this paper, we incorporate the island confinement method into PAWS to speed up PAWS for solving any type of SAT. We show through experiments that, the resulted algorithm, PAWSI, betters PAWS in solving the hard graph coloring and AIS problems.

The rest of this paper is organized as follows. Section 2 introduces the SAT. Section 3 presents the PAWS algorithm based on the source code taken from the author. Section 4 introduces the ICM which we incorporate into PAWS to speed up PAWS. Section 5 presents PAWSI, our algorithm after incorporating the ICM into PAWS. Section 6 shows the results of running PAWS and PAWSI and compares between them. The last section gives conclusion remarks.

2   SAT

A SAT problem has n *(Boolean variables)/variables*: $x_1,...,x_n$ [10]. For each variable x_i, there exist two *literals*, $\bar{x}_i$ (the negative form) and x_i (the positive form). Each variable can take the value of either *true* (1) or *false* (0). When x_i = true the literals $\bar{x}_i$ and x_i are false and true respectively and when x_i = false the literals $\bar{x}_i$ and x_i are true and false respectively. A *clause* or a *constraint* is a disjunction of literals which is true (*satisfied*) when at least one of its literals is true. The SAT problem is a conjunction of a set of clauses.

The SAT problem consists of finding an assignment to all variables of a propositional formula ϕ, expressed in *conjunctive normal form* (CNF) so that all clauses of ϕ is satisfied [10]. An *valuation* or a *state* is a complete assignment to each variable the value of either true or false. A *solution* is an valuation that satisfies all the clauses. A *solution space* of a SAT problem s is a set of all solutions of s. *Flipping a literal x or $\bar{x}$* means flipping the variable x by changing its current value either from true to false or false to true.

Example 1. given a SAT problem which has the set of variables: $\{x_1, x_2, x_3, x_4\}$, and the set of clauses $\{c_1, c_2, c_3, c_4\}$, where $c_1 \equiv x_1 \vee \overline{x_2} \vee \overline{x3} \vee x_4$, $c_2 \equiv x_2 \vee \overline{x3}$, $c_3 \equiv x_2 \vee x_3 \vee x_4$, and $c_4 \equiv x_3 \vee x_4 \vee x_2$.

3   PAWS

The Pure Additive Weighting Scheme (PAWS) is now one of the best *dynamic local search* (DLS) algorithm in the additive weighting category [7]. PAWS is one of the current state-of-art techniques for solving SAT. The DLS algorithm is the local search algorithm that adjusts the weights of the clauses, the noise value, and/or the value of the *smooth probability* (SP) during the process of executing the local search algorithm. The SP is the process of decreasing the weights of the clauses during the process of executing the local search algorithm. Figure 1 shows PAWS as taken from [15]. In this figure, PAWS include all the lines that do not start with the minus sign. PAWS works as follows. It gives each clause in a SAT problem a weight. Initially, it generates a random starting point (*i.e. a random valuation*) and sets each clause's weight to 1. In a search for a solution,

PAWS makes a series of *local search moves* from the current valuation to a *better (best < 0) or equal neighbour (best = 0)* valuation. This neighbour valuation becomes the current valuation after moving to it. PAWS repeats this process of moving from the current valuation to a neighbour valuation until it either finds a solution or the time is over. The neighbour valuation of a valuation x is the valuation that results from flipping a single variable v from x. Valuation x is better than or equal to valuation y, if the sum of the weights of the unsatisfied clauses in x is less than or equal to the sum of the weights of the unsatisfied clauses in y respectively. The best neighbour of x is a better neighbour of x that has the minimum sum of the weights of the unsatisfied clauses among the neighbours of x. Initially, the current valuation is the random starting point. PAWS moves to the best neighbout valuation of the current valuation if there is any better neighbour valuation. It moves to a best neighbour by flipping one of the best literals from the *best* set if *best* is not empty. All the literals in *best* must appear in the unsatisfied clauses of the current valuation. Whenever PAWS encounters a situation where there is no better neighbour valuation, it will either move to an equal neighbour valuation with probability P_{flat} or it will increase the weights of the currently unsatisfied clauses and make smoothing if the number of times clause weights increased exceeds a certain number, Max_{inc}. If PAWS does not find a solution within a *cutoff* flips, it restarts the search. It repeats this up to a number of tries (*tries*), where *tries* is a parameter.

4   The Island Confinement Method

The ICM is based on an observation: a solution of a SAT S must lie in the intersection of the solution space of all clauses of S [2]. Solving S thus amounts to locating this intersection space [2]. In addition, the solution space of any subset of clauses in S encloses all solutions of S [2]. Fang et. al. [2] introduce the notion of the *island constraints*. We say that a conjunction of constraints is an island if we can move between any two valuations in the conjunction's solution space using a fine sequence of local moves without moving out of the solution space [2]. The constraints comprising the island are island constraints [2]. Furthermore, Fang et. al. [2] and Fang et. al. [5] introduce two theorems when a set of clauses forming an island. The first theorem species that the set of clauses forming an island when there is no literal and its complement appearing in these clauses. Fang et. al. [2], [3] and Kilani [4] use this theorem to incorporate the ICM into the DLM [11], [12], [13] and ESG [14] algorithms. However, Fang et. al. [2], [3] and Kilani [4] use the SATs translated from the *binary constraint satisfaction problems*. Every instance of these SATs has two parts. The set of clauses in the first and second parts contains all the literals in the positive and negative forms respectively. The first part does not contain any negative form for any variable and the second part does not contain any positive form for any variable. Fang et. al. [2], [3] and Kilani [4] use the second part as island constraints.

PWAS()
- generate random starting point
+generate random starting point from the island
    for each clause c_i **do** set clause weight $w_i \leftarrow 1$
    while solution not found and not timed out **do**
        $best \leftarrow \infty$
-     **for** each literal x_{ij} in each false clause f_i **do**
+   **for** each free literal x_{ij} in each false clause f_i **do**
            $\Delta w \leftarrow$ change in summed weight of false clauses caused by flipping x_{ij}
            if $\Delta w < best$ **then** $L \leftarrow x_{ij}$ and $best \leftarrow \Delta w$
            else if $\Delta w = best$ **then** $L \leftarrow \cup x_{ij}$
        end for
        if $best < 0$ **then** randomly flip $x_{ij} \in L$
        else if $best = 0$ and probability $\leq P_{flat}$ **then** flip $x_{ij} \in L$
        else
+   **if** island trap or probability $\leq P_1$ **then**
+   **if** probability $\leq P_2$ free the best literal from unsatisfied clauses
+   **else** free the second best
          for each false clause f_i **do** $w_i \leftarrow w_i + 1$
          if # times clause weights increased % $Max_{inc} = 0$ **then**
            for each clause $c_i | w_j > 1$ **do**: $w_j \leftarrow w_j - 1$
          end if
        end if
    end while

Fig. 1. PAWS: All the lines that do not start with the plus sign and PAWSI: All the lines that do not start with the minus sign

5   PAWSI

We need to define the set of island constraints before incorporating ICM into PAWS. As we mentioned in the previous section that the first theorem species that the set of clauses forming an island when there is no literal and its complement appearing in these clauses. Therefore, we have developed the algorithm shown in figure 2 to find the island clauses. This algorithm finds the set of clauses in which no literal and its complement occurring in in these clauses. Initially, it stores all the clauses and the literals of the SAT problem in $IslandClauses$ and $literals$ respectively. Then, it calculates the number of occurrences of each literal (*i.e. form literals*) in these clauses (*i.e. IslandClauses*). It finds the smallest occurrence literal Lit_1 after that. It removes all the clauses from $IslandClauses$ in which Lit_1 occurs. Finally, it removes Lit_1 and $\overline{Lit_1}$ from $literals$. It repeats these steps until $literals$ becomes empty.

FindIslandClauses()
   $IslandClauses$ = all clauses in the SAT problem
   $literals$ = all the literal in the SAT problem
   cls = all clauses in the SAT problem
   while $literals$ is not empty **do**
     for each literal l_i in the SAT problem **do** $Count_{li} = 0$
     for each clause $c_i \in cls$ **do**
       for each literal $x_i \in c_i$ **do**
         $Count_{x_i} = Count_{x_i} + 1$
       end for
     end for
     $bestLitSet = \{k \mid k \leq Count_y, \forall\ y \in literals\}$
     Lit_1 = choose randomly one litral from $bestLitSet$
     $clLit_1$ = all the clauses in wich Lit_1 occurs
     $IslandClauses = IslandClauses - clLit_1$
     $literals = literals - Lit_1$
     $literals = literals - \overline{Lit_1}$
   end while
   return $IslandClauses$

Fig. 2. FindIslandClauses()

We incorporate the ICM into PAWS in order to speed up PAWS. We name the new algorithm PAWSI. Figure 1 shows PAWSI. In this figure, PAWSI includes all the lines that do not start with the minus sign. Initially, PAWSI starts from an initial valuation inside the island. This initial valuation satisfies all the island clauses. Simply, we can do this by passing by each island clause, choosing one of its literals, and making it true. Similar to PAWS, PAWSI moves from the current valuation to a better or equal neighbour valuation by flipping the best *free variable* x from the unsatisfied (or false) clauses. A free variable is a variable once flipped the search remains inside the island (*i.e. no island clause is violated*). The remaining search steps are the same as in PAWS.

PAWSI reaches *an island trap* during the search process. An island trap happens when there is no neighbour valuation for the current valuation that is inside the island. In other words, flipping any literal from the unsatisfied clauses moves the search outside of the island by violating at least one island clause. In this case, PAWSI *frees* one of the variables from the unsatisfied clauses. To free a varaible, x, we need to flip the set of variables, $freeme_x$, from the satisfied clauses which makes x not free. By flipping all the variable from $freeme_x$, x becomes free.

6   Experiments

We got the source code of PAWS from the author through a personal communication and we incorporate the ICM into this source code to produce PAWSI. PAWS is implemented using a C language under Linux or Unix platform. The time function used calculates the sum of the user time and the system time.

PAWS has four parameters: $cutoff$, $tries$, P_{flat}, and Max_{inc}. We use the default parameters' values, $P_{flat} = 0.15$ and $Max_{inc} = 10$, as provided by the source code. We use the $cutoff = 20,000,000$ and $tries = 1$ since we noticed that PAWS's performance degraded while running the instances taken with the default values of $cutoff$ and $tries$.

We use a PC with Pentium III 800 MHz and 256 MB memory to get the results.

We run PAWS and PAWSI for each instance for 100 runs and each run is terminated if it reaches 3,000 seconds of CPU time without finding an answer. We test PAWSI using the benchmarks Thornton [15] used while creating PAWS. Thornton uses the instances: blocks world, graph coloring, AIS, small random 3-SAT, and large random 3-SAT. Initially, we experiment with the graph coloring and the AIS problems. We avoid using the randomly generated instances since the ratio of the number of the island clauses to the total number of clauses in these instances does not exceed 40%. Therefore, confining the search within the island clauses of these instances does not improve the search.

Tables 1 and 3 show the results of running PAWS and PAWSI. Each of these tables shows: the success ratio of the 100 runs, and the average CPU time in seconds and the average number of flips for the success runs. In addition, table 3 shows the values for the P_1 and P_2 parameters for each instance after tuning It is clear that PAWS has a $100/100$ success ratio for all the instances except for g125n-17c $(3/100)$ and g250-29c $(0/100)$ while PAWSI obtains a $100/100$ success ratio for all the instances.

Table 2 shows the result of running $FindIslandClauses()$. For each instance, it shows the number of clauses, the number of island clauses, the ratio of the number of the island clauses to the total number of clauses, and the CPU time in seconds used to find the island clauses. It is clear that $(99+)\%$ and $(70+)\%$ of the hard graph coloring and the AIS problems are island clauses respectively. The last column shows the total time taken, ttt, to solve each instance, where ttt is equal to the time taken by PAWSI plus the time taken by $FindIslandClauses()$. Note that ttt for each instance is far better than PAWS's time for solving the same instance of all the hard graph coloring problems instances and the ais12 instance. But, *ttt* is more (slightly worse) than PAWS's time for solving the ais8 instance (0.067 compare to 0.0469).

Table 1. The result of PAWS algorithm using the parameters: cuttoff = 20,000,000, tries = 1, P_{flat} = 0.15 and Max_{inc} = 10

Instance	success	Average Time	Average Flip
The hard graph-coloring problems			
g125n-17c	3/100	2,345.22	13,560,633
g125n-18c	100/100	11.09	21,621
g250n-15c	100/100	5.50	2,231
g250n-29c	0/100	-	-
The AIS problems			
ais8	100/100	0.0469	13,025
ais10	100/100	0.497	94,599
ais12	100/100	10.13	1,666,626

Table 2. The Result of running FindIslandClauses

Instance	Number of clauses	Number of island clauses	(Number of island clauses)/(Number of clauses)	CPU Time (s)
The hard graph-coloring problems				
g125n-17c	66,272	66,147	0.998	2.35
g125n-18c	70,163	70,038	0.998	2.527
g250n-15c	233,965	233,715	0.998	15.24
g250n-29c	454,622	454,372	0.999	31.403
The AIS problems				
ais8	1,520	1,110	0.73	0.025
ais10	3,151	2,332	0.74	0.06
ais12	5,666	4,193	0.74	0.06

Table 3. The result of PAWSI algorithm

Instance	success	Average Time CPU (s)	Average Flip	P_1	P_2	PAWSI time + FindIslandClauses time
The hard graph-coloring problems						
g125n-17c	100/100	44.4	2,040,700	10	90	46.75
g125n-18c	100/100	0.20	22,721	10	90	2.727
g250n-15c	100/100	1.04	9,781	10	90	16.28
g250n-29c	100/100	95.61	1,189,401	10	10	127.013
The AIS problems						
ais8	100/100	0.042	8,374	5	5	0.067
ais10	100/100	0.34	51,542	5	5	0.4
ais12	100/100	4.7	544,003	5	5	4.76

7 Conclusion and Future Work

In this paper, we incorporate the island confinement method into PAWS to speed up PAWS. We show through experiments that, the resulted algorithm, PAWSI, betters PAWS in solving the graph coloring and the AIS problems.

We test PAWSI using the benchmarks Thornton [15] used while creating PAWS. Thornton uses the instances: blocks world, graph coloring, AIS, small random 3-SAT, and large random 3-SAT. Initially, we run PAWSI for the graph coloring and the AIS problems. The work in progress to extend our algorithm to the remaining benchmark instances Thornton used.

Acknowledgments. We would like to thank the anonymous reviewers for their comments and Thornton for emailing us the PAWS's source code. Besides, we would like to thank the staff of our faculty for their support and help while doing this research and for the Hashemite University for providing us the environment to do this research.

References

1. Balint, A., Fröhlich, A.: Improving Stochastic Local Search for SAT with a New Probability Distribution. In: Strichman, O., Szeider, S. (eds.) SAT 2010. LNCS, vol. 6175, pp. 10–15. Springer, Heidelberg (2010)
2. Fang, H., Kilani, Y., Lee, J.H., Stuckey, P.J.: The island confinement method for reducing search space in local search methods. Journal of Heuristics 13(6), 557–585 (2007)
3. Fang, H., Kilani, Y., Lee, J., Stucky, P.: Reducing Search Space in Local Search for Constraint Satisfaction. In: Proceeding of the American Association for Artificial Intelligence, pp. 200–207 (2002)
4. Kilani, Y.: Speeding up Local Search by Using the Island Confinement Method. Ph.D. Thesis, Faculty of Information Science and Technology, University of Kebangsaan Malaysia, Malaysia (2007)
5. Fang, H., Kilani, Y., Lee, J., Stucky, P.: The Island Confinement Method for Reducing Search Space in Local Search Methods. Technical report, University of Melbourne, Department of Computer Science and Software Engineering (2006), http://www.cs.mu.oz.au/pjs/papers/joh2006.pdf
6. Tompkins, D.A.D., Hoos, H.H.: UBCSAT: An Implementation and Experimentation Environment for SLS Algorithms for SAT and MAX-SAT. In: Hoos, H.H., Mitchell, D.G. (eds.) SAT 2004. LNCS, vol. 3542, pp. 306–320. Springer, Heidelberg (2005)
7. Pham, D., Thornton, J., Gretton, C., Sattar, A.: Combining Adaptive and Dynamic Local Search for Satisfiability. Journal on Satisfiability, Boolean Modeling and Computation, 4:149–4:172 (2008)
8. Davis, M., Logemann, G., Loveland, D.: A Machine Program for Theorem proving. Communications of the ACM 5(7), 394–397 (1962)
9. Selman, B., Levesque, H., Mitchell, D.: A New Method for Solving Hard Satisfiability Problems. In: Proceeding of the American Association for Artificial Intelligence, pp. 440–446 (1992)

10. Audemard, G., Katsirelos, G., Simon, L.: A Restriction of Extended Resolution for Clauses Learning SAT Solvers. In: Proceeding of the Twenty-Fourth AAAI Conference on Artificial Intelligence, pp. 15–20 (2010)
11. Wu, Z., Wah, B.: An Efficient Global-Search Strategy in Discrete Lagrangian Methods for Solving Hard Satisfiability Problems. In: Proceeding of the 17th National Conference on Artificial Intelligence, pp. 310–315 (2000)
12. Wu, Z., Wah, B.: Trap Escaping Strategies in Discrete Lagrangian Methods for Solving Hard Satisfiability and Maximum Satisfiability Problems. In: Proceeding of the 16th National Conference on Artificial Intelligence, pp. 673–678 (1999a)
13. Wah, B.W., Wu, Z.: The Theory of Discrete Lagrange Multipliers for Nonlinear Discrete Optimization. In: Jaffar, J. (ed.) CP 1999. LNCS, vol. 1713, pp. 28–42. Springer, Heidelberg (1999b)
14. Schuurmans, D., Southey, F., Holte, R.: The exponentiated subgradient algorithm for heuristic boolean programming. In: Proceeding of the International Joint Conference on Artificial Intelligence, pp. 334–341 (2001)
15. Thornton, J.: Clause Weighting Local Search for SAT. Journal of Automated Reasoning 35(1-3), 97–142 (2005) ISSN:0168-7433

Hypergraph Distributed Adaptive Design Supported by Hypergraph Replication

Leszek Kotulski[1] and Barbara Strug[2]

[1] Department of Automatics, AGH University of Science and Technology
Al. Mickiewicza 30, 30 059 Krakow, Poland
kotulski@agh.edu.pl
[2] Department of Physics, Astronomy and Applied Computer Science,
Jagiellonian University, Reymonta 4, Krakow, Poland
barbara.strug@uj.edu.pl

Abstract. In this paper a hypergraph transformation model is used for distribution and adaptation in computer aided design. The application of the theoretical results ina graph distribution toolkit proposed as a multi-agent framework is also considered. To assure the efficiency of the system it should be implemented as a parallel multiagent system. The hypergraph distribution and partial replication, allowing for the parts of a hypergraph to be managed by agents, is also presented. The approach is illustrated by an example from the domain of floor layout design.

Keywords: computer aided design, adaptive design, hypergraph transformations, replication, distributed grammar systems.

1 Introduction

Distributed model of computing is more and more popular, especially with a rapid development of the Internet and availability of distributed development platforms. Such a model is also very useful in the domain of computer-aided design. Many design problems can be divided into a number of smaller tasks, either totally independent or only occasionally exchanging pieces of information or contributing its capabilities to a common object being designed. At the same time research into proposing a formal model of such a cooperative distributed design is rather scarce.

This paper deals with a linguistic approach to distributed design. The formal model of computer-aided design is based on hypergraph structures for which a lot of research has been done, both in context of design [2], and in a more general aspects.

A complex design problem can be divided into smaller, more approachable, subproblems. In this paper we introduce a distributed design system using graph distribution and local hypergraph transformation rules. Searching for each sub-problem solution is supported by one local system. Solving the whole problem requires the ability of local systems to communicate and cooperate when needed [3–6].

L. Rutkowski et al. (Eds.): ICAISC 2012, Part II, LNCS 7268, pp. 671–678, 2012.

Previous approach to solving the problem of cooperation strategy is presented in [9–11, 16]. In this paper we take a different approach; the system communication is realized by a specially introduced agents and uses the notion of complementary graphs [12] and conjugated hypergraph grammars [13]. These concepts, supported by the multi-agent GRADIS framework, will be briefly reviewed.

The presented hypergraph grammars generate a set of hypergraphs representing design task solutions satisfying the given design criteria. The proposed approach is illustrated by the example of designing floor layouts for large building and internal arrangements of rooms.

2   Hypergraph Representation

Our approach to hypergraphs is based on a formal model presented in [17]. A hypergraph consists of hyperedges and nodes. Hyperedges of the hypergraph are labelled by names of the components or relations. Hyperedges representing components are undirected. Hyperedges representing to asymmetric relations are directed. Hypergraph nodes express potential connections between hyperedges. To each hyperedge a sequence of source and target nodes is assigned. The number of all nodes assigned to a hyperedge specifies its type. As a hypergraph can be seen as a hyperedge on the higher level of detail, the external nodes, which determine the type of a hypergraph, are also specified.

To represent features of components and relations between them, attributing of hyperedges and nodes is used. Values assigned to attributes specify the design requirements which should be met by solutions.

In Fig. 1 a hypergraph representing a layout of a floor with three flats is depicted. Hyperedges representing components are drawn as rectangles and labelled with names of elements they represent. The layout consists of components representing spaces (i.e flat 1, flat 2 , flat 3 and a hall) and other elements like walls, doors. Relational hyperedges depicted as circles labelled acc denote the fact that given components are adjacent, al - denotes the fact that a walls are aligned and in - the being inside relation. It can be noted that even for a relatively small design the number of hypergraph atoms is large. And if we would like to represent the whole building of which these floor constitutes a part the number of atoms would have to be multiplied.

Let [i] denote the interval $\{1 \ldots i\}$ for $i \geq 0$ (with $[0] = \emptyset$). Let $\Sigma_E = \Sigma_C \cup \Sigma_R$, where $\Sigma_C \cap \Sigma_R = \emptyset$, and Σ_V be fixed alphabets of hyperedge and node labels, respectively. Let A_V and A_E denote sets of node and hyperedge attributes, respectively.

Definition 1. *An attributed hypergraph over* $\Sigma = \Sigma_E \cup \Sigma_V$ *is a system* $G = (E_G, V_G, s_G, t_G, lb_G, ext_G, att_V, att_E)$, *where:*

1. $E_G = E_C \cup E_R$, *where* $E_C \cap E_R = \emptyset$, *is a finite set of hyperedges, where elements of* E_C *represent object parts, while elements of* E_R *represent relations,*

2. V_G *is a finite set of nodes,*

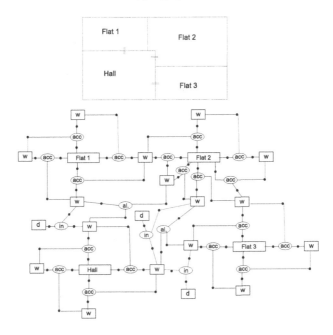

Fig. 1. A floor layout and its hypergraph representation

3. $s_G : E_G \to V_G^*$ and $t_G : E_G \to V_G^*$ are two mappings assigning to hyperedges sequences of source and target nodes, respectively,
4. $lb_G = (lb_V, lb_E)$, where:
   - $lb_V : V_G \to \Sigma_V$ is a node labelling function,
   - $lb_E : E_G \to \Sigma_E$ is a hyperedge labelling function, such that $\bigvee e \in E_C \; lb_E(e) \in \Sigma_C$ and $\bigvee e \in E_R \; lb_E(e) \in \Sigma_R$,
5. $ext_G : [n] \to V_G$ is a mapping specifying a sequence of hypergraph external nodes,
6. $att_V : V_G \to P(A_V)$ and $att_E : E_G \to P(A_E)$ are two functions assigning sets of attributes to nodes and hyperedges, respectively.

In the paper we consider undirected graphs so $\bigvee e \in E_C \; s_G(e) = t_G(e)$,

Hypergraphs representing structures of design solutions are generated by hypergraph grammars. Let us denote by L_H a set of attributed hypergraphs and define $\pi : L_H \to \{TRUE, FALSE\}$ as a design predicate.

A hypergraph grammar is composed of a set of hypergraph edges with terminal and non-terminal labels, a set of hypergraph nodes, a set of productions and an axiom being its initial hypergraph.

Each grammar production is of the form $p = (l, r, \pi)$, where

- l contains only one attributed hyperedge,
- r is an attributed hypergraph with the same number of external nodes as the number of external nodes of l,
- π is a design predicate determining the production applicability.

As mentioned above, the example shows just one flat, but in real situation we may need to design a building containing tens of similar flats. The respective hypergraph representing such a building would be a very large one. Working on such a massive structure requires large computational time and resources and is not very efficient. At the same time transformations performed on different parts of such a hypergraph are independent.

3   Replicated Complementary Hypergraphs

For the efficient application of the hypergraphs transformation we will try to partition the centralized graph G into the set of subgraphs G_i, called *replicated complementary graphs* (RCHGs). Next, the complementary graphs are distributed to different locations. Transformation of each subgraph G_i will be controlled by its Local Graph Transformation Agent (LGTA$_i$); in this section we will introduce the formal definition of RCHGs.

To maintain the consistency between centralized graph G and the set of distributed graphs, some hyperedges should be replicated and placed in the proper complementary graphs. Graphically, we will mark them by a double circle.

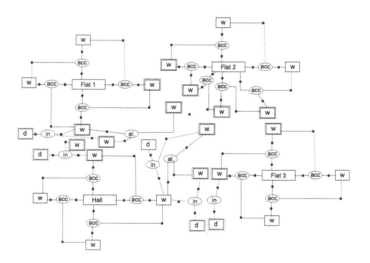

Fig. 2. Four complementary hypergraphs

Let G be a hypergraph and $\{G_i\}$ be a set of hypergraphs, then we will use the following notation:

- Replicas$(G_i) \subset E_{C_i}$ is a set of all elements representing object parts of the graph G_i that are shared with another local graph, i.e for which replicas exist;
- Private$(G_i) \subset E_{C_i}$ is a set of all elements representing object parts of the graph G_i that belong only to the graph G_i.

- $v \xrightarrow{G} w$ means that $v, w \in E_C$ and there exists $a \in E_R$, $\alpha, \beta \in V_G$ such that $\alpha \in s_G(v) \cap s_G(a)$ and $\beta \in s_G(w) \cap s_G(a)$.
- $v \xrightarrow[+]{G} w$ means that there exist $u_1, u_2, ..., u_k \in G$ and $v = u_1$ and $u_k - w$ and $u_p \neq u_q$ for $p \neq q$ and $u_p \xrightarrow{G} u_{p+1}$ for $p < k$; the sequence of hyperedges $(u_1, u_2, ..., u_k)$ will be called the prof of an acyclic connection between v and w.
- all sequences which are the profs of an acyclic connection between v and w will be called $\mathsf{Path}(G_i, v, w)$, and the set of all hyperedges belonging to $\mathsf{Path}(G_i, v, w)$ will be called $\mathsf{PHEs}(G_i, v, w)$

Then we can formally define a RCHGs.

Definition 2. *A set of graphs* $G_i = (E_{G_i}, V_{G_i}, s_{G_i}, t_{G_i}, lb_{G_i}, ext_{G_i}, att_{V_i}, att_{E_i})$, $i = 1, 2, ... k$, *is a replicated and complementary form of hypergraph* G *iff there exists a set of injective homomorphisms* $m_i : G_i \to G$ *such that:*

1. $\bigcup_{i=1,...k} m_i(G_i) = G$
2. $\forall i, j \in \{1, ... k\} : m_i(E_{C_i}) \cap m_j(E_{C_j}) = m_i(\mathsf{Replicas}(G_i)) \cap m_j(\mathsf{Replicas}(G_j))$
3. $\forall i \in \{1, ... k\}$
   $\mathsf{Border}(G_i) = \{v \in \mathsf{Replicas}(G_i) : \exists w \in \mathsf{Private}(G_i) \text{ and } v \xrightarrow{G_i} w\}$
4. $\forall w \in \mathsf{Private}(G_i) \; \forall v \in \mathsf{Private}(G_j) \; \forall (u_1, u_2, ..., u_k) \in \mathsf{PHEs}(G, w, v) \Rightarrow$
   $\exists b \in \mathsf{Border}(G_i) \text{ and } \exists p : m_i(b) = u_p$

Hypergraph G_i *is also referred to as a complementary or a local hypergraph.*

For example hypergraph G depicted in fig 1 can be split into four complementary hypergraphs. This operation generates a number of border hyperedges. One of possible results is depicted in fig 2.

Two issues can be observed in this figure. First, only hyperedges representing object components are replicated, according to the rules introduced above. Secondly, there is more than one possibility of splitting, in the figure it can be noted that two elements representing doors are replicated, while the third one is a private element to one of the complementary hypergraphs.

4   Operation on Complementary Hypergraphs

When we apply productions to complementary hypergraphs a consistency must be preserved. If a production applied to one of complementary hypergraphs affects only the set of private elements it can be applied locally and supervised by the Local Transformation Control System.

On the other hand some of the productions applied to such a hypergraph may involve border of this hypergraph. In this case there is a need to make each hyperedge involved in a transformation private to the hypergraph to which the production is applied. To convert a border hyperedge into a private one we have to incorporate the replicas of border hyperedge together with its embedding in the complementary hypegraph it is replicated in. Such an operation "moves" the borderline, as some of the embedding hyperedge will have to be replicated thus generating new set of border hyperedges.

More formally these operations are defined in the following way:

Incorporate(v, i) - for any replicated hyperedge $v \in E(C_i)$ this operation moves boundaries between complementary hypergraphs in such a way, that all hyperedges w (existing in another complementary hypergraphs) that are connected with any replica of v, say v' (i.e. $v' \xrightarrow{G_i} w$), are replicated and those new replicas are added to G_i together with the nodes and edges creating the connection w with v' (i.e. a, α, β from def. of $v' \xrightarrow{G_i} w$). Then replicas v' are removed from another complementary graphs (i.e. v becomes a private node in G_i). Sometimes the hyperedge incorporation may cause splitting another complementary hypergraph into few subgraphs; if any of those fragments consists of a single isolated hyperedge (being the replicated one) then we remove it, otherwise a new agents are created to maintain new complementary hypergraphs. Note that removing such replicated isolated hyperedge doesn't impact the consistency of RCHGs because other replicas stil exist in RCHGs.

Neighborhood(v, G, k) - for any hyperedge $v \in V(G_i)$ it returns the hypergraph B such that $\forall w \in V(B)$ distance between w and v is not greater than k (i.e. $\exists p \in$ Path(G, v, w) and number of hyperedges representing objects in p is less or equal to k). Determining of B requires a recursive cooperation of agents maintaining complementary hypergraphs.

Similarly as for complementary graphs [14] we can show that these operation have the polynomial complexity of considered both in a context of agents algorithms complexity and number of exchanged messages.

In case of design system we need to perform operations on the design structure in response to changing conditions and/or requirements. One of the simplest change that may occur would consist in moving doors from Hall to Flat 2. It will require the application of the production which involves elements belonging to the set of border hyperedge (walls) it will require several steps to be performed. These elements are shown in fig 3. The elements drawn with a dotted line will be removed from the final hypergraph, and the ones denoted with the bold black line will be added.

1. The border hyperedges representing walls of flat 1 aligned with the walls of the hall will be incorporated into the complementary hypergraph representing hall (it is made by the execution of the Incorporate(...) operation for the hyperedge labelled "W" that is in connection with the hyperedge representing removed door). This operation will move the border to the element representing flat2. The place of the new borderline is sketched with a thick black line in fig 3.

2. As all the elements involved in the application of the production are now private so the production can be performed by the Local Transformation System.

3. After this the complementary hypergraph representing flat 2 has to be expanded to move the borderline in such a way that the splitting occurs alongside the walls (it is made by the execution of the Incorporate(...) operation for the hyperedge labelled as "Flat2").

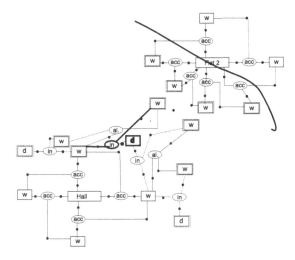

Fig. 3. Elements of the complementary hypergraphs affected by the production responsible for moving the doors.

It can be observed that also the transformation requires number of steps it involves only two of the complementary hypergraphs. The other hypergraphs can be at the same time modified by other transformations and can even be stored on other computers without any interference from the production described here.

5   Conclusions

In the example presented here a high level view of the floor layout is used. Each of the flats can be divided into smaller spaces representing rooms, bedrooms, kitchen, bathrooms etc. It can further be expanded to include such elements as furniture, fireplaces, tv sets, kitchen and bathroom appliances and other elements.

In such a detailed representation we can use the incorporate/expand approach to test different positions of shared elements like doors. But we can also optimize the use of some elements. For example the positions of kitchens and baths in different flats will affect the number of water pipes that have to be installed. By limiting their number we can force the adjacency of spaces containing appliances demanding access to water pipes.

As a hypergraph representing such a detailed view of the layout will rapidly grow splitting it can largely improve efficiency of such a system in practice thanks to the possibility parallel execution of the RCHGs.

The proposed solution has to fulfill two additional conditions (i) new, *parallel* representation has to be equivalent to a centralized description in entire lifetime of a system and (ii) the complexity of migrations from centralized to distributed description and back again, have to be polynomial. The concept of replicated complementary graphs applied in GRADIS platform and presented in the paper satisfies those requirements. We proved that both the migration between centralized and distributed form of system description and all core procedures underlying RCGs environment have polynomial complexities. Those considerations include also the message exchange in the multiagent environment.

References

1. Rozenberg, G.: Handbook of Graph Grammars and Computing By Graph Transformation, vol. 1-3. World Scientific (1997-1999)
2. Grabska, E., Palacz, W.: Hierarchical graphs in creative design. MG & V 9(1/2), 115–123 (2000)
3. Csuhaj-Varju, E., Dassow, J., Kelemen, J., Paun, G.: Grammar systems. A grammatical approach to distribution and cooperation (1994)
4. Kelemen, J.: Syntactical models of cooperating/distributed problem solving. Journal of Experimental and Theoretical AI 3(1), 1–10 (1991)
5. Martin-Vide, C., Mitrana, V.: Cooperation in contextual grammars. In: Proc of the MFCS 1998 Workshop on Grammar Systems, Opava, pp. 289–302 (1998)
6. Simeoni, M., Staniszkis, M.: Cooperating graph grammar systems. In: Grammatical Models of Multi-Agent Systems, pp. 193–217 (1999)
7. Engelfriet, J., Rozenberg, G.: Node Replacement Graph Grammars, 3–94 in [1]
8. Ehrig H., Heckel R. Löwe M., Ribeiro L., Wagner A.: Algebraic Approaches to Graph Transformation - Part II: Single Pushout and Comparison with Double Pushout Approach. In: [1], pp. 247–312
9. Grabska, E., Strug, B.: Applying Cooperating Distributed Graph Grammars in Computer Aided Design. In: Wyrzykowski, R., Dongarra, J., Meyer, N., Waśniewski, J. (eds.) PPAM 2005. LNCS, vol. 3911, pp. 567–574. Springer, Heidelberg (2006)
10. Grabska, E., Strug, B., Ślusarczyk, G.: A Graph Grammar Based Model for Distributed Design. In: Artificial Intelligence and Soft Computing, pp. 440–445. EXIT, Warszawa (2006)
11. Kotulski, L., Strug, B.: Distributed Adaptive Design with Hierarchical Autonomous Graph Transformation Systems. In: Shi, Y., van Albada, G.D., Dongarra, J., Sloot, P.M.A. (eds.) ICCS 2007. LNCS, vol. 4488, pp. 880–887. Springer, Heidelberg (2007)
12. Kotulski, L.: GRADIS – Multiagent Environment Supporting Distributed Graph Transformations. In: Bubak, M., van Albada, G.D., Dongarra, J., Sloot, P.M.A. (eds.) ICCS 2008, Part III. LNCS, vol. 5103, pp. 644–653. Springer, Heidelberg (2008)
13. Kotulski, L., Fryz, L.: Conjugated Graph Grammars as a Mean to Assure Consistency of the System of Conjugated Graphs. In: Proceedings of RELCOMEX 2008, pp. 9–14. IEEE (2008)
14. Kotulski, L.: Distributed Graphs Transformed by Multiagent System. In: Rutkowski, L., Tadeusiewicz, R., Zadeh, L.A., Zurada, J.M. (eds.) ICAISC 2008. LNCS (LNAI), vol. 5097, pp. 1234–1242. Springer, Heidelberg (2008)
15. Kotulski, L., Sedziwy, A.: Agent framework for decomposing a graph into the subgraphs of the same size. In: WORLDCOMP 2008 (FCS 2008), Las Vegas (2008)
16. Kotulski, L., Strug, B.: Parallel Graph Transformations in Distributed Adaptive Design. In: Proc. GCM-ICGT 2008, Leicester (2008)
17. Minas, M.: Concepts and Realization of a Diagram Editor Generator Based on Hypergraph Transformation. Science of Computer Programming 44, 157–180 (2002)

Extended CDC vs Other Formalisms – The Comperative Analysis of the Models for Spatio-temporal Reasoning

Jedrzej Osinski

Faculty of Mathematics and Computer Science,
Adam Mickiewicz University, Poznan, Poland
josinski@amu.edu.pl

Abstract. Spatio-temporal reasoning is a well recognized branch of artificial intelligence with an increasing significance in whole modern computer science. In this paper we compare the recently introduced XCDC formalism with other qualitative techniques: classic CDC, Allen's interval calculus, n-block algebra, topological models (RCC-5 and RCC-8), internal cardinal directions (ICD-5 and ICD-9) and the spatio-temporal patterns. We also introduce the methods of the conversion of the basic relations expressed in the previous models to the structures of the XCDC formalism.

Keywords: spatio-temporal reasoning, qualitative calculus, XCDC.

1 Introduction

Qualitative techniques for spatio-temporal representation and reasoning (which make abstraction from an actual quantitative knowledge) are important in artificial intelligence and widely applied for describing spatial relations between objects, computing positions (localizing objects), analyzing relationship between temporal intervals or for assessing similarity between spatial scenes. They are commonly used in many specialized systems implemented in different areas: language processing, route planning, picture processing, security, user interface design, etc. Starting from Allen's interval algebra presented in 1983 there have been constructed many further formalisms representing different aspects of time and space: cardinal directions determined in a particular system of coordinates (both external and internal), topological models (describing the relations between the boundaries and the interiors of a given objects), also the patterns for spatio-temporal situations as well as mixed solutions. In this paper we compare the XCDC (eXtended CDC) formalism recently introduced in [8] with the most popular and widely recognized formalisms. As the algorithms' complexity is similar for all the discussed models, the comparison will be accomplished from the point of view of the representational capabilities of this formalisms. In particular we will show how the relations of the classic models can be represented in the language of XCDC structures.

L. Rutkowski et al. (Eds.): ICAISC 2012, Part II, LNCS 7268, pp. 679–687, 2012.

Let us start from the definition of the Cardinal Direction Calculus (CDC), originally proposed in [4], which is a widely known technique of qualitative calculus for spatial reasoning. The key idea of that formalism is based on dividing the plane around the minimal bounding rectangle of a reference object into nine regions named after the geographical directions: NW, N, NE, W, O (central region which refers to the minimal bounding rectangle itself), E, SW, S and SE. This areas, called direction tiles, are closed, unbounded (except for O), their interiors are pairwise disjoint and their union is the whole plane. It is worth noticing that this classical model can be extended in different aspects, e.g. in [3] we can find reference to the four bordering lines on A at the top, bottom and both sides. Directions between the reference object A and target object B are represented in a 3 x 3 direction-relation matrix denoted by dir(A,B) which we define as follows:

$$dir(A, B) = \begin{bmatrix} f(NW(A) \cap B) & f(N(A) \cap B) & f(NE(A) \cap B) \\ f(W(A) \cap B) & f(O(A) \cap B) & f(E(A) \cap B) \\ f(SW(A) \cap B) & f(S(A) \cap B) & f(SE(A) \cap B) \end{bmatrix},$$

$$where f(x) = \begin{cases} 0, & if\ Interior(X) \neq \emptyset \\ 1, & if\ Interior(X) = \emptyset \end{cases}.$$

In addition let us define the alternative (but equivalent) notation of this relations as an expression $R_1:...:R_k$ such that:

1. $1 \leq k \leq 9$,
2. $R_k \in$ NW,N,NE,W,O,E,SW,S,SE,
3. $R_i \neq R_j$ for every i, j such that $1 \leq i, j \leq k$ and $i \neq j$.

We also define U_{dir} symbol which concerns the sum of all 9 basic relations, i.e. $U_{dir} :=$ NW:N:NE:W:O:E:SW:S:SE.

Now we can define the XCDC (eXtended CDC) which is based on two modifications. Firstly, we describe the spatial relation between objects A and B from two independent perspectives using the pair (instead of one) of direction-relation matrices in which the reference and target object exchange their roles, i.e. we create the structure [dir(A,B), dir(B,A)]. In the second stage of the extension we define the 3-dimensional Cartesian coordinate system with three axes:

 - N* - a spatial extension in the geographical direction from south to north,
 - E* - a spatial extension in the geographical direction from west to east,
 - T - a temporal span (pointing the passage of time).

To distinguish a geographic direction from the element of a matrix, we add the symbol * to the former (i.e. N* denotes the geographic north direction, while N describes a direction-relation matrix). With a 3D representation we can describe situations using three main projections (see Fig. 1): on the N*-E* plane, on the T-N* plane and on the T-E* plane. Finally we define the relation between two spatio-temporal objects A and B as follows:

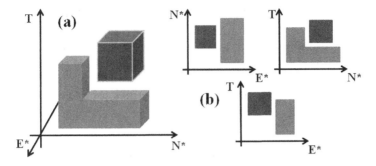

Fig. 1. The example of a spatio-temporal relation (a) and the corresponding projections according to the XCDC formalism (b)

$$TS(A, B) = [dir_{N^*-E^*}(A, B), dir_{N^*-E^*}(B, A), dir_{T-N^*}(A, B),$$
$$dir_{T-N^*}(B, A), dir_{T-E^*}(A, B), dir_{T-E^*}(B, A)],$$

where $dir_{X-Y}(A, B)$ denotes a direction-relation matrix for the projection on the X-Y plane.

2 XCDC vs CDC

The XCDC formalism in comparison with classic CDC model:

- Is characterized by a higher representational capability in a spatial aspect. Using two direction-relation matrices instead of one allows to analyze a situation from two independent perspectives in which the reference and target object exchange their roles. That implies more precise mapping of a real-world relationship also indicating the size comparison between objects. This problem was carefully discussed in [9].
- Provides the representation of the internal cardinal direction relations which describe the situation when a target object is located inside a reference one (also discussed in [9]).
- Takes into consideration the temporal aspect what allows to represent relations between time intervals.
- Allows to describe the changes of spatial relation in time appearing in a dynamic environment. That provides the mechanism for a complex spatio-temporal representation of the relationship between objects like people, groups of people, places, artifacts and events.

It is important to mention that the set of relations in the CDC model is a proper subset of the set of the XCDC structures, i.e. the XCDC formalism is an extension of CDC. In other words, there are no such a relation in CDC which could not be represented in XCDC and, on the other hand, there exist relations in XCDC which are not representable in the CDC formalism. The first assumption is easy to verify: for any direction-relation dir(A,B) representing a spatial relation in the CDC model we can assign the structure TS(A,B)=[dir(A,B), U_{dir}, U_{dir}, U_{dir}, U_{dir}, U_{dir}] of the XCDC formalism which, as can be noticed, describes the same spatial relationship without losing any information. The proof of the second part is also elementary if we compare the potential number of structures in both models: 2^{3*3} in CDC and 2^{6*9} in XCDC, and apply Dirichlet's box principle - it is impossible to represent all the XCDC structures using only a single 3 x 3 binary matrix.

3   XCDC vs Allen's Calculus and n-Block Algebra

The Allen's calculus originally introduced in [1] was the first formalism to represent qualitative relations between temporal intervals independently from a low precision, knowledge uncertainty or a different level of granularity. Allen presented 13 basic relations B_{int} which can be treated as equivalence classes in the set of intervals defined by their beginnings and ends: < ('X before Y', reverse relation: >), = ('X equal Y'), m ('X meets Y', reverse relation: mi), o ('X overlaps Y', reverse notation: oi), d ('X during Y', reverse relation: di), s ('X starts Y', reverse relation: si), f ('X finishes Y', reverse notation: fi). Each of these relation can be described in the XCDC model as shown in Tab. 1. The two matrices referring to the projection on the $N^* - E^*$ is U_{dir} because the temporal relation does not contain any information about the spatial relation between given objects. For the same reason the next two pairs are equal as it does not matter which of the spatial axes we analyze. The only two case when the Allen's relations are indistinguishable in the XCDC model (relations 'o' and 'm') are connected with the boundary of the minimal bounding rectangle which is not analyzed in XCDC. If necessary it can be extended according to the solution in [3] which was mention before. However it is important to analyze whether such a extension is appropriate to a particular application: too precise data may increase the complexity, cause mistakes based on imprecise input or problems with a conversion from and to a natural language. Let us now discuss the n-block algebra presented in [2] which is an extension of the classic Allen's model into many dimensions. We analyze this formalism for n=2 (when it is called a rectangle algebra) so the set of relations can be defined as $B_{rec} := \{(X, Y) : X, Y \in B_{int}\}$. It is easy to notice that there are 13*13 = 169 basic relations. Let us analyze Fig. 2a which

Table 1. The conversion from Allen's calculus to the XCDC structures

Allen's relation	$dir_{N^*-E^*}(A, B)$	$dir_{N^*-E^*}(B, A)$	$dir_{T-N^*}(A, B)$ $dir_{T-E^*}(A, B)$	$dir_{T-N^*}(B, A)$ $dir_{T-E^*}(B, A)$
A < B, B > A	U_{dir}	U_{dir}	SW:S:SE	NW:N:NE
A = B	U_{dir}	U_{dir}	W:O:E	W:O:E
A m B, A o B	U_{dir}	U_{dir}	W:O:E:SW:S:SE	NW:N:NE:W:O:E
A mi B, A oi B	U_{dir}	U_{dir}	NW:N:NE:W:O:E	W:O:E:SW:S:SE
A d B, B di A	U_{dir}	U_{dir}	W:O:E	U_{dir}
A s B, B si A	U_{dir}	U_{dir}	W:O:E	NW:N:NE:W:O:E
A f B, B fi A	U_{dir}	U_{dir}	W:O:E	W:O:E:SW:S:SE

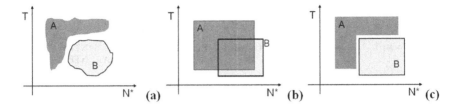

Fig. 2. (a) Real-world situation, (b) the representation in the rectangle calculus and (c) the XCDC formalism

shows a real-world situation which can be described with the following two sentences: *Fire (event A) is spreading across the area. A group of tourists (denoted as B) was successfully evacuated before the fire reached the place where they had been staying.* We calculate the minimal bounding rectangles mbb(A) and mbb(B) for both of the objects. In the 2-block algebra we have: mbb(A) (oi,o) mbb(B), because horizontally mbb(A) overlaps mbb(B) while vertically mbb(A) is overlapped by mbb(B) (compare Fig. 2b) - there is a possibility of generating a false message which could cause a danger consequences, e.g. it seems that some tourists were trapped in the burning area and that a rescue team needs to be sent. In the XCDC model (limited to the projection on the $T - N^*$ plane only) we have: $[dir_{T-N^*}(A, B), dir_{T-N^*}(B, A)] = [\text{O:E:S:SE, NW:N:W}]$. Although we lose the information about the shape of the objects we still know the exact spatial relation (see Fig. 2c).

4   XCDC vs RCC-8 and RCC-5

We will now compare the XCDC formalism with the topological model which describes the relation between two spatial regions (of the same dimension) making abstraction from the actual cardinal directions. Starting from the relation 'X connects with Y' the set of eight basic relations (see Fig. 3) has been introduced (first in [10]): DC(A,B) ('A disconnected from B'), EC(A,B) ('A externally connected to B'), PO(A,B) ('A partially overlapping B'), EQ(A,B) ('A equal to B'), TPP(A,B) ('A tangential proper part of B'), TPPI(A,B) ('A has tangential proper part B'), NTPP(A,B) ('A nontangential proper part of B'), NTPPI(A,B) ('A has nontangential proper part B'). The model is called RCC-8 - Region Connection Calculus and allows to formulate complex theorems as well as to reason about a specific relation (using both composition rules and the hierarchical structure of this model). It is easy to notice that it is impossible to represent all the XCDC relations in the RCC-8 model (just compare the number of possible structures in the both formalisms). However every relation in RCC-8 can be described in XCDC as shown in Tab. 2. Again we need to remain that in the XCDC model we do not analyze the bounder lines around the minimal bounding rectangle (see discussion above) - that is way we assign the same matrix interpretations to the pairs of RCC-8 relations: EC and PO, TPP and NTTP, TPPI and NTPPI. This problem does not appear if we take into the consideration

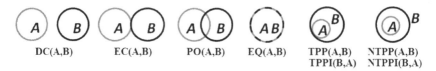

Fig. 3. The basic relations of the RCC-8 model

Table 2. The conversion from RCC-8 and RCC-5 to the XCDC structures

RCC-8	RCC-5	$\mathrm{dir}_{N^*-E^*}$ (B,A)	$\mathrm{dir}_{N^*-E^*}$ (A,B)	$\mathrm{dir}_{T-N^*}(B,A)$ $\mathrm{dir}_{T-E^*}(B,A)$	$\mathrm{dir}_{T-N^*}(A,B)$ $\mathrm{dir}_{T-E^*}(A,B)$
DC(A,B)	DR(A,B)	NW:N:NE:W :E:SW:S:SE	NW:N:NE:W :E:SW:S:SE	NW:NE:W :E:SW:SE	NW:NE:W :E:SW:SE
EC(A,B) PO(A,B)	PO(A,B)	U_{dir}	U_{dir}	U_{dir}	U_{dir}
TPP(A,B) NTPP(A,B) TPPI(B,A) NTPPI(B,A)	PP(A,B) PPI(B,A)	O	U_{dir}	N:O:S	U_{dir}
EQ(A,B)	EQ(A,B)	O	O	N:O:S	N:O:S

the reduced model called RCC-5 presented in [6] which operates on five basic relations (Tab. 2): DR (disjointedness),PO (partially overlapping) PP (proper part), PPI (strict containment), EQ (equal). In this case we can talk about the conversion function from RCC-5 into the XCDC formalism - the eXtended CDC model fully covers the representational capabilities of RCC-5. It is also worth mentioning that in RCC-8 we can construct further relations being the logical sums of the basic ones, e.g. PP(X,Y) is equivalent to the logical sum TPP(X,Y) $\vee$ NTPP(X,Y). What is interesting we can transfer this property to the XCDC representation of RCC-8 relations according to the conversion table. Let us define M $\oplus$ N as a logical sum of the corresponding elements in the 3 x 3 matrices (or combinations of such matrices) M and N, e.g. NW:N $\oplus$ NE = NW:N:NE. Then we have PP(X,Y)=

$$[O, U_{dir}, N:O:S, U_{dir}, N:O:S, U_{dir}]\oplus[O, U_{dir}, N:O:S, U_{dir}, N:O:S, U_{dir}]$$

$$= [O \oplus O, U_{dir} \oplus U_{dir}, N:O:S \oplus N:O:S, U_{dir} \oplus U_{dir}, N:O:S \oplus N:O:S,$$

$$U_{dir} \oplus U_{dir}] = [O, U_{dir}, N:O:S, U_{dir}, N:O:S, U_{dir}].$$

Similarly we can calculate the XCDC representation for other topological relations: PPI (has proper part), P (part of), PI (has part), O (overlaps), C (connects with), DC (discrete from), U_S (the sum of all the relations).

5   XCDC vs ICD

Apart from the conventional cardinal direction relations there exist Internal Cardinal Direction (ICD) relations which are used to describe the situation when one object/region contains another object (or objects). This formalism was carefully analyzed in [7] where also three ICD models called ICD-5 (see Fig. 4a), ICD-9 (see Fig. 4b) and ICD-13 were introduced. These models are characterized by a different degree of details. To choose the one that fit best our particular application it is necessary to analyze two aspects: the scale of the container objects and the spatial distribution characteristics of target objects. The ICD-5 and ICD-9 relations can be represent as the XCDC structures as shown in Tab. 3.

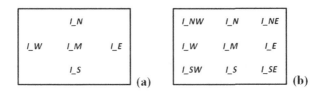

Fig. 4. The ICD models: ICD-5 (a) and ICD-9 (b)

Table 3. The conversion from ICD-5 and ICD-9 to the XCDC structures

ICD-5	
I-N	[O, W:O:E:SW:S:SE, N:O:S, NW:N:W:O:SW:S, N:O:S, U_{dir}]
I-S	[O, NW:N:NE:W:O:E, N:O:S, N:NE:O:E:S:SE,N:O:S, U_{dir}]
I-W	[O, N:NE:O:E:S:SE, N:O:S, U_{dir} ,N:O:S, N:NE:O:E:S:SE]
I-E	[O, NW:N:W:O:SW:S, N:O:S, U_{dir}, N:O:S, NW:N:W:O:SW:S]
ICD-9	
I-N	[O, O:S, N:O:S, NW:N:W:O:SW:S, N:O:S, N:O:S]
I-S	[O, N:O, N:O:S, N:NE:O:E:S:SE, N:O:S, N:O:S]
I-W	[O, O:E, N:O:S, N:O:S, N:O:S, N:NE:O:E:S:SE]
I-E	[O, W:O, N:O:S, N:O:S, N:O:S, NW:N:W:O:SW:S]
I-NW	[O, O:E:S:SE, N:O:S, NW:N:W:O:SW:S, N:O:S, N:NE:O:E:S:SE]
I-NE	[O, W:O:S:SW, N:O:S, NW:N:W:O:SW:S, N:O:S, NW:N:W:O:SW:S]
I-SW	[O, N:NE:O:E, N:O:S, N:NE:O:E:S:SE, N:O:S, N:NE:O:E:S:SE]
I-SE	[O, NW:N:W:O, N:O:S, N:NE:O:E:S:SE, N:O:S, NW:N:W:O:SW:S]

6   XCDC vs Spatio-temporal Patterns

Hazarika and Cohn discuss in [5] the spatio-tempral relations between objects referring to the concept of RCC-8. They also introduced the spatio-temporal patterns describing changes in spatial relation which refer to the different categories of movement. We will now show how these patterns can simply expressed in the language of the XCDC structures. According to Hazarika and Cohn, a single 'one piece' spatial entity X can identify with one of the three patterns (we can recognize them in the XCDC model by analyzing properties of the $M:=dir_{T-N*}(Y, X)$ or $M:=dir_{T-E*}(Y, X)$ depending on which spatial direction we describe) - see Fig. 5a: IMB_X (Immobility - the object occupies the same space at all times; the sum of the values in each of the column in M equals 0 or

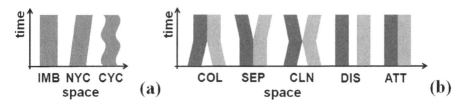

Fig. 5. Spatio-temporal patterns: (a) single objects and (b) two objects

Table 4. The conversion of the spatio-temporal patterns into the XCDC structures (D $\in \{N^*, E^*\}$)

	$dir_{T-D}(Y,X)$	$dir_{T-D}(X,Y)$		$dir_{T-D}(Y,X)$	$dir_{T-D}(X,Y)$
COL_{XY}	NW:N:W:O:SW	N:NE:O:E:SE	DIS_{XY}	NW:W:SW	NE:E:SE
SEP_{XY}	NW:W:O:SW:S	NE:O:E:S:SE	ATT_{XY}	NW:W:SW:N:O:S	N:O:S:NE:E:SE
CLN_{XY}	NW:W:O:SW	NE:O:E:SE			

3, e.g. N:O:S, NW:W:SW:NE:E:SE), NYC_X (Non-Cyclicity - the object never takes the same path twice; the sum of the values in each of the column in M equals 1, e.g. NW:O:SE), CYC_X (Cyclicity - the object takes the same path more than once; the sums of the values in the columns in M equal 0, 1 and 2, however in any order, e.g. NW:O:SW (2,1,0), N:E:S (0,2,1)). There are introduced also the patterns which involve mutual relationship between two objects (see Fig. 5b): COL_{XY} (Coalescence - coming together for a period), SEP_{XY} (Separation of two object), CLN_{XY} (Collision - coming into contact and separating again), DIS_{XY} (Disjointness), ATT_{XY} (Attachment). Tab. 4 shows how these patterns can be represented in XCDC in one of the plane: $T - N^*$ and $T - E^*$. It is important to notice that a paticular situation is independent for both of the planes, e.g. the same object can be described, analyzing them from two different perspectives, by the patterns COL_{XY} and ATT_{XY}.

7   Conclusion

We have compared the representional capabilities of the XCDC formalism with other widely used models. The results show that the XCDC can be treated as a general solution applicable in many systems. It is a single qualitative technique combining the valuable properties of CDC, Allen's calculus, block algebra, ICD, RCC-5 (and RCC-8) and spatio-temporal patterns.

References

1. Allen, J.F.: Maintaining Knowledge about Temporal Intervals. Artificial Intelligence and Language Processing 26(11), 832–843 (1983)
2. Balbiani, P., Condotta, J., Farinas del Cerro, L.: A model for reasoning about bidimensional temporal relations. In: Colin, A.G., Schubert, L., Shapiro, S.C. (eds.) Proceedings of 6th International Conference on Principles of Knowledge Representation and Reasoning (KR 1998), pp. 124–130. Morgan Kaufmann (1998)

3. Cicerone, S., Di Felice, P.: Cardinal directions between spatial objects: the pairwise-consistency problem. Information Sciences 164(1-4), 165–188 (2004)
4. Goyal, R.K., Egenhofer, M.J.: Cardinal directions between extended spatial objects. IEEE Transactions on Knowledge and Data Engineering (2001)
5. Hazarika, S.M., Cohn, A.G.: Qualitative Self-Localization using a Spatio-Temporal Ontology: A Preliminary Report. In: International Joint Conference on Artificial Intelligence - Workshop on Spatial and Temporal Reasoning with Agents' Focus (2001)
6. Jonsson, P., Drakengren, T.: A Complete Classication of Tractability in RCC-5, Research Notes. Journal of Artificial Intelligence Research 6, 211–221 (1997)
7. Liu, Y., Wang, X., Jin, X., Wu, L.: On Internal Cardinal Direction Relations. In: Cohn, A.G., Mark, D.M. (eds.) COSIT 2005. LNCS, vol. 3693, pp. 283–299. Springer, Heidelberg (2005)
8. Osinski, J.: Extending the Cardinal Direction Calculus to a Temporal Dimension. In: Chad Lane, H., Guesgen, H.W. (eds.) Proceedings of the 22nd Florida Artificial Intelligence Research Society Conference, Sanibel Island, Florida, USA, May 19-21, pp. 141–142. AAAI Press (2009)
9. Osinski, J.: Using Extended Cardinal Direction Calculus in Natural Language based Systems. In: Rutkowski, L., Scherer, R., Tadeusiewicz, R., Zadeh, L.A., Zurada, J.M. (eds.) ICAISC 2010, Part II. LNCS (LNAI), vol. 6114, pp. 606–613. Springer, Heidelberg (2010)
10. Randell, D.A., Cohn, A.G., Cui, Z.: An interval logic for space based on 'connection'. In: Neumann, B. (ed.) ECAI 1992 Proceedings of the 10th European Conference on Artificial Intelligence, pp. 394–398. John Wiley and Sons, Inc., New York (1992)

Interval Probabilities of State Transitions
in Probabilistic Automata

Henryk Piech and Olga Siedlecka-Lamch

Czestochowa University of Technology,
Dabrowskiego 73
h.piech@adm.pcz.czest.pl

Abstract. Working principle of the probabilistic automaton is based on the state transition probability [4], [6]. Construction of the automaton depends on its purpose. We assume that all transitions probabilities are constant[3]. In situations where low levels of information (entropy) suggest assurance solutions, we use interval probabilities (remembering that the sum of the probabilities of transition to the given state must remain equal to 1). This variant generates additional problems, which are: how to prevent the redundancy of the probabilities sum; the physical interpretation of this situation; undervaluing of the probabilities sum; determine the criteria of the structure and parameters optimization (minimization) relative to the semantic resources of formal languages described by the automaton; change in the level of information entropy.

Keywords: probabilistic automata, probabilistic algorithms, interval analysis.

1   Interval Variant of Probabilistic Automata

A finite reactive probabilistic automaton is a tuple $PA = (Q, \Sigma, \delta, q_0, F)$, where Q is a finite set of states, Σ is a finite set of input symbols, $\delta : Q \times \Sigma \mapsto \mathcal{D}(Q)$ is a function of partial transition, $q_0 \in Q$ is an initial state, $F \subseteq Q$ is a set of final (accepting) states [6]. Shortly, we call it a probabilistic automaton. After each step, a probabilistic automaton is in a superposition of states, and satisfies the condition $\sum_{q \in Q} \delta(q_i, \sigma)(q) = 1$ [5].

The probability of achieving different states may vary during the execution of various tasks, that are usually associated with artificial intelligence (evolution, control of a colony of ants, a random effects of neighborhood, etc.), statistical experiments, mass support, etc. The simplest way to describe similar situations is to use interval probabilities. We propose interval form of the condition of transition function :

$$\sum_{q \in Q} \delta(q_i, \sigma)(q) = [\underline{p_\sigma(i)}, 1] \tag{1}$$

what should be interpreted as an interval with lower and upper limit $\underline{p_\sigma(i)}$ equal to one. The estimation of the lower limit, does not have to be treated as the sum of lower limits of probabilities.

L. Rutkowski et al. (Eds.): ICAISC 2012, Part II, LNCS 7268, pp. 688–696, 2012.

This variant of automaton can be represented by matrices, which desribe the state of transition probabilities intervals, where $pr_\sigma(i,j)$ means probability of transition from state i to state j after reading σ(underline - lower bound, overline - upper bound):

$$\begin{pmatrix} \underline{pr_\sigma(1,1)} & \underline{pr_\sigma(1,2)} & \cdots & \underline{pr_\sigma(1,n)} \\ \underline{pr_\sigma(2,1)} & \underline{pr_\sigma(2,2)} & \cdots & \underline{pr_\sigma(2,n)} \\ \vdots & \vdots & \ddots & \vdots \\ \underline{pr_\sigma(n,1)} & \underline{pr_\sigma(n,2)} & \cdots & \underline{pr_\sigma(n,n)} \end{pmatrix} = \underline{pr_\sigma}, \qquad \begin{pmatrix} \overline{pr_\sigma(1,1)} & \overline{pr_\sigma(1,2)} & \cdots & \overline{pr_\sigma(1,n)} \\ \overline{pr_\sigma(2,1)} & \overline{pr_\sigma(2,2)} & \cdots & \overline{pr_\sigma(2,n)} \\ \vdots & \vdots & \ddots & \vdots \\ \overline{pr_\sigma(n,1)} & \overline{pr_\sigma(n,2)} & \cdots & \overline{pr_\sigma(n,n)} \end{pmatrix} = \overline{pr_\sigma}, \quad (2)$$

In the simplest variant lower bound for i-th state is expressed as $\underline{p_\sigma(i)} = \sum_{j=1}^{n} \underline{pr_\sigma(i,j)} \leq 1$. For upper bound we should save the limitation typical for a determinism:$\overline{p_\sigma(i)} = \sum_{j=1}^{n} \overline{pr_\sigma(i,j)} = 1$. We can create a general matrix:

$$\begin{pmatrix} \Delta pr_\sigma(1,1) & \Delta pr_\sigma(1,2) & \cdots & \Delta pr_\sigma(1,n) \\ \Delta pr_\sigma(2,1) & \Delta pr_\sigma(2,2) & \cdots & \Delta pr_\sigma(2,n) \\ \vdots & \vdots & \ddots & \vdots \\ \Delta pr_\sigma(n,1) & \Delta pr_\sigma(n,2) & \cdots & \Delta pr_\sigma(n,n) \end{pmatrix} = \Delta pr_\sigma, \qquad (3)$$

Individual rows (which relate to specific states) can be illustrated with the help of a diagram of transition to the states ranked according to: 1) numbers, 2) level of probability of transition to another state, 3) the size of the transition probability interval. The third option is selected and shown in fig. 1. Transitions by the individual states can be illustrated graphically by ordering states because of different criteria:

- any sequence, including the possibility of reaching the individual states (the first part of fig. 2),
- according to the maximum probability (upper, middle or lower limits) of the transition to another state (the second part of fig. 2),

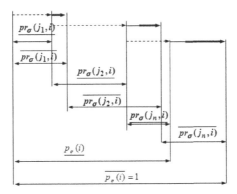

Fig. 1. Diagram of probability intervals

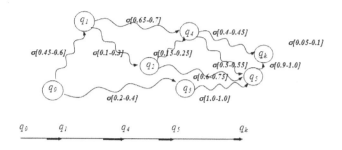

Fig. 2. State transitions in PA

- by decreasing the variance of probabilities (upper, middle or lower limits) of the transition state,
- by decreasing the variance intervals of probabilities of the state transition.

The product of the lower/upper values of probabilities, regarded here as the lower/upper level of probability of the way, is: $PP_low(0,1,4,5,k) = \prod_{i=1,i\in\{0,1,4,5,k\}}^{k-1} \underline{pr_\sigma(i,i+1)} = 0,45 * 0,65 * 0,5 * 0,9 = 0,10125$ and $PP_up(0,1,4,5,k) = \prod_{i=1,i\in\{0,1,4,5,k\}}^{k-1} \overline{pr_\sigma(i,i+1)} = 0,6*0,7*0,55*1 = 0,231$. The interval probability value of a choice of given way is equal: $PP(0,1,4,5,k) = [0,10125;0,231]$. Our example associated with the formation of the most likely chosen road is presented in the form of polyline connecting elements of the matrices $\underline{P_\sigma}$ and $\overline{P_\sigma}$ (fig. 3). We need to determine the probability of transition of all roads in the automaton, in real example, we reject these unattainable. $PP(path_1) = 0(path_1 = \{0,k\}); \quad PP(path_i) = 0(path_i = \{0,1,2,3,k\})$ etc. Thus, only six roads will be taken into account: $PP(0,1,4,5,k) \neq 0; PP(0,1,4,k) \neq 0; PP(0,1,2,4,k) \neq 0; PP(0,1,2,4,5,k) \neq 0; PP(0,1,2,5,k) \neq 0; PP(0,1,3,5,k) \neq 0.$

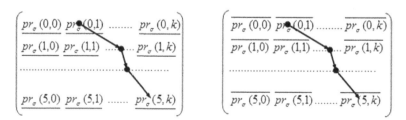

Fig. 3. Elements forming the most probable way :(0,1,4,5,k)

2   Consistency of Probabilities Matrix

The sum of elements in rows in matrices in equation 2 are equal to 1. In the proposed convention, we assume that eigenvector can be estimated on the base of the sum of the elements in columns after the normalization procedure:

$$v(i,j) = \sum_{i=1}^{n} pr_\sigma(i,j)/\sum_{i=1}^{n}\sum_{l=1}^{n}\overline{pr_\sigma(i,l)}, \quad \overline{v(i,j)} = \sum_{i=1}^{n}\overline{pr_\sigma(i,j)}/\sum_{i=1}^{n}\sum_{l=1}^{n} pr_\sigma(i,l). \quad (4)$$

We propose the following method of estimating the interval matrix consistency:

1. The procedure of creating consistency vector with help of the bounded probability matrix:

$$u1 = \underline{Pr_\sigma} * \overline{v}, \quad u2 = \overline{Pr_\sigma} * \underline{v}, \quad (5)$$

2. Procedure of division of relevant elements of vector $u1$ by elements $\overline{v}$ and $u2$ by $\underline{v}$:

$$d1(j) = u1(j)/\overline{v(j)}, \quad d2(j) = u2(j)/\underline{v(j)}, \quad (6)$$

3. Procedure of summing relevant differences $d1$ and $d2$ as a measure of inconsistency of matrix:

$$CI = \sum_{j=1}^{n}|d1(j) - d2(j)|. \quad (7)$$

For example, based on the data presented in figure 2 we calculate the lower and upper values of eigenvectors (fig. 4).

Lower values of eigenvector elements

states	0	1	2	3	4	5	k	sum
0	0	0,45	0	0,2	0	0	0	
1	0	0	0,1	0	0,65	0	0	
2	0	0	0	0	0,15	0,6	0	
3	0	0	0	0	0	1	0	
4	0	0	0	0	0	0,5	0,4	
5	0	0	0	0	0	0	0,9	
k	0	0	0	0	0	0	0	
sum	0	0,45	0,1	0,2	0,8	2,1	1,3	4,95
v low	0,00	0,09	0,02	0,04	0,16	0,42	0,26	1,00

Lower values of eigenvector elements

states	0	1	2	3	4	5	k	sum
0	0	0,6	0	0,4	0	0	0	
1	0	0	0,3	0	0,7	0	0	
2	0	0	0	0	0,25	0,75	0	
3	0	0	0	0	0	1	0	
4	0	0	0	0	0	0,55	0,45	
5	0	0	0	0	0	0	1	
k	0	0	0	0	0	0	0	
sum	0	0,6	0,3	0,4	0,95	2,3	1,45	6
v_up	0	0,10	0,05	0,07	0,16	0,38	0,24	1,00

Fig. 4. Example - bounded values of eigenvector elements

We start from counting values of vectors U and D (respectively the first and the second step of the algorithm). Results are presented in fig. 5.

Total differences between $d1$ and $d2$ form are treated as a measure of probability bounds inconsistency (fig. 6).

It generates the problem: if we can correct these bounds, how should we do it when the level of inconsistency is given? In this situation, we can offer a few different rules, for example:

- the possibility of correcting only lower limits,
- the correction of selected borders while maintaining the unity of the sum of upper limits of state transitions probabilities,
- the correction of selected limits of preset intervals,
- the limits correction relating to the selected states.

stage	v_low	u1	d1	v_up	u2	d2
0	0,00	0,07	x	0,00	0,06	x
1	0,09	0,12	1,31	0,10	0,11	1,08
2	0,02	0,36	17,75	0,05	0,25	5,08
3	0,04	0,42	10,50	0,07	0,38	5,75
4	0,16	0,35	2,18	0,16	0,29	1,82
5	0,42	0,26	0,62	0,38	0,22	0,57
k	0,26	0,00	0,00	0,24	0,00	0,00

Fig. 5. Elements of vectors U and D

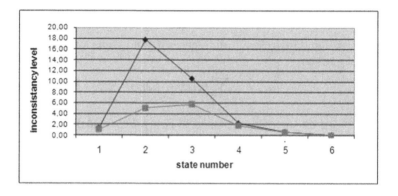

Fig. 6. The scale of probability bounds inconsistency CI

Choosing a lower adjustment of Excel optimizer (Solver), we find the following values of the lower limits of state transitions probabilities (fig. 10).

The total scale of inconsistency for values we found decreased from 18.063 to 0.2942 (for the first variant of mentioned types of corrections). The values of the elements of vectors v_low, v_up, U and D after the lower limits correction and the differences - components of the inconsistency are presented in fig. 8.

The corrections levels are presented on fig. 9.

If we regard only two modification possibilities taking into account maximal positive and maximal negative corrections, then with help of Solver we found the solution presented in fig. 10. Total correction decreases from 18.063 to 3.98.

Results obtained after the chosen transition, taking into account maximal positive and maximal negative corrections are presented in fig. 11.

The correction of selected borders while maintaining the unity of the sum of upper limits of state transitions probabilities is a very interesting variant. In this case we obtain the set of new upper bounds (fig. 12) and the rest of results are in fig. 13.

The total correction decreases from 18.063 to 2.18. We can show in the diagram the dependency of correction levels for state transitions, when upper bounds will be corrected (fig. 14).

state	0	1	2	3	4	5	k		sum
0	0	0,547	0	0,365	0	0	0		0,912
1	0	0	0,3	0	0,7	0	0		1
2	0	0	0	0	0,25	0,679	0		0,929
3	0	0	0	0	0	0,992	0		0,992
4	0	0	0	0	0	0,411	0,432		0,843
5	0	0	0	0	0	0	0,883		0,883
k	0	0	0	0	0	0	0		
									5,559
sum	0	0,547	0,3	0,365	0,95	2,082	1,315	5,559	
v_low	0,00	0,10	0,05	0,07	0,17	0,37	0,24	1,00	

Fig. 7. Lower values of the eigenvector after the lower bounds correction

v_low	u1	d1	v_up	u2	d2	|d1(j)-d2(j)|
0,00	0,09	x	0,00	0,08	x	x
0,10	0,14	1,38	0,10	0,13	1,26	0,121
0,05	0,32	6,00	0,05	0,30	6,00	0,000
0,07	0,37	5,70	0,07	0,38	5,70	0,000
0,17	0,31	1,83	0,16	0,26	1,66	0,173
0,37	0,24	0,63	0,38	0,21	0,56	0,075
0,24	0,00	0,00	0,24	0,00	0,00	0,000
						suma
						0,294

Fig. 8. Results obtained after lower bound corrections

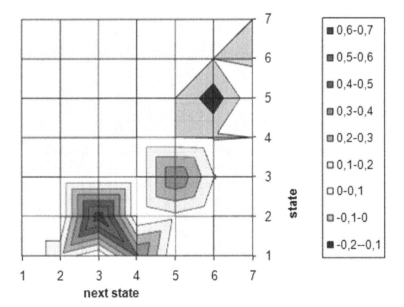

Fig. 9. The correction levels for state transitions

state	0	1	2	3	4	5	k		sum	norm
0	0	0.45	0	0.2	0	0	0		0.65	0.14
1	0	0	0.276	0	0.65	0	0		0.926	0.20
2	0	0	0	0	0.15	0.6	0		0.75	0.16
3	0	0	0	0	0	1	0		1	0.22
4	0	0	0	0	0	0	0.4		0.4	0.09
5	0	0	0	0	0	0	0.9		0.9	0.19
k	0	0	0	0	0	0	0			
									4.626	1.00
sum	0	0.45	0.276	0.2	0.8	1.6	1.3	4.626		
w low	0.00	0.10	0.06	0.04	0.17	0.35	0.28	1.00		

Fig. 10. Lower values of state transition probabilities after lower bounds corrections in states transitions:$(1 \to 2)$ and $(4 \to 5)$

w_low	u1	d1	w_up	u2	d2		$\lvert d1(j)\text{-}d2(j) \rvert$
0.00	0.08	x	0.00	0.06	x		x
0.10	0.14	1.43	0.10	0.12	1.17		0.26
0.06	0.30	5.08	0.05	0.25	5.08		0.00
0.04	0.35	8.00	0.07	0.38	5.75		2.25
0.17	0.32	1.83	0.16	0.10	0.61		1.22
0.35	0.28	0.81	0.38	0.22	0.57		0.25
0.28	0.00	0.00	0.24	0.00	0.00		0.00
							sum
							3.98

Fig. 11. Results obtained after lower bound corrections for chosen state transitions:$(1 \to 2)$ and $(4 \to 5)$

stany	0	1	2	3	4	5	k		sum	norm
0	0	0.79	0	0.21	0	0	0		1	0.17
1	0	0	0.1	0	0.9	0	0		1	0.17
2	0	0	0	0	0.4	0.6	0		1	0.17
3	0	0	0	0	0	1	0		1	0.17
4	0	0	0	0	0	0.6	0.4		1	0.17
5	0	0	0	0	0	0	1		1	0.17
k	0	0	0	0	0	0	0			
									6	1.00
sum	0	0.79	0.1	0.21	1.3	2.2	1.4	6		
w up	0	0.13	0.02	0.03	0.22	0.37	0.23	1.00		

Fig. 12. Upper values of state transition probabilities after upper bounds corrections

w_low	u1	d1	w_up	u2	d2	$|d1(j)-d2(j)|$
0,00	0,08	x	0,00	0,07	x	x
0,09	0,15	1,62	0,13	0,14	1,08	0,54
0,02	0,32	15,80	0,02	0,25	15,15	0,65
0,04	0,42	10,50	0,03	0,37	10,50	0,00
0,16	0,36	2,23	0,22	0,28	1,28	0,95
0,42	0,26	0,62	0,37	0,21	0,57	0,05
0,26	0,00	0,00	0,23	0,00	0,00	0,00
						sum
						2,18

Fig. 13. Results obtained after upper bound corrections

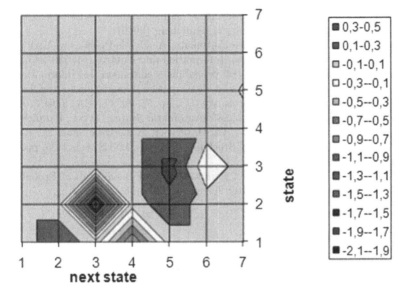

Fig. 14. The correction levels for state transitions

Comparing diagrams in figures 9 and 14 we can see, that the proposition of maximal positive corrections for the lower bound modification are located in the maximal negative correction for the upper bounds modification (transition from state 1 to 2).

3   Conclusions

The use of interval analysis and optimization lets get close to the level of consistency of probabilistic matrix taking into account not only their range but also the levels.

The most effective variant of the algorithm for optimizing the boundaries of state transitions probabilities, is a variant of the correction of lower limits, while maintaining value of upper limits.

When correcting lower limits, places where biggest positive corrections where made correspond to largest negative corrections, when adjusting the upper limits.

The use of consistency of state transitions probabilities matrix can be used to build the effective parameters of the automaton, corresponding to the given formal language.

References

1. Kozen, D.C.: Automata and Computability. Springer, New York (1997)
2. Piech, H., Bednarska, U.: Iterative Method for Improving Consistency of Multi-attribute Object Judgments Performed by Teams of Decision Makers. In: Jedrzejowicz, P., Nguyen, N.T., Howlet, R.J., Jain, L.C. (eds.) KES-AMSTA 2010. LNCS, vol. 6071, pp. 150–159. Springer, Heidelberg (2010)
3. Paz, A.: Introduction to Probabilistic Automata. Academic Press, New York (1971)
4. Rabin, M.O.: Probabilistic automata. Information and Control (6), 230–245 (1963)
5. Siedlecka, O.: Minimization of reactive probabilistic automata. In: Information Science and Computing" - Algorithmic and Mathematical Foundations of the Artificial Intelligence. International Book Series, vol. (1), pp. 75–80. ITNEA, Sofia (2008)
6. Sokolova, A., de Vink, E.P.: Probabilistic Automata: System Types, Parallel Composition and Comparison. In: Baier, C., Haverkort, B.R., Hermanns, H., Katoen, J.-P., Siegle, M. (eds.) Validation of Stochastic Systems. LNCS, vol. 2925, pp. 1–43. Springer, Heidelberg (2004)
7. Wu, S.H., Smolka, A., Stark, E.W.: Composition and Behaviours of Probabilistic I/O automata. Theoretical Computer Science (176), 1–38 (1997)

A New Method to Construct of Interpretable Models of Dynamic Systems

Andrzej Przybył and Krzysztof Cpałka

Czestochowa University of Technology,
Department of Computer Engineering, Poland
{andrzej.przybyl,krzysztof.cpalka}@kik.pcz.pl

Abstract. The paper presents a new method to create model of nonlinear dynamic systems which gives a real opportunity for the interpretation of accumulated knowledge. By combining methods of control theory with fuzzy logic rules a good accuracy of the model can be achieved with use of a small number of fuzzy rules.

1 Introduction

In the process of designing automatic control systems is very important to have an accurate model of the controlled process. In a literature a lot of methods to create models of that processes is presented. Unfortunately, available models are very approximate or uninterpretable (working as a black box) in typical case. Moreover, usually they are not appropriate for real-time working because of their complex structure. As a result they are not useful to create a hardware emulator responsible for emulation of some kind of industrial processes, which may not be tested during experiments, because the tests are too expensive or they may be dangerous to human health or life (e.g. metallurgical, chemical or live processes, tests connected with a work of nuclear reactor or in some cases with motion control).

In the paper the authors present new method, which will be able to work in the real-time and it will be enough accurate for mapping in details many nonlinear dynamic systems, e.g. industrial processes or natural phenomena. It will be able to obtain the model by the non-invasive observation, transparent for the monitored process. In a case of industrial process modeling, data will be collected by the analysis of the packets, which are sent in the real-time in the Ethernet network ([11]).

In the commonly used modeling method, which models the industrial nonlinear dynamic systems, the applied intelligent systems were used as a "black box" or as a "gray box" models. It should be noted, that the systems in many cases replaced commonly used and reputable solutions from the classic control theory. The authors would like to create new hybrid method, which will be used to support that solutions from control theory, but it will also make available the knowledge, which describes mechanism of the model work.

The idea of our method is such that in the modeling of nonlinear systems take advantage of computational intelligence systems. We propose the neuro-fuzzy

L. Rutkowski et al. (Eds.): ICAISC 2012, Part II, LNCS 7268, pp. 697–705, 2012.

systems, because the knowledge contained in them is interpretable. In literature various neuro-fuzzy systems have been developed (see e.g. [1], [2], [15]). They combine the natural language description of fuzzy systems and the learning properties of neural networks. The task of intelligent systems is not modeling input-output dependencies. In this approach a large number of rules is required. This implies that the rules are becoming illegible. In our approach an intelligent system is used to generate the coefficients of the matrices of the state-vector equation. Recently several evolutionary algorithms have been proposed for designing and learning of neuro-fuzzy systems. In this paper for learning the system we use an evolutionary strategy (μ, λ) and data obtained from the observation of the real object.

This paper is organized into six sections. In the next section an idea of the proposed modeling method is presented. In Section 3 we describe neuro-fuzzy system for nonlinear modeling. Section 4 shows the evolutionary generation of the interpretable models of dynamic systems and Section 5 presents experimental results. Conclusions are drawn in Section 6.

2   Idea of the Proposed Modeling Method

Modeling of the systems is a widely developed area. In the literature many topics connected with modeling issue are considered. In the last years, besides classic solutions, modeling solutions based on the artificial neural networks and fuzzy logic rules are presented ([6]-[8], [12]-[18]). It should be noted, that most of the papers which use above-mentioned methods relates to the phenomena, that can be simply described by "input-output" type transposition

$$\mathbf{y} = F(\mathbf{u}), \tag{1}$$

where $\mathbf{y}$, $\mathbf{u}$ - are vectors of input and output signals. In reality most of physical phenomena are dynamic and state of them is not only depended on input of current signals, but also on their prior states. Inclusion in the input vector $\mathbf{u}$ of historical data (i.e. prior values of inputs and/or outputs) enables consideration of dynamic dependences in the designed model. However, in the general case that model may be too complex and uninterpretable, what makes it usefulness in the practice. This disadvantage is a characteristic of modeling by artificial neural networks and also modeling based on the fuzzy rules, which input vector was enlarged by the historic data. Another way of modeling is the use of the state variables technique. State of the dynamic object model may be comprehensively described by vector of state variables, which has an appropriate size [9]. Vector of state variables describes completely a state of the object, what means, that knowledge about it at time t, and knowledge about input signals (vector $\mathbf{u}$) at the next moments, with known model of the object, gives a complete knowledge about the object behavior. The model in a linear case is described as follows

$$\frac{d\mathbf{x}}{dt} = \mathbf{A}\mathbf{x} + \mathbf{B}\mathbf{u}, \tag{2}$$

where $\mathbf{A}$, $\mathbf{B}$ - are system output matrices of an appropriate size. Output signals $\mathbf{y}$ are connected with the vector of state variables and input signals $\mathbf{u}$ by the following way

$$\mathbf{y} = \mathbf{C}\mathbf{x} + \mathbf{D}\mathbf{u}, \tag{3}$$

where $\mathbf{C}$, $\mathbf{D}$ are output and transfer matrices of an appropriate size.

Description of the models in a subspace of state variables has an acclaimed position and it is a part of modern control theory. It should be noted, that systems modeled by presented approach may be divided into stationary and non-stationary. In the non-stationary models a coefficients of matrix, which describe the model, change in the time function. In the stationary models the coefficients are constant. Furthermore, it should be noted, that presented dependences refer to only a subset of real objects - i.e. linear objects, what restricts area of use of the models to description of simply physics phenomena or restrict accuracy of the modeling. In a more general case - i.e. for non-linear objects, equation (2) takes a form

$$\frac{d\mathbf{x}}{dt} = F\left(\mathbf{x}, \mathbf{u}\right), \tag{4}$$

where F is a non-linear dependency in the function of state variables and input signals. However, it is very hard to obtain and analyze the non-linear models. Practical use of these models is also very hard. It is, because most of the known design methods of automatic control theory refers only to linear models. Modeling of the non linear objects and phenomena is much more complicated. However, it should be noted that many physical phenomena may be described by linear approximation (2) of non-linear dependency (4) around actual operating point with a good accuracy [9]. Operating point changes over time during the process. However, a local re-determination of linear approximation in any new point is possible. For the discretization with the suitable short time step T that solution is enough accurate, even if the first order approximation is used, i.e.

$$\mathbf{x}\left(k + 1\right) = \mathbf{I} + \mathbf{A}\left(k\right)\mathbf{x}\left(k\right) \cdot T + \mathbf{B}\left(k\right)\mathbf{u}\left(k\right) \cdot T, \tag{5}$$

where $\mathbf{I}$ is the identity matrix with the appropriate size. Designed models will refer to continuous objects noted as discrete form with time step T, connected with the current time t by the dependency $t = kT$, where $k = 1, 2, ...$ Modeling with use of the dynamic phenomena description as state variables and fuzzy rules will be based on the canonical form of the state equations [9]. This approach is not only comfortable in use but also necessary because of ambiguity, which is an effect of many alternative possibilities of state variables chose.

Presented method of modeling allows to use of a lot of methods elaborated for analysis and design of linear model, also in use of the non-linear objects. Certainly the analysis of non-linear model have to be performed for all operating points, which are important from practical point of view.

Advantage of the numerical linear models, if they are possessed, is possibility of analysis by good known methods of control theory. Methods based on the input-output model and fuzzy rules or neural networks have other advantage, which is simplicity. Especially, the methods based on the fuzzy rules enable interpretation of knowledge, which was automatically obtained by experiment, during the observation of the real object. Interpretability of the model of any object is the result of possibility of obtainment of the knowledge about physical processes of modeled object. This is an attribute of the objects based on the fuzzy rules, which are described as linguistic form.

This notation is legible and interpretable especially if the number of the fuzzy rules is small. However, it is very difficult to get enough accuracy of the designed dynamic object model for the system with small number of rules. Moreover, the model described by this notation is not directly useful for the design of the control systems of the modeled process. That is, because existing and good elaborated methods of the control theory connected with the design of automatic control systems are related to objects described by the state equations or transfer function [9]. In the paper we propose elaboration of new modeling method, in which will be connected advantages of both described techniques: numeric modeling by the local linear approximation of non-linear object and fuzzy rules allow to practical interpretation of new received knowledge. In the proposed solution obtainment of accurate model of non-linear object (performed by fuzzy rules) and analysis of the model by techniques developed for linear models are possible, so the solution allows on automatic building of the object model based on the fuzzy rules. The structure designed by this approach connects advantages of both model types: classic (numeric) and fuzzy. Notation described by legible fuzzy rules will allow to reach conclusions about dependencies between observed input and output values.

It should be noted that some publications show a small usefulness of the methods based on the fuzzy logic theory in practical use of the most demanding real-time application. This is because of relatively high computational complexity in comparison with other solutions. However, correctly designed algorithm (based on the algebraic equations with support of small number of fuzzy rules) and adjusted for hardware realization, e.g. in the FPGA structures, eliminates described disadvantages and allows to real use of high potential of the novel soft-computing methods.

The proposed solution uses the fuzzy rules to generate the coefficients of matrices (Fig. 1), which are in algebraic notation of equations (4). The coefficients define the model. If the model is non-linear or non-stationary, the coefficients of matrices will change over time function or selected state variables function. The dependency between selected matrix coefficients will be described by the fuzzy rules in an interpretable way (Fig. 1).

Form and number of the fuzzy rules will be automatically selected in the procedure of minimization of properly defined objective function, with use of the evolutionary algorithm. If the approximate linear model is available, it will be used as a initial model, which will be improved in the next steps of algorithm.

The approach proposed in (Fig. 1) has not been described in the literature yet. In paper [10] a little similar conception of the authors has been only presented. The conception was successfully used in the project of adaptive observer of state

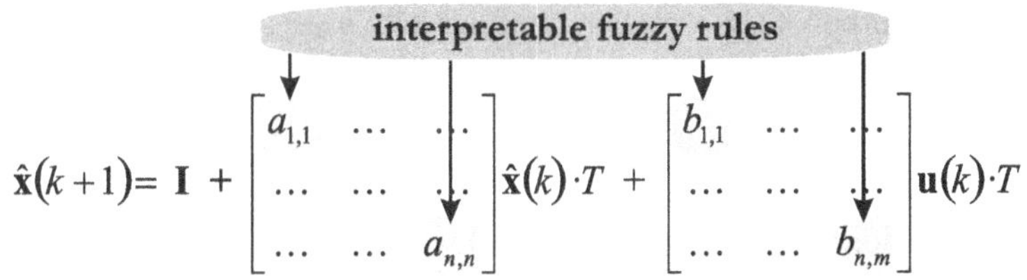

$$\hat{\mathbf{x}}(k+1)= \mathbf{I} + \begin{bmatrix} a_{1,1} & \cdots & \vdots \\ \cdots & \cdots & \vdots \\ \cdots & \cdots & a_{n,n} \end{bmatrix} \hat{\mathbf{x}}(k) \cdot T + \begin{bmatrix} b_{1,1} & \cdots & \vdots \\ \cdots & \cdots & \vdots \\ \cdots & \cdots & b_{n,m} \end{bmatrix} \mathbf{u}(k) \cdot T$$

interpretable fuzzy rules

Fig. 1. Idea of the modeling method based on the fuzzy logic rules and modeling technique with use of dynamic state object variables

variables of induction motor. Received results confirm very well qualities of this solution. The results confirm also rightness of the presumptions of new algorithm development.

3   Intelligent System for Nonlinear Modeling

We consider a multi-input, multi-output neuro-fuzzy system for nonlinear modeling (see e.g. [2], [3], [12]), mapping $\mathbf{X} \to \mathbf{Y}$, where $\mathbf{X} \subset \mathbf{R}^n$ and $\mathbf{Y} \subset \mathbf{R}^m$. The fuzzy rule base of the system consists of a collection of N fuzzy IF-THEN rules in the form

$$R^k : \left[\text{IF } x_1 \text{ is } A_1^k \text{ AND} \ldots \text{AND } x_n \text{ is } A_n^k \text{ THEN } y_1 \text{ is } B_1^k \text{AND} \ldots \text{AND } y_m \text{ is } B_m^k \right], \tag{6}$$

where $\mathbf{x} = [x_1, \ldots, x_n] \in \mathbf{X}$, $\mathbf{y} = [y_1, \ldots, y_m] \in \mathbf{Y}$, $A_1^k, A_2^k, \ldots, A_n^k$ are fuzzy sets characterized by membership functions $\mu_{A_i^k}(x_i)$, $i = 1, \ldots, n$, $k = 1, \ldots, N$, whereas B_j^k are fuzzy sets characterized by membership functions $\mu_{B_j^k}(y_j)$, $j = 1, \ldots, m$, $k = 1, \ldots, N$.

Each of N rules (6) determines fuzzy sets $\bar{B}_j^k \subset \mathbf{Y}$ given by

$$\mu_{\bar{B}_j^k}(y_j) = \mu_{A_1^k \times \ldots \times A_n^k \to B_j^k}(\bar{\mathbf{x}}, y_j) = \mu_{\mathbf{A}^k \to B_j^k}(\bar{\mathbf{x}}, y_j) = T\left\{ \tau_k(\bar{\mathbf{x}}), \mu_{B_j^k}(y_j) \right\}, \tag{7}$$

where $T\{\}$ is a t-norm and $T\left\{ \tau_k(\bar{\mathbf{x}}), \mu_{B_j^k}(y_j) \right\}$ denotes a inference operator in the Mamdani-type system (see eg. [12]). As a result of aggregation of the fuzzy sets $\bar{B}_j^k$, we get set B_j' with membership function given by

$$\mu_{B_j'}(y_j) = \underset{k=1}{\overset{N}{S}}\left\{ \mu_{\bar{B}_j^k}(y_j) \right\}. \tag{8}$$

The defuzzification is realized by the COA method defined by the following formula

$$\bar{y}_j = \frac{\sum\limits_{r=1}^{N} \bar{y}_{j,r}^B \cdot \mu_{B_j'}\left(\bar{y}_{j,r}^B \right)}{\sum\limits_{r=1}^{N} \mu_{B_j'}\left(\bar{y}_{j,r}^B \right)}, \tag{9}$$

where $\bar{y}_{j,r}^B$ are centers of the membership functions $\mu_{B_j^r}(y_j)$, i.e. for $j = 1, \ldots, m$ and $r = 1, \ldots, N$, we have

$$\mu_{B_j^r}\left(\bar{y}_{j,r}^B\right) = \max_{y_j \in \mathbf{Y}}\left\{\mu_{B_j^r}(y_j)\right\}. \tag{10}$$

In our investigation we used the system (10) to produce the values of coefficients of matrix $\mathbf{A}$ of the equation (4) as shown in Fig. 1.

4   Evolutionary Generation of the Interpretable Models of Dynamic Systems

We used the evolutionary strategy in the process of creating the interpretable model of the dynamic processes (μ, λ). The purpose of this is to obtain the parameters of system described in the previous section. In the process of evolution we assumed, that:

- In a single chromosome $\mathbf{X}_{ch}^{\mathrm{par}}$, according to the Pittsburgh approach, a complete linguistic model is coded in the following way

$$\begin{aligned}
\mathbf{X}_{ch}^{\mathrm{par}} &= \begin{pmatrix} \bar{x}_{1,1}^A, \sigma_{1,1}^A, \ldots, \bar{x}_{n,1}^A, \sigma_{n,1}^A, \bar{y}_{1,1}^B, \sigma_{1,1}^B, \ldots, \bar{y}_{m,1}^B, \sigma_{m,1}^B, \ldots \\ \bar{x}_{1,N}^A, \sigma_{1,N}^A, \ldots, \bar{x}_{n,N}^A, \sigma_{n,N}^A, \bar{y}_{1,N}^B, \sigma_{1,N}^B, \ldots, \bar{y}_{m,N}^B, \sigma_{m,N}^B \end{pmatrix}, \\
&= \left(X_{ch,1}^{\mathrm{par}}, X_{ch,2}^{\mathrm{par}}, \ldots, X_{ch,L}^{\mathrm{par}}\right)
\end{aligned} \tag{11}$$

where $ch = 1, \ldots, \mu$ for parent population or $ch = 1, \ldots, \lambda$ for the temporary population and $L = 2N(n+m)$ denotes length of the chromosome (11). In the paper the following parameters of this system are determined in the process of evolution: parameters $\bar{x}_{i,k}^A$ and $\sigma_{i,k}^A$ of input fuzzy sets A_i^k, $k = 1, \ldots, N$, $i = 1, \ldots, n$, and parameters $\bar{y}_{j,r}^B$ and $\sigma_{j,r}^B$ of output fuzzy sets B_j^k, $k = 1, \ldots, N$, $j = 1, \ldots, m$.
- Each neuro-fuzzy system has a number of outputs equal to the number of matrix $\mathbf{A}$ coefficients. Fitness function is based on the differences between output signals generated by the created model at step $k+1$ and corresponding reference values. Starting values for the model are the reference values at step k

$$\mathrm{ff}\left(\mathbf{X}_{ch}\right) = \sqrt{\frac{1}{2Z}\sum_{z=1}^{Z}\begin{pmatrix} \left(x_1(z+1) - \hat{x}_1(z+1)\right)^2 + \\ \left(x_2(z+1) - \hat{x}_2(z+1)\right)^2 \end{pmatrix}}. \tag{12}$$

- Genes in chromosome $\mathbf{X}_{ch}^{\mathrm{par}}$ which correspond to the input fuzzy sets $A_i{}^k$, $k = 1, \ldots, N$, $i = 1, \ldots, n$, $(\bar{x}_{i,k}^A$ and $\sigma_{i,k}^A)$ and genes which correspond to the output fuzzy sets B_j^k, $k = 1, \ldots, N$, $j = 1, \ldots, m$ $(\bar{y}_k^B$ and $\sigma_k^B)$ were initialized on the basis of the method described in [3].

Detailed description of the evolutionary strategy (μ, λ), used to modify the parameters of the neuro-fuzzy system (9), can be found in [3].

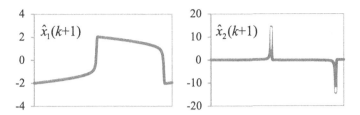

Fig. 2. Output signals for the van der Poll oscillator, used as reference values of the created model

5   Experimental Results

In our work we considered the van der Pol oscillator [4], which is used in the medicine as the model of the heart beat. We have attempted to identify that model on the basis of the reference data, which were generated using the adequate differential equation

$$\frac{d^2 x}{dt^2} + \alpha \left(x^2 - 1 \right) \frac{dx}{dt} + \omega^2 x = 0, \tag{13}$$

where α, ω are oscillator parameters, and $x(t)$ is a reference value of the modeled process as a function of time. We used the following state variables: $x_1(t) = x(t)$, $x_2(t) = dx(t)/dt$. In such a case the system matrix $\mathbf{A}$ of the equation (2) takes the following form

$$\mathbf{A} = \begin{bmatrix} 0 & 1 \\ -\omega^2 & -\alpha \left(x_1^2 - 1 \right) \end{bmatrix} = \begin{bmatrix} 0 & 1 \\ a_{21}(\mathbf{x}) & a_{22}(\mathbf{x}) \end{bmatrix}. \tag{14}$$

The goal of the modeling was to recreate the unknown parameters $a_{21}(\mathbf{x})$, $a_{22}(\mathbf{x})$ in such a way that the model reproduces the reference data as accurately as possible. Of course in a general case analytical dependencies, which were used to generate the reference data are not known. However, the proposed method allows us to reconstruct these dependencies in the form of a set of interpretable fuzzy rules (9). This is possible on the basis of the analysis of measurable outputs of the modeled process. In our case, the measurable output signals are $x_1(k)$ and $x_2(k)$. They are used as reference values for the outputs. Output signals generated by the created model $\hat{x}_1(k)$ and $\hat{x}_2(k)$ are compared with their reference values and the error of the model is calculated (12).

In our simulations we use neuro-fuzzy system (9) with Gaussian membership functions and algebraic triangular norms. The evolution process is characterized by the following parameters: $\mu = 10$, $\lambda = 500$, $p_m = 0.077$, $p_c = 0.770$, and the number of generations $= 100000$ (for details see e.g. [3]).

Neuro-fuzzy system obtained in evolutionary learning is characterized by 3 or 5 rules, 2 inputs ($\hat{x}_1(k)$ and $\hat{x}_2(k)$) and 2 outputs ($a_{2,1}(k)$ and $a_{2,2}(k)$). The experimental results are depicted in Table 1 (average RMSE for system with 3 and 5 rules) and presented on the Fig. 3.

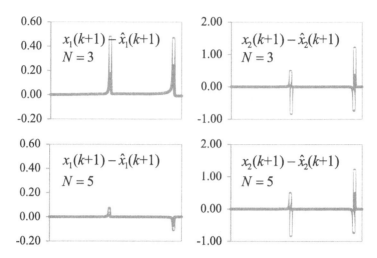

Fig. 3. Simulation results of the obtained neuro-fuzzy models in a case of a) three and b) five fuzzy rules used in the model

Table 1. Accuracy of the nonlinear modeling obtained in our simulations

Number of rules	Average RMSE
$N = 3$	0.0035
$N = 5$	0.0007

6 Summary

In the paper a new method to create model of nonlinear dynamic systems was proposed. The novelty was the combination of the method of control theory and fuzzy rules, which enables to obtain good accuracy of the model using a small number of fuzzy rules. That model gives the potential possibility to the interpretation of accumulated knowledge. The simulation shows the fully usefulness of the proposed method.

References

1. Casillas, J., Cordon, O., Herrera, F., Magdalena, L. (eds.): Interpretability Issues in Fuzzy Modeling. Springer (2003)
2. Cpałka, K.: A New Method for Design and Reduction of Neuro-Fuzzy Classification Systems. IEEE Transactions on Neural Networks 20(4), 701–714 (2009)
3. Cpałka, K.: On evolutionary designing and learning of flexible neuro-fuzzy structures for nonlinear classification. Nonlinear Analysis Series A: Theory, Methods and Applications 71 (2009)
4. Żebrowski, J., Grudziński, K.: Observations and modeling of unusual patterns in human heart rate variability. Acta Physica Polonica B 36(5), 1881–1895 (2005)
5. Korytkowski, M., Rutkowski, L., Scherer, R.: From Ensemble of Fuzzy Classifiers to Single Fuzzy Rule Base Classifier. In: Rutkowski, L., Tadeusiewicz, R., Zadeh, L.A., Zurada, J.M. (eds.) ICAISC 2008. LNCS (LNAI), vol. 5097, pp. 265–272. Springer, Heidelberg (2008)

6. Nowicki, R.: Rough Sets in the Neuro-Fuzzy Architectures Based on Monotonic Fuzzy Implications. In: Rutkowski, L., Siekmann, J.H., Tadeusiewicz, R., Zadeh, L.A. (eds.) ICAISC 2004. LNCS (LNAI), vol. 3070, pp. 510–517. Springer, Heidelberg (2004)
7. Nowicki, R.: Rough Sets in the Neuro-Fuzzy Architectures Based on Non-monotonic Fuzzy Implications. In: Rutkowski, L., Siekmann, J.H., Tadeusiewicz, R., Zadeh, L.A. (eds.) ICAISC 2004. LNCS (LNAI), vol. 3070, pp. 518–525. Springer, Heidelberg (2004)
8. Nowicki, R.: Nonlinear modeling and classification based on the MICOG defuzzification. Journal of Nonlinear Analysis, Series A: Theory, Methods & Applications 71, e1033–e1047 (2009)
9. Ogata, K.: Modern Control Engineering. Prentice Hall (2001)
10. Przybył, A.: Doctoral dissertation: Adaptive observer of induction motor using artificial neural networks and evolutionary algorithms (in Polish). Poznan University of Technology (2003)
11. Przybył, A., Smolag, J., Kimla, P.: Real-time Ethernet based, distributed control system for the CNC machine (in Polish). Electrical Review 2010-2 (2010)
12. Rutkowski, L., Cpałka, K.: Flexible neuro-fuzzy systems. IEEE Trans. Neural Networks 14(3), 554–574 (2003)
13. Rutkowski, L., Przybył, A., Cpałka, K.: Novel Online Speed Profile Generation for Industrial Machine Tool Based on Flexible Neuro-Fuzzy Approximation. IEEE Transactions on Industrial Electronics 59(2), 1238–1247 (2012)
14. Scherer, R.: Boosting Ensemble of Relational Neuro-fuzzy Systems. In: Rutkowski, L., Tadeusiewicz, R., Zadeh, L.A., Żurada, J.M. (eds.) ICAISC 2006. LNCS (LNAI), vol. 4029, pp. 306–313. Springer, Heidelberg (2006)
15. Scherer, R.: Compact and transparent fuzzy models and classifiers through iterative complexity reduction. International Journal of Neural Systems 20(5), 381–388 (2010)
16. Scherer, R.: Neuro-fuzzy Systems with Relation Matrix. In: Rutkowski, L., Scherer, R., Tadeusiewicz, R., Zadeh, L.A., Zurada, J.M. (eds.) ICAISC 2010. LNCS (LNAI), vol. 6113, pp. 210–215. Springer, Heidelberg (2010)
17. Starczewski, J., Rutkowski, L.: Interval type 2 neuro-fuzzy systems based on interval consequents. In: Rutkowski, L., Kacprzyk, J. (eds.) Neural Networks and Soft Computing, pp. 570–577. Physica-Verlag, Springer Company, Heidelberg, New York (2003)
18. Starczewski, J., Rutkowski, L.: Connectionist Structures of Type 2 Fuzzy Inference Systems. In: Wyrzykowski, R., Dongarra, J., Paprzycki, M., Waśniewski, J. (eds.) PPAM 2001. LNCS, vol. 2328, pp. 634–642. Springer, Heidelberg (2002)

Hybrid Anticipatory Networks

Andrzej M.J. Skulimowski

AGH University of Science and Technology, Chair of Automatic Control,
Decision Sciences Laboratory, al. Mickiewicza 30, 30-050 Kraków, Poland
ams@agh.edu.pl

Abstract. This paper presents a theory of hybrid anticipatory networks that generalizes earlier models of consequence anticipation in multicriteria decision problems. We assume that the decision maker takes into account the anticipated outcomes of future decision problems linked by the causal relations with the present decision problem. This can be represented by a multigraph, where decision problems are modeled as nodes linked causally and by one or more additional anticipation relations. These types of multigraphs are termed anticipatory networks. Hybrid anticipatory systems may contain additional models of random and non-cooperative game decisions. Constructive solution methods for decision problems modeled by anticipatory networks are discussed as well. Further, we present a generalization of hybrid anticipatory networks, known as superanticipatory systems. In the final section we discuss some of their applications in the design of decision-making rules in autonomous robotic systems and in filtering technology development scenarios.

Keywords: Anticipatory networks, decision theory, multicriteria optimization, analysis of consequences, superanticipatory systems.

1 Introduction

The introduction of anticipatory networks as models of future consequences in a decision-making process was inspired by the idea formulated in [6] as "*To use anticipated future consequences of a decision as a source of additional preference information in multicriteria decision problems*". The exploration of such anticipatory feedback is possible owing to the following assumptions:

1. A decision maker is responsible for solving a decision problem which corresponds to the starting node of the anticipatory network.
2. There exist estimates (forecasts or foresight scenarios) of future decision problem formulations, their solution rules, decision makers' preferences and of the relations binding their anticipated outcomes with the current problem.
3. The decision maker knows the causal structure of future decision problems that are modeled by the other nodes of the network, in particular the way in which problem parameters are influenced by solutions to preceding decision problems.

The first and third assumptions allow us to model the impact of a decision to-be-made on any subsequent problem in the network. The second assumption is a basis for

L. Rutkowski et al. (Eds.): ICAISC 2012, Part II, LNCS 7268, pp. 706–715, 2012.
© Springer-Verlag Berlin Heidelberg 2012

defining anticipatory relations, which describe the *present* interests in the *future* outcomes that depend on *present* decisions.

The usual approach used in decision theory is to model the consequences of the decision with just one value, called utility [1,2,6]. The utility refers implicitly to the future, and in multicriteria decision problems it indicates how the values of multiple optimization criteria should be assessed. The assumption that there may exist multiple measures of utility led in [6] to an anticipatory model of consequences in a sequence of multicriteria decision problems. This was expanded in a series of later papers [8,10] to a theory of new networks, called *optimizer networks,* which model the optimization problems and their temporal environment. An *optimizer* O acts on a set of feasible decisions U and on a preference structure P and selects a subset $X \subset U$ according to P and to a fixed set of optimization criteria F that are characteristic for this optimizer. The optimization problems modeled as the optimizers have the form

$$(F:U \to E) \to min(P) \qquad (1)$$

where P is a general preference structure in the sense of Yu and Leitmann [12] defined as $P := \{\pi(u) \subset U: u \in U\}$ and such that if $v \in \pi(u)$ and $w \in \pi(v)$ then $w \in \pi(u)$. Usually E is a vector space with a partial order $\leq_\theta$ introduced by a convex cone θ, and

$$\pi(u) := \pi(u,\theta) = \{v \in U: F(v) \leq_\theta F(u)\}.$$

A *free optimizer* O may select any solution u_0 from U that is nondominated with respect to P and F in (1), i.e. u_0 belongs to the set

$$\Pi(U,F,P) := \{u \in U: [\forall v \in U: F(v) \leq_\theta F(u) \Rightarrow v=u]\}. \qquad (2)$$

O is then uniquely characterized by U, F, and P and may be denoted as a 3-tuple $O := (U,F,P)$. If the admissible solution set in an optimizer O may be different from $\Pi(U,F,P)$ and equal to $X \subset \Pi(U,F,P)$, we will denote it as $O := (U,F,P,X)$. X will be interpreted as the required solution set that defines the optimization principle applied to F in the problem (1).

In addition to their optimizing capabilities, the optimizers may influence each other, forming thus networks with essentially new properties compared to the former theory of linked multicriteria decision problems [6,10]. In particular, in feed-forward networks of optimizers, constraints and preference structures in some optimizers are causally linked to the solutions of other problems and may depend on their preference structures. Thus, in a network of optimizers, the parameters of actual instances of optimization problems to-be-solved depend on the results of solving other problems in the network.

An influence relation r represented by the network of optimizers may be defined as

$$O_1 \, r \, O_2 \iff \exists(\varphi:X_1 \to 2^{U_2}) \text{ such that } X_2 = \varphi(X_1), \qquad (3)$$

where $O_1 := (U_1,F_1,P_1,X_1)$, $O_2 := (U_2,F_2,P_2,X_2)$, and φ is the multifunction that defines the influence of the solutions to O_1 on the set of admissible decisions in O_2. Influence relations linking preference structures may be defined analogously, using multifunctions from X_1 to the family of preference structures in U_2 to modify P_2. If r is acyclic it will be termed a *causal influence relation*. The term *causal network* will refer to the graph of a causal influence relation. In a causal network of optimizers the function φ influences the constraints in O_i by outputs from the problems preceding O_i in r.

This paper presents a theory of hybrid anticipatory networks that generalizes the above outlined model of consequence anticipation in multicriteria optimization. Motivated by real-life problems, apart from optimizers, the hybrid networks may contain nodes related to non-cooperative game solutions and those describing random decisions. In addition, the situations where the decision is pre-determined, e.g. by optimizing a single criterion on a fixed set, or by using a deterministic decision-making algorithm, are modeled as separate "algorithmic decision" units in the causal network.

To sum up, similarly as in [6,8,10] we assume that while making the decision at the starting node of the anticipatory network, the decision maker takes into account forecasts concerning the parameters of future decision problems, anticipation of future decision makers' behavior, the forecasted causal dependence relations linking the parameters of decision problems in the network, and the anticipatory relations pointing out which future outcomes are relevant to decision making at the specified causally-preceding problems. There exists an additional preference structure at the starting problem O_0 that specifies the solution subsets to future problems that are regarded as required (or desired in a relaxed formulation of the problem) by the decision maker at O_0.

Moreover, it is assumed that an additional preference structure concerning future decision problems may occur at other nodes of the network as well. This led us to the introduction of so-called *superanticipatory systems* (cf. Sec. 3 and [8]). Recall that a system is *anticipatory* in the sense of Rosen [5,4] iff it contains a model of itself and of the outer environment, and its future extrapolation. By definition, a superanticipatory system is an anticipatory system that contains a future model of at least one other anticipatory input-output system whose outcomes may influence decisions at a causally-preceding problem by an anticipatory feedback relation. It will be observed that most anticipatory networks are superanticipatory systems because decisions at future nodes can be based on similar anticipatory principles as those applied at the current node.

The next Secs. 2 and 3 will show the basic properties of anticipatory networks and propose a method of solving the corresponding decision problems, network transformations and computing, so that the additional preferences concerning the required (or desired) future decisions are taken into account at the starting node.

2   Basic Properties and Structure of Hybrid Anticipatory Networks

As pointed out in the preceding section, we will construct anticipatory networks with nodes modeling different types of future decision problems. Apart from optimization problems we can also model the choice of a mixed strategy in games with conflicts that may eventually lead to Nash equilibria, subset selection problems, pre-determined, random or irrational decisions. Hybrid anticipatory networks may contain nodes of all types, but their structure is similar to networks of optimizers as the nodes are connected by edges modeling causal and anticipatory relations. All nodes in an anticipatory network will be termed *decision units* (DU), while optimizers and non-cooperative game units will be additionally termed *controllable*.

Similar to the free optimizers defined in Sec.1, the decision units of all kinds produce an output decision based on the inputs fed by units preceding them in the causal order. In Fig.1 below we present the schemes of the most important decision problems that can be modeled as nodes in hybrid anticipatory networks.

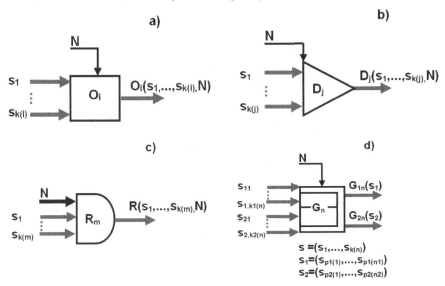

Fig. 1. The basic decision units that may occur in a hybrid anticipatory network: simple box (a) - multiple-input optimizer with output possibly influenced by the states of nature N, triangle (b) - the pre-determined algorithmic decision unit, where the decision may additionally depend on the states of nature N, rounded box (c) – random decision is selected based on known inputs and an output distribution function, subdivided box (d) – 2-player non-cooperative game unit

The inputs in all units presented in Fig.1 depend on the outputs from other units except the initial node, which has no inputs unless it is influenced by the external environment (the nature) N. This dependence may have the form of a multifunction φ that defines the influence relation r (3), or another influence relation that e.g. modifies the preference structure in an optimizer or the information set in a game unit. The influence relations are characteristics of edges that link the DUs, but they always depend on the output from their starting node. Every decision unit has two functions:

(i) first, it transforms (aggregates) the input signals into the mapping that modifies the parameters of the decision problem to be solved by this DU; this transformation is a characteristic feature of a particular DU;

(ii) second, it solves its decision problem with modified parameters and produces the output, which can be identified with the solution of the DU's characteristic problem; the output is unique except the game units, where the number of outputs equals the number of players.

For instance, the aggregation of input signals represented by multifunctions $\varphi_1, \ldots, \varphi_k$ that restrict the choice of an admissible decision at a decision unit O by imposing additional constraints (3) may be defined as an intersection $\varphi = \varphi_1 \cap \ldots \cap \varphi_k$, i.e. if U is the decision set at O and the outputs at the decision units causally preceding O are $x_1, \ldots, x_k$ then

$$\varphi(x_1, \ldots, x_k) = \varphi_1(x_1) \cap \ldots \cap \varphi_k(x_k) \subset U.$$

In general, aggregations can be defined by arbitrary Boolean and algebraic operations, depending on the modeling purposes.

We will say that a decision unit O is *active*, if a decision-maker that performs a free choice [9] can be associated with O. Otherwise it is termed *passive*. The operations of the decision units are summarized in the following Tab.1.

Table 1. The properties of the decision units occurring in anticipatory networks

Decision unit	Type	Internal parameters	Output function(s)
Multicriteria optimizer	active	The feasible decision set U, the (vector) criterion F, the preference structure P	A single optimal solution or a subset of $\Pi(U,F,P)$
n-Player game unit	active	Strategy sets for all players, information sets, payoff functions	The values of payoff functions G_i for all players
Algorithmic decision unit	passive	The function D or a (deterministic) algorithm that calculates the value of the output function D on the set U	A unique value of D on $V \subset U$, or a subset of $D(U)$ determined by the inputs
Random Decision Unit	passive	Probability distributions describing the random decision generation	A random number or a random subset
Other units	active or passive	Different uncertainty model parameters (fuzzy, possibilistic, fuzzy-random variables etc.) and decision sets	Different types of outputs, depending on the specificity of the decision unit

The influence relations form the causal graph Γ, where the nodes are decision units O and the edges correspond to the general relation R defined as *"there exist an influence relation between two nodes"*. Although each DU has one output, different influence relations may depend on this output, so any node can influence many nodes. We will assume that the graph $\Gamma = (O,R)$ is a directed acyclic graph (DAG). The paper [10] contains the discussion of the transitivity of R, and of potential causal graphs with loops that might correspond to so-called strong anticipatory systems [3].

As already mentioned in Sec.1, an anticipatory network is a multigraph, which contains additional anticipatory feedback relations. They can be defined as follows:

Definition 1. Suppose that Γ is a hybrid causal network consisting of optimizers, game units and other DUs shown in Fig.1. Assume that an active decision unit O_i in Γ precedes another one, O_j in the causal order R. Then the *anticipatory feedback relation* between O_j and O_i in Γ is a requirement f imposing certain condition(s) on the anticipated output from O_j when regarded as influenced by the decision made at O_i. ∎

By Def. 1, the existence of an anticipatory feedback between O_j and O_i means that:

(i) the decision maker at O_i is able to anticipate the decisions to be made at O_j;

(ii) the results of this anticipation are to be taken into account when selecting the decision at O_i.

Throughout this paper we will assume that the requirement f in Def.1 specifies certain subset $\{V_{ij}\} \subset U_j$ that contains decisions available at O_j, that the decision-maker at O_j should consider when selecting the decision to satisfy the decision maker at O_i. Usually, this assumption means that reaching certain levels of criteria or payoff functions F_j on V_{ij}, is of special importance to the decision maker at O_i. Such levels can be defined as reference sets [7].

Now we can formulate the formal definition of the hybrid anticipatory network.

Definition 2. A *hybrid anticipatory network* is a hybrid causal network with at least two active decision units and with an additional anticipatory feedback relation.   ∎

In addition, we will assume that the initial node in an anticipatory network must always be an optimizer. Anticipatory networks with both types of relations as well as forecasts and scenarios regarding the future decision units and influence relation parameters form an information model, which can be applied to solve decision problems at the initial nodes or to model the decision-making processes.

An example of a hybrid anticipatory network is given in Fig.2.

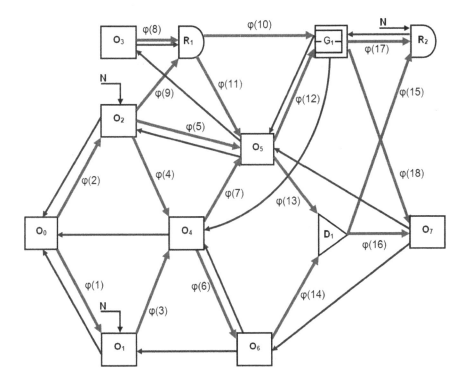

Fig. 2. An example of a hybrid anticipatory network: simple black boxes denote the optimizers, subdivided double boxes – the conflicting game decision units, triangles - the pre-determined algorithmic decisions, rounded elements – random decisions. Red arrows denote causal relations and temporal order; narrower blue lines – anticipatory information feedback

Let us observe that the anticipatory network shown in the above figure does not pre-determine neither its decision-theoretic interpretation nor the solution method. The latter depends on the fact whether the network is asynchronous, i.e. only the time order, and not its absolute values, are relevant. Additionally, the input aggregation functions at DUs should be specified. A more elaborated taxonomy of anticipatory networks is left to future research.

In the next section we will provide an outline description of the method of solving the anticipatory networks for the decision problems with finite sets of alternatives.

3   Solving Hybrid Anticipatory Networks

Below we present a short overview of the solution methodology proposed in [10] to solve the above-defined class of problems, assuming that

(i)   The initial decision problem $O_0=(U,F,P)$ is a multicriteria decision making problem with a finite number of alternatives U,

(ii) The goal of the decision maker at the initial node O_0 is to consider all causal relations and anticipatory feedbacks in the network to select a single compromise decision or to confine the selection of a compromise decision to a possibly minimal subset of U,

(iii) In case where the satisfaction of all anticipatory feedback conditions yields no admissible solution, the decision maker accepts compromise solutions that satisfy certain relaxed condition (here we assume that the relaxation is based on a proximity measure to the subsets V_{ij}). Furthermore, the decision maker requires that the satisfaction of the anticipatory feedback conditions at the decision units in a closer future has a priority over feedback conditions at later moments,

(iv) The inputs to the same decision unit in the network manifest their influence simultaneously,

(v)   For the clarity's sake, all decision unit parameters are assumed deterministic.

Definition 3. A hybrid anticipatory network is termed *solvable* if the process of considering all future information feedback results in selecting a non-empty solution set at the starting problem (or to each of the starting problems).   ∎

The general idea of algorithms used to solve anticipatory networks is be based on analysing cycles in the common network of causal and anticipatory feedback relations. Specifically, simple cycles, i.e. cycles, which do not contain other cycles, are replaced by a synthetic decision unit with a reduced set of admissible decisions and updated links to the remaining units in the network. The process is repeated until all cycles are solved and the network is reduced to a single simple cycle.

For decision problems with discrete sets of alternatives the analysis is performed on sequences of decisions at consecutive DUs ordered causally from the initial node to those having no successors. They are termed *admissible chains*, while those of them which fulfil all anticipatory feedback conditions are termed *anticipatory chains* (of decisions). Constructive solution algorithms for the networks of optimizers, based on dynamic programming have been given in [10]. Their construction assures that the above outlined procedure is convergent and yields a decision recommendation based on anticipated consequence scenarios.

The assumptions (i)-(v) above allow to formulate the following decision problem with relaxed anticipatory feedback requirements. Its solution for the optimizer networks is given in [10].

Anticipatory Decision-Making Problem (ADMP). For a hybrid anticipatory network Γ with finite decision sets find the set of all admissible chains $(u_1,...,u_n)$ that maximize the function

$$g(u_0,...,u_n):=\Sigma_{i\in J(0)}h(u_i,q(0,i))w_{0i} \tag{4}$$

and such that for all i, $1\leq i<n$, the truncated admissible chain $(u_i,...,u_n)$ maximizes

$$g(u_i,...,u_n):=\Sigma_{j\in J(i)}h(u_j,q(i,j))w_{ij}, \tag{5}$$

where $J(i)$, $i=0,1,...,n$, denote the indices of decision units in Γ, which are in the anticipatory feedback relations with O_i, h is defined as

$$h(u_i,q(i,j)):=\left\|F_{i-1}(u_i)-q(i,j)\right\|, \tag{6}$$

and w_{ij} are positive coefficients corresponding to the relevance of each anticipatory feedback relation between the decision units O_i and O_j. ∎

The decision making principle at O_0 implied by solving the above problem is to select this decision $u_0 \in U$ that is the first element of an admissible chain satisfying (4)-(6). It turns out that taking into account anticipatory feedback conditions can lead to a considerable reduction of the number of compromise alternatives at the initial problem.

To solve the above presented discrete problem numerically, we have developed an application in Matlab, which consists of the following components:

1. A database W that contains all potential criteria, payoff functions, admissible alternatives for all decision stages U_i, $i=0,...k$, and all other components of decision units. It allows a data interchange with spreadsheets, definition of new units and a modification of those already stored in the database.
2. A graphical editor that makes possible an interactive construction of causal and anticipatory feedback networks. Each anticipatory network can be stored as a "problem file" that allows for its further processing and modifications.
3. A graphical module to define the multifunctions φ_i that describe the causal relations between a solution admitted and the scope of admissible decisions in some future problems. The same editor allows us to directly point out the elements of the sets V_{ij} that define the anticipatory feedback relations.
4. An analytic interface makes it possible to define all the graphs used in the problem solution in the form of lists of successors/predecessors, define the reference values q_i for the criteria or payoff functions that determine the sets $\{V_{ij}\}_{i\in I, j\in J}$, the functions $h(u_i,q_i)$ and coefficients w_{ij} that occur in problem (ADMP).
5. An analytic machine that implements dynamic programming algorithms given in [10] calculates the anticipatory chains, compromise solutions and their consequences in multicriteria anticipatory problems.

To conclude this section, let us observe that in the above presented approach to solving anticipatory networks we have assumed that the anticipation is a universal principle governing the solution of optimization problems at all stages. In particular, future decision makers modelled at the starting decision node O_0 can in the same way take into account the network of their relative future optimizers when making their decisions. Thus, the model of the future of the decision-maker at O_0 contains models of future agents including their respective future models. This has motivated us to introduce the notion of superanticipatory systems [8], that are direct generalizations of anticipatory systems in the sense of Rosen [5].

Definition 4. A *superanticipatory system* is an anticipatory system that contains at least one model of another future anticipatory system beyond itself.   ∎

In addition, one can introduce the notion of a grade of superanticipatory system, namely a superanticipatory system is of grade K if it contains the model of a superanticipatory system of grade $K-1$. Anticipatory systems, which are not superanticipatory are assigned grade 0. One can observe that an anticipatory network containing a chain of K decision units, each one linked with the initial node O_0 and with all its causal predecessors in the same chain by an anticipatory feedback is an example of a superanticipatory system of grade K.

4   Discussion

This paper presents the fundamental ideas concerning hybrid anticipatory networks, the basic methods for solving them, and their extension, known as superanticipatory systems. From among a variety of anticipatory network architectures we have selected and analysed in more detail those that could be used to solve real-life problems in autonomous robot motion planning and to filter scenarios in technological foresight based on the identification of future decision-making processes and on anticipating their outcomes. Filtering plausible outcomes from each decision unit allows us to reduce the set of plausible action scenarios described as a chain of decisions and their implementation processes. This approach can also assist in planning the actions of cooperating autonomous robotic systems. Other applications include multi-stage resource allocation, predictive control of partitioned systems [11] and technological roadmapping.

Game-theoretic decision models that lead to mixed random strategies turned out to be a practical extension of anticipatory networks based on the multicriteria optimization principles presented in [10] for a situation where two non-cooperative future decision makers influence the same decision unit. *Scenarios* and *forecasts* can be used simultaneously to support decisions in hybrid anticipatory networks. Forecasts are an imminent component the model presented here, as the parameters of all future decision problems and the links between them need to be predicted. Scenarios can be external event-driven. When included in solution models, they allow us to generate decision rules that take into account the dependence of the next-stage problems-to-be-solved on the causally preceding problems as well as on potential outcomes of the external events considered.

The networking of future decision-making problems compelled us to introduce superanticipatory systems. The superanticipatory approach can change the paradigms of decision theory, where the decision is usually selected with a simple model of consequences. Our approach will require the decision maker to gather substantial information about anticipated future consequences, future decision problems and future decision makers. However, available information about the future has often been neglected or oversimplified due to the lack of appropriate models. The author believes that the theory presented in this paper and in [10] merits further research, such as an analysis of networks with iterative decision units, different inference models and multiple anticipatory feedback relations. The solution methodology for large anticipatory networks may require new, more efficient numerical methods as well, while evolutionary computational models seem particularly promising. Finally, detailed studies of real-life applications may provide clues as regards further directions of research on anticipatory networks and their applications.

Acknowledgement. The author is grateful for the support of the research project No. WND-POIG.01.01.01-00-021/09: "Scenarios and development trends of selected information society technologies until 2025" funded by the ERDF within the Innovative Economy Operational Programme, 2006-2013, and carried out by the International Centre for Decision Sciences and Forecasting, Progress & Business Foundation, Kraków, Poland (www.ict.foresight.pl).

References

1. Beardon, A.F., Candeal, J.C., Herden, G., Induráin, E., Mehta, G.B.: The non-existence of a utility function and the structure of non-representable preference relations. J. Math. Econ. 37(1), 17–38 (2002)
2. Debreu, G.: Theory of value. Wiley, New York (1959)
3. Dubois, D.M.: Mathematical Foundations of Discrete and Functional Systems with Strong and Weak Anticipations. In: Butz, M.V., Sigaud, O., Gérard, P. (eds.) Anticipatory Behavior in Adaptive Learning Systems. LNCS (LNAI), vol. 2684, pp. 110–132. Springer, Heidelberg (2003)
4. Nadin, M.: Annotated Bibliography. Anticipation. Int. J. General Systems 39(1), 35–133 (2010)
5. Rosen, R.: Anticipatory Systems - Philosophical, Mathematical and Methodological Foundations. Pergamon Press, London (1985)
6. Skulimowski, A.M.J.: Solving Vector Optimization Problems via Multilevel Analysis of Foreseen Consequences. Found. Control Engrg. 10(1), 25–38 (1985)
7. Skulimowski, A.M.J.: Methods of Multicriteria Decision Support Based on Reference Sets. In: Caballero, R., Ruiz, F., Steuer, R.E. (eds.) Advances in Multiple Objective and Goal Programming. Lecture Notes in Economics and Mathematical Systems, vol. 455, pp. 282–290. Springer, Heidelberg (1997)
8. Skulimowski, A.M.J.: Anticipatory Networks and Superanticipatory Systems. In: 10th International Conference on Computing Anticipatory Systems, CASYS 2011, Liège, August 8-13 (2011)
9. Skulimowski, A.M.J.: Freedom of Choice and Creativity in Multicriteria Decision Making. In: Theeramunkong, T., Kunifuji, S., Sornlertlamvanich, V., Nattee, C. (eds.) KICSS 2010. LNCS (LNAI), vol. 6746, pp. 190–203. Springer, Heidelberg (2011)
10. Skulimowski, A.M.J.: Anticipatory Network Models of Multicriteria Decision-Making Processes. Int. J. Systems Sci. 43 (in print, 2012)
11. Skulimowski, A.M.J., Schmid, B.F.: Redundancy-free description of partitioned complex systems. Mathematical and Computer Modelling 16(10), 71–92 (1992)
12. Yu, P.L., Leitmann, G.: Compromise Solutions, Domination Structures and Salukvadze's Solution. Journal of Optimization Theory and Applications 13(3), 362–378 (1974)

A Question Answer Approach
to Building Semantic Memory

Basawaraj[1], Janusz A. Starzyk[1,2], and Marek Jaszuk[2]

[1] School of Electrical Engineering and Computer Science, Ohio University, Athens OH, USA
{Basawaraj.Basawaraj.1,starzykj}@ohio.edu
[2] University of Information Technology and Management, Rzeszow, Poland
mjaszuk@wsiz.rzeszow.pl

Abstract. Semantic memory is an integral part of intelligent systems dealing with natural language processing (NLP). Building these memories is a challenging task. Different approaches have been proposed and tested, using a variety of corpuses. The corpora used to build the semantic memories vary from well structured to highly unstructured. The more structured a corpus, the easier it is to build a semantic memory using it. This is because a structured corpus delivers the NLP system more knowledge about the language and its grammar. In this paper we show how a question answering based approach can be used in learning of concepts and building the semantic memory.

Keywords: semantic memory; concepts; question answering.

1   Introduction

Interaction between humans and computers has been researched since the early days of modern computers, with the goal being to use natural language for such interactions. An intelligent agent should be able to both understand and generate meaningful statements in natural language to successfully interact with humans. REQUEST and PLANES were some of the earlier successful attempts. REQUEST, a question answering (QA) system developed in the mid 1970's, employed grammar based analysis and could answer questions posed in plain, but restricted, English using a formatted database [1]. Similarly, PLANES was another QA system that could answer questions posed in English using a relational database consisting of aircraft maintenance and flight information data [2]. QA systems have come a long way since then. Modern QA systems, using information retrieval (IR) and information extraction (IE) techniques such as those shown in [3] and [4] have been very successful at answering questions posed in natural language. QA systems such as [5], [6] have been successful in answering factoid questions but have not been shown to succeed at answering questions requiring contextual analysis. Some researchers, want to improve the performance of search techniques by helping users better formulate their queries by providing a list of possible questions related to the topic being searched and thus guiding them towards fulfilling their need [7]. For a review of the state of the art in QA refer

L. Rutkowski et al. (Eds.): ICAISC 2012, Part II, LNCS 7268, pp. 716–723, 2012.
© Springer-Verlag Berlin Heidelberg 2012

to [8]. [9] provides a very good analysis of the problems with the present direction of QA research. For a QA system to be able to succeed in answering questions on complex context, something that humans are capable of, its working should be grounded in cognitive principles.

Memory is central to human cognition and semantic memory plays a major role in it. Semantic memory stores the knowledge about the world and learned relationships [10]. Concepts are created, managed, and related to one another through activation of the semantic memory. Relations between them are context dependent. Concepts and their relations play a major role in human cognition and their absence would severely handicap us. In this work we propose a simple approach that uses question answering to build a semantic memory.

2   Question Answering Approach to Knowledge Acquisition

The approach in most NLP systems has been to use statistical processing to solve the problems faced. This is not the approach that humans take. Humans solve problems based on the world knowledge that they have acquired during their lifetime. There is a very good, though not complete, understanding about how humans acquire language skills. This understanding of human language skills should be used by NLP systems in hope to achieve context understanding of the human speech.

NLP systems use large databases and use them to build their semantic memories. Humans do not do so; they start from forming simple relations and then build on them as they acquire more knowledge. A child does not start building its semantic memory by reading an encyclopedia; it does it by observing others and by asking or answering simple questions. It uses such interactions to learn relationships and form concepts, for example it learns that the pronouns *she* and *he* refer to the names of a female and male respectively. The proposed approach uses a similar approach to building semantic memory. Our system has access to a database that it can use to answer the questions posed to it, but building the semantic memory and learning the grammar of the language is done while answering questions. This approach was first suggested in [11].

Though most NLP systems tend to use a semantic memory that is build by statistically processing a large corpus of text, this need not be so. [12] shows an approach in which knowledge is acquired and semantic memory grows through dialogues or QA. In this case the system can not only ask questions but also verifies information before writing it to the memory.

3   System Organization

The organization of the QA system is shown in figure 1. The system consists of: a) Input Unit, b) Output Unit, c) Dataset, d) Working Memory, e) Semantic Memory, and f) Episodic Memory.

The **input** and **output units** are used by the user to interact with the system. The **dataset** consists of the documents that are to be used to find the answers. The **working memory** is sequential in nature. It reads the user inputs and documents in the dataset. It converts the documents into paragraphs, sentences and finally into words or phrases. These words or phrases then activate nodes in the semantic memory that represent them. It can also read in the user feedback for a generated answer. The user feedback is a reward signal that is used to train/improve the system. The working of this is explained later.

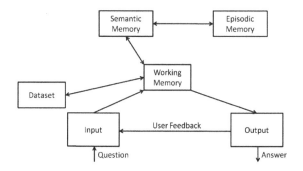

Fig. 1. The System Organization

When the documents are read by the working memory, the system extracts the words from the file and activates the corresponding nodes in the semantic memory. Fig. 2 shows the different stages that the working memory goes through when the system is dividing the document read from the dataset into words. Fig. 2 shows the example of a single paragraph in a document, created for testing the algorithm, but it can be extended to documents of any size.

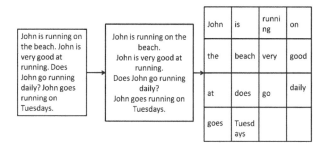

Fig. 2. Document being broken into words in the working memory

The **semantic memory** and the **episodic memory** consist of Long-Term Memory (LTM) cells [13] capable of remembering sequences of vectors.

There are four types of nodes in the semantic memory, shown in Fig. 3. The first kind are the sensory nodes representing the basic sensory activation, i.e., characters in the alphabet that are activated only when the particular character is received on the input. The second kind are the sequence nodes that are activated only if all their inputs are activated in the correct order. They are illustrated by word or sentence nodes.

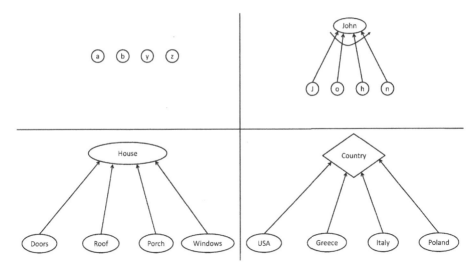

Fig. 3. Four types of nodes. Clockwise from top-left: basic characters, sequence, set and concept nodes.

The third kind are those nodes that have no requirement about the order of their inputs and are activated if all or most of their inputs are activated. They are called set nodes and are winner-take-all (WTA) nodes. The nodes of the last kind are activated if any one of their input is activated. They are called concept nodes. The sentence nodes do not store the actual sentence; they only store the locations of the words (in the order in which they occur) that constitute the sentence. Thus all nodes in the semantic network can be activated depending on activities of their inputs and rules for activation specified by the type of node. The level of activation of the nodes is calculated in accordance with the LTM recognition mechanism discussed in [13], with modifications to account for the three types of nodes discussed here.

4   Building Semantic Memory

The proposed approach is based on understanding of learning in humans. That is, we start with learning simple sentences and move to complex sentences whose meaning depends on context. Consider the scenario where the system has no prior knowledge, except for the paragraph read in Fig. 2, and the following question is asked: "*Where is John?*". The system generates an answer based on the activations that the question leads to in the semantic and episodic memories. The working memory breaks down the question into the words {*where, is, John*} and activates *is* and *John* nodes in the semantic memory. The nodes are activated considering the order of inputs (in case of word and sentence nodes) and the number of inputs according to the LTM recognition mechanism discussed in [13]. The organization of the paragraph from Fig. 2 in the semantic memory with the activations[1] (in brackets) due to this is shown in Fig. 4.

---

[1] Activations shown in the figure are simplified for representational purpose.

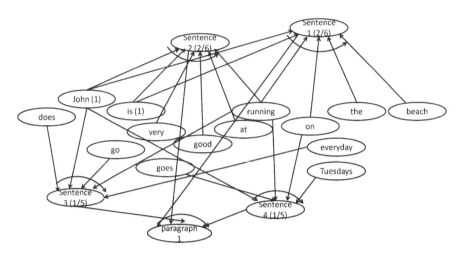

Fig. 4. Nodes and their activations

As, at this point, the system has no prior knowledge. It looks for the sentence that has the highest activation and returns this sentence as the answer[2]. If more than one sentence has the same activation, as in this case, the system gives one of them as the answer. Assume it gives sentence 1, "*John is running on the beach*", as the answer. Now the user has the option to accept the answer, ask for another, accept the answer but with modifications (the corrected answer has to be given to the system) or give the answer. The users can provide a reward signal if they desire. If the users feel that the first answer is false or not appropriate they can ask for the second best answer. If they feel that even the second best answer is incorrect or not appropriate then the system expects them to provide the answer.

In the present case assume that the user accepts the answer, but with modifications: "*John is on the beach*". The system, using this question-answer pair, builds its knowledge and generalizes it as follows:

1. Analyze this question answer pair: (shown in Fig. 5)

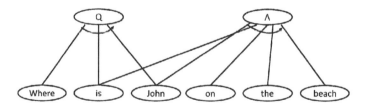

Fig. 5. Question Answer (QA) pair

    a.   Find parts / words that are common to both question and answer: {John, is}, and link them to both question and answer.

---

[2] For simplification have shown sentence activation equal to number of activated inputs.

b. Find parts that are different and form a relation ('R' in Fig. 6):{where | "on the beach"}.

In Fig. 6, 'S' is a sequence node and is activated only if all its inputs: {on, the, beach}, are activated. The 'R' nodes are used to show a relationship between a question and its related answer (e.g., *where - place*).

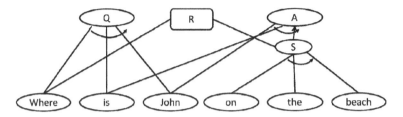

Fig. 6. Relations and categories from the QA pair

2. Form a general relation about the format of the questions and answers for future use {"where *is* **something**" -> "**something** *is* **somewhere**"}. This means that whenever the system is asked a question starting with "where is" followed by a noun, it knows that the answer starts with the noun (**something**) followed by *is* and a place phrase (**somewhere**).

3. To make use of general relation obtained in 2 in even broader sense we first find the sentence S_A with the highest activation when a correct answer **A** is played. Next we align S_A and **A**, determine their matching parts and find differences. The categories of differences show acceptable deviation from previously learned answer format. For instance if,

A = "John is in the park", and

S_A = "My brother John is playing in the park with his friends",

then the system learns that for every question of the type "where *is* **something**" the sentence containing the answer can have additional words in it, i.e., the sentence can be of the type: "*some phrase* **something** *is some phrase* **somewhere** *some phrase*", and the acceptable format of the answer contains: **something** followed by *is* and there is a place phrase (**somewhere**) at the end. Only the simplest case of the answer within a single sentence has been shown here. The analysis, however, can be extended to answer spreading over multiple sentences, paragraphs etc.

Now if a new question of the same type, say "Where is Jim?" is asked, the system searches for sentence containing the words {Jim, is} in the required order to find the best answer. If more than one sentence has them, then it looks for the best match based on its knowledge. Assume that there are two sentences: a) "Jim is sleeping", and b) "Jim is in the park", that matches this criterion. In such cases the system uses its knowledge (about the relation: {"where" | "on the beach"}) and finds that the previously seen relation is more similar to the second sentence and thus gives it as the answer.

The system now finds relations between the new question answer pair and appropriately modifies the sequence node 'S' (Fig. 7). Hence the system learns that its inputs can be concepts, node 'C' in Fig. 7. The concept nodes are activated if any one of their inputs is activated.

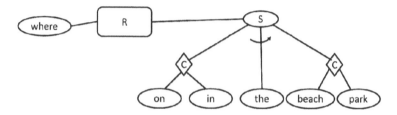

Fig. 7. Relations and categories from additional QA pairs

Fig. 7 shows that by answering two simple questions of the type: *where is somebody?*, the system is able to form the concept of *place*, learn the relation: {*where | place*}, and also the grammatically correct form of referring to *somebody is* in a *place*. Similarly to the above relation the system learns a variety of concepts, correct grammatical structures and relations in addition to the different types of questions that it can answer.

The 'R' nodes introduced in Fig. 6 are used to specify a variety of relations and their interpretation changes accordingly. The connections between 'R' nodes and the concepts that they are connected to are bidirectional. Thus activation on any one of the node connected to an 'R' node will affect all other nodes connected to the 'R' node. Thus in Fig. 6 if the concept *where* is activated it activates the concept *place* (*on the beach* in the above example). These 'R' nodes are also used to connect 'synonyms' to show equivalence relationship, thus if one of the concepts is activated (or inhibited) all its synonyms are activated (or inhibited). Similarly, they are also used to connect 'antonyms' (using inhibition links) so if one concept is activated its antonyms are inhibited.

5   Discussion and Future Work

A well structured semantic memory is necessary for systems to succeed in NLP tasks, but building associative semantic memory that can consistently provide unambiguous answers to user's questions is difficult. The proposed semantic memory consists only of concept nodes and the links between them. Using these simple elements, the system is able to represent the knowledge it has gained through question answering. Since the method is very general, it can be applied to any language. Consider the example: *dog chases cat*, a simple and grammatically correct sentence in English. But this form: *noun verb noun*, would be considered grammatically incorrect in many other languages. As the proposed method uses examples to learn the grammar of a language, it is very flexible, and can be applied to any language in open learning environment without specific rule based grammar.

The proposed method is capable of creating the semantic memory structure and algorithm to retrieve associated information from the memory given a query input, so one can use everyday examples to build the memory. The proposed approach can be used to train the system to learn both formal and colloquial form of a language.

We will use this work to test the datasets [14] from now discontinued QA Track from the annual TREC conference and compare the accuracy of our method to those of others. We are also working on extensions that could allow the proposed method to solve the four challenges presented by Jackendoff and discussed in [15]. Our method is able to create and modify relations between different concepts based on the questions, and their answers. Thus, if suitably trained, this approach can be used to retrieve documents and extract information from multi-lingual sources in addition to translating them.

References

1. Plath, W.J.: Request – Natural Language Question-Answering System. IBM Journal of Research and Development 20, 326–335 (1976)
2. Waltz, D.L.: An English language question answering system for a large relational database. Commun. ACM 21, 526–539 (1978)
3. Robertson, S.E., et al.: Okapi at TREC-3. In: Third Text REtrieval Conference (TREC-3), pp. 109–126, http://trec.nist.gov/pubs/trec3/t3_proceedings.html
4. Buckley, C., et al.: Using clustering and super concepts within SMART: TREC 6. In: Sixth Text Retrieval Conference (TREC-6), pp. 107 – 124, http://trec.nist.gov/pubs/trec6/t6_proceedings.html
5. Katz, B., Lin, J.: REXTOR: A System for Generating Relations from Natural Language. In: ACL 2000 Workshop of Natural Language Processing and Information Retrieval (NLP&IR), http://groups.csail.mit.edu/infolab/publications/Katz-Lin-ACL00.pdf
6. Bill, E., Dumais, S., Banko, M.: An Analysis of the AskMSR Question-Answering System. In: Conf. Empirical Methods in Natural Language Processing (EMNLP 2002), pp. 257–264 (2002), http://research.microsoft.com/en-us/um/people/sdumais/EMNLP_Final.pdf
7. Kotov, A., Zhai, C.: Towards natural question guided search. In: World Wide Conference (WWW 2010), pp. 541–550 (2010), http://sifaka.cs.uiuc.edu/czhai/pub/www10-quse.pdf
8. Mittal, S., Mittal, A.: Versatile Question Answering Systems: Seeing in Synthesis. Int. J. Intelligent Information and Database Systems 5, 119–142 (2011)
9. Ferrucci, D., et al.: Towards the Open Advancement of Question Answering Systems. IBM Research Report RC24789 (2009)
10. Tulving, E.: Organization of Memory: Quo Vadis? In: Gazzaniga, M.S. (ed.) The Cognitive Neurosciences, pp. 753–847. The MIT Press, Cambridge (1995)
11. Starzyk, J.A.: Basawaraj.:Self-Organizing Neural Network for Question Answering. In: 13th Intl Conf on Cognitive and Neural Systems (ICCNS), Boston University, Boston (2009)
12. Szymanski, J., Duch, W.: Semantic Memory Knowledge Acquisition Through Active Dialogues. In: 20th Intl Joint Conf Neural Networks (IJCNN), pp. 536–541. IEEE Press, New York (2007)
13. Starzyk, J.A., He, H.: Spatio-Temporal Memories for Machine Learning: A Long-Term Memory Organization. IEEE Transactions on Neural Networks 20, 768–780 (2009)
14. Text REtrieval Conference (TREC), http://trec.nist.gov/
15. van der Velde, F., de Kamps, M.: Neural blackboard architectures of combinatorial structures in cognition. Behavioral and Brain Sciences 29, 37–108 (2006)

Enhanced Approach of Traffic Profiling for Dimensioning of Mobile Wireless Networks

Mateusz Sztukowski[1,3], Henryk Maciejewski[2], and Andrzej Cader[3]

[1] Nokia Siemens Networks,
Wrocław, Poland
`mateusz.sztukowski@nsn.com`
[2] Institute of Computer Engineering, Control and Robotics,
Wroclaw University of Technology,
ul. Wybrzeże Wyspiańskiego 27, 50-370 Wrocław, Poland
`Henryk.Maciejewski@pwr.wroc.pl`
[3] Social Acadamy of Science,
Institute of Information Technology, Łódź, Poland
`acader@swspiz.pl`

Abstract. This paper presents enhanced approach to profiling traffic in mobile packet services such as HSDPA. Deriving accurate and meaningful profiles of traffic generated by packet services can greatly improve dimensioning of the infrastructure for packet mobile networks. Traffic profiles are derived by clustering of daily aggregates of the traffic volume. In this work we propose a new definition of distance between the clustered vectors of daily aggregated traffic. This enhancement allows to derive clusters with desired characteristics in terms of both similar shape of the daily traffic profile and similar busy hour characteristics of each profile. The proposed method is used to obtain traffic profiles from several mobile networks in Europe and Asia. We discuss the differences in characteristics of profiles obtained as a function describing BTS in the context of load shape and its busy hour.

Keywords: Traffic profiling, clustering, mobile networks, packet services, HSDPA.

1 Introduction - Formulation of the Problem

Mobile network operators have recently observed rapid growth of packet services (PS) share in the traffic, which in some networks amounts to over 99% of the total traffic. This leads to difficulties in estimation of the offered traffic and in dimensioning of networks. Previously, with voice services dominating in the network, it was enough to estimate the daily maximum (or Busy Hour, BH) traffic for every NodeB. The traffic aggregated from several NodeB's at the RNC (Radio Network Controller) level could then be estimated by summing up BH traffic over all NodeB's. However, as PS traffic shows high dispersion of BH for different NodeB's or different user groups, etc, this approach leads to significant over-estimation of traffic at RNC. This is schematically shown in Fig. 1, where

L. Rutkowski et al. (Eds.): ICAISC 2012, Part II, LNCS 7268, pp. 724–732, 2012.

the left side illustrates the actual traffic aggregated at an RNC, while on the right the RNC traffic estimated by summing BH traffic over NodeB's is shown. This implies that for proper estimation of the aggregated traffic, the complete distribution of traffic should be considered rather then the BH traffic.

This work builds on our previous developments [8,6] where we proposed the original idea to use data driven profiles of traffic volume to improve dimensioning of the networks. We introduced there a measure of dispersion of BH in the group of cells, referred to as the *Load Distribution Factor* (LDF). We defined LDF as the ratio of the sum of busy hour traffic calculated over all cells in the group (denoted A, Fig. 1) and the maximum traffic generated by the group of cells (denoted B, Fig. 1), ie. $LDF = A/B$. We showed that machine learning (clustering) can be successfully used to derive traffic profiles and that using these profiles significant reduction in over-dimensioning of packet services networks can be achieved. However, one of major shortcomings of our previous methods was rather simple definition of similarity between vectors of traffic aggregate volume. Namely we used correlation based distance which implied that resulting clusters were quite similar in terms of the overall shape, however the time of daily maximum traffic (or *busy hour*) in cells clustered together often showed too much dispersion. Although similarity in shapes of profiles makes it easier to interpret and identify the profiles, some dispersion in busy hours still leads to unnecessary over dimensioning of the network. This problem motivated the research reported in this paper. We proposed an enhanced approach to clustering where we at the same time control similarity in shapes of profiles clustered together and similarity in terms of the the busy hour. To achieve this we formulate the new definition of distance between the traffic aggregate vectors. We demonstrate characteristics of traffic profiles obtained with this method based on real data from several mobile networks from Europe and Asia.

In the following section we discuss how accurate traffic profiles can be used to improve dimensioning of packet services infrastructure. Next we formulate the proposed approach to clustering of the traffic volume characteristics. Finally in section 4 we demonstrate performance of the method based on a comprehensive analysis of real mobile operator data.

2 Traffic Profiling for More Accurate Dimensioning of Packet Networks

Inaccuracy in network dimensioning discussed in this paper considers impact of busy hour dispersion between BTS serving HSDPA service on aggregation node in the network i.e. RNC. The issue is not directly related to the fact that such situation exists but to the scale and variety (LDF between 2-5) for various operators as presented in [8,6]. The LDF equal 2 means two times smaller offered traffic to be considered when dimensioning network elements. The offered traffic is the key parameter in dimensioning process and taking into account some simplification it can result with 2 times smaller capacity requirements for Iub interface or especially RNC. For this reason the extremely big variety where LDF

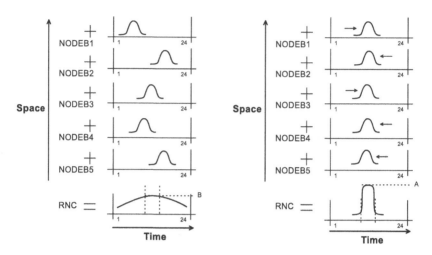

Fig. 1. Illustration of the Load Distribution Factor (LDF). LDF is defined as the ratio of the A and B.

can reach even 5 has significant impact on estimations of necessary capacity for interfaces and network elements and thus final prices. The variety of LDF is still unpredictable, currently there are no clear indicators enabling prediction what the LDF depends on and how it will evolve in time with the network or service growth.

Traffic profiling is a key part of wider research work that should help by identifying needed predictors. General concept behind bases on definition of LDF itself and on assumptions that profiles from single BTSs indicate LDF in the same was as few profiles derived from and valid for the whole network.

Going forward, analyzing of derived traffic profiles opens new possibilities to get additional knowledge about the network. Even number and shape of profiles is already an important information and can be used i.e. to optimize planning of maintenance breaks or many others.

The idea is to use this opportunity to get knowledge about relationship between particular BTS and the profile it belongs. Answer for question what network parameters decide about membership of particular BTS to a profile is also indirect answer for another key question in the context of this research work, what parameters LDF depends on. Identification of these parameters is the goal of the research. Quality of knowledge about relationships between two elements (BTS and its load profile) depends directly on quality of the profiles. For this reason proposed enhancement improving quality measures is so important point in this research.

In [8,6] it has been presented that traffic load of BTSs serving HSDPA service can be well profiled. Then it has been assumed that similarity between two load profiles can be defined as correlation. It enabled to significantly reduce the LDF quality measures but the value of LDF still remains relatively high. For this reason additional research has been started how to improve the profiling algorithm and this paper presents the results of proposed improvements.

LDF characterizes first of all dispersion of busy hours between BTSs as a result of those various traffic load profiles. It has been assumed that if load profiles will be clustered then LDF will be reduced. For this reason application of correlation algorithm between load vectors was fully justified but still in many cases caused the issue as presented before. After reviewing the assumptions, we considered that BH itself as a key parameter for LDF and should be taken into account in the definition of similarity. It results that similarity distance between two nodes will consists of two elements, similarity in the sense of shape and similarity in the sense of the busy hour value.

3   Proposed Enhancement of Traffic Profiling

3.1   Derivation of Daily Aggregates of the Traffic Volume

Performance monitoring data of UMTS network include several thousands of various parameters. In this research focus has been limited to RNS (Radio Network System) compound of NodeBs (UMTS Base Stations with its cells) connected to single RNC (Radio Network Controllers). RNC aggregates transport traffic and measurements data from multiple NodeBs (up to several hundreds) and takes care about control of radio resources. It is one of the key measurement points collecting data in i.e. 20-second intervals (depending on the counter) and additionally updating whenever connection will be released or active set will be changed. For this research single performance parameter has been selected presenting information about amount of transferred volume (in Bytes) from SRNC (Serving RNC) to NodeB on MAC-d layer. The parameter characterizes usage of HSDPA service and includes data with hourly aggregation on single cell level. Several counters create measurement sets where necessary parameter can be derived from. Such measurements have been collected for several European and Asian mobile operators for at minimum two weeks period. Sample measurement records that were source for any further calculation have been presented in Table 1.

From this table (several millions of records) HSDPA usage parameter has been derived and transformed to the format that will allow applying data mining techniques. Resulting table represents 24 hours load profiles for each cell in the network and for single averaged day, as shown in Table 2.

To avoid obvious differences in load profiles only working days have been taken into account. The last point to prepare data for traffic profiling was noise eliminations. Context of network dimensioning enforces special requirements what

Table 1. Sample from the traffic monitoring database

Data	Time	Granularity [min]	RNC	WBTS	WCEL	HSDPA Usage [bytes]	
9/9/2011	10:00	60	23	3	1	22984123	...
9/9/2011	10:00	60	23	3	2	13984123	...
9/9/2011	11:00	60	23	4	1	14213621	...

Table 2. Example of aggregate traffic vectors representing daily traffic profile of each cell

Cell ID (RNC_NodeB_Cell)	Hour 0	Hour 1	...	Hour 23
23_3_1	32984122	36455982	...	10345296
23_3_2	11074749	26479315	...	8345883
24_3_1	43264907	44823577	...	34335821

kind of NodeBs or its cells should be taken into account. The key requirement was to assure a maturity of considered network elements. It means that only network elements generating significant load should be taken into account. Based on experience and review of available networks the minimum level per single cell has been set at 2Mbytes / hour. In some cases it reduced even 50% of all cells but only 2% of overall traffic measured on RNC.

3.2 Clustering Method

Technical details pertaining to the clustering method will be explained using the following notation. Let V denote the set of vectors of daily traffic profile for all cells in the network (elements of this set are illustrated in Table 2). Elements of a vector $v = [v_0, v_1, \ldots, v_{23}] \in V$ represent total volume transfered in consecutive hours. Definition of distance between vectors $u, v \in V$ is defined as:

$$d(u, v) = (1 - w) \cdot d_{shape}(u, v) + w \cdot d_{BH}(u, v) \tag{1}$$

where $d_{shape}(u, v) = \frac{1}{2}(1 - cor(u, v))$ is the component of distance related to similarity of shapes of daily traffic profiles, and the d_{BH} is the component of distance introduced in order to favour clustering together cells which are close in terms of their busy hour (ie., realize maximum daily traffic at or near the same hour). The weight $w \in [0, 1]$ is used to balance the effect of shape-related and BH-related similarity in the final clustering. To calculate the d_{BH} we first determine the busy hour BH_u, BH_v of u and v, ie., the hour of maximum daily traffic in corresponding cells, ie., $v_{BH_v} = \max_{i=0,\ldots,23} v_i$, $u_{BH_u} = \max_{i=0,\ldots,23} u_i$. Then the d_{BH} component is defined as:

$$d_{BH}(u, v) = \frac{1}{12} \min(|BH_u - BH_v|, 24 - |BH_u - BH_v|) \tag{2}$$

According to this definition, distance between two busy hours BH_u, BH_v is maximum (equal 1) if they are 12 hours apart, where we consider hours 0 and hour 23 adjacent. E.g., for $BH_u = 1$ and $BH_v = 22$, $d_{BH} = 3$ (and not 21 hours).

Additionally, when calculating the d_{shape} component, we limit the vectors u, v to the period of hours 8-23. In this way we exclude night hours, where traffic in different cells is very similar, and thus d_{shape} is focused on daily traffic where differences in profiles are of highest interest.

In hierarchical clustering of V we used different linkage functions (ie., definitions of intercluster distance), such as average (AVG), flexible beta, or the Ward method.

4 Profiling of Traffic in Sample Networks

4.1 Empirical Results

The empirical study consisted in clustering the set V defined in the previous section, where elements of V represent all cells in the network. We conducted a comprehensive study with (i) different number of disjoint clusters generated from results of hierarchical clustering, (ii) different linkage functions, and (iii) different values of weight $0 \leq w \leq 1$ in eq. 1. We did this based on real monitoring data from several mobile networks in Asia and Europe.

We use the following measures to evaluate quality of results of clustering of the set of cells V into m disjoint clusters. Let $CLUS = \{C_1, \ldots, C_m\}$ denote the set of clusters generated from V. Let LDF_V denote the the LDF measure calculated for the set of all cells V. For each of the clusters C_i we calculate the LDF measure, denoted LDF_{C_i}, and the share of the total traffic comprised in cluster C_i, denoted w_i. Notice that the LDF_{C_i} represents the dispersion of the BH within cluster C_i, while the LDF_V represents dispersion of BH in all cells in the network. Once the traffic is modelled by m traffic profiles defined by clusters $C_1, \ldots, C_m$, then dispersion of the BH can be estimated by $LDF_{CLUS} = \sum_{i=1,\ldots,m} w_i LDF_{C_i}$. We can then estimate improvement in terms the LDF measure realized by clustering $CLUS$ as:

$$LDF_{IMP} = \frac{LDF_V - LDF_{CLUS}}{LDF_V - 1} \qquad (3)$$

We introduce additional measure to estimate compactness of clusters C_1, $\ldots, C_m$ in terms of similarity of vectors v clustered together in each of the clusters: $STD_{CLUS} = \sum_{i=1,\ldots,m} w_i STD_{C_i}$, where $STD_{C_i} = \mathrm{mean}(s_0, s_1, \ldots, s_{23})$ with s_i calculated as standard deviation of the traffic in hour i for all cells in cluster C_i. If we calculate this measure also for set V (denoted STD_V) then:

$$STD_{IMP} = \frac{STD_V - STD_{CLUS}}{STD_V} \qquad (4)$$

can be used to express improvement in terms of compactness of clusters.

In Fig. 2 we depict typical relationship of LDF_{IMP} and STD_{IMP} as a function of the weight w in eq. 1. These plots were obtained for $m = 8$ clusters based on data from two mobile operators in Asia and Europe, however very similar relationship is observed for a number of datasets from other operators/regions.

In Table 3, we summarize improvement in LDF obtained when clustering as proposed in [8,6], ie. comparing cells only in terms of similarity in traffic profile shape ($w = 0$ in Eq. 1) – column 2 of the table. In column 3 we show results of the proposed method, ie. when both shape and BH terms are used when comparing cells.

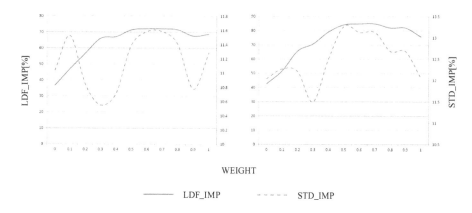

Fig. 2. LDF_{IMP} and STD_{IMP} as a function of the weight w in Eq. 1

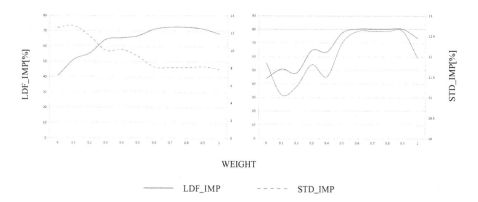

Fig. 3. LDF_{IMP} and STD_{IMP} as a function of the weight w in Eq. 1 – untypical scenarios

Table 3. Improvement in LDF when cells are compared by traffic profile shape only $(w = 0)$, and when both shape and BH are considered (Best LDF_{IMP})

Operator	LDF_{IMP} for $w = 0$	Best LDF_{IMP}	# of clusters
1	29.82	67.55	8
2	40.75	72.36	8
3	61.56	79.14	8
4	36.61	72.08	8
1	19.56	56.17	6
2	37.17	59.23	6
3	50.57	69.21	6
4	33.65	59.31	6

4.2   Discussion

In Fig. 2 we observe that including the BH term in the definition of distance used to compare cells (ie. using $w > 0$) brings significant improvement in terms of the LDF. This effect could be expected, since by using $w > 0$ we explicitly request that clustering groups cells with adjacent busy hours. However, we also observe that for w around 0.5-0.6 we also seem to get more compact clusters in terms of shapes of cell profiles (as $STD_{IMP}(w = 0.5)$ is significantly higher than $STD_{IMP}(w = 0)$). This result is quite surprising, as $w = 0$ requests clustering only based on profile shapes. Apparently, including additional term in Eq. 1 related to BH can bring further improvement also in terms of similarity of shapes of cells in clusters. This result is interesting and important both from the perspective of reduced over-dimensioning of the network (due to better LDF_{IMP}) and better interpretability of the clusters (ie. traffic profiles) obtained (due to more compact clusters, as shown in the STD_{IMP} measure).

Relationship similar to the one in Fig. 2 is observed in majority of networks we analyzed. However, in some projects we observe somewhat different behaviour of LDF_{IMP} and STD_{IMP} – as illustrated in Fig. 3. On the left we observe that improving LDF leads to deterioration in cluster compactness – which may lead to problems in interpretability and future identification of clusters. On the right of Fig. 3 an opposite effect is shown, as observed in one of the projects. Here improvement in one measure closely correlates with improvement in the other, with a wide plateau in maximum. This is a very desirable behaviour, unfortunately quite uncommon.

5   Conclusions

In this work we presented an enhanced method of clustering traffic profile vectors which represent cells in a mobile network that carry the HSDPA service. In our first approaches to traffic profiling through clustering cells, we compared cells only in terms of similarity in profile vectors (we used correlation-based distance to focus on similarity of shapes of daily profiles). This resulting clusters show much better concentration of busy hour, as compared to the original set of all sets. Thus based on the traffic model defined by clusters, it is much easier to correctly estimate the offered traffic. However, the clusters still show relatively high value of LDF, which translates into too much dispersion in busy hours, and consequently into possible over dimensioning of the network. The enhancement proposed in this word consists of clustering in terms of both shape of traffic profile and proximity of the busy hour. As expected, this brings further improvement in concentration of busy hour in resulting clusters, hence less network over dimensioning. However, we also found that in many cases we at the same time improve in consistency of cells clustered together, ie. cells show more similar daily traffic profiles which makes interpretation and further identification of resulting clusters easier.

References

1. 3GPP TS 25.401, Technical Specification Group Radio Access Network: UTRAN Overall Description
2. Foster, I., Kesselman, C.: The Grid: Blueprint for a New Computing Infrastructure. Morgan Kaufmann, San Francisco (1999)
3. Han, J., Kamber, M.: Data Mining: Concepts and Techniques, 2nd edn.
4. Leung, K.K., Massey, W.A., Whitt, W.: Traffic Models for Wireless Communication Networks. IEEE Journal on Selected Areas in Communications 12(8) (1994)
5. Li, X., Bigos, W., Goerg, C., Timm-Giel, A., Klug, A.: Dimensioning of the IP-based UMTS Radio Access Network with DiffServ QoS Support. In: Proc. of the 19th ITC Specialist Seminar on Network Usage and Traffic (ITC SS 19), Technische Universität Berlin, and Deutsche TelekomLaboratories (2008)
6. Maciejewski, H., Sztukowski, M., Chowanski, B.: Traffic Profiling in Mobile Networks Using Machine Learning Techniques. In: Snasel, V., Platos, J., El-Qawasmeh, E. (eds.) ICDIPC 2011, Part I. CCIS, vol. 188, pp. 132–139. Springer, Heidelberg (2011)
7. McGregor, A., Hall, M., Lorier, P., Brunskill, J.: Flow Clustering Using Machine Learning Techniques. In: Barakat, C., Pratt, I. (eds.) PAM 2004. LNCS, vol. 3015, pp. 205–214. Springer, Heidelberg (2004)
8. Sztukowski, M., Maciejewski, H., Chowanski, B., Koonert, M.: Dimensioning of Packet Networks Based on Data-Driven Traffic Profile Modeling. In: Proc. of the First European Teletraffic Seminar (ETS 2011), Poznan (2011)

Author Index